OECD Competition Assessment Reviews: Romania

OECD
BETTER POLICIES FOR BETTER LIVES

Please cite this publication as:
OECD (2016), *OECD Competition Assessment Reviews: Romania*, OECD Publishing, Paris.
http://dx.doi.org/10.1787/9789264257450-en

ISBN 978-92-64-25742-9 (print)
ISBN 978-92-64-25745-0 (PDF)

Photo credits: © Craitza/Shutterstock.com.

Corrigenda to OECD publications may be found on line at: *www.oecd.org/about/publishing/corrigenda.htm*.

Foreword

Since joining the European Union (EU) in 2007, Romania's economy has made remarkable progress. In 2015, the country achieved one of the highest growth rates of all EU Member States, at 3.7%. This growth is supported by exports, mainly to the EU and strong domestic demand. Local consumption has been significantly strengthened by rising wages, low interest rates, low fuel prices and VAT reductions on food items. Meanwhile, the deficit reduction is contributing to greater macroeconomic stability.

In comparison to many countries, Romania has recovered well from the global financial crisis. Yet the rate of Romanian GDP growth has not returned to the high levels achieved from 2000 to 2008, which peaked at over 8%, while the country continues to confront important economic and social challenges. A quarter of the population is still living below the national poverty line and in rural areas this reaches 70% of the population. Important challenges remain in eliminating the gaps between Romania and other economies, in particular structural problems, such as weak competitiveness. Enhancing competition is essential to improving economic performance.

Against this backdrop, the Romanian government asked the OECD to conduct an assessment of regulatory constraints on competition in three key sectors of the Romanian economy: construction, freight transport and food processing. Together, these three sectors account for just over 12% of GDP and almost 10% of employment.

By scrutinising 895 pieces of legislation, the OECD Competition Assessment Project identified 227 problematic regulations and 152 provisions where changes could be made to foster competition. It is never possible to quantify entirely the benefits arising from enhanced competition, but OECD calculations estimate that the total effect from rising expenditure, increased turnover and lower prices for the Romanian consumer could be in the region of EUR 434 million per year, equivalent to 0.27% of GDP.

Full implementation of the recommendations resulting from the assessment would do much to enhance the competitiveness of the Romanian economy, stimulate productivity and promote economic growth and job creation.

I congratulate the Romanian Competition Council and the Romanian Chancellery on the efforts they have undertaken to reinforce competition law. These are courageous, necessary steps towards building a better future for all Romanians.

Angel Gurría
Secretary-General, OECD

Acknowledgements

This report is the result of a collective effort which started several months ago, but came to fruition when the Competition Assessment of Laws and Regulations in Romania project was formally launched in October 2014 in Bucharest, Romania under the auspices of the President of the Romanian Competition Council (RCC), Bogdan Chiritoiu, and the Secretary of State of the Romanian Chancellery Radu Puchiu.

Our particular thanks go to the RCC which supported the project from its inception, contributed staff to work part-time with the project team and provided us with office space for the duration of the project.

We would like to thank the members of the High-Level Committee who participated in meetings to discuss the findings of the report: Iulian Matache, former Minister, Ministry of Transport; Marius Humelnicu, Secretary of State, Ministry of Transport; Mihai Busuioc, Deputy General Secretary, Ministry of Regional Development and Public Administration; Daniel Botănoiu, Secretary of State, Ministry of Agriculture and Rural Development, Elena Tatomir, General Director, Ministry of Agriculture and Rural Development; Viorel Morarescu, previously General Director, Ministry of Agriculture and Rural Development; Attila Gyorgy, Secretary of State, Ministry of Public Finance, Dragos Ungureanu, Counsellor, Ministry of Public Finance; Mariana Voicu, Director for Industrial Policies and Environment, Ministry of Economy, Commerce and Relations with the Business Environment; Elena Mehedintu, Director, National Environmental Protection Agency; Nicusor Ciocanea, ex-Deputy General Director, National Sanitary Veterinary and Food Safety Authority; Mrs. Lenuta Ichim, Vice-president, National Sanitary Veterinary and Food Safety Authority; Paul Silviu Anghel, General Director, National Authority for Consumer Protection; Laura Maria Radut, Chief of Service, National Authority for Consumer Protection; Cătălin Homor, Acting General Director, National Company of Motorways and Roads; Anghel Tanasescu, Counsellor of the General Director, National Company of Motorways and Roads; Laszlo Ladanyi, General Secretary, National Agency for Public Procurement; Iuliana Chilea, Director, Directorate for Standardization, Romanian Standards Association; Adina Silvia Ionescu, Director, Directorate for Monitoring the Market of Products for Construction, State Inspectorate for Construction; Elena Sava, Chief of Service, National Authority for Mineral Resources; Mircea Costineanu, Minister Counsellor, Ministry of Foreign Affairs. The members of the High-Level Committee will be responsible for the dissemination and advocacy of the recommendations in this report.

The following senior experts also participated in the High-Level Committee meetings: Marius Alban, Counsellor for European Affairs, Ministry of Transport; Diana Mladin, Personal Adviser to the Secretary of State Marius Humelnicu, Ministry of Transport; Adrian Dobrescu, Superior Counsellor, General Directorate for Food Industry, Ministry of Agriculture and Rural Development; Codruta Paliu, European Affairs Counsellor, General Directorate for the Food Industry; Ministry of Agriculture and Rural Development, Catalin

Bohaltea, Construction Inspector, State Inspectorate for Construction; Cristian Paul Stamatiade, Chief of Service for Construction Regulations; Mihaela Bontea, Superior Counsellor, General Directorate for Regional Development and Infrastructure, Ministry of Regional Development and Public Administration; Aurelia Mogoşiu, Deputy Director, National Agency for Public Procurement; Eduard Badea, Chief of Service Regulation, National Agency for Public Procurement; Georgeta Briciu, Counsellor, Animal Food Safety Directorate, National Sanitary Veterinary and Food Safety Authority; Daniela Lulea, Counsellor, Romanian Standards Association; Raluca Antonescu, Senior Commissary, National Authority for Consumer Protection; Florina Sora, Superior Expert, National Authority for Mineral Resources; Dragos Negoita, Director, Chancellery of the Prime Minister; Cristina Amarazeanu, Chief of Service, EC Financing Contracts, National Company of Highways and Roads; Aurelian Nastasia, Engineer, EC Financing Contracts.

For outstanding co-ordination throughout the project we would like to thank Radu Puchiu, Secretary of State of the Romanian Chancellery who ensured the co-ordination of the various and disparate bodies involved in the project.

In addition, we would like to thank the following ministerial experts who participated actively in the project by providing information, advice and feedback throughout the project: Simona-Laura Alban, Counsellor for European Affairs, Road Transport Directorate, Ministry of Transport; Marius-Eugen Alban, Counsellor for European Affairs, Road Transport Directorate, Ministry of Transport; Mariana-Stefania Colonelu, Railway Transport Directorate, Ministry of Transport; Cristian Dobritoiu, Legal Counsellor, Sea Transport Service, Ministry of Transport; Codruta Paliu, European Affairs Counsellor, General Directorate for Food Industry, Ministry of Agriculture and Rural Development; Adrian Dobrescu, Superior Counsellor, General Directorate for Food Industry, Ministry of Agriculture and Rural Development; Mihaela Bontea, Superior Counsellor, General Directorate for Regional Development and Infrastructure, Ministry of Regional Development and Public Administration; Cristian-Paul Stamatiade, Chief of Service for Construction Regulations, Ministry of Regional Development and Public Administration; Mariana Voicu, Director, Directorate for Industrial Policies and Competitiveness, Ministry for Economy, Commerce and Relations with the Business Environment; Marioara Capra, Director, Technical Directorate, National Company of Motorways and Roads; Cristina Amarazeanu, Chief of Service, EC Financing Contracts, National Company of Motorways and Roads; Victor Candea Muntean, Chief of Service, Inspectorate of State in Constructions; Catalin-Ionel Bohaltea, construction inspector, Inspectorate of State in Constructions; Alecsandra Cozachievici, Chief of Service, Non-animal Food Safety Directorate, National Sanitary Veterinary and Food Safety Authority; Georgeta Briciu, Counsellor, Animal Food Safety Directorate, National Sanitary Veterinary and Food Safety Authority; Laura Maria Radut, Chief of Service, National Authority for Consumer Protection; Raluca Alexandra Antonescu, Senior Commissary, National Authority for Consumer Protection; Elena Maria Sava, Head of Department, National Authority for Mineral Resources; Florina Sora, Senior Adviser, European Affairs Compartment, National Authority for Mineral Resources; Iuliana Chilea, Director, Romanian Standards Association; Daniela Lulea, Counsellor, Romanian Standards Association; Aurelia Mogosiu, Deputy Director, National Agency for Public Procurement.

We would also like to thank

Construction: the Association of Producers of Construction Materials (APMCR), the Romanian Association of Construction Contractors (ARACO), the Romanian Society of

Construction Law (RSCL), the Professional Association of Roads and Bridges from Romania (APDP), the Federation of Building Materials Industry (PATROMAT), the Construction Employers Association (PSC), the Romanian Register of Urban Planners (RUR), the National Institute for Research and Development in Building, Urbanism and Sustainable Territorial Development (URBAN-INCERC) .

Transport: the Romanian Association of Rail Freight Transport (ATFER), the National Union of Road Hauliers from Romania (UNTRR), the Association for Transport of Dangerous Goods (ATMP), the Consţanta Port Business Association (Organizatia Patronala "Operatorul Portuar" Consţanta).

Food Processing: the Romanian Association of Milk Industry Owners (APRIL), the Romanian Employers Federation in the Food Industry (Romalimenta), the Association of Organic Agriculture Operators – Bio România (Association "Bio-Romania"), the National Committee for Grading Consumption Seeds (CNGSC).

Others: the American Chamber of Commerce (AmCham Romania), the Anticorruption National Directorate (DNA), the Directorate for Investigating Organised Crime and Terrorism Offences (DIICOT).

The opinions expressed in the report do not necessarily reflect the views of the abovementioned organisations or individuals.

The OECD *Competition Assessment Toolkit* was developed by the Working Party No. 2 of the Competition Committee with the input of members of many delegations to the OECD, both from member and non-member jurisdictions. The materials were drafted at the OECD Secretariat under the leadership of Sean F. Ennis, Senior Economist at the Competition Division.

The report was edited by Michael Saller, Project Leader and Senior Competition Expert at the OECD Competition Division in the Directorate for Financial and Enterprise Affairs.

The project team in Bucharest consisted of Michael Saller, Project Leader, and Federica Maiorano, Senior Economist, both from the OECD Competition Division; Anca Atomi, Daniela Eleodor, Mariana Irimia, Diana Vărzaru, Didona Nistor, Mirela Dobrotă, Marian Ivan, Ruxandra Coman, Nicolaie Moroianu, Claudia Bajanaru, all competition inspectors from the RCC. The project team was led by Michael Saller from the OECD and Anca Atomi from the RCC, with Daniela Eleodor acting as the project manager. The team was supported by external consultants Deloitte Consultanta SRL and attorneys at law Reff & Asociatii (Construction, Food processing), Musliu şi Asociaţii (Transport), Andreas Reindl (Food Processing) and Christos Genakos (Quantitative Analysis). Olaf Merk, Lorenzo Casullo and Raimonds Aronietis from the OECD International Transport Forum also contributed to the report.

Specialist advice on competition assessment was provided by colleagues at the OECD Competition Division in the Directorate for Financial and Enterprise Affairs: John Davies, Head of the Competition Division, Sean Ennis, Senior Economist, and Despina Pachnou, Policy Analyst.

The report was edited for publication by Barbara Zatlokal.

Table of contents

Acknowledgements 5
Preface by Radu Puchiu 17
Preface by Bogdan M. Chiriţoiu 19
Acronyms and abbreviations 21
Executive summary 25

Chapter 1. Assessment and recommendations 29
1.1. The benefits of competition 30
1.2. Key findings from the Competition Assessment project in Romania 33
1.3. Main restrictions identified and recommendations 34
1.4. Quantification of the recommendations 40
1.5. Conclusion: Overall benefits from removing the regulatory barriers to competition 41
Notes 42
References 43

Chapter 2. Construction 45
2.1. Economic overview of the Romanian construction sector 46
2.2. Restrictions to competitiveness in construction 70
2.3. Mining 88
2.4. Environmental law 91
2.5. Public procurement 93
Notes 105
References 109
Annex 2.A1. Public procurement: Number of submitted/accepted offers 110
Annex 2.A2. Parking places 117
Annex 2.A3. Regulated prices of sand and rock products 122

Chapter 3. Transport 127
3.1. Economic overview of the Romanian freight transport sector 128
3.2. Restrictions to competitiveness in road freight transport 148
3.3. Restrictions to competitiveness in rail transport 161
3.4. Restrictions to competitiveness in maritime transport 173
Notes 188
References 193
Annex 3.A1. Plates 195
Annex 3.A2. Copy of road transport licence 197
Annex 3.A3. Braking energy 199

Annex 3.A4. Pilotage services . . . 202
Annex 3.A5. Towing services . . . 207
Annex 3.A6. Waybills and records of incoming-outgoing wood transport . . . 209

Chapter 4. Food processing . . . 211
4.1. Economic overview of the Romanian food processing sector . . . 212
4.2. Restrictions to competitiveness in food processing . . . 245
Notes . . . 259
References . . . 262
Annex 4.A1. Staff qualifications . . . 263

Annex A. Methodology . . . 269

Annex B. Legislation screening by sector . . . 275

Tables

1.1. Legal provisions analysed by sector . . . 34
1.2. Synthesis of positive effects quantified by item . . . 41
2.1. Global Competitive Rank . . . 47
2.2. Structure of the civil engineering industry . . . 52
2.3. Top 10 players in the civil engineering construction industry . . . 52
2.4. Top 10 players in construction of roads and railways sector . . . 54
2.5. Structure of roads and railways construction activities . . . 55
2.6. Gross profit in the construction of roads and railways sector . . . 55
2.7. Top 10 players in the construction of utility projects sector . . . 58
2.8. Structure of construction of utility projects activity . . . 59
2.9. Gross profit in the construction of utilities projects sector . . . 59
2.10. Top 10 players in the construction of other civil engineering projects sector . . . 60
2.11. Structure of construction of other civil engineering projects activity . . . 61
2.12. Gross profit in the construction of other civil engineering projects sector . . . 61
2.13. Top 10 companies in the construction materials industry . . . 62
2.14. Main results of the construction materials sectors . . . 63
2.A1.1. Estimated consumer benefit components for one and two additional acceptable offers . . . 116
2.A1.2. Estimated consumer benefits per year (2014) in EUR . . . 116
2.A2.1. Projects to build underground parking places with 2 levels . . . 118
2.A2.2. Projects to build underground parking places with 3 levels . . . 118
2.A2.3. Division of cities by category (Colliers) . . . 119
2.A2.4. Cost of land (2010) . . . 119
2.A2.5. Cost of parking place with and without land costs . . . 120
3.1. Length of the Romanian road network . . . 130
3.2. Top 10 players in the road freight sector . . . 132
3.3. Top 10 players in the rail freight sector . . . 138
3.4. International freight shipping operators . . . 143
3.5. Top 10 players in the inland waterway freight sector . . . 145
3.A1.1. Total number of plates by category of vehicle (2014) . . . 195
3.A1.2. Registered road freight vehicles with maximum weight > 3.5 tonnes . . . 196
3.A1.3. New vehicles registered for freight transport in 2015 . . . 196

3.A2.1. Copies of road freight transport licence (end of year: 2012-14)............. 198
3.A3.1. Revenues from sales of goods of CFR Electrificare 199
3.A3.2. Estimated revenues from traction energy of CFR Electrificare for 1 year 200
3.A3.3. Railway traffic in Romania in the period 2006-14 by type of train 200
3.A3.4. Estimated revenues from traction energy for freight trains of CFR Electrificare .. 200
3.A4.1. Pilotage tariffs throughout different ports in Europe by gross tonnage....... 202
3.A4.2. Pilotage market value in the period 2012-14 204
3.A4.3. Price elasticities of 10% change in port dues............................ 205
3.A5.1. Towing tariffs throughout different ports in Europe by gross tonnage 207
3.A6.1. Number of waybills and records sold in 2014-15.......................... 209
3.A6.2. Revenues of Imprimeria Națională obtained from the sale of waybills and records 209
3.A6.3. The estimated benefits from the liberalisation of printing waybills and records 210
4.1. Top 10 food retailers in Romania based on 2014 turnover.................. 215
4.2. Structure of the processing and preserving of meat and meat products subsector.. 224
4.3. Top 10 players in the processing and preserving of meat and meat products subsector.. 226
4.4. Structure of the bakery and farinaceous products subsector 227
4.5. Top 10 players in the manufacture of bakery and farinaceous products subsector.. 228
4.6. Structure of the manufacture of dairy products subsector 230
4.7. Top 10 players in the manufacture of dairy products subsector............. 232
4.8. Structure of the manufacture of grain mill products, starches and starch products subsector 233
4.9. Top 10 players in the manufacture of grain mill products, starches and starch products subsector....................................... 235
4.10. Structure of the processing and preserving of fruit and vegetables subsector.. 236
4.11. Top 5 players in the processing and preserving of fruit and vegetables subsector.. 237
4.12. Structure of the manufacture of vegetable and animal oils and fats subsector .. 238
4.13. Top 5 players in the manufacture of vegetable and animal oils and fats subsector.. 240
4.14. Structure of the manufacture of the prepared animal feeds subsector....... 240
4.15. Top 5 players in the manufacture of prepared animal feeds subsector....... 241
4.16. Top 5 players in the processing and preserving of fish, crustaceans and molluscs subsector... 243
4.17. Structure of the manufacture of other food products subsector 244
4.18. Top 5 players in the manufacture of other food products subsector 246
4.A4.1. Cost of obtaining a compulsory food hygiene certificate (EUR) 264
4.A4.2. Annual costs of compliance (EUR)...................................... 265
4.A4.3. Annual cost savings if 15% of the personnel are exempt from obtaining the certificate (EUR).. 266
4.A4.4. Annual cost savings if 20% of the personnel are exempt from obtaining the certificate (EUR).. 266

Figures

1.1. Competition and growth 30
2.1. Global Competitive Index: Score for quality of overall infrastructure (2014) .. 47
2.2. Global Competitive Index: Score for quality of roads (2014) 48
2.3. Global Competitive Index: Score for quality of railroad infrastructure (2014) 48
2.4. Gross value added construction industry 49
2.5. Evolution of main indicators in the civil engineering and construction materials industries 49
2.6. Relationship between several institutions for issuance of technical approvals and ETAs 51
2.7. Total length of road network in Romania (km) 53
2.8. Total length of motorway network in Romania (km) 53
2.9. Total length of railway network in use in Romania (km) 54
2.10. Evolution of main indicators (base year 2008) in the construction of roads and railways sector 56
2.11. Number of settlements with public water distribution networks 57
2.12. Number of settlements with public sewage networks 57
2.13. Number of settlements with natural gas distribution networks 58
2.14. Evolution of main indicators (base year 2008) in the construction of utilities projects sector 59
2.15. Evolution of main indicators (base year 2008) in the construction of other civil engineering projects sector 62
2.16. Evolution of the number of companies in construction materials sectors 64
2.17. Evolution of the number of employees in construction materials sectors 64
2.18. Evolution of turnover (million EUR) in construction materials sectors 65
2.19. Relationship of the main institutions involved in public procurement activity .. 67
2.20. Construction sector procurement: volume and share in GDP and government expenditure 69
2.21. Share of construction spending in total public procurement 70
2.A1.1. Discount of award price compared to estimate price (%) 111
2.A1.2. Term for submitting offers (days) 112
2.A1.3. Number of offers submitted 112
2.A1.4. Number of offers accepted 112
2.A1.5. Estimated value of the contract in RON 113
2.A1.6. Terms for submitting offers – offers submitted 114
2.A1.7. Estimated contract value – offers submitted 114
2.A1.8. Offers accepted – price discount 114
2.A1.9. Offers submitted – price discount 115
2.A2.1. Influence of number of building levels and price of land on total cost per parking place 121
2.A3.1. Sand and rock active licences and permits 123
2.A3.2. Average price of sand 0-4 mm (Romanian producers and Commodities Exchange, RON equivalent) 124
3.1. Transport sector, GVA (millions of EUR, % of GDP) 128
3.2. Evolution of GVA and GDP in the transport sector, 2006-14 (%) 129
3.3. Modal split of inland freight transport in 2014: % of inland freight volume and value 129

3.4. Modal split of freight transport in 2014: % of overall freight volume and value 130
3.5. Road infrastructure investment (millions of EUR) 131
3.6. Investment in road transport infrastructure as a % of GDP 131
3.7. Sector regulation indicator for road freight transport, 2013 132
3.8. Total road freight transport in Romania 133
3.9. Road freight transport in Romania, volume of goods carried by road (thousands of tonnes) 134
3.10. International road freight transport across different markets in Europe, volume of goods carried by road (thousands of tonnes) 134
3.11. Rail infrastructure investment (millions of EUR) 136
3.12. Investment in rail transport infrastructure as a % of GDP 136
3.13. Access charges for freight trains for the year 2014 (EUR/tonne-km) 137
3.14. Sector regulation indicator for rail transport, 2013 138
3.15. Total rail freight transport in Romania 139
3.16. Rail freight transport in Romania, volume of goods carried by rail (thousands of tonnes) 140
3.17. International rail freight transport across different markets in Europe, volume of goods carried by rail (thousands of tonnes) 140
3.18. Structure of the maritime industry 141
3.19. Maritime freight transport in Romania 144
3.20. Total volume of maritime freight transport in Romania (thousands of tonnes) 144
3.21. Total inland waterway freight transport in Romania 145
3.22. Inland waterway freight transport in Romania, volume of goods carried (thousands of tonnes) 146
3.23. International inland waterway freight transport across different markets in Europe, volume of goods carried (thousands of tonnes) 147
3.24. Maritime freight transport across different markets in Europe, volume of goods carried (thousands of tonnes) 147
3.25. Pilotage tariffs in different ports throughout Europe 178
3.26. Towage tariffs in different ports throughout Europe 182
3.A4.1. Pilotage tariffs throughout different ports in Europe 203
3.A4.2. Volume of goods handled in different ports in Europe in 2014 203
3.A5.1. Towing tariffs throughout different ports in Europe 207
4.1. Food processing: Value added at factor cost (millions of EUR) and % of GDP . . 213
4.2. Share of value added of food processing in total manufacturing 213
4.4. Consumer Price Index in the food industry 214
4.3. Value added at factor costs of each subsector 214
4.5. Evolution of main indicators in the food processing sector 216
4.6. Imports, exports and trade balance in the food processing sector 216
4.7. Prices for 1kg of white bread, loaf, across Europe (2014) 217
4.8. Prices for 1kg of fillets, chicken breast, across Europe (2014) 217
4.9. Prices for 1L of fresh, unskimmed milk across Europe (2014) 218
4.10. Household consumption expenditure in EU on food products (absolute terms, per capita, in EUR) in 2013 (2012 for Romania) 218

4.11. Household consumption expenditure in EU on food products (percentage of total household expenditure) in 2013 (2012 for Romania) ... 219
4.12. Evolution of tonnes of meat from cattle, pigs, sheep, goats and poultry in Romania (thousands of tonnes) ... 224
4.13. Production of meat, meat products and tinned meat (thousands of tonnes) ... 225
4.14. Exports of processed meat (thousands of EUR) ... 225
4.15. Evolution of main indicators (base year 2008) in the processing and preserving of meat and production of meat products subsector ... 227
4.16. Production of confectionery and pastry products (thousands of EUR) ... 228
4.17. Evolution main indicators (base year 2008) in the manufacture of bakery and farinaceous (flour-based) products subsector ... 229
4.19. Milk production in Romania (thousands of litres) ... 230
4.18. Evolution of number of milk cows in Romania (thousands of head) ... 230
4.20. Production of fresh milk products, cheese products and butter ... 231
4.21. Exports of dairy products (thousands of EUR) ... 231
4.22. Imports of dairy products (thousands of EUR) ... 232
4.23. Evolution of main indicators (base year 2008) in the manufacture of dairy products subsector ... 233
4.24. Production of wheat and rye flour (thousands of tonnes) ... 234
4.25. Exports of main grain mill, starches and starch products (thousands of EUR) ... 234
4.26. Evolution of main indicators (base year 2008) in the manufacture of grain mill products, starches and starch products subsector ... 235
4.27. Imports of fruit and vegetables (thousands of EUR) ... 236
4.28. Production of tinned fruit and vegetables (tonnes) ... 237
4.29. Evolution of the main indicators (base year 2008) in the processing and preserving of fruit and vegetables subsector ... 238
4.30. Production of vegetable oils (thousands tonnes) ... 239
4.31. Exports of main vegetable and animal oils and fats (thousands EUR) ... 239
4.32. Evolution of main indicators (base year 2008) in the manufacture of vegetable and animal oils and fats subsector ... 240
4.33. Evolution of main indicators (base year 2008) in the manufacture of prepared animal feed subsector ... 241
4.34. Production of processed fish products (thousands of EUR) ... 242
4.35. Exports of processed fish, crustaceans and molluscs (thousands of EUR) ... 243
4.36. Evolution of the indicators (base year-2008) in the processing and preserving of meat and production of meat products subsector ... 244
4.37. Sugar beet production (thousands of tonnes) ... 245
4.38. Exports of main products from the manufacture of other food products subsector (thousands of EUR) ... 245
4.39. Evolution of main indicators (base year 2008) in the manufacture of other food products subsector ... 246
A.1. Changes in consumer surplus ... 272

Follow OECD Publications on:

http://twitter.com/OECD_Pubs

http://www.facebook.com/OECDPublications

http://www.linkedin.com/groups/OECD-Publications-4645871

http://www.youtube.com/oecdilibrary

http://www.oecd.org/oecddirect/

This book has...

StatLinks

A service that delivers Excel® files from the printed page!

Look for the *StatLinks* at the bottom of the tables or graphs in this book. To download the matching Excel® spreadsheet, just type the link into your Internet browser, starting with the *http://dx.doi.org* prefix, or click on the link from the e-book edition.

Preface

by Radu Puchiu

Romania ranks amongst European countries with the most important economic growths over the past years, and this new favourable economic context should be capitalised through investments, with a view to stimulating prosperity and economic development. This inter-institutional partnership between the Competition Council and the Government of Romania concerning the "*Analysis of the impact of the regulations in force over the competition environment in key three sectors of Romanian economy*", under the auspices of OECD thus is an investment with important long-term benefits.

The project strengthens inter-institutional co-operation in the field of the Regulatory Impact Analysis and helps developing the central administration's skills to formulate public policies that foster competition.

It also lays the premises for a sound legislative reform in the three sectors representing the subject of the project, i.e. agri-food processing, transports, and constructions, and implicitly it leads to the strengthening of the competitiveness of Romanian economy. It becomes even more important considering that Romania needs competitiveness in the current European, regional, and global environment.

I would like to congratulate you on this first sectoral partnership between Romania and OECD, concluded upon the initiative of the Competition Council. This project is, beyond all doubt, an example of successful partnership that we desire to replicate in other fields of interest for Romania.

I see this project not only as an important contributor towards the improvement of sectoral legislation, but also as an opportunity to reassert our strong interest in going further in our collaboration with the OECD.

I firmly believe that we will continue to benefit from OECD of such high quality sectoral analyses accompanied by recommendations, because they have a considerable impact on economic development.

Radu Puchiu

Secretary of State,
Chancelery of the Prime Minister,
Romania

Preface

by Bogdan M. Chiriţoiu

The Competition Council's mission is to make markets function well for consumers, undertakings and the economy and it entitles the Council to recommend amendments to laws with an anti-competitive impact. Nevertheless, creating a competitive environment means a joint effort from all stakeholders – companies and authorities – to ensure citizens' welfare, in their position as end consumers of goods and services.

In recent years, the Competition Council has become more involved in the legislative area, with a more pregnant focus on its role as an advisor to state institutions – the Government, the Parliament, regulators, and local public authorities – for drawing up regulations, so as not to restrict competition.

The experience gathered in this area has shown us that the elimination of barriers to competition from regulations can lead to a decrease of prices, diversification of services and a higher customer switching rate, which, most certainly, benefits consumers.

In this context, I consider an important step for the national economy that, in partnership with the Romanian Government and the OECD, we conducted the project "*Competition Assessment of laws and regulations in three sectors of the Romanian economy*". Thus, we concentrated our efforts on improving the legislation in three sectors having a significant weight in the national economy and an important impact on Romania's economic development: food processing, freight transport and constructions. Next, we will provide all support required for the implementation of the OECD Recommendations so that they would produce benefits over the Romanian economy as soon as possible.

At the same time, I need to mention that this endeavor represents a continuation of the commitments assumed by Romania, as an Associate country to the OECD Competition Committee to assimilate the Recommendations and Guidelines of this elite Organization in the area of competition and not only.

The co-operation between the Competition Council, the Romanian Government and the OECD has led to a transfer of know-how from the OECD to the central administration in Romania.

I hope that this successful project will continue in other areas of the national economy, as it is our intention to reach a legislative system oriented towards economic efficiency and promotion of the general public interest.

Bogdan M. Chiriţoiu
President of the Competition Council,
Romania

Acronyms and abbreviations

AADR	Agency for Romanian Digital Agenda
AAOPFR	Romanian Association of Inland Ship Owners and Port Operators
AETR	European Agreement Concerning the Work of Crews of Vehicles Engaged in International Road Transport
AFDJ	Lower Danube River Administration Galati A.A.
AFER	Romanian Railway Authority
ALT	Abnormally low tender
ANAF	National Agency for Fiscal Administration
ANAP	National Agency for Public Procurement
ANR	Romanian Naval Authority
ANRM	National Agency for Mineral Resources
ANRMAP	National Regulatory and Monitoring Authority for Public Procurement
ANRSC	Regulatory Authority for Pubic Transport Community Services
ANSVSA	National Sanitary Veterinary and Food Safety Authority
APDM	National Company Maritime Danube Ports Administration S.A. Galati
APPA	Professional Association of Mineral Aggregates Producers
APTE2002	Transport Heritage Association Europe 2002
ARACO	Romanian Construction Entrepreneurs Association
ARILOG	Romanian-Italian Association of Logistics and Management
ARR	Romanian Road Transport Authority
ARSVOM	Romanian Agency for Saving Life at Sea
ARTRI	Romanian Association of International Road Transport
ASRO	Romanian Standards Association
ATFER	Association of Romanian Railway Transport Operators
ATRC	Road Hauliers in Construction Association
ATRT	Transylvania Road Hauliers Association
BAT	Best available techniques
CA	Court of Auditors
CAGR	Compound Annual Growth Rate
CC	Competition Council
CEE	Central and Eastern Europe
CENAFER	National Centre for Railway Qualification and Training
CERONAV	Romanian Maritime Training Centre
CFR Marfa	Freight Rail Transport Operator (state owned)
CNADNR	Romanian National Company of Motorways and National Roads
CNCAN	National Commission for Nuclear Activities Control
CNSC	National Council for Solving Complaints
CSF	Railway Supervision Council

CTPC	Standing Technical Council for Construction
DFR SA	Romanian Railway Company (infrastructure administrator),
EBRD	European Bank for Reconstruction and Development
EGO	Emergency Government Ordinance
EIB	European Investment Bank
EIF	European Investment Fund
ERA	European Railway Agency
ERRU	European Register of Road Transport Undertakings (database)
ERTMS	European Railway Traffic Management System
ETA	European Technical Assessment
EU	European Union
FCMG	Fast-moving consumer goods
FORT	Federation of Romanian Transport Operators
FRAND	Fair, reasonable and non-discriminatory
FS	Ferrovie dello Stato
GDP	Gross domestic product
GMO	Genetically modified organisms
GMP	Genetically modified organism
GO	Government Ordinance
GVA	Gross value added
HACCP	Hazard Analysis Critical Control Point
ICECON	Research Institute for Construction Equipment and Technology
ICT	Information and communication technology
INCERTRANS	Research Institute for Transport
INS/NSI	National Institute of Statistics
ISC	Construction State Inspectorate
ISCTR	State Inspectorate for Road Transport Control
MARD	Ministry of Agriculture and Rural Development
MARPOL	International Convention for Prevention of Pollution from Ships
MDRAP	Ministry of Regional Development and Public Administration
MEPC	Marine Environment Protection Committee
MEWF	Ministry of Environment, Waters and Forests
MLPTL	Ministry of Public Works, Transport and Housing
MoE	Ministry of Economy, Commerce and Relations with Business Environment
MoF	Ministry of Finance
MoT	Ministry of Transport
n.e.c.	Not elsewhere classified
NACE	Statistical Classification of Economic Activities in the European Community
NACP	National Authority for Consumer Protection
NAMMD	National Agency for Medicine and Medical Devices
NCES	National Committee for Emergency Situations
NCNAC	National Commission for Nuclear Activity Control
NEPA	National Environmental Protection Agency
NGO	non-governmental organisation
NIS	National Institute of Statistics
NLc	Nederlandse Loodsencorporatie
NTRO	National Trade Register Office

OLFR	Romanian Railway Licensing Body
PAIA	Payment and Agriculture Intervention Agency
PATROCONS	Employers Association of Manufacturers
PATROMAT	Employers Federation of Building Materials
PMRI	Product Market Regulation Indicator (OECD)
R&D	Research and development
RAR	Romanian Automotive Registry
RAS	Romanian Academic Society
RCC	Romanian Competition Council
RFC7	Rail Freight Corridor 7
RRA	Romanian Road Authority
SAR	Romanian Academic Society
SCI	State Construction Inspectorate
SEAP	Electronic System of Public Procurement
SPS Agreement	Agreement on Application of Sanitary and Phytosanitary Measures (WTO)
SUMAL	Integrated Informational System of Tracking Wood Materials
SVA	Sanitary-Veterinary Authorisation
SVFSNA	Sanitary-Veterinary and Food Safety National Authority
TAB	Technical assessment body
TEN-T	Trans-European Transport Network
TESA	Technical, economic and socio-administrative (personnel)
TIR	Transports Internationaux Routiers
UCVAP	Unit for the Coordination and Verification of Public Procurement
UNECE	United Nations European Commission for Europe
UNTRR	National Union of Romanian Road Hauliers
USER	Freight Forwarders Association
VAT	Value added tax
WTO	World Trade Organization

Executive summary

The OECD was asked by the Romanian government to carry out an independent policy assessment to identify rules and regulations that may hinder the competitive and efficient functioning of markets in three sectors: construction (including public procurement and building materials), freight transport and food processing.

The project proceeded in four stages. Stage 1 defined the exact scope of all three sectors. A list of all sector-relevant legislation was collected with the help of government experts. This list consisted of 895 pieces of legislation, such as laws, (emergency) government ordinances, government decisions and ministerial orders. In Stage 2 this legislation was screened to identify potential competition barriers using the OECD's *Competition Assessment Toolkit*. The review included both national provisions and pieces of legislation transposing EU directives as all three sectors are to a significant extent regulated by EU directives and regulations. We identified 227 potential restrictions of competition (95 in construction, 85 in transport and 47 in food processing). Additionally, we prepared an economic overview for each sector which contained important economic indicators such as output, employment and price trends. In Stage 3 we researched the policymakers' objective for each provision. An in-depth analysis was carried out qualitatively and, when possible subject to availability of data, also quantitatively. In Stage 4 we developed recommendations for those provisions which were found to restrict competition, taking into account EU legislation and relevant provisions in comparable countries, notably EU Member States. Finally, we held several workshops with ministerial experts and members of the Romanian Competition Council (RCC) to build up competition assessment capabilities in the Romanian administration.

As a result of this work the report makes 152 recommendations on specific legal provisions.

Summary of the legal provisions analysed by sector

	Construction	Freight transport	Food processing
Legislation scanned	162	566	167
Prima facie restrictions found	95	85	47
Recommendations made	**72**	**46**	**34**

If the recommendations detailed in this report are implemented, benefits to consumers in Romania and to the Romanian economy should increase in all three sectors. Throughout the project, we have tried to identify the sources of those benefits and, where possible, provide quantitative estimates. More specifically, if our recommendations are implemented, the OECD has calculated a positive effect on the Romanian economy of around

EUR 434 million. This estimated amount stems from a small number of issues which we were able to quantify, so that the final benefits from full implementation could be larger.

In addition, the rationalisation of the body of legislation in these sectors will also positively affect the ability of businesses to compete in the longer term, provided that the recommendations are implemented fully. As a result, we consider that the cumulative, long-term impact on the Romanian economy of lifting all the restrictions identified as harmful, including those that were more technical in nature, will be significant. In this report we do not attempt to estimate this effect.

Key recommendations by sector

Construction

- Draft application guidelines for those legal provisions from procurement legislation, which are currently applied discretionarily by the contracting authorities and reduce the number of participants in public tenders;
- Apply the tender procedure for the concession of terrains to developers building houses for young people under the age of 35, to reduce the risk of differential treatment of competing developers;
- Abolish the maximum prices for sand and gravel;
- Exempt from the obligation to obtain a building permit all stalls which are directly affixed to the ground, without foundations or platforms and that only need to be supplied with electricity;
- Remove the national interdiction to execute construction or maintenance works in the coastal areas of the Black Sea, in seaside resorts and the area of tourist beaches, between 15 May and 15 September;
- Implement a code of conduct to eliminate conflicts of interest when professional associations are involved in the decision-making process and control the activity of public authorities;
- Abolish outdated restrictions with respect to the location of professional schools or medical centres;

Freight transport

- Abolish unnecessary authorisations identified in the road freight sector, such as the authorisation to repair, adjust, reconstruct and dismantle vehicles and the certificate of professional competence for "abnormal load transport" (transport of goods with vehicles exceeding the applicable dimension and/or weight limits) drivers.
- Abolish the requirement for road transport freight operators to display on their vehicles a plate containing information on the dimensions and maximum weight authorised for the vehicle.
- Modify the requirements for obtaining a copy of the transport licence.
- Modify unclear provisions regarding access to railway infrastructure and the independence of the infrastructure manager in order to prevent possible discrimination of CFR SA against private operators.
- All tariffs set by the port authorities should be supervised and approved *ex ante* by an independent regulatory body.

- Port safety services, such as pilotage and towage, should not be granted directly by the port authority, but instead they should be tendered in an open and transparent procedure.

Food processing

- Eliminate 10 m^2 minimum areas in stores for the sale of bread and grant operators greater flexibility with respect to the conditions in which they sell bread, so long as they can ensure food safety.
- Apply rules concerning staff training.
- Review licence regimes in order to provide clear deadlines by which authorities must decide on applications for licences, and to ensure that the process of reviewing licence applications is free from potential conflict of interest.
- Review control regimes to eliminate double controls by different authorities.
- Clarify ambiguous legislative provisions to remove uncertainty for market operators and reduce the potential for arbitrary decisions and corruption.
- Repeal outdated legislation, especially domestic rules that are redundant in the light of EU regulations with the same regulatory content that became effective when Romania joined the European Union.

Chapter 1

Assessment and recommendations

This assessment identifies distortions to competition in Romanian legislation and proposes recommendations for the removal of regulatory barriers to competition in three key areas of the Romanian economy: construction, freight transport and food processing. The 227 potential regulatory restrictions that were identified were analysed, and the report makes 152 specific recommendations. Among the benefits from increased competition will be lower prices and greater choice and variety for consumers as a result of entry of new, more efficient firms or from new forms of production in existing firms. This report identifies the sources of those benefits and, where possible, provides quantitative estimates. If the particular restrictions that have been quantified are lifted and the expected effects are realised, the OECD has calculated a positive effect for the Romanian economy of around EUR 434 million.

The Romanian Competition Assessment of Laws and Regulations project has identified and evaluated regulatory barriers in the sectors of construction including public procurement, freight transport and food processing, and pinpoints the necessary steps required to remove these restrictions in order to stimulate the emergence of a more competitive environment for Romanian businesses. This section outlines some of the key economic benefits that arise from competition. It then summarises the main recommendations for regulatory change and their expected benefits, both to the Romanian consumer and to the Romanian economy.

1.1. The benefits of competition

One of the main reasons to pursue pro-competitive regulatory reforms is to benefit the economy. When customers can choose between different providers of goods they benefit, and so does the economy as a whole. Their ability to choose forces firms to compete with each other. Choice and variety for consumers is a good thing in itself but, most importantly, firms that operate in competitive markets experience faster productivity growth than firms in less competitive environments. Although it is hard to measure the effect of, for example, changes in competition law on economic growth, there is solid evidence in support of each of the relationships shown below.

This has been confirmed in a large number of empirical studies, both on an industry and on a firm level.

Figure 1.1. **Competition and growth**

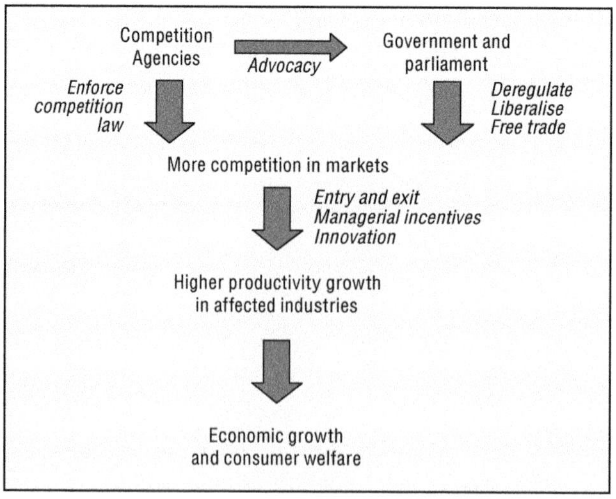

Source: OECD (2013), *Factsheet on Competition and Growth*, OECD Working Party 2 on Competition and Regulation.

Improving productivity on a widespread scale enhances economic growth. Other benefits from competition can also be important. These include lower consumer prices, greater consumer choice and better quality of products and services, more employment, greater investment in R&D, and faster adoption of innovations by firms that are close to the technology frontier.

The primary reason that competition stimulates productivity seems to be that it allows more efficient firms to enter and gain market share at the expense of less efficient firms. Increased productivity from competition may arise as a result of both static and dynamic gains. Static gains follow from eliminating inefficiencies as the monopolists facing competitive pressures cease to live the "comfortable life". Dynamic efficiency improvements arise, for example, because competition improves the ability of owners or the financial market to monitor managers, by enhancing opportunities for comparing performance, enhancing the incentive to innovate to gain market share or because competition leads managers to work harder to maintain profits (Nicoletti and Scarpetta, 2003).

The productivity impact of competitive rivalry has been studied empirically with event studies of large regulatory changes, analyses of cross-country or cross-sectoral regulatory differences and their impact on competition or productivity, and detailed firm-level analyses of productivity. In all these studies, there is ample evidence that productivity increases when competitive forces are augmented.

Box 1.1. **Empirical evidence for productivity gains from lifting regulatory barriers to competition**

In Australia, broad efforts to revise laws to promote competition, which took place in the 1990s, have delivered significant benefits. In 2005 the Productivity Commission examined the effects of selected pro-competitive reforms and calculated that, by enhancing productivity in particular sectors, they had boosted Australia's GDP by about 2.5% above levels that would have otherwise prevailed. Moreover, those reforms examined were only a selection of all reforms, suggesting that the 2.5% figure is likely to be a conservative estimate (Sims, 2013; Productivity Commission, 2005). The studies on Australia are consistent with the positive relationship between competition policy and productivity. Sims (2013), the OECD (2006) and the Productivity Commission (2005) attribute Australia's performance turnaround to pro-competitive reforms, including those from the National Competition Policy's regulatory reviews as well as from other reforms, such as tariff reductions that increased international competition. Australia's productivity performance went from being one of the worst in the OECD to one of the top performers during the period of the National Competition Policy reforms.

Policies liberalising industries that were previously regulated monopolies (especially utilities) also provide clear natural experiments on the effects of competition. For example, in the US electricity industry, Fabrizio et al. (2004) find that private electricity generators facing competition had 5% higher productivity than privately-owned generators facing no competition. Cahuc and Kamarz (2004) find that after deregulating the road transport sector ("trucking") in France, employment levels in road transport increased at a much faster rate than before deregulation, with employment growth increasing from 1.2% per year between 1981 and 1985 to 5.2% per year between 1986 and 1990. Between 1976 and 2001, total employment in the road transport sector doubled, from 170 000 to 340 000.

Davies et al. (2004) note the significant price effects from deregulation that had the effect of introducing competition, such as the introduction of low-cost airlines within Europe.

Box 1.1. Empirical evidence for productivity gains from lifting regulatory barriers to competition *(cont.)*

Taking the opposite approach, Haskel and Sadun (2009) look at an increase in regulation, finding that increased regulation of retailing in the United Kingdom from 1996 reduced total factor productivity growth in retailing by about 0.4% per year. More generally, Cincera and Galgau (2005) find that tighter regulation that reduced entry into European markets raised mark-ups and lowered labour productivity growth.

Source: OECD compilation.

Direct measurement of the effects of competition

The conclusion that increased competition generates high productivity is supported by detailed studies of industries and individual firms. For example, Nickell (1996) states that the evidence he examined suggests that "competition, as measured by increased numbers of competitors or by lower levels of rents, is associated with a significantly higher rate of total factor productivity growth." Building upon and deepening Nickell's work, Disney, Haskell and Heden (2003) use data on 140 000 separate businesses and conclude that "market competition significantly raises both the level and growth of productivity". Blundell, Griffith and Van Reenen (1999), by examining a set of data on manufacturing firms in the United Kingdom, find a positive effect from product market competition on productivity growth.

OECD research has also provided substantial evidence that product market deregulation can result in increased growth. Mechanisms identified include shifting resources from less efficient to more efficient providers through the process of competition and lifting restrictive regulation that was holding back the take-up of information and communication technology (ICT) (Nicoletti and Scarpetta, ; Conway et al., 2006). Looking at 15 countries and 20 sectors, Bourlès et al. (2010) find that eliminating regulatory restrictions on competition in upstream sectors would enhance multi-factor productivity growth by 1% to 1.5% a year.

In a cross-country comparison of anti-competitive regulatory restrictions using the OECD's Product Market Regulation (PMR) index,[1] Arnold, Nicoletti and Scarpetta (2011) find that product market regulations that restrict competition are associated with reduced total factor productivity of firms. They sample evidence from 100 000 firms in 10 European countries, finding that anti-competitive regulations may particularly restrict the firms that are on a path to catching up with the most productive firms in their industry. Competition ensures that firms catch up more quickly to reach the technological frontier within their sector.

In Japan, work by Michael Porter and others demonstrated that it was those industries exposed to international competition that experienced rapid productivity growth, while those that operated in protected domestic markets stagnated. For example, Sakakibara and Porter (2001) conclude that "local competition – not monopoly, collusion or a sheltered home market – pressures dynamic improvement that leads to international competitiveness". Other economists have confirmed the findings. For example, Okada (2005) finds that "competition, as measured by lower level of industrial price-cost margin, enhances productivity growth, controlling for a broad range of industrial and firm-specific characteristics."

Ospina and Schiffbauer (2010) use firm-level observations from the World Bank Enterprise Survey database, and find that "countries that implemented product-market reforms had a more pronounced increase in competition, and correspondingly, in productivity: the contribution to productivity growth due to competition spurred by product-market reforms is around 12% to 15%".

A detailed study of management practices in more than 10 000 firms from 20 countries finds that those firms facing more product market competition have better management practices and, in turn, higher productivity. In high competition cases, firm management practices tended to be concentrated around best practices. In contrast, when competition was less intense, a "fat tail" of firms with poor management practices was found even while some firms were well managed. Competition is a mechanism that incites firms to improve their management practices (Bloom et al., 2012).

To sum up, anti-competitive regulations that hinder entry into and expansion in markets may be particularly damaging for the economy because they reduce pressures to increase productivity and ultimately limit economic growth. Revising regulations to ensure they are pro-competitive, and lifting any barriers identified, can unleash rivalry that makes firms become more productive and, when widespread, can generate aggregate increases in economic growth.

Removing regulatory barriers to competition was the overall aim of the competition assessment project carried out by the OECD with the support of the Romanian Competition Council (RCC). The rest of the chapter outlines the main findings from the project.

1.2. Key findings from the Competition Assessment project in Romania

The main aim of the Competition Assessment of Laws and Regulations in Romania project is to improve competition in three sectors of the Romanian economy – construction, freight transport and food processing – through the removal of regulatory barriers. These three sectors had a combined gross value added (GVA) of 12.4% (construction: 6.29%[2] [total NACE group F], Transport: 5.08%, Food processing: 0.98%[3]) of GDP by output in 2014 (2013 for Food processing as it is the last available year).

In 2014 freight transport generated a turnover of approximately 5.08% of GDP (by output), whereas transport, including passengers, generated a GVA of 5.11% of Romania's GDP (GDP by GVA).

These three sectors represented 401 281 jobs (Construction: 111 568 jobs[4] in selected subsectors of NACE groups F and B, Transport: 133 100 jobs, Food processing[5] 156 613 jobs[6] or 10.3% of total employment in Romania in 2014 (the total number of employees in Romania in 2014 was 3 887 461, of which 401 281 were in the three analysed sectors[7]). Lifting the restrictions to competition in these sectors is therefore likely to have a significant positive economic impact, both in the short term and in the long term.

The outcomes discussed in this section were reached by identifying regulatory barriers to competition, assessing their impact in terms of harm to competition, and suggesting specific recommendations to lift the restrictions. This is not an economic impact assessment. It is a methodical analysis of the legislative texts related to the sectors under analysis.

The work has led to the identification of **227** regulatory restrictions found in the original 895 legal texts selected for assessment. In total, the report makes **152 specific recommendations** to mitigate harm to competition. These are all available in Annex B to this report.

Table 1.1. **Legal provisions analysed by sector**

	Construction	Freight transport	Food processing
Legislation scanned	162	566	167
Prima facie restrictions found	95	85	47
Recommendations made	**72**	**46**	**34**

Source: OECD analysis.

1.3. Main restrictions identified and recommendations

Below we briefly summarise the restrictions found, as well as our main recommendations in the construction, freight transport and food processing sectors. Those will be discussed in detail in the specific chapters.

Construction

The construction sector is of high importance in the development of the Romanian economy, as it generated a GVA of EUR 9.4[8] billion (total NACE group F) in 2014, representing 6.29% of Romanian GDP in 2014 and employing approximatively 1 115 000 people in the same year[9] (selected subsectors of NACE groups F and B). Of the total turnover generated in 2014 by the companies that are active in this sector (selected subsectors of NACE groups F and B), 66.7% was generated by the construction of roads and railways subsector, 17.0% by the construction of utility projects subsector and the rest of 16.2% by the construction of other civil engineering projects subsector.

The main issues and recommendations in the construction sector are as follows:

- **Limitation of the number of participants in public tenders.** A smaller number of participants in tenders reduces competition and leads to higher prices for the contracting authorities. We identified several provisions which, if applied discretionarily by the contracting authorities, might limit the number of participants in public tenders. Such restrictions include the possibility of starting negotiations without prior publication of the participation notice, the limitation of participants to public procedures based on prior experience, and setting deadlines for submitting the tenders at the minimum threshold provided by the law which might be too short in case of more complex projects. These issues arise not from the legislation but from the practice of the contracting authority, due to the broad discretion they are granted by the law. Our recommendation is to draft guidelines to give market participants and contracting authorities a sufficient level of predictability and transparency with respect to the application of legal provisions. A lower award price may lead to savings of approximately EUR 418 million.
- **Provisions in construction legislation derogating from procurement legislation.** We identified various provisions granting exceptions to procurement legislation, such as that no tender procedure is needed for the concession of terrains to developers building houses for young people under the age of 35 or in order to lease private terrains owned by public authorities if they are to be used by the initial owner of a building for extending the existing building on nearby terrains. We recommend abolishing these exceptions and applying the usual tender procedure.
- **Maximum prices for gravel and sand** are set by the Ministry of Finance (MoF) for each individual producer and are adjusted yearly based on a consumer price index. We recommend abolishing the maximum price for sand and gravel as it might lead to horizontal effects of producers aligning to the maximum price.

- **Unclear provisions that give unguided discretion for public authorities.** We found several provisions in Romanian legislation that do not contain definitions of important notions and leave far-reaching discretion to the public authorities without any guidelines. These provisions allow authorities to discriminate between competitors, giving some of them cost advantages over others which might lead to an unpredictable business environment for private investors. Such provisions include the manner of granting parking places on public land or the manner in which the State Construction Inspectorate (SCI) carries out its control activity. We recommend defining and clarifying these provisions.
- **Street sale through stalls.** Construction works for placing stalls, without foundations or platforms and which only need to be supplied with electricity, for the distribution and trading of newspapers, books and flowers are exempted from the obligation to obtain a building permit. Restricting the products that vendors are allowed to sell in stalls may potentially limit the development of businesses and consumer choice. We recommend extending the exemption to all such stalls independently of their purpose.
- **Construction works in coastal areas.** Currently, it is forbidden to execute construction or maintenance works between 15 May and 15 Septembers in the coastal areas of the Black Sea, in seaside resorts and areas of tourist beaches. By applying automatically, without a prior assessment, irrespective of the execution period, location, risk of adverse health and safety of persons made by the local public authority, this interdiction interferes with the business activity of undertakings. We recommend abolishing this provision. Any temporal restrictions to build should be decided at a local community level.
- **Conflict of interests likely.** We identified various provisions which might lead to potential conflicts of interest between competing undertakings (or potential competitors), mainly due to the involvement of professional associations in the decision-making process of the competent public authorities. For example, members of professional associations collaborate with the public authorities, providing technical expertise, and thus contributing to the decisions undertaken by the authorities. Members of professional associations may even control the activity of other competitors, by being subsequently involved in the controls carried out by the SCI. The same issue arises with respect to the composition of the Standing Technical Council for Construction (CTPC), where competitors are in a position to decide on their competitors' activities. We recommend establishing a complete, clear and accessible set of conflict rules to be followed by professional associations. The implementation of an ethical code of conduct should be mandatory for each professional association involved in decisions made by public bodies. Also, the legislation should be amended by mentioning independence rules so as to avoid possible conflict of interest.
- **Obsolete legislation.** We found two types of obsolete legislation: Some restrictions have been superseded by more recent legislation but have not been explicitly removed from the body of legislation. Another type of obsolete legislation contains restrictions that are outdated by nature, but are still formally in force. Among these are: professional schools have to be built within 1 000 metres (m) of a housing area, medical assistance for chronic diseases should be located outside town areas, regardless of the type of disease. The OECD recommends that all such provisions should be abolished or, where new legislation has been enacted, to specifically repeal the outdated provisions.

- **Environmental law.** The issues identified in this field arise from a lack of clear national guidelines and rules, especially with regard to the wide discretion granted to the environmental authorities in the authorisation process of the economic operators subject to the industrial emissions legislation. For example, environmental authorities may impose stricter authorisation conditions for the economic operators in the field of industrial emissions than the ones established as best practice at the European level but without clear guidelines as to when this can be done. We recommend drafting guidelines in order to provide authorities with clear criteria for the application of the identified provisions.

The full analysis and recommendations for the construction sector including public procurement are set out in Chapter 2.

Freight transport

Freight transport plays an important role in the Romanian economy, generating a turnover of approximately 5% of gross domestic product in 2014 and employing around 133 000 people. The modal split of freight transport in 2014 in terms of volume was 60.9% for road, 16.2% for rail, 13.9% for maritime, 8.89% for inland waterways and 0.01% for air. Romania's indicator for road transport in the OECD Product Market Regulation indicator shows that it is one of the most regulated in the European Union, while Romania's rail transport is one of the most liberalised rail transport markets.

The main issues and recommendations in the transport sector are as follows:

Road transport

- **Authorisations.** We found various authorisations that may unnecessarily limit the number of operators and may increase costs. For example, the authorisation for repairing, adjusting, reconstructing and dismantling of vehicles should be abolished. Instead, the garage should be checked by the Romanian Automotive Register (RAR) in order to prove that its manager possesses a certificate of professional studies or a degree issued by the RAR and that its employees have certificates of professional studies.
- **Local taxes.** Local authorities impose additional taxes for the use of national roads that cross municipalities and for the use of local and county roads they manage. These taxes generally lack transparency. Also, it is difficult for road freight transporters to pay such taxes, as currently there does not seem to be an efficient tax payment system in place. We recommend introducing an appropriate legal framework in order to ensure the transparency and efficiency of the payment system for local road taxes. A good measure might be the publication of all road taxes on the websites of the Ministry of Transport (MoT) and Ministry of Regional Development and Public Administration (MDRAP). Furthermore, an online payment system of taxes or a system which involves payment with mobile phones should be introduced.
- **Plates for trucks.** We recommend that the provision requiring road transport freight operators to display on their vehicles a plate containing information on the size and maximum weight authorised for the vehicle to be abolished. Instead, compliance of the transport operators with the rules on weight and dimensions can be achieved through documentation such as the vehicle identity card or the periodical technical inspection certificate, which should be carried by the vehicle driver. We estimate that the benefits for road freight transport operators of abolishing the plate requirement for vehicles with a maximum weight greater than 3.5 tonnes (t), would be approximately EUR 1.14 million a year.

- **Copy of transport licence.** Road transport operators must obtain a copy of the transport licence for each vehicle in their fleet, which must be renewed annually. We recommend that the provisions should be modified and the copy be issued for the same period of time as the duration of the licence to which it refers, i.e., 10 years. The benefits of freight transport operators from modifying the provision are estimated to be around EUR 7.1 million a year.

Rail transport

- **Access to railway infrastructure and the independence of the infrastructure manager.** We found various unclear provisions and a lack of definitions for relevant terms which might lead to discrimination against private operators. For example, for railway infrastructure capacity allocation, the relevant provision simply mentions that the Romanian railway company, CFR SA, has the right to reject a path allocation requested by railway operators when statistics related to freight transport operating on that route show an under-use below 20% for the timetable in place. Another provision refers to access to the railway infrastructure: when dealing with a request for access to some facilities and services, such as a power supply system, fuel supply, freight terminals, etc., the infrastructure manager CFR SA can reject such requests if there are alternative options in the market. These "alternative options" are not defined. We recommend that all these provisions shall be made clearer and definitions should be given to provide further guidance to railway operators.
- **No recommendation concerning CFR Marfă's privatisation.** Privatisation may represent the best opportunity to address issues of possible discrimination because splitting ownership of the infrastructure manager and the rail freight operator would eliminate any incentives for CFR SA to favour its affiliated freight rail company, CFR Marfă. However, there is no clear conclusion in the existing economic literature on whether full vertical separation is necessarily more suitable than other structural approaches and whether there is a one-size-fits-all solution. Nevertheless, evidence on rail freight privatisation seems to point in a positive direction.

Inland waterway and maritime freight transport

- **The lack of transparency in the calculation of tariffs** charged by port authorities may lead to abuses as there is a risk that the tariffs may be disproportionate to the economic value of the services provided. We recommend that port authorities set their charges based on a transparent cost-based approach. Furthermore, port authorities' autonomy in setting charges should be balanced by allowing an independent regulatory body the right to supervise these charges. For that, we recommend that an independent supervisory body approve *ex ante* all tariffs set by the port authorities.
- **Pilotage and towage services** should not be granted directly by the port authority, but instead they should be tendered in an open competitive procedure. The introduction of a more transparent procedure would ensure more reliable, better quality services for freight shippers and lower costs for the port authority, which is the contracting authority for these services. We estimate that the introduction of tendering procedures in granting the right of operating pilotage and towage services by the port authority to economic operators would generate savings for the port authority and further for freight shippers, if the port authority passes on the savings to its customers, of approximately EUR 6.5 million a year.

- Moreover, the provisions requiring a certain number of pilots or tugboats should be abolished. The law should not impose a minimum number of pilots or tugboats per port, but instead require a minimum service level, such as a maximum ship waiting time. The required service level must also be transparent, non-discriminatory, objective and relevant to the category and nature of the port services concerned.
- **Lack of transparency and unguided discretion.** We found several provisions in Romanian law that grant significant discretion to the Romanian Naval Authority (ANR) when carrying out its tasks. These provisions may lead to discrimination between market participants. For example, the provisions regarding the compliance of Romania with its flag state obligation should be modified in order to state the activities that the ANR is entitled to carry out in order to verify compliance with safety rules by Romanian vessels. Also, we found that the powers of the ANR to suspend or to withdraw the licence of a supplier of liquid fuels for travel by sea may lead to more advantageous treatment of some bunkering companies. We recommend the relevant provision be amended in order to clearly establish the instances in which a warning is proportional and adequate, as well as the instances that require the suspension or withdrawal of the company's authorisation.

The full analysis and recommendations for the freight transport sector are set out in Chapter 3.

Food processing

The food processing sector generated a GVA of EUR 1.4 billion in 2013. This represents approximately 1% of total GVA across all economic sectors in Romania, and approximately 10% of the GVA generated by the manufacturing sector. Processing and preserving of meat, bakery and farinaceous products, and dairy products are the most significant subsectors, representing a combined output of approximately 65% of total sector output. Since the financial crisis in 2008/09, the sector has undergone significant restructuring and increased productivity, as the number of firms as well as the number of employees have decreased, while revenues recovered after a sharp drop and today exceed 2008 levels. Despite this trend toward consolidation, the sector remains fragmented. The top 10 firms represent approximately one-third of the sector's total revenues.

The Food processing sector also represents an important activity of the Romanian economy. In 2014, the sector employed a total of 156 613 people.[10] From the total GVA generated in the sector in 2013, 31.5% came from the processing and preserving of meat and production of meat products activity (EUR 0.44 billion), 25.5% from the manufacture of bakery and farinaceous products (EUR 0.36 billion), 12.0% from the manufacture of other food products activity (EUR 0.17 billion) and 10.3% from the manufacture of dairy products (EUR 0.14 billion).

Compared with other EU Member States, food prices in Romania are quite low. Household consumption expenditure for food items in absolute terms is among the lowest among all EU Member States. However, in terms of percentage of total household expenditure, households in Romania spend a higher share on food products than households in any other EU Member State. Thus, even moderate efficiency gains that could result from regulatory reforms in this sector would provide measurable benefits to Romanian households and could benefit the less well off in particular.

The main recommendations in the food processing sector are as follows:

- **Modalities of sale and food preparation.** We found various provisions in Romanian law and regulations limiting the production or sale of food products. For example, bakery products must be sold in specially designated, separated areas of stores that, as regards bread, must be at a minimum 10 m^2. Such restrictions impose costs on market participants and can create entry barriers for new players. We recommend amending existing rules to grant operators greater flexibility with respect to selling conditions, so long as food safety can be ensured.
- **Staff Training.** We identified one instance where Romanian law imposes training and examination requirements for all staff handling food products. Staff qualifications must be attested by a certificate issued after completion of a training course and passing of an exam. The course and exam, which costs approximately EUR 20 per person, must be repeated every three years. These rules impose costs on market participants including not only the fees for course and examination but also the costs of absent personnel that go beyond what appears necessary to attain the legitimate policy goals of ensuring a high level of food safety. We recommend applying these rules in a more targeted fashion only to those employees that could in fact pose risks to food safety because they come into direct contact with foodstuffs. We have estimated that excluding personnel which are not involved in activities that imply direct contact with foods (such as technical and administrative personnel), would result in a total cost saving of between EUR 0.53 million and EUR 0.73 million annually
- **Licensing requirements.** We found several instances where market operators must obtain licences before they take up activities, and the conditions under which such licences can be granted can lead to a restriction of competition. This includes, for example, instances where licences must be obtained from state authorities, but regulations do not clearly spell out by when the authorities must act on the application of a licence. This also includes the situation where a licence for operators of storage facilities for edible seeds that is required to obtain deposit certificates must be approved by a commission where the incumbent operators (who would compete with the new licence holder) represent more than half of the commission members. In such a situation, decisions may reflect the interests of incumbents rather that the public interest in creating liberal market access. We recommend reviewing licence regimes in order to provide for clear deadlines by which authorities must decide on applications for licences, and to ensure that the process of reviewing licence applications is free from potential conflicts of interest.
- **Control regimes.** We found several instances where control regimes concerning operators in the food processing sector can harm competition. These include controls for compliance with the same legal requirements by two different authorities that may use different standards to assess legal compliance and control regimes or that use unclear terms and therefore create unnecessary uncertainty for market players. It also includes rules concerning the inspection of food products on the Romanian border, where in practice the authorities require importers to keep their goods in (more expensive) refrigerated trucks for several days while the analysis of food products is carried out. These control regimes impose costs on market players. We recommend amending control regimes to eliminate costs for market players that are not necessary to achieve the policy goals related to the control of food products.

- **Discrimination based on nationality.** We identified one instance where Romanian laws related to the testing of animal feeds impose higher costs on importers than on domestic producers. This situation results in discrimination of certain market players and could be an entry barrier for foreign producers. We recommend eliminating the discrimination of importers of animal feed products.
- **Rules encouraging competitor collaboration.** We found one instance in which rules concerning voting rights in milk producer associations which may encourage association members to exchange commercially sensitive information about each individual member's milk production or production capacity. Exchanging this information may help members to reach an understanding of how future production should be allocated among them, or it could be used to monitor compliance with an already established understanding of how production should be allocated among members. We recommend amending association rules so that voting shares are established in light of historic production data, and that only the association has access to individual member production information.
- **Ambiguity in legislative provisions.** We have identified instances where rules related to the handling and selling of food products include unnecessarily ambiguous terms. Frequently, the norms seek to establish exceptions for smaller operators from generally applicable rules for the relevant sector. They therefore pursue the legitimate policy goal of avoiding an unnecessary regulatory burden on small market players as the risk to public health posed by small operators is limited. However, ambiguity in rules creates uncertainty for operators as the scope of the rules remains unclear and leaves unnecessary discretion to the authorities and, in the worst case, may encourage corruption. We recommend amending existing laws and regulations to use clear legal terms and to remove uncertainty for market operators.
- **Outdated legislation.** We have found several instances in which rules contained in domestic legislation are redundant in light of EU regulations with the same regulatory content that became effective when Romania joined the European Union. The domestic rules typically predate EU accession. We recommend abolishing redundant domestic norms to create greater legal certainty.

The full analysis and recommendations for the food processing sector are set out in Chapter 4.

1.4. Quantification of the recommendations

It was not possibly to quantify the effects of all the restrictions identified, either because of a lack of data, or because of the nature of the regulatory change. However, it is clear from the above that the ramifications for the Romanian economy in terms of long-term positive economic effects on productivity and growth will be significant, provided all the recommendations are implemented in full.

More specifically, if the particular restrictions that have been identified during the project and quantified are lifted, the OECD has calculated a positive effect for the Romanian economy of around EUR 434 million. This amount stems from a few issues that we were able to quantify – in other words, the full effect on the Romanian economy is likely to be even larger. The amount is the total of the estimated resulting positive effects on consumer surplus in the sectors analysed as a result of removing current regulatory barriers to competition.

Although only a small number of the restrictions could be fully quantified, we consider that the cumulative, long-term impact on the Romanian economy of lifting all of the restrictions identified as harmful, including those that were more technical in nature (for instance, regulations on foodstuffs), should not be underestimated. The rationalisation of the body of legislation in these sectors will also positively affect the ability of businesses to compete in the longer term, provided that the recommendations are implemented fully. Finally, by removing obsolete or redundant legislation, investors face a more transparent and less uncertain business environment.

Table 1.2 below summarises the quantifiable effects of lifting the regulatory barriers to competition for selected obstacles.

Table 1.2. **Synthesis of positive effects quantified by item**

Sector	Number of provisions affected	Consumer benefit/year
Construction/ public procurement	8	418.0
Estimated effect of stimulating an average of one additional acceptable bid per procurement procedure		418.0
Freight transport	**9**	
Plates	1	1,1
Copy of licence	1	7,1
Breaking energy	1	0.9
Pilotage services	2	3.4
Towing services	2	3.1
Waybills and registers of input-output wood material	2	0.3
Food processing	**1**	
Staff qualification	1	0.7
Total	18	434

Note: Some of the issues identified and analysed are related to the expected consumer benefit included in the table. The expected consumer benefit of EUR 418 million reflects the effect of stimulating, on average, one additional accepted bid in every procurement procedure.

1.5. Conclusion: Overall benefits from removing the regulatory barriers to competition

The present chapter summarises the main findings and recommendations resulting from the analysis of almost 900 legal provisions. If our recommendations are fully implemented, benefits to consumers in Romania and to the Romanian economy should arise in all three sectors, and throughout the economy as a whole through dynamic effects.

Throughout this report, we have sought to identify the sources of those benefits and, where possible, provide quantitative estimates. Because the benefits of competition arise from innovative actions by many private sector agents – perhaps not even operating in the market just now – any such estimates are highly uncertain and must be regarded as providing, at best, orders of magnitude for the likely effects. Moreover, the aim of the report is to assess the harm to competition, and the expected benefits to consumers from lifting barriers. It was not always possible to quantify the effects of lifting all the restrictions because in many cases it was not possible to measure them. Out of the small number of issues we were able to quantify we find total effects in the range of **EUR 434 million**, arising from efficiency gains and lower prices on goods and services for consumers. But the positive effects on the Romanian economy over time are likely to be far greater.

Such benefits generally take the form of lower prices and greater choice and variety for consumers. Often this will result from the entry of new, more efficient firms, or from existing suppliers finding more efficient forms of production under competitive pressure. As noted earlier, more competitive markets result in faster productivity growth over a longer timescale, but we do not attempt to estimate this effect.

The rest of this report describes the results of the assessment in the three sectors. For each of the provisions or groups of provisions that were identified as potentially harmful, the report describes the nature of the restriction, the harm it causes to competition, the policymakers' objective and the recommendations and associated benefits that the OECD has identified.

Annex A to the report describes in detail the methodology followed in the process, both to screen the laws and regulations, and also to assess the harm to competition from the restrictions, as well as the benefits to the Romanian economy and to consumers from removing the barriers to competition.

Annex B to the report provides, line by line, a summary of all the regulations identified, to help the reader identify the law or article that was analysed, as well as a summary description of all the analyses carried out.

Notes

1. The OECD Indicators of Product Market Regulation (PMR) are a comprehensive and internationally comparable set of indicators that measure the degree to which policies promote or inhibit competition in areas of the product market where competition is viable. They measure the economy-wide regulatory and market environments in 30 OECD countries in (or around) 1998, 2003 and 2008, and in another four OECD countries (Chile, Estonia, Israel and Slovenia) as well as in Brazil, China, India, Indonesia, Russia and South Africa around 2008; they are consistent across time and countries. More information is available at: *www.oecd.org/eco/reform/indicatorsofproductmarketregulationpmr.htm.*
2. This includes total NACE group F (Romanian National Institute of Statistics, *http://statistici.insse.ro/shop/index.jsp?page=tempo3&lang=en&ind=CON104H* (accessed on 11 February 2016) and Deloitte calculations.
3. Source: Eurostat, codes: sbs_na_ind_r2 and nama_gdp_c (accessed on 11 February 2016), and Deloitte calculations.
4. Source: Eurostat, codes: sbs_na_ind_r2 and nama_gdp_c (accessed on 11 February 2016), and Deloitte calculations.
5. Despite the fact that the Food Processing sector generates the highest turnover and employs the largest number of people of the three sectors presented in this report, Food Processing also has the smallest percentage contribution to GDP of the three in 2013 (0.98%). This is mainly because Food Processing is a low value added industry compared to other sectors of the economy. A large share of the turnover generated by the sector corresponds to intermediate consumption / purchase of inputs and therefore most of the value is transferred to input producers situated further up in the value chain of the food industry, including to agriculture.
6. Ibid.
7. ibid.
8. Romanian National Institute of Statistics, *http://statistici.insse.ro/shop/index.jsp?page=tempo3&lang=en&ind=CON104H* (accessed on 11 February 2016) and Deloitte calculations.
9. National Agency for Fiscal Administration (ANAF): *www.anaf.ro/indicatori/indfinanciari.html* (accessed on 16 March 2016) and Deloitte calculations.
10. ANAF, *www.anaf.ro/indicatori/indfinanciari.html* (accessed on 16 March 2016) and Deloitte calculations.

References

Arnold, J.M., G. Nicoletti and S. Scarpetta (2011), "Does Anti-Competitive Regulation Matter for Productivity? Evidence from European Firms", *IZA Discussion Paper* No. 5511, Institute for the Study of Labor, Bonn.

Bloom, N., C. Genakos, R. Sadun and J. van Reenen (2012), "Management practices across firms and countries", *Academy of Management Perspectives*, 26/1, pp. 12-33.

Blundell, R., R. Griffith and J. van Reenen (1999), "Market Share, Market Value and Innovation in a Panel of British Manufacturing Firms", *Review of Economic Studies*, Vol. 66, pp.529-554.

Bourlès, R. et al. (2010), "Do Product Market Regulations in Upstream Sectors Curb Productivity Growth? Panel Data Evidence for OECD Countries", *Banque de France Working Paper* No. 283.

Cahuc, P. and F. Kramarz (2004), "De la précarité à la mobilité : vers une Sécurité sociale professionnelle", report to ministre de l'Économie, des Finances et de l'Industrie et au ministre de l'Emploi, du Travail et de la Cohésion sociale, France.

Cincera, M. and O. Galgau (2005), "Impact of market entry and exit on EU productivity and growth performance", *Economic Paper* No. 222, European Commission DG for Economic and Financial Affairs, Brusssels.

Conway, P. et al. (2006), "Regulation, Competition, and Productivity Convergence", *OECD Economics Department Working Paper* No. 509, OECD, Paris.

Davies, S. et al. (2004), "The Benefits from Competition: Some illustrative UK cases", *DTI Economics Paper* 9, UK Department of Trade and Industry. Available at: *www.berr.gov.uk/files/file13299.pdf.*

Disney, R., J. Haskell and Y. Heden (2003), "Restructuring and productivity growth in UK manufacturing", *The Economic Journal*, Vol. 113, pp. 666–694. *http://onlinelibrary.wiley.com/doi/10.1111/1468-0297.t01-1-00145/pdf*

Fabrizio, K., N. Rose and C. Wolfram (2004), "Does Competition Reduce Costs? Assessing the Impact of Regulatory Restructuring On US Electric Generation Efficiency", Center for the Study of Electricity Markets, *Working Paper* 135R, University of California Energy Institute.

Haskel, J. and R. Sadun (2009), "Regulation and UK Retailing Productivity: Evidence from Microdata", *IZA Discussion Paper* No. 4028, Institute for the Study of Labor, Bonn.

Meyer, M. and J. Vickers (1997), "Performance Comparisons and Dynamic Incentives", *Journal of Political Economy*, 105/3, pp. 547-81.

Nickell, S. (1996), "Competition and Corporate Performance", *Journal of Political Economy*, 104/4, pp. 724-746. Available at: *www.jstor.org/stable/10.2307/2138883.*

Nicoletti, G. and S. Scarpetta (2003), "Regulation, Productivity and Growth: OECD Evidence," *Economic Policy*, 2003, Vol. 18, pp. 9-72.

OECD (2013), *Factsheet on Competition and Growth*, OECD Working Party 2 on Competition and Regulation, OECD Publishing, Paris. *www.oecd.org/officialdocuments/publicdisplaydocumentpdf/?cote=DAF/COMP/WP2(2013)11&docLanguage=En.*

OECD (2006), *OECD Economic Surveys: Australia 2006*, OECD Publishing, Paris, available at: *http://dx.doi.org/10.1787/eco_surveys-aus-2006-en.*

Okada, Y. (2005), "Competition and Productivity In Japanese Manufacturing Industries", *Journal of the Japanese and International Economies*, Vol. 19, pp. 586-616.

Ospina, S. and M. Schiffbauer (2010), "Competition and Firm Productivity: Evidence from Firm-Level Data", *IMF Working Papers*, 10/67, International Monetary Fund, Washington.

Productivity Commission (2005), *Review of National Competition Policy Reforms*, Inquiry Report No. 33.

Sakakibara, M. and M. Porter (2001), "Competing at home to win abroad: Evidence from Japanese Industry", *Review of Economics and Statistics*, 83/2, pp. 3310-322.

Sims, R. (2013), "Driving prosperity through effective competition", speech to The Mexico Forum, 8 January 2013, available at: *www.accc.gov.au/system/files/The%20Mexico%20Forum%202013%20-%20Driving%20prosperity%20through%20effective%20competition_0.pdf.*

Chapter 2

Construction

The Construction sector is important, both as the creator of infrastructure for other sectors and as a great source of employment (over 1.1 million people in 2014). It is also a major contributor of GVA (EUR 9.4 billion in 2014). Among its major constraints are unclear procurement practices with unguided discretion by public authorities, caps on prices for major components such as gravel and sand and constraints on specific types of business such as market stalls and tourist constructions. Potential conflict of interest with public authorities, obsolete legislation and laws that have not kept up with recent EU legislation, such as those governing the environment have also led to wide discretion granted to authorities.

2.1. Economic overview of the Romanian construction sector

General Overview

Definition of the relevant sectors and areas of investigation

The construction sector can be defined and segmented into submarkets using various criteria:

Statistical and financial definitions are largely related and rely on the European standard classification system (NACE) which groups all core construction activities under group F (consisting of F41 Construction of buildings, F42 Civil engineering and F43 Specialized construction). A number of construction-related activities which could be considered as part of the wider construction sector[1] fall outside the scope of NACE Group F but rather are dispersed into other NACE Groups such as B Mining and Quarrying, C Manufacturing, G Wholesale and Retail Trade or M Professional, Scientific and Technical Activities.

For the purpose of this study, **depending on the availability of information, report objectives and relevant market,** the analysis focusses on a list of NACE groups and codes which have been identified as relevant for each subsector analysed. An adapted business approach to defining the construction sector was used to define the relevant sectors/market according to the NACE classification.[2] This study will attempt to focus on the areas of interest consisting of NACE group F42 Civil Engineering[3] and its subsectors as well as identified subsectors relating to construction materials from groups B Mining and Quarrying and C Manufacturing.[4]

International Comparisons

According to the World Economic Forum, the *Global Competitiveness Report 2015-2016*, Romania is ranked 91st on the competitive index on quality of overall infrastructure, with a score of 3.6 on a scale from 1 to 7 (Table 2.1). Looking at the second pillar that is focussed specifically on infrastructure, on the quality of roads, Romania is in 120th place, and on the quality of railroad infrastructure in 62nd place.

In comparison with the other 27 EU countries (Figure 2.1, Figure 2.2 and Figure 2.3), Romania is placed last on the quality of overall infrastructure and the quality of railroad infrastructure, whereas the European leader is the Netherlands. On the quality of railroad infrastructure Romania is ranked as second-last in Europe, the country scoring the lowest in this area being Croatia; the European leader in this category is Spain.

Development of the constructions sector

The overall construction sector's importance for the Romanian economy is highlighted by the **gross value added** (GVA) of the sector (as a percentage of total gross domestic product [GDP]). From 2005 until 2007 construction intensified and the construction sector's contribution to GDP reached over 9%. However, the situation changed

Table 2.1. **Global Competitive Rank**[1]

Indicator	Rank of 144
Quality of infrastructure overall	91
Quality of roads	120
Quality of railroad infrastructure	62

1. The World Economic Forum calculated the scores for the above-mentioned indicators by sending a questionnaire to different respondents from all targeted countries. Respondents included companies from the main sectors of the economy (agriculture, manufacturing industry, non-manufacturing industry, and services), representing private, public and foreign companies. The companies include small companies (<50 employees), small-medium companies (50-150 employees), large-medium companies (151-1000 employees) and large companies (>1 000 employees). The respondents also include private, public and foreign companies. The respondents were asked to assess the quality of the overall infrastructure with the question: "How would you assess general infrastructure (e.g., transport, telephony and energy) in your country?", the quality of roads: "How would you assess the quality of roads?" and the quality of railroad infrastructure: "In your country, how would you assess the quality of the railroad system?" The respondents were given a range of scores for each question, from 1 (implying extremely underdeveloped – among the worst in the world) to 7 (meaning extensive and efficient – among the best in the world) and the final score for each indicator was calculated as a weighted average from the scores representing the responses.

Source: World Economic Forum, *Global Competitiveness Report* (2015-16), *http://reports.weforum.org/global-competitiveness-report-2015-2016/.*

Figure 2.1. **Global Competitive Index: Score for quality of overall infrastructure (2014)**

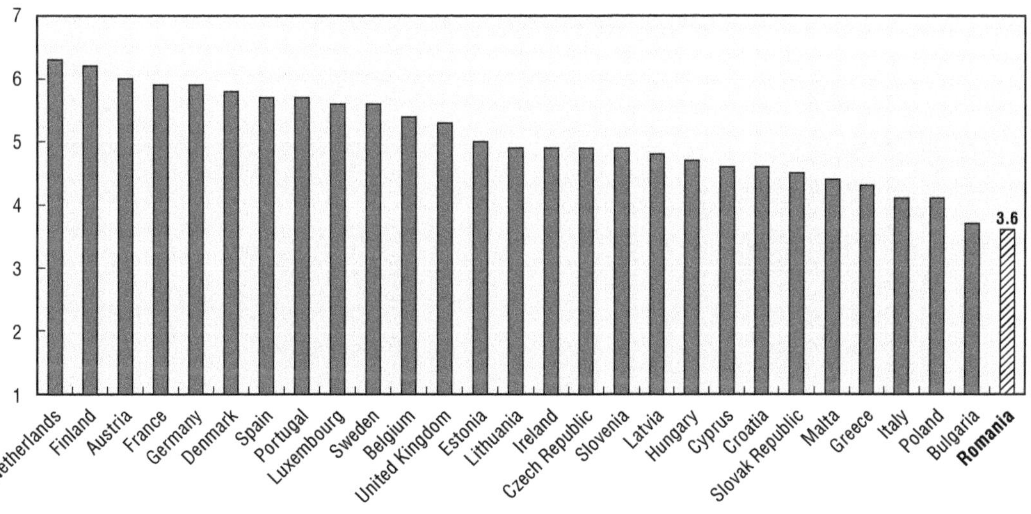

Source: World Economic Forum, Global Competitiveness Report (2015-16), *http://reports.weforum.org/global-competitiveness-report-2015-2016/.*

StatLink http://dx.doi.org/10.1787/888933361134

in 2008 as a consequence of the economic and financial crisis as a slowdown of the overall real estate business, adjustment in value of real estate and budget balance issues emerged. In 2009, however, the sector reached a peak in its contribution to national GDP (10.23%), but followed a decreasing trend the years after (until 2015).

The reduction of the GVA as a percentage of GDP was accompanied by a drop of revenues in the roads and railways sector, a decrease of fixed assets and a reduction in public spending in this sector (Coface, 2015). Even though the sector is still recovering and certain subsectors are still struggling to return to pre-crisis levels, others have seen **slow growth resuming in the last few years**.

Figure 2.2. **Global Competitive Index: Score for quality of roads (2014)**

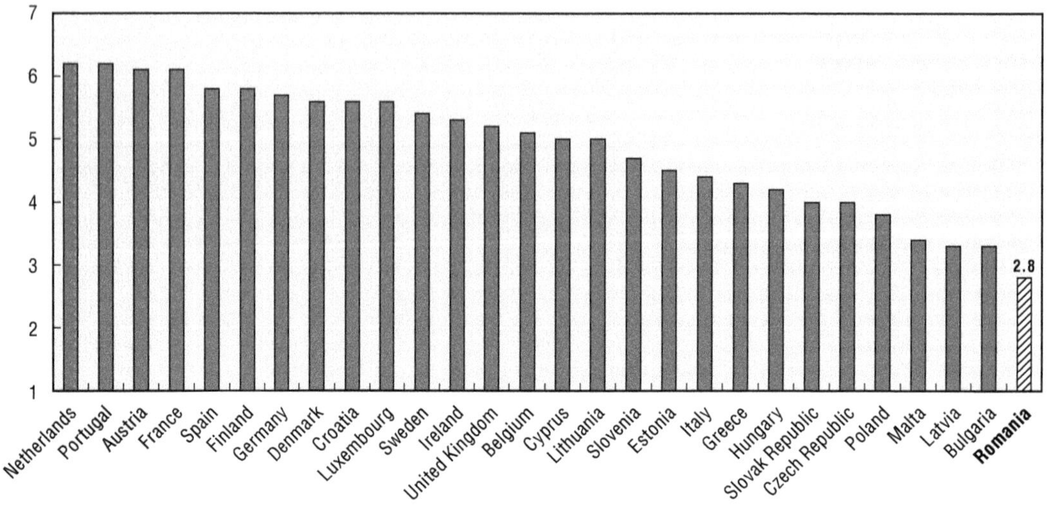

Source: World Economic Forum, *Global Competitiveness Report (2015-16)*, *http://reports.weforum.org/global-competitiveness-report-2015-2016/*.

StatLink http://dx.doi.org/10.1787/888933361142

Figure 2.3. **Global Competitive Index: Score for quality of railroad infrastructure (2014)**

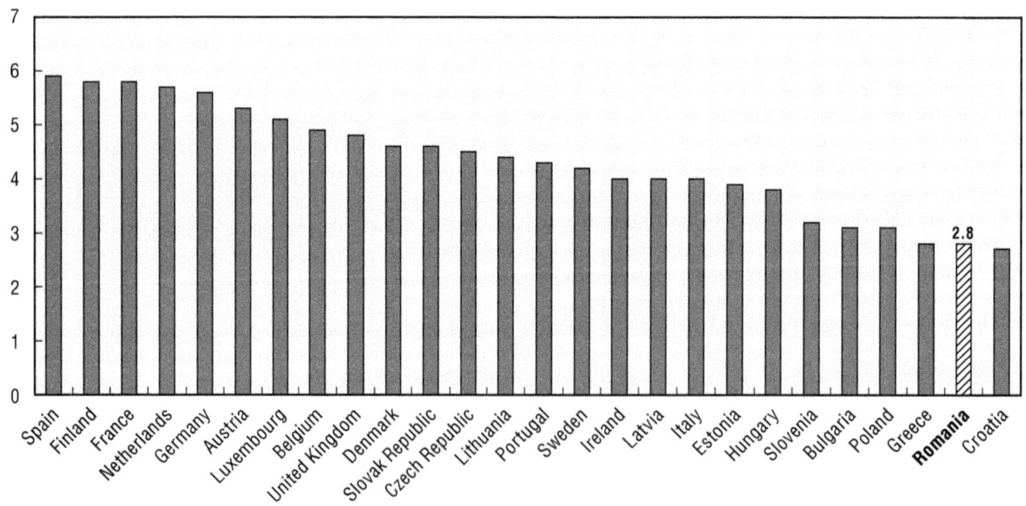

Source: World Economic Forum, *Global Competitiveness Report (2015-16)*, *http://reports.weforum.org/global-competitiveness-report-2015-2016/*.

StatLink http://dx.doi.org/10.1787/888933361155

The construction of roads and railways has seen a steady increase in the number of companies active on the market since 2010 but subsector turnover and number of employees only increased between 2010 and 2012 and contracted in 2013 (Figure 2.5).

The Construction of utility projects subsector was relatively stable from 2008 to 2013 but has seen slight improvements in turnover throughout the period. The Construction of other civil engineering projects subsector has seen the most dramatic continued decrease in numbers of companies, employees and turnover.

Figure 2.4. **Gross value added construction industry**

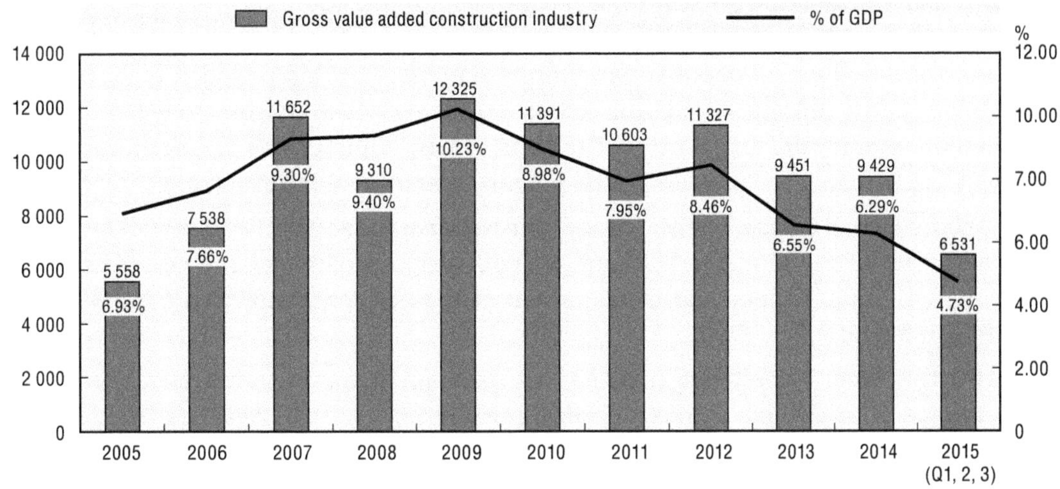

Source: National Institute of Statistics and Deloitte calculations.

StatLink http://dx.doi.org/10.1787/888933361162

Figure 2.5. **Evolution of main indicators in the civil engineering and construction materials industries**

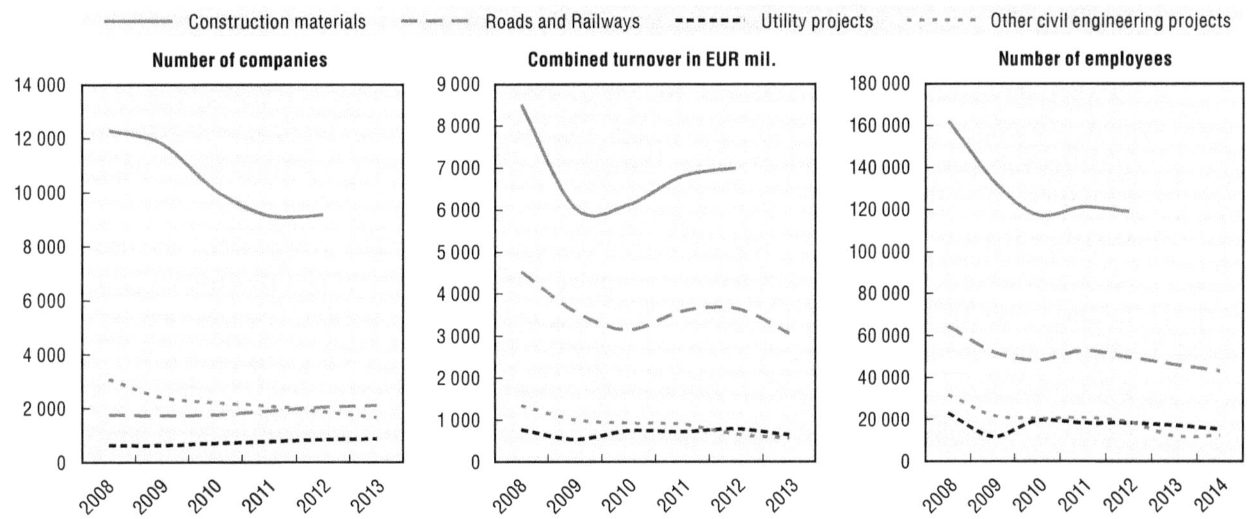

Source: ANAF.

StatLink http://dx.doi.org/10.1787/888933361175

Relevant government authorities and associations

In Romania the main government authorities involved in regulating, managing and supervising construction activity (including the area of construction materials) are the following:

- The ***Ministry of Regional Development and Public Administration*** (MDRAP) carries out, as appropriate, together with the line ministries, government policy in the following areas of activity: regional development, cohesion and spatial development, cross-border, transnational and interregional co-operation, discipline in construction, spatial planning, urban planning and architecture, habitation, housing, residential buildings, thermal rehabilitation of buildings, real estate and urban planning management and development, public works, construction, central and local public administration, decentralisation, reform and administrative-territorial reorganisation, taxation and regional and local public finance, dialogue with the associative structures of local public administration authorities, development of public community services, state aid provided to local public administration authorities, industrial parks, public service management, planning, co-ordination, monitoring and control of the use of non-reimbursable financial assistance provided to Romania by European Union programmes in its areas of activity[5].

- ***Romanian National Company of Motorways and National Roads*** (CNADNR) is working under the authority of the Ministry of Transport with responsibility for the administration, exploitation, maintenance and development of the national roads and motorways on Romanian territory;[6]
- ***Construction State Inspectorate*** (ISC) has as its main scope to verify and ensure the observance of applicable urban planning regulations and the legal requirements to assure the quality of construction work and materials.[7]
- The ***Ministry for Environment, Waters and Forests*** promotes a unitary, coherent environmental policy, setting itself some major targets to comply with the *acquis communautaire* for the environment, increasing energy efficiency, promoting the renewable sources of energy and the ecological rehabilitation of the historically polluted areas or coastal erosion.[8]
- ***Standing Technical Council for Construction*** (CTPC) is composed of qualified specialists who are part of organisations involved in introducing construction materials onto the market; its main responsibilities are: applying Romanian legislation in regard to *acquis communautaire* to construction materials, managing and supervising conformity certification of construction materials, managing and supervising technical agreement activity for construction and construction materials.[9]
- ***National Agency for Mineral Resources*** (ANRM) has as its main responsibilities the administration of hydrocarbon resources (petroleum and natural gas resources) and mineral resources (public property), concluding agreements for mining concessions, for petroleum extraction and exploitation permits and monitoring compliance with petroleum agreements and with permits and licences.[10]
- ***National Commission on Seismic Engineering*** is composed of technical experts and specialists in the construction domain. The main activities of the Commission are: it technically approves the recondition interventions on constructions considered vital for the society of which the functionality during and after an earthquake has to be fully assured, it approves the interventions for buildings considered as high seismic risk.[11]

The ***Social Dialogue Commission*** is part of the Ministry of Regional Development and Public Administration and has a consulting role. Its main responsibilities are to inform and consult its social partners about the legislative initiatives and to ensure social partnerships between the administration, employers' associations and trade unions (in order to ensure permanent communication of issues derived from the main activity of the Ministry of Regional Development and Public Administration).[12]

The industry players are organised in various associations, especially:

- Federation of Building Materials Industry (PATROMAT)
- Professional Association of Mineral Aggregates Producers (APPA)
- Romanian Construction Entrepreneurs Association (ARACO)

- Patronal Association of Constructors (PATROCONS)

In Europe, ***technical assessment bodies*** (TABs) are designated for technical assessment of construction materials and for issuing the **European Technical Assessment** (ETA). In Romania, the following institutions make up the TAB:

- **The National Institute for Research and Development in Construction, Urban Planning and Sustainable Spatial Development** "URBAN-INCERC"
- **The Research Institute for Construction Equipment and Technology** (ICECON)
- **The Research Institute for Transport** (INCERTRANS)

Moreover, the Body responsible for standardisation of construction in Romania is the ***Romanian Standards Association*** (ASRO) which is a non-governmental private legal entity of public interest. The main responsibilities of ASRO consist of developing, approving and managing documentation and editing, publishing and disseminating information related to national and international standards.[13]

The chart below describes the process and parties involved in issuing technical approvals and ETAs for construction materials:

Figure 2.6. **Relationship between several institutions for issuance of technical approvals and ETAs**

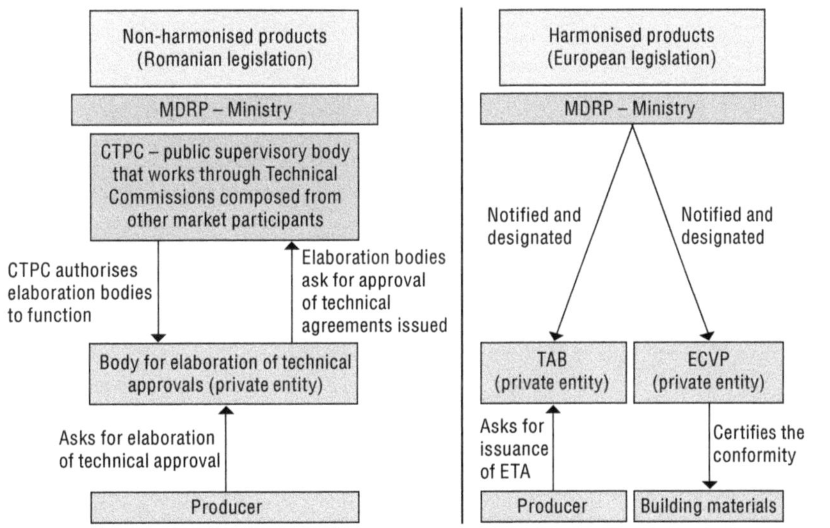

Source: Deloitte calculations.

Civil Engineering

Overview

The construction of roads and railways accounts for approximately 66.7% of the turnover of the overall civil engineering sector. In second place is the construction of utility projects with approximately 17% of turnover in the sector and the last contribution to the cumulated turnover is in construction of other civil engineering projects.

In the **Civil engineering** sector the supply generally consists of a diversified group of private companies, both Romanian owned and international, which often partner together and engage in subcontracting to execute complex projects. The following table presents the top ten companies in the civil engineering construction industry, in terms of 2014 turnover:

Table 2.2. **Structure of the civil engineering industry**

Sector	Code		Turnover 2014 (EUR mil.)
Construction of roads and railways	F 421	Abs.	2 564.31
		Percentage	*66.72%*
Construction of utility projects	F 422	Abs.	654.7
		Percentage	*17.04%*
Construction of other civil engineering projects	F 429	Abs.	624.24
		Percentage	*16.24%*
Total	F 42	*Abs.*	*3 843.25*
		Percentage	*100%*

Source: ANAF and Deloitte calculations.

Table 2.3. **Top 10 players in the civil engineering construction industry**

No.	Company	NACE Code	Description NACE	Turnover 2014 (EUR mil.)	Total market share 2014[1]
1	HIDROCONSTRUCTIA SA	F 4291	Construction of water projects	116.27	3.03%
2	DELTA ANTREPRIZA DE CONSTRUCTII SI MONTAJ 93 SRL	F 4211	Construction of roads and motorways	113.05	2.94%
3	SOCIETATEA FILIALA DE INTRETINERE SI SERVICII ENERGETICE "ELECTRICA SERV" S.A.	F 4222	Construction of utility projects for electricity and telecommunications	85.82	2.23%
4	TANCRAD SRL	F 4211	Construction of roads and motorways	70.14	1.82%
5	STRACO GRUP SRL	F 4211	Construction of roads and motorways	68.39	1.78%
6	FCC CONSTRUCCION SA BARCELONA SUCURSALA BUCURESTI	F 4211	Construction of roads and motorways	68.24	1.78%
7	TEHNOSTRADE SRL	F 4211	Construction of roads and motorways	66.06	1.72%
8	ELECTROMONTAJ SA	F 4222	Construction of utility projects for electricity and telecommunications	53.86	1.40%
9	EURO CONSTRUCT TRADING 98 SRL	F 4211	Construction of roads and motorways	53.30	1.39%
10	MAX BOEGL ROMANIA SRL	F 4211	Construction of roads and motorways	67.48	1.76%
TOTAL				***3 843.25***	***19.84%***

1. References to "market characteristics", "market shares" or "markets" in general, included in this report, do not reflect the same definitions used for purposes of applying competition law.

Source: ANAF, Credit Info and Deloitte calculations.

Table 2.3 demonstrates that the top ten companies in the industry account for approximately 20% of the total turnover generated in the entire civil engineering construction subsector, of which 13.18% comes from the Construction of roads and railways sector (more specifically, from the Construction of roads and motorways subsector), 3.63% from the utility construction sector (construction of utility projects for electricity and telecommunications subsector) and 3.03% from other civil engineering projects (however, this turnover comes from only one company).

Construction of roads and railways

Description of the subsector. The construction of roads and railways capitalises on sizable amounts allocated from the state budget and other financing sources (Competition Council, 2013), such as government loans, European funds and funds provided by international development organisations such as the European Bank for Reconstruction and Development (EBRD), the European Investment Bank (EIB), the European Investment Fund (EIF), the World Bank, etc. It is an auction market where companies have to participate in auctions organised by state authorities; the state accounts for most of the demand for these projects, and previous experience, recommendations and scale requirements for participating in auctions are requested by typical tender books. Complex projects spanning long periods of time expose the sector to delays and cancellations and lead to frequent subcontracting and/or partnering. The high cost of transportation of building materials favours local suppliers.

For the **Construction of roads and railways** subsector demand is generally represented either by the National Company of Motorways and National Roads of Romania (CNADNR), CFR SA (for railway infrastructure), local government or state owned public transportation companies (tram networks). Private sector demand for roads and railways is limited though there are infrequent small scale projects for private beneficiaries.

The main driver of demand for construction of roads and railways is government policy in the infrastructure/transportation sector – the pipeline of projects.

The total road network of Romania (Figure 2.7) increased by 4 469 km between 2007 and 2014 or 5.5% while the motorway network (Figure 2.8) increased by 402 km in the same interval – representing a growth of a 143%.

Figure 2.7. **Total length of road network in Romania (km)**

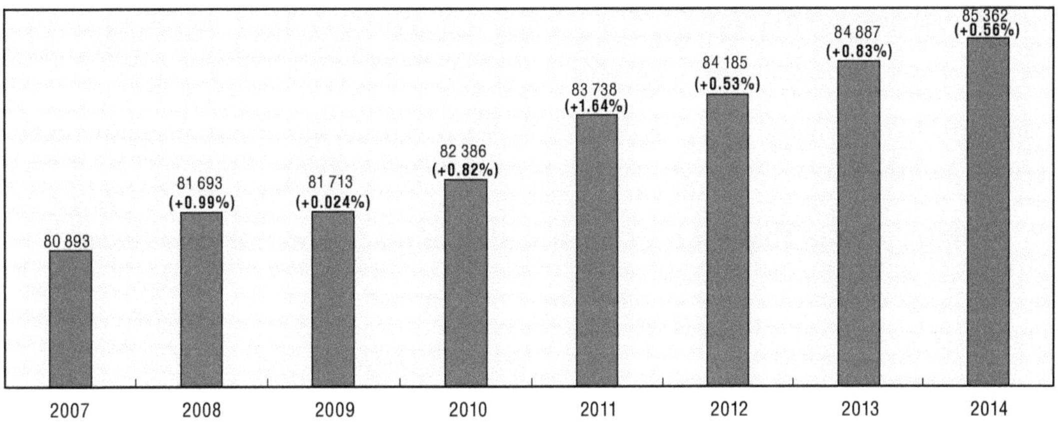

Source: National Institute of Statistics.

StatLink http://dx.doi.org/10.1787/888933361186

Figure 2.8. **Total length of motorway network in Romania (km)**

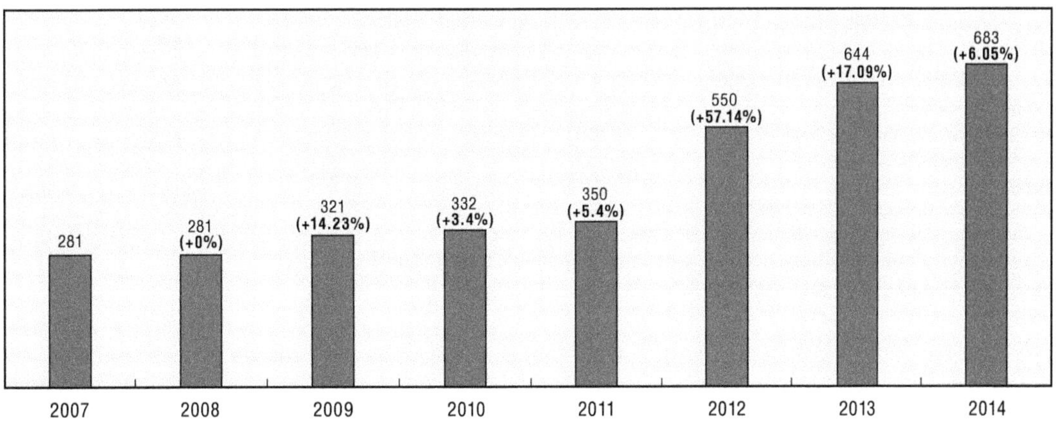

Source: National Institute of Statistics.

StatLink http://dx.doi.org/10.1787/888933361198

On the other hand, the length of railways in use (Figure 2.9) did not experience any changes from 2007 until 2014. Even if in some years there has been some variation in this indicator, in 2014 it returned to the same level as in 2007, namely 10 777 km of railways in use.

Figure 2.9. **Total length of railway network in use in Romania (km)**

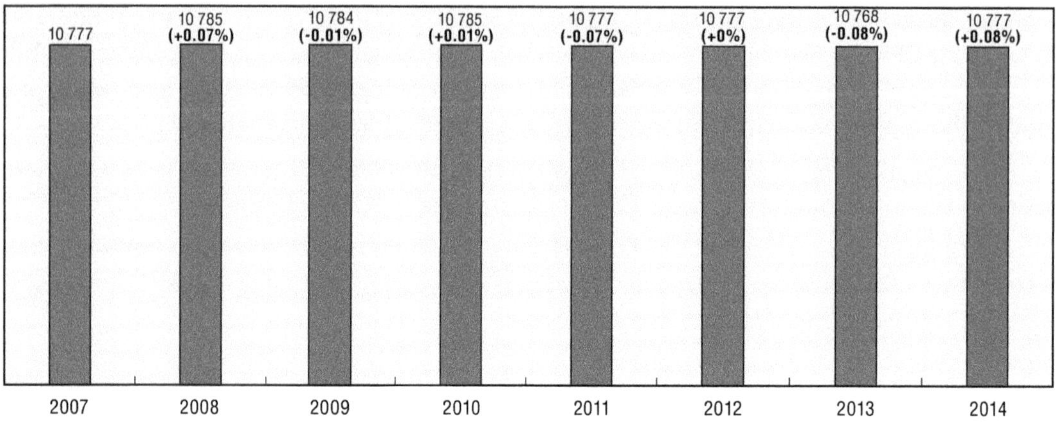

Source: National Institute of Statistics.

StatLink http://dx.doi.org/10.1787/888933361206

Subsector characteristics. The top ten companies in terms of turnover in the **Construction of roads and railways** sector[14] are presented in the following table:

Table 2.4. **Top 10 players in construction of roads and railways sector**

No.	Company	NACE Code	Description NACE	Turnover 2014 (EUR mil.)	Market share 2014[1]
1	DELTA ANTREPRIZA DE CONSTRUCTII SI MONTAJ 93 SRL	C 4211	Construction of roads and motorways	113.05	4.41%
2	TANCRAD SRL	C 4211	Construction of roads and motorways	70.14	2.74%
3	STRACO GRUP SRL	C 4211	Construction of roads and motorways	68.39	2.67%
4	FCC CONSTRUCCION SA BARCELONA SUCURSALA BUCURESTI	C 4211	Construction of roads and motorways	68.24	2.66%
5	TEHNOSTRADE SRL	C 4211	Construction of roads and motorways	66.06	2.58%
6	EURO CONSTRUCT TRADING 98 SRL	C 4211	Construction of roads and motorways	53.30	2.08%
7	MAX BOEGL ROMANIA SRL	C 4211	Construction of roads and motorways	50.98	1.99%
8	DIFERIT SRL	C 4211	Construction of roads and motorways	45.09	1.76%
9	ANTREPRIZA DE REPARATII SI LUCRARI A R L CLUJ SA	C 4211	Construction of roads and motorways	42.41	1.65%
10	IMPRESA PIZZAROTTI & C SPA ITALIA SUCURSALA CLUJ	C 4211	Construction of roads and motorways	40.20	1.57%
TOTAL				**617.86**	**24.09%**

1. References to "market characteristics", "market shares" or "markets" in general, included in this report, do not reflect the same definitions used for purposes of applying competition law.

Source: ANAF, Credit Info and Deloitte calculations.

The top ten[15] companies in the Construction of roads and railways sector (Table 2.4) account for 24.1% of the sector's turnover. The highest share in this sector is held by "DELTA ANTREPRIZA DE CONSTRUCTII SI MONTAJ 93 SRL", which contributed to the turnover of the Construction of roads and railways sector by 4%.

Table 2.5 shows that the most important activity in the construction of roads and railways is represented by the construction of roads and motorways, with over 95% of the turnover of the sector coming from this activity (ratio quite stable in the last 3 years), representing EUR 1 732 m in 2014.

Table 2.5. **Structure of roads and railways construction activities**

Sector	Code		Turnover 2014 (EUR mil.)	Employees 2014
Construction of roads and motorways	F 4211	Abs.	1 732.7	27 683
		Percentage	*95.97%*	*91.40%*
Construction of railways	F 4212	Abs.	53.9	2 346
		Percentage	*2.98%*	*7.75%*
Construction of bridges and tunnels	F 4213	Abs.	18.87	259
		Percentage	*1.04%*	*0.86%*
Total	**F 421**	**Abs.**	***1 805.5***	***30 288***
		Percentage	***100%***	***100%***

Note: For companies with a turnover higher than EUR 50 000 and more than 50 employees in 2014.
Source: Credit Info and Deloitte calculations.

In terms of gross profit (Table 2.6), in 2014 the construction of roads and motorways registered EUR 24.6 m, representing 94% of the gross profit of the sector. In the last three years, gross profit in the sector has experienced a downward trend from 2012 until 2014, with the only exception being in the construction of railways where in 2014 the subsector registered a cumulated positive gross profit after two years of losses.

Table 2.6. **Gross profit in the construction of roads and railways sector**

Sector	Code	Gross profit 2012 (EUR mil.)	Gross profit 2013 (EUR mil.)	Gross profit 2014 (EUR mil.)
Construction of roads and motorways	F 4211	100.20	95.14	24.62
Construction of railways	F 4212	-3.29	-4.55	1.60
Construction of bridges and tunnels	F 4213	3.60	1.30	0.10
Total	***F 421***	***100.50***	***91.90***	***26.32***

Source: Credit Info and Deloitte calculations.

In roads and railways construction, in 2014, 10.7% of the enterprises accounted for 80% of the turnover from the sector.[16]

The development of the sector points to an increasing trend from 2008 until 2013 regarding the number of companies in Europe. Romania follows the same trend with the exception of 2011 when there was a brief drop in this indicator. However, the general trend between 2008 and 2013 was a reduction in the number of employees in this sector in both Europe and Romania (with the exception in Romania in 2011 where the number of employees increased by 6.8% compared to 2010, despite the reduction in the number of companies in the same year).

Construction of utility projects

Description of the subsector. Construction of utilities often relies on financing from local budgets and external financing from the European Union (which runs programmes and national programmes in the area of transportation, environment, regional and rural

Figure 2.10. **Evolution of main indicators (base year 2008) in the construction of roads and railways sector**

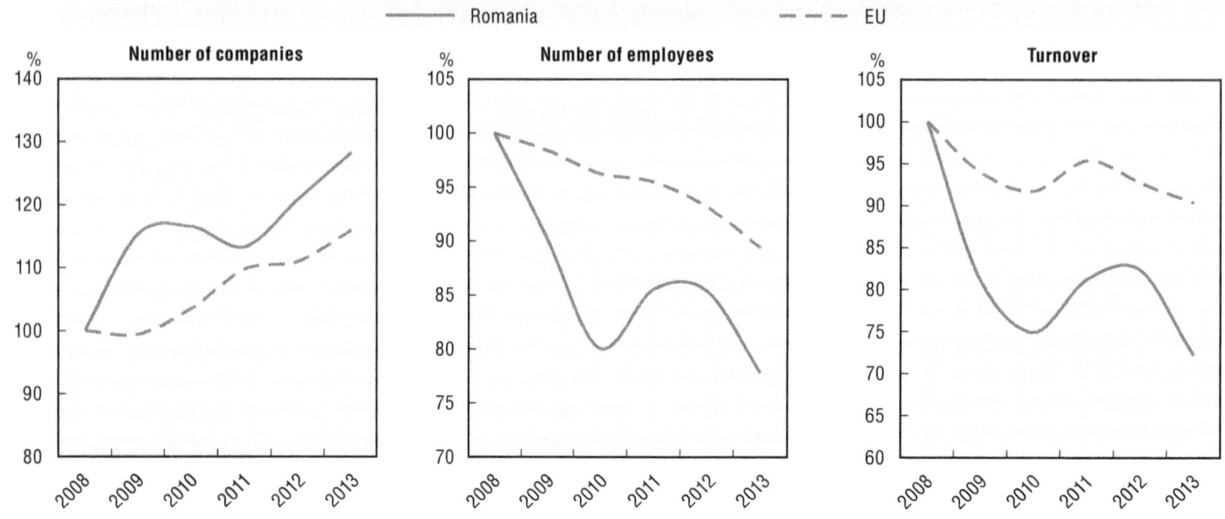

Source: Eurostat and Deloitte calculations.

StatLink http://dx.doi.org/10.1787/888933361217

development, large projects programme etc.), international development organisations (e.g. EBRD, EIB, EIF, World Bank) or the banking system. Local policies to extend network coverage to address availability gaps as well as government policy in the energy and utilities sector are key for these projects. It is also an auction market where companies have to participate in auctions organised by state authorities by following the general procurement procedure. This is frequently the case because the state is often the ultimate beneficiary, including where distribution networks are leased to private companies (due to the practice of granting concessions of networks to private operators rather than selling/ transferring these, even for new projects).

In the **Construction of utility projects** subsector both supply and demand can be represented by the same companies. For example, in some cases Transgaz acts as a beneficiary of construction of utilities projects, in other cases it can act as a supplier. In general, subsector demand consists of both private and state companies mainly in the production, transportation and distribution chains for natural gas, electricity, petroleum products, water and sewage, telephones, TV and data.

Major state-owned companies include Transgaz (gas transportation), Transelectrica (electricity transportation), Conpet (transportation of petroleum products), water companies owned by public administrations and even public data projects such as the Netcity project in Bucharest. Private beneficiaries include natural gas distributors (GDF Suez and EON), electricity distributors (Electrica regional companies, Enel regional companies, CEZ, EON), private water companies (e.g. Apanova), etc.

The main drivers of demand for the construction of utility projects include the following: government, local authority and state company policies to cover any utilities availability gaps and to develop new capabilities in the energy and utilities sectors; available external funding including available EU funds; and foreign direct investment.

Access to public utilities has been slowly improving as 298 towns and villages in the rural area gained public water distribution networks between 2007 and 2013 (Figure 2.11).

Figure 2.11. **Number of settlements with public water distribution networks**

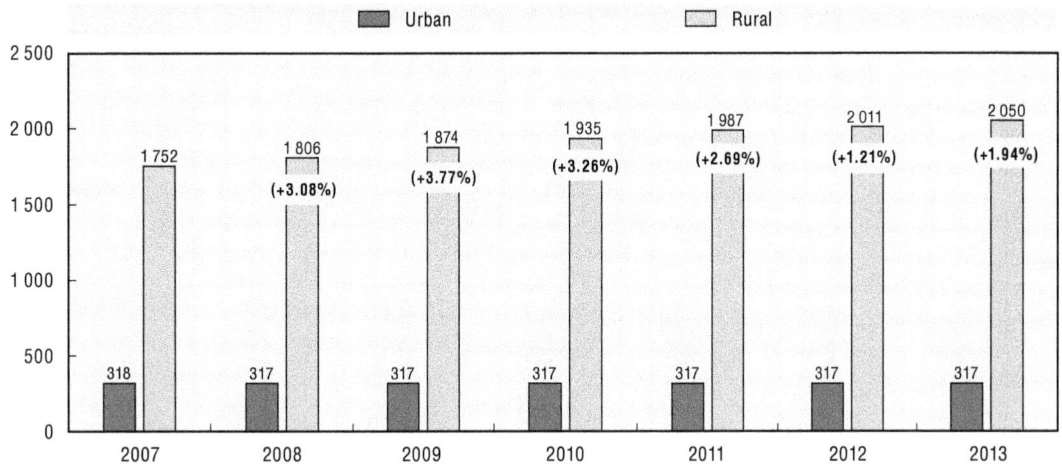

Note: Urban settlements are defined according to Romanian statistical standards which identify all municipalities and cities as urban settlements and all villages and communes as rural settlements.
Source: National Institute of Statistics.

StatLink http://dx.doi.org/10.1787/888933361224

As well, 246 rural towns and villages and one urban town gained public sewage networks in the same time period (Figure 2.12), 94 towns and cities had natural gas distribution networks built (Figure 2.13) and the overall number of households with an internet connection improved from 31% to 56%. Further extensions of utilities networks were completed in the period.

Figure 2.12. **Number of settlements with public sewage networks**

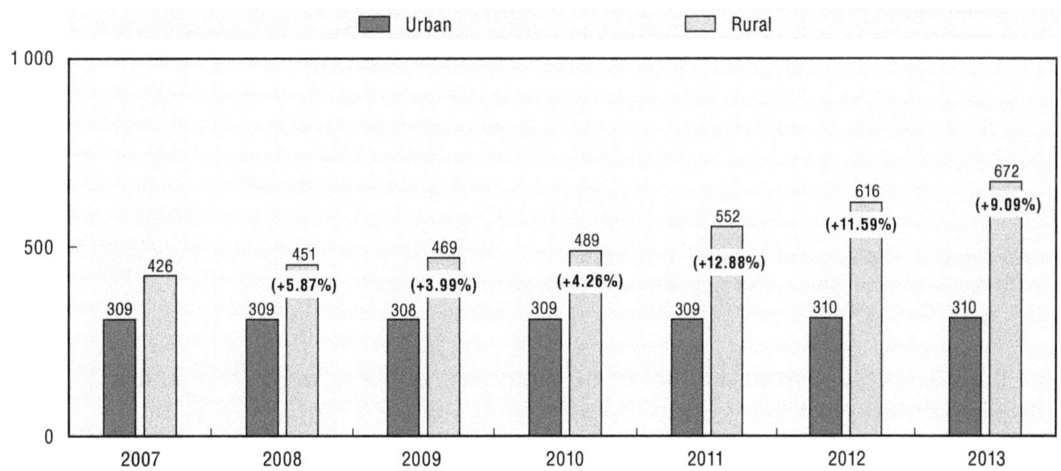

Source: National Institute of Statistics.

StatLink http://dx.doi.org/10.1787/888933361231

Subsector characteristics. The top ten companies in terms of turnover in the **Construction of utility projects** sector[17] are presented in the following table:

In the construction of utility projects sector, the main players (presented in Table 2.7) account for 44.92% of the total turnover from construction of utilities projects. The top company, "SOCIETATEA FILIALA DE INTRETINERE SI SERVICII ENERGETICE 'ELECTRICA SERV' S.A.", contributed 13.11% to the turnover of sector followed by "ELECTROMONTAJ SA" with 8.23%.

Figure 2.13. **Number of settlements with natural gas distribution networks**

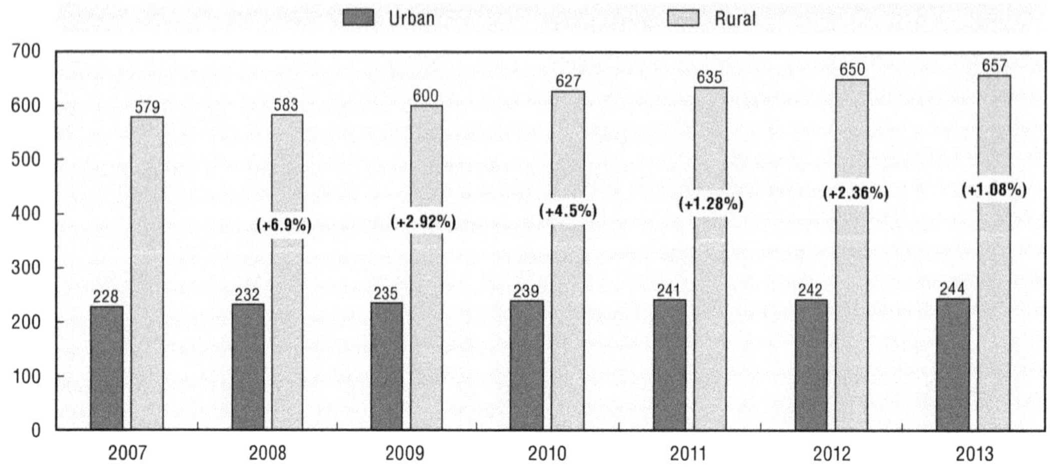

Source: National Institute of Statistics.

StatLink http://dx.doi.org/10.1787/888933361246

Table 2.7. **Top 10 players in the construction of utility projects sector**

No.	Company	NACE Code	Description NACE	Turnover 2014 (EUR mil.)	Market share 2014 [1]
1	SOCIETATEA FILIALA DE INTRETINERE SI SERVICII ENERGETICE "ELECTRICA SERV" S.A.	C 4222	Construction of utility projects for electricity and telecommunications	85.82	13.11%
2	ELECTROMONTAJ SA	C 4222	Construction of utility projects for electricity and telecommunications	53.86	8.23%
3	CONDMAG SA	C 4221	Construction of utility projects for fluids	39.03	5.96%
4	INSPET SA	C 4221	Construction of utility projects for fluids	38.20	5.83%
5	COMESAD RO SA	C 4221	Construction of utility projects for fluids	17.81	2.72%
6	CAMUSAT ROM-TELECOMUNICATII SRL	C 4222	Construction of utility projects for electricity and telecommunications	17.02	2.60%
7	IRIDEX GROUP CONSTRUCTII SRL	C 4221	Construction of utility projects for fluids	11.88	1.82%
8	T.A.G.C.M. DUNĂREA SOCIETATE PE ACŢIUNI	C 4221	Construction of utility projects for fluids	11.19	1.71%
9	ALPENSIDE SRL	C 4221	Construction of utility projects for fluids	10.07	1.54%
10	AL STOM COMPANY SRL	C 4221	Construction of utility projects for fluids	9.17	1.40%
TOTAL				***294.06***	***44.92%***

1. References to "market characteristics", "market shares" or "markets" in general, included in this report, do not reflect the same definitions used for purposes of applying competition law.

Source: ANAF, Credit Info and Deloitte calculations.

Table 2.8 presents the structure of the financial results from the companies active in the construction of utility projects sector. There are two main activities in this sector, namely construction of utility projects for fluids (53% of the sector's turnover) and construction of utility projects for electricity and telecommunications (47% of the total turnover of the sector).

The gross profit of the companies involved in construction utility projects registered a cumulated loss in 2014 for construction of utility projects for electricity and telecommunications of EUR 1.19 m (Table 2.9). However, the loss was compared to the one previous year. In the construction of utility projects for fluids, gross profit amounted to EUR 7.65 m, and this indicator followed an increasing trend over the last three years.

From 2008 until 2013, the number of companies active in the construction of utility projects has followed an increasing trend, with the only exception in 2011 when the

Table 2.8. **Structure of construction of utility projects activity**

Sector	Code		Turnover 2014 (EUR mil.)	Employees 2014
Construction of utility projects for fluids	F 4221	Abs.	231.58	4 079
		Percentage	*53.25%*	*37.87%*
Construction of utility projects for electricity and telecommunications	F 4222	Abs.	203.3	6 691
		Percentage	*46.75%*	*62.13%*
Total	**F 422**	**Abs.**	**434.88**	**10 770**
		Percentage	***100%***	***100%***

Note: For companies with a turnover higher than EUR 50 000 and more than 50 employees.
Source: Credit Info and Deloitte calculations.

Table 2.9. **Gross profit in the construction of utilities projects sector**

Sector	Code	Gross profit 2012 (EUR mil.)	Gross profit 2013 (EUR mil.)	Gross profit 2014 (EUR mil.)
Construction of utility projects for fluids	F 4221	5.13	7.54	7.65
Construction of utility projects for electricity and telecommunications	F 4222	4.39	-4.55	-1.19
Total	*F 422*	*9.51*	*2.99*	*6.46*

Source: Credit Info and Deloitte calculations.

number of active companies was lower than in 2010. In Europe, the situation was not the same, as the evolution of the number of companies in this sector did not follow a clear trend. However, the evolution of the number of employees shows a general personnel reduction in Romania, while in Europe the number of employees working in the construction of utility projects remained relatively stable.

Figure 2.14. **Evolution of main indicators (base year 2008) in the construction of utilities projects sector**

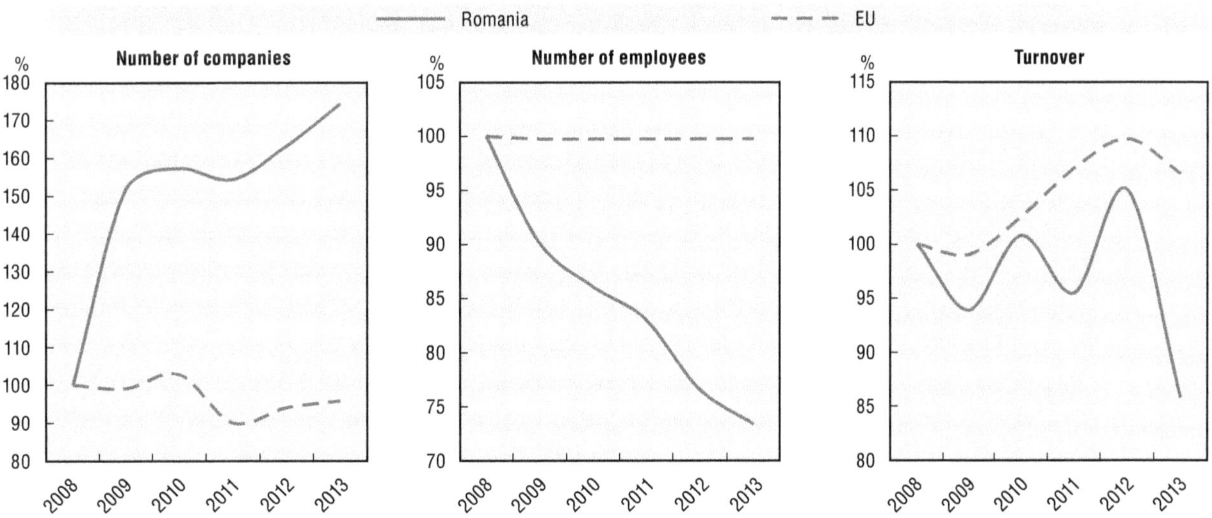

Source: Eurostat and Deloitte calculations.

StatLink http://dx.doi.org/10.1787/888933361257

Construction of other civil engineering projects

Description of the subsector. In the **Construction of other civil engineering projects** subsector demand consists of state companies and administrations relating to waterways, port management, flood prevention (for port infrastructure, dredging, dykes), both state and private companies and private or state companies for industrial construction work excluding chemical plants and refineries.

The main drivers of demand for **Construction of other civil engineering projects** include general economic and industrial sector growth, government policy in the infrastructure/water transportation sector and available external funding including available EU funds.

Subsector characteristics. The top ten companies in terms of turnover in the **Construction of utility projects** sector[18] are presented in the following table:

Table 2.10. **Top 10 players in the construction of other civil engineering projects sector**

No.	Company	NACE Code	Description NACE	Turnover 2014 (EUR mil.)	Market share 2014 [1]
1	HIDROCONSTRUCTIA SA	C 4291	Construction of water projects	116.27	18.63%
2	ROMELECTRO SA	C 4299	Construction of other civil engineering projects	32.61	5.22%
3	KREMSMUELLER ROMANIA SRL	C 4299	Construction of other civil engineering projects	24.93	3.99%
4	IREM CONSTRUCŢII GENERALE SRL	C 4299	Construction of other civil engineering projects	14.65	2.35%
5	LESCACI COM SRL	C 4291	Construction of water projects	10.76	1.72%
6	PETROCONST SA	C 4299	Construction of other civil engineering projects	10.60	1.70%
7	LUCA PREST SRL	C 4299	Construction of other civil engineering projects	10.24	1.64%
8	ISAF-SOCIETATE DE SEMNALIZARI SI AUTOMATIZARI FEROVIARE SA	C 4299	Construction of other civil engineering projects	9.52	1.52%
9	S.U.C.T. SA	C 4299	Construction of other civil engineering projects	8.42	1.35%
10	SOCOT SA	C 4291	Construction of water projects	8.05	1.29%
TOTAL				***246.05***	***39.42%***

1. References to "market characteristics", "market shares" or "markets" in general, included in this report, do not reflect the same definitions used for purposes of applying competition law.

Source: Credit Info and Deloitte calculations.

Table 2.10 shows that the top ten companies in the construction of other civil engineering projects sector account for 39.42% of the sector's turnover. Out this percentage, 21.64% of the market share comes from the construction of water projects, while the rest – 17.78% – comes from construction of other civil engineering projects. "HIDROCONSTRUCTIA SA" alone contributed to the total turnover of the sector by 18.63%, as the main player in the sector.

Based on data on the top ten constructors, Table 2.11 shows that the main subactivity in 2014 was the construction of water projects, representing almost 60% of the total turnover of this activity. Also, 66% of the employees are working in this area.

With regards to gross profit (Table 2.12), the construction of water projects suffered a loss of EUR 34.14 m in 2014. The construction of other civil engineering projects reached a low total profit of EUR 83 606. For each subsector the trend of the previous three years was a decrease in gross profit, the most significant reduction being in 2014.

Table 2.11. **Structure of construction of other civil engineering projects activity**

Sector	Code		Turnover 2014 (EUR mil.)	Employees 2014
Construction of water projects	F 4291	Abs.	185.71	5 218
		Percentage	*59.42%*	*66.31%*
Construction of other civil engineering projects	F 4299	Abs.	126.80	2 651
		Percentage	*40.58%*	*33.69%*
Total	**F 429**	**Abs.**	**312.51**	**7 869**
		Percentage	***100%***	***100%***

Note: For companies with a turnover higher than EUR 50 000 and more than 50 employees in 2014.
Source: Credit Info and Deloitte calculations

Table 2.12. **Gross profit in the construction of other civil engineering projects sector**

Sector	Code	Gross profit 2012 (EUR mil.)	Gross profit 2013 (EUR mil.)	Gross profit 2014 (EUR mil.)
Construction of water projects	F 4291	8.70	3.43	-34.24
Construction of other civil engineering projects	F 4299	7.06	6.29	0.08
Total	***F 429***	15.76	9.72	-34.16

Source: Credit Info and Deloitte calculations.

Between 2008 and 2013 the number of companies involved in the construction of other civil engineering projects (in Romania) decreased (on average) – Figure 2.15, the only increase being in 2010 compared to 20.8% in 2009, followed by a drop of 22% in 2011. In Europe the evolution of the number of companies show a decreasing trend from 2009 until 2013. The number of employees in Romania also fell over the same period, by more than the number of companies. The only year when there were more people employed in this subsector than the previous year was 2011 (but it was followed by a higher drop in 2012). The turnover of the companies also suffered a reduction from year to year between the period 2008 to 2013, for both Romania and the European average.

Construction materials

Overview

Construction materials generally represent inputs for the construction industry and as such there is a significant overlap between demand for construction materials and supply of construction works. Demand for building materials is mainly driven by the construction sector and ultimately by the overall state of the economy. The nature of both production and consumption of most building materials contributes to this close link between local building materials and the construction sector as a whole (including construction of residential and commercial buildings and specialised construction).

Demand for building materials also originates from sources such as international demand, especially in the case of high value added construction materials, construction materials which can easily be transported over long distances and certain products such as those derived from wood, glass and plastics, and from "do it yourself" construction, renovation and repair activities. Imports of construction materials also play a role in satisfying demand for the products mentioned above.

Figure 2.15. **Evolution of main indicators (base year 2008) in the construction of other civil engineering projects sector**

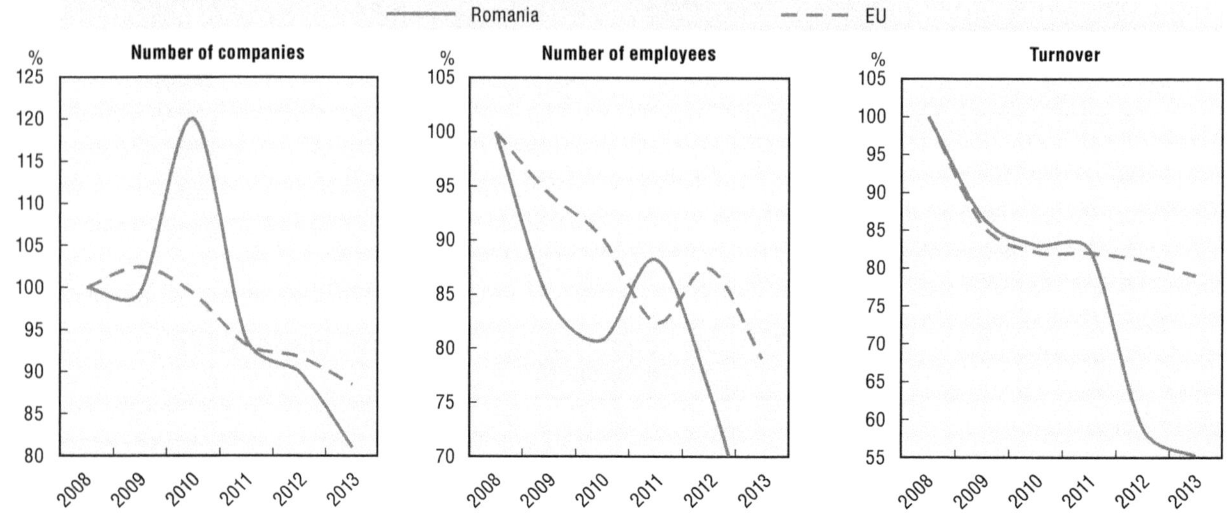

Source: Eurostat and Deloitte calculations.

StatLink http://dx.doi.org/10.1787/888933361260

Sector characteristics

The sector is highly dependent on the development of the construction industry which provides demand for construction materials. It is a largely local market due to high transportation costs – building materials are generally supplied to construction companies in relative vicinity of the manufacturing facilities. However, some construction materials are more easily transported and have a higher value, and are therefore suited to transportation over long distances e.g. wood, glass or high value added products. Construction materials represent a diversified subsector consisting of a wide range of products resulting from processing of outputs from various materials/resources industries (e.g. metals, glass, chemical, forestry).

The top ten companies in the construction materials industry[19] (in term of the turnover from 2014) are the following:

Table 2.13. **Top 10 companies in the construction materials industry**

No.	Company	NACE Code	Description NACE	Turnover 2014 (EUR mil.)
1	EGGER ROMANIA SRL	C 1621	Manufacture of veneer sheets and wood-based panels	297.76
2	KRONOSPAN SEBES SA	C 1621	Manufacture of veneer sheets and wood-based panels	253.17
3	Holcim (Romania) SA	C 235	Manufacture of cement, lime and plaster	219.23
4	CARPATCEMENT HOLDING SA	C 235	Manufacture of cement, lime and plaster	171.59
5	LAFARGE CIMENT (ROMANIA) SA	C 235	Manufacture of cement, lime and plaster	155.50
6	HENKEL ROMANIA SRL	C 236	Manufacture of articles of concrete, cement and plaster	132.06
7	KRONOSPAN ROMANIA SRL	C 1621	Manufacture of veneer sheets and wood-based panels	112.64
8	SAINT-GOBAIN GLASS ROMANIA SRL	C 2311	Manufacture of flat glass	70.76
9	ADEPLAST S.A.	C 236	Manufacture of articles of concrete, cement and plaster	67.63
10	SAINT-GOBAIN CONSTRUCTION PRODUCTS ROMANIA SRL	C 236	Manufacture of articles of concrete, cement and plaster	67.48

Source: ANAF, Credit Info and Deloitte calculations.

Data for the last complete available year from Eurostat are presented in Table 2.14 (2012). Incomplete data for 2014 is referred to in the analysis below depending on availability.

Table 2.14. **Main results of the construction materials sectors**

Sector description	NACE Code	Number of companies 2013	Number of employees 2013	Turnover (EUR mil.) 2013
Quarrying of stone, sand and clay	B081	828	7 431	316.8
Manufacture of wood and of products of wood and cork, except furniture; manufacture of articles of straw and plating materials	C16	1 444	20 347	1 757.1
Manufacture of chemicals and chemical products	C20	164	3 818	280
Manufacture of other non-metallic mineral products	C23	1 959	26 241	2 006
Manufacture of fabricated metal products, except machinery and equipment	C25	3 164	39 233	1 525
TOTAL		***7 559***	***97 070***	***5 884***

Note: The data presented are for 2012 as it is the last available year with complete information from Eurostat.
Source: Eurostat.

In 2014, there were 846 companies in the **quarrying of stone, sand and clay** activity, representing a 2.17% increase compared to 2013.[20] The total number of active companies for this activity followed a decreasing trend from 2009 until 2013. In 2013 there were 7 431 people employed in this area, a relatively stable value between 2010 and 2013 (in 2010, however, there was a 14% drop). The turnover generated by these companies followed a general increasing trend after a sharp contraction in 2009, reaching EUR 355 m in 2014.

In the **manufacture of wood and products of wood and cork, except furniture, manufacture of articles of straw and plating materials** subsector the total number of companies in 2013 was 1 444.[21] The number of companies has decreased every year since 2008, resulting in a total reduction of 45.8% over the period 2008 to 2013. On the other hand, the number of employees has decreased only in the first two years after 2008, but more people were employed in 2011, 2012 and 2013 compared to the previous period, reaching 20 337 employees in 2013. The companies in the three activities considered relevant in this study generated a total turnover of EUR 1 757 m in 2013, following an increasing trend from 2009 on.

In the **manufacture of chemicals and chemical products** subsector, the number of active companies was 162 in 2014, showing a 1.2% decrease compared to 2012.[22] The number of employees was 3 818 people in 2013, decreasing by almost 1.5% from the previous year. The turnover generated by the companies operating in this area was relatively stable over the period 2010-2014, reaching EUR 311 m in 2014.

For the relevant activities operating in the **manufacture of other non-metallic mineral products** subsector, there were 1 959 active companies in 2013, employing 26 241 people and generating a turnover of EUR 2 006 m. The evolution of the number of companies shows in 2012 the first year of superior value compared to the previous year, after three consecutive years of reduction. The number of employees registered a cumulated reduction of 35% over the period 2008-2013, and the turnover decreased by 40% from 2009 until 2012.

In 2014, there were 3 279 companies operating in the **manufacture of structural metal products** subsector, representing a 3.63% increase compared to 2013.[23] The total number of active companies for this activity followed a decreasing trend from 2009 until 2013. In 2013 there were 39 223 people employed in this area. The 3 279 companies generated a cumulated turnover of EUR 1 513 m, a value lower than in 2013.

Figure 2.16. **Evolution of the number of companies in construction materials sectors**

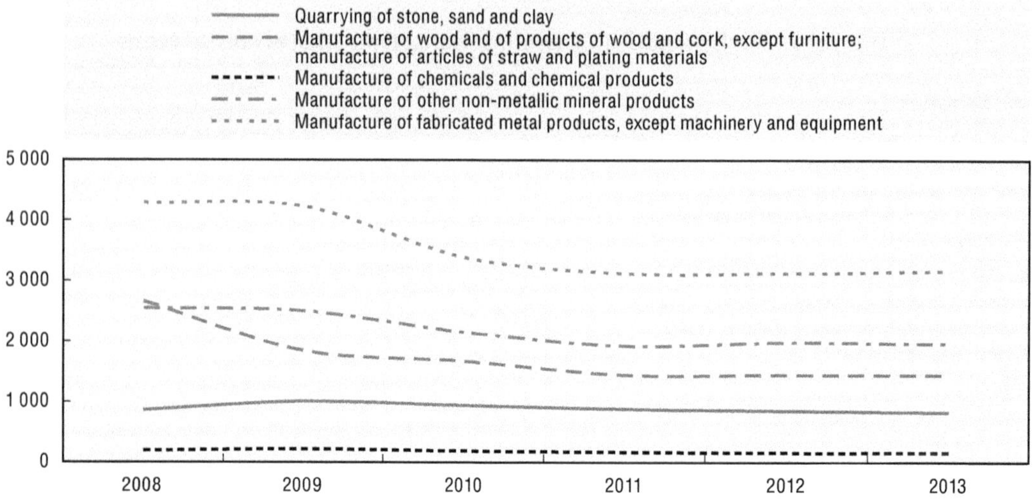

Source: Eurostat and Deloitte calculations.

StatLink http://dx.doi.org/10.1787/888933361276

Figure 2.17. **Evolution of the number of employees in construction materials sectors**

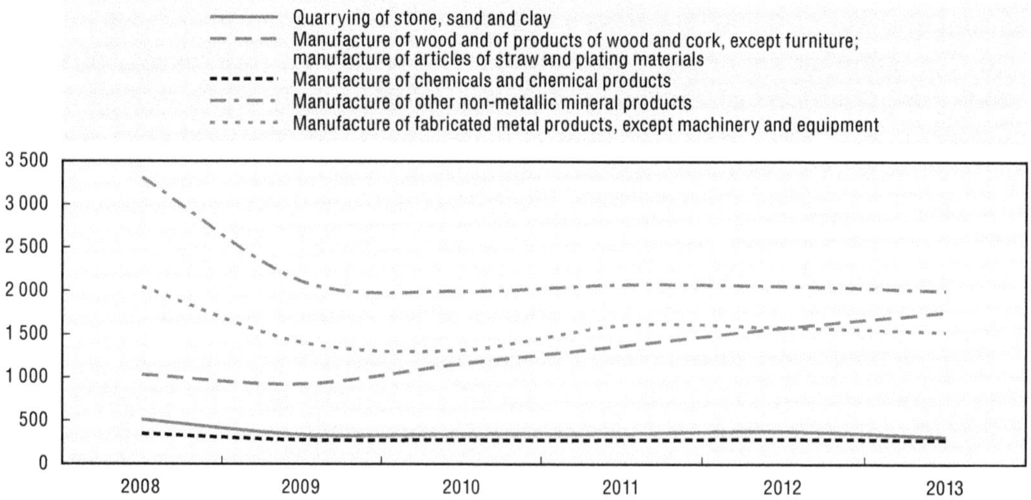

Source: Eurostat and Deloitte calculations.

StatLink http://dx.doi.org/10.1787/888933361286

Public Procurement

Relevant legislation

The field of public procurement in Romania is currently regulated in primary legislation by a single act: Government Emergency Ordinance (GEO) No. 34/2006 on the award of public procurement contracts, public works concession contracts and concession of services,[24] which implements EU Directives 2004/17/EC and 2004/18/EC in public procurement and concessions.

Figure 2.18. **Evolution of turnover (million EUR) in construction materials sectors**

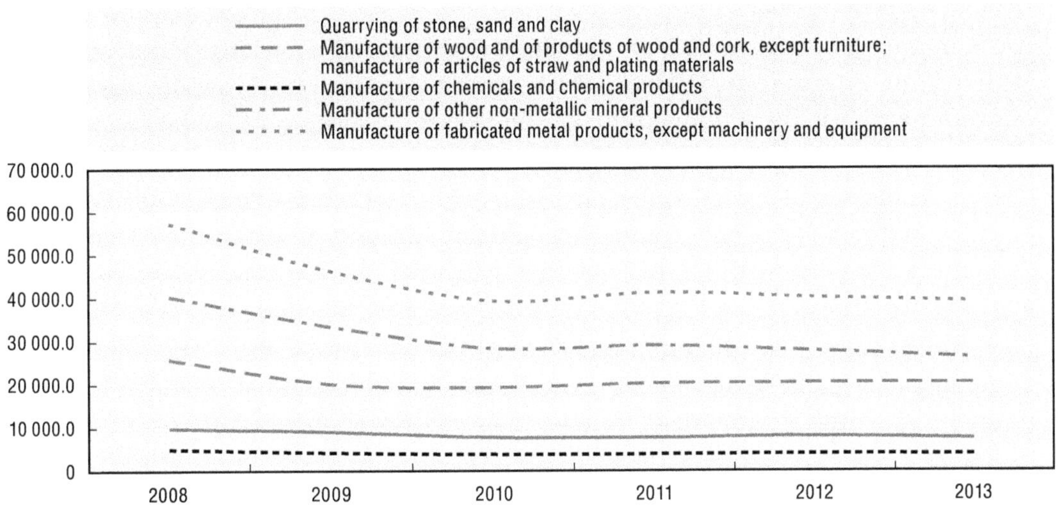

Source: Eurostat and Deloitte calculations.

StatLink http://dx.doi.org/10.1787/888933361291

Secondary legislation details the implementation in specific areas, including procurement and operational aspects of the general sector, utilities sector, concessions and electronic procurement.

The public tender procedures are regulated in the former EU Directives on procurement, respectively open tender, restricted tender, competitive dialogue, negotiated procedures, frameworks agreements and dynamic purchasing system. The deadlines set within the procedures, including those regarding the submission of offers or contestations, the timeframe for requesting clarifications and the obligation of contracting authorities to respond to requests, comply with the provisions of the directives.

Also, the thresholds for publication of the different announcements regarding the public procurement procedures, such as the tender announcement, tender documentation or awarding announcement, in the national and European publication systems, implement the provisions of the EU Directives.

Relevant government authorities

Central functions of the public procurement system are fulfilled by the following institutions:

- ANRMAP (***National Regulatory and Monitoring Authority for Public Procurement)*** is the institution managing the public procurement system in Romania, with the fundamental role of defining, promoting and implementing the public procurement policy. The institution has a legislative function, offers advisory and operational support and performs *ex ante* evaluation of the tender documentation and *ex post* control.
- UCVAP (***Unit for the Coordination and Verification of Public Procurement)*** is an institution under the Ministry of Finance responsible for the *ex ante* verification of the procedures for awarding public procurement contracts, public works concession and service concessions by the contracting authorities;
- CNSC (***National Council for Solving Complaints***) is an independent body with administrative-jurisdictional activity, which has jurisdiction to hear appeals made in the award of public

procurement procedures before the contract is concluded. In exercising its powers, the Council takes decisions.

- AADR (***Agency for Romanian Digital Agenda***) is a specialised public institution under the Ministry for Information Society which aims to operate nationwide systems for eGovernment. It is the administrator of the Electronic System of Public Procurement (Sistemul Electronic de Achizitii Publice – S.E.A.P.).
- ***Court of Auditors*** is an operationally independent body within the Court of Accounts. The Court of Auditors is the only competent national authority to conduct external public audits in accordance with EU and national legislation, performing system audits and audits of operations.
- ***Competition Council*** is an autonomous body, which administers and implements Competition Law and which aims to protect, maintain and stimulate competition and a normal competitive environment, in order to promote the interests of consumers.
- ***Courts of appeal*** are courts in the constituency within which several tribunals and specialised courts operate. They represent the second instance for settlement of disputes in the matter of public procurement.

In addition, the management authorities and the implementation bodies which are charged with managing EU funds can also issue opinions on the conformity of a procurement procedure.

The steps of a public procurement procedure are as follows:

1. The contracting authority asks for approval of the tender documentation from ANRMAP.
2. After obtaining ANRMAP`s approval, the contracting authority publishes tenders above the legal threshold in the Electronic System of Public Procurement (SEAP).

   The procurement directives define a variety of procurement procedures. The basic characteristics of the most common ones are:

   - In an open procedure any business may submit a tender.
   - In a restricted procedure any business may ask to participate, but only those who are pre-selected will be invited to submit a tender. This saves time and money for both businesses and buyers.
   - In a negotiated procedure the public authority invites at least three businesses with whom it will negotiate the terms of the contract. This procedure can take place with or without prior publication. Most contracting authorities can use this procedure only in a limited number of cases.
   - The competitive dialogue is often used for complex contracts where the public authority cannot define the technical specifications at the outset.
3. Bidders submit their offers online or offline.
4. UCVAP performs *ex ante* verification of the procedures for awarding public procurement contracts.
5. The contracting authority designates a winner of the procedure.
6. Any interested third party can appeal the result of the procedure in the first instance with CNSC and in the second instance with the Court of Appeal.
7. A contract is signed between the contracting authority and the economic operator(s).
8. ANRMAP, the Competition Council and the Court of Auditors can verify various aspects of the procurement procedure after the contract is signed/finalised.

Figure 2.19. **Relationship of the main institutions involved in public procurement activity**

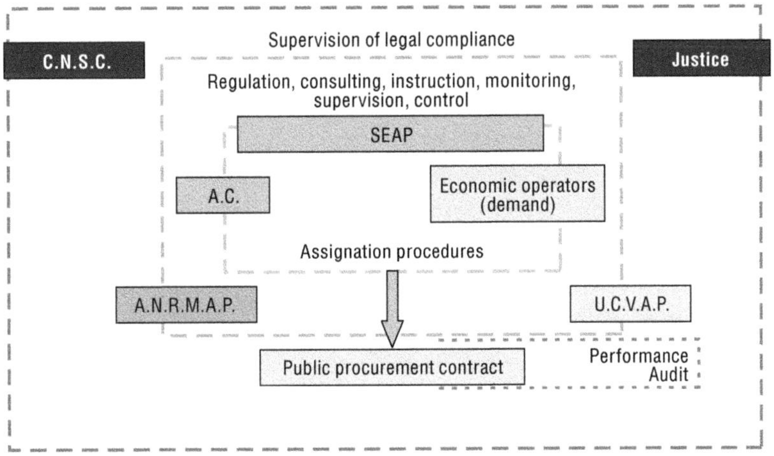

Source: *ANRMAP (2012)*, "Sistemul de achizitii publice din Romania" (Romanian Public Procurement System), *http://romaniacurata.ro/wp-content/uploads/2012/04/Sistemul-de-achizitii-publice.pptx.*

Following the issuance of three new EU Directives in 2014 on public procurement, respectively Directives 2014/23/EU, 2014/24/EU and 2014/25/EU, the national legislation in force is due to change. The transposition of the new EU Directives into Romanian legislation is planned to be made through four pieces of primary legislation that are, at the moment of writing this report, subject of public debate (one piece of legislation dealing with classical procurement, one dealing with utilities, one dealing with concessions and public private partnership and one piece of legislation dealing with appeals). Also, the national strategy on public procurement is subject to public debate.

Following the enactment of Government Emergency Ordinance No. 13/2015 on the set-up, organisation and functioning of the ***National Agency for Public Procurement*** ("ANAP") in May 2015, ANRMAP and UCVAP shall be dissolved and their attributions will be undertaken by ANAP, which is an institution subordinated to the Ministry of Public Finance. However, until the issuance of the methodological norms for the functioning of ANAP, ANRMAP and UCVAP shall continue to perform their attributions.

General problems of public procurement in Romania

According to the European Commission's Single Market Scoreboard,[25] the overall performance of the Romanian public procurement system is below average, with a poor score for two out of the three dimensions[26] (bidders' participation, accessibility and effectiveness of the procedure).

In Romania, public procurement is currently carried out by thousands of decentralised contracting authorities (in accordance with the National Strategy on Public Procurement[27] in the period 2007-14, an annual average of 7 300 public contracting authorities conducted online and offline procurement procedures using SEAP or direct commitment with values below or above the thresholds set by EU law).

According to the National Strategy on Public Procurement, some of the main deficiencies of the national procurement system are:

- lack of integrated functionality and co-operation among responsible authorities;

- emphasis on regulation and control functions within the system, leading to a lack of involvement of the contracting authorities; and
- insufficient orientation of involved institutions towards an efficient use of public funds, but rather towards compliance with procedures.

The National Strategy on Public Procurement (2015) states that there is a generalised perception that deficiencies of the system are imposed primarily on the persons involved in the procedure who are punished as individuals, instead of identifying and solving the shortcomings of the system. This perception determines risk avoidance behaviours through which implementing best practice is replaced by an emphasis on the literal application of the rules and using just judgment is replaced by a mechanical approach. Some of the consequences are:

- the widespread use of the criterion "the lowest price", even if significant intellectual services or complex works are required;
- a focus on detailed technical specifications instead of performance specifications; or
- a focus on qualification criteria in the evaluation of technical proposals.

Ultimately, the consequences are detrimental to obtaining a good price-quality ratio and the effective use of public procurement in promoting public policies.

Therefore, despite validation by *ex ante* control of procurement procedures applied by contracting authorities, some issues can be challenged and held to be illegal at a later stage (*ex post* control, auditing), obliging the contracting authority to bear penalties/related financial corrections. In the absence of a common approach, *ex post* control is carried out by various institutions (ANRMAP, Court of Auditors) analysing the same items (documents/procedures), determining the contracting authority to adopt the option with minimal risk when awarding contracts.

Moreover, due to the requirement to justify in detail the award criterion "the most advantageous offer economically", contracting authorities are discouraged from using this criterion and prefer to rely on the criterion of "the lowest price", even when it is not appropriate to use it, because it is perceived as the most secure in the event of subsequent checks. Such an approach substantially restricts the development of strategic procurement policies and leads to losses of efficiency in the use of public funds.

According to the same strategy mentioned above, due to the widespread use of the criterion "the lowest price", reflected in substantial differences between the estimated price and the contract price, current market conditions in Romania determine economic operators to compete strongly on the price criteria which has an adverse effect on ensuring sustainable and efficient use of public funds ("value for money").

According to the CNSC Activity Report[28] of 2014, out of over 18 000 procedures published in SEAP, 20% were appealed in first instance, out of which 40% referred to construction contracts. Thus, according to the National Strategy on Public Procurement the large number of appeals was perceived by the administration more as an abuse of the economic operators rather than as an indicator of the lack of capacity in the public procurement system. Legislative solutions envisaged, respectively the guarantee of good conduct, were repealed by the Constitutional Court[29] and are also subject to an infringement procedure before the European Court of Justice.

According to a recent report of the Romanian Academic Society,[30] because of an unclear, unstable, and overregulated legislative framework worsened by sometimes contradictory implementation of the rules and a lack of administrative capacity, contracting authorities and economic operators end up being sanctioned both by national monitoring and control bodies and corresponding EU institutions via financial corrections. Furthermore, public projects are placed on hold until contestations and legal disputes are settled in courts, thus leading to a waste of public resources. Nevertheless, putting on hold public procurement projects is not mandatory according to national legislation, but is left for the decision of the CNSC and the courts.

In 2013, the Romanian Competition Council issued a report following a sector inquiry on the construction market of roads and highways. The competition authority scrutinised the said market and identified certain factual situations which could trigger competition issues, as we describe below:

- partnerships between companies active on the market with the view of participation in tenders;
- sub-contracting of part of works awarded to a contractor following completion of tender procedure;
- increase of initial cost of works after the tender procedure through addenda to the contract until in the end the final cost overtakes the initial one.

Relevance of public procurement for the Romanian construction sector

According to a report of the Romanian Academic Society,[31] public spending in the construction sector accounts for 58% of total public procurement. More precisely, public spending in construction reached nearly EUR 7 billion in 2007, peaked at EUR 11.6 billion in 2009 and one year later dropped to EUR 6 billion. Afterwards it surged again to EUR 10.6 billion (2011) and in the following two years it settled to around EUR 9.1 billion. Public procurement in the construction sector follows the same trend as total public procurement. The year 2009 represents the peak, both in absolute value and in percentage share of GDP and the share of total government expenditure.

Figure 2.20. **Construction sector procurement: volume and share in GDP and government expenditure**

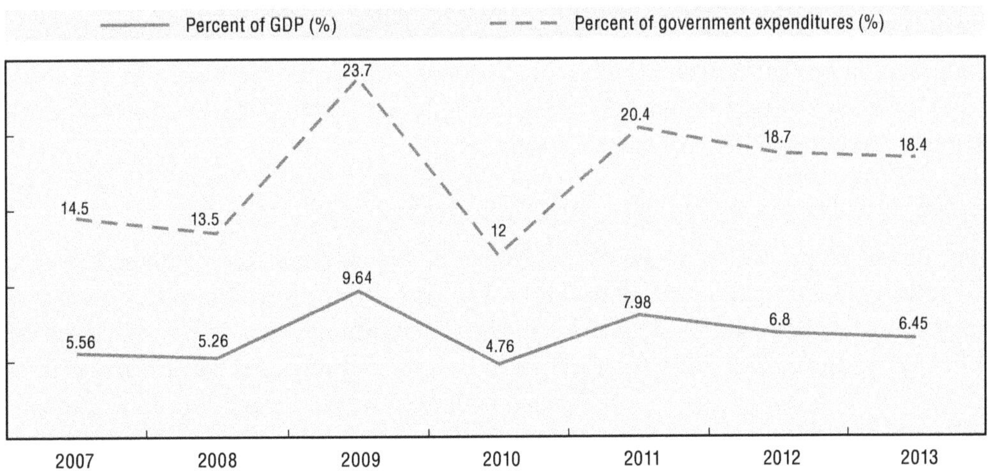

Source: Romanian Academic Society (SAR) (2015) Romanian public procurement in the construction sector. Corruption risks and particularistic links (30 March 2015): *http://anticorrp.eu/publications/report-on-romania/*. Construction procurement constitutes a significant share of total procurement, as shown in the figure below.

StatLink http://dx.doi.org/10.1787/888933361308

Figure 2.21. **Share of construction spending in total public procurement**

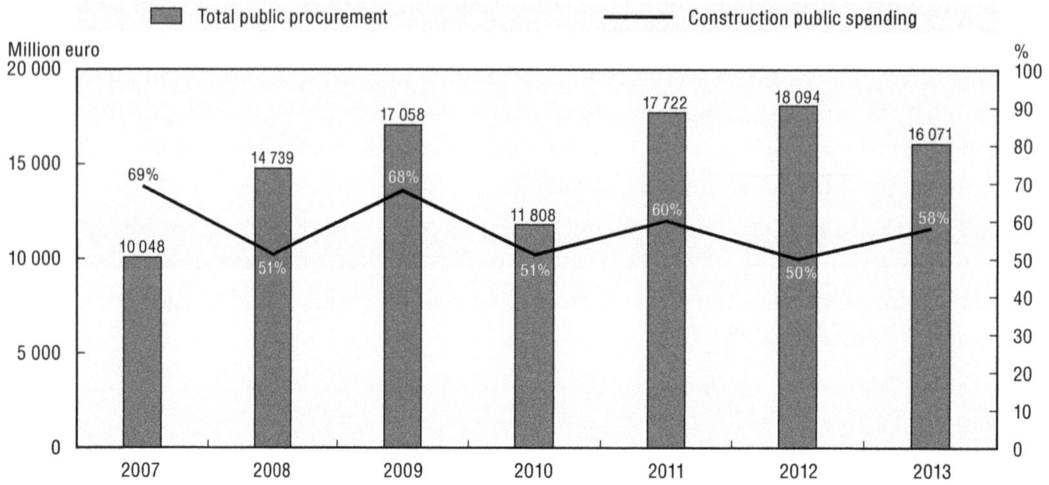

Source: Romanian Academic Society (SAR) (2015) Romanian public procurement in the construction sector. Corruption risks and particularistic links (30 March 2015): *http://anticorrp.eu/publications/report-on-romania/*.

StatLink http://dx.doi.org/10.1787/888933361316

The corruption report prepared by SAR (2015) reveals that the award criterion for **construction procedures** over EUR 1 m was in 46.3% of the cases "the lowest price". Instead, contracts receiving European funding were awarded at "the lowest price" in 37.4% of the cases, the rest being awarded based on "the most economically advantageous" criterion.

Among the most frequent public authorities awarding works public procurement contracts over EUR 1 m (SAR, 2015), there were five entities that signed over 100 contracts from 2007 to 2014: the Romanian National Company of Motorways and National Roads (CNADNR: 444 contracts), the Bucharest City Hall (118 contracts), the National Housing Agency (110 contracts) and two gas national companies (over 100 contracts). Bucharest road and public domain administrations followed closely (under 100 contracts).

The National Strategy on Public Procurement mentions some of the main deficiencies identified during implementation of works contracts, such as: the transfer of responsibility for authorisation of works from the contracting authority to the supplier, thus leading to significant delays in execution of contracts; lack of flexibility of technical indicators used in the procurement procedure; barriers in subcontracting after the award of the contract, low quality of works performed due to tight financing; addenda to contracts in order to satisfy the real needs of the contracting authority.

2.2. Restrictions to competitiveness in construction

According to the OECD paper "Competition in the construction Industry" (2008), the construction industry plays a fundamental role in the economy and development of every country. Its significance stems from the creation of structures and infrastructures on which every other industry depends, as well as making a major contribution in generating employment. The report describes the construction sector in general as a fragmented industry that is prone to cartel activity. This fragmented structure also exists in Romania, as described in the Economic overview above. According to the report, the following features encourage cartel formation: i) a lack of differentiation in product delivery among construction firms, ii) a lack of transparent bidding procedures, iii) the large number of clients, and iv) the need for subcontracting of works (OECD, 2008).

Unclear provisions

In the revised construction legislation we identified several unclear provisions that give public authorities far-reaching discretional powers unguided by any requirements or guidelines. This discretion might lead to possible abuses among market participants if interpreted by public authorities on a case-by-case basis. Also, the provisions granting discretionary powers to public authorities result in regulatory uncertainty for market participants.

The restrictions that have been identified come from two types of legal provisions: i) a lack of definition of the important notions used in the legislation, or a lack of clear criteria that can be objectively applied by the authorities when taking a decision, and/or ii) far-reaching powers/discretion granted to local authorities. Based on these provisions, authorities can make administrative decisions on a case-by-case basis and may come to different conclusions or interpretations in similar situations, thus favouring one competitor and discriminating against another. This may lead to additional costs for market participants and to an unpredictable business environment for private investors.

Although administrative decisions may sometimes require discretion and the flexible exercise of judgement and decision, legislation should be clear enough not to allow any practical discrimination between undertakings that are active in the same market. Although we do not recommend excessive regulation of all possible situations that might arise in practice, we suggest eliminating the lack of clarity in legislation, either by clarifying the provisions or by giving examples and/or guidelines with clear and objective criteria on how the legislation should be interpreted. Additionally, previous decisions of the authorities on the same subject should be published on its website. Thus, while administrative discretion remains for public administrations, such measures would ensure a higher degree of transparency and reduce unpredictability for the business environment.

Granting parking places on public land

Description of the obstacle. According to Article 33 of Annex 1 of Government Decision No. 525/1996 for approving general urbanism regulation, when requesting a building permit for execution of construction works for a building that, by its purpose requires parking places, the building permit can only be obtained if a minimum number of parking places are placed outside the public grounds (i.e., on private land). Exceptionally, local public authorities can allow the building of parking places on public land.

Two issues arise as regards this legal provision:

- It is not clear whether the requirement refers solely to new buildings. The legal provision may also be interpreted in the sense that the existence of a sufficient number of parking places is required by the authorities each time a building permit is required for construction works to an existing building (or when the owner changes the existing purpose of the building to a new one);
- It is not clear whether the local authorities may use public land to grant parking places at their sole discretion.

In order to establish the conditions under which such provisions apply, several cities have concretised the general norm through decisions of their local councils. For example, the Local Council of Bucharest, through Decision 66/2006,[32] established that the obligation to have parking spaces for new buildings is not applicable for the city centre and buildings not having access to roads. Moreover, developers building outside the central area of the city have the option to build only 80% of the parking places necessary, provided that they pay the public authority a fee of EUR 10 000 for each parking place not built. The fees collected are deposited by the public authority in a fund for building parking spaces on public land.

Other local authorities, such as Brasov,[33] Cluj-Napoca[34] and Pitesti,[35] have issued similar local council decisions establishing how the parking places available (residential or not) will be assigned to natural persons or legal entities.

Harm to competition. The wording of the legal provision may lead to an arbitrary application of the law on a case-by-case basis, thus leading to heterogeneous practices across various cities or even inside the same city.

First, it is not clear if the obligation to ensure parking places outside public land applies only to newly-built constructions. It seems to be at the sole discretion of local authorities in each city to decide when and where such a requirement is applicable. If interpreted in the sense that parking places are also necessary in each case where a building permit is required for construction work to an existing building or when the owner changes its current purpose to a new one, the owners of existing buildings might be prevented from performing such works (of course, only if the existing building does not have the minimum number of parking places).

Second, due to lack of any clear objective criteria for granting parking places, one undertaking might receive parking places on public land (in exchange for an amount to be paid below the real costs of building a parking space) while another would need to invest significant funds in building its own parking places.

The analysis presented in Annex 2.A2 leads to the conclusion that the cost of each parking space differs from area to area and from city to city. The main influential factor that causes these differences to occur is the cost of land. The range of costs for each parking place (also including the cost of land) is between EUR 2 644 and EUR 49 024 (in central Bucharest). However, on average, the cost per parking place is EUR 11 574 for a ground floor option, EUR 15 121 for the two floors of underground parking and EUR 13 777 for three floors of underground parking. The cost per parking place calculated on each scenario is equivalent to the cost advantage/benefit of a private investor for each parking place granted by the local public authority through the exception identified.[36]

Policy maker's objective. The objective of the provision is to provide a solution for the lack of sufficient parking places by allowing public land to be used for the necessary parking places.

Recommendation. We recommend amending the legislation in the sense that the requirement to ensure parking places in order to obtain the building permit is applicable only when erecting new buildings. Furthermore, in order to avoid discretionary application of the legislation by public authorities, the possibility of granting parking places on public land should be limited solely to areas such as city centres, protected areas or areas in which the buildings have no direct access to roads. Each city hall would then establish which areas fall under the exception.

Lack of clear/objective criteria to be used in the control activity of the State Construction Inspectorate

Description of the obstacle. In Romania, the State Construction Inspectorate (SCI) is responsible for controlling and inspecting construction activities, thus ensuring compliance of constructions with the legislation in force, the quality of the construction works and the uniform application of legal provisions in the field. SCI decides on the type of control applicable to each construction process (including the type of control in case of verification of a quality management system), taking into account the complexity of the works. The control applied may be either a regular one (planned control of all important documents and operations which is carried out on the basis of a prior established agenda) or a random one (unplanned control of selective documents and operations).

The legislation in force does not prescribe any criteria for SCI when deciding to pursue random control.

Harm to competition. Due to a lack of clear criteria when assessing the type of control applicable, SCI might discriminate between competing undertakings on the market. There is only limited predictability for the subjects of the random control activities. Those operators subject to random control need to allocate supplementary time resources for controls by SCI.

Policy maker's objective. The lawmaker has allowed SCI to decide on the type of control applicable to each construction process during the execution phase in order to use its resources efficiently and to prioritise. According to SCI, a "system procedure" could be implemented containing criteria on the type of control (a "system procedure" provides general rules in comparison to an "operational procedure" which provides detailed criteria).

Recommendation. Implement a "system procedure" to be used by the SCI when assessing the complexity of the works and deciding when to apply random controls.

Annexes subject to a demolition permit

Description of the obstacle. Article 8 of Law No. 50/1991 regarding authorisation for the execution of construction works establishes the obligation to obtain a demolition permit prior to any demolition, removal or dismantling, partial or total, of a construction. The constructions that are subject to a demolition permit are not clearly defined in this piece of legislation, as the lawmaker also included the installation annexes in the notion of constructions, a notion which is not explained in the law.

Harm to competition. Lack of definition for installation annexes to constructions, might trigger arbitrary application of the provision by public authorities, on a case-by-case basis. In practice, this would result in discrimination among market participants as the authorities might come to different interpretations when issuing the building permit.

Policy maker's objective. The demolition permit should guarantee that demolitions of constructions are performed in a safe manner, both for the construction and for the population. The object of the provision is to discourage any potentially dangerous demolition works without obtaining a demolition permit, by including in the buildings subject to demolition permit a broad category of assets of the building.

Recommendation. We recommend to define the installation annexes to construction that are subject to a demolition permit, taking into account what affects the structural stability of buildings.

Different treatment of undertakings in comparable situations

Under the revised legislation, we identified several provisions that limit services/sales of goods without an objective justification. Especially, by limiting the categories of products that can be sold in specific places, by interfering with the business activity of the undertakings depending on their location or by establishing a different treatment towards undertakings active on the market depending on their size, there might be discrimination between undertakings in comparable situations.

Street sales from stalls

Description of the obstacle. According to Article 1 of Law No. 50/1991 regarding authorisation for the execution of construction work, the execution of construction work is possible only after obtaining a building permit. Among the exceptions to this rule, according to Article 11 of the same law, construction work for placing stalls for the distribution and trading of newspapers, books and flowers is exempt from the obligation to obtain a building permit. This exception is applied in cases where the stalls are affixed directly to the ground, do not have foundations or platforms, and are not supplied with any public utilities except electricity.

Harm to competition. Restricting the products that vendors are allowed to sell in stalls may potentially limit the development of businesses of market participants and may also limit consumer choice. These restrictions affect three groups: i) the vendors who already have the respective stalls are restricted to trading only newspapers, books and flowers; ii) the undertakings that are interested in street trading of products other than newspapers, books and flowers do not benefit from the exception, resulting in potentially higher costs for them compared to the "preferred traders" and iii) consumers have access to a more limited variety of products.

Our research in other EU Member States (for example Austria) showed that the differentiation of construction regulations is based on the size of the project but not on the categories of products sold.

Policy maker's objective. The objective of this provision is to reduce the administrative burden for simple constructions with low complexity. We have not identified the reasons why only stalls selling books, flowers and newspapers are covered by the exception.

We identified street trading regulations in municipalities in Austria, Germany and in the United Kingdom. Street trading provisions in London, for example, foresee an application in writing, including information on the time, date and location of the envisaged street sale, to a local district council. An application may be rejected, among other reasons, if the stall would cause interference or inconvenience to street users or if there are convictions for previous behaviour (e.g. the failure to pay fees or misusing the licence) making a seller unsuitable to hold a licence.

Recommendation. We recommend extending the exemption from the obligation to obtain a building permit to also include all stalls which are directly affixed to the ground, without foundations or platforms and that only need to be supplied with electricity.

However, keeping in mind environmental and public safety considerations together with the public's right to use the street, we recommend that each city hall issues a public policy with respect to street trading and the conditions under which such businesses may be permitted to operate without a building permit.

The availability of spaces to be used for street trading should be a decision for each city hall and each city hall should implement limits in order to ensure that the undertakings carrying out commercial activities on public land are not abusing this right. It should ensure that vendors are not transforming such stalls into actual stores and that environmental and public safety considerations together with the public's right to use the street are observed.

Thus, the legislation should provide, for example, the following types of limitations for a stall erected on public land:

- It shall not lead to, or cause, congestion or block pedestrian traffic on the sidewalk (establishing thus maximum sizes of the stall).
- Commercial activities would involve a short transaction period necessary for completing the sale or rendering the service.
- It shall not cause undue noise or offensive odours.

Construction work in coastal areas

Description of the obstacle. According to Law No. 597/2001 regarding certain protection and authorisation measures of construction in the coastal areas of the Black Sea, in seaside resorts and tourist beach areas, it is prohibited to carry out construction or maintenance works between 15 May and 15 September. Starting in 2014, works within a project financed with non-reimbursable external funds, on-going works, seasonal works, urgent works and works that do not affect touristic activities are exempt from the abovementioned prohibition, and are therefore allowed.

Harm to competition. This provision interferes with the business activity of undertakings due to the fact that the interdiction to carry out construction or maintenance works in coastal areas is applicable automatically, without prior assessment of the execution period, location to risk the health and safety of persons made by the local public authority.

In addition, the legal provision discriminates between undertakings carrying out economic activity inside the interdiction zone and those located outside the interdiction zone (i.e. resorts in the mountains or at historical sites) for which there is no such prohibition.

Finally, the large number of exceptions may allow circumvention of the application of the interdiction, considering that the interdiction is not applicable for a project financed with non-reimbursable external funds, on-going works, seasonal works, urgent works or works that do not affect tourist activities.

Policy maker's objective. The objective of the provision is to keep construction works from interfering with tourist activity during the full occupancy season in coastal areas.

International comparison did not reveal regulations similar to the Romanian legislation on works in tourist areas. In the EU Member States investigated, for example in Croatia, hotels and similar tourist buildings may only be constructed within special spatial areas and have to be built in accordance with regional and municipal zoning plans (thus, rules are established at a local level). In addition, further spatial zoning rules apply to construction in most parts of the coastal area and islands.

In Romania, when issuing a building permit, the local authorities have the power to analyse each case and to regulate the periods when construction can be carried out or prohibited in cases where such construction works may damage the health of the population.[37]

Recommendation. We recommend to abolish Article 6 of Law No. 597/2001. Any restriction to build should only be established when necessary at the local community level rather than at the national level. Each public authority has the capacity to establish when a construction could affect tourist activities and thus to regulate the time periods when construction can be carried out or prohibited.

Fire protection authorisation

Description of the obstacle. Government Decision No. 1739/2006 for approving the types of constructions for which fire protection authorisation should be obtained establishes that buildings under a specific size (determined in consideration of the number of square metres [m^2] of a building and type and the purpose of a building) do not need a fire protection permit.

A fire protection permit certifies the implementation of fire safety measures provided by the law. This permit is mandatory, as a functioning condition, for undertakings owning buildings who carry out their activity in these buildings.

Harm to competition. This provision might create advantages for those enterprises owning small-size buildings.

Policy maker's objective. Most probably, the lawmaker has considered that small buildings are easier to evacuate.

Recommendation . We recommend abolishing this exception and making fire protection authorisation compulsory for all buildings, irrespective of their size.

Conflict of interest

Description of the obstacle

We have identified several provisions in the revised legislation which might lead to potential conflict of interest between competing undertakings (or potential competitors), mainly due to the involvement of professional associations in the decision-making process of the competent public authorities. Members of professional associations, usually experts in their field, participate and collaborate with public authorities, providing technical expertise, and thus contributing to the decisions taken by the authorities and even control the activity of other competitors, and are subsequently involved in the control carried out by the SCI. Thus, competitors are in a position to (potentially) directly affect competing undertakings. This risk is increased even more by the fact that the national competent authority for controls in the construction sector, the SCI, works together with professional associations on multiple levels.

Romanian law does not provide mechanisms and rules to determine, manage or avoid possible conflict of interest for these specific scenarios.

Examples of the involvement of professional associations in the construction field.

All construction works must be verified by quality experts in all phases of construction. In accordance with Article 23 of Decision No. 925/1995 approving the regulation of verification and technical expertise of quality of projects, execution work and construction, the certificate of the quality experts can be suspended/cancelled by the Ministry of Regional Development and Public Administration (MDRAP), based on a report prepared by a group of three experts. One member of the group must be an expert recommended by a professional association active in the field.

A similar situation was identified in the legislation regarding the measures undertaken to mitigate the seismic risk of existing buildings. According to Government Ordinance No. 20/1994 on measures to mitigate the seismic risk of existing buildings, intervention works to buildings containing a seismic risk are carried out by state authorities (MDRAP) based on a technical solution issued by a designer. Technical solutions are also reviewed by the National Commission for Seismic Risk, a technical body set up by the authority with a consultative role. This commission analyses the technical solution and advises MDRAP, the authority that approves the technical solution. Members of the commission also include experts appointed by professional associations and representatives of employers' unions in the field. Even though formally MDRAP is not obliged to consider the input received from the National Commission for Seismic Risk when deciding whether to approve or not the technical solution, it is likely that MDRAP follows the advice of the National Commission for Seismic Risk (as its members are the ones providing technical input and expertise).

Additionally, the SCI also works with professional associations in order to develop expertise, prepare research reports and issue technical solutions.

Finally, professional associations also collaborate with public authorities in the field of energy performance of constructions. According to Emergency Ordinance No. 18/2009 for increasing the energy performance of housing blocks, representatives of professional associations in the field of energy performance (such as energy auditors) collaborate with technical committees when approving local programmes for increasing the energy performance of housing blocks. A possible conflict of interest might arise as the energy auditors would be subsequently involved in the control procedure of the SCI. Two provisions are provided in the current legislation:

- According to Article 31 of Law No. 372/2005 regarding energy performance of buildings, specialists appointed by professional associations in the construction field participate in the checks carried out by the SCI.
- According to Article 16 of Order No. 3152/2012 approving Control procedures regarding the unitary application of the legal provisions regarding energy performance of buildings and the control of heating/air conditioning systems, the professional associations of construction designers, plumbing engineers, energy auditors, architects and technical experts in air conditioning/heating systems participate in the checks carried out by the SCI.

Thus, energy auditors contribute in the first instance to the technical committees in creating the rules which they then also control by participating in checks together with the SCI.

Harm to competition

In all the cases above, market participants decide on the matters of their competitors. There is a danger of foreclosure of competition, a dictation of the interests of the professional associations, especially against newcomers or so-called mavericks, which aggressively compete in a market, and the possible exchange of sensitive information between competitors. Another negative consequence could be the implementation of unnecessary administrative barriers due to a tendency to standardise interests and actions in cases where the members of private associations may influence the attitude of the public authorities and the legislation in their favour.

Policy maker's objective

The involvement of professional associations in the decision-making process of the authorities could prove to be beneficial as they come with high expertise. The lawmaker established such a procedure due to a lack of their own experts working in public administration.

Recommendation

We recommend amending the national legislation in order to establish a complete, clear and accessible set of conflict rules to be followed by professional associations. The implementation of an ethical code of conduct should be mandatory for each professional association involved in public decisions. The code of conduct should cover at least rules regarding identification of what constitutes a conflict of interest (i.e., an expert who is part of a technical commission or committee controlling or analysing the issuance of a permit for a competitor), the disclosure procedure and the obligation to abstain from actively participating in the decision-making process of the authority in case of conflict. As a result of this recommendation, each representative of a professional association taking part in a government decision would have the necessary knowledge and tools to disclose the potential conflict of interest and, if this is the case, refrain from actively participating in the activity of the technical commission or committee in question. Such codes of conduct are also implemented in other fields in other Romanian sectors (see, for example, Law No. 7/2004 regarding the code of conduct applicable to public servants or Regulation No. 5/1995 on the code of ethics and conduct of the members and staff of the National Securities Commission).

It might also be helpful (although not a legal measure) to hire more independent experts for the internal structures of public authorities, which would mitigate the risk of conflict of interest. Also, compliance training within the associations and ministries might be helpful. However, this as well as the hiring of experts may be difficult to implement in practice, from the perspective of both the number of experts available and the increased costs for public authorities.

Opportunity notice

Description of the obstacle

In Romania, the functions of an area (such as housing, services, production, circulation, green spaces and public institutions) and the coefficient of utilisation of a terrain (the part of the land that can be used for buildings) are mentioned in planning regulations.

When a private investor wishes to build but the project is not compatible with existing planning regulations, he/she may request a derogation from the existing planning regulations already approved for the respective area. For that purpose, the investor prepares and submits to the public authority (i.e., the local council) a technical document generally called an "opportunity study". After analysing the opportunity study, the planning and the Territory Arrangement Department within the city hall can issue the opportunity notice. Often, this department is advised by a consultative technical commission (such consultative commissions do not exist in every municipality). The opportunity notice also needs to be approved by the mayor of the municipality. Based on the opportunity notice, the local council can then issue a new zonal urbanistic plan.[38]

We identified the following issues in relation to this process:

- As described, the decision of the planning and territory arrangement department within the city hall that issues the opportunity notice is often based on the input given by a consultative technical commission. Each city hall can decide through a local council decision if it wants to set up such a consultative technical commission or not. The technical commission i) has no clear criteria when it advises on the opportunity study prepared by the investor and ii) it is not organised in the same manner in all localities.
- Upon amendment and based on the opportunity notice, the initial coefficient of terrain usage[39] may be exceeded by a maximum of 20%. This limitation applies to all lands except those located in an area with an economic purpose, such as industrial parks, technological parks, supermarkets, hypermarkets, commercial parks, service areas and other similar areas. There are two issues related to this matter: i) for those excepted areas there is no limitation of percentage by which the initial coefficient of land usage may be exceeded, and ii) the notion of "similar areas" is not defined.

Harm to competition

Considering that the consultative technical commissions are not organised in the same manner in all counties and that there are no clear criteria when giving input for changing existing urbanistic plans, this might lead to arbitrary advice in granting the opportunity notices.

As regards the coefficient of land usage:

- The lack of a definition for the notion of "similar areas" may lead to an uneven application of the law by the local authorities and discrimination may take place between market participants.
- The possibility for the land located in areas designated to be of economic interest should have different coefficients of land usage.

Lawmaker's objective

We have not identified any objective concerning the organisation of the consultative technical commission. As regards land usage, according to the official recital, the objective is to allow economic and industrial development in certain areas in accordance with local economic interests.

Recommendation

The legislation should be amended in order to ensure that the technical commissions have the same organisational structure in all localities. Also, MDRAP should prepare a checklist and clear elements should be taken into consideration by the consultative technical commission when advising the planning and territory arrangement department within city hall with respect to the opportunity study.

In order to limit possible differing interpretations of "similar areas", we recommend either defining the notion of "similar areas" or eliminating it from the exception. In all cases, the lawmaker should set a threshold for the changes that can be made to the usage coefficient for land located in areas destined for economic activity.

Technical approvals

General description of legal framework

Technical approval, also called a technical agreement, is a favourable technical assessment regarding the use of new products, procedures or equipment for which there are no national standards or other official technical regulations in force, or the existing standards or rules are not completely suitable for the products, procedures or equipment. Technical approvals are required for a wide range of products including building materials.

The applicable legislation and issuance mechanism is different for harmonised or non-harmonised products:

- ***For non-harmonised products***, the technical approvals are elaborated by specialised entities which must be Romanian legal persons or associations of Romanian legal persons. The elaboration entities are private companies. According to data from the Standing Technical Council for Construction (CTPC) website,[40] there are currently 12 such entities active on the market. The elaboration entities must be authorised by the CTPC, a public supervisory body under MDRAP. The CTPC also approves the technical approvals issued by elaboration entities.
- ***For harmonised products***, EU legislation (mainly EU Regulation No. 305/2011 setting forth harmonised conditions for the marketing of construction products and repealing Council Directive 89/106/EEC) is directly applicable in Romania. In this case, the technical approval that is to be obtained by each manufacturer and applicable at the European level is called a European Technical Assessment (ETA). It is elaborated by technical assessment bodies (TABs). TABs are private Romanian entities notified to MDRAP, as providing this type o work. According to data from the CTPC website,[41] there are currently three such entities active on the market.

For further reference, please see Figure 2.6Relationship between several institutions for issuance of ETAs in Section 2.1 of this chapter.

Issues identified in the relevant legislation with respect to technical approvals for building materials

We identified several restrictions to competition. One of them consists of the composition of the CTPC and the participation of competitors in the authorisation process of the elaboration entities. The CTPC is formed, among others, of representatives appointed specifically by such existing elaboration entities. This means that the entities elaborating technical approvals are in a position to influence the decision of the CTPC according to their own interests. This is an issue of conflict of interest, similar to that described in Section 2.2.3 above. For such cases, we also recommend that national legislation be amended in order to establish a complete, clear and accessible set of conflict rules to be followed by the CTPC.

The other issues we identified with respect to technical approvals refer to prolongation or amendments of technical approvals and the distribution of contracts of entities elaborating technical approvals whose activity was suspended:

Amendment or extension of technical approvals

Description of the obstacle. An extension or an amendment of a technical approval can only be requested of the competent body that elaborated the initial technical approval. Only strict exceptions are allowed, for example if the issuing competent body no longer exists or if its activity was suspended by the competent authority.

Harm to competition. An undertaking intending to amend the initial technical approval or to prolong its duration is not free to choose the body that will make such amendments. This restriction thus affects competition between private companies authorised by the CTPC to elaborate technical approvals.

Recommendation. We recommend that this provision should be abolished.

Distribution of contracts concluded with a suspended entity which elaborated technical approvals

Description of the obstacle. If the activity of an entity elaborating technical approvals is suspended for any reason, the CTPC may discretionarily distribute the contracts of the suspended entity to other entities which elaborates technical approvals if the manufacturer (solicitor) cannot wait for the delay caused by the suspension of activity (suspension of activity lasts from three to six months). The law provides no criteria for the CTPC's allocation of the suspended entity's contracts to other entities. The opinion of the undertaking requesting the elaboration is not requested.

Harm to competition. Considering that the CTPC may discretionarily distribute the contracts to other entities that elaborate technical approvals, without criteria and without having to ask the producer, there is a risk of abuse and discrimination. Moreover, considering that representatives of the elaborating bodies are members of the CTPC, the distribution of contracts may be dictated by the representatives' own interests.

Recommendation. We recommend that the company requesting the elaboration of technical approval should be consulted when the project is allocated to another entity. The final decision on the allocation should remain with the solicitor and not with the CTPC.

Unclear provisions regarding the duration of validity of a technical approval

Description of the obstacle. The validity of a technical approval is three years but it may be extended by the CTPC to five years for certain products, services or equipment that are "safe" and "without risks". The provision does not define these notions.

Harm to competition. The unclear wording of the provision triggers the risk of abuse and discrimination in practice. Moreover, there is no predictability among the elaborating entities with respect to the application of this legal provision.

Recommendation. The national legislation should be amended so that it clearly defines the notion of products, services and equipment "without risk" and the notion of "safe" products, services and equipment.

Different criteria in evaluating the entities authorised to elaborate technical approvals

Description of the obstacle. The CTPC assesses the activity of entities elaborating technical approvals. Among others, the number of previously issued technical approvals is a criterion taken into consideration by the CTPC when determining whether or not to prolong or preserve the authorisation. Such a criterion is used in practice, but it is unclear how much this aspect counts when a decision is taken not to renew an authorisation.

Harm to competition. Taking into consideration the lack of guidelines in deciding whether to prolong or preserve the authorisation of entities elaborating technical approvals, this provision is likely to create an unjustified barrier to entry for newly-authorised entities, as well as for small ones.

Recommendation. We have identified two options:

- Abolish the provision that mentions the number of previously issued technical approvals as information to be provided to the CTPC when deciding on renewal of the authorisation to function.
- Amend the national legislation to mention explicitly that such information is required solely for statistical purposes and is not taken into consideration by the CTPC when assessing the activity of entities elaborating technical approvals.

Unclear provision with respect to the duration of the mandate of technical assessment bodies for harmonised building materials

Description of the obstacle. As described above, for harmonised building materials, TABs are the competent entities in elaborating the technical approval (i.e., ETA, as defined above). According to Article 6 para. (3) of Order No. 2142/2013 approving Procedures for designating the Technical Assessment Bodies for construction products, the duration of appointment of TABs by MDRAP is "generally" unlimited. The national law fails to provide criteria in order to assess whether the appointment is limited or not.

Harm to competition. This provision is likely to trigger the risk of discrimination and abuse, considering that national law practically allows the CTPC to discretionarily decide when to grant an unlimited designation for certain TABs. Thus, this provision is likely to favour the TABs with an unlimited mandate, considering that the designation procedure involves several stages of preparation and audit, which involves additional costs.

Recommendation. We have identified two possible options:

- to expressly stipulate cases in which the appointment is limited in time; and
- to amend the national legislation and to eliminate the word "generally" from the text of the legal provision, so that all appointments of TABs are granted for an unlimited period of time.

Regulatory burden

While legislation is essential for achieving policy objectives and creating benefits for businesses and society, it can also generate regulatory costs and burdens on businesses. In order to ensure competitiveness in a globalised world, to adjust to new social challenges and to achieve the purpose of a policy more efficiently and effectively, legislation and the regulatory cost and burden arising from it must be constantly revised and improved (European Commission, 2014).

We have identified several provisions of the legislation that constitute an administrative burden on businesses. These regulations do not have a direct bearing on competition; nonetheless, they constitute burdens on businesses and clearly affect the general environment. Two examples are provided below.

- The law establishes the obligation of obtaining a building permit or a demolition permit for any type of construction prior to commencement of works by the developer. The entire process of obtaining a building permit is bureaucratic as it involves submission of a significant amount of documentation, part of which includes documents issued by other state authorities involved in the process.

- The planning certificate is an informative document issued by the local public authorities ascertaining, among others, how land and existing constructions can be used in accordance with existing planning regulations. The planning certificate also informs the applicant of the approvals and notices necessary to obtain a building permit. The issuance of a planning certificate serves informational purposes and contains conditions that need to be observed in terms of construction work, green space requirements and classification as a historical monument.

In order to reduce the administrative burden on businesses, we recommend the use of all electronic means available and the elimination from the application dossier of all documents already in the possession of a state authority.

Strategies for reducing the administrative burden as well as various reports on the same issue have been prepared by the Romanian authorities responsible.[42] According to MDRAP, initiatives are currently being undertaken to simplify the bureaucracy and to implement e-government systems for issuing building and demolition permits as well as planning certificates. However, there are several conditions to be fulfilled at the local level in order to make the systems functional, such as the necessary IT resources and the availability of sufficient human resources with the required abilities.

Outdated legislation

We have identified several pieces of legislation that no longer correspond to the current socio-economic context of Romania. Those provisions contain unjustified restrictions or outdated rules no longer applicable in practice. Some of these provisions are left over from Romania's communist era. Outdated legislation should be abolished.

Examples of outdated legislation

Location of constructions used for service provision outside industrial areas

Description of the obstacle. According to Annex No. 1, section 1.3.7 of Government Decision No. 525/1996 approving the general urbanism regulation, it is forbidden to locate constructions used for services in industrial areas – except for services provided in buildings integrated with other purposes. Instead, buildings destined for service provision can only be built in central, commercial, residential or recreational areas. For example, within an industrial area, a car wash, shop or canteen could not be built if it was not integrated with other existing facilities.

Harm to competition. Although industrial activities should not be carried out in residential or service areas, it is not clear why the reverse should not be possible.

Policy maker's objective. The objective of the regulation might be to preserve the health of the labour force in service provision. Most probably, the provision comes from communist era Romania when there should have been dedicated areas for each purpose.

Recommendation. Amend legislation in order to allow service provision in industrial areas as long as specific health and safety regulations for each activity are observed.

Location of professional schools

Description of the obstacle. According to Government Decision No. 525/1996 approving the general urbanism regulation, professional schools can only be built within 1 000 metres of housing areas and neighbourhoods.

Harm to competition. Operators wanting to build a school outside a housing area are prevented from doing so.

Policy maker's objective. The provision establishes a maximum distance to be travelled by students. However, the limitation seems excessive considering the rapid expansion of cities and the means of transport available to the population in order to move around.

Recommendation. We recommend abolishing this provision.

Location of specialised medical centres

Description of the obstacle. According to Annex 1, point 1.7.4 of Government Decision No. 525/1996 approving the general urbanism regulation, specialised medical assistance for functional recovery, chronical diseases, psychiatric diseases and disabled persons need to be located in out-of-town areas. The law does not differentiate between contagious and non-contagious chronic diseases such as cancer.

Harm to competition. This provision is likely to affect private investors providing specialised medical assistance, which may have to bear additional costs for assuring all required treatment of conditions outside city areas, where access to utilities or transportation is limited. This is the opposite of other medical service providers located within the boundaries of a city. In addition, providers of services already located within the boundaries of a city are prevented from developing their businesses by also offering services for chronic diseases.

Policy maker's objective. This restriction is destined to protect healthy citizens and to offer an appropriate environment for the recovery of the sick, which is easier to achieve if the facility is located outside urban areas and is close to green spaces. Most probably, the provision comes from Romania's communist era when there should have been dedicated areas for each purpose.

Our research has shown that there are no limiting regulations on the location of medical centres in out-of-town areas in the regulations of other EU Member States.

Recommendation. The provision should be amended in order for the restriction to apply solely to contagious diseases if they require medical isolation, or if specific medical equipment used in curing the disease presents a risk to the surrounding population.

Export ban on timber and related products

Description of the obstacle. Since 1991, the export of timber and related products has been forbidden for all private agents, except companies or other entities under the Ministry of Resources and Industry (original name). Such entities are required to obtain a licence from the government. Following discussions with the business community, this limitation (imposed by Government Decision No. 1364/1990 prohibiting the export of raw or semi-finished wood products) we know that this is no longer applied in practice and that the export of timber is possible, in accordance with Article 35 of the Treaty of Functioning of the European Union – prohibition of export bans or equivalent.

However, we have identified a draft of a law regulating the export ban with respect to wood products which is currently under the legislative process of the Parliament.[43] The proposed law mentions as its objective the preservation of Romanian forests, which are currently being illegally exploited on a large scale. Also, the preamble of the proposed law specifies a limited applicability of the export ban for five years.

Harm to competition. The provision qualifies as an export ban, which triggers fragmentation of the market for trading timber. In addition, by granting the possibility of exporting solely to state-owned companies, a legal monopoly is created for those undertakings with a negative impact on pricing. Although it seems that the law is not applied in practice, keeping it in force might create legal uncertainty for undertakings.

Policy maker's objective. None of the ministries asked could explain the interdiction in the existing piece of legislation. However, the proposed law mentions as its objective the preservation of Romanian forests which are currently being illegally exploited on a large scale.

Our international research found no obstacles to the trade of timber in the European Union. Currently, Bulgaria only foresees an automatic licence mechanism by registration for the export of raw timber.

Recommendation. Abolish Government Decision No. 1364/1990. With regard to the new proposal of law currently under the legislative process, we recommend that the lawmaker reconsider the necessity of such a measure.

Powers granted to the General Inspectorate for Emergency Situations in relation to cases of unfair competition

Description of the obstacle. According to Article 19 of Order No. 607/2005 approving the control methodology regarding the monitoring of the market of construction products designed to protect constructions against fire, the General Inspectorate for Emergency Situations has the responsibility for solving unfair competition complaints.

Harm to competition. This provision infringes the provisions of Competition Law No. 21/1996 and Law No. 11/1990 regarding unfair competition, which provide for the exclusive attributions of the Romanian Competition Council (RCC) in this field. The RCC is best placed to decide on such cases.

Also, according to the Romanian legislative system, an order issued by the ministry cannot infringe a law of a superior force. The existence of such legal provisions may create uncertainty regarding the state authorities' competency in solving competition issues among market participants.

Recommendation. This provision should be abolished. Complaints of unfair competition should be solved in accordance with Competition Law No. 21/1996 and Law No. 11/1990 regarding unfair competition.

Not-published legislation, double legislation

Double legislation

In the revised technical legislation in the construction field we have identified several pieces of legislation which are not published in the *Official Gazette* of Romania. We also found cases where, although legislation was published, it is not generally available and a separate fee must be paid in order to obtain it. Moreover, we identified several pieces of legislation in force regulating the same object. This might affect the activity of economic operators and create legal uncertainty considering that it is unclear which piece of legislation should be followed.

Double legal framework on technical approvals. There are two pieces of legislation in force with the same object of regulating the legal framework, main elements, methodology and organisation on technical approval in the construction field. They are Order No. 1889/2004 approving certain procedures for technical approvals in the construction field, and Annex 5 of Government Decision No. 766/1997 approving certain regulations regarding quality in construction (Regulation on the technical approval of products, processes and equipment in construction). Considering that the content of the two pieces of legislation does not seem to be completely identical, the national legislation should be unified into one legislative act.

Double control activities. Annex 4 of Government Decision No. 766/1997 approving certain regulations regarding the quality of constructions regulates the same control activity as mentioned under Order No. 847/2014 approving the Procedure regarding control activities performed for enforcing the legal provisions related to the current and specialised monitoring of the serviceability of constructions. However, the control activities pertain to two different authorities, namely specialists of MDRAP and SCI. This uncertainty regarding the applicable legislation creates legal uncertainty and affects the activity of economic operators in complying with the legal requirements. The national legislation should be amended to establish a sole control authority.

Double legislation regarding ETA. Two pieces of legislation are in force regulating the European technical approval for construction products. Order No. 2190/2004 has the same objective as EU Regulation No. 305/2011 setting forth harmonised conditions for the marketing of construction products and repealing Council Directive 89/106/EEC. Similarly, Government Decision No. 622/2004 approving the conditions to introduce construction products onto the national market has the same objective as European Regulation No. 305/2011 setting forth harmonised conditions for the marketing of construction products and repealing Council Directive 89/106/EEC. Therefore, dual pieces of legislation are in force creating legal uncertainty for companies active in the field. According to the policy makers' objective, the national legislation was no longer applied once the European legislation came into force. We recommend that the part of the national legislation related to the harmonised technical approvals should be abolished to eliminate uncertainty regarding the applicable piece of legislation.

Legislation not published

We have identified several pieces of legislation which are not published in the *Official Gazette* of Romania. Moreover, sometimes pieces of legislation have been published but they are not easily available and it is necessary to pay a separate fee in order to obtain them. Some of these pieces of legislation are only contained in construction bulletins. Thus, the legislation in force is unclear for companies active in the field which may create legal uncertainty for undertakings willing to enter the market. Moreover, even if the interested undertakings find the legislation in a construction bulletin, it remains unclear for them whether these provisions have been replaced or if they are still in force. For example, Order No. 615/2003 approving the technical regulation "Regulation regarding the organisation and conduct of traffic surveys, origin, destination. Preparing data for processing" (revision DD 506 – 1988), having indicator DD 506 – 2001, was published in the *Official Gazette* of Romania (only the order was published, not the Annex containing the actual regulation). According to a list published by MDRAP on its website containing the technical enactments in force as of 1 January 2016 (the list was revised on 9 February 2016), the abovementioned regulation, with the identification DD 506-2001, was replaced by another regulation (DD 506-2015), in accordance with Decision No. 155/02.12.2015 of the National Company for Highways and National Roads of Romania. Neither the decision nor the new regulation were published in the *Official Gazette* of Romania, but only in a construction bulletin.

We recommend that all relevant provisions should also be published on the dedicated website of MDRAP in order to make the information easily available to all market participants.

Approval of neighbours

Description of the obstacle

Among the documents that must be submitted when applying for a building permit is the neighbours' approval· A neighbour`s approval is required in the following situations:

- when erecting a new construction adjacent to another building or in their immediate neighbourhood, if there are necessary measures for protecting such adjacent/ neighbouring buildings;
- when construction works which are necessary for changing the purpose of an existing building are performed; and
- when erecting new buildings having a different purpose from the surrounding buildings (e.g., erecting an office building while the surrounding buildings have a residential purpose).

Harm to competition

The obligation to have the neighbours' approval with respect to the purpose of a building creates uncertainty in the market and raises a barrier to entry onto the market for any potential investor. According to discussions held with the business community, such provisions sometimes lead to abuses in practice, in cases where neighbours request money for the approval or use it to keep competitors away. The neighbours' discretionary power not to allow an investment is contrary to the principles of economic freedom and competition. In practice, it would require significant time and costs for the undertakings to challenge the ungrounded refusal of neighbours to give their approval.

Policy maker's objective

The objective of the provision is to ensure that the neighbours have been informed about the construction works to be performed in their vicinity and have given their consent that their living environment will not be affected by the works. The lawmaker's intention was to protect existing owners from potential abuses/discomfort caused by incompatibilities between the pre-existing and proposed function. (e.g., a building is built to be used for concerts around a building used for personal purposes, office buildings or educational purposes – in general quiet activities).

International research shows that in Austria and Germany, for example, the challenging of a building permit does not have a suspensive effect on the permit itself. In addition, due to the exposure to abuse, i.e., the raising of unreasonable objections by neighbours to delay the project, it is worth noting that the Austrian law was changed in January 2015 and is now limited to instances where the neighbour is directly affected by the building project.

Recommendation

We recommend keeping the obligation to request the neighbours' approval in the cases described above. However, for those situations where the investor does not obtain the neighbours' approval, he should still be able to apply for the building permit. It is then up to the local authority to decide, taking account (but not being bound by) the neighbour's opinion.

2.3. Mining

Description of the legislative framework

Mining activities in Romania include prospecting, exploration, development, exploitation, preparation/processing, concentration, commercialisation of mining products, conservation and closure of mines, including work related to restoration and rehabilitation of the environment. The authority responsible in the field of mineral resources is the National Authority for Mineral Resources.

The right to perform mining activities is granted to an investor through:

- ***exploration licences*** – granted for identification of the deposits, their quantitative and qualitative assessment and determining the technical and economic exploring conditions;
- ***exploitation licences or permits*** – granted for all activities performed underground and/or above ground for the extraction and processing of mineral resources; and
- ***prospecting licences or permits*** – granted for all studies and surface operations carried out to identify the existence of the possible accumulation of mineral resources.

Interested undertakings or the authority responsible can take the initiative for commencing the process for conceding rights for prospecting, exploring or exploiting. Concession rights are granted following a competition where the interested entities have to demonstrate their technical and financial capabilities.

Prolongation of a mining licence

According to Article 20 of Law No. 85/2003 on mines, an exploitation licence can be granted for up to 20 years and may be extended for consecutive periods of a maximum of five (5) years each, without a maximum number of extensions foreseen by the legislation.

Possible harm to competition comes from the fact that, without foreseeing a maximum duration in time for the exploitation licence, other undertakings could be prevented from entering the market for an infinite time.

The lawmaker's objective is to ensure the continuity of investment. Mining requires large investments. The holder of the licence who discovered a deposit of mineral resources is carrying out mining activities at its own risk and cost. If the discovery is very significant it may require a long period of production until the mineral resources are depleted and investment costs are amortised.

In order to avoid preventing other interested undertakings from entering the market and in order to ensure predictability, we recommend amending the legislation and stipulating a maximum number of prolongations that can be granted by the authorities responsible before a new competition for awarding the licences has to take place.

Foreign entities performing mining activities in Romania

Mining activities may be carried out by Romanian companies, which are registered according to the law and are specialised and certified to perform mining operations. Foreign companies may also be granted mining permits and licences. However, according to Article 23 of Law No. 85/2003, the foreign company which has obtained the right to perform mining activities, must set up and maintain a subsidiary in Romania for the entire duration of the concession within ninety (90) days of the date when the licence entered into effect.

The harm of this provision to competition resides in the fact that additional administrative barriers are created for foreign undertakings when they have to open a subsidiary in Romania.

The lawmaker`s objective is that mining activities are large operations which must be monitored on a daily basis. Also, proper communication between the state and the investor should be ensured. However, the interdiction is not justified from a fiscal point of view, as neither a subsidiary, nor a branch is sufficient to declare a permanent establishment with the fiscal authorities.

In order to reduce additional administrative barriers for current and potential investors, we recommend amending the provision to allow any type of representation of foreign entities in Romania, not necessarily a subsidiary.

Financial guarantees when performing mining activities

At the end of the mining process, all mining operations must include activities for closure and post-closure (e.g., greening activities). In order to ensure that those obligations under the permit are fulfilled, undertakings performing mining activities have to establish a financial guarantee.

According to Articles 6 and 8 of Order No. 202/2881/2348/2013 of the National Agency for Mineral Resources, undertakings performing mining activities that involve closure and post-closure activities with a values below RON 4 000 000 (as estimated at the moment when the mining permit was granted) must establish a financial guarantee which can be provided exclusively in the form of a bank deposit. No other form of guarantee is accepted, such as a bank letter of guarantee or an insurance policy. The amount of the guarantee shall be put into an account established by the National Agency for Mineral Resources (ANRM).

The harm to competition is that a high volume of liquidities is blocked for those subject to this obligation, considering that only a bank deposit is accepted for performing the specific activities mentioned despite other forms of guarantees being available. This is likely to discriminate against small companies.

The provision is in line with EC Directive 2006/21 concerning the management of waste from extractive industries and with EC Decision 335/2009 on technical guidelines for the establishment of the financial guarantee. Directive 2006/21 foresees under Article 14 that the competent authority shall, prior to the commencement of any mining operations, require a financial guarantee (e.g., in the form of a financial deposit, including industry-sponsored mutual guarantee funds) or equivalent, in accordance with procedures to be decided by the EU Member States, ensuring that all the obligations under the permit will be fulfilled, including those relating to closure and post-closure of the waste facility.

We recommend amending the legislation in order to allow all legal types of guarantees (bank deposit, guarantee letter, insurance policies) to allow small companies to access the market.

Maximum price for gravel and sand

Description of the obstacle

The maximum prices for sand and gravel[44] are set based on provisions of GEO No. 36/2001 regarding regulated prices and tariffs, confirmed by the Competition Office (original name).

The maximum price for sand and gravel products is set separately for each producer and adjusted yearly based on the consumer price index. Maximum prices are only set for raw materials and do not cover materials mixed with other products used in construction.

At the end of 2014 there were 731 companies registered in Romania with the primary NACE[45] code 8.1.2 "Operation of gravel and sand pits; mining of clays and kaolin", of which 489 were active, with a total turnover[46] in 2014 of EUR 190.8 mln equivalent. We identified 759[47] active licences and permits for sand and rock exploitation in Romania (a company can have more than one permit or licence for several exploitation sites). On average, there are 19 exploitation sites per county.

Sand and gravel are also traded on the commodities market, thus establishing a transparent price.

There is currently a project on the agenda of the parliament to eliminate the maximum price for sand and rock.[48] By the date of release of this report, the project had not yet been voted upon.

Harm to competition

Maximum prices for rock and sand create the risk of having all producers align to the maximum price, thus creating a horizontal effect.

Policy maker's objective

According to the Ministry of Public Finance[49] local monopolies can occur through the heterogeneous dispersion of undertakings producing sand and gravel. In addition, this category of products has a significant impact on the cost of public works.

We undertook an international comparison in order to identify price regulations relating to sand and rock products but did not find any price regulations affecting rock and sand products in other EU Member States.

Recommendation

We recommend abolishing the maximum price for sand and gravel. Price caps can only be justified in exceptional cases and when there is evidence that an organisation is exploiting its market power. The analysis presented in Annex 2.A3 below shows that such a situation does not exist in Romania.

2.4. Environmental law

In addition to the revised legislation relevant to the construction field, we identified a number of provisions in environmental law that affect companies across sectors, including companies in the construction sector. The issues here mostly arise from a lack of clear national guidelines and rules, especially with regard to the wide discretion granted to environmental authorities (i.e., environmental territorial authorities subordinated to the National Environmental Protection Agency – NEPA) in the authorisation process of economic operators subject to the industrial emissions legislation. Often, the wide discretion seems to be the result of an improper transposition of European directives, i.e., the text of some directives was adopted into national law more or less identically, without specifying important terms and notions.

Unguided discretion when imposing stricter authorisation conditions for economic operators in the field of industrial emissions

Description of the obstacle

Directive 2010/75 of the European Parliament and of the Council on industrial emissions[50] was transposed into the national legislation through Law No. 278/2013 on industrial emissions. Directive 2010/75 defines the concept of BAT conclusions ("best available techniques conclusions") containing the best available techniques, their description, information to assess their applicability, the emission levels associated with the best available techniques, associated monitoring, associated consumption levels and, where appropriate, relevant site remediation measures for certain fields involving industrial emissions.

BAT conclusions introduce a minimum binding standard for the EU Member States. According to Directive 2010/75, Member States may establish rules under which their national competent authorities may set stricter permit conditions than those described in the BAT conclusions. Article 14 of Law No. 278/2013 expressly provides the possibility that the competent authority may impose permit conditions which are stricter than those described in the BAT conclusions. However, the law does contain rules to be followed by the competent authorities when imposing such stricter conditions. Thus, it seems that authorities have unguided discretion to decide on a case-by-case basis.

Harm to competition

Due to a lack of clear guidelines and a predetermined set of rules adopted at the national level for when the competent authority may impose authorisation conditions stricter than the conditions resulting from BAT conclusions, the risk arises of market foreclosure and discrimination among market participants.

Recommendation

The national legislation should provide objective and transparent criteria for determining the situations in which the competent authority may impose stricter permit conditions than the conditions resulting from BAT conclusions.

Legitimate interest to challenge decisions of the competent authority in the field of industrial emissions

Description of the obstacle

Annex 4 of Law No. 278/2013 on industrial emissions, transposing Directive 2010/75, establishes rules regarding the obligation of the environmental authorities to make available to the public a wide range of information and data during the authorisation process of an economic operator. Article 25 of the same law provides that any interested third party having a "legitimate interest" may appeal the decisions, omissions, or any other acts of the competent authority in the field of industrial emissions. However, the law does not define "legitimate interest".

Harm to competition

Failing to establish specific examples of what constitutes a legitimate interest of a third party in the field of industrial emissions gives the authority and the relevant courts of law wide discretion in appreciating the legitimacy of claims of third parties.

Policy maker's objective

Directive 2010/75 states expressly that Member States must establish what constitutes a sufficient interest and breach of a right in the relevant field to allow the affected third party to challenge decisions, omissions, or any other acts of the competent authority.

Recommendation

The lawmaker should issue clear guidelines with examples stating when a third party has a legitimate interest in challenging a decision regarding industrial emissions.

Restrictive emission limits for certain air pollutants depending on the geographical area

Description of the obstacle

According to Article 57 par. 3 of Law No. 104/2011 on ambient air quality, in the areas where emissions in the air for certain pollutants exceed the thresholds contained in the legislation in force, the environmental authority will impose more restrictive emission limits than those previously existing "for these pollutants", based on studies assessing their environmental impact.

Harm to competition

The wording of this provision is unclear concerning the subjects of the new emission limits for "these pollutants", with two possible interpretations. One would be that the more restrictive conditions are imposed only on new pollutants. Another possible interpretation would be that more restrictive conditions may also be imposed on old pollutants (in this case, the thresholds contained in the environmental authorisation of the economic operators may also be modified).

Recommendation

The national legislation should be amended in order to clarify how and to what type of pollutants the restriction applies.

Unclear criteria with respect to the procedure of the environmental impact of certain projects

Description of obstacle

Order No. 863/2002 on the approval of methodological guidelines applicable to the framework procedure for evaluating environmental impact does not provide clear criteria to be followed by the environmental authority when deciding to initiate the evaluation procedure in case of projects with a potential impact on the environment.

After the economic operator submits certain data and information regarding its project to the environmental authority, the competent authority has to decide whether the project will go to the evaluation procedure or not. In order to take such a decision, the authority fills in a control list consisting of prepared questions based on the data provided by the economic operator. The possible answers for the economic operator are "Yes", "No", "Not applicable" or "Unclear". Then the authority decides if the project must go to the evaluation procedure or not. The legislation does not provide clear criteria to be followed by the authority when taking such a decision. Order No. 863/2002 establishes that even a single "Yes" answer in the control list could trigger the decision to submit the project for further evaluation.

Harm to competition

Failing to provide clear and objective criteria for the authorities to follow in the screening stage triggers the risk of discrimination and possible abuse by the authority when deciding which projects should be further evaluated. Those operators subject to the evaluation procedure need to allocate supplementary time resources and this further evaluation might create additional costs.

Recommendation

The procedure for evaluating the environmental impact should be amended to include clear criteria for the authority when deciding which projects to further evaluate. It should also provide a minimum threshold for determining when an evaluation is mandatory. It might also be helpful to publish the decisions of the competent authority for each project on its website in order to create transparency and predictability for the undertakings active on the market.

2.5. Public procurement

Public procurement in Romania

In Romania, public procurement is mainly regulated by Government Emergency Ordinance No. 34/2006 on the awarding of public procurement contracts, public works concession contracts and concession of services (GEO No. 34/2006). GEO No. 34/2006 transposed the provision of Directive 2004/17/EC co-ordinating the procurement procedures of entities operating in the water, energy, transport and postal services sectors and Directive 2004/18/EC on the co-ordination of procedures for the awarding of public works contracts, public supply contracts and public service contracts (former EU Directives on public procurement). Besides GEO No. 34/2006, secondary legislation regarding procurement is also applicable (e.g., Government Emergency Ordinance No. 54/2006 on the regime of public assets concession contracts) and relevant provisions in other construction framework laws (e.g., Law No. 50/1991 authorising the execution of construction works and Government Emergency Ordinance No. 18/2009 for increasing the energy performance of housing blocks).

In 2014, in order to simplify the public procurement procedures and to make them more transparent and flexible, three new EU directives for the reform of the public procurement system were adopted: Directive 2014/23/EU on the awarding of concession contracts, Directive 2014/24/EU on public procurement and Directive 2014/25/EU on procurement by entities operating in the water, energy, transport and postal services sectors.[51] Romania is currently in the process of transposing the new EU directives. The enactment will be made through four new bills, regulating classical procurement, sectoral procurement, concessions and appeal procedures. These bills have recently been adopted by the Senate and were sent for approval to the Chamber of Deputies (the decision-making chamber of the parliament). The bills are available on the Chamber of Deputies' website.[52]

While the following analysis focusses on identifying problems within the legislation in force, it also deals with the provisions of new drafts of public procurement legislation, as some of the identified issues would be resolved by the enactment of these new bills.

Generally speaking, public procurement in Romania is in line with the EU framework legislation. However, national authorities face serious practical problems, including corruption, as detailed below. According to the Transparency International Corruption Perceptions Index, on a scale from 0 to 100, (0 being highly corrupted and 100 very clean) Romania averaged a score of 46 for the year 2015 in terms of public perception relating to the corruption level in general and it was the 58th ranked country (out of 168 participant countries) for perceived transparency. Romania has one of the lowest scores among EU Member States (tied with Greece).

According to a report prepared by the Romanian Academic Society (RAS) in 2016, one of the major problems of public procurement in Romania is the allocation of public contracts to certain companies who benefit from governmental favouritism. This study showed that for the period between 2007 and 2013, one agreement out of seven was granted to companies that have formally donated money to one or more political parties.

Romania is taking steps to improve the environment in public procurement. While legislative measures have already been taken in order to ensure more transparency during the procurement procedure and to block the awarding of contracts to preferred companies, the Romanian Competition Council (RCC) is actively involved in national efforts to fight procurement fraud. As of the date of this report (March 2016), a proposed bill regarding conflict of interest rules for civil servants in public procurement was adopted by the Chamber of Deputies and sent for approval to the Senate. This bill is available on the Chamber of Deputies' website.[53] In addition, in March 2016, GEO No. 34/2006 was amended in the sense that the contracting authorities are now obliged to use electronic means for carrying out procurement procedures in at least 60% of cases for the year of 2016 (the threshold for 2017 is at least 80%, while starting with 2018, the use of electronic means becomes completely mandatory). The introduction of electronic means will also increase the possibility of monitoring public agreements after their awarding as the related addenda will also be publicly available. Currently, not all addenda to initial agreements are published in SEAP (electronic database as defined in the Economic overview).

Fighting bid rigging is a priority for the RCC. Bid rigging qualifies as an anti-competitive practice, which is prohibited and sanctioned by Competition Law No. 21/1996. The OECD has published various materials on collusion and bid rigging, including *Guidelines for Fighting bid rigging in Public Procurement* (2009) and *Recommendations on Fighting Bid Rigging in Public Procurement* (2012).

The issues identified upon review of the legislation and following consultation with market participants are presented below.

Limitation of the number of participants

As shown in the Economic overview above, according to the European Commission's Single Market Scoreboard, the overall performance of the Romanian public procurement system is rated as below average. One of the reasons for that was bidder participation, and especially the high numbers of tenders with only one bidder. According to the report prepared by the RAS in 2016, mentioned above, for the period between 2007 and 2013, public tenders with a single participant took place in 21.4% of the cases. This means that one public contract out of five has been granted to the sole participant of the tendering process.

A limited number of participants in public procedures affects competition between market participants and, as a consequence, prices on the market and the quality of the work/services/supply provided.

In the revised legislation, we identified certain provisions which, applied discretionary by the contracting authorities, might be the cause for the limited number of participants in public tenders. For example, the contracting authorities may restrict access to economic operators by imposing certain participation conditions (such as prior experience) on a case-by-case basis. Another example is the practice of setting the deadlines for submitting the tenders by the contracting authorities at the minimum threshold provided by the law. Some market participants claim they are too short, particularly in the case of more complex projects. Although these issues are not linked to the legal provisions in force but to the practices of the contracting authority, this is possibly due to the unguided powers granted to contracting authorities. In all these cases our recommendation is to draft guidelines to give market participants and contracting authorities a sufficient level of predictability and transparency with respect to the application of legal provisions.

Estimates of the benefits if particular restrictions identified below are lifted (quantitative analysis)

We performed a quantitative analysis to investigate possible relationships between various features of procurement procedures and the outcomes of these procedures as indicated in Annex 2.A1. The regression analyses were run on a number of variables constructed from a set of completed procurement procedures meeting predefined criteria. The results suggest that there is more competition where participants submit more offers (or more offers are accepted by the public authority) as this leads to a larger discount of the award price from the original estimated price. Also, a larger contract value and more days available for preparing bids are correlated with a higher number of offers submitted. By extrapolating the results of the analysis to all construction procedures in 2014, and accepting a number of assumptions, it is estimated that the total savings resulting from a decreased award price can amount to approximately EUR 418 mln by stimulating, on average, one additional acceptable bid in construction procurement procedures. Similarly, two additional offers could yield approximately EUR 871 mln in savings.

Situations in which the contracting authority starts negotiations without prior publication of a participation notice

Description of the obstacle. According to Article 122 letter c) of GEO No. 34/2006, the contracting authority may start negotiations for the tender procedure without the prior publication of a participation notice in cases of extreme urgency, resulting from unforeseeable situations which cannot be the result of misconduct of the contracting authority. Moreover, in cases of force majeure or duly justified cases, the contracting authority may order the beginning of the works/services in parallel with the initiation of the negotiation, without the prior publication of a participation notice procedure (i.e., before the execution of the procurement contract).

This provision is similarly contained in the newly-proposed public procurement legislation under Article 104 par. 1 and par. 4 of the bill regulating classical procurement.

Harm to competition. Considering that the notions of "extreme urgency" and "duly justified cases" are not properly defined in legislation, the contracting authorities have broad power to decide, on a case-by-case basis, when to apply the exception (thus avoiding the publication of the participation notice). Following discussions with market participants, it is our understanding that, in practice, the contracting authorities use the lack of definitions in order to avoid procurement even in cases where, in reality, the situation provoking the application of the exception does not result from an unforeseeable situation.

Policy maker's objective. The objective of the provision is to eliminate bureaucratic procedures and to reduce waiting time in cases of extreme urgency and resulting from unforeseeable situations. This is in line with Art. 32 of Directive 2014/24. According to the National Agency for Public Procurement (ANAP), there are some materials containing guidance for contracting authorities to apply this provision. There is a document published on ANAP website[54] regarding the general applicability of Article 122, mentioned above, but it does not provide adequate instructions or concrete examples for contracting authorities and market participants as regards the application of these exceptional situations.

Recommendation. We recommend one of the following options:

- The legislation (and the new proposed legislation) should define more clearly the notions of "extreme urgency" and "duly justified cases" to mitigate and restrain the discretionary power of the contracting authorities.
- Draft guidelines with examples of situations which may be considered as "extreme urgency" or "duly justified cases", based on European and national case law and practical experiences from the past. Such guidelines would give procurement authorities and market participants predictability with respect to the application of these provisions. Ensure that such materials are published on ANAP's website and applied in practice by all contracting authorities.

Time limits for submission of offers

Description of the obstacle. The Romanian public procurement legislation currently in force provides various deadlines for the tender procedures (e.g., minimum time limit for submission of the participation request, for sending the invitation request, for submission of offers). For example,[55] for an open procedure, the minimum term for submission of offers is 20 days/52 days, depending on the estimated value of the agreement. Though these are minimum deadlines, in practice they are often applied by the Romanian contracting authorities as fixed terms without considering the complexity of each project. These deadlines, if strictly applied in practice, may lead to potential impediments for economic operators in submitting sound offers, especially for undertakings participating in more complex projects or for small companies. Also, following discussions with market participants, we understand that there are offers submitted within this timeframe which are of low quality.

The newly-proposed public procurement legislation establishes even shorter minimum terms than the current ones, in accordance with Directive 2014/24.[56] For example, according to Directive 2014/24.[57] the minimum term for an open procedure was reduced to 35 days (by comparison, the term is to 52 days according to the legislation in force), a term which can be even further shortened in certain instances by up to 20 days to a minimum of 15 days.

Harm to competition. Since in practice the contracting authorities frequently use minimum terms as fixed ones rather than establishing appropriate terms considering the specifics of each project, many economic operators may be prevented from submitting sound offers for more complex projects. If the contracting authorities used longer deadlines when necessary, more offers could be submitted. Thus, the competition between economic operators would intensify, prices would drop and/or the quality of the works performed would improve.

Policy maker's objective. The deadlines prescribed by the law are minimum periods to be respected by the contracting authority, which may be extended, depending on the complexity of the contract and the time required for drawing up and submitting bids. According to ANAP, considering the multitude of public procedures undertaken annually and the particularities of the documentation for each tender, it is difficult to implement generally applicable rules when setting the deadlines.

Recommendation. We recommend drafting instructions giving practical examples (taken both from national and international practice) for contracting authorities to show how deadlines should be set in accordance with the complexity of the contract and the project. These instructions should be a useful tool for contracting authorities in further setting such deadlines.

Limitation of participants in the awarding procedure based on experience

Description of the obstacle. According to Article 188 of GEO No. 34/2006, for certain public procurement agreements, the contracting authority may request that economic operators submit proof of their prior professional experience in the last three years (for supply and service agreements) or in the last five years (for works agreements). The contracting authorises may request professional experience as a condition of participation considering the nature and complexity of the public agreement. Thus, the contracting authorities are free to decide whether to request professional experience or not on a case-by-case basis.

Harm to competition. Discretionary power is granted to contracting authorities which are allowed to request proof of professional experience, on a case-by-case basis, depending on the complexity of the public agreements. Due to a lack of any guidance when taking the decision as to whether to request proof of professional experience or not, the contracting authorities decide on a case-by-case basis when to apply the provisions. Therefore, contracting authorities might take different decisions in similar situations. This may qualify as a barrier to entry onto the market and leads to an unpredictable business environment for private investors.

Policy makers' objective. The purpose of the provision is to ensure the proper experience of the bidders and to diminish the risk of non-fulfilment or inappropriate execution of the contract. The provision is in line with Annex XII of Directive 2014/24.

Recommendation. Guidelines should be published to give market participants and contracting authorities a sufficient level of predictability and transparency with respect to the situations in which contracting authorities may require proof of professional experience. According to ANAP, they are currently working on drafting instructions regarding requests for proof of professional experience.

Non-application of procedures under GEO No. 34/2006 for contracting authorities located outside Romania

Description of the obstacle. The general thresholds provided by GEO No. 34/2006 are as follows:

- For supply and servicing agreements below EUR 30 000 the contracting authority has no obligation to apply a public procedure; (for works agreements, the threshold is EUR 100 000).
- For supply and servicing agreements above EUR 30 000 and below EUR 130 000, the contracting authority has the obligation to apply a public procedure, including calls for tenders; (for works agreements the range is between EUR 100 000 and EUR 5 000 000).
- For supply and servicing agreements above EUR 130 000, the contracting authority has the obligation to apply a public procedure, excluding calls for tenders; (for works agreements the threshold is EUR 5 000 000)

As an exception to the above, the public procurement procedure is not applicable for "structures of the contracting authority functioning outside Romania" (including undertakings which qualify as contracting authorities because they are state owned) when the value of the public procurement agreement is lower than: a) EUR 130 000 for a supply agreement; b) EUR 130 000 for a servicing agreement; and c) EUR 5 000 000 for a works agreement.

This exception might allow the following scenario: a state-owned company which qualifies as a contracting authority requires the performance of services (which are carried out exclusively on the territory of Romania) through a subsidiary set up in another state. In such a case the general public procurement procedures under GEO No. 34/2006 would not be applicable.

The procedure for performing works outside the territory of Romania is not governed by European directives but needs to be established at the national level.

However, GEO No. 34/2006 does not provide clear criteria to be applied by the "structures of the contracting authority functioning outside Romania" when awarding an agreement without applying a public tender, such as conditions to be met by the economic operators (i.e., qualification, reputation, experience, or guidelines for the contracting authorities to be followed when choosing the economic operator). GEO No. 34/2006 solely provides very general principles to be followed (e.g., non-discrimination, equal treatment for the participants, transparency).

In a similar manner, the same procedure is also provided in the new proposed public procurement legislation. While the current procedure governed by GEO No. 34/2006 solely provides general principles to be followed when awarding contracts below the aforementioned thresholds, the new proposed public procurement legislation expressly states that below the thresholds (i.e., when the public procedures are not applicable), methodological norms (which have not been issued yet) will further establish rules covering general principles such as transparency or equality. It remains to be seen whether this issue will be properly addressed and resolved in the new legislation, considering that at the date of writing of this report, the methodological norms have not yet been elaborated.

Harm to competition. State-owned companies qualify as contracting authorities under national legislation even if their market activities are similar to other private undertakings. In situations where the objective of the agreement concluded by a contracting authority located outside Romania (supply, service, or works) is to be carried out exclusively on the territory of Romania, this provision is likely to cause discrimination between economic operators in terms of costs and timeline. Undertakings that do not have a subsidiary abroad are obliged to follow the procurement procedure under GEO No. 34/2006 when exceeding the general thresholds (EUR 30 000 for a supply or servicing agreement and EUR 100 000 for a works agreement) or applying the procedure of a request for offers. However, undertakings with a subsidiary abroad can purchase the work/services if the value of the agreement is under EUR 130 000 (for a supply or servicing agreement) or EUR 5 000 000 (for a works agreement) through that subsidiary, thus avoiding the application of GEO No. 34/2006.

Policy maker's objective. The exception is motivated by the difficulty of carrying out a request for an offer outside national territory.

Recommendation. The national legislation should be amended, so that the same thresholds apply in all situations involving public money, including to contracting authorities located outside Romania, when the objective of the procedure is the acquisition of works and/or services to be delivered within Romania.

Addenda

The need to conclude addenda usually comes from faults of the contracting authority in estimating the requirements of the works, or is the result of unforeseeable circumstances which incur additional costs.

In 2013, the RCC undertook a sector inquiry in the construction market of roads and highways. During this inquiry, the RCC also investigated the importance of addenda. According to its final report, for 96 contracts of road construction and services works 203 addenda were concluded in the period between June 2010 and June 2011, out of which 23 were modified in terms of value. Of the 23 contracts with a modified value, for 9 the value increased by between 10% and 40%; for 8 the value increased by almost 50%; and for 2 of them the value increased by more than 50%. Prior to 2011, the limit for concluding addenda was 50% of the initial value of the agreement. The contracts examined by the RCC were from this period.

According to Article 122 of GEO No. 34/2006, after awarding a public agreement the contracting authority may conclude an addendum to the agreement with the winner of the procedure having as its objective the modification of the price of the agreement up to 20% of the initial value, subject to certain conditions. Addenda can be concluded following direct negotiations between the authority and the economic operator, without an obligation to apply an additional public procurement procedure. However, if the value of the addenda is more than 20% of the initial value of the agreement, the contracting authority has the obligation to award the addenda only through a public procurement procedure.

National rules regarding the conclusion of addenda contained in the national legislation seem to be clear and, at least in theory, do not leave room for abuse. The small derogation allowed (concluding addenda without a public procedure if the value of the addenda is less than 20% of the initial value) seems fair and can be easily justified by the need to complete the public contract in a timely manner without incurring significant delays for such small amendments.

Derogation as regards addenda in case of intervention works to enhance the performance of buildings.

Description of the obstacle. According to Article 15 of the methodological norms of Emergency Ordinance No. 18/2009 for increasing energy performance of housing blocks, the contracting authority and the winner of the awarding procedure may conclude addenda to the agreements if the value of the addenda does not exceed the value of the initial agreement by more than 10%. This provision derogates from general procurement procedure rules, according to which additional works/services could be awarded directly to the initial winner without an additional public procedure if the value of the additional works does not exceed 20% of its initial value.

Harm to competition. The derogation from the general public procurement legislation may lead to delays in executing the work.

Policy maker's objective. We did not find a reason why the threshold is 10% instead of the usual 20%.

Recommendation. This derogation should be abolished. Awarding of agreements in the field of intervention works to enhance the energy performance of residential buildings should be governed exclusively by GEO No. 34/2006.

Unusually low price

The issue of abnormally low tenders (hereinafter referred to as ALTs) is widely recognised as a major problem in public procurement (OECD, 2015). At the European level, Directive 2014/24 puts an explicit obligation on contracting authorities in Member States to ask the bidders to explain the price or costs contained in a tender in situations where tenders "appear to be abnormally low in relation to the works, goods or services". The EU framework provides guidance as to which elements of a tender may be subject to further inquiry. For example, the contracting authority may request further explanations regarding the economics of the manufacturing process, of the services provided or of the construction method, the technical solutions chosen, or the originality of the work, supplies or services.[58] However, the EU framework does provide further indications for determining the basis upon which a tender may "appear" abnormally low.

The reasons bidders submit ALTs may vary, depending, for example, on the fact that each of them might have a different quality of information at the bidding stage. Another reason might be uncertainty about the components of the overall cost of serving an agreement, since the contractor may find out that the "true" cost of performing the contract differs from its initial estimate, especially if the bid was submitted on the basis of a forecast that was too optimistic – the "winner's curse" (OECD, 2015).

Description of the obstacle

GEO No. 34/2006 establishes that an offer is classified as having an unusually low price if the price contained in the offer is lower than 80%, excluding VAT, of the estimated value of the agreement. In this case, the contracting authority has the obligation to request further information (including, for example, information on prices, stocks, salary, and organisation) and clarifications from the economic operator. Upon consultation with market operators, it is our understanding that in practice the contracting authorities do not challenge the justifications received from market participants and do not reject ALTs.

According to newly-proposed legislation in the field of public procurement, the contracting authority will reject an ALT only when the proof submitted by the economic operators does not justify the low price level/proposed costs, taking into consideration the clarifications offered during the investigation. However, the new legislation does not provide any criteria for rejection of a bid and no threshold is provided under which the offer is presumed to be abnormally low (Directive 2014/24, similarly, does not provide such thresholds).

Harm to competition

Considering that in practice the contracting authorities do not reject the justifications and are still awarding the project to the bidder offering the lowest price, this may facilitate price dumping. Companies might win with non-sustainable offers which cannot be implemented or will require amendments to the contract later on.

Policy maker's objective

This current practice of the contracting authorities may be the result of a lack of specific and objective criteria to justify the rejection of an offer. Authorities might also fear a potential challenge of the rejection decision by an economic operator.

Recommendation

The national legislation should be amended to provide the contracting authorities with clear criteria and examples of when to reject an offer based on a lack of justification of an abnormally low price. The objective of the proposed recommendation is to allow contracting authorities to reject an offer due to a greatly underestimated price. Such offers are unlikely to cover the costs necessary and thus in practice are unlikely to be implemented.

Subcontracting

Description of obstacle

According to Article 225 letter a) of GEO No. 34/2006, the contracting authority may impose on the concessionaire the obligation to subcontract 30% of the value of the concession agreement for public works to a third party. The legislation does not provide for the following clarifications: i) if the contracting authority can impose such an obligation in the situation where the company can perform the work by itself and ii) if the company itself decides who will be the third party for the subcontract work or services or whether such third parties are imposed by the contracting authority.

No similar provision has been identified in the newly-proposed legislation in the field of public procurement.

Harm to competition

The unclear wording of the legislation grants to the contracting authority an arbitrary power as regards the request for subcontracting 30% of the value of the agreement. This may prejudice economic operators that have the capabilities to provide the service or perform the work themselves. Additionally, in cases when the authority determines who will be the third party, the economic operator is not be free to choose its subcontractor. However, upon discussions with market participants, we understand that there have been no situations where the contracting authorities have imposed a third party.

Policy maker's objective

The provision transposes Article 60 from Directive 2004/18/CE. The objective of this provision is to allow small and medium-sized enterprises access to public works concession agreements.

Recommendation

Considering that the new proposed legislation in the field of public procurement does not provide a similar restriction, and provided that it is enacted as such, we make no further recommendation.

Other critical provisions

We identified several additional issues in general construction law that had an impact on public procurement procedures. These provisions identified often set derogations from the general tender procedure. Our recommendation is to abolish them and to apply the normal tender procedure.

Exception with respect to concession agreement of land which is to be used by the concessionaire to build houses for people under the age of 35

Description of the obstacle. A concession is an agreement according to which a natural or legal person can obtain a right to exploit a good owned by the state in exchange of a fee. Generally, under Law No. 50/1991, the concession of land belonging to the state should be conducted through a public tender. However, according to Article 15 letter c) of Law No. 50/1991, no public tender procedure is required for concession of land which is to be used by the concessionaire to build houses for young people under the age of 35.

Harm to competition. This provision is likely to create advantages for real estate developers building houses to be sold/rented to young people as opposed to other real estate developers. Large and valuable areas can be leased to developers without any public tender procedure. There is a risk of discrimination, corruption, concession and under-pricing while providing no guarantee that the real estate developers will pass on their cost savings to the young people.

Policy maker's objective. The objective of this provision resides in a social policy meant to encourage real estate developers to build houses which will subsequently be sold/rented to young people under the age of 35.

Recommendation. This provision should be abolished and the tender procedure should be introduced as indicated under Law No. 50/1991.

Exception with respect to concession agreement of land which is used by the initial owner of a building for extending the existing building on nearby land

Description of the obstacle. Article 15 letter e) sets another exception to the rule according to which the concession under Law No. 50/1990 is made through a public tender procedure. No public procurement procedure is foreseen in order to lease private terrain owned by public authorities if they are to be used by the initial owner of a building for extending the existing building on nearby land. For example, an undertaking owning a building may ask for a concession on an adjacent land belonging to public authorities for extending the existing construction.

Harm to competition. An undertaking wanting to prevent a competitor from developing its business might buy/lease property around the land owned by the competitor and then concede the nearby land directly from the public authority.

The public entity might concede the adjacent land at a lower price compared to the price which would have been paid in case a public procedure applied. There is also a certain risk for corruption, as in all cases in which a derogation from tender procedure is permitted without solid grounds.

Policy maker's objective. The objective of this provision is to allow an existing company to expand on nearby land.

Recommendation. We identified two possible options in order to remedy the issue described above:

- One option is to abolish this provision and apply the tender procedure as indicated under Law No. 50/1991. This avoids lease under pricing and granting of preferential rights.
- A second option is to grant the owner of the existing building a special pre-emption right and to match the best offer under the tender procedure. In this case, only if a new participant is offering a higher price than the neighbour, should the new participant win the tender.

Restricted access to information regarding tender procedures for land in private ownership of the state

Description of the obstacle. According to Article 16 of Law No. 50/1991 regarding authorisation of construction works execution, information regarding tender procedures for land in the private ownership of the state or of the municipality is to be disclosed by the city hall only by publishing it at its headquarters and in two major newspapers 20 days prior to the procedure. No reference is made to the requirement to publish the information online or to use other means of communication.

Harm to competition. Currently the information is available only through local communication means so that undertakings located outside the city may not have access to such information and might not be aware of future tender procedures. Thus, the number of potential bidders might be reduced.

Policy maker's objective. Tender procedures were duly publicised at the time of enactment of the legal provision. However, traditional communication channels have changed, making newspapers and notice boards less used/relevant as communication channels.

Recommendation. This provision should be amended in order to extend it to other means of communication, including the online environment (including the city hall's web site, where possible).

Restriction with respect to the commercial relationship between general contractors and subcontractors

Description of the obstacle. According to Article 12 of Emergency Ordinance No. 84/18.09.2003 for the establishment of the National company for highways and roads in Romania, for the execution of works contracts covering construction, rehabilitation, expansion or modernisation of roads (and also the execution of addenda to such contracts), the general contractor must constitute a pledge in favour of its subcontractors or suppliers having as object any amounts due by the National Company for Highways and National Roads in Romania ("CNADR") to the general contractor. The amounts to be recovered by subcontractors or suppliers consist of the value of the works/services they have provided to the general contractor. No other form of guarantee is allowed (such as a bank guarantee).

Harm to competition. This provision interferes with commercial contracts between general contractors and subcontractors who may in practice use different commercial measures in order to protect their interests. In addition, the measure of not allowing insurance policies as a form of guarantee is seen by the business community as an excessive financial guarantee in certain cases.

Policy maker's objective. The objective of the provision is to protect subcontractors and suppliers from delivering works/goods and not being paid for them. The pledge established by the general contractor would confer on the subcontractors the same assurances as those received by the general contractor. Setting a pledge in favour of the subcontractors covering the sums owed by CNADR to the general contractor gives the subcontractors certainty that they will receive the amounts the general contractor owes them under their contractual relationship.

Recommendation. Keep the provision as it is in order to ensure that the work of the subcontractor is guaranteed. Additionally, the provision should be amended to allow all types of commercial guarantee instruments to be used in the commercial relationship between general constructors and their subcontractors.

Awarding criterion in the field of intervention works on buildings with seismic risk

Description of the obstacle. Intervention works in buildings with a seismic risk are carried out by state authorities based on a technical solution issued by a designer. During the public procurement procedure for drafting technical solutions, according to Article 83 of the Methodological Norms for the application of Government Ordinance No. 20/1994 on measures to mitigate the seismic risk of existing buildings, the criterion of the lowest price should be used exclusively. Also, according to Article 55 of the same enactment, the same criterion is to be used during the public procedure for the acquisition of technical expertise concerning the buildings. Thus, the second criterion under the procurement legislation, the economically most advantageous bid, is automatically excluded.

Harm to competition. In accordance with European Legislation, the national framework legislation on public procurement provides two criteria when awarding a public procurement agreement: the lowest price and the criterion of the economically most advantageous tender. The provision limiting the criterion solely to the lowest price derogates from this generally applicable legal regime. For example, operators who have new technology and who would be able to make the economically most advantageous offer are at a disadvantage. The provision is also likely to affect the quality of the performance, as the economic operators would look to utilise cheaper solutions in order to cut costs, which might not be appropriate when it comes to seismic risks.

Policy maker's objective. Considering that the costs are supported by public resources, the state wanted to limit the financial effort of the contracting authority.

Recommendation. This provision should be amended to allow both the criteria that are foreseen by general public procurement legislation.

Notes

1. For instance taking into consideration close interdependencies between players along the construction industry value and supply chains and also vertically integrated companies.
2. A large share of companies and most of the larger ones generally feature diversification of their activities and are required by the Registry of Commerce and other relevant authorities and regulations to identify their main activity NACE code as well as to list all other secondary NACE codes for their diversified operations. This leads to a situation where companies may have several divisions, each contributing significantly to the overall results of the company, while it is not possible to match the contribution/weight of all NACE codes into the company's activity or total revenue. This is because financial results of companies are generally attributed to the main NACE code of the company.
3. The following NACE codes are considered as part of the construction sector: F4211 Construction of roads and motorways, F4212 Construction of railways and underground railways, F4213 Construction of bridges and tunnels, F4221 Construction of utility projects for fluids, F4222 Construction of utility projects for electricity and telecommunications, F4291 Construction of water projects, F4299 Construction of other civil engineering projects n.e.c.
4. The following NACE codes are considered as part of the construction materials sector: B0811 Quarrying of ornamental and building stone, limestone, gypsum, chalk and slate, B0812 Operation of gravel and sand pits; mining of clays and kaolin, C1621 Manufacture of veneer sheets and wood-based panels, C1622 Manufacture of assembled parquet floors, C1623 Manufacture of other builders' carpentry and joinery, C2030 Manufacture of paints, varnishes and similar coatings, printing ink and mastics, C2311 Manufacture of flat glass, C2331 Manufacture of ceramic tiles and flags, C2332 Manufacture of bricks, tiles and construction products, in baked clay, C2351 Manufacture of cement, C2352 Manufacture of lime and plaster, C2361 Manufacture of concrete products for construction purposes, C2362 Manufacture of plaster products for construction purposes, C2363 Manufacture of ready-mixed concrete, C2364 Manufacture of mortars, C2365 Manufacture of fibre cement, C2369 Manufacture of other articles of concrete, plaster and cement.
5. *www.mdrap.ro/en/ministerul/prezentare*.
6. *www.cnadnr.ro/pagina.php?idg=49*.
7. *www.isc-web.ro/*.

8. *www.mmediu.ro/.*
9. *www.ctpc.ro/.*
10. *www.namr.ro/prezentare-anrm/atributii/.*
11. Government Emergency Ordinance (GEO) No. 20/1994.
12. The Social Dialogue Commission is composed of: 1) representatives of the ***Ministry of Regional Development and Public Administration***; 2) representatives of ***employers' associations*** (such as the General Union of Romanian Industrialists (UGIR), the National Council of Small and Medium Sized Private Enterprises in Romania (CNIPMMR), the Employers' Confederation Concordia); 3) representatives of ***trade unions*** (such as the National Confederation of Free Trade Unions of Romania (CNSLR Fratia), the National Trade Union Bloc (BNS), the National Trade Union Confederation Cartel ALFA, the Democratic Trade Union Confederation of Romania (CSDR), the National Trade Union Confederation – Meridian); 4) representatives of ***associative structures of local public administration authorities*** (the National Union of County Councils of Romania (UNCJR), the Romanian Municipalities Association (AMR), the Association of Romanian Towns (AOR), the Association of Romanian Communes (ACoR)); 5) a representative of the ***Ministry of Labor, Family and Social Protection of Romania.***
13. *www.asro.ro/engleza2005/default_eng.html.*
14. Top companies in terms of turnover from 2014.
15. Only companies with their main NACE code corresponding to construction of roads and railways were included in this ranking. Other major construction companies which have participated and were selected in procurement processes for major roads and railways projects, which have primary NACE codes such as F 41 Construction of buildings are not included in the ranking, but they should be taken into consideration while looking at the market. Such companies include: STRABAG SRL, SPEDITION UMB, ASTALDI - branch Romania Bucharest, EURO COSNTRUCT TRADING 98, BOG'ART, VEGA 93.
16. According to ANAF data.
17. Top companies in terms of turnover from 2014.
18. Top companies in terms of turnover from 2014.
19. Considering the NACE codes mentioned in Chapter 2.1.1 "Definition of the relevant sectors and areas of investigation".
20. According to Eurostat data.
21. According to Eurostat data.
22. According to Eurostat data.
23. According to Eurostat data.
24. Between 2006 and 2015, GEO no. 34/2006 was amended and supplemented by a total of 20 acts. Currently, GEO no. 34/2006 includes procurement chapters of the utilities and concessions sector, separate chapters on the remedies system and the applicable penalties and offenses in the field. In terms of scope, GEO no. 34/2006 regulates the procurement above and below the thresholds for publication in the Official Journal of the European Union.
25. *http://ec.europa.eu/internal_market/scoreboard/performance_per_policy_area/public_procurement/index_en.htm.*
26. The indicators set out in the Single Market Scoreboard reflect how the different Member States are performing in key aspects of public procurement. While they offer a simplified picture, they nevertheless show basic aspects of countries' procurement markets. All indicators are based on notices published in the Tenders Electronic Daily (TED) database under directives 2004/17/EC and 2004/18/EC. The overall performance is a weighted average of the three performance indicators. Triple weight is given to both the bidder participation and accessibility indicators, as compared to the procedural efficiency indicator (normalized to 0 – 100%). Scores above 90% are marked green, while those between 90% and 80% are marked yellow and those below 80% are marked red.

    "Performance" measures the extent to which purchasers obtain good value for money. The indicators – bidder participation, accessibility and efficiency – measure important influences on public procurement performance in a way that is transparent, readily comprehensible and comparable.
27. National Strategy on Public Procurement elaborated by the Romanian Ministry of Finance in the context of the transposition of the new EU Directives on Public Procurement, published on 31/07/2015 on *www.mfinante.ro/proiecteachizitii.html?&pagina=acasa.*

28. CNSC Activity report for 2014, page 6, *www.cnsc.ro/raport-de-activitate/*.
29. Constitutional Court Decision no. 5/15th of January 2015.
30. Romanian public procurement in the construction sector. Corruption risks and particularistic links, *http://anticorrp.eu/publications/report-on-romania/*.
31. Romanian public procurement in the construction sector. Corruption risks and particularistic links, page 13, *http://anticorrp.eu/publications/report-on-romania/*.
32. Bucharest Municipality Local Council Decision no. 66/2006, regarding the approval of the norms for ensuring a minimum number of parking places for new constructions and decorations authorised on the territory of Bucharest Municipality and of the prospects necessary for a proper functioning of the thoroughfares, *http://acteinterne.pmb.ro/legis/acteinterne/acte_int/afisint.php?f=16937*.
33. Brasov Municipality Local Council Decision no. 927/2006 regarding the approval of the Regulation for assigning parking places from the residential parking lots established within the city.

    www.brasovcity.ro/documente/public/regulamente/parcare/Regulament%20de%20atribuire%20a%20locurilor%20de%20parcare.pdf.
34. Cluj-Napoca Municipality Local Council Decision no. 25/2010, regarding the approval of the regulation for tenancy of terrain for parking places, garages or awnings situated on the public or private domain of the Municipality *www.primariaclujnapoca.ro/doc/administratie/Regulament%20serviciu%20parcari.pdf*.
35. Pitesti Municipality Local Council Decision no. 185/2012 regarding the approval of the regulation for assigning parking places in residential parking lots in the city *www.primariapitesti.ro/portal/arges/pitesti/portal.nsf/All/FC4F3327FDCF862CC2257AD00050201F/$FILE/HCL%20185-privind%20aprobarea%20Regulamentului%20pentru%20atribuirea%20in%20folosinta%20a%20locurilor%20de%20parcare%20situate%20in%20parcarile%20de%20resedinta%20amenajate%20in%20Municipiul%20Pitesti.pdf*.
36. No official records could be identified concerning the exact number of parking places subject to the exception mentioned under the legislation.
37. See Order no. 119/2014 for the approval of Norms of hygiene and public sanitation regarding the living environment of the population.
38. An urbanistic plan is a document regulating land planning and development of localities. The zonal urbanistic plan regulates in detail the urbanistic development of an area inside a locality (thus covering all functions: housing, services, production, circulation, green spaces, public institutions, etc.).
39. The coefficient of terrain usage is the ratio between the built surface and the surface of the parcel of land included in the reference territorial unit.
40. The information was updated on 23 May 2014. Available at: *www.ctpc.ro/bdsni.html*.
41. Available at: *www.ctpc.ro/bdsni.html*.
42. *www.sgg.ro/index.php?politici_publice_documente*.
43. *www.cdep.ro/pls/proiecte/upl_pck.proiect?cam=2&idp=14945*.
44. Description of the Department for state aid, unfair practices and regulated prices, *http://discutii.mfinante.ro/static/10/Mfp/rof2013/4_9_674_2013.pdf*.
45. The NACE Code is a pan-European classification system which groups organisations according to their business activities.
46. Source: ANAF *www.anaf.ro/indicatori/indfinanciari.html*, Deloitte calculations.
47. Source: ANRM *www.namr.ro/resurse-minerale/licentepermise-active/* (accessed 22 February 2016), Deloitte calculations.
48. PL-x nr. 522/2015, Draft law to repeal a position of the Annex to Government Emergency Ordinance No. 36/2001 on the regulated prices and tariffs that are established with the approval of the Competition Office (Proiect de Lege pentru abrogarea unei poziţii din anexa la Ordonanţa de urgenţă a Guvernului nr.36/2001 privind regimul preţurilor şi tarifelor reglementate, care se stabilesc cu avizul Oficiului Concurenţei) *www.cdep.ro/pls/proiecte/upl_pck.proiect?cam=2&idp=14645*, accessed on 9 March 2016.
49. Point of view of the Romanian government regarding various legislative initiatives, *www.cdep.ro/proiecte/2015/500/20/2/12%20PVG%2026%2010%202015.pdf*.

50. Directive 2010/75/EU of the European Parliament and of the Council of 24 November 2010 on industrial emissions (integrated pollution prevention and control).

51. Directive 2014/23/EU of the European Parliament and of the Council of 26 February 2014 on the award of concession contracts; Directive 2014/24/EU of the European Parliament and of the Council of 26 February 2014 on public procurement and repealing Directive 2004/18/EC; and Directive 2014/25/EU of the European Parliament and of the Council of 26 February 2014 on procurement by entities operating in the water, energy, transport and postal services sectors and repealing Directive 2004/17/EC.

52. *www.cdep.ro/pls/proiecte/upl_pck.proiect?cam=2&idp=15471*, *www.cdep.ro/pls/proiecte/upl_pck.proiect?cam=2&idp=15472*, *www.cdep.ro/pls/proiecte/upl_pck.proiect?cam=2&idp=15473*, *www.cdep.ro/pls/proiecte/upl_pck.proiect?cam=2&idp=15474*.

53. *www.cdep.ro/pls/proiecte/upl_pck.proiect?cam=2&idp=15159*.

54. *www.anrmap.ro/web/public/puncte-de-vedere/-/asset_publisher/nVxyj1ceeqMD/content/cand-poate-fi-aplicata-procedura-de-negociere-fara-publicare-prealabila-a-unui-anunt-de-participare-ce-se-intampla-daca-necesitatea-achizitionarii-ser?redirect=http%3A%2F%2F www.anrmap.ro%2Fweb%2Fpublic%2Fpuncte-de-vedere%3Fp_p_id%3D101_INSTANCE_nVxyj1ceeqMD%26p_p_lifecycle%3D0%26p_p_state%3Dnormal%26p_p_mode%3Dview%26p_p_col_id%3Dcolumn-1%26p_p_col_count%3D1*.

55. GEO No. 34/2006 provides with different deadlines for the same procedure depending on the estimated value of the contracts. (e.g., as stated above, the minimum term of an open procedure is currently 20 days for contracts below the thresholds and 52 days for contracts above the thresholds – for which the participation notice is published in the Official Journal of the European Union).

56. The terms provided in Directive 2014/24 are applicable only for public contracts with an estimated value over certain thresholds. Under these thresholds, the Member States are free to decide the terms and deadlines.

57. Article 27 of Directive 2014/24.

58. Article 69 par. 2 of Directive 2014/24.

References

Academic Society of Romania (2016), *Analysis and Forecast Annual Report – Romania*. Available at: *http://sar.org.ro/wp-content/uploads/2016/02/RAPORT-SAR-2016.pdf*.

Coface (21 April 2015). Sectorul Autohton de Lucrari de Constructii a Drumurilor si Autostrazilor.

Competition Council (2013), "Sectorial research on the road and motorway construction market report".

High Level Group on Administrative Burdens (2014), "Final report of Cutting Red Tape in Europe", *http://ec.europa.eu/smart-regulation/refit/admin_burden/docs/08-10web_ce-brocuttingredtape_en.pdf*.

National Strategy on Public Procurement (published on 31st July 2015): *www.mfinante.ro/proiecteachizitii.html?&pagina=acasa*, and *www.cnadnr.ro/pagina.php?idg=49*.

OECD (2015), *Hearing on Auction and Tenders: Further issues*, , Working Party No.2 on Competition and Regulation, OECD, Paris.

OECD (2012), *Recommendations on Fighting Bid Rigging in Public Procurement*, OECD, Paris. *www.oecd.org/daf/competition/fightingbidrigginginpublicprocurement.htm*.

OECD (2009), *Guidelines for Fighting bid rigging in Public Procurement*, OECD, Paris OECD (2008), *Competition in the construction industry*, Directorate for Financial and Enterprise Affairs Competition Committee, OECD, Paris.

Romanian Academic Society (SAR) (2015), "Romanian public procurement in the construction sector. Corruption risks and particularistic links", 30 March 2015). Available at: *http://anticorrp.eu/publications/report-on-romania/*. Details on data used can be found in section D8.1.5 Chapter II, 1. *General view – The public procurement market*: "The necessary information on the specific national level indicators was obtained through a FOIA request sent to the National Authority for Regulating and Monitoring Public Procurement (ANRMAP) which answered in over 30 calendar days. Furthermore, although several projects had been publicly announced, until the completion of this country report, no Public-Private Partnerships (PPPs) were signed. Therefore, the following analysis of national level data on procurement relies entirely on the registered public procurement contracts in SEAP, the e-procurement portal. However, at least a third of public institutions did not use SEAP back in 2007. The number of users has gradually increased and, by the end of 2014, 14 721 contracting authorities were registered in SEAP (up from 9 591 in 2007)."

Romanian Competition Council (2013), *Sector inquiry on the construction market of roads and highways*, Available at: *www.consiliulconcurentei.ro/uploads/docs/items/id8693/raport.pdf*.

Romanian Standards Association, *www.asro.ro/engleza2005/default_eng.html*.

Schwab, K. (2014), *The global competitiveness report 2010-2011*, Geneva: World Economic Forum.

Single market Scoreboard: *http://ec.europa.eu/internal_market/scoreboard/performance_per_policy_area/public_procurement/index_en.htm*.

Standing Technical Council for Construction (CTPC): *www.ctpc.ro/*.

Transparency International (2015), *Corruption perceptions index*, available at: *www.transparency.org/cpi2015#results-table*.

ANNEX 2.A1

Public procurement: Number of submitted/accepted offers

The key objective of the quantitative analysis for the various issues identified in relation to public procurement procedures for construction works is to investigate possible relationships between various features of procurement procedures and the outcomes of these procedures.

Method and indicators

Information regarding the procurement procedures was manually extracted from the SEAP[1] system in order to build the input database for the analysis. Approximately 50 procedures were identified and relevant data was extracted for these procedures.

Sample criteria:

- tender procedure announcement between 1 January 2013 and 31 December 2014
- only works contracts
- CPV[2] code corresponding to road construction works (45233120-6)
- open tender procedure type
- tender procedure finalised
- contract value registered in SEAP system
- excluded works related to sidewalks, urban furniture, etc.

Indicators:

- estimated value of the agreement in Romanian leu (RON)
- number of offers submitted
- number of suitable offers submitted
- final price of the winning bid
- days available for preparing documentation and submitting bid
- discount of the winning price from the original estimate (% winning price/estimated price)

The main method used is linear regression analysis investigating the relationship between the constructed variables.

Outliers are identified for each variable based on maximum and minimum cut-off values determined using a rule. Any values over or below two standard deviations from the mean are considered to be outliers and are excluded from each indicator pair used in the analysis. Overall, 10 procurement procedures from the 50 identified have at least one outlier and the actual number of data points used in the analysis varies between 44 and 48 depending on the outliers present in the dependent and independent variables defined in each case.

Regression framework and hypotheses

The following hypotheses were formulated:

- There should be a positive relationship between number of days given to submit offers and number of offers submitted (more time to prepare offers = more competition).
- There should be a positive relationship between number of days given to submit offers and number of offers accepted (more time to prepare offers = more competition).
- There should be a positive relationship between offers submitted and award price discount compared to initial price estimate (more competition = lower price)
- There should be a positive relationship between offers accepted and award price discount compared to initial price estimate (more competition = lower price)
- A higher estimated contract value results in more competition and thus a larger price discount (larger value = more competition = lower price).

Descriptive statistics

Descriptive statistics and the frequency distribution of values for the main variables used are presented below. Identified outliers are coloured in orange.

Figure 2.A1.1. **Discount of award price compared to estimate price (%)**

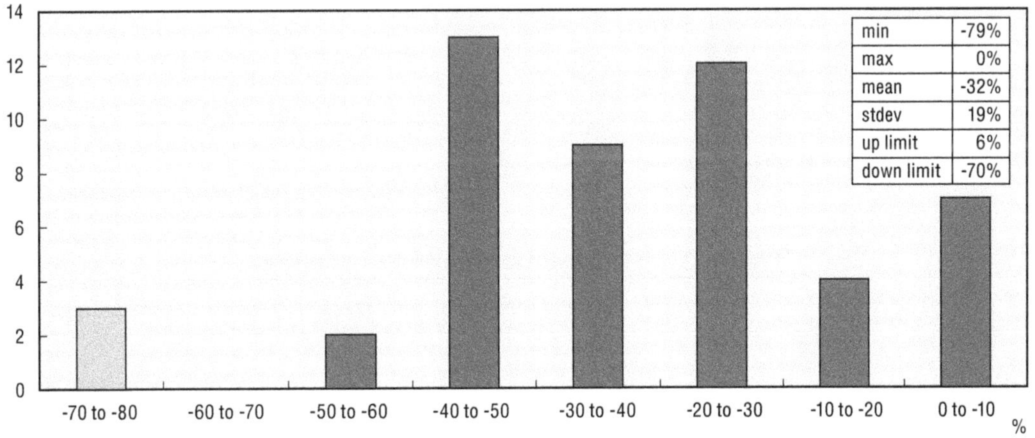

Source: Data extracted from *www.e-licitatie.ro/*, Deloitte Analysis.

StatLink http://dx.doi.org/10.1787/888933361322

Figure 2.A1.2. **Term for submitting offers (days)**

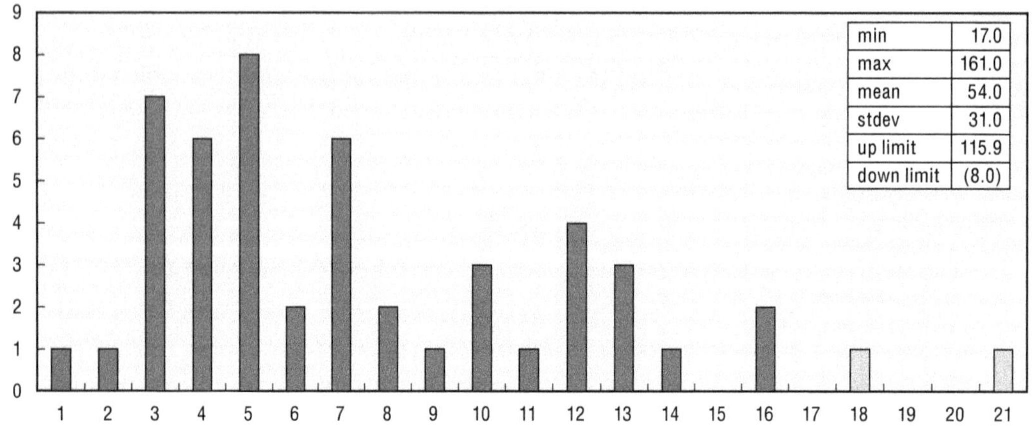

Source: Data extracted from *https://www.e-licitatie.ro/*, Deloitte Analysis

StatLink http://dx.doi.org/10.1787/888933361333

Figure 2.A1.3. **Number of offers submitted**

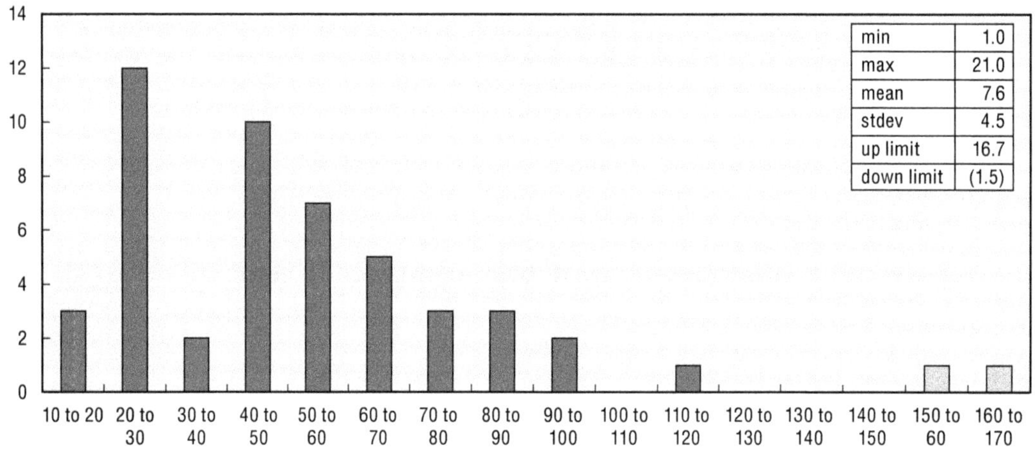

Source: Data extracted from *www.e-licitatie.ro/*, Deloitte Analysis.

StatLink http://dx.doi.org/10.1787/888933361348

Figure 2.A1.4. **Number of offers accepted**

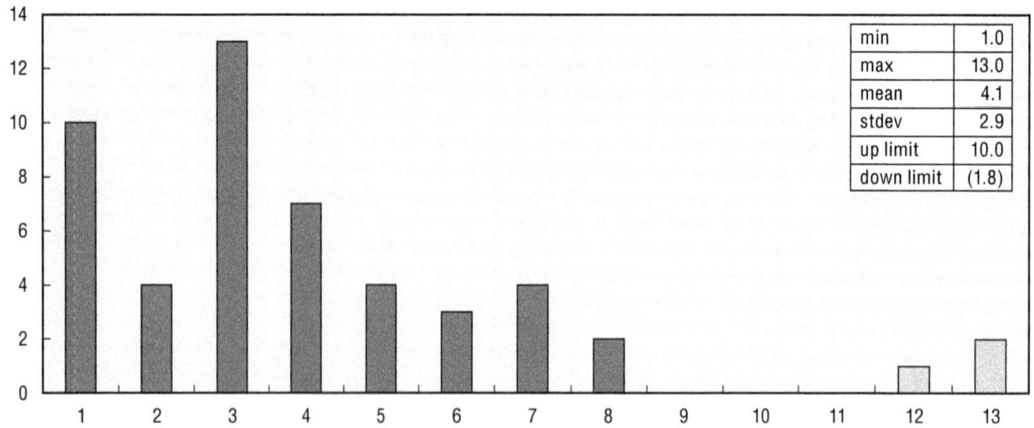

Source: Data extracted from *www.e-licitatie.ro/*, Deloitte Analysis.

StatLink http://dx.doi.org/10.1787/888933361352

Figure 2.A1.5. **Estimated value of the contract in RON**

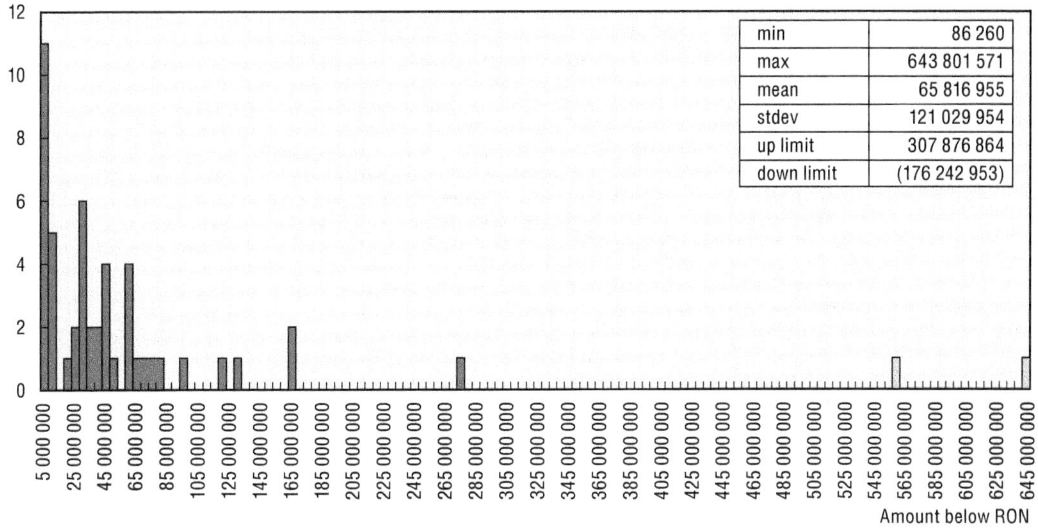

Source: Data extracted from *www.e-licitatie.ro/*, Deloitte Analysis.

StatLink http://dx.doi.org/10.1787/888933361360

Results

The estimated value of the contract is correlated with the number of offers submitted, the number of offers accepted and the days available for submitting offers. Furthermore, the estimated value of the contract in the sample exhibits Skewness and Kurtosis[3] and is not close to a normal distribution. Considering this, the value of the contract cannot be used to control for the anticipating effect of higher value contracts (more competition, more time to prepare bids, more offers submitted and accepted); the relationship between the variables are be investigated separately but care should be exercised in interpreting the results.

Results

- More days available to submit offers results in a higher number of offers being submitted (for every extra day available to submit offers, 0.095 additional offers are submitted) and explains 34.6% of the variation (N = 46).
- A higher estimated contract value results in more offers submitted but does not result in more offers accepted or an improvement in the quality (% accepted from those submitted) and explains 16.7% of the variation of offers submitted (N = 46).
- A higher number of offers submitted results in a larger discount of the final award price compared to the estimated price (for every additional offer submitted, a further 2.1% discount is observed) and explains 28.1% of the variation (N = 45).
- A higher number of offers accepted results in a larger discount of the final award price compared to the estimated price (for every additional offer accepted, a further 4.4% discount is observed) and explains 34% of the variation (N = 44)
- The number of days available to submit offers does not result in a higher number of offers accepted.
- The estimated value of the contract does not result in a larger discount of the award price.

Figure 2.A1.6. **Terms for submitting offers – offers submitted**

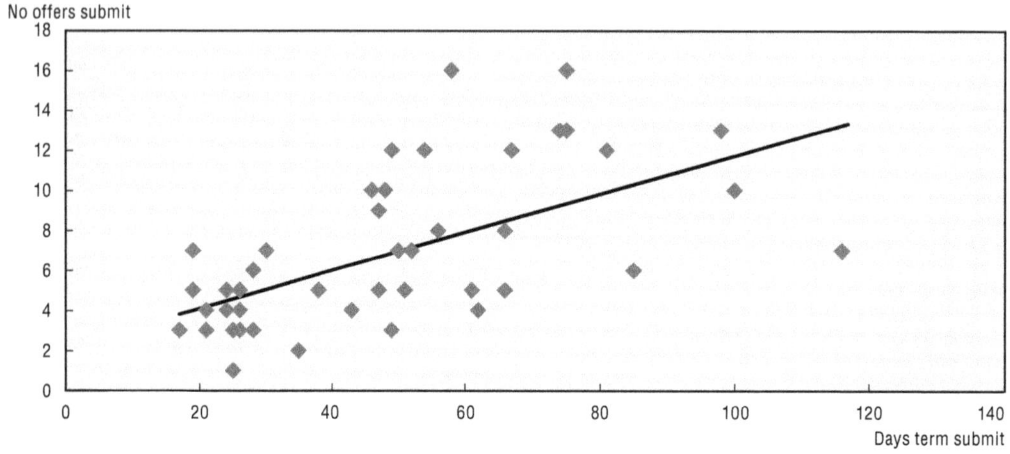

Source: Deloitte Analysis.

StatLink http://dx.doi.org/10.1787/888933361377

Figure 2.A1.7. **Estimated contract value – offers submitted**

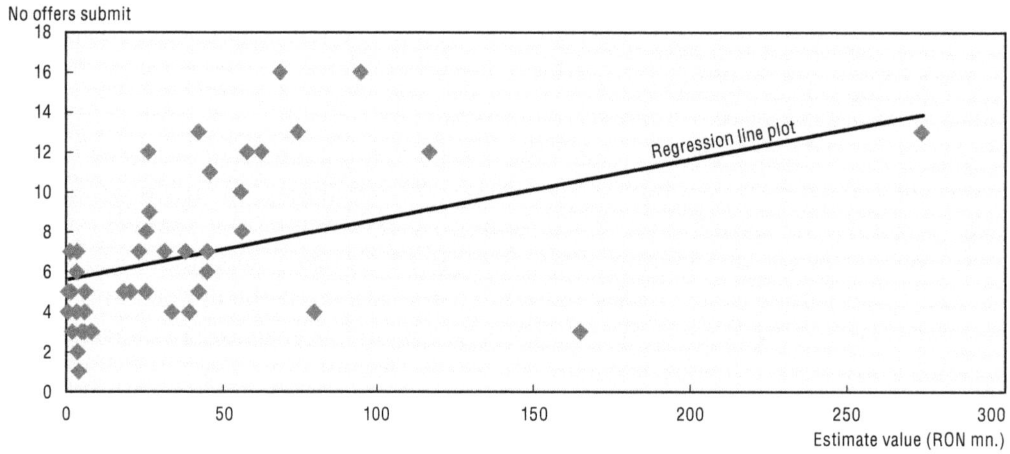

Source: Deloitte Analysis.

StatLink http://dx.doi.org/10.1787/888933361384

Figure 2.A1.8. **Offers accepted – price discount**

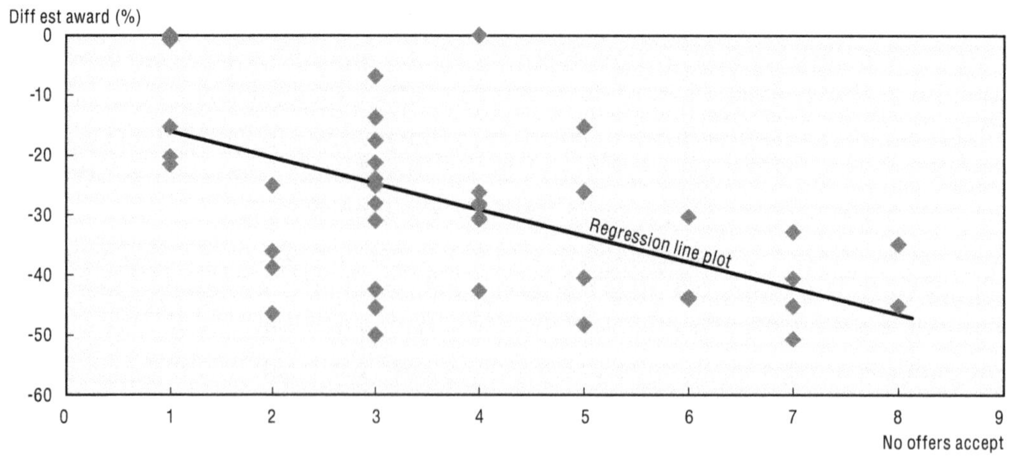

Source: Deloitte Analysis.

StatLink http://dx.doi.org/10.1787/888933361392

Figure 2.A1.9. **Offers submitted – price discount**

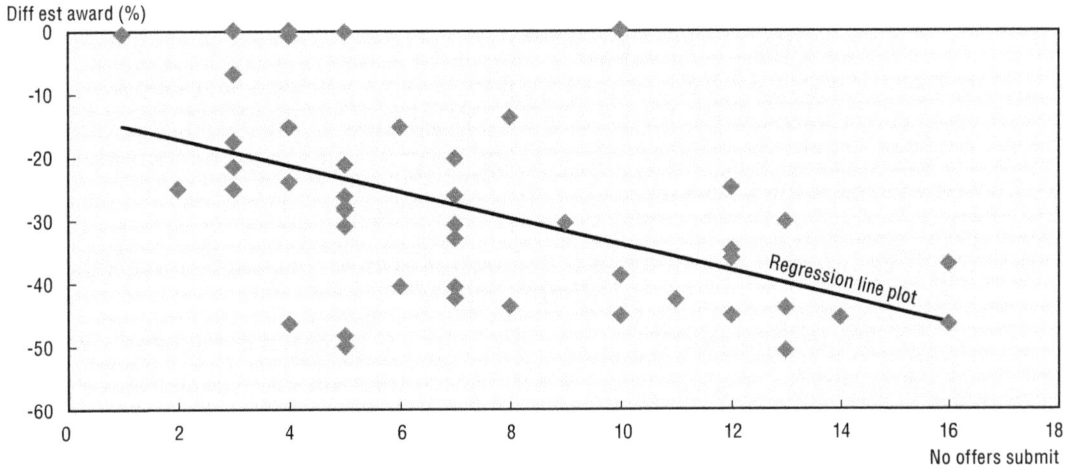

Source: Deloitte Analysis.

StatLink http://dx.doi.org/10.1787/888933361403

Conclusion

- More competition in the form of more offers submitted and more offers accepted does lead to a larger discount of the award price from the original estimated price. This is especially true for offers accepted by the contracting authority.
- A larger contract value and more days available for preparing bids do lead to a higher number of offers submitted but do not lead to a higher number of offers accepted.

Consumer benefits

Having predicted that for each additional accepted offer in a public procurement procedure a higher price discount can be obtained and assuming that the benefit of the lower awarded price is transmitted to the final consumers, consumer benefits are estimated using the following formula:

$$CB = \left(\rho + \frac{1}{2} | \epsilon | \rho^2\right) R_r$$

where:

- CB: standard measure of consumer harm
- ρ:percentage change in price related to restriction
- R: sector revenue
- |∊|: absolute value of elasticity of demand

As the absolute value of elasticity of demand is unknown, this index is assumed to take the value of 2. In this case, the consumer benefits formula can be simplified as follows:

$$CB = \left(\rho + \rho^2\right) R_r$$

For estimating the consumer benefits several assumptions are made. First, the effect of additional accepted offers on the award price discount for roads sample is the same as for the entire volume of public procurement in construction. In this case we can calculate the consumer benefit for both the public procurement procedures regarding road construction and any other public procurement procedure in the construction industry.

Moreover, the yearly volume of road related public procurement is estimated by dividing the sum of the contracted value of the procedures included in the sample by two, as the sample included both 2013 and 2014 procedures.

Moreover, the consumer benefits are calculated in four separate cases, by taking into consideration the cases of both one and two additional accepted offers, and road construction procedures and total construction procurement procedures. In the four cases the input data used is the following:

Table 2.A1.1. **Estimated consumer benefit components for one and two additional acceptable offers**

	One additional accepted offer		Two additional accepted offers	
	Road construction procedures	Total construction procedures	Road construction procedures	Total construction procedures
ρ^1	4.40%	4.40%	8.80%	8.80%
R^2	150 581 229	9 100 000 000	150 581 229	9 100 000 000

1. Estimated from the regression analysis for one additional offer, multiplied by two for two additional offers.
2. In EUR, calculated as a sum of the contracted value included in the sample for road construction procedures and taken from the Romanian Academic Society Report for value of total construction procedures (Romanian public procurement in the construction sector. Corruption risks and particularistic links, *http://anticorrp.eu/publications/report-on-romania)*.

Source: Deloitte Analysis.

The estimated benefits per year using the input data from the table presented above are the following:

Table 2.A1.2. **Estimated consumer benefits per year (2014) in EUR**

		Procrement procedures included in sample (N = 50)	Total construction procedures
Additional offers	1	6 917 099	418 017 600
	2	14 417 249	871 270 400

Source: Deloitte Analysis.

Notes

1. Electronic Public Tender System
2. Common Procurement Vocabulary (for public procurement in the European Union)
3. Skewness is a measure of symmetry, or more precisely, the lack of symmetry. A distribution, or data set, is symmetric if it looks the same to the left and right of the center point. Kurtosis is a measure of whether the data are heavy-tailed or light-tailed relative to a normal distribution.

ANNEX 2.A2

Parking places

Decision No. 525/1996 for approving the general urbanism regulation, Art. 33 of Annex 1.

When requesting a building permit for a construction which, through its purpose requires parking places, the building permit can only be obtained when the parking places are placed outside the public area. Exceptionally, the public area can be used for the necessary parking places should the local public authorities agree.

The **key objective** of the quantitative analysis of the issue is to estimate the value of the advantage or benefit of building owners being offered public spaces by local public authorities according to the identified exception in comparison to the building owners who are required to build parking spaces according to the general applicable regulations in order to obtain the building permit.

To estimate this benefit, a **case study** focussing on a number of parking projects in key cities of Romania is presented. In the first step, an estimated average cost of building one parking place excluding the cost of land is calculated by dividing the estimated average capital expenditure of a number of parking projects identified (excluding the estimated cost of land for the project) by the average parking capacity of these projects. In the second step, the estimated price of land is added to the estimated cost of building a parking place in order to quantify the total advantage/benefit obtained per parking space in key cities.

Assumptions

The main **assumptions** that are considered refer to aspects such as expropriation versus buying the land, scope of the new building for which the building permit is required, and the desired quality of the parking places to be built. First, the cost of buying the land for construction is considered to be equivalent to the cost of expropriation. In case of private investors that build new parking places to comply with the requirement for obtaining a building permit, the correspondent cost of expropriation is the same as for buying land for construction. For the purpose of this study, these two costs are considered to be equivalent, lowering the risk of lack of comparability between investments made by public authorities in building parking places and the ones made by public investors. Second, construction costs are considered to be equivalent regardless of the scope of building of the parking places. Even if the building for which the building permit is required is to be an office building, a commercial building, etc.; the final purpose is not considered to be an influential factor on the cost of building a parking place. Third, the objective of the analysis is to quantify the cost of fulfilling the requirement to build parking places regardless of the quality of those parking places. Moreover, the cost of building a parking place is influenced only by the number of storeys and the cost of the land; all other costs that make up the total cost of a parking place are considered to be identical regardless of factors such as location. Lastly, we consider the cost of building a parking place on the ground by a private investor to be equivalent to those built by public authorities.

Cost of a parking space excluding land

The costs of building parking places vary based on a number of factors such as the cost of land, number of levels above or underground, location where the facility is to be built (city and location within the city), whether it is a purpose built parking facility or a parking section integrated into a larger real estate project, etc. In this analysis, we decided that the best approach to estimating the cost of building a parking space is to investigate the cost of underground public parking projects since a large number of public and private parking projects are built underground. Also, the estimated cost of land (where available, whether an estimated cost of acquiring the land or an assumed value of expropriations required) was excluded from the cost calculation in order to make the costs comparable. This is because the large variation in the cost of land can often make underground or overground parking spaces built on multiple levels cheaper compared to building simple parking spaces on the ground.

A differentiation will be made between building a parking space with several floors, and building the same number of parking places on the ground (ground level). The cost of building the parking place on land (ground level) are calculated using the costs spent by Bucharest's District 3 City Hall on building parking places on streets.

Several underground parking projects in Bucharest were used. The source of data is the Bucharest City Hall, Parking strategy in Bucharest Municipality. The main characteristics of the parking places are shown in Table 2.A2.1 and Table 2.A2.2.

Table 2.A2.1. **Projects to build underground parking places with 2 levels**

Location	Investment cost (EUR)	Number of parking places	Cost / parking place (EUR)
Baneasa Esplanade Railway Station	1 336 704	100	13 367
Dorobanti Square	3 467 374	360	9 632
Walter Maracineanu Square	1 805 097	276	6 540
		AVERAGE	***9 846***

Source: Deloitte Analysis.

Table 2.A2.2. **Projects to build underground parking places with 3 levels**

Location	Investment cost (EUR)	Number of parking places	Cost / parking place (EUR)
Free Press Square	5 745 695	1 633	3 518
Charles de Gaulle Square	15 625 111	831	18 803
Alba Iulia Square	18 528 146	2 190	8 460
		AVERAGE	**10 261**

Source: Deloitte Analysis.

The average values for building one parking place (for each case: 2 or 3 levels underground) are used as a **cost per parking place excluding land**. Therefore, the cost per parking place excluding land for an underground parking with 2 floors is EUR 9 846 and the cost per parking place excluding land for an underground parking with 3 floors is EUR 10 261.

Assuming that the parking is built on land (ground level), the costs per parking place, without taking into consideration the cost of land, are considered to be equal to the estimated cost of Bucharest's District 3 City Hall project to build public parking places on public roads. In this case, the cost per parking place is calculated through the following formula:

$$cost\ per\ parking\ place\ excluding\ land$$
$$= \frac{total\ amount\ invested\ in\ parking\ places\ on\ land\ by\ Bucharest's\,District3\ City\ Hall}{total\ number\ of\ parking\ places\ built}$$
$$= \frac{35350000\ \text{EUR}\ (1)}{34508} = \text{EUR}1024\ per\ parking\ place$$

(1) *www.gandul.info/financiar/parcarea-pe-familie-in-bucuresti-30-000-de-euro-948292.*

Cost of land

The cost of land differs by city and by area within the city. A report published by Colliers in 2011 estimates the average price per square metre (m^2) of building land in the main Romanian cities, by differentiating between central, semi-central and peripheral areas in each city. According to Colliers, the division of cities between the abovementioned categories are the following:

Table 2.A2.3. **Division of cities by category (Colliers)**

Primary	Secondary	Tertiary
Brasov	Bacau	Alba Iulia
Cluj Napoca	Galati	Botosani
Consţanta	Iasi	Focsani
Craiova	Ploiesti	Piatra Neamt
Timisoara	Sibiu	Targu Jiu

Source: Colliers (2011), *Romania Retail Market Analysis*, Colliers International.

The cost of land per parking place is added to the cost of land without parking places to calculate the total cost of a parking place in each situation (area/city). The cost of land per each area in Bucharest is provided by Colliers (2015)*Romania Market Review*. Ranges of cost of land per each area in each city by Colliers 2011 *Romania Retail Market Analysis*, and the mean value of the range is used. For comparability purposes, the cost of land used is the one in 2010, the same year for which the study case data is provided.

Table 2.A2.4. **Cost of land (2010)**

cost of land per m^2 (EUR)	Central	Semi-central	Peripheral
Bucharest	2 000	700	200
Primary (Brasov, etc.	450	300	125
Secondary	375	225	100
Tertiary	250	150	67.5

Source: Colliers (2015), *Romania Market Review* and Colliers (2011), *Romania Retail Market Analysis*, Colliers International.

Cost of a parking place including land

It is considered that each parking place has a dimension of 24 m^2. Each parking place in Romania must have around 20 m^2, to which an additional 20% is added as land that is necessary for accessing the parking place (20 m^2*1.2 = 24 m^2 per parking place).

In the case of a parking garage on several floors, the cost of the land is distributed over the number of floors, resulting in a lower cost of land per parking place. Therefore, the cost of land per parking place is calculated by the following formula:

$$cost\ of\ land\ per\ parking\ place(ground\ floor) = land\ per\ parking\ place * cost\ of\ land\ per\ sqm$$

$$cost\ of\ land\ per\ parking\ place\ (X\ floors) = \frac{cost\ of\ land\ per\ parking\ place(ground\ floor)}{X\ floors}$$

where X represents the number of floors, in our case 2 or 3; land per parking place is 24 m^2 and the cost of land per m^2 is, as shown in Table 2.A2.4 above, differing by each area/city.

The estimated cost per parking place is calculated as a sum between the cost of land per parking place and cost of the parking place without land (which is EUR 1 024 if the parking is on the ground floor, EUR 9 846, if the parking has 2 floors and EUR 10 261 if the parking has 3 floors).

The total cost per parking place resulting from the calculations above is presented below (together with its two main components: cost per parking place without land and cost of land per parking place).

Table 2.A2.5. **Cost of parking place with and without land costs**

		Central			Semi-central			Peripheral		
		ground floor	2 floors	3 floors	ground floor	2 floors	3 floors	ground floor	2 floors	3 floors
Bucharest	**Total cost per parking place**	**49 024**	**33 846**	**26 261**	**17 824**	**18 246**	**15 861**	**5 824**	**12 246**	**11 861**
	cost per parking place without land	1 024	9 846	10 261	1 024	9 846	10 261	1 024	9 846	10 261
	cost of land per parking place	48 000	24 000	16 000	16 800	8 400	5 600	4 800	2 400	1 600
Primary (Brasov, Cluj Napoca, Consţanta etc.)	**Total cost per parking place**	**11 824**	**15 246**	**13 861**	**8 224**	**13 446**	**12 661**	**4 024**	**11 346**	**11 261**
	cost per parking place without land	1 024	9 846	10 261	1 024	9 846	10 261	1 024	9 846	10 261
	cost of land per parking place	10 800	5 400	3 600	7 200	3 600	2 400	3 000	1 500	1 000
Secondary (Bacau, Galati, Iasi etc.)	**Total cost per parking place**	**10 024**	**14 346**	**13 261**	**6 424**	**12 546**	**12 061**	**3 424**	**11 046**	**11 061**
	cost per parking place without land	1 024	9 846	10 261	1 024	9 846	10 261	1 024	9 846	10 261
	cost of land per parking place	9 000	4 500	3 000	5 400	2 700	1 800	2 400	1 200	800
Tertiary (Alba Iulia, Botosani, Focsani etc.)	**Total cost per parking place**	**7 024**	**12 846**	**12 261**	**4 624**	**11 646**	**11 461**	**2 644**	**10 656**	**10 801**
	cost per parking place without land	1 024	9 846	10 261	1 024	9 846	10 261	1 024	9 846	10 261
	cost of land per parking place	6 000	3 000	2 000	3 600	1 800	1 200	1 620	810	540

Source: Deloitte calculations.

It is also worth noting that the cost of building a parking place including land is generally lower for parking spaces built on the ground/alongside public roads. However, in certain areas such as Bucharest semi-central or Bucharest Central it can be much more efficient to build underground or overground parking on multiple levels to dilute the exceptionally high cost of land in these areas.

Conclusion

The main conclusion that can be drawn from the analysis is that the cost of each parking space differs from area to area and from city to city. The main factor influencing these differences is the cost of land. Therefore, in most central areas (except for the tertiary cities) the cost of building a parking space overground is lower than building it at ground level, as opposed to the peripheral areas. The range of costs per parking place (also including the cost of land) is between EUR 2 644 (peripheral areas in tertiary cities) and

Figure 2.A2.1. **Influence of number of building levels and price of land on total cost per parking place**

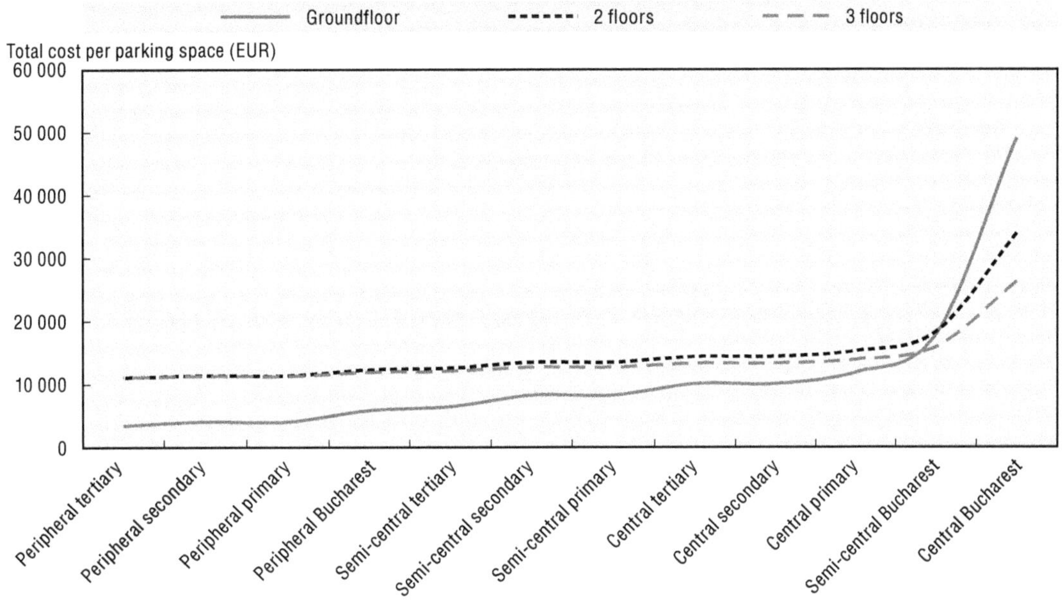

Source: Deloitte calculations.

StatLink http://dx.doi.org/10.1787/888933361411

EUR 49 024 (in central Bucharest). However, on average, the cost per parking place is EUR 11 574 for the ground floor option, EUR 15 121 for the two-floor underground parking option and EUR 13 777 for the three-floor option for an underground parking place.

The implication of the analysis in the issue identified is that the cost per parking place calculated in each scenario is equivalent to the cost advantage/benefit of a private investor for each parking place granted from the local public authority through the exception identified.

ANNEX 2.A3

Regulated prices of sand and rock products

Objective

Sand and rock products are subject to price ceilings which are set individually for producers by the Ministry of Finance and are indexed annually based on the Consumer Price Index. The framework legislation on which sand and rock products are based are assigned price caps following the argument that price caps should be set for products in markets featuring "natural monopolies".

Based on generally accepted economic theory, a price ceiling is a maximum price limit which can be set either below or above the free market equilibrium price. In case the price ceiling is set below the equilibrium price where supply and demand match for a certain product or product category, the price is "bound" by the ceiling, i.e. the price ceiling keeps the price below the equilibrium. If the price ceiling is set above the equilibrium price then the price is not "bound" by the ceiling and can generally stay below the ceiling.

Binding price ceilings can keep the price permanently at a lower level than the equilibrium price, while non-binding ceilings can allow a certain level of competition in the market but can also prevent local or temporary price increases due to local monopolies or special circumstances. (In such a case the price ceiling becomes binding in a certain area and for a certain amount of time.)

Natural monopolies describe a situation where a monopoly emerges in a certain industry due to its high operating costs and the investment required, leaving smaller players unable to compete.

The objective of the analysis regarding sand and rock products is to explore the binding or non-binding nature of the price ceilings set in Romania. This is done by benchmarking prices and investigating qualitative market features.

Producer overview and concentration

At the end of 2014 there were 731 companies registered in Romania (489 active) with the primary NACE code[1] 8.1.2 "Operation of gravel and sand pits; mining of clays and kaolin" with a total turnover in 2014 of EUR 190.8 m[2] equivalent.

Producer concentration is also considered because price ceilings can have a binding effect limited in time and area, therefore providing price protection at local level. We identified 759[3] active licences and permits for sand and rock exploitation in Romania (licences and permits identifying exploitation sites; a company can have more than one permit or licence for several exploitation sites) with an average of approximately 19 sites per county. There is only one

Figure 2.A3.1. **Sand and rock active licences and permits**

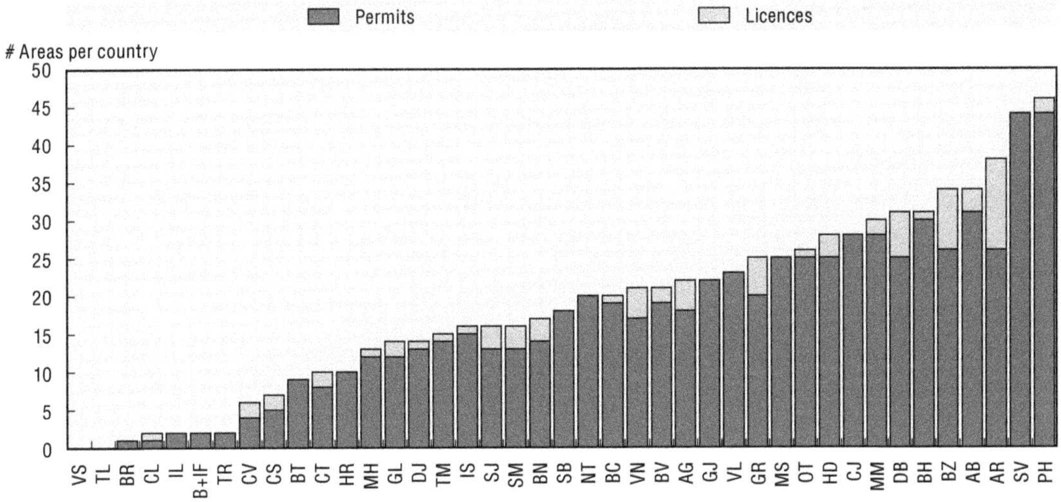

Source: National Agency for Mineral Resources (ANRM), *www.namr.ro/resurse-minerale/licentepermise-active/*, Deloitte Calculations.

StatLink http://dx.doi.org/10.1787/888933361425

county with a single sand and rock exploitation site while two others have none, suggesting that in these areas there may be lower competition between producers.

The figure provides an overview of counties where there is a significantly lower number of sand and rock exploitation sites than the national average of 19, suggesting that in these areas there may be lower competition between producers. However only one county has a sngle sand and rock exploitation site while two others have none.

Data collection

Data on actual market prices were collected from a number of sources for one basic product category (natural sand, 0-4 mm grain):

- Prices offered by Romanian producers of sand and rock producers (most recently available, desk research) which are subject to price ceilings – 6 prices.[4]
- Prices at the Romanian Commodities Exchange which should not be subject to the price ceilings (2015 prices, desk research) – 10 prices.[5]
- Prices offered by producers of sand and rock producers in Poland, Czech Republic and Moldova (most recently available, desk research) – 12 prices.[6]

Assumptions and limitations

An effort was made to identify most recent prices and prices for comparable products, however some differences were observed in the nature of the sand product (source, grain size). It is assumed that the sand products identified are comparable.

In Romania different price ceilings are set for sand and rock products while the price benchmark only focusses on one product category for which data could be collected. Care should be exercised in generalising the conclusions to all sand and rock product categories.

A legislation scan to identify price regulations relating to sand and rock products in EU Member States was performed. No other price regulation affecting rock and sand products directly was identified and it is assumed that no such regulation exists in the European

Union except in Romania. Price comparability may be hindered by local regulations, taxes (excep VAT) and royalties.

Aggregated financial and business statistics of companies classified under NACE code 8.1.2 "Operation of gravel and sand pits; mining of clays and kaolin" provide a general view of the sector. However, there is no complete overlap with the "relevant market" due to a number of factors:

- Aggregated data takes into consideration companies with their primary NACE code 8.1.2, however sand and gravel is also produced as a secondary activity by other companies, especially in the case where sand and rock products are inputs for other value added products such as autoclaved aerated concrete (AAC) or concrete.
- The price ceiling applies to sand and rock products whereas the NACE code 8.1.2 also takes into consideration additional related construction materials such as clay and kaolin.

Price benchmark

The prices collected were for one product category (natural sand for construction ranging from 0 to 4 mm grain size), sold in bulk (either by ton or cubic metre, converted to tonnes for comparability), excluding transportation costs[7] and VAT. The prices were converted into RON using the exchange rate as of 3 February 2016.

The average prices for each price source is presented below:

Figure 2.A3.2. **Average price of sand 0-4 mm (Romanian producers and Commodities Exchange, RON equivalent)**

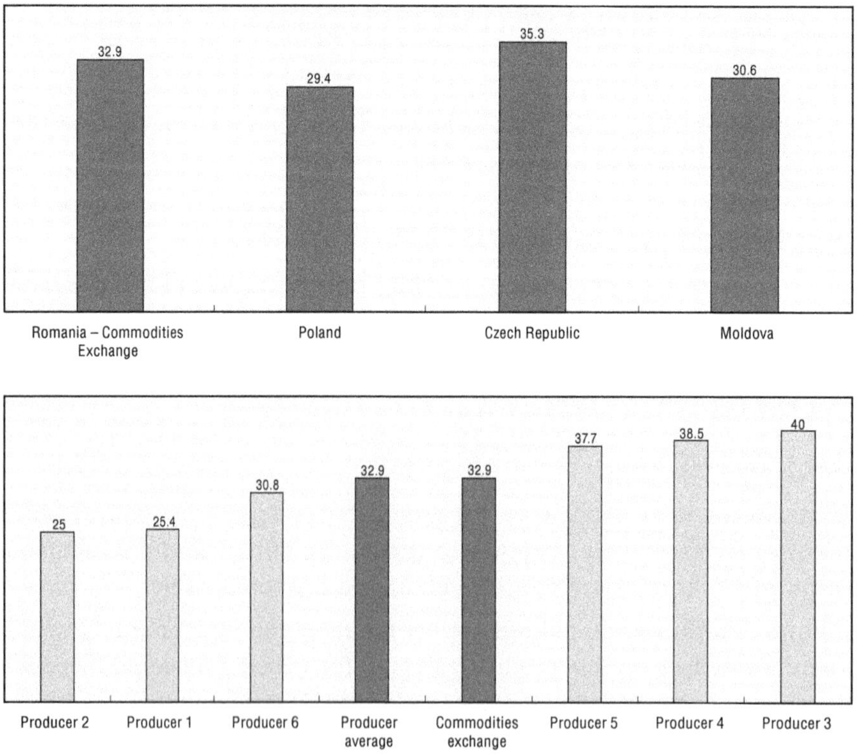

Source: As detailed in data collection section, Deloitte analysis.

StatLink http://dx.doi.org/10.1787/888933361431

Results

Assuming that the price ceiling had a binding effect on the prices offered by sand and rock producers in Romania, it is expected that: 1) prices offered by producers should be lower than prices at the Commodities Exchange and 2) prices offered by producers and at the Commodities Exchange in Romania should be lower than in other countries in the region. Benchmarked average prices show that the price of the sand product analysed is very similar in Romania (producers vs. Commodities Exchange) and also between countries in the region, suggesting that the price is not bound or not substantially bound by the ceiling.

Conclusions

The price benchmark performed suggests that overall the price of sand products in Romania is not bound by the ceiling. It is however possible that the price is bound in certain areas and for certain amounts of time due to the highly local nature of the market, especially in areas with a low number of producers.

It is also expected, with price ceilings set below the equilibrium, for certain features of the market to be exhibited, e.g. shortages due to reduced supply and suppliers forming long-term relationships with preferred customers. While we have not found evidence of these, the features of the market should be further investigated in order to test these features at the local level, especially in cases where the maximum price set is below the prices of goods traded at the Commodities Exchange.

Despite the lack of evidence of the binding effect of the price cap, it is obvious that in most counties there is a relatively high number of sand and rock producers with an average number of exploitation sites of 19 per county. Only one county has a single exploitation site licence or permit and two have none. Natural monopolies in the sand and rock producers market are therefore a rare occurrence and the need for a national price cap mechanism cannot be supported to protect against these cases. A comprehensive analysis at the local level may reveal genuine local monopolies where price caps may be justified, but price caps at the national level are not supported by the current geographic distribution of over 700 companies active in the sector.

Notes

1. The NACE Code is a pan-European classification system which groups organisations according to their business activities.
2. ANAF, *www.anaf.ro/indicatori/indfinanciari.html*, Deloitte calculations.
3. ANRM, *www.namr.ro/resurse-minerale/licentepermise-active/* (accessed 22 February 2016), Deloitte calculations.
4. *www.geiger.ro*, *www.viarock.ro*, *malidcom.ro*, *www.betonix.ro*, *www.preturibeton.ro*, *www.transportnisip-balastru.ro* (accessed on 3 February 2016).
5. *www.brm.ro/licitatii/preturi-de-tranzactionare/* (accessed on 3 February 2016).
6. *www.siegl.cz*, *www.a-cervenka.cz*, *www.miroslavsmid.cz*, *http://makler.md*, *http://construct.md*, *http://fmc.md*, *www.cennik-budowlany.pl*, *www.jft.com.pl*, *olx.pl*, *www.jatech.pl*, *www.kzek.pl*, *www.piasekbudowlany.pl* (accessed on 3 February 2016).
7. Transportation costs are not regulated and therefore there is a risk of price collusion indirectly increasing the price of sand and rock products while the baseline price remains below the price cap.

Chapter 3

Transport

The various types of transport (road, rail and maritime) together generate a turnover of about 5.08% of Romania's GDP and employs about 133 100 people. Although Romania's road transport is among the most regulated in the European Union, its rail transport is one of the most liberalised rail transport markets. Road transport is constrained by unnecessary documentation, such as authorisations for vehicle repair, complicated payment of local taxes, display of vehicle plates and copies of transport licences. Rail transport suffers from unclear provisions relating to private and public railway infrastructure and the ambiguous position of Romania's state-owned rail freight operator in regard to private operators. Inland waterway and maritime transport is constrained by the lack of transparency in tariff calculation, a lack of open competition for pilotage and towage services and undue discretion given to the Romanian Naval Authority (ANR) regarding compliance of market participants with state regulations.

3.1. Economic overview of the Romanian freight transport sector

The freight transport sector includes activities related to the following transport modalities: road, rail, inland waterways, maritime and support activities for transport such as warehousing.[1] The freight transport sector plays an important role in the country's economy, generating a turnover of approximately 5.08% of gross domestic product (GDP) in 2014 and employing 133 100 people. Figure 3.1 shows that in 2014 the transport sector (including passengers) generated a gross value added (GVA) of approximately EUR 7.6 billion, representing 5.11% of Romania's GDP. In 2014, Romania's gross domestic product reached EUR 148.7 billion.

Figure 3.1. **Transport sector, GVA (millions of EUR, % of GDP)**

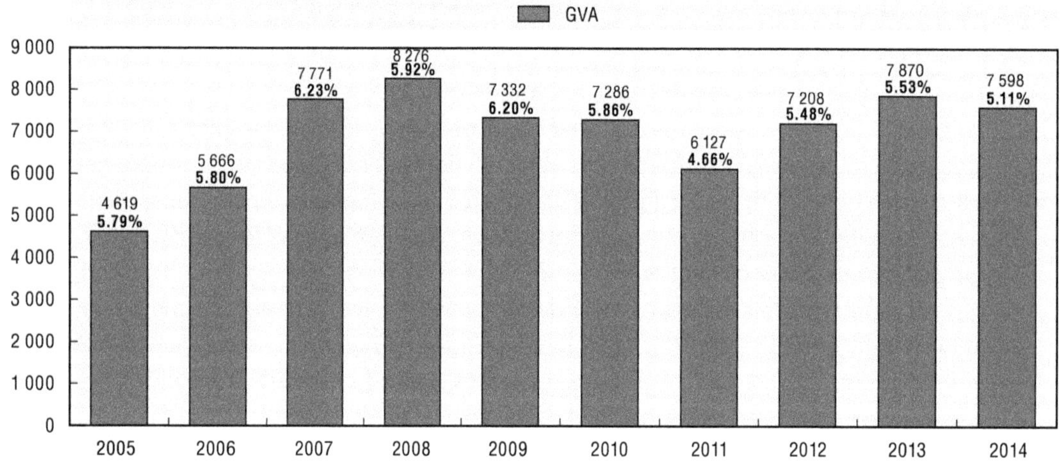

Source: Eurostat, National Accounts aggregates by industry (database), *http://bit.ly/1Wn1OhH*, GDP and main components (database), *http://bit.ly/1dBAzYR* (accessed on 26 January 2016).

StatLink http://dx.doi.org/10.1787/888933361448

Figure 3.2 shows the relationship between the evolution of Romanian transport's GVA and GDP.

According to Romania's NIS, there were approximately 133 100 people employed in the freight industry in 2014, working for a total of 25 125 firms, of which 24 892 were operating in the road transport sector. Most of the companies are either small or medium-sized. Approximately 91% of these companies have 1 to 10 employees, 8% have 10 to 50 employees while the remaining companies exceed 50 employees. Employment in the freight transport sector has increased by approximately 12% from 2008 to 2014, although this increase relates exclusively to the road transport sector.

Figure 3.3 compares the modal split of Romanian inland freight transport in volume and value. In volume terms, the split was 70.84% for road, 18.83% for rail and 10.33% for inland waterways. In value terms, the split was 89.63% for road, 9.11% for rail and 1.26% for inland waterways.

Figure 3.2. **Evolution of GVA and GDP in the transport sector, 2006-14 (%)**

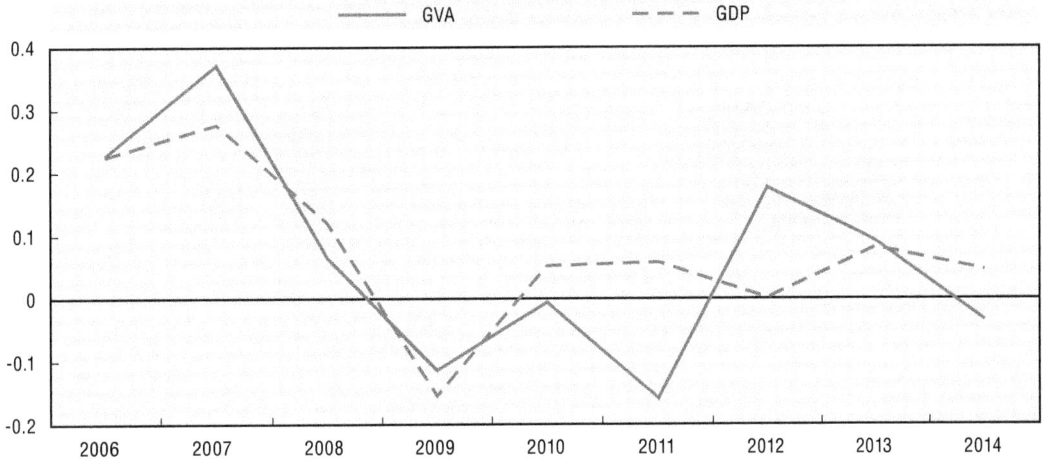

Source: Eurostat, National Accounts aggregates by industry (database), *http://bit.ly/1Wn1OhH*, GDP and main components (database), *http://bit.ly/1dBAzYR* (accessed on 26 January 2016) and Musliu şi Asociaţii calculations.

StatLink http://dx.doi.org/10.1787/888933361455

Figure 3.3. **Modal split of inland freight transport in 2014: % of inland freight volume and value**

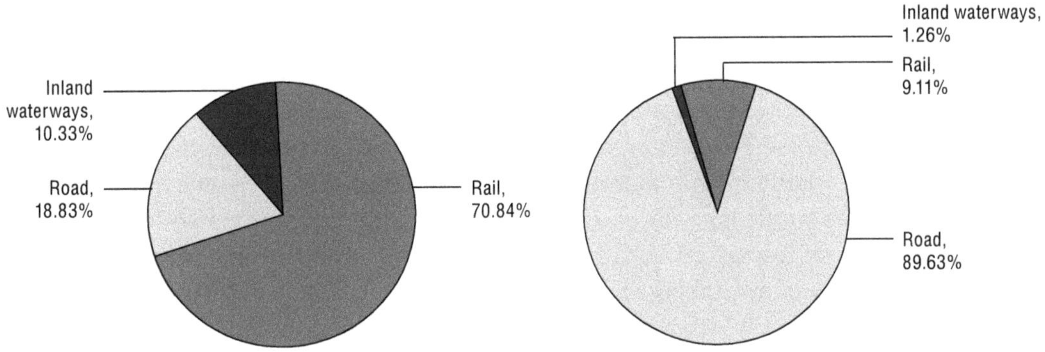

Source: NIS, *Goods transport, by mode of transport* (database), *http://bit.ly/21a7Nxe* (accessed on 26 January 2016) and Musliu şi Asociaţii calculations.

StatLink http://dx.doi.org/10.1787/888933361468

Figure 3.4 shows the overall modal split of freight transported within and outside Romania including maritime and air transport in 2014. In volume terms, this was 60.95% road, 16.2% rail, 13.95% maritime, 8.89% inland waterways and 0.01% for air. In value terms, the split was 88.54% road, 9% rail, 1.25% inland waterways, 0.98% maritime and 0.23% air.

Road freight transport

Definition

The road freight transport sector refers to the transportation of goods between economic enterprises and between enterprises and consumers, including bulk goods and goods requiring special handling, such as refrigerated and dangerous goods.[2]

Transport can be for own-account (e.g. freight transportation between establishments belonging to the same firm) and for hire or reward. In Romania, road transport is the principal modality of moving freight, representing 70.84% of all inland freight transport volumes.

Figure 3.4. **Modal split of freight transport in 2014: % of overall freight volume and value**

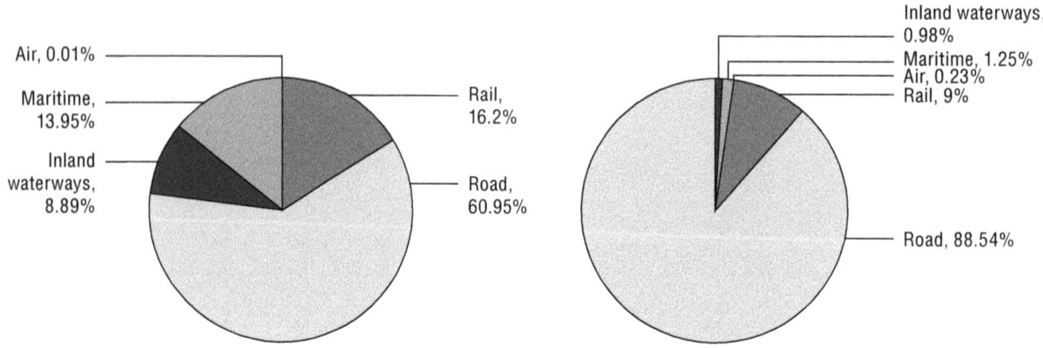

Source: NIS, *Goods transport, by mode of transport* (database), *http://bit.ly/21a7Nxe* (accessed on 26 January 2016) and Musliu şi Asociaţii calculations.

StatLink http://dx.doi.org/10.1787/888933361476

Infrastructure

The total length of the road network is 85 362 km as shown in Table 3.1. The roads are uniformly distributed along the country, the only exception being the Bucharest-Ilfov region which has a much higher density of public roads and where the majority of business is concentrated. Over the last eight years, the Romanian road network has grown by almost 12 000 km. However, there are still gaps in the highway system and connections between regions are still insufficient. The poor infrastructure is reflected in the length of the country's road network, notably with respect to motorways and national roads. The network of motorways and national roads represents only 20% of the entire network, as shown in Table 3.1 below. In addition, approximately 90% of the national road network is made up of roads with only one traffic lane for each direction and with very low speed limits (average 66 km/h). This has an impact on both freight delivery time and safety. These roads do not ensure the possibility of overtaking local agrarian vehicles and thus reduce safety for heavy freight transport vehicles, which are the major users of the national road network.[3]

Table 3.1. **Length of the Romanian road network**

Road type	Kilometres	Percentage
Motorways	683	0.80
European national roads	6 269	7.34
Other national roads	10 320	12.09
County roads	35 505	41.59
Municipal roads	32 585	38.17
Total	85 362	100

Source: NIS, *Length of public roads* (database), *http://bit.ly/1Q5VxDi*, (accessed on 26 January 2016).

According to the National Union of Romanian Road Hauliers,[4] to reach the European Union (EU) average of road network of motorways, Romania should build another 3 150 km of road.

Nevertheless, Romania has made a significant investment in its road transport infrastructure over the past 4 years, although the trend and size of such investment differs significantly in Central and Eastern European (CEE) countries compared to Western European countries, as shown in Figure 3.5.

Figure 3.5. **Road infrastructure investment (millions of EUR)**

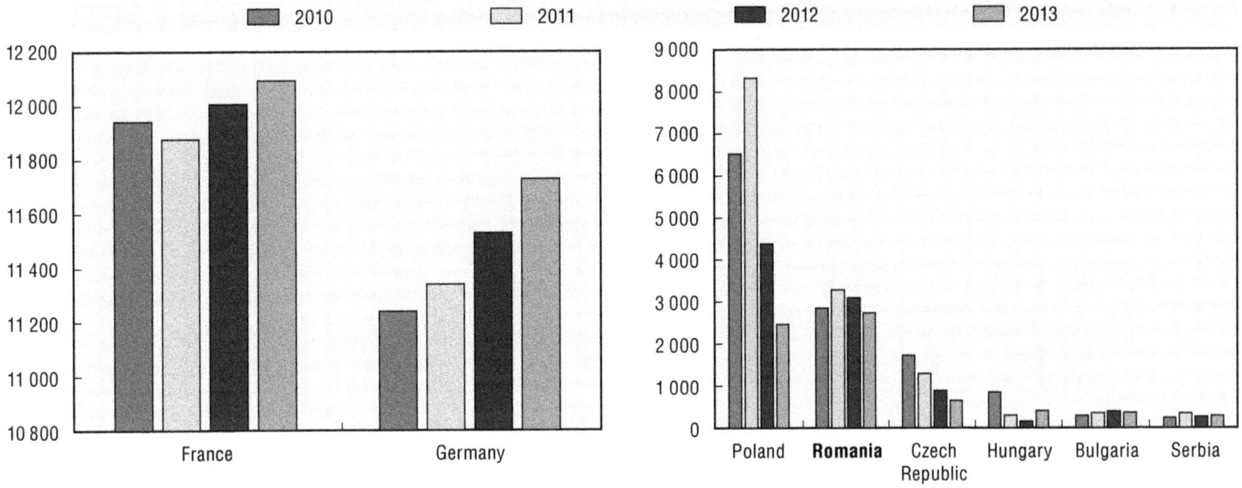

Source: OECD, *Statistics, Infrastructure investment* (Database), *http://bit.ly/1ObFyBD* (accessed on 26 January 2016).

StatLink http://dx.doi.org/10.1787/888933361485

Figure 3.6. **Investment in road transport infrastructure as a % of GDP**

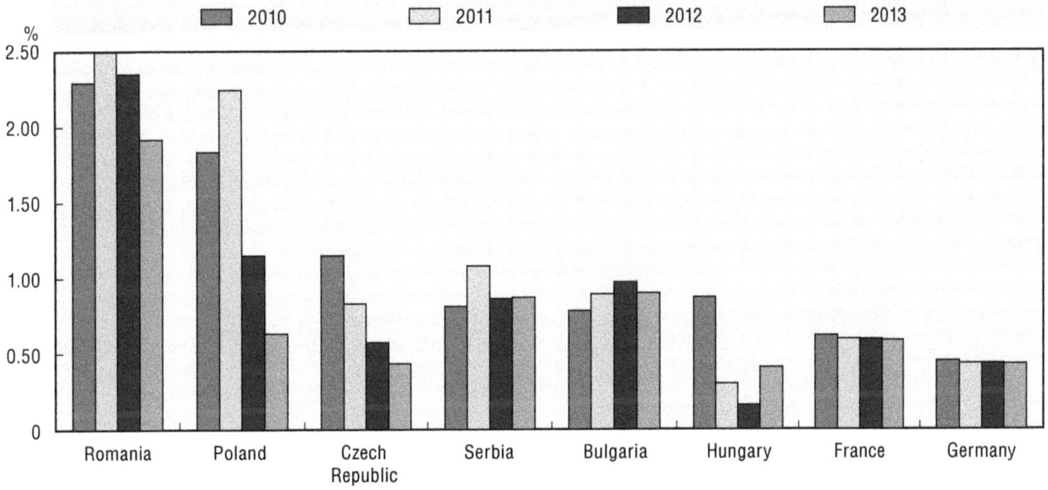

Source: OECD, *Statistics, Infrastructure investment* (Database), *http://bit.ly/1ObFyBD* (accessed on 26 January 2016) and Eurostat, *GDP and main components* (database), *http://bit.ly/1dBAzYR* (accessed on 26 January 2016).

StatLink http://dx.doi.org/10.1787/888933361495

International comparison

The Romanian road freight industry sector is dominated by competition in prices and quality of service. Two broad categories of road freight regulation exist in OECD countries:[5] i) rules on traffic and vehicles and ii) rules on access to the marketplace. The first category includes the Highway Code, labour issues, carriage of hazardous substances and traffic restrictions. The second category covers mainly market access restrictions and price regulations. The main issues targeted by road freight regulation relate to safety, impact on the environment and use as well as maintenance of the infrastructure.

Figure 3.7 illustrates a comparison between Romania and other EU countries over regulatory constraints in road freight transport. According to the OECD's Product Market Regulation Indicator (PMRI),[6] Romania's road freight industry is one of the most regulated in the EU.

Figure 3.7. **Sector regulation indicator for road freight transport, 2013**

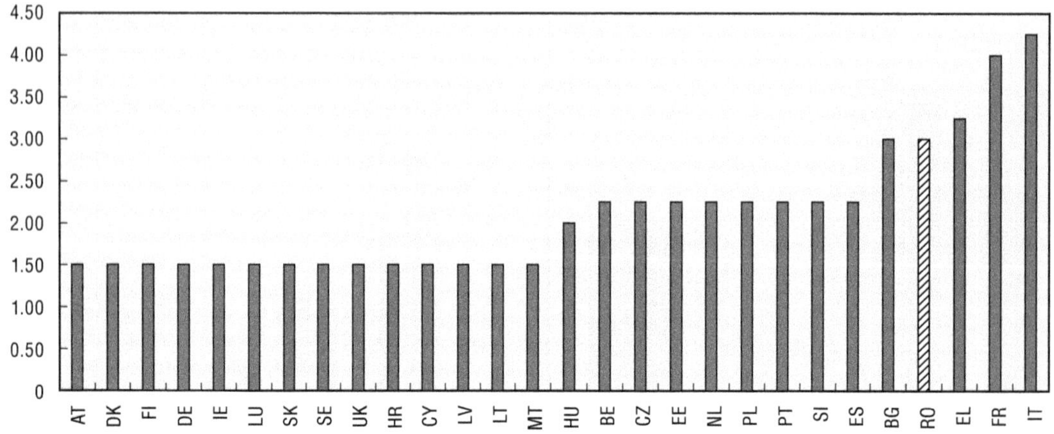

Source: OECD PMRI, *http://bit.ly/1VzCOE4.*

StatLink http://dx.doi.org/10.1787/888933361503

Subsector characteristics

According to Romania's NIS, the overall value of the road freight transport sector in 2014 was about EUR 6.8 billion and accounted for about 4.56% of Romania's GDP. In the same year, employment reached approximately 117 200 people with 24 892 firms operating in this sector. The industry mainly consists of small companies, with about 91% of companies having 1 to 10 employees, 8% having 10 to 50 employees and only 1% having more than 50 employees. Over the last five years, the number of firms active in road freight has increased by approximately 10%, while employment has grown by 33%.

According to the Ministry of Finance (MoF), the largest players in road freight transport in the year 2014, expressed in turnover's terms, were as follows:

Table 3.2. **Top 10 players in the road freight sector**

	Company	Turnover 2014 (EUR)	Market share 2014 [1]
1.	Carrion Expedition	84 470 278	1.29%
2.	Transcondor	71 821 717	1.06%
3.	Duvenbeck Logistik	56 198 953	0.83%
4.	Total NSA	44 060 449	0.65%
5.	International Lazar Company	42 025 159	0.62%
6.	Dunca Expeditii	40 707 529	0.60%
7.	Dumagas Transport	38 351 009	0.56%
8.	Hartl Carrier	30 373 115	0.45%
9.	J.T. Grup Oil	30 351 680	0.45%
10.	Dianthus Company	29 896 260	0.44%

1. Calculated as a percentage of total turnover in the road freight transport sector. References to "market share" or "markets" in general, included in this report, do not reflect the same definitions used for purposes of applying competition law.

Source: Ministry of Finance, *http://bit.ly/1QxjYPO* and Musliu şi Asociaţii calculations.

Road freight transport in Romania is a very fragmented subsector, characterised by the predominance of small firms.

The most important trade associations in road freight transport are: the National Union of Romanian Road Hauliers (UNTRR),[7] Romanian Association of International Road

Transport (ARTRI),[8] Federation of Romanian Transport Operators (FORT),[9] Transport Heritage Association Europe 2002 (APTE2002),[10] Transylvania Road Hauliers Association (ATRT),[11] Road Hauliers in Construction Association (ATRC),[12] Freight Forwarders Association (USER)[13] and Romanian-Italian Association of Logistics and Management (ARILOG).[14]

Figure 3.8 illustrates the evolution of Romanian road freight transport over the last decade (2005-14). This sector exhibits a sharp decrease during the outbreak of the global financial crisis, with a post-crisis gradual increase. The annual growth rate of goods transported by road decreased from +9.2% in 2006 to -0.3% in 2014. In value terms, the Compound Annual Growth Rate (CAGR) has fallen from +27% before the crisis to +12% in the period between 2009 and 2014.

Figure 3.8. **Total road freight transport in Romania**[1]

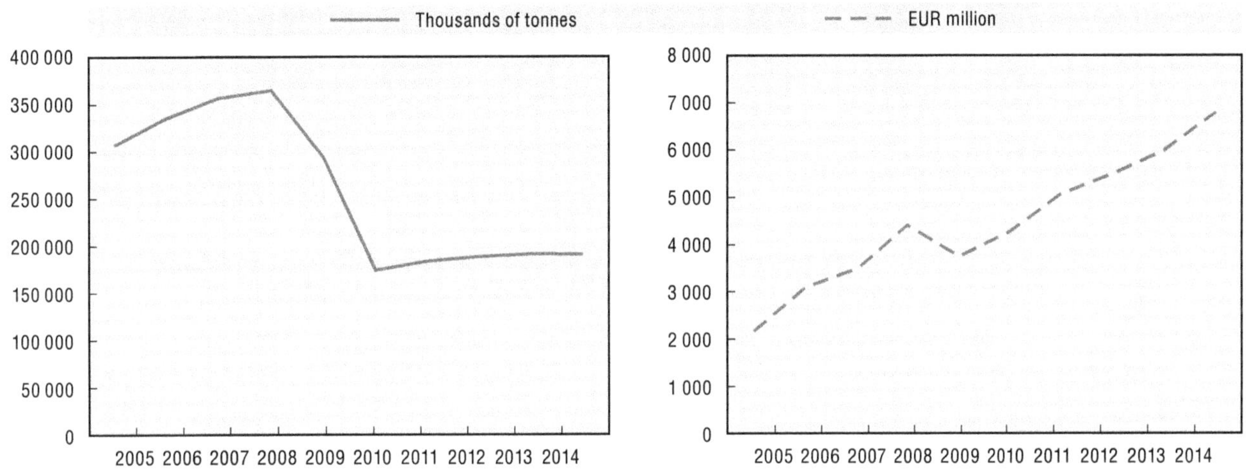

1. The data on volume represents inland traffic whereas that on value also corresponds to freight road transport services provided by Romanian companies abroad. This may explain why over the crisis period, turnover increased whereas volume decreased.

Source: NIS, *Goods transport, by mode of transport* (database), *http://bit.ly/21a7Nxe* (accessed on 26 January 2016).

StatLink http://dx.doi.org/10.1787/888933361518

Road freight transport is the second transport modality used for import and export in Romania, following maritime transport. As shown in Figure 3.9, about 13.4% of the volume of goods transported by road in 2014 represented international transport. Transit transport is very low due to the lack of an efficient infrastructure. Indeed, Romania has not yet taken advantage of its status as a transit country for the southern regions of Eastern Europe.

According to the NIS, the main categories of goods that were transported by road in 2014 were: metal ores and other mining products (32.16%), non-metallic mineral products (19.8%), food products (8.98%), agriculture products (6.17%), wood and products of wood and cork (5.26%), secondary raw materials and municipal waste (3.24%), basic metals (3.05%) and coke and refined petroleum products (2.31%). Demand is therefore driven mainly by the following industry sectors: extraction, quarry, cement, food, agriculture and forestry.

International road transport

As shown in Figure 3.10, compared to other EU countries, Romania operates small volumes of international traffic, including incoming, outgoing and transit international freight transport. Transit volumes are particularly small even if compared to other CEE countries, namely Hungary, Poland and the Czech Republic.

Figure 3.9. **Road freight transport in Romania, volume of goods carried by road (thousands of tonnes)**

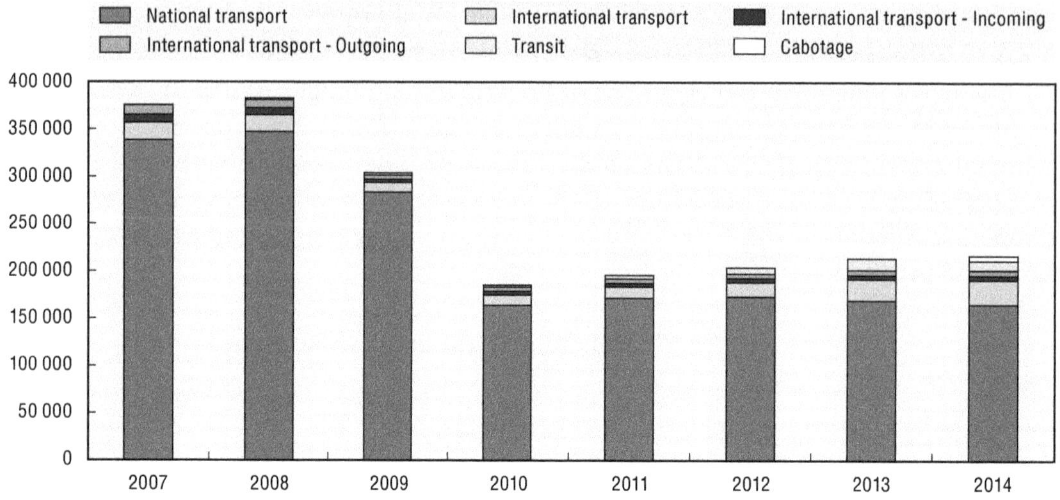

Source: Eurostat, *Summary of annual road freight transport by type of operation and type of transport* (database), *http://bit.ly/1yussbN* (accessed on 26 January 2016).

StatLink http://dx.doi.org/10.1787/888933361521

Figure 3.10. **International road freight transport across different markets in Europe, volume of goods carried by road (thousands of tonnes)**

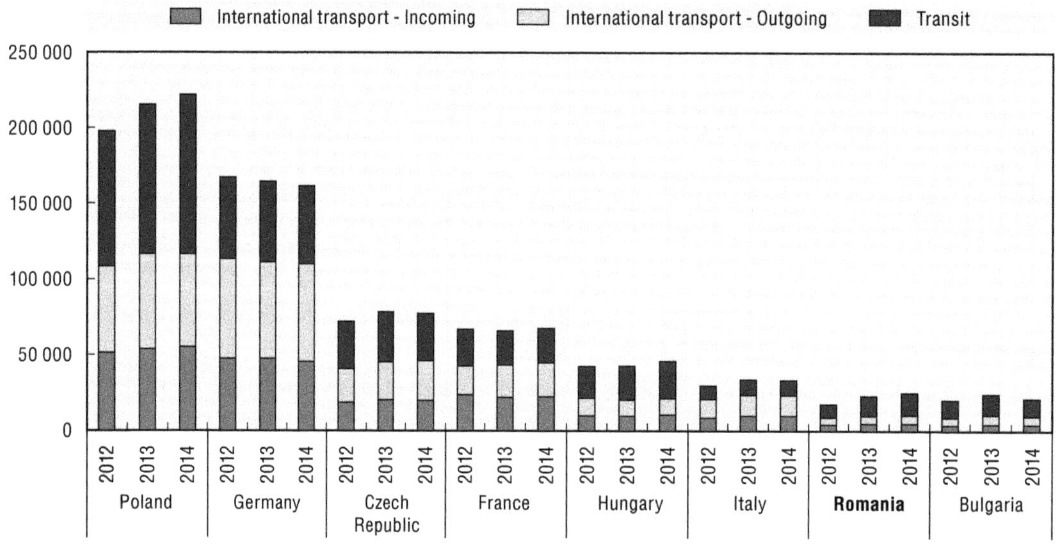

Source: Eurostat, *Summary of annual road freight transport by type of operation and type of transport* (database), *http://bit.ly/1yussbN* (accessed on 26 January 2016).

StatLink http://dx.doi.org/10.1787/888933361539

Relevant government authorities

The **Ministry of Transport** (MoT) is the central body of the state administration in charge of transport policy. The Ministry is responsible for regulation, economic policy and international agreements in the area of transport.

Other regulatory powers with respect to road transport are as follows:

- ***Romanian Automotive Register*** (RAR) is a technical specialised body designated by the MoT as the competent authority in the field of road vehicles, road safety, environmental protection and quality assurance. The RAR has the following main tasks: granting national approval and certification of conformity for classes as well as individual road vehicles; licensing technical inspection stations and overlooking their activity.[15]

- ***State Inspectorate for Road Transport Control*** is a permanent technical specialised body under the MoT monitoring compliance with national and international regulations in road transport, mainly regarding: the conditions for carrying out road transport activities; the training required to obtain a driving licence; road safety and environmental protection; technical conditions of road vehicles; tonnage and/or maximum size allowed on public roads.[16]
- ***Inter-ministerial Council for Road Safety*** is a Government advisory body without a legal personality. Its main tasks consists of developing strategies for national road safety and priority actions for implementing these strategies; assessing the impact of road safety policy and coordinating research and communication related to road safety.[17]
- ***Romanian Road Authority*** is a technical specialised body of the MoT. Its main activities are: delivering licences for road transport activities and professional certifications of specific transport personnel; evaluating the impact of state policies on road safety, through carrying out road safety audits, safety inspections, training activities, certification and professional training of road safety auditors.[18]
- ***Regional and Municipal Councils*** control regional roads and may apply taxes in addition to the RO-vignette[19] as well as establishing traffic rules and speed limits affecting freight hauliers, given that regional and municipal roads make up approximately 80% of the entire Romanian national road network.

Rail freight transport

Definition of the relevant sectors and ares of investigation

Rail freight refers to freight, cargo or goods transported by railways and does not include parcels or baggage transport services associated with railway passenger services.[20]

Infrastructure

The Romanian rail network is operated by Compania Naţională de Căi Ferate "CFR" (National Railway Company "CFR") and covers the majority of urban and economic centres. It is connected to the European rail network by the railway administrations of neighbouring countries, namely Hungary, Serbia, Bulgaria, Moldova and Ukraine.

The network consists of approximately 20 000 km of track, with a railway route length of 10 777 km,[21] of which around 37% is electrified (compared with the EU27 average of 52%).[22] A significant proportion (72%) of the rail network is single track type; the EU27 average is 59%.

The length of Romania's railway network has been constant over the last years. Due to the lack of maintenance funds, the technical parameters of the public railway infrastructure suffer continuing damage. This leads to a reduced quality of the services provided, one of them being a reduced speed for commercial freight trains (approximately 28.3 km/h). This affects the delivery time of rail freight transport which in Romania is significantly slower than road freight transport and explains the preference expressed by the business sector for road. The average delivery time of a container by rail normally exceeds that by road, due to the condition of the infrastructure and delays in the transferring/handling of containers from terminals.[23]

As shown in Figure 3.11, notwithstanding the above problems, Romania has made little investment in upgrading its rail infrastructure from 2010 to 2013.

Figure 3.11. **Rail infrastructure investment (millions of EUR)**

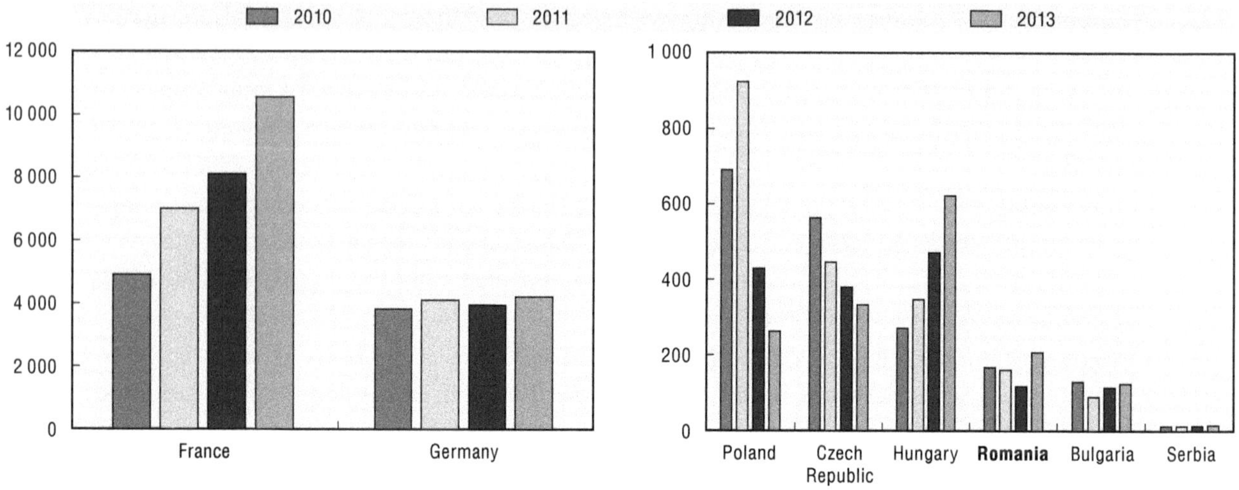

Source: OECD, *Statistics, Infrastructure investment* (Database), *http://bit.ly/1ObFyBD* (accessed on 26 January 2016).

StatLink http://dx.doi.org/10.1787/888933361540

Figure 3.12. **Investment in rail transport infrastructure as a % of GDP**

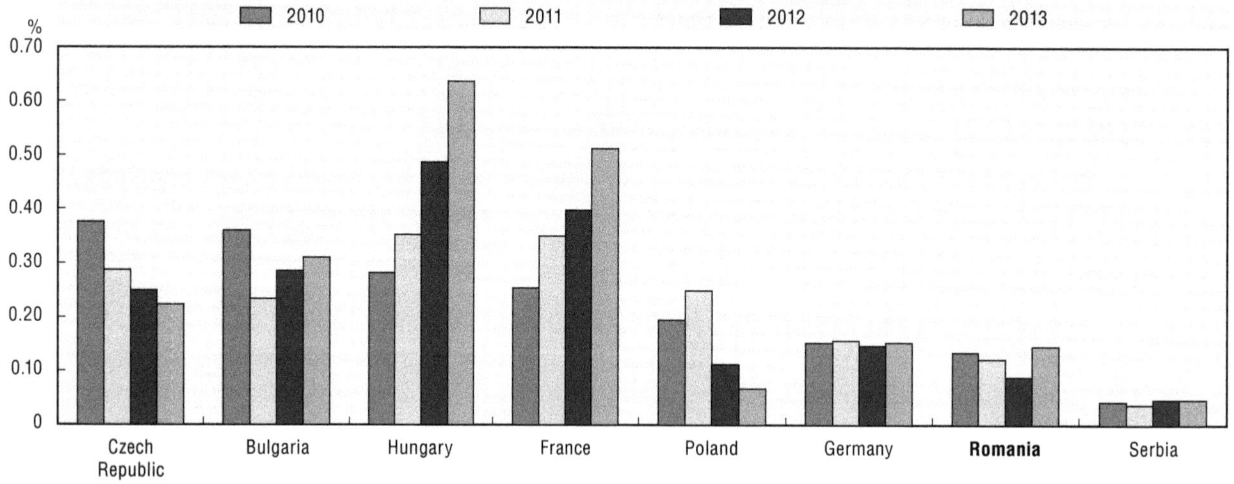

Source: OECD, *Statistics, Infrastructure investment* (database), *http://bit.ly/1ObFyBD* (accessed on 26 January 2016) and Eurostat, *GDP and main components* (database), *http://bit.ly/1dBAzYR* (accessed on 26 January 2016).

StatLink http://dx.doi.org/10.1787/888933361558

An important element affecting access to the marketplace is the infrastructure access fee. Calculating and levying this fee is the responsibility of the infrastructure manager, in line with EU legislation. The methodology for calculating this fee is based on the following charges: distance run, gross tonnage, traffic type (freight or passenger), route of movement, class of traffic section and its electrification systems for supplying traction.[24]

In order to have access to the railway infrastructure, railway transport operators must conclude an infrastructure access contract with the National Railway Company "CFR". The access contract establishes the rights and obligations of CFR and railway transport operators concerning infrastructure capacity allocation and utilisation.

Figure 3.13 below shows that Romania has one of the highest railway infrastructure access fees among EU countries.

Figure 3.13. **Access charges for freight trains for the year 2014 (EUR/tonne-km)**

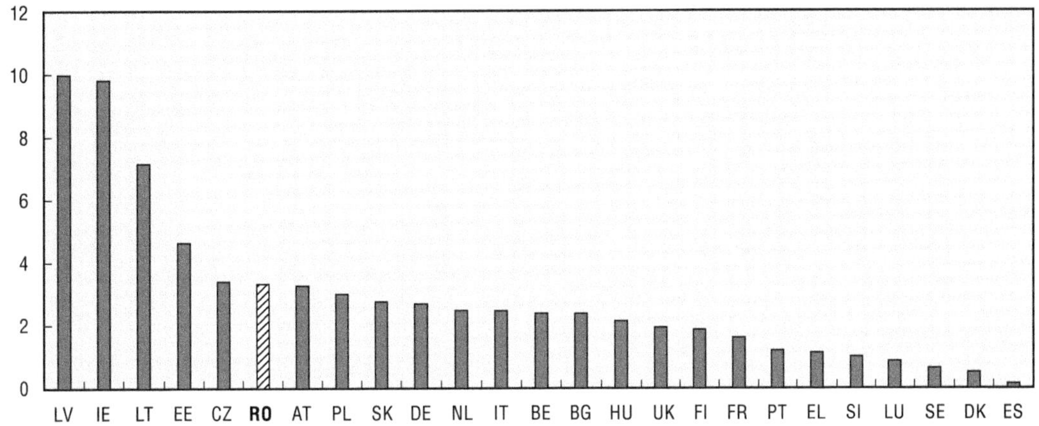

Source: European Commission (2014), *Fourth report on monitoring development in the rail market*, Report from the Commission to the Council and the European Parliament, 13.06.2014, *http://bit.ly/1PMs4OR.*

StatLink http://dx.doi.org/10.1787/888933361566

Liberalisation of the transport sector started in 1998 when the National Company of Romanian Railways, the old state-owned monopoly, was split into five independently-administered companies: CFR SA (dealing with infrastructure), CFR Călători (the operator of passenger trains), CFR Marfă (freight railway transport company), CFR Gevaro (services linked with restaurant cars) and SAAF (dealing with excess rolling stock to be sold, leased or scrapped). Following the introduction of open access to the monopoly infrastructure,[25] competition among rail freight operators has increased over time. The market share of CFR Marfă has dropped from 100% in the year 2000 to just under 35% at the end of 2014.[26] New entrants are therefore controlling more than half of this market.

In 2013, the MoT tried to privatise the national company CFR Marfă by selling off 51% of its share capital. Grup Feroviar Român, the second largest company operating in this sector, fulfilled all stages of the tender procedure and became the only qualified company to submit a tender for purchasing CFR Marfă in accordance with the conditions established by the MoT. The share purchase agreement between the MoT and Grup Feroviar Român was signed on 2 September 2013.[27] The Romanian government set 13 October 2013 as the deadline for completion of privatisation of CFR Marfă, but in the end the transaction has not gone through.

International comparison

Figure 3.14 shows a comparison across EU markets of the degree of regulation in rail transport developed by the OECD.[28] According to the OECD's PMRI, Romania is one of the countries with the most liberalised rail transport in the EU.

Subsector characteristics

The freight transport sector is undergoing a severe structural crisis. Since 2008, about 10 000 jobs have been lost in this subsector.[29] In 2013, the freight rail transport subsector generated an overall value of approximately EUR 680 million providing employment to

Figure 3.14. **Sector regulation indicator for rail transport, 2013**

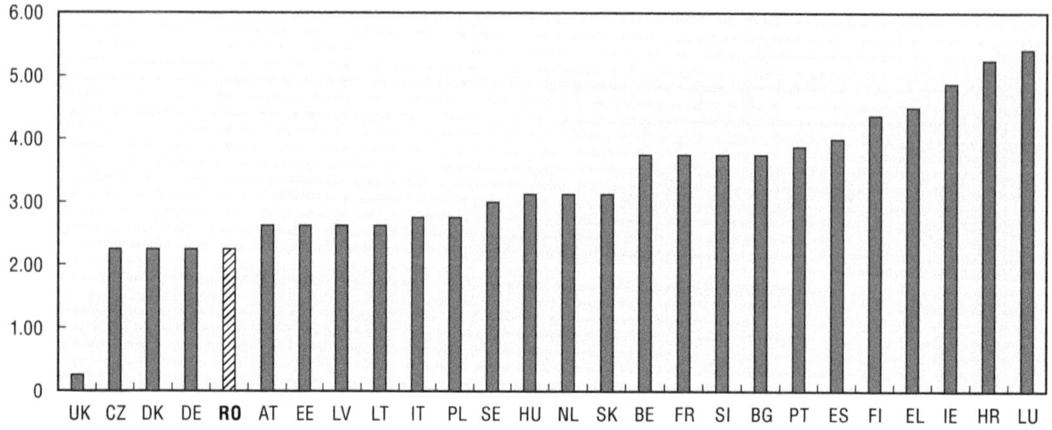

Source: OECD PMRI, *http://bit.ly/1VzCOE4.*

StatLink http://dx.doi.org/10.1787/888933361571

approximately 16 400 people.[30] In 2014, the same subsector generated an overall value of approximately EUR 603 million providing employment to approximately 13 500 people.[31]

The major player in this subsector is CFR Marfă, the former monopolist. Since 2001, an important number of private companies have entered the marketplace. According to data published by AFER (Romanian Railway Authority) on 31 December 2015, there are 23 railway freight operators, in addition to the state-owned CFR Marfă.

According to AFER and the MoF, the main rail freight companies in 2014, in terms of revenues, were as follows:

Table 3.3. **Top 10 players in the rail freight sector**

	Company	Turnover 2014 (EUR)	Market share 2014 [1]
1.	CFR Marfă	204 988 026	33.95%
2.	Grup Feroviar Român	154 700 480	25.62%
3.	Unicom Tranzit	55 301 189	9.16%
4.	Transferoviar Grup	37 967 410	6.29%
5.	DB Schenker Rail Romania	35 517 082	5.88%
6.	Rail Force	16 807 328	2.78%
7.	Servtrans Invest	12 398 216	2.05%
8.	Cargo Trans Vagon	11 661 097	1.93%
9.	Vest Trans Rail	11 479 457	1.90%
10.	Trans Expedition Feroviar	10 519 547	1.74%

1. Calculated as a percentage of total turnover of rail freight transport sector. References to "market shares" or "markets" in general, included in this report, do not reflect the same definitions used for purposes of applying competition law.

Source: AFER, Ministry of Finance, *http://bit.ly/1QxjYPO* and Musliu şi Asociaţii calculations.

Competition in the Romanian rail freight subsector has increased over the past 10 years. In the year 2000, CFR Marfă was the only company in this sector whereas in 2009 there were 12 companies operating in the market and in 2015 this number increased to 24 companies. The incumbent company CFR Marfă has constantly lost market share in favour of competing private companies.

The most important trade associations in the rail freight sector are the Association of Romanian Railway Transport Operators[32] and the Association of Romanian Railway Industry.[33]

Figure 3.15 illustrates the evolution of rail freight transport over the last decade in Romania (2005-14), both in volume and in value terms. The rail freight transport recorded significant declines in the last 9 years, with the volume of goods transported by rail dropping from approximately 69 million tonnes in 2005 to approximately 50 million tonnes in 2014, representing a CAGR of -2.9%. In value terms, over the same period, the decline of the CAGR was -2.7%. This decline comes in the context of a constant increase in road freight transport volumes in Romania.

Figure 3.15. **Total rail freight transport in Romania**

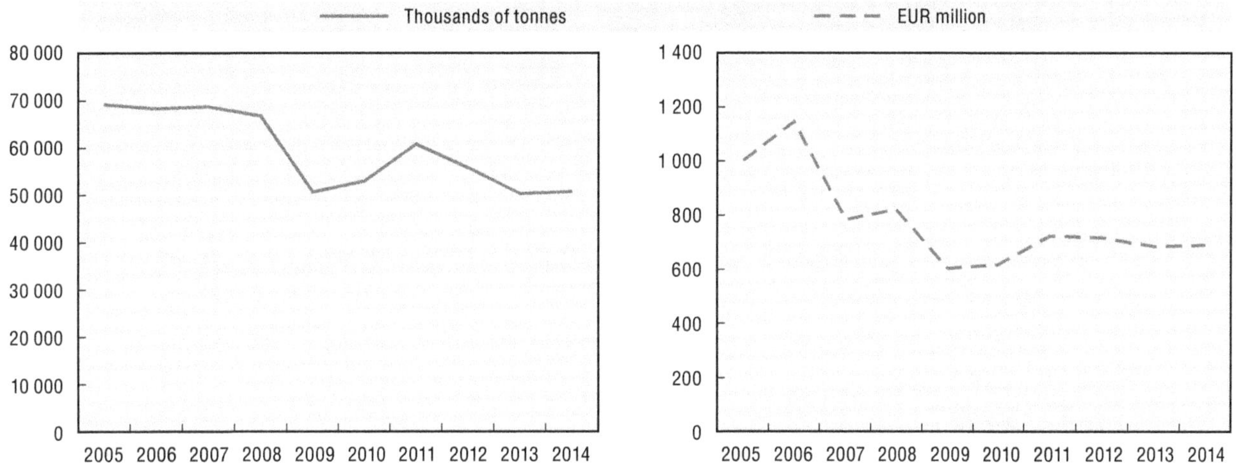

Source: NIS, *Goods transport, by mode of transport* (database), *http://bit.ly/21a7Nxe* (accessed on 26 January 2016).

StatLink http://dx.doi.org/10.1787/888933361588

Figure 3.16 illustrates the structure of railway freight transport. National transport represents the biggest share (over 80%) of total freight transport. The poor state of the railway transport infrastructure and the high infrastructure access fees lead to insignificant volumes of international transit. Import and export represents a small part of the total railway freight transport – below 20% since 2008.

According to the NIS, the main categories of goods that were transported by rail in 2014 were: coal and lignite, crude petroleum and natural gas (35.71%), coke and refined petroleum products (29.51%), products of agriculture (6.42%), chemicals (5.52%), metal ores and other mining products (5.04%), basic metals (4.95%), non-metallic mineral products (2.74%) and wood and products of wood and cork (2.71%). Therefore, the major demand operators come from the following industry sectors: energy, agriculture and extraction.

International rail transport

International railway transport is negligible in Romania, compared to other European countries, confirming the weak attraction of Romania's infrastructure for international traffic. This conclusion is in sharp contrast with the fact that Romania is located at the crossroads between three trans-European network corridors going from west to east and from south to north.[34]

Figure 3.16. **Rail freight transport in Romania, volume of goods carried by rail (thousands of tonnes)**

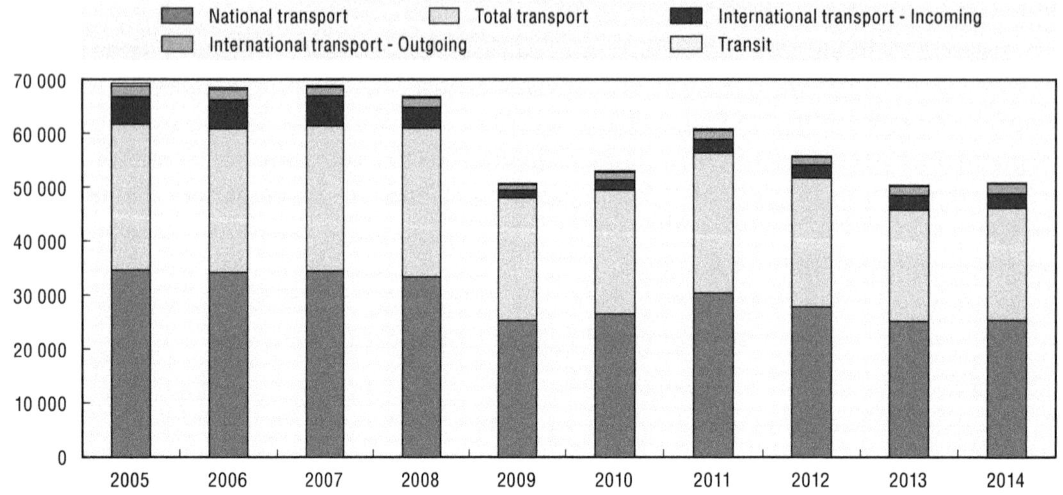

Source: Eurostat, *Railway transport – Goods transported, by type of transport* (database), *http://bit.ly/1yussbN* (accessed on 26 January 2016).

StatLink http://dx.doi.org/10.1787/888933361593

Figure 3.17. **International rail freight transport across different markets in Europe, volume of goods carried by rail (thousands of tonnes)**

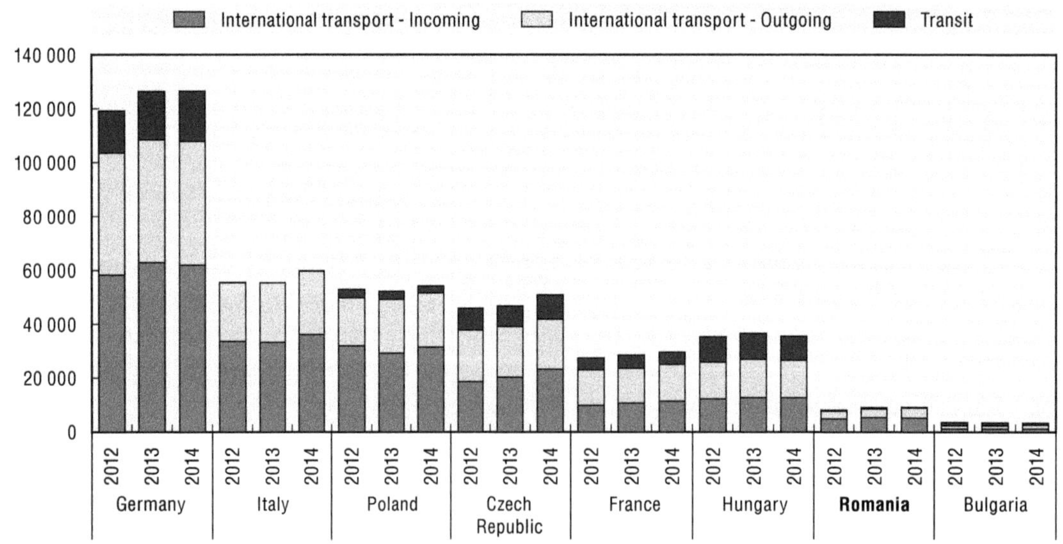

Source: Eurostat, *Railway transport – Goods transported, by type of transport* (database), *http://bit.ly/1yussbN* (accessed on 26 January 2016).

StatLink http://dx.doi.org/10.1787/888933361601

Relevant government authorities

The following regulatory authorities are responsible for developing the rail freight national policy:

- ***Railway Supervision Council (CSF)*** is the national authority monitoring railway service markets which intervenes when discrimination occurs notably with respect to access to infrastructure. The CSF may investigate, either on its own initiative or following a complaint, situations such as refusal of access or tariff discrimination implemented by the infrastructure administrator or railway transport operators. The CSF has authority to issue reasoned decisions and implement appropriate remedies.[35]

- ***Romanian Railway Authority (AFER)*** is a technical body within the MoT, overseeing safety authorisations and licences related to the railway infrastructure administrator or rail transport operators. It also monitors the respect of the conditions needed for interoperability of the conventional and high speed trans-European railway system.[36]
- ***Romanian Railway Licensing Body (OLFR)*** is the national authority designated for issuing licences for rail transport operators.[37]
- ***National Centre for Railway Qualification and Training (CENAFER)*** is a national specialised body under the MoT, designed to ensure the regular professional training and testing of the staff carrying out typical activities in railway transport, in order to ensure safe conditions for circulation, transport security and railway services quality.[38]

Inland waterway and maritime freight transport

Definition

Water freight transport refers to goods transported on waterways by using various means such as boats, steamers, barges, ships, etc. Goods are carried to different places by these means both within and outside the country. When the goods are transported inside the country on rivers and canals, transport is referred as "inland waterway transport". "Maritime transport" refers to movement of goods on ships on the sea and is carried out on fixed routes, linking a large number of origin and destination points in separate countries. Maritime transport therefore plays an important role in the development of international trade.

Ports in maritime and inland waterway transport serve as infrastructure to a wide range of customers including freight shippers, ferry operators and private boats. One of the main functions of ports is facilitating domestic and international trade of goods, often on a large scale.

Figure 3.18. **Structure of the maritime industry**

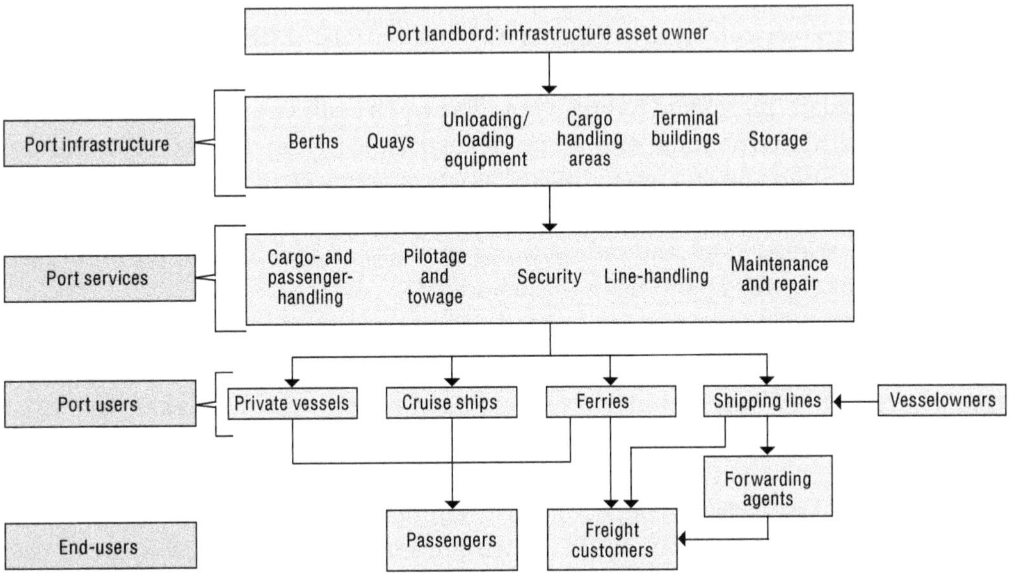

Source: OECD (2011), *Competition in ports and port services, http://bit.ly/1oDSwU2.*

Some shipping services as well as shipping related activities taking place in ports are provided by the port administration under monopoly conditions, while others are subject to competition.[39] Shipping related activities include safety services such as port pilotage and towing, activities related to ship operation[40] and other shipping auxiliary activities.[41]

Infrastructure

The naval infrastructure in Romania consists of maritime ports, river-maritime ports and river ports. There are three maritime harbours along the Black Sea, namely Constanța, Mangalia and Midia. These ports are directly linked to the Danube-Black Sea Canal, which ensures connection between the Black Sea and the river Danube, the Poarta Albă-Midia Năvodari Canal and, indirectly, with the "Mihail Kogălniceanu" Airport located 20 km away from Constanța.

The Port of Constanța is the main Romanian sea port, playing a significant role as the transit node for the landlocked countries in central and south-eastern Europe. It has connections with all means of transport: railway, road, inland waterways and air. The volume of goods handled here represents more than 95% of the commodities handled in all maritime ports in Romania, with a total volume of 55.64 million tonnes in 2014 (of which 43.05 million tonnes corresponded to maritime transport and 12.58 million tonnes corresponded to river transport).[42]

The Port of Constanța has gradually become one of the main distribution centres serving central and eastern Europe, having the fourth largest port surface in the EU, ranked just after Rotterdam, Antwerp and Marseille.[43]

The Port of Constanța has also an advantageous geostrategic position, being located at the intersection of the Pan-European Transport Corridor No. IV, which goes from Dresden/ Nuremberg to Istanbul (road and railway), with the Pan-European Transport Corridor No. VII, which connects the North Sea to the Black Sea by the Rhine-Main-Danube Canal. This port therefore links two European trade poles, Rotterdam and Constanța, creating an inland waterway transport route from the North Sea to the Black Sea. In the southern part of the port, Constanța also has a river area, which makes it a river-maritime port.

The Danube River can be divided into two structurally different sectors: the River Danube and the Maritime Danube. Several ports situated along the Maritime Danube, namely Brăila, Galați, Tulcea and Sulina, allow access for both river and maritime vessels, so they serve both international and inland transport. However, the lack of multimodal facilities for these ports represents a major obstacle in terms of alignment of port logistics to international transport, notably with respect to shipment of containers. Moreover, connections to national roads and rail networks are slow and inefficient. All these factors limit the volume of traffic operating in these ports.[44]

The inland waterway network is composed of the Danube, secondary navigable branches of the Danube and navigable canals. The navigable inland waterways have a total length of about 1 779 km, of which 1 647 are navigable rivers and lakes and 132 are navigable canals. The Danube River has a length in or along the border of Romania of about 1 075 km so is considered an important transport corridor. Romania has 30 inland river ports.[45] Most of these ports have a poor infrastructure when compared to modern logistic requirements, with obsolete equipment, which prevents the efficient transport of goods. Also, these ports have inefficient connections with other transport modalities. These issues are reflected in the reduced volumes of cargo in these ports.[46]

According to the MoT Master Plan for the transport sector, investments are necessary to modernise and upgrade the Romanian inland waterway infrastructure. Indeed, following Bulgaria, Romania has the lowest investment rate on the Danube river infrastructure of all the Danube countries based on the length of its section of this river.[47]

Subsector characteristics

Maritime freight transport. Maritime transport is the most important modality of international freight transport in Romania. Approximately 60% of the goods imported and exported by Romania in 2014 were transported by sea, followed by road and inland waterways.

According to the NIS, in 2014 maritime freight transport generated overall revenues equal to EUR 75.3 million, with 284 people employed. In addition, in 2014 all shipping-related activities generated an overall value of EUR 366 million, with approximately 240 active firms and about 5 320 people employed.

As shown in the table below, freight shipping operations in Consţanta are mainly run by international shipping companies, whereas Romanian ship owners have gradually disappeared.

Table 3.4. **International freight shipping operators**

	Company	Local Agent
1.	APM-Maersk Danemarca	Maersk Romania
2.	Mediterranean Shipping Company Elvetia	MSC Romania Shipping
3.	CMA CGM Franta	CMA CGM Romania
4.	Hapag-Lloyd Germania	Hub Dacia
5.	Evergreen Line	Bosphorus Shipping Agency Romania
6.	CSCL China Shipping Container Lines Co. Ltd	China Shipping Romania Agency Co. Ltd.
7.	Hanjin Shipping Korea	Arkas Dacia
8.	Hamburg Süd Group, **APL**	Economu International Shipping Agency
9.	Yang Ming Line China	Team Logistic Specialists
10.	UASC (United Arab Shipping Company)	Formag Romania
11.	K-Line (Kawasaki Kisen Kaisha) Japonia	Kapital Leading Transport Romania
12.	EMES	Romar Shipping Agency

Source: Port of Consţanta website, *http://bit.ly/1ojYSYZ.*

The maritime freight transport had a sharp decrease during the outbreak of the global financial crisis, reaching a positive evolution in terms of volume in the last five years, with a CAGR of approximately +4%. Figure 3.19 shows the evolution of maritime freight transport during the period between 2005 and 2014.

Figure 3.20 shows that Romania has suffered from the economic downturn which is reflected in the drop in imports. Since 2008, the volume of goods imported has been constantly decreasing.

According to the NIS, the main categories of goods that were transported by sea in 2014 were: agricultural products (33.36%), coal and lignite, crude petroleum and natural gas (18.53%), coke and refined petroleum products (10.05%), metal ores and other mining and quarrying products (8.39%), basic metals (5.41%), chemicals (5.19%), secondary raw materials and municipal wastes (3.05%), wood and products of wood (1.34%), non-metallic mineral products (1.31%) and food products (1.24%). Demand is therefore coming mainly from the following industry sectors: agriculture, energy, extraction and chemicals.

Figure 3.19. **Maritime freight transport in Romania**

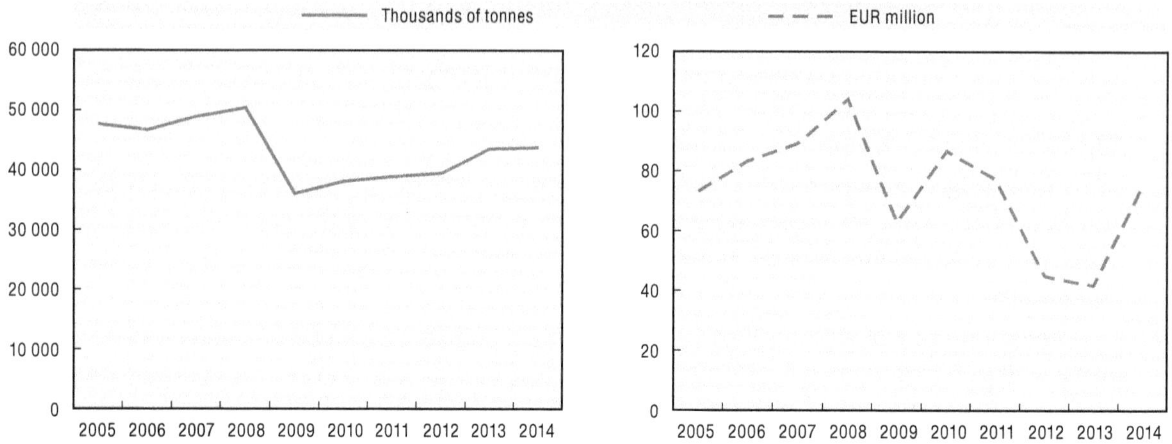

Source: NIS, *Goods transport, by mode of transport* (database), *http://bit.ly/21a7Nxe* (accessed on 26 January 2016).

StatLink http://dx.doi.org/10.1787/888933361613

Figure 3.20. **Total volume of maritime freight transport in Romania (thousands of tonnes)**

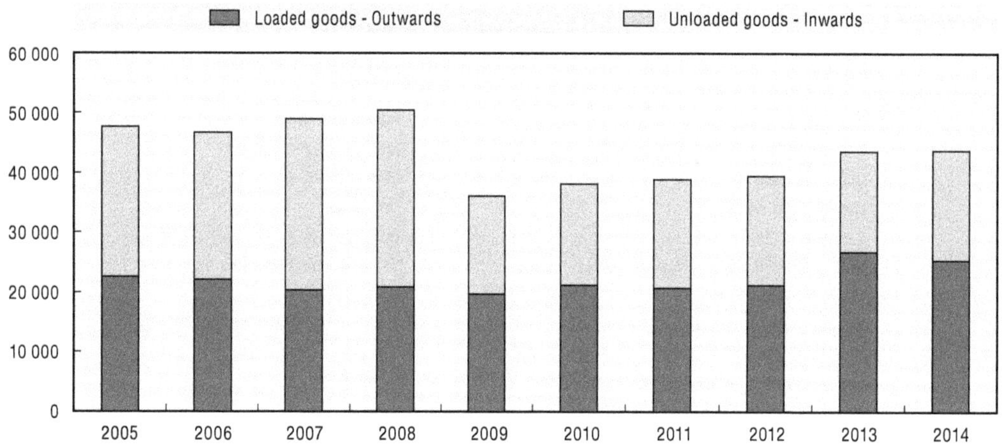

Source: Eurostat, *Maritime transport – Goods* (database), *http://bit.ly/1yussbN* (accessed on 26 January 2016).

StatLink http://dx.doi.org/10.1787/888933361626

Inland waterway freight transport. According to the NIS, inland waterways freight transport generated an overall value of about EUR 95.5 million in 2014. Employment in this sector reached 1 719 people in the same year. There are 90 active companies in inland waterway freight transport, of which 75 % have 1 to 10 employees, 15% have 11 to 50 employees, and the remaining 10% exceed 50 employees. The number of active firms active in inland waterway freight transport decreased from 112 in 2008 to 90 in 2014 and the employment recorded a decrease of -17% in the same period.

The major player in this sector is Compania De Navigaţie Fluvială Română NAVROM S.A., with an annual volume of over ten million tonnes of goods transported. NAVROM operates towards both internal routes such as Galaţi, Consţanta, Cernavodă, Medgidia, Mahmudia, etc. and external routes such as Ukraine, Serbia, Hungary, Austria and Germany. NAVROM is the incumbent company in the inland waterway freight sector, having being privatised by the Romanian government in 1998.[48]

According to the NIS, the first ten inland waterway freight companies in 2014 were:

Table 3.5. **Top 10 players in the inland waterway freight sector**

	Company	Turnover 2014 (EUR)	Market share 2014[1]
1.	Compania de Navigaţie Fluvială Română Navrom	50 336 957	52.68%
2.	Romnav	5 923 150	6.2%
3.	Trading Line	3 803 618	3.98%
4.	Navrom Portservice	2 751 801	2.88%
5.	Beo Trade Com	2 535 468	2.65%
6.	Danubtrans	1 833 225	1.92%
7.	DSSG Fluvial	1 782 832	1.87%
8.	Euro Bevrachting Logistics	1 562 806	1.64%
9.	Spet Shipping	688 303	0.72%
10.	Compania de Navigaţie Fluvială Giurgiu Nav	293 401	0.31%

1. Calculated as a percentage of total turnover of the inland waterway freight transport sector. References to "market shares" or "markets" in general, included in this report, do not reflect the same definitions used for purposes of applying competition law.

Source: Ministry of Finance, *http://bit.ly/1QxjYPO*and Musliu şi Asociaţii calculations.

The above table shows a highly concentrated subsector in which the largest company, NAVROM, holds a market share of over 50%. Moreover, there is significant disparity between NAVROM's market share and the remaining companies.

Figure 3.21 shows the evolution of inland waterway transport over the period 2005-14.

Figure 3.21. **Total inland waterway freight transport in Romania**

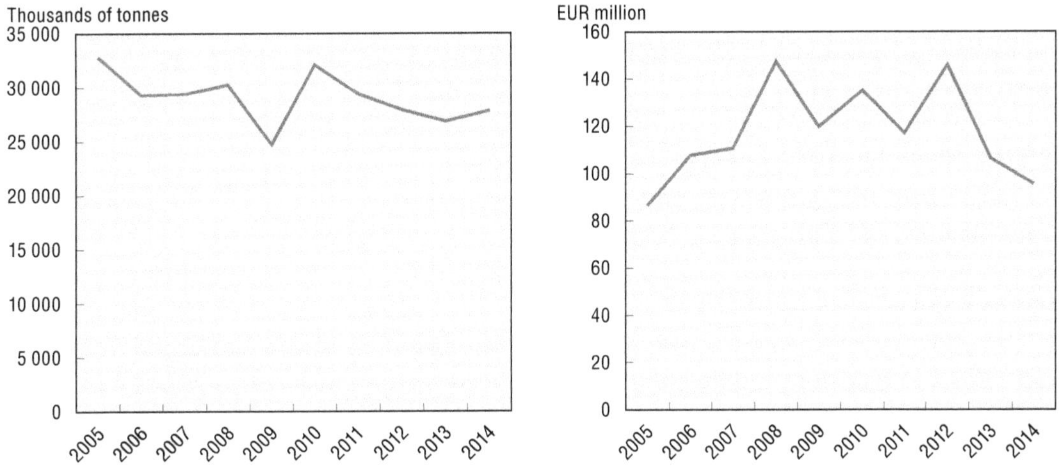

Source: NIS, *Goods transport, by mode of transport* (database), *http://bit.ly/21a7Nxe* (accessed on 26 January 2016).

StatLink http://dx.doi.org/10.1787/888933361639

After a fast recovery and a significant increase in inland waterway freight transport in 2010, the volume of goods handled by inland waterways registered a constant decline in the period from 2011 to 2014, with a CAGR of -3.4%.

On the Danube, three types of transport operate: i) internal, ii) transit and iii) import/export. International transport represents a significant share (28% in 2010, 20% in 2011, 33% in 2012, 36% in 2013 and 32% in 2014) of the total volume of goods transported by inland waterways. Transit has an important share (over 15% in the period between 2009 and 2014), showing that the Danube River is an advantageous transport modality and represents an efficient alternative to rail and road transport.

Figure 3.22. **Inland waterway freight transport in Romania, volume of goods carried (thousands of tonnes)**

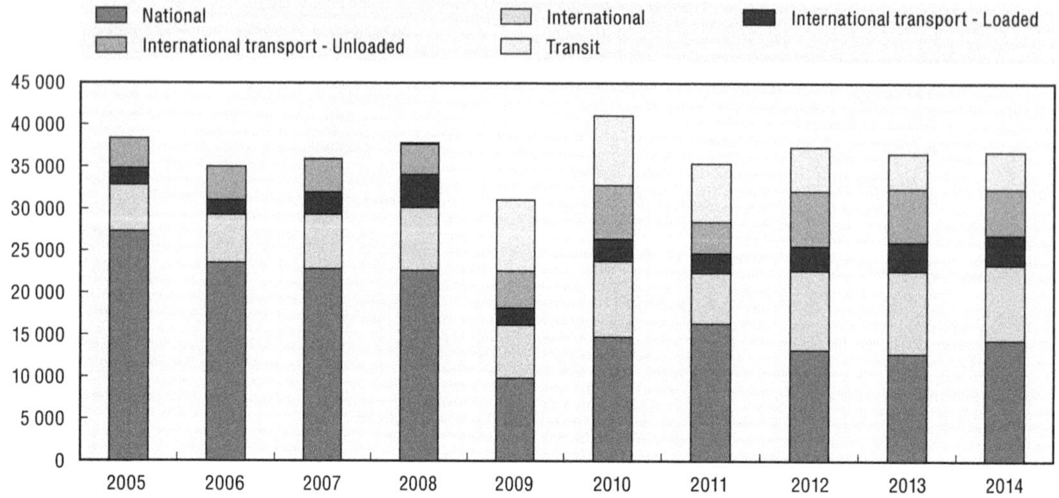

Source: Eurostat, *Inland waterways transport by type of vessel* (database), *http://bit.ly/1yussbN* (accessed on 26 January 2016).

StatLink http://dx.doi.org/10.1787/888933361643

According to the NIS, the main categories of goods that were transported in 2014 by inland waterways were: metal ores and other mining products (44.97%), products of agriculture (31.18%), coal and lignite, crude petroleum and natural gas (8.09%), chemicals (5.69%), coke and refined petroleum products (4.7%) and basic metals (2.76%). Hence, demand is driven by the following industry sectors: extraction, energy, agriculture and chemicals.

International maritime transport

As shown in Figures 3.23 and 3.24, inland waterway and maritime transport in Romania have not reached a significant scale.

Relevant government authorities

The MoT is the main authority responsible for regulation, authorisation, co-ordination and control in maritime and fluvial transport. The Ministry is also responsible for ensuring the functionality of harbours and other naval transportation infrastructure.

Under its subordination there are several entities with specific tasks:

- ***Romanian Naval Authority*** (ANR) is the state authority responsible for navigation safety. Its main tasks are: elaboration and submission for approval to the MoT of draft legislation and binding rules; implementation of rules, regulations and international conventions in Romanian legislation; inspection, registration and recording of Romanian-flagged vessels; recording and certification of seafarers; technical supervision, classification and certification of ships.[49]
- ***National Company Maritime Danube Ports Administration S.A. Galaţi*** works under the MoT and operates as port authority for the ports whose infrastructure was leased by the MoT, namely Galaţi, Brăila and Tulcea.[50]
- ***National Company Fluvial Danube Ports Administration S.A. Giurgiu*** acts as port authority within its area of activity. It is responsible for managing the port land, harbour limits and

Figure 3.23. **International inland waterway freight transport across different markets in Europe, volume of goods carried (thousands of tonnes)**

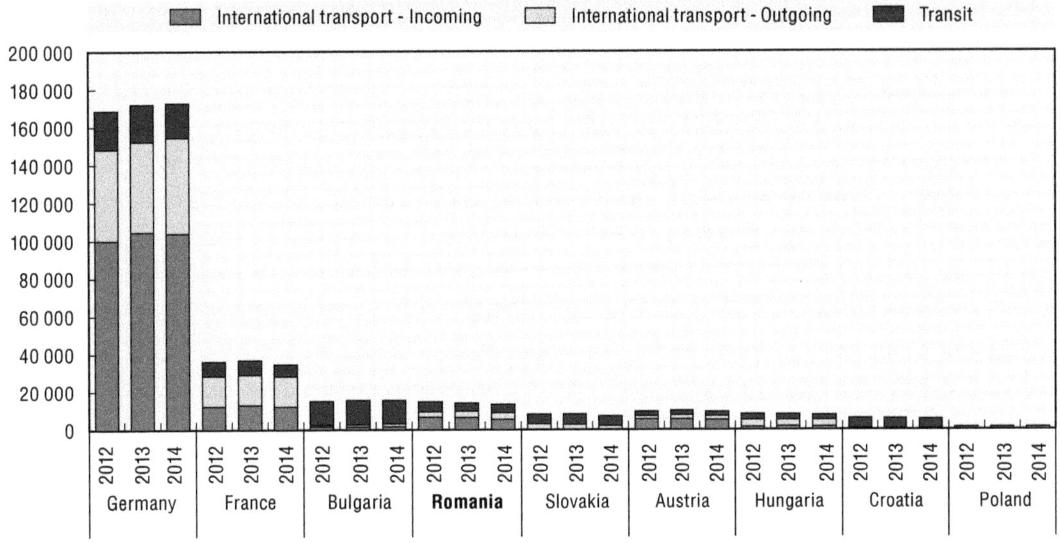

Source: Eurostat, *Inland waterways transport by type of vessel* (database), *http://bit.ly/1yussbN* (accessed on 26 January 2016).

StatLink http://dx.doi.org/10.1787/888933361650

Figure 3.24. **Maritime freight transport across different markets in Europe, volume of goods carried (thousands of tonnes)**

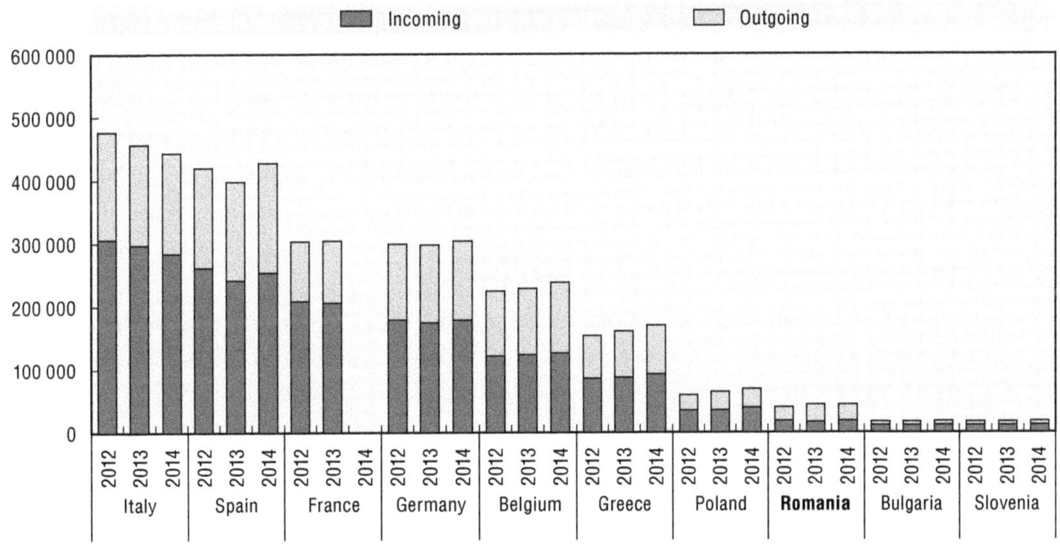

Source: Eurostat, *Maritime transport – Goods* (database), *http://bit.ly/1yussbN* (accessed on 26 January 2016). No data available for France, 2014.

StatLink http://dx.doi.org/10.1787/888933361663

port infrastructure established by MoT for the following river ports: Bechet, Călăraşi, Calafat, Cernavodă, Cetate, Corabia, Drobeta Turnu Severin, Giurgiu, Orşova, Olteniţa, and Moldova Veche.[51]

- ***National Company Navigable Canals Administration S.A. Consţanta*** is a national company subordinated to the MoT which acts as port authority according to legal regulations and statutes along the Danube-Black Sea Canal and the Poarta Albă-Midia Năvodari Canal and in the ports located in this area.[52]

- ***National Company Maritime Ports Administration S.A. Consţanta*** is a joint stock company assigned by the MoT to develop activities of national public interest in its capacity as a port administration. The company fulfils the port authority functions for Consţanta, Midia, Mangalia and Tomis Marina ports.[53]
- ***Lower Danube River Administration Galaţi A.A.*** operates as an autonomous administration under the MoT and serves as a waterways authority on the Romanian Danube sector. Its main tasks are to ensure minimum depth navigation by providing dredging, ensuring coastal and floating signals, conducting topographic measurements, performing construction and repair works to ensure navigation conditions, ensuring pilotage of ships on the Danube stretch between Brăila and Sulina and in the ports situated in this sector and providing the water transport infrastructure to all companies in the sector.[54]
- ***National Company of Naval Radio Communications "Radionav" S.A*** is a company that works under the MoT and provides radio communication services related to maritime operations and navigation safety.[55]
- ***Romanian Maritime Training Centre*** (CERONAV) is a public institution that provides theoretical and practical training to staff of sea, river, harbour and oil platforms in accordance with national legislation, international regulations and training standards set by various accredited bodies. As a national body, CERONAV fulfils the obligations of the Romanian state arising from international conventions and agreements relating to staff preparation and training.[56]
- ***Romanian Agency for Saving Life at Sea*** (ARSVOM) is a specialised technical body under the MoT, responsible for searching and saving human lives at sea and intervening in case of casualties generated by pollution.[57]

The main trade associations in the inland waterway freight transport are: Romanian Association of Inland Ship Owners and Port Operators (AAOPFR); Romanian Association of Ship owners; Romanian Ship Agents and Brokers Association; Romanian Naval League; and, Employer Organization "Port Operator" Consţanta.

3.2. Restrictions to competitiveness in road freight transport

The road freight sector has historically been a highly regulated sector. In the last decades many OECD countries have significantly liberalised their road freight sector. According to a report by the OECD (2000), "*Competition Issues in Road Transport*", the results of the liberalisation have been almost entirely positive, such as reduction of operators' costs, improved efficiency and innovative new services development. For example, in the United Kingdom deregulation has promoted the development of new types of logistics services, such as distribution contractors providing road haulage as part of an integrated package of logistics service.

The same study by the OECD finds that as of 1998, among the main remaining regulatory constraints in road freight were the complete prohibition of cabotage, pricing, or entry regulations enforced by professional bodies, price control, competition law exemption for road freight, criteria other than the technical, financial and safety criteria considered in granting a licence/permit/concession, regulatory competence to limit the capacity or the number of competitors and reservation of certain freight for rail transport.

Although in 2016 we did not find those obstacles identified within the Romanian road freight transport sector, Romania's road freight industry remains one of the most regulated in the European Union, as shown in the economic overview (Koske et al., 2014).

Description of the European legal framework

Most *road freight transport* regulations in Romania are based on European legislation, as they either directly implement European regulations, or transpose European directives. The main *pieces of European legislation* are the following:

- **European Regulation No. 1071/2009** setting the provisions with which undertakings must comply in order to gain access to the occupation of a road transport operator.
- **European Regulation No. 1072/2009** on common rules for access to the international road haulage market lays down the provisions to be complied with by undertakings that wish to operate on the international road haulage market and on national markets other than on their own (cabotage). It includes provisions relative to the documents to be issued to such undertakings in order to obtain a Community licence. Finally, it also sets down provisions regarding the sanctioning of infringements and co-operation between Member States. The purpose of the regulation is to improve the efficiency of road freight transport by reducing the number of empty trips in international transport operations.
- **European Directive No. 96/53** laying down the maximum authorised dimensions for certain road vehicles circulating within the Community, the maximum authorised dimensions in national and international traffic and the maximum authorised weights in international traffic. The directive also ensures that Member States cannot restrict vehicles that comply with these limits from performing international transport operations within their territories.
- **Directive No. 2003/59/EC** on the initial qualification and periodic training of drivers of certain road vehicles for the carriage of goods or passengers. As part of the overall effort to increase safety on European roads, the directive establishes the mandatory initial qualification and periodic training requirements for drivers.

Authorisations

Authorisations required for the provision of services might represent legal barriers to entry on the market. In general, authorisations should ensure consumer protection. However, often the requirements of authorisations are stricter than necessary for consumer protection and can unnecessarily reduce consumer choice. Also, they may make it more difficult, expensive and time-consuming for new companies to enter a market.

The authorisation for repairing, adjusting, reconstructing and dismantling of vehicles

Description of obstacle. Article 122 (m) of the Government Emergency Ordinance No. 195/2002 regarding the traffic on public roads states that the repairing, adjusting, reconstructing and dismantling of vehicles are to be undertaken only by authorised operators. The authorisation is granted by the Romanian Automotive Register (RAR), the technical specialised body designated by the Ministry of Transport (MoT) as the competent authority in the field of road vehicles, road safety, environmental protection and quality assurance.

In order to obtain this authorisation, vehicle repair garages must provide the following documents: i) a copy of the certificate, issued by the RAR, attesting the professional ability of the garage manager, ii) the "criminal record" of the economic operator's manager, iii) a copy of the company registration certificate issued by the National Trade Register Office, iv) a copy of the tax registration certificate issued by the National Agency for Fiscal Administration, v) a copy of the certificate of incumbency issued by the National Trade Register Office with the corresponding activity field, and vi) a list of the equipment used for providing the service. The opening of a garage is subject to an authorisation tax with the amount depending on the number of technical activities planned to be carried out in it.

In addition, for the authorisation to be maintained, the vehicle repair garages must annually obtain a visa. The visa is granted by the RAR after checking the technical ability of the vehicle repair garages by verifying the existence and conformity of the equipment used for performing the garages' activities. The vehicle repair garages must pay an annual tax for the abovementioned audit of their technical ability.

Harm to competition. The authorisation requirement constitutes an administrative burden that may reduce the number of operators and raise administrative costs.

Policymakers' objective. The objective of the provision is to ensure public safety on the roads.

Legal frameworks from other European countries such as France, the United Kingdom and Spain do not require an authorisation in order to run a vehicle repair garage.

In France, starting up a garage is subject to proving the professional qualifications of the person who leads the activity of the operator. Such a person must possess a certificate of professional competence, a certificate of professional studies, a degree or the equivalent of a degree issued by a national directory of professional certifications, or have three years of relevant experience working in the European Economic Area.

Also, French legislation establishes the obligation of garages to be registered in the National Register of Professions. In order to be enrolled in the abovementioned register, the manager of the garage must have attended a preparatory course that is organised by the regional Chamber of Commerce and Industry.

For the registration, the manager of the garage must submit the following documents: i) a statement of intent to create the garage, ii) a statement concerning any (or no) criminal record of the manager iii) the certificate granted by the Chamber of Commerce and Industry attesting to the completion of the preparatory course, iv) a copy of the identity card of the manager.

In the United Kingdom, there seems to be no obligation for the manager of a garage or for the employees directly involved in repairing vehicles to pass an exam or to have a diploma in order to prove their professional qualifications. To convince customers that the garage is reputable, the garage owner joins a trade association with codes of practice that have been approved by the Trading Standards Institute or a trading-standards approved scheme such as "Buy With Confidence". The membership inspection regime to which garages voluntarily submit ensures that they are monitored in terms of their premises, equipment, technical training, customer care and operation of the code of practice and of their individual ability to quickly remedy any problem, as it arises, to their customers' satisfaction.

Recommendation. We recommend that the provisions be repealed. The obligation to obtain an authorisation in order to run a vehicle repair garage is disproportionate to the envisaged aim of public safety on roads. The quality of the repairs performed by the garages could be ensured by requiring the manager of the garage to possess a certificate of professional studies or a degree issued, for instance by the RAR, in case the manager does not have a certificate of professional studies. Also, the employees directly involved in repairing, adjusting, reconstructing and dismantling vehicles should have a certificate of professional studies.

Moreover, the policymakers' objective – public safety on the roads – is supposed to be achieved through periodic technical inspection. According to Government Ordinance No. 81/2000[58] all vehicles and trailers must be inspected at regular intervals by the RAR or by bodies authorised by the RAR. The ordinance provides a basis for checking that vehicles throughout Romania are in a roadworthy condition and meet the same safety standards as when they were first registered.

Therefore, no authorisation should be required for the garage to operate. Instead, the garage should be checked by the RAR in order to prove that its manager possesses a certificate of professional studies or a degree issued by the RAR and that its employees have certificates of professional studies.

Certification of drivers

Description of obstacle. According to Article 1 of Annex 5 of MoT Order No. 1214/2015 on the approval of norms establishing the conditions for obtaining a professional attestation by road transport staff, in order to transport goods with vehicles exceeding the applicable dimension and/or weight limits, so-called "abnormal load transport", drivers must obtain a certificate of professional competence. This provision only applies to drivers who use vehicles registered in Romania for transport.

An abnormal vehicle is one that due to its construction exceeds at least one of the maximum dimensions of axle, bogie or total weights (for unloaded vehicles) authorised by Directive No. 96/53/EC and national legislation. The legal dimensions and weights vary between countries, and between regions within a country.[59]

The abnormal load transport certificate for drivers is required in Romania in addition to the general certificate, called the "certificate of professional competence".

Harm to competition. The professional certificate for abnormal load transport affects drivers and operators, provides less flexibility in replacing the drivers for these types of transport because an operator needs a driver with an additional certificate in order to transport goods in abnormal vehicles. Also, the provision increases the administrative burden of road transport operators. Moreover, the provision applies only to those drivers who perform transport operations with vehicles registered in Romania. Therefore, besides the additional cost and administrative burden, it discriminates in favour of foreign transport operators with drivers operating vehicles registered in other countries. We did not find a similar requirement in any other European Union Member States.

Policymakers' objective. There is no official recital for this particular provision. However, it seems that the objective of the provision is to ensure public safety on roads.

The relevant Romanian provision exceeds the requirements of European legislation. Thus, in order to enhance road safety in Europe by ensuring a common level of training and the achievement of the necessary skills and competences for professional drivers, European Directive No. 2003/59 requires a mandatory initial qualification and periodic training for truck drivers, with both attested by the certificate of professional competence. The directive does not require an additional certificate of professional competence for drivers in order to carry out road transport of goods with vehicles exceeding applicable length or weight limits.

Recommendation. The provision requiring an abnormal load transport certificate for drivers should be abolished. Professional qualification requirements concerning abnormal load can be addressed in the initial training undertaken for obtaining the certificate of professional competence. In other EU Member States, such as the United Kingdom and Spain, there is no obligation to obtain a certificate of professional competence for "abnormal load transport". Thus, the courses related to the abnormal load should be part of the general course. This abolition will harmonise Romanian legislation with that of other EU Member States.

Conformity certificates for superstructures fitted on vehicles transporting dangerous goods

Description of obstacle. Currently only one undertaking in Romania, IPROCHIM SA, is entrusted with issuing certificates of conformity with respect to superstructures fitted on vehicles transporting dangerous goods, and transporting packaging containing dangerous goods. The list, which includes only IPROCHIM, was issued by the Ministry of Economy (MoE) and approved by the Order of the MoE No. 971/2014.

Any undertaking aiming to perform the activity of issuing certificates must first submit a request to the MoE proving that it fulfills the conditions stipulated by Order No. 2737/2012 of the MoE.[60]

In our understanding, all these conditions are clear and non-discriminatory. Thus, theoretically, any legal person established in Romania and registered in the Trade Register who proves that they can perform specific tasks regarding conformity assessment and inspection of specialised superstructures, should be appointed and designated by the MoE as a certificate-issuing body.

The main shareholder of IPROCHIM SA is the MoE, which owns 72.99% of its shares. The ministry is also in charge of authorising the operators who wish to issue such certificates of conformity. This creates a certain conflict of interest resulting from the fact that the MoE acts as a regulator, operator, and the authority empowered to authorise operators. In practice, requests for authorisation have been submitted by undertakings interested in acting as a certificate-issuing body which did not receive an official response, although, according to Romanian legislation, the MoE should answer within 30 days of receiving an application.

Harm to competition. IPROCHIM SA currently holds a monopoly in the market, leading to higher costs for transport operators who need to obtain a certificate of conformity with respect to superstructures.

Recommendation. Given that the conditions for authorising the performance of this activity set forth in Order No. 2737/2012 of the MoE are clear and non-discriminatory, and considering that operators whose application was rejected or not answered may challenge this decision in court, no recommendation concerning the relevant provisions is given. However, the MoE needs to act in a diligent manner in the light of its potential conflict of interest when receiving requests for authorisations submitted by undertakings interested in acting as a certificate-issuing body.

Transport manager

Description of obstacle. Article 15 of the Methodological Norms approved by Order No. 980/2011 of the MoT,[61] which regulates the criteria that must be fulfilled by an undertaking in order to become a road transport operator, both on its own account and for hire/reward, requires the applying undertaking to have professional competence.

Undertakings shall thus appoint a transport manager who must have a certificate of competence, fulfill the requirement of good repute, permanently manage the transport activities of the undertaking and must be an employee, director, owner, shareholder or manager of the undertaking. Additionally, the transport manager must reside in the European Union. Finally, this article provides that a natural person can be a transport manager only within one single undertaking.

The requirements of the Romanian legislation are in line with European Regulation No. 1071/2009 – but the obligation of the transport manager to lead only one single undertaking is more stringent.

Thus, according to Article 4 of European Regulation No. 1071/2009, transport managers can either be direct employees or persons so closely linked to the business that they have a real, direct connection with the operator. They can also be independent third parties, such as transport consultants, in the case where the operator does not have a transport manager with a genuine link to the undertaking. According to Article 4 para. (2), a transport manager who does not have a genuine link to the undertaking may serve up to four separate transport operators, as long as their combined fleet does not exceed 50 vehicles. The European regulation provides that Member States may decide to lower the number of undertakings and/or the size of the total fleet of vehicles which the manager may manage.

However, even if the Member States can determine the maximum number of transport operators led by a manager, the Romanian provision makes no link to the total combined fleet of operators, which seems to be the relevant criterion.

Policymakers' objective. There is no official recital for the provision. It should ensure the quality of transport manager services, since, if a transport manager works for several separate undertakings at the same time, he may not always be available to brief drivers (e.g. on the characteristics of the goods transported, or on the route to choose to avoid delays or additional charges) or to respond to the client's demands.

Harm to competition. Romanian transport managers are prevented from expanding their business by covering more than one undertaking. This also raises costs for Romanian undertakings, especially for the small ones, which must bear the cost of hiring their own transport manager.

Recommendation . We recommend modifying the relevant Romanian legislation by inserting the provision from the EU legislation, where transport managers can cover up to 4 undertakings and up to 50 vehicles.

More restrictive provisions than those in the EU regulation are not justified, notably due to the fact that Romanian freight hauliers generally have small fleets, so managers can carry out their tasks for more than one operator.[62] If the restriction is lifted, the costs of the services performed by a transport manager may drop when he operates as an independent transport manager, and can provide services for more undertakings.

Local taxes

Description of obstacle

Local authorities in their capacity as managers of national roads that cross a municipality can impose additional taxes to those established by the government for using the Romanian national road network (the Romanian vignette).

Local and county councils also charge fees for the use of the local and county roads that they manage.

Harm to competition

These additional taxes increase the costs and administrative burden of road transport operators. There are frequent complaints that these taxes are not levied in a transparent manner and can lead to uncertainty and discrimination of some operators in relation to others. Also, it is *difficult and time-consuming for freight hauliers to pay such taxes,* as currently there is no efficient tax payment system in place.

As for fee transparency, access to information is often difficult. Most of these taxes are published on the websites of municipalities. However, in practice most of those websites are not well-organised. Also, often the decisions of the municipalities concerning the taxes are published together with other decisions, making it difficult to find them and to calculate the amount to be paid. Theoretically, for operators to find out whether they must pay a tax in a certain locality, they would need to study all local or county council decisions, as there is no official centralised system dealing with local taxes. As a consequence, road transport operators usually only learn of these taxes when they have to transit that locality and are being sanctioned by the competent authorities.

These taxes usually cannot be paid at major points-of-sale for road transport operators (e.g. gas stations), but only on the premises of city halls and county councils. To pay the fees, drivers are forced to leave their vehicles in a parking space and go to the city hall/local council during their operating hours. Generally, no 24/7 service is provided for fee payment, and fees cannot be paid by using a typical means of payment, such as the internet, telephone, etc. Thus, road transport operators in transit suffer a considerable disadvantage when compared to local transporters; they are often stuck in traffic until they obtain the authorisation, or become offenders for reasons difficult to control.

The absence of a transparent and efficient charging system leads to an additional administrative burden, and a differential treatment of market players.

The amount of local road taxes is sometimes even higher than the cost of the national vignette. For instance, the vignette for the national road network (totalling approximately 15 000 km) which consists of roads of normal European carrying capacity of 11.5 tonnes/axle and a total capacity of 40 tonnes, costs EUR 1 210 (RON 5 363) annually, compared to, for instance, Consţanta County, which has county roads with a lower carrying capacity totalling about 800 km in length and an annual fee of EUR 1 400 (RON 6 300).[63] The fact that local fees are often much higher than the national vignette is also confirmed by the MoT in *Romania's General Transport Master Plan, issued* in 2015.

Policymakers' objective

The main objective of local taxes is the regulation of local traffic and to avoid congestion in municipalities. Taxes are also aimed at ensuring investment in the infrastructure and its maintenance and thus a high level of road quality and safety, providing drivers with an appropriate network of national, county and local roads.

Recommendation

We do not recommend abolishing local road taxes. However, we recommend that the Romanian government introduce an appropriate legal framework to ensure the transparency and efficiency of the payment system for local road taxes. Local authorities should also find a way to ensure transparency of the tax requirements, notably by making the application of these taxes more transparent for hauliers. County and local councils need to publish these charges and make them easily accessible since they are likely to apply not only to local operators, but also to operators coming from other regions of Romania, as well as from abroad. In particular, in order to ensure easy access for foreign operators, the information related to local taxes should also be made available in English.

To guarantee transparency of local taxes, a good measure might be to publish all road taxes on the websites of the MoT, and the Ministry of Regional Development and Public Administration. Also, an efficient payment system of taxes could be introduced through a new legal framework.

An efficient payment system might involve online payment or payment by mobile phone, as is currently implemented in cities such as London and Milan – but also in Romania. For example, payment for the toll bridge at the Feteşti-Cernavodă station on the A2 Bucureşti-Consţanta highway, introduced by Emergency Government Ordinance No. 8/2015 that ensures tax payment, is made by means of a closed-circuit television (CCTV) system, which records the licence plate of each vehicle entering and exiting the perimeter of the city.

Spare parts for tachographs

Description of obstacle. According to Order No. 181/2008 of the MoT,[64] undertakings authorised to perform the installation, repair and/or verification of tachographs and speed limit devices must use only spare parts provided by the manufacturer of those tachographs and speed limit devices, or by suppliers appointed by the manufacturer.

Harm to competition. This provision is likely to eliminate other producers of spare parts for tachographs and speed limit devices. It may also raise costs for transport operators, as it prevents competition on the spare parts aftermarket.

Policymakers' objective

There is no official recital for this particular provision. A speed limitation device is a piece of equipment used to limit the top speed of a vehicle. A tachograph is a device intended for installation in road vehicles to display, record, print, store and automatically or semi-automatically output details of the movement, including the speed of such vehicles, and details of certain periods of activity of the drivers. A tachograph, moreover, provides information to the road traffic inspection authority regarding the transport operators' compliance with the regulations, mainly observance of working hours and possible overwork in the road transport industry. The regulation should ensure road safety and prevent accidents. Taking into consideration the importance of these devices for road safety, it is mandatory to eliminate every possibility of their manipulation by the operators. Sometimes, tachographs are manipulated to enable drivers to drive longer and take less rest. If the spare parts aftermarket were to be opened, it might lead to an increased risk of manipulation of these devices.

Moreover, even if the tachograph spare parts aftermarket were to be opened, its impact on competition and on the transport operators' costs would be reduced as the tachographs generally have a longer life span than that of the trucks; because of this the volume of the spare parts aftermarket for tachographs is relatively small.

Recommendation. Even though this restriction is likely to exclude other producers of spare parts for tachographs and speed limit devices, and may raise costs for *freight hauliers*, the restriction seems proportional to the objective served, namely to promote road safety by avoiding the manipulation of these devices. Thus, no recommendation is made.

Waybills for transport and registration of incoming-outgoing wood material

European Regulation No. 995/2010, laying down the obligations of operators who place timber and timber products on the market, states that illegal logging is a pervasive problem within the European Union. "It poses a significant threat to forests as it contributes to the process of deforestation and forest degradation, which is responsible for about 20% of global CO_2 emissions, threatens biodiversity, and undermines sustainable forest management and development. This also includes the commercial viability of operators acting in accordance with applicable legislation. It also contributes to desertification and soil erosion, and can exacerbate extreme weather events and flooding. In addition, it has social, political, and economic implications, often undermining progress towards good governance, and threatening the livelihood of local forest-dependent communities, and it can be linked to armed conflicts."[65] Combatting the problem of illegal logging in Romania has been a subject of ongoing concern in recent years.

Description of obstacle

According to Government Decision No. 470/2014 for the approval of Norms regarding the origin, movement, and sale of timber materials, the storage regime of timber materials, and the regime of round timber processing plants, as well as of measures for the implementation of European Regulation 995/2010. The undertakings that perform the activity of sale and transport of wood material must obtain specific waybills for the transport and register of the input-output of such materials. Both the waybills and the records are to be printed and sold only by the Imprimeria Naţională S.A., a state-owned company.

The waybills for the transport of wood materials are documents under a special regime, provided with specific security elements, are printed in blocks with 150 sheets, consisting of 50 sets of three sheets each, on carbonless copy paper, with the security elements applied on the first copy. The characteristics of the security elements contained in the waybills are established on the basis of a protocol with the Imprimeria Nationalǎ. The characteristics of the security elements are not made public. An Integrated Informational System of Tracking Wood Materials (SUMAL) was established for the traceability of timber harvested from the woods and to provide statistical information.

The waybill is issued by the operator who sells and transports wood material at the point of origin of transport. The operator must upload the standardised information in the SUMAL application, either online or using any electronic terminal that runs this application; this terminal must necessarily exist at the point of origin of the transport. The information uploaded refers among others to the series and number of the waybill for the transport of the wood materials, the point of unloading of the timber, the vehicle registration number and the species, type and volume of the timber. After receiving the information, SUMAL generates a unique code, as well as the date, hour, minute and second of the registration. The law requires that the unique code generated by SUMAL is written on the waybill. The unique code, as well as the date, hour, minute and second of the registration are also recorded in the register of input-output wood materials kept by the operator. The unique code attests to the legal origin of the transported timber. The registers of input-output wood materials are documents under a special regime they are printed in blocks with 100 sheets. The legal provisions do not stipulate whether the registers contain security elements.

Harm to competition

The provisions set up a monopoly in the printing forms of the waybills and the records of incoming-outgoing wood materials. The purchase of those required waybills and registers may therefore lead to higher costs for operators that sale and transport wood material.

Policymakers' objective

The objective of the provision is to prevent illegal deforestation and smuggling of Romanian wood. However, the monopoly position held by Imprimeria Naţională on printing waybills and registers of input-output wood materials is not fulfilling the policymakers' objective, namely to prevent illegal deforestation and smuggling of Romanian wood. Instead, this monopoly leads to higher costs for the operators who sell and transport wood material. The waybills also do *not need* to be printed with security elements as the unique code generated by the application SUMAL attests to the legal origin of the transported timber.

Recommendation

We recommend opening the market and allowing both the waybills and records of incoming-outgoing wood material to be printed by any company willing to perform such an activity.

Opening the market for the issuing of waybills for transport and records of incoming-outgoing wood materials, an activity which is currently performed exclusively by Imprimeria Naţională, should lead to a reduction in the price of waybills and records. The benefits arising from opening the market and liberalising the provision of this service are estimated to be worth approximately EUR 0.3 mln a year.

Geographic restrictions

Auditors of road safety

Description of obstacle . Law No. 265/2008[66] stipulates that the appointment of road safety auditors/inspectors is made for territorial areas and gives preference to individuals residing in those areas or close to those areas where the auditor/inspector needs to be appointed.

Road safety auditors/inspectors are professional individuals in charge of verifying road construction projects in terms of safety. They also periodically check the existing road infrastructure.

Harm to competition. These provisions create an entry barrier and favour auditors residing in the area where road infrastructure should be inspected in relation to auditors from other areas.

Policymakers' objective. The law implements European Directive No. 2008/96 on road infrastructure safety management, which requires the establishment and implementation of procedures relating to road safety impact assessment, road safety audit, the management of road network safety, and inspections by Member States. Although the Directive stipulates the criteria for the appointment of road safety auditors, it makes no reference to territorial criteria.

There is no official recital for these specific restrictions. However, this may be necessary in order to make the deployment of auditors/inspectors' activities more efficient in terms of costs and time.

Recommendation. This restriction exceeds the Directive No. 2008/96/EC requirements, and the appointment of road safety auditors/inspectors should not be linked to the geographical residence of the auditor/inspector. We recommend abolishing the provisions.

Additional tariffs

Description of obstacle. According to Government Ordinance No. 43/1997 on the road regime, as further amended and supplemented, managers of national roads apply tariffs in addition to the Romanian vignette to authorise access to the national road network for vehicles registered in a foreign country that is not a member of the European Union. These tariffs are established through bilateral agreements between Romania and third countries.

The provision authorises Romania to charge differential tariffs to third country hauliers as opposed to Romanian and EU hauliers. It may therefore lead to discriminatory treatment of third country hauliers.

Harm to competition. These provisions discriminate in favour of national and EU transport operators against those from a non-EU country.

Policymakers' objective. During bilateral talks with third countries, Romania negotiates these additional tariffs together with the number of authorisations which are granted to third country hauliers, taking into consideration the interests of Romanian hauliers.

Recommendation. Even though this restriction is likely to create an entry barrier that discriminates against operators who are not members of European Union, it is our understanding that this restriction is justified for reasons of public interest. Thus, no recommendation for change is made for the specific provision.

Regulatory burden

Plate

Description of obstacle. Government Ordinance No. 27/2011 on road transport, as further amended and supplemented, provides that *own-account transport operators, and* transport operators who *transport* goods for hire or *reward* using a vehicle with a maximum permitted weight above 3.5 tonnes, are required to display on their vehicles a plate containing information related to the dimensions and maximum weight authorised for the vehicle. The plate must be displayed if vehicles do not have a manufacturer's plate or the manufacturer's plate does not contain the necessary information.

According to MoT Order No. 980/2011 if the vehicle has a trailer and/or a semi-trailer, it is necessary to have a plate for each trailer in addition to the plate for the vehicle.

In order to obtain the plate it is necessary that the dimensions and maximum weight of the vehicles, trailers and semi-trailers are established. This activity is currently performed exclusively by the RAR. According to the RAR website, there are two ways of establishing the dimensions and maximum weight: i) for vehicles without a towing device the dimensions and weight are established by the RAR based on the information from its database and the vehicle identity card and ii) for vehicles with a towing device, trailers and semi-trailers, the dimensions and weight are established by measuring them. In this case, each of them are measured separately. Thus, not all the vehicles are measured. However, in both the abovementioned cases, fees are received by the RAR.

Policymakers' objective. In Romania as well as in Europe, heavy goods vehicles must comply with certain rules on weight and dimensions, for road safety reasons, and to avoid damaging roads, bridges and tunnels. These rules are established by European Directive No. 96/53 and Romanian legislation.[67]

The obligation to display a plate is required by Romanian law so that law enforcers can verify the compliance of the transport operators with the abovementioned legislation.

Harm to competition. Article 6 of European Directive No. 96/53 authorises Romania to opt for a regulatory system whereby information related to the vehicle's dimensions and maximum weight is included on a plate. However, the same article from the directive stipulates that the information can also result from "a single document issued by the competent authorities of the Member State in which the vehicle is registered or put into circulation. Such a document shall bear the same headings and information as the plates."

The requirement to display on vehicles a plate containing information related to the dimension and maximum weight authorised for the vehicle applies for all operators established in Romania. It represents an unnecessary burden for road transport operators and may also lead to a rise in costs for national operators compared to EU operators, who do not have such an obligation.

The total cost generated by the obligation to display such a plate on vehicles is approximately EUR 55 per vehicle. As mentioned above, if the vehicle has a trailer and/or a semi-trailer, it is necessary to have a plate for each, thus adding a EUR 55 charge for each additional trailer or semi-trailer. Approximately EUR 45 of this sum corresponds to the fee charged by the RAR for measuring the vehicle's dimensions. The difference corresponds to the price of the plate. When the provision came into force in January 2014, in order to comply with the plate requirement Romanian transport operators had to purchase these plates, generating an estimated total cost of around EUR 6.3 million.

Recommendation. We recommend repealing this provision. The objective of the provision to verify the compliance of transport operators with the rules on weights and dimensions can be achieved through documentation, such as the vehicle identity card or the periodical technical inspection certificate, which should be carried by the vehicle driver. The vehicle identity card is the single document by which the vehicle is registered and put into circulation. It is issued by the RAR and contains the same headings and information as those appearing on the plate (the manufacturer's name, identification number, dimensions and weight of the vehicle). The transport operator should keep the original vehicle identity card or a certified copy of it in case the operator is not the owner of the vehicle (for instance, in case of a lease). The periodical technical inspection certificate is issued automatically and free of charge by the RAR or by a body authorised by the RAR to perform periodical technical inspection. It is issued after the performance of the mandatory technical inspection that can include also measuring the vehicles. The periodical technical inspection certificate does not currently contain information referring to the vehicle's dimensions and weight, but it can be inserted by the issuer. Both the vehicle identity card and the periodical technical inspection certificate should also be kept for trailers and semi-trailers. Carrying an identity card or a periodical technical inspection certificate by the vehicle driver would be in line with EU legislation regarding the vehicle's dimensions and maximum weight.

According to our estimates, the benefits for road freight transport operators of abolishing the plate requirement for vehicles with maximum weight > 3.5 tonnes, would be approximately EUR 1.14 mln a year.

Copy of transport licence

Description of obstacle. According to MoT Order No. 980/2011 approving the Methodological Norms on the application of the provisions regarding the organisation and performance of road transport and related activities established by Government Ordinance No. 27/2011 on road transport, as further amended and supplemented, road transport operators must obtain a copy of the transport licence for each vehicle in their fleet, which must be renewed annually, although the road freight transport licence issued to transport operators is valid for a period of 10 years.

A copy of the transport licence must be carried on the vehicle on all journeys, and must be presented to any enforcement official upon request. Each copy states the registration number of the vehicle, and cannot be used for any other vehicle in the same transport operator's fleet.

Harm to competition. The requirement to obtain a copy of the licence for transport of goods by road for hire or reward is in line with Article 4 of EU Regulation 1072/2009. However, the fact that this copy costs approximately EUR 58 per vehicle per year and that it applies only to one registered vehicle increases the costs for hauliers established in Romania. Also, the provision increases the administrative burden for transport operators, as they must obtain a copy every year.

Policymakers' objective. The transport of goods by road, both on own account and for hire or reward, should be conditional on the possession of a transport licence. For hire or reward transport the licence is called a "Community licence", and for own-account transport the licence is called a "transport certificate". Transport operators are required to have a copy of the licence for each vehicle in their fleet. According to point 9 of EU Regulation 1072/2009, the obligation to carry a copy of the transport licence should facilitate effective controls by enforcement authorities regarding the compliance with the authorisation requirement of transport operators.

Research indicates that in some European countries the validity of a copy of the Community licence has the same validity as the licence itself. For example, in Estonia, a copy of the licence is **issued for 10 years** if the applicant does not require it for a shorter period, and not for longer than the term of validity of the Community licence (10 years). In the United Kingdom and Spain the Community licence is issued for a five-year period, as well as a copy of the Community licence, and it is not specific to one vehicle – it does not contain the vehicle registration number. Also, in Spain a copy costs EUR 5.99 for five years.[68]

Recommendation. We recommend that the provisions should be modified. There is no need to impose an annual renewal of the copy when the licence is issued for a 10-year period. The copy should be issued at the same time as the licence, and it should be made available for the same period of time as the duration of the licence to which it refers, i.e. 10 years. Although we agree that the number of copies should be the same as the number of vehicles in the operator's fleet, there is no reason to require specific copies for the registration number of the vehicle. This requirement increases the administrative burden on the operator. For instance, when a truck is sold and another is bought instead, the operator is not able to use the same copy of the licence and he must obtain a new one with a new registration number. Moreover, the cost of the copy should not exceed the administrative cost of issuing it.

The benefits arising from modifying this provision should have a significant impact on costs for freight transport operators, and may lower the overall cost of freight transport services if these savings are passed on to the customer. Moreover, the extension of validity of the licence copy for the entire duration of the transport licence, i.e. up to 10 years, will remove an unnecessary administrative burden for freight transport operators.

The benefits of freight transport operators from modifying the provision are estimated to be around EUR 7.1mln a year.

Legislation not published

Description of obstacle

According to MoT Order No. 980/2011, approving the Methodological Norms on the application of the provisions regarding the organisation and performance of road transport and related activities established by Government Ordinance No. 27/2011 on road transport, as further amended, one of the requirements for obtaining a transport licence is to have good repute. The State Inspectorate for Road Transport Control (ISCTR) is in charge of enforcing this requirement.

The requirement of good repute is in line with Article 6 of Regulation 1071/2009/EC. However, the ISCTR enforcement procedure to verify compliance with the good repute requirement has not been published. According to MoT representatives, the ISCTR enforcement procedure is established in a document entitled "Ediţia I, Revizia 0 – Cod PO 89" recorded with the ISCTR under No. 2508/30.01.2014 and refers to an internal administrative procedure that does not need to be published. Infringements of good repute are recorded in a local database and should be reported in the European Register of Road Transport Undertakings (ERRU) database.

Recommendation

The ISCTR procedure related to compliance with the requirement of good repute of transport operators should be published, to enable the monitoring of the ISCTR's exercise of power, and to enable operators to present their view in face of a potentially negative decision.

3.3. Restrictions to competitiveness in rail transport

Description of the European legal framework

Rail freight transport in Romania is governed to a significant degree by European legislation. In this section, the main pieces of European legislation will be briefly summarised before restrictions in national Romanian laws are discussed to describe the wider legal framework.

The EU legislation on rail transport aims to achieve the creation of a single, efficient and competitive market for rail throughout Europe, through opening rail markets, promoting competition, tackling barriers to market entry, harmonisation of technical specifications (inter-operability) and harmonisation of safety standards and certification.

Directive No. 91/440/EEC on the development of the European Union's railways is the main measure that the European Union has taken to increase competitiveness in rail transport. The Directive distinguishes between the provision of transport services and the operation of infrastructure, identifying the necessity for these two areas to be managed separately in order to facilitate further development and efficiency of the European Union's railways. The Directive covers particularly four areas of policy: 1) the independence of railway undertakings with regard to management, administration and internal control over administrative, economic and accounting matters, thereby holding assets, budgets and accounts separate from those belonging to the State; 2) the separation of infrastructure management and transport operations; 3) the reduction of debt and improvement of finances and 4) access rights to railway infrastructure.

Since 2000, those principles have been progressively implemented through the adoption of three successive packages of EU legislation and the recast of the First Railway Package.[69]

In 2001, the European Commission issued the First Railway Package to be implemented by the Member States by 15 March 2003.[70] This was the first step in liberalising the railway sector through the introduction of open access on the Trans-European Rail Network on a non-discriminatory basis.

The Second Railway Package was proposed in January 2002 by the European Commission, introducing full open access for freight throughout the European Union, by amending EU Directive 91/440 starting 1 January 2007. The Trans-European Rail Freight Network was expanded to include the entire network of a Member State, and not just designated "freight corridors". Access to that network was available both for international freight services and domestic freight services. The Second Railway Package also enhanced safety and inter-operability, primarily by establishing the European Railway Agency (ERA) to supervise technical standards.[71]

The Third Railway Package was issued in October 2007. It introduced open access rights for international rail passenger services (including cabotage) by 2010.

Directive No. 2012/34/EU establishing a single European railway area was issued as a separate piece of legislation to any railway package, recasting the First Railway Package with the merger of the three directives in force, Directives No. 91/440/EEC, No. 95/18/EC and No. 2001/14/EC, and their successive amendments. The core provisions of Directive No. 2012/34/EU set out the requirements and procedures for i) the allocation of railway infrastructure capacity, ii) the methods of calculation and collection of infrastructure charges and iii) the requirement for infrastructure managers to grant non-discriminatory access to railway undertakings operating on the European railway network.

Also, Directive No. 2012/34/EU stipulates that a single and independent national regulatory body for the railway sector should be established in each Member State,[72] and that the regulatory body should have the necessary organisational capacity in terms of human and material resources, proportionate to the importance of the rail sector in the Member State.

In 2013, proposals for a Fourth Railway Package were released. The Package was adopted by the European Council in December 2015, but as of writing this report (March 2016) has not yet been approved by the European Parliament.

The proposed Fourth Railway Package aims to ensure that public service contracts deliver the best possible value for money, by restricting their size and ensuring that they cannot be granted directly without justification. The new rules would also ease market entry for new rail service operators, by giving them fairer access to infrastructure. It would also simplify procedures for certifying the safety of new rolling stock and gradually transfer certification responsibilities to the ERA. In addition, planned measures to ensure the independence of infrastructure managers would centre on path allocation and infrastructure charging. Member States may decide to allow these to be carried out by an independent body, and an infrastructure manager could outsource functions. Rules to ensure the independence of staff and management would be simplified.

Access to infrastructure

In 1998 the old vertically integrated state-owned monopoly railway company SNCFR was split up. As a result, CFR Marfă S.A. was established as a state-owned rail freight transport operator while railway infrastructure is currently managed by the state-owned national rail company CFR SA. At the moment of writing this report, 23 other private companies operate on the Romanian freight transport market, in addition to the state-owned CFR Marfă. Following Ministry of Transport (MoT) Order No. 461/2003,[73] CFR Marfă is the owner of 26 freight terminals.

The main problems identified in the rail sector are access to infrastructure and the independence of the infrastructure manager, CFR SA, when making decisions related to path allocation and the way CFR SA deals with its obligations to grant equitable and non-discriminatory access to infrastructure. We also identified unclear conditions for accessing certain facilities or services and a lack of definition of key concepts. In particular, capacity allocation, access to infrastructure and essential services (such as power supply, etc.), as well as the level of charges for using infrastructure and other essential services, might lead to discriminatory treatment in favour of the state-owned company CFR Marfă.

Unclear conditions for capacity allocation

Description of obstacle. According to Article 7 of the Regulation on Railway Infrastructure Capacity Allocation, approved by Government Decision No. 1696/2006, any request for infrastructure capacity allocation is subject to financial and technical analysis carried out by the infrastructure manager, CFR SA. CFR SA has the right to reject a path allocation requested by railway operators when statistics related to freight transport operating on that route show an under-use below 20% for the timetable in place. This right of refusal and the threshold are also mentioned in the CFR SA Network Statement – Article 7 para. 1) (b) of Annex XV. There are no further details to facilitate calculation of the under-utilisation rate by railway undertakings or to ensure a suitable level of predictability in relation to the CFR SA decision-making process.

Harm to competition. Possible discrimination against private operators could occur due to the fact that the provision is too vague, simply mentioning CFR SA's right to refuse a path allocation and the 20% threshold, without offering any guidance and transparency about the infrastructure manager's decision-making process. Any CFR SA refusal to grant access to the railway infrastructure may represent a serious limitation to the provision of services or even market entry. The insufficient legal provision may encourage CFR SA to favour CFR Marfă over its competitors.

Policy objective. The provision aims to transpose Article 27 para. 2) of Directive No. 2001/14/EC, which states that the railway infrastructure manager is entitled to optimise the use of the infrastructure and may terminate a route allocation in case a railway's operator utilisation rate is underperforming compared to the operational plan ("use it or lose it principle"). The provision therefore should deal with minimising sub-optimal use of capacity.

International comparison. Similar considerations are made by capacity allocation bodies across the EU – e.g. in the United Kingdom, the infrastructure manager, Network Rail, considers whether the entry of a new operator affects the timetable of existing services and could potentially lead to sub-optimal use of capacity.[74] Still, no estimated percentage of an underperformance utilisation rate is stipulated within the UK Network Code, but there is a clear description of what qualifies as a failure-to-use case that may justify the rejection of capacity allocation based on sub-utilisation.[75] Accordingly, a rejection is justified, e.g. any time the access beneficiary fails to make use of a train slot[76] which has been included in the working timetable[77] and which relates to the quantum access right.[78]

Recommendation. We recommend making the provision clearer. Railway undertakings should be provided with guidelines, included both in Government Decision No. 1696/2006 approving the Regulation on Railway Infrastructure Capacity Allocation and in the CFR SA Network Statement. Those guidelines should describe in detail i) instances that can be accounted for to trigger the 20% underperformance threshold by the infrastructure manager, and ii) instances which fall outside the application of this threshold since they do not fall under the responsibility of the railway operator. Acceptable reasons for under-utilisation may include seasonal factors, e.g. commodities for which demand varies during the course of the year, non-economic issues beyond the railway undertaking's control, a strike or other industrial action. However, these instances should be quantified to the best possible extent in order to facilitate calculation of the underutilisation rate by railway undertakings.

Unclear conditions for accessing facilities or services

Description of obstacles. According to Article 5 para. (1) of Government Ordinance No. 89/2003 on the allocation of railway infrastructure capacity and the levying of charges for the use of railway infrastructure and safety certification, when dealing with a request for access to some facilities and services,[79] such as a power supply system, fuel supply, freight terminals, etc., the infrastructure manager can reject such requests if there are alternative options in the market. These "alternative options" are not specified or defined.

In addition, Article 18 para. (3) of Emergency Government Ordinance No. 12/1998 on freight railway transport and the reorganisation of the Romanian National Railways Company states that access to infrastructure and services provided in terminals and ports linked to the railway infrastructure can be restricted when there are "viable alternatives" in the market. Again, no definition of "viable alternative" is provided.

Harm to competition. The absence of any explanation of what an "alternative option"/ "viable alternative" may be and how it should be assessed makes the provisions unclear and leaves significant discretion to the infrastructure manager, CFR SA. Thus, CFR SA can easily favour CFR Marfă over its competitors by simply limiting their access to essential infrastructure and services.

Policy objective. The provision in Government Ordinance No. 89/2003 was supposed to transpose Article 5 of Directive No. 2001/14/CE, aiming at efficient allocation of capacity. However, there is no justification for the lack of a definition for "alternative options"/ "viable alternatives", in either the provisions of Government Ordinance No. 89/2003 or the provisions of the Emergency Government Ordinance No. 12/1998.

International comparison. A definition of "alternative option" can be found in other EU national legislation, e.g. in Section 2.23 *et seq.* of the UK Guidance on Appeals to the Office of Rail Regulation under the Railways Infrastructure. The UK Guidance provides several assessment parameters for establishing an alternative option, such as commercial viability and availability, and gives examples for a non-viable alternative (e.g. when using another facility is certain to increase the operator's costs, so that the rail freight transporter wanting to use the facility could no longer perform the transport at a competitive price).

Recommendation. We recommend making both provisions clearer, so that an unambiguous definition of "alternative option"/"viable alternative" can be provided as further guidance to rail freight transporters. The definition should be in line with Directive No. 2012/34/EU, notably Article 3 para. (10) and Article 13, providing the meaning of "viable alternatives" and the conditions of access to services. This definition should be made available in the CFR SA Network Statement, in accordance with Article 27 and Annex IV of Directive 2012/34/EU.

Other essential facilities

Description of obstacle. Government Decision No. 581/1998 on setting up the National Railway Company "CFR SA", Annex No. 1 Article 19 subparagraph (o) allows the CFR SA board of administration to approve tariffs for specific services, other than those related to infrastructure access, including, for example, freight terminals, train path preparation, storage on CFR's land and train path reservation, etc.[80]

Access tariffs for such services are established unilaterally by CFR SA. They can give rise to some form of discrimination against operators competing with CFR Marfă, as CFR SA and CRF Marfa belong to the same holding group.

Furthermore, since CFR Marfă was established (in 1998), 26 CFR SA terminals have been used by CFR Marfă free of charge, before ultimately being transferred to CFR Marfă (in 2003). CFR Marfă therefore has the possibility to limit or even completely prevent access to its terminals or to discriminate by using unfair terms against private freight operators.

Harm to competition. CFR SA may use its discretion to grant CFR Marfă undue advantages over its competitors. The restriction of competition on the freight transport market could be quite serious due to the fact that CFR Marfă owns a large number of terminals[81] that it received from CFR SA.

Freight terminals are generally difficult or impossible to replicate by the market, so it is unlikely that a viable alternative can be found. If either CFR SA or CFR Marfă decide to subject access to their own terminals to unfair and/or discriminatory charges, this may lead to a serious restriction of competition in the rail freight transport market.

The Romanian Competition Authority has fined CFR Marfă in the past for i) applying dissimilar and far higher tariffs to equivalent transactions with other private trading parties compared to state-owned ones (e.g. CFR Călători, the state-owned passenger rail operator, which was provided with services within CFR Marfă terminals) and ii) refusal to deal and conclude contracts with private rail operators for services within CFR Marfă terminals.[82]

Policy objective. The objective of the provision is not officially described in the provision. However, CFR SA tariffs are claimed to be the same for every transport operator. Regarding CFR Marfă tariffs, there is no official justification.

International comparison. In our research into European experience, we found some discriminatory practices related to charging. A number of cases have been dealt with by German competition and regulatory authorities in which the German infrastructure manager (which is part of the German incumbent holding group) was accused of having introduced discriminatory charges. For instance, the competition authority found that the charging system TPS 1998 allows for charges for DB Regio to be 25%-40% lower than that of its competitors. The German regulator also pinpointed the use of "regional factors" in track access charging (i.e. definition of charges applicable to specific parts of the rail network) which were discriminatory against competitors of the incumbent. [83]

Another case concerns DB Energie, the Deutsche Bahn (DB) subsidiary responsible for providing electricity to the rail network. DB Energie applied volume discounts that favour DB operating subsidiaries since only they benefit from the maximum discount available. As a result, competing rail undertakings paid electricity charges 15-20% higher than those paid by DB. In February 2012 BNetzA, the German rail regulator, required that DB Energie reduce the fee by 23%, which it has agreed to do. However, DB Energie did not keep its promise to abolish the discriminatory discount system as of 1 January 2013.[84]

Italy seems to have faced the same situation as Romania regarding the infrastructure manager (RFI) and the incumbent rail operator (Trenitalia) being under the same state ownership and regarding the assignment to the latter of a large number (61) of freight terminals due to a contract between RFI and Trenitalia in 2002.

In the Report on the Separation between the Railway Infrastructure Management Company and Train Operators (2003),[85] the Italian Competition Authority highlighted the potential distortion of competition stemming from the fact that other facilities, such as freight terminals and maintenance infrastructures, are owned directly and/or managed by Trenitalia, Italy's state-owned rail operator.

Recommendation. We recommend that CFR SA publishes guidelines explaining the methodology it uses to calculate its tariffs, notably with reference to the costs related to each of its essential services. Also, as long as terminal ownership by CFR Marfă continues and as long as CFR Marfă is a state-owned company, CFR Marfă should be under the same obligation as CFR SA to grant access to its terminals to competing railway operators. Notably, both CFR SA and CFR Marfă should grant fair, transparent and non-discriminatory conditions for accessing their terminals ("FRAND terms").[86] This would be in line with Article 10 of Directive No. 2012/34/EU which provides that railway undertakings must be granted the right to access the railway infrastructure in all Member States for the purpose of operating all types of rail freight services under equitable, non-discriminatory and transparent conditions.

Compliance with FRAND terms should be ensured by an independent regulatory body, such as the Rail Supervisory Council. As Directive No. 2012/34/EU requires (Article 56 para. (5), the national regulatory body shall have the necessary organisational capacity in terms of human and material resources, which shall be proportionate to the importance of the rail sector in the Member State. In addition, the Romanian Rail Supervisory Council capabilities need to be strengthened as to be in line with Directive No. 2012/34/EU requirements.

Privatisation of CFR Marfă

The National Rail Freight Company CFR Marfă is a wholly state-owned company operating as a separate subsidiary from CFR SA within a holding structure under the authority of the Ministry of Transport. Privatisation of CFR Marfă was planned for 2013[87] and then again for 2015,[88] but neither transaction has taken place. According to the Minister of Transport, a new attempt to sell may take place in 2017.[89]

We do not make any recommendation (neither for nor against) concerning the planned privatisation of CFR Marfă. Though privatisation and ownership separation would likely solve the access and discrimination problems described above, and might additionally accelerate investment into infrastructure, we see that there are other issues which the Romanian government needs to take into account when making its decision, especially: EU legislation does not require ownership separation; various models from full ownership separation to vertical separation exist in OECD countries; economic studies dealing with the benefits of ownership separation are not clear-cut and do not necessarily provide "a better solution".

Ownership separation likely to solve access and discrimination issues

According to the OECD (2013), Recent Developments in Rail Transportation Services, a vertical integration model provides incentives for the vertically integrated company to foreclose competitors and to favour its own transport operator, which might harm competition. It also places a burden on regulators and competition authorities to prevent or remedy such conduct. Experience shows that in a holding structure these forms of discrimination are not readily eliminated by the requirement for non-discriminatory access (OECD, 2013). Furthermore, if a good level of institutional separation is not achieved, deliberate favouring by the infrastructure manager of a sister company or a national operator can occur (OECD, 2013).

For Romania, CFR Marfă's privatisation may provide the opportunity to address discrimination issues existing in the related Romanian legal framework and solve them simultaneously with the transfer of CFR Marfă to the private sector. Splitting ownership of the infrastructure manager and the rail freight operator would eliminate any incentives for CFR SA to favour its affiliated company, CFR Marfă, through practices aimed at either refusing access or charging unfair prices for essential services such as allocation of tracks, or access to traction services or energy supply.

Investment in infrastructure

As mentioned in the Romanian General Transport Master Plan,[90] the Romanian public rail infrastructure has been suffering from continuous degradation, but the privatisation process could improve the allocation of resources and reduce reliance on public funds.

Additionally, privatisation could result in divesting CFR Marfă of the terminals it owns so as to eliminate discriminatory behaviour by CFR Marfă.[91] Across the EU, overall, freight terminals, marshalling yards and storage sidings seem to be mostly owned and managed by incumbents' holdings (in particular in large freight markets such as those in Germany, Austria, Poland, Lithuania and Latvia), except in the United Kingdom and the Netherlands – where the independent infrastructure manager predominantly owns them. In Portugal, Bulgaria, Luxembourg and Slovakia, they are state-owned, but managed by the infrastructure manager.[92]

Ownership separation not required by EU law

EU legislation does not require separation of ownership. However, it requires that the manager of the rail infrastructure must be independent from any railway undertakings when performing essential functions and that it must keep separate financial accounts and grant access to rail infrastructure in a non-discriminatory manner.

Directive No. 2012/34/EU aims to limit the possibilities of discrimination by increasing the level of transparency obligations on infrastructure managers when settling the conditions of access to railway infrastructure. Railway undertakings must be granted, under equitable, non-discriminatory and transparent conditions, the right to access the railway infrastructure in all Member States for the purpose of operating all types of rail freight services.

The Fourth Rail Package aims to ensure that infrastructure managers can perform all the functions needed to run the infrastructure in an optimised, efficient and non-discriminatory manner. Since this is the simplest and most efficient solution to create a level playing field among transport operators, the Commission proposes an institutional separation of infrastructure management and transport operations. However, where Member States wish to maintain existing holding structures with ownership of the infrastructure manager, the Commission proposes the introduction of strict safeguards to protect the independence of the infrastructure manager with a process of verification by the Commission to ensure that a genuine level playing field for all railway undertakings is put in place.

Various models in OECD member countries

A variety of forms of vertical separation exist among OECD member countries, ranging from mere separation of accounts within a vertically integrated entity to full structural separation. Some countries, such as Sweden[93] and the United Kingdom, have implemented full structural separation. Other countries have organised infrastructure and operations into separate subsidiaries within a holding company structure (e.g. Germany and Italy), while outside Europe, most railways are vertically integrated (e.g. U.S. and Mexico).

In Italy, around the year 2000 the state-owned monolith Ferrovie dello Stato (FS) was transformed into a holding company, comprising an infrastructure manager (Rete Ferroviaria Italiana – RFI) and an operator responsible for freight and passenger services (Trenitalia). Furthermore, a law was issued[94] that granted all EU railways operators open access to the Italian railway infrastructure, thus depriving Trenitalia of the monopoly it had so far enjoyed on both freight and passenger services.

The UK rail industry has experienced several reforms. The rail sector in the United Kingdom comprises an infrastructure manager, Network Rail (which was a private company with state guarantee, brought back into public sector hands in 2015), an independent economic and safety regulator, the Office of Rail and Road, and private railway undertakings which provide passenger and freight services, most of them subsidiaries of public rail companies such as Deutsche Bahn (German national rail operator), SNCF (French national rail operator), ND (Dutch national rail operator).

Facing increasing costs, the government initiated a Rail Value for Money Study completed in 2011. It highlighted that, compared to other European railways, the UK rail industry was found to show a significant efficiency gap, with rail costs that should have been 20-30% lower (the focus was on infrastructure management costs).[95]

Economic literature

Regarding the impact of structural separation on the rail sector, there is no evidence in the economic literature (Mizutani and Uranishi, 2013) that either structural separation increases competition compared with a holding company model, or that structural separation improves rail's modal share[96] compared with a holding company model (Van de Velde, 2012). As for the overall impact of restructuring on costs, the issue is more complicated. For example, Mizutani and Uranishi (2013) suggests that effects of structural separation change according to the train density of the railway organisation. Where there is lower train density, it seems that structural separation reduces costs, whereas at high levels of train density it increases costs.

Nevertheless, evidence on rail freight privatisation seems to be positive. A country-by-country analysis clearly indicated that the Member States which were the first to reform their railways by introducing competition in the rail freight transport sector recorded the biggest increases in volume between 1995 and 2004: the United Kingdom (70%), the Netherlands (67%) and Austria (36%), countries where the main operator was the incumbent following privatisation. Analysing the share of this volume handled by the incumbent undertaking, it emerged that, in the United Kingdom, EWS[97] accounted for 70% and three other undertakings shared the remainder and in the Netherlands, Railion Nederland accounted for 85% of the volume and 6 other undertakings shared the rest (European Commission, 2006).

In the United Kingdom, Pollitt and Smith (2002) estimate that, after taking account of scale effects, the rail industry has achieved efficiency savings of 13% (or 2% per annum) since privatisation. Lodge (2013) writes that freight operating companies reduced their unit costs by 35% between 1998-1999 and 2008-2009 and traffic increased by 50% since privatisation with half the number of locomotives and two-thirds of the wagons used at the time moving a greater volume of goods (Lodge, 2013).

Conclusion

Due to major differences in market circumstances across countries, a clear conclusion has not yet been reached on whether full vertical separation is better than other structural approaches.

Braking energy and traffic management signalling system

Description of obstacles

When a train brakes, electrical energy is produced by the braking traction (also known as regenerative braking). The generated electricity can be recovered and used both internally by the train for operating auxiliary systems (e.g. to power lights, air conditioning, door opening and closing) and externally: this electricity can be sent back to the grid and used by other trains (Railway Handbook, 2015).

Worldwide, we are seeing an increase in the number of trains equipped with technology to recover electrical energy from braking (Railway Handbook, 2015).

Harm to competition

Romania lacks a legal framework enabling the regenerative braking to be metered and discounted. The lack of a regulatory framework discriminates against those operators that have invested in new technology in their locomotives. For these operators, the absence of the possibility of using braking energy generates no savings in electricity costs.

Policymakers' objective

There is no official justification for the absence of regulating braking energy, either within legislation on transport or on energy legislation.

International comparison

A good example of a legal framework for regenerative braking discounts, which can be legally claimed by rail transport operators, can be found in the United Kingdom, whereby Article 8 of the Traction Electricity Rules[98] issued by the Office of Rail Regulation[99] stipulates that a train operator operating a regenerative braking system for any of its vehicles is entitled to receive a regenerative braking discount. Network Rail, the UK's infrastructure manager, decides the level of regenerative braking discount to be applied to each train operator.

However, most European countries do not seem to have a specific legal framework on compensation for braking energy.

Need for upgrade of railway infrastructure

The introduction of a legal framework needs to be supported by an adequate upgrade of railway infrastructure including the metering devices, dedicated storage facilities and regenerative inverters necessary to exploit the electricity produced by this form of braking. Regenerative braking energy may, in principle, be generated by trains running on the Romanian rail network, at least with respect to those routes that are part of the Trans-European Transport Network (TEN-T) corridors of Romania. As these routes have already been electrified,[100] they are theoretically suitable to absorb regenerative braking energy.[101] Still, infrastructure upgrading and development for braking energy is also needed in order to exploit the electricity produced by braking, requiring adequate metering devices, dedicated storage facilities or regenerative inverters.

Upgrading infrastructure for braking energy is not the only upgrade the Romanian railway infrastructure required as a part of the EU railway network. At the European level, the deployment of the European Railway Traffic Management System (ERTMS) is a priority, aiming to ensure the inter-operability of the EU railway system. Currently there are more than 20 train control systems across the European Union. Each system is stand-alone and non-interoperable, and therefore requires extensive integration and engineering effort, raising total delivery costs for cross-border traffic. This restricts competition and hampers the competitiveness of the European rail sector compared to road transport, by creating technical barriers to international journeys. As a single European train control system, ERTMS is designed to gradually replace the existing incompatible systems throughout Europe.[102]

As ERTMS has not yet been fully deployed in Romania, with the exception of the Feteşti- Consţanta corridor, foreign locomotives may need a second signalling system when running trains in Romania. In addition, Romanian locomotives cannot easily run abroad. This affects the ability of both foreign and Romanian operators to compete, increasing their operating costs. Introducing ERTMS would allow market entry into Romania and

Romanian operators to be able to compete abroad, as in other EU Member States implementing ERTMS is an ongoing process.[103]

Recommendation and benefits

We recommend creating an appropriate legal framework whereby metering regenerative braking legally entitles rail transport operators to reduce their electricity costs. Compensation for regenerative braking energy could be introduced in Romanian Law on Energy No. 123/2014 or in a separate piece of legislation.

As explained in Annex 3.A3, we estimate that the expected annual energy savings for freight operators from introducing a framework for compensation of braking energy would be worth around EUR 0.9 million, based on previous experience. Further savings could be achieved for railway companies active in passenger transport if the appropriate technology is installed. The overall outcome is uncertain as trains equipped with braking technology can be significantly heavier and thus increase wear and tear on rail tracks. Therefore, an overall reduction in charges for these trains is not a given even if a system is introduced to account for energy savings.

Due to the fact that the regenerative braking issue is not just a regulatory matter but also a matter of investment, it is up to the Romanian legislator and public executive bodies in charge to decide on whether the legal framework is to be issued before, or coupled with the required infrastructure upgrade. It is also to be considered that investment costs would be high in order to install an appropriate railway system that allowed the recovery of braking energy and might even be higher than the recovered costs. As there may be other important priorities regarding investments in the railway sector, such as the sustainability of national infrastructure, and investment resources might be limited, an appropriate system for braking energy should be taken into consideration in the medium to long term.

Discrimination based on nationality

Description of obstacles

Article 5 and Article 6 of Annex 1 of MoT Order No. 410/1999[104] stipulate the requirement of having Romanian legal personality in order to obtain authorisation for testing and certifying railway products.

A similar nationality condition can be found in the mandatory requirements that must be met in order to operate as a railway transport operator. According to Article 1 para. (9) of Government Emergency Ordinance No. 12/1998, undertakings are required to be registered as a Romanian legal person in order to obtain a transport license issued by the MoT.

Harm to competition

Those provisions may discriminate against foreign companies, acting as a barrier to entry to the market and as they are contrary to Directive No. 95/18/EC and Directive No. 2001/13/EC establishing a common license for the European rail freight network.

Justification

We have found no justification for requesting undertakings to have Romanian legal personality, either for testing and certifying rail products or for engaging in rail transport activities. However, CFR SA claims that there is no discrimination.

Paragraph 2.2.2 of the CFR SA Network Statement provides that there should be no discrimination against foreign operators. Still, both MoT Order No. 410/1999 and the Government Emergency Ordinance no 12/1998 have primacy over the Network Statement under Romanian law.

Recommendation

We recommend amending the provision to enable operators registered in the European Union to legitimately operate in Romania without being subject to the requirement to register in Romania.

Other problems

Legislation transparency

Description of obstacles. In order to verify transport safety, railway products are tested by authorised laboratories. These laboratories are authorised by AFER, the Romanian Railway Authority. The conditions for the authorisation are mentioned in the Annexes to Order No. 410/1999,[105] issued by the MoT. However, the mentioned Annexes are not published and they can be obtained only by request from AFER.

Similarly, Article 4 para. (2) of the Regulation on Railway Infrastructure Capacity Allocation, approved by Government Decision No. 1696/2006, refers to the issuing of a MoT Order establishing the conditions for granting CFR SA special rights to allocate public railway infrastructure. As no such Order has been published, it is still unclear whether it was ever issued.

Harm to competition. The lack of transparency may lead to unclear conditions for operators and increase administrative costs.

Justification. We found no justification for the non-publication of the Annexes to Order No. 410/1999, or for not publishing the Order mentioning which special rights are granted to CFR SA.

Recommendation. We recommend that the regulatory framework be more transparent and approachable. The Annexes to Order No. 410/1999 should be published in order to make all the authorisation requirements known to interested operators. To this end, the Annexes should be published both in the *Official Gazette* and on AFER's website.

The Order of the Ministry of Transport establishing the conditions for granting CFR SA special rights to allocate public railway infrastructure, if issued, should also be published in the *Official Gazette*.

Licence renewal

Description of obstacle. In order to ensure the safety of rail transport, railway products are only tested by authorised independent laboratories. Although these laboratories are authorised by AFER for a 10-year period, the authorisation is subject to a mandatory renewal every two years at the end of which these independent testing laboratories need to show they still fulfill all the authorisation requirements, as requested by Article 4 para. (2) of Annex No. 1 of Order No. 410/1999.

Harm to competition. The rather short period of two years may act as an administrative burden which reduces the incentive for independent testing laboratories to invest resources into entering or staying in the business, since there is a risk that their authorisation will not be renewed at the end of the two-year period. Other EU Member States such as Italy have already adopted a five-year renewal term.

Justification. We found no justification for the two-year period.

Recommendation. We recommend extending the renewal period to five years which would be in line with Article 10 of Commission implementing Regulation (EU) No. 402/2013.

3.4. Restrictions to competitiveness in maritime transport

Ports for maritime and inland waterway transport serve as an infrastructure for a wide range of customers, including freight shippers, ferry operators and private boats. One of the main functions of ports is facilitating domestic and international trade of goods, often on a large scale. Several services are necessary for the functioning of a port, such as: provision of transport infrastructure, technical-nautical services (pilotage, towage and mooring), operational infrastructure and equipment, cargo handling and ancillary (or general) services (Cullinane, 2010).

Ports all over the world are organised in various ways. As stated in the guidelines issued by the European Commission, COM (2007) 616, the structure of port management varies considerably across the European Community. In most cases, ports are managed by public entities, which can be designated as port "authorities", while in some countries they are entirely private businesses, which own the port land. Moreover, in some countries shipping activities taking place in ports are being provided by the port administration under monopoly conditions, while in others they are subject to competition. In Romania, maritime and inland ports are administered by national companies owned by the Ministry of Transport, appointed as port authorities.

Box 3.1. **Port organisational structure – Port of Constanța, Romania**

The Port of Constanța, the main Romanian sea port and the largest one on the Black Sea in terms of area, plays a significant role as the transit hub for the landlocked countries in Central and South Eastern Europe.

- The ports Midia and Mangalia are located close to Constanța Port. They are part of the Romanian maritime port system co-ordinated by Compania Națională Administrația Porturilor Maritime S.A.
- The port authority is responsible for the management and development of the port infrastructure for the Romanian maritime ports Constanța, Midia and Mangalia. It also provides safety services (pilotage, towing) through specialised and authorised private operators.
- In addition, several private operators handle cargo and invest in machinery and superstructures.
- Significant freight volume is handled in the Port of Constanța, while passenger traffic is occasional.
- The Port of Constanța, as well as the four river maritime ports in Romania – Brăila, Galați, Sulina and Tulcea – are part of the Trans-European Transport Network (TENT).

Description of the European legal framework

The current European framework encompasses several initiatives regarding the establishment of a port services policy. In recent times, the Commission proposed a directive on Market Access to Port Services, issued several guidelines on port services and, recently, in 2013, proposed a regulation which, in an adapted fashion, is currently being debated in the European Parliament.

Even if the Commission proposal might not be eventually adopted by the European Parliament, we consider it a good initiative to establish a framework for the organisation of port services and for financial transparency of ports whose principles the Romanian government might take into account when reforming its national law.

Also, other European legislation relevant to this report provides rules regarding ship inspection and survey organisations, as well as compliance of Member States with flag state requirements.

The European Commission Regulation Proposal on market access to port services and financial transparency of ports

Compared with other transport sectors, there is no European legislation on port services, either with regard to access to port services or to infrastructure charging. The European Commission has considered several proposals regarding a harmonised ports policy beginning with a Green Paper published on this subject in 1997. In 2001, the Commission proposed a Directive on Market Access to Port Services, the proposal being rejected by the European Parliament in 2003. Furthermore, in 2004, the Commission came forward with a second proposal on the Directive on Market Access to Port Services which was also eventually turned down by Parliament.

In 2007, following a wide consultation of stakeholders, in order to better understand the port sector, the Commission adopted guidelines which provide a framework and a number of related actions for implementation. The Communication on a European Ports Policy (2007) outlined the main issues identified at that time: i) the threats of port performance and hinterland connections; ii) expanding capacity while respecting the environment; iii) the need to modernise ports; iv) the lack of clarity and transparency of public financing and market access restrictions and v) issues on work in ports.

As the soft measures laid down by the Commission in 2007 in its guidelines on fair market access and transparency had almost no impact, in 2013, along with its communication on EU ports, the Commission proposed simultaneously to the European Parliament and Council a regulation designed to establish a framework on market access to port services and financial transparency of ports (European Commission, 2013). With it the Commission attempts to correct significant disparities in the performance of ports in the Trans-European Transport Network (TEN-T). The Commission proposes new rules in order to guarantee the freedom to provide services in these ports through the introduction of more transparent procedures for hiring service providers for eight port services[106] in the sea ports within the TEN-T. The Commission also proposes to give port authorities more autonomy on infrastructure charging, provided this is done transparently. Adoption of the proposed regulation was scheduled for 2014, but has been delayed. This is an ongoing legislative process, with the Commission proposal still being debated in the European Parliament.[107]

(ii) European rules governing ship inspection and survey organisations, as well as compliance of Member States with flag state requirements

European legislation also provides rules and standards for ship inspection and survey organisations. Inspections and surveys refer to control activities that are mandatory for ships under the existing maritime international conventions.[108] Directive 2009/15/EC establishes measures to be followed by the Member States in their relationship with organisations entrusted with the inspection, survey and certification of ships for compliance with the international conventions on safety at sea and prevention of marine pollution.

Moreover, under European Regulation No. 391/2009, it is mandatory for survey organisations to fulfill minimum criteria to obtain or to continue to enjoy community recognition. According to Article 3 of the abovementioned regulation, recognition should be granted to organisations that fulfill the criteria established in Annex 1 of the regulation. Recognised ship inspection and survey organisations shall provide their services throughout the European Union.

Another piece of relevant European legislation in the field of maritime transport policy is Directive 2009/21/EC which aims to ensure that Member States comply with their obligations as flag states, to enhance safety and to prevent pollution from ships flying the flag of a Member State.

Finally, Directive 2006/87/EC establishes technical requirements for inland waterway vessels referring to shipbuilding, safety clearance, freeboard and draught marks, manoeuvrability, steering system, engine design and electrical equipment, etc.

Investigation of the Romanian Competition Council into port services performed in the ports administered by Compania Naţională Administraţia Porturilor Maritime S.A.

In 2012, the Romanian Competition Council (RCC) launched an investigation into the port services market with regard to the pilotage and towage services performed in the ports administered by Compania Naţională Administraţia Porturilor Maritime S.A. At the time of writing (March 2016), the investigation is ongoing. According to the RCC press release,[109] the investigation covers several practices that may constitute a breach of competition law. First, the investigation analyses a possible abuse of its dominant position by the Consţanta port authority through the imposition of access criteria on pilotage and towage services markets and by applying dissimilar treatment to trading parties with regard to the leasing conditions of port land infrastructure, thereby placing them at a competitive disadvantage. Second, the investigation also refers to two possible anti-competitive agreements: the first one concerns a possible collusion between towage operators that perform the services through the creation of a joint venture, the only one performing these services, while the second one concerns a market-sharing agreement on the pilotage services market.

Pilotage services

Description of the pilotage services sector

Pilotage is a service provided by a pilot with local knowledge and skills which enable him to conduct navigation and manoeuvring of the vessel into and approaching the harbour (OECD, 2011). Pilotage of seagoing ships in Romania is a safety service regulated by Government Ordinance No. 22/1999 and performed under state control for all ships, irrespective of the flag they fly. According to Article 48 of the same law, it must be offered without discrimination in terms of duration, quality and tariffs. The conditions under which economic operators can obtain authorisation to provide ship pilotage services are covered by the Order of the Ministry of Transport No. 547/2014.

According to Article 50 of Government Ordinance No. 22/1999, such services may be based on three different legal arrangements: they may either be provided by the port authority through its own pilots or through specialised operators based on a non-discriminatory agreement between the port authority and the operators (in this case, the port authority outsources the services to specialised operators) or by concession agreements. Currently, the pilotage services in the ports administered by Compania Naţională Administraţia Porturilor Maritime S.A. are provided to freight shippers by the port authority, which has concluded service agreements with four private operators. Nevertheless, pilotage services are managed and billed to freight shippers directly by the port authority. The port authority also sets the timetable for the provision of pilotage services in the three maritime ports.

Authorisation for private pilotage operators

Description of the obstacle. Article 2 of the Order of the Ministry of Transport No. 547/2014 states that the Ministry of Transport, through the Romanian Naval Authority, authorises economic operators to perform pilotage services. Further, it sets out that the port administration and/or authorities managing maritime canals may perform pilotage services without an authorisation, unlike private operators, for which an authorisation by the Ministry of Transport is mandatory.

Harm to competition. The provision may offer state-owned port authorities an unfair competitive advantage as they do not need an authorisation. One can conclude that it is not necessary for port authorities to fulfill the conditions stipulated in Annex 1 of the abovementioned order regarding the authorisation requirements for pilotage operators and port authorities are not verified to that effect. Moreover, the possibility of coexistence of two forms of pilotage service provision to vessels by the port administration and by private parties may lead to a wide range of potential abuses of market power, such as refusal to supply and/or excessive pricing. Thus, port authorities (state operators) and private operators should not be subject to different legal and administrative regimes when performing the same services in competition.

Policy makers' objective. The justification for these provisions may be that port authorities are required by law to ensure pilotage services, having the alternative to provide pilotage services either directly themselves or through third parties.

Recommendation. Pilotage services should be provided either directly by the port authority or through a third party provider, but not by both. When being outsourced, the services agreement to the private operator should be granted through a tendering procedure subject to fair and non-discriminatory terms.

Our recommendation refers to public tendering and its aim is the introduction of competition for the right to provide pilotage services and therefore to enter the market, so the competition is for the market itself.

Number of pilots required

Description of the obstacle. In order to be authorised by the Ministry of Transport through the ANR, pilotage service providers must have a minimum number of pilots employed per port. Article 1 of the Annex regarding criteria for pilotage operator authorisation set by the Order of the Ministry of Transport No. 547/2014 requires companies to have a minimum of 8 pilots in Consţanta, 4 pilots in Midia and 2 pilots in Mangalia. However, the port authority Compania Naţională Administraţia Porturilor Maritime S.A. has unilaterally established additional, more restrictive, terms and conditions for the provision of pilotage services. For example, for the ports of Consţanta, Mangalia and Midia, it requires that companies have at least 21 pilots servicing those three ports, without the companies being able to serve only one port. These additional criteria are established through the framework services agreement, approved by the board of directors of Compania Naţională Administraţia Porturilor Maritime S.A. Consequently, an operator who might obtain an authorisation for pilotage services under the conditions required by the abovementioned Order of the Ministry of Transport, will in practice not be able to conclude a service agreement with the port authority if it does not additionally fulfill its stricter criteria.

Harm to competition. The minimum number of 21 pilots set by the port authority, which is higher than the minimum number required by the Order of the Ministry of Transport, constitutes an entry barrier for smaller operators who do not have such a large number of pilots at their disposal.

The number of pilots has also been subject to an investigation by the RCC with regard to possible abuse of their dominant position by Compania Naţională Administraţia Porturilor Maritime S.A. At the time of writing (March 2016), the investigation is ongoing.

A comparison with other ports indicates that the tariffs for pilotage services charged in Romanian maritime ports are 2 or 3 times higher than those charged in other EU ports handling a comparable total volume of goods (gross weight), such as Barcelona, Valencia, Genoa and Koper.

Policy makers' objective. The objective of a minimum number of pilots is that pilotage services should be provided non-stop, 24 hours a day, 7 days a week.

Recommendation and benefits. Further to the above, we recommend the following:

The current provision requiring a certain number of pilots should be abolished. The law should not impose a minimum number of pilots per port, but instead require a minimum service level, such as a maximum ship waiting time for pilots to be on board. Each pilotage company shall make its own assessment and shall make its own decision regarding the number of pilots necessary to reach the required service level.

Moreover, pilotage services shall not be granted directly by the port authority, but instead they should be tendered in an open procedure. The introduction of a more transparent procedure like this would ensure more reliable, better quality services for freight shippers and lower costs for the port authority, which is the contracting authority for pilotage services. For the port authority savings to be passed on to freight shippers, the port authority should implement a cost-based approach in the pricing process of the pilotage services provided by it. The required service level must also be transparent, non-discriminatory, objective and relevant to the category and nature of the port services concerned.

Figure 3.25. **Pilotage tariffs in different ports throughout Europe**

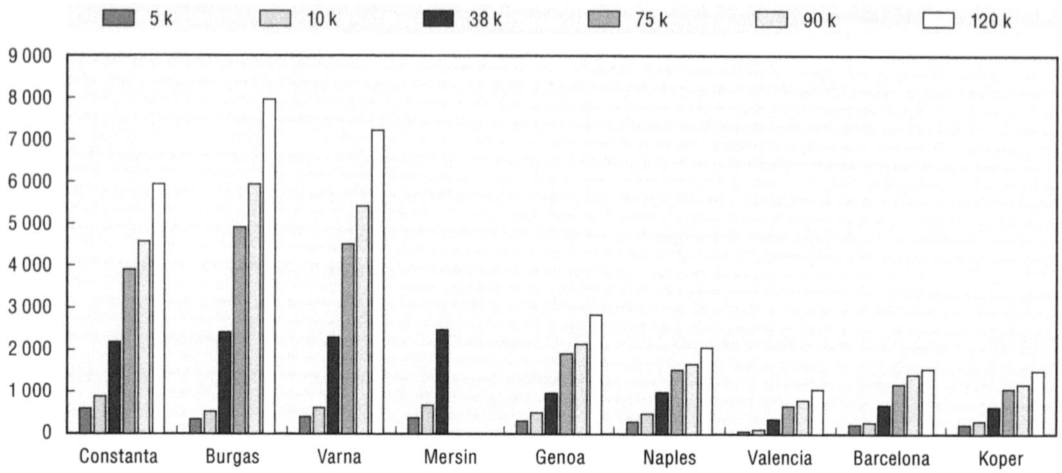

Note: For Burgas and Varna, an average tariff has been determined based on the tariffs of the two port areas of Burgas/the five port areas of Varna. For Mersin an average between the tariffs for container vessels and the tariffs for other cargo vessels is also used. For Valencia and Barcelona, the tariffs used are the maximum rates set by the port authorities.

Source: Relevant port websites: *http://bit.ly/1QJpHw6*, *http://bit.ly/1TLkDxw*, *http://bit.ly/1V9lEik*, *http://bit.ly/2522pvA*, *http://bit.ly/21tjHwV*, *http://bit.ly/1YVR8bM*, *http://bit.ly/21tkMoC*, *http://bit.ly/1TLmxOJ* accessed on 7 January 2016,

StatLink http://dx.doi.org/10.1787/888933361670

We estimate that the introduction of tendering procedures in granting the right of operating pilotage services by the port authority to economic operators would generate savings for the port authority, which is the contracting authority for pilotage services, and further savings for freight shippers, if the port authority were to pass on the savings to its customers, of approx. EUR 3.4 million (mln) a year, as shown in Annex 3.A4. Moreover, the establishment of an independent regulatory body to monitor the activity of the port authority when setting pilotage tariffs may contribute to a further reduction in these tariffs.

Inland ports

Description of the obstacle. According to Article 51 of Government Ordinance No. 22/1999, pilotage of seagoing ships in the ports of Sulina, Tulcea, Galaţi and Brăila is provided by the Autonomous Administration "Administraţia Fluvială a Dunării de Jos" Galaţi by its own pilots, by pilots authorised by the Autonomous Administration "Administraţia Fluvială a Dunării de Jos" Galaţi under a contract for services concluded or by a concession agreement.

The same provision provides that pilotage of ships on the Danube route between Brăila and Sulina are performed in accordance with Article 31 and Article 33 regarding pilotage services of the 1948 Belgrade Convention, ratified by Romania under Decree 298/1948. The abovementioned articles of the Belgrade Convention state that pilotage of vessels is provided by pilots who "*depend on port administrations*", and that they are "*recruited from among the citizens of the Danube country members of the Administrations concerned*".

Harm to competition. The possibility of the coexistence of two forms of pilotage services provision to vessels by the port administration and by private parties may lead to a wide range of potential abuses of market power, such as a refusal to supply and/or excessive pricing. "Administraţia Fluvială a Dunării de Jos" Galaţi may abuse its exclusive rights granted by the law in order to operate pilotage and harbour manoeuvres. It may also reduce the number of authorised operators and/or their incentive to compete against its own services.

The provisions of the Belgrade Convention should be applied by the signatory states in accordance with the realities of the present times, in the light of the *Treaty on the Functioning of the European Union*. However, the condition regarding the pilot's nationality should not be applicable as it is a discriminatory condition in the recruitment process.

Policy makers' objective. The justification for Article 51 of Government Ordinance No. 22/1999 may be that port authorities are required by law to ensure pilotage services, having the alternative to provide pilotage services either directly themselves or by third parties.

Also, the provision is in line with the Convention regarding the regime of navigation on the Danube, signed in Belgrade on 18 August 1948, ratified by Romania under Decree No. 298/1948.

Recommendation. We recommend that the provision is amended so that pilotage services are either offered by the port authority or outsourced to private companies. When outsourced, the right to provide pilotage services shall be granted through a tendering process under fair and non-discriminatory terms. The port authority should not act both as regulator and service provider in the same port.

Tariffs for pilotage services

Description of the obstacle. Currently, vessels flying the Romanian flag benefit from large discounts on pilotage tariffs compared to foreign-registered vessels. Regarding the pilotage service provided in the ports of Consţanta, Midia and Mangalia by the port authority, the price list available on the port authority website[110] indicates that pilotage tariffs will be reduced by 50% for ships registered in Romanian maritime ports.

Harm to competition. Discounts granted to vessels flying the Romanian flag violate the principle of non-discrimination based on the grounds of nationality established by EU law.

Policy makers' objective. There is no objective justification for the port authority to apply tariffs on a discriminatory basis.

Recommendation. The pilotage tariffs should be set by port authorities based on a transparent cost-based approach. Further, the autonomy of port authorities in setting these tariffs should be balanced by allowing an independent regulatory body the right to supervise them, see below.

To the same effect, to discourage excessive or discriminatory tariffs and to avoid the abuse of the market power of ports, in some countries regulators intervene and set prices. For example, in the Netherlands, pilots are organised in a corporation called Nederlandse Loodsencorporatie (NLc) and do not compete with each other. The Netherlands Authority for Consumers and Markets sets the annual pilotage tariffs based on a tariff proposal submitted by the NLc following an assessment in order to establish whether or not the tariffs are unreasonably high.[111]

Towage services

Description of the towage services sector

Towage is a service provided by tug boats which move larger ships that either should not or cannot power themselves (OECD, 2011). According to Article 47 of Government Ordinance No. 22/1999, towage of seagoing ships in ports is a safety service and is performed under state control for all ships, irrespective of the flag they fly, without discrimination in terms of duration, quality or tariffs. Towage ensures the safe conduct of shipping and port manoeuvres. The conditions under which economic operators can obtain authorisation to provide ship towage services are covered by the Order of the Ministry of Transport No. 548/2014.

Currently, towage services in Romania are provided by the port authority through a services agreement with one single company, which is a joint venture formed by the previous three largest towage operators in the market.

A study prepared for the Directorate-General Transport and Mobility of the European Commission[112] indicated pilotage and towage as the most problematic of port services, having the lowest scores for satisfaction as measured by survey responses. Moreover, price was most frequently mentioned as a challenge for these port services.

In the towage sector, there have been cases of anti-competitive behaviour. For example, the Competition Protection Office of the Republic of Slovenia sanctioned the public limited company and port authority Luka Koper for abusing its dominant position in the market for the organisation of port services. Luka Koper had refused to grant access to the Port of Koper to other private operators to perform towage and mooring activities, resulting in the exclusion of all competition in the markets for towage and mooring services in the Port of Koper (OECD, 2011). In 2007, the Portuguese Competition Authority uncovered a cartel between towage services operators that fixed prices, divided customers and established a monitoring and compensation mechanism in the Port of Setúbal. The price-fixing resulted in significantly higher price levels than those before the cartel (OECD, 2011).

Authorisation for private towage operators

Description of the obstacle. Article 2 of the Order of the Ministry of Transport No. 548/2014 states that the Ministry of Transport, through the ANR, authorises economic operators to perform towage services. Furthermore, the same provision stipulates that the port administration may operate towage services for maritime vessels without authorisation, unlike private operators for whom an authorisation by the Ministry of Transport is mandatory.

Harm to competition. This provision may offer state-owned port authorities an unfair competitive advantage as they do not need an authorisation. One can conclude that it is not necessary for port authorities to fulfill the conditions stipulated in Annex 1 of the abovementioned order regarding the authorisation requirements for towage operators, and port authorities are not verified to that effect. Moreover, the possibility of the coexistence of two forms of towage service provision to vessels by the port administration and by private parties may lead to a wide range of potential abuses of market power, such as refusal to supply and/or excessive pricing.

Policy makers' objective. The justification for these provisions may be that port authorities are required by law to ensure towage services, with the possibility of providing towage services either directly themselves or by concluding services agreements with private operators.

Recommendation. Port authorities and private operators should not be subject to different legal and administrative regimes when performing the same competing service. We do not recommend that towage services should be provided in competition, but rather that towage services should be provided by the port authority, as is currently the case, for safety and security reasons. The provision should be amended so as to allow towage services to be either provided directly by the port authority or to be outsourced. When outsourced, the services agreement with private operators should be granted through a tendering process subject to fair and non-discriminatory terms.

Number of tugboats required

Description of the obstacle. Article 1 and Article 2 of the Annex to the Order of the Ministry of Transport No. 548/2014 set out criteria to be fulfilled in order to be authorised as a towage operator by the Ministry of Transport, through the ANR. One of the criteria is that an operator needs to have a minimum number of tugboats for each category of vessels requesting authorisation. The vessel categories are defined depending on the length of the vessel and its maximum gross tonnage. An operator may require authorisation for one or more vessel categories. For example, the provisions require at least one tugboat with a hook traction strength of a minimum of 5 tonnes for towage of vessels up to 120 metres in length and weighing 1 000 tonnes; 4 tugboats for towage vessels over 250 metres, etc. Although the abovementioned order is in force, the port authority Compania Naţională Administraţia Porturilor Maritime S.A. unilaterally established additional terms and conditions for the provision of towage services in its ports. For the ports of Constanţa, Mangalia and Midia, the port authority requires companies to have at least 17 towage vessels servicing these three ports, without the companies being able to serve only one port. These additional criteria are established through the framework services agreement, approved by the board of directors of Compania Naţională Administraţia Porturilor Maritime S.A. Consequently, an operator who might obtain an authorisation for towage services under the conditions required by the abovementioned Order of the Ministry of Transport, will in practice not be able to conclude a service agreement with the port authority if it does not additionally fulfill its stricter criteria.

Harm to competition. The minimum number of tugboats set by the port authority, which is higher than the minimum number required by the Order of the Ministry of Transport, constitutes an entry barrier to smaller operators who do not have such a large number of tugboats at their disposal. Moreover, large investments are required in order to acquire tugboats.

The minimum number of tugboats has also been subject to an investigation by the Romanian Competition Council with regard to a possible abuse of dominant position by Compania Naţională Administraţia Porturilor Maritime S.A. At the time of writing (March 2016), the investigation is ongoing.

Figure 3.26 shows that the towage tariffs charged in the Port of Consţanta are similar to those charged in other ports throughout Europe. Actually, in some cases, tariffs charged in the Port of Consţanta are below the average tariffs charged by other ports.

Policy makers' objective. The objective of a minimum number of tugboats is that towage services should be provided non-stop, 24 hours a day, 7 days a week. Also, this specific number of tugboats is requested in order to ensure safe navigation.

Recommendation and benefits. The current provision regarding the minimum number of tugboats should be abolished. Instead, a minimum service level should be required by law, such as the maximum ship waiting time for a tugboat. Consequently, each towing operator shall make its own assessment and shall make its own decision regarding the number of tugboats necessary to reach the required service level.

Figure 3.26. **Towage tariffs in different ports throughout Europe**

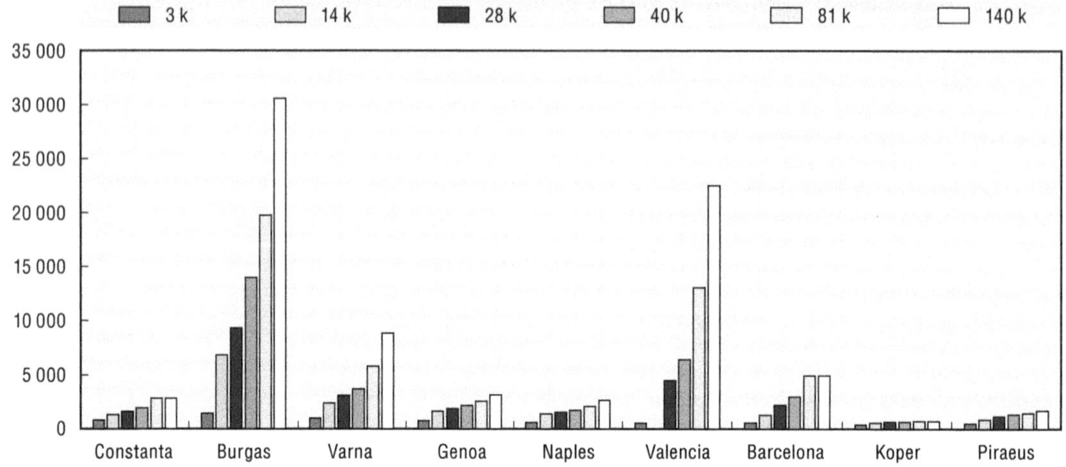

Note: For Burgas and Varna, an average tariff has been determined based on the tariffs of the three port areas of each port. For Valencia and Barcelona, the tariffs used are the maximum rates set by the port authorities.
Source: http://bit.ly/1U4laew, http://bit.ly/1QUCX3H, http://bit.ly/1S1UYNQ, http://bit.ly/1QV3QG7, http://bit.ly/1MkqOkv, http://bit.ly/1Pa4Gcs, http://bit.ly/1QUETcD, http://bit.ly/1WnzIDl (accessed on 7 January 2016).
StatLink http://dx.doi.org/10.1787/888933361689

Towage services shall not be granted directly by the port authority, but instead they should be open to public tender. Introducing a public tendering procedure for towage services is estimated, as shown in Annex No. 3.A5, to generate savings of approx. EUR 3.1 mln a year for the port authority, which is the contracting authority for towage services. This would also be further savings for freight shippers, if the port authority were to pass on the savings to its customers. For the benefits to be passed on to freight shippers, the port authority should implement a cost-based approach in the pricing process of the towage services it provides and the tariffs should also be validated by an independent regulatory body.

Tariffs charged by port authorities

The tariffs covered in this section refer to tariffs on ships that visit Romanian ports for using the port infrastructure (so-called port tariffs).

Generally, ports are considered as having market power or even as being essential facilities. There is a risk that port authorities may abuse their power against their customers, for example by refusing access to infrastructure, to supply a service or to limit the number of competitors in a certain market in which it is also active. Port authorities might also have the power to set their own dues and tariffs for the use of port infrastructure or for other services provided by them above a competitive level. However, the main customers of freight ports tend to be major shipping lines which are often organised into shipping conferences and consortia. This increases their scale and potentially gives them considerable countervailing buying power.[113]

Description of the obstacle

Article 37 of Government Ordinance No. 22/1999 gives port authorities the power to set tariffs for the use of port infrastructure and for other services provided by them. The same article states that tariffs are set by the administration in a non-discriminatory way and that tariff setting is based on the substantiation rules drawn up by the administration.

Currently the ANR with competences regarding port services is part of the Ministry of Transport. The port authorities are also owned by the same Ministry of Transport.

Harm to competition

The lack of transparency in the calculation of the tariffs charged by port authorities may lead to abuses as there is a risk that the tariffs they charge may be disproportionate to the economic value of the services provided.

Supervision of port authorities might not be efficient as the Romanian Naval Authority is insufficiently independent from the port authority, both belonging to the Ministry of Transport. The lack of independence of the regulatory body and the existing conflict of interest may lead to distortions of competition in this sector.

Policy makers' objective

There is no objective justification for the lack of transparency in the calculation of the tariffs charged by port authorities.

Recommendation

We recommend that port authorities set their charges based on a transparent cost-based approach. Furthermore, the autonomy of port authorities in setting charges should be balanced by allowing an independent regulatory body to supervise these charges. For that, we recommend installing an independent supervisory body which has to approve *ex ante* all tariffs set by the port authorities.

The establishment of an independent regulatory body is in line with The Proposal for a Regulation of the European Parliament and of the Council Establishing a Framework on Market Access to Port Services and Financial Transparency of Ports issued by the European Commission in 2013.[114] Article 17 of the adapted version of the proposed regulation states that Member States shall ensure that effective mechanism are in place to handle complaints for all the maritime ports covered by this regulation and, to that and, Member States shall designate one or more bodies which shall be legally distinct from, and functionally independent of, any managing body of the port or providers of port services. Regarding the pricing of port services and port infrastructure tariffs, Articles 13 and 14 of the proposed regulation stipulate that the port service provider shall make available to the independent supervisory body, in the event of a formal complaint and upon request, detailed information on the elements serving as a basis to determine the tariff structure and level, as well as the methodology used for setting those tariffs.

Moreover, the proposed regulation expressly stipulates that, in the event that a Member State retains ownership or control of ports or port managing bodies, it shall ensure an effective structural separation between the functions relating to the supervision and monitoring of the regulation and the activities associated with that ownership or control of the port. The independent supervisory body shall exercise its powers impartially and transparently and with due respect to the right to conduct business freely.

The right to issue compliance certificates with technical rules for shipbuilding

Description of the obstacle

Article 25 of Government Ordinance No. 42/1997 on civil navigation stipulates that compliance with mandatory technical rules for shipbuilding is established by certificates issued by the ANR or by organisations that have concluded agreements with the Ministry of Transport to this effect. Article 26 of the same ordinance stipulates that the Ministry of Transport annually approves and publishes the list of organisations appointed to inspect, survey and issue compliance certificates for ships flying the Romanian flag. However, even if Government Ordinance No. 42/1997 states that the ministry establishes the criteria for choosing the organisations with whom it concludes agreements, the ordinance does not set out any criteria to be fulfilled by those organisations.

European Regulation No. 391/2009 establishes the criteria to be fulfilled by recognised organisations to inspect, survey and issue certification for ships in terms of compliance with the international conventions on maritime safety and the prevention of marine pollution. Only organisations that have gained European Commission recognition under the regulation are allowed to carry out ship inspections and survey activities, as well as issue certificates of compliance within the European Union. The European Commission draws up a list of such recognised organisations and publishes it periodically in the *Official Journal of the European Union.*

Harm to competition

In the absence of clear criteria for the appointment of such institutions, the ANR, which is owned by the Ministry of Transport and acts as both regulator and operator of the market, may distort competition by regulating access to the market, prohibiting the entry of new competitors and charging supra-competitive fees for its services.

The fact that the Ministry of Transport does not publish in a transparent way the criteria applied to select organisations with which it enters into agreements for the delegation of the right to issue certificates of compliance of ships, cannot have any objective justification. The lack of transparency of these criteria reduces competition in the market for certificates of compliance of vessels flying the Romanian flag.

Policy makers' objective

The provision is in line with European Regulation No. 391/2009. However, Romanian legislation does not specify further criteria that the Ministry of Transport considers when concluding an agreement with a recognised organisation for inspection, survey and certification of ships flying the Romanian flag.

Recommendation

The criteria for the appointment of organisations in charge of issuing certificates of compliance with shipbuilding rules should be incorporated in the law and should be fair and non-discriminatory. We recommend that the law is amended by having set the conditions to be met by a recognised organisation to conclude a contract with the Ministry of Transport in order to issue certificates of compliance of ships flying the Romanian flag and to operate in Romania. Those criteria should not be more stringent than those set out in European Regulation No. 391/2009 as they may represent a market entry barrier, thus limiting the number of recognised organisations active in Romania.

Unguided discretion

Use of Romanian flag

Description of the obstacle. Article 3 para.1 of the Order of the Ministry of Transport and Infrastructure No. 250/2011 on the compliance by Romania with its flag state obligations stipulates that before allowing a ship which has been granted the right to fly the Romanian flag to operate, the ANR shall take the measures it considers appropriate to ensure that the ship in question complies with the applicable international rules and regulations, especially by verifying the safety records of the ship by all reasonable means and, if necessary, by consulting with the "losing" flag state (the state under which the ship is no longer registered) in order to establish whether any outstanding deficiencies or safety issues identified by the latter remain unresolved. Nevertheless, the provision does not state expressly the measures to be taken and the means of control in order to ensure the ship's compliance with international ship safety rules, as well as the instances in which the ANR shall consult with the losing flag state.

Harm to competition. The ANR enjoys significant discretion when carrying out this task. This may lead to abuse of power by placing some market operators at a competitive disadvantage in comparison with others. For example, the authority may apply different measures to ship owners in equivalent situations, thereby leading to significant differences of administrative and operative costs for shipowners.

Policy makers' objective. The objective of the provision is to harmonise the national legislation with European legislation. This provision aims to transpose Article 4 of European Directive No. 2009/21/EC on compliance with flag state requirements. However, discretion granted to Member States by European legislation needs to be specified by national law, which has not been done in Romania.

Recommendation. We recommend to amend the provision in order to indicate the activities that the ANR is entitled to carry out in order to verify compliance with safety rules by vessels.

Inspection of maritime vessels flying the Romanian flag

Description of the obstacle. Article 6 para. 1 of the Order of the Ministry of Transport and Infrastructure No. 249/2011 on the inspection, technical supervision and certification of maritime vessels flying the Romanian flag and carrying out international voyages, establishes that the ANR may suspend or terminate the agreement concluded with a recognised authorised organisation in charge of inspecting vessels if it considers that the recognised organisation can no longer be authorised to carry out the tasks even though this organisation meets the minimum criteria established for such activity under Annex 1 of European Regulation No. 391/2009.

Organisations recognised under European Regulation No. 391/2009 are authorised to perform inspection, technical supervision and certification for vessels flying the Romanian flag through agreements concluded by the ANR.

Harm to competition. The Romanian legal provision establishes the sanction of suspending or terminating the agreement of an organisation authorised to provide inspection services of Romanian-flagged vessels, without specifying the conditions under which this can be done. This may lead to a lack of transparency, predictability and possible abuses by the ANR.

Policy makers' objective. The objective is to harmonise the national legislation with European legislation. The provision aims to transpose Article 8 of Directive No. 2009/15/EC, which gives the Member States the possibility to suspend or withdraw authorisation, where a Member State considers that a recognised organisation can no longer be authorised to carry out the tasks on its behalf.

Recommendation. The provision should be amended in order to specify the instances in which the ANR is entitled to suspend or terminate the mandate of an organisation authorised to provide inspection services of Romanian-flagged vessels.

Bunkering oil

Description of the obstacle. According to Article 49 of Methodological Norms of 11 September 2007 for the enforcement of the provisions of Appendix VI to the International Convention for the Prevention of Pollution from Ships (MARPOL) 1973, enforced by Government Decision No. 1105/2007, the ANR has the power to suspend the licence of a supplier of liquid fuels for seagoing ships if it is proven that they have supplied improper liquid fuel which does not fulfill the qualitative requirements regarding air pollution as well as to withdraw the authorisation in case of more than one infringement. Article 50 further provides that if an authority included in the MARPOL list[115] establishes that an inadequate fuel has been supplied from Romania, the ANR may, before suspending or withdrawing its authorisation, warn the supplier to adopt remedies in order to bring the fuel within the designated parameters. The ANR may require the supplier to prove that the remedial measure has been taken and may also suspend or withdraw the authorisation of the liquid fuel supplier if it does not apply remedial measures, continues to supply inadequate liquid fuel or cannot prove that it has applied remedial measures.

Harm to competition. This provision may lead to more advantageous treatment for some bunkering companies. It grants the ANR significant discretion as to whether a company may only be warned or whether its licence should be suspended or withdrawn for supplying inadequate fuel.

Policy makers' objective. The actions of the ANR (warning, suspending or withdrawing the licence) are issued depending on the gravity and the repeatability of the situations in which an improper liquid fuel has been provided. The authority, however, aims to remedy the quality of the improper liquid fuel provided by the bunkering companies and to suspend or withdraw the licence only in cases where remedial measures are not carried out.

Recommendation. We recommend that the relevant provision (Article 50 para. 2) be amended in order to clearly establish the instances in which a warning is the proportional and adequate measure to be taken, as well as the instances that require the suspension or withdrawal of the company's authorisation.

Other problems

Crewing agencies

Description of the obstacle. Crewing agencies carry out the recruitment and placement of crew on vessels. Economic operators wishing to act as crewing agencies must receive an authorisation from the ANR. According to Article 2, para. 3 subparagraph f) from the Annex of Government Decision No. 83/2003, as a condition for authorisation, they must prove that they have already concluded a services agreement or a pre-contractual agreement with a shipowner.

Harm to competition. The requirement to have concluded an agreement or a pre-contractual agreement with a shipowner may discourage entry into the market by those new economic operators who have the required professional competence to act as crewing agencies but who do not have an agreement or a pre-contractual agreement with a ship-owner. This is a kind of chicken and egg dilemma because it is also difficult to get a contract with a shipowner without being a recognised agency.

Policy makers' objective. There is no objective justification for a crewing agency to have an agreement concluded with a shipowner prior to authorisation. According to the Ministry of Transport, the condition aims to be a protection measure for the crew from bankruptcy or liability. However, this justification is rather related to another condition for crewing agencies' authorisation stipulated by the same provision: the establishment of a permanent financial guarantee in the amount of a minimum of USD 100 000.

Recommendation. The contract requirement should be abolished. There is no match between the requirement and the policy objective since shipowners can always cause liability to crew even if the latter has been employed through an authorised crewing agent.

Derogations from technical requirements for inland waterway vessels

Description of the obstacle. Article 7 of the Order of the Ministry of Transport No. 1447/2008 establishing technical requirements for inland waterway vessels gives the ANR the power to grant derogations from the application of all or part of the provisions of the abovementioned order concerning technical requirements for certain categories of inland waterway vessels, depending on vessel capacity. Technical requirements refer to shipbuilding, safety clearance, freeboard and draught marks, manoeuvrability, steering system, engine design and electrical equipment, etc.

Harm to competition. The derogation may grant preferential treatment to some operators in comparison with others.

Policy makers' objective. The objective is to harmonise national legislation with European legislation. This provision is in line with Article 7 of Directive No. 2006/87/EC. The directive enables the Member State to grant derogations to certain categories of vessel, but the Romanian law transposing the directive does not specify any criteria to be met in order to obtain derogation.

Recommendation. The provision regarding the derogations should be amended in order to expressly state the conditions required to be fulfilled by a market operator in order to be granted derogation from the provisions of this order.

Exclusive right of CFR Marfă

Description of the obstacle. In order to co-ordinate the traffic of maritime and inland waterway vessels, to establish the entry/exit order and the transit of vessels, as well as the allocation of berths in the ports of Galaţi, Brăila and Tulcea, co-ordination commissions for the movement of vessels have been established.

The Order of the Ministry of Transport No. 251/2011 sets out the founding of the co-ordination commissions for each port and their structure. The measures established by the commissions are mandatory for all economic operators performing services in the ports of Galaţi, Brăila and Tulcea, such as transport operators, loading/unloading operators, pilotage and towage operators, etc.

Article 5 of the Order of the Ministry of Transport and Infrastructure No. 251/ 2011 on establishing the commissions for the co-ordination of maritime and inland waterway vessel movement in the ports of Galaţi, Brăila and Tulcea stipulates that economic operators who provide loading and unloading services in the ports of Brăila, Galaţi and Tulcea must establish their plan for loading and unloading rail wagons on a daily basis with CFR Marfă, the state-owned rail freight operator.

There are currently other rail freight operators operating in the ports of Galaţi, Brăila and Tulcea in addition to CFR Marfă. Unlike CFR Marfă, they are not involved in scheduling the activities of loading and unloading of wagons but have to comply with the timetable established by their competitor, CFR Marfă.

Harm to competition. Other railway operators may be disadvantaged by the fact that the timetable for loading and unloading rail wagons in the ports mentioned is established by CFR Marfă, their competitor.

Policy makers' objective. This exclusive right to establish the timetable for loading and unloading rail wagons should ensure a more efficient use of port logistics and also guarantee railway transport services safety within the port. Most likely, this provision has been maintained over time since the successor of CFR Marfă, the National Company of Romanian Railways, has historically been the only railway freight operator in the market.

Recommendation. We recommend that the provision should be abolished. The timetable for loading and unloading rail wagons should be established by committees co-ordinating the movement of maritime and inland waterway vessels in the ports of Galaţi, Brăila and Tulcea, so that all rail freight operators transporting goods in these ports benefit from equivalent and non-discriminatory conditions.

Notes

1. NACE codes covered by this study are: H49.2 – Freight rail transport; H49.4 – Freight transport by road and removal services; H50.2 – Sea and coastal freight water transport; H50.4 – Inland freight water transport; H52 –Warehousing and support activities for transportation. The following NACE codes are not covered by this report: H49.1 – Passenger rail; H49.3 – Other passenger land transport; H49.5 – Transport via pipeline; H50.1 – Sea and coastal passenger water transport; H50.3 – Inland passenger water transport; H51 – Air transport; H52.2.3 – Service activities incidental to air transportation; H53 – Postal and courier activities.
2. This definition is taken from OECD, Competition Issues in Road Transport, 2000.
3. Source: The General Transport Master Plan of Romania.
4. The National Union of Romanian Road Hauliers, Road Transport Market, 2008-2015.
5. OECD Economic Studies No. 32, 2001/I, Regulatory Reform in Road Freight.
6. In order to compare regulatory approaches in several countries, the OECD has developed quantitative indicators over various aspects of regulation (on a scale from 0 to 6 from least to most restrictive of competition) which aim to measure the degree of the impact of a regulatory restriction on market mechanisms. The OECD's PMRI for road freight transport was constructed by aggregating detailed information on regulation in relation to two criteria: barriers to entry and price regulation.
7. *www.untrr.ro*.
8. *www.artri.ro*.

9. *www.fort-romania.ro.*
10. *www.apte2002.ro.*
11. *www.atrt.ro.*
12. *www.atrc.ro.*
13. *www.user.ro.*
14. *www.arilog.ro.*
15. *www.rarom.ro.*
16. *www.isctr-mt.ro.*
17. *www.cisr.ro.*
18. *www.arr.ro.*
19. The RO-vignette is a tax charged on motor vehicles for using the national road infrastructure.
20. This definition is taken from the Freight Transport for Development Toolkit: Rail Freight, The International Bank for Reconstruction and Development/The World Bank, 2009.
21. A route can have one, two or more tracks. The length of the railway route is determined by the length of a single line between stations; i.e. even if a route is characterised by several lines, multi-way lines are considered as one line.
22. Source: NIS.
23. Source: The General Transport Master Plan of Romania.
24. See Government Decision No. 73/2012 regarding the approval of the National Railway Company "CFR" Activity Contact for the period 2012-2015.
25. See Government Decision No. 581 of 10 September 1998 regarding the establishment of the National Railway Company "CFR" – S.A. through the reorganisation of the National Company of Romanian Railways.
26. Source: AFER, MoF.
27. Following the adoption of Government Decision No. 46/2013 on the approval of the privatisation strategy of the national company CFR Marfă and the implementation of Government Decision No. 526/2013 for approval of the main conditions of the contract for the transfer of the ownership of a block of the share capital of CFR Marfă.
28. This indicator was constructed by aggregating detailed information on regulation of rail transport based on four criteria: barriers to entry, public ownership, vertical integration and market structure.
29. In 2008 this sector counted 23 462 employees (source: NIS), compared to 13 500 in 2014 (source: MoF).
30. Source: NIS.
31. Source: MoF.
32. *www.atfer.ro.*
33. *www.asifrom.ro.*
34. Pan-European Corridor IV (road and rail) connecting western and southern Europe crossing Bucharest and linking Constanţa via road and rail; Pan-European Corridor VII – the Danube connecting western and eastern Europe; Pan-European Corridor IX connecting northern and southern Europe – crossing Bucharest and linking Constanţa via railway.
35. Its competences and tasks are established by Government Emergency Ordinance No. 21/2011; *www.consiliulferoviar.ro.*
36. Its competences and tasks are established by Government Decision No. 626/1998 and by Government Decision No. 1561/2006; *www.afer.ro.*
37. OLFR is organised and functions according to the provisions of Law No. 55/16.03.2006 on railway safety and of Government Decision No. 1561/01.11.2006, modifying and completing the Government Decision No. 626/1998 on organising and functioning of the Romanian Railway Authority; *www.afer.ro/olfr/.*
38. CENAFER is established by Government Ordinance No. 58/2004; *www.cenafer.ro.*
39. See Art. 19 of Government Ordinance No. 22/1999.

40. Loading/unloading, storage, handling, mooring, sorting, labelling, palletising, ship broker services, bunkering, ship's stores cleaning.

41. Port infrastructure maintenance, signalling, dredging, shipping surveillance, dredging extraction, ship repairs and ship supply.

42. Source: Annual Report Port of Constanţa, 2014.

43. Source: Constanţa Port Operator.

44. Source: The General Transport Master Plan of Romania.

45. The Romanian inland waterways ports are: Murfatlar, Medgidia, Cernavodă, Călăraşi, Olteniţa, Giurgiu, Corabia, Bechet, Calafat, Drobeta Turnu Severin, Orşova, Moldova Veche, as well as the local ports Drencova, Gruia, Cetate, Turnu Măgurele, Zimnicea, Hârşova, Turcoaia, Măcin, Gura Arman, Isaccea, Mahmudia, Ovidiu, Chilia Veche, Feteşti, Tişoviţa, Rast, Baziaş, Luminiţa.

46. Source: The General Transport Master Plan of Romania.

47. Romania allocates EUR 11 300 per km a year for maintenance of the section of the Danube for which it is responsible, compared with a budget of EUR 250 000 per km allocated by Austria. See MoT General Transport Master Plan of Romania.

48. See Government Decision No. 140 of 23 March 1998 on the approval of companies privatisation strategy for the year 1998.

49. ANR is organised according to the provisions of Government Decision no. 1133/2002 and Government Ordinance No. 42/1997 on maritime transport and inland waterway, as amended; *http://portal.rna.ro*.

50. *www.romanian-ports.ro*.

51. *www.apdf.ro*.

52. *www.acn.ro*.

53. The National Company Maritime Ports Administration S.A. Constanţa is a company set up through Romanian Government Decision No.517/1998, altered and completed by Government Decision No. 464/2003, through the reorganisation of the former Autonomous Enterprise "Constanţa Port Administration"; *www.portofconstantza.com/apmc/*.

54. In accordance with the provisions of Government Decision No. 492/2003 and with the international conventions and agreements to which Romania is a party; *www.afdj.ro*.

55. It is established by Government Decision No. 525/1998; *www.radionav.ro*.

56. Subordinated to the Ministry of Transport and works under the provisions of Government Decision No. 33/2003 and Government Decision No. 449/2003; *www.ceronav.ro*.

57. ARSVOM is a public institution with a legal personality founded by Government Decision No. 33/2004 and approved with amendments by Law No. 337/2004; *www.arsvom.ro*.

58. Government Ordinance No. 81/2000 on the registered road vehicle certification of compliance with the technical norms on road safety, environmental protection and category of use according to their destination, through periodic technical inspection.

59. According to Government Ordinance No. 43/1997 and the information posted on the website of the International Transport Forum, in Romania the legal dimensions and weights are the following:

Permissible maximum weights of lorries (in tonnes)

Weight per non-drive axle	Weight per drive axle	Lorry 2 axles	Lorry 3 axles	Road train 4 axles	Road train 5 axles and +	Articulated vehicle 5 axles and +
10	11.5	18	25/26 (46)	36	40	40/44 (13)

Permissible maximum dimensions of lorries

Height	Width	Length		
		Lorry or trailer	Road train	Articulated vehicle
4 m	2.55 m	12 m	18.75 m	16.50 m

60. MoE Order No. 2737/2012 on the procedure related to the appointment of institutions performing checks on superstructure built on top of vehicles transporting dangerous goods, as well as packaging.
61. MoT Order No. 980/2011 on the application of the provisions regarding the organisation and performance of road transport and related activities established by the Government Ordinance (GO) No. 27/2011 on road transport, as further amended and supplemented.
62. As shown in the economic overview, the Romanian road freight sector in 2014 mainly consisted of small companies, with about 91% of companies having less than 10 employees.
63. According to information received from the National Union of Romanian Road Hauliers.
64. Order No. 181/2008 of the MoT on the approval of Regulations concerning the conditions for installation, repair and verification of tachographs and speed limitation devices, as well as for the authorisation of the economic operators performing such activities.
65. European Regulation No. 995/2010 laying down the obligations for operators who place timber and timber products on the market.
66. Law No. 265/2008 on the management of traffic safety on road infrastructure and Order No. 358/2012 on the approval of Guidelines related to measures to improve traffic safety on road infrastructure, implementing Directive 2008/96/EC on road infrastructure safety management.
67. Government Ordinance No. 43/1997 on the road regime, as further amended and supplemented.
68. *http://bit.ly/1RwcGGA*.
69. Directive No. 2012/34/EU establishing a single European railway area.
70. The First Railway Package includes i) Directive No. 2001/12/EC amending Directive No. 91/440/EEC on the development of the Community's railways, ii) Directive No. 2001/13/EC amending Directive No. 95/18/EC on the licensing of railway undertakings, and iii) Directive No. 2001/14 for infrastructure capacity allocation and charging, and safety certification.
71. The Second Railway Package includes: i) Directive No. 2004/51 further amending Directive No. 91/440/EEC; ii) Directive No. 2004/49/E on safety on the Community's railways; iii) Directive No. 2004/50/EC amending inter-operability Directives No. 96/48/EC and 2001/16/EC; and iv) Regulation No. 881/2004 establishing a European railway agency.
72. Since 2011, Romania has fulfilled the requirement of establishing an independent regulatory body, as the Rail Supervisory Council is no longer a part of the Ministry of Transport, but under the aegis of the Romanian Competition Council.
73. The full title is Order of MLPTL (the Ministry of Public Works, Transport and Housing) No. 461/2003.
74. Network Rail must observe The Network Code, Part J – Changes to Access Rights, Article 4, regarding the failure to use cases.
75. According to Article 4.1.1 UK infrastructure manager Network Code, Part J.
76. A train slot is a licence that allows its holder, a railway company, to run a train on a specific section of track at a specific time.
77. The working timetable shows all movements on the rail network including freight trains, empty trains and those coming in and out of depots. It also includes the unique identification code for each train, and intermediate times for journeys, including which stations a train is not scheduled to stop at.
78. A quantum access right means any right under an access agreement in respect of a number (or quantum) of train slots in any specified period (including rights to train slots in respect of additional trains or relief services), and includes part of such a right.
79. The facilities are mentioned in Annex 2 of Government Ordinance No. 89/2003.
80. Tariffs for specific services are covered by Annex 23, List and Level of the Charges for Related Activities and Other Activities, to the CFR Network Statement.
81. According to CFR Marfă's website and as mentioned in The Romanian General Transport Master Plan, Chapter 5, Railway Transport (point 8.1.28), CFR Marfă owns 26 freight terminals.
82. Romanian Competition Council Decision No. 119/2006, upheld by the Romanian Supreme Court of Justice.
83. Commission staff working document impact assessment accompanying the document Proposal for a Directive of the European Parliament and of the Council amending Directive 2012/34/EU.

84. Ibid.
85. *http://bit.ly/1nqL4KM.*
86. FRAND is an abbreviation for "fair, reasonable and non-discriminatory".
87. *http://bit.ly/1oE5j8Y.*
88. *http://bit.ly/1Ssmsit; http://bit.ly/1o52Ung.*
89. *http://bit.ly/1QDuejn.*
90. The Romania General Transport Master Plan, Chapter 5, Railway Transport.
91. It should be noted that in Romania ownership and management of the intermodal terminals were transferred from the infrastructure manager to CFR Marfă, creating an atypical situation unlike that in many other European countries, as results from Diomis – Evolution of intermodal rail/road traffic in Central and Eastern European Countries by 2020, page 26.
92. Report from the Commission to the Council and the European Parliament – Fourth report on monitoring development of the rail market, 2014.
93. Sweden has managed to introduce intra-modal competition for the provision of most services.
94. Law 388/2000.
95. Realising the Potential of GB Rail -Final Independent Report of the Rail Value for Money Study-Detailed Report notably page 30 and page 31.
96. A modal share is the percentage of travelers using a particular type of transportation or number of trips using said type; in freight transportation, this may be measured in mass.
97. EWS is the former UK rail freight company, sold to Deutsche Bahn in 2007.
98. *http://bit.ly/1T4b5Og.*
99. Office of Rail and Road, as of writing this report (March 2016).
100. According to Eurostat, about 40% of the total railway network has been electrified.
101. CFR SA Network Statement 2015 indicates that 99% of the rail network is electrified on Pan European Corridor IV and 87% of the rail network is electrified on Pan European Corridor IX.
102. According to *www.ertms.net/*, the ERTMS Benefits Section.
103. The European Commission is currently following a "corridor-based approach", with Romania included in Rail Freight Corridor 7 (RFC7). Corridor 7 has been defined to run through the Prague-Vienna/Bratislava-Budapest-Bucharest-Constanța and Vidin-Sofia-Thessaloniki-Athens axis According to the Implementation Plan of Rail Freight Corridor 7 "Orient Corridor" based on Regulation (EU) No. 913/2010 of the European Parliament and of the Council of 22 September 2010 concerning a European rail network for competitive freight. The management board of RFC7 considers investment planning along the corridor a very important matter and an investment plan has been drawn up, including a deployment plan for ERTMS. ERTMS requires an infrastructure update before it can be introduced to the whole territory of Romania, not only within the Romanian part of RFC7.
104. MoT Order No. 410/1999 on the authorisation for testing and certifying railway products used in construction activities, upgrade, operation, maintenance and repair of rail infrastructure and rolling stock, railway and subway.
105. Ibid.
106. Pilotage, towing, mooring, dredging, bunkering, cargo handling, passenger services, waste reception facilities.
107. *http://bit.ly/1LtTxD7.*
108. According to Article 2 of Directive 2009/15/EC, "international conventions" means the International Convention for the Safety of Life at Sea of 1 November 1974, (SOLAS 74) with the exception of chapter XI-2 of the Annex thereto, the International Convention on Load Lines of 5 April 1966 and the International Convention for the Prevention of Pollution from Ships of 2 November 1973 (Marpol), together with the protocols and amendments thereto, and the related codes of mandatory status in all Member States, in their up-to-date version.
109. Romanian Competition Council, press release, November 2012, *http://bit.ly/1oqNGcS.*
110. *http://bit.ly/1QJpHw6*, accessed on 17 February 2016.

111. Authority for Consumers & Markets' website, *http://bit.ly/1oxc9gj*.

112. PwC (2013), Study aimed at supporting an impact assessment on: "Measures to enhance the efficiency and quality of port services in the EU", submitted to: European Commission Directorate-General for Mobility and Transport Unit B3 Ports & Inland Navigation, page 42, *http://bit.ly/1QJnEbd*.

113. The global container shipping sector is a concentrated one, with the five largest container shippers having a cumulated market share of almost 50%, according to Statista (2016), leading the ship operator's share of the world liner fleet as of 18 January 2016: *http://bit.ly/1Ws2ORL*.

114. *http://bit.ly/1QllKmP*.

115. 153 states are currently signed up to thenotes MARPOL Protocol (1973/1978), *https://imo.amsa.gov.au/public/parties/marpol78.html*.

References

Access to Port Services, COM/2001/0035, OJ C 154E, 29.5.2001, p. 290-296.

ATENCO (2001), *Analysis of the cost structures of the main TEN ports*, Public Final Report, Project funded by the European Commission under the transport RTD programme of the fourth Framework programme.

Brunet, E., Guérin-Schneider and F. Bonnet (2002), "Impact of a new legislation on the water market and competition in France" in *Water Science and Technology: Water Supply*, École nationale du genie rural, des eaux et des forêts (ENGREF) *Working Paper*, IWA Publishing.

Cullinane K. (ed.) (2010), "International Handbook of Maritime Economics", Edinburgh Napier University, UK.

DB *Schenker Environmental Report*, 2012.

Drew, J. and C.A. Nash (2011), "Vertical separation of railway infrastructure – does it always make sense?", Institute for Transport Studies, University of Leeds, *Working Paper* 594, Leeds, UK.

ECMT (2007), *Competitive Tendering of Rail Services*.

European Commission (2013), *Proposal for a Regulation of the European Parliament and of the Council establishing a framework on market access to port services and financial transparency of ports*, COM/2013/0296, *http://bit.ly/1QllKmP*.

European Commission (2013), *Communication from the Commission – Ports: An engine for growth*, COM/2013/0295.

European Commission (2007), *Communication from the Commission – Communication on a European Ports Policy*, COM/2007/0616.

European Commission (2007), COM (2007) 616 final – *Communication on a European Ports Policy* (2007)

European Commission (2006), COM(2006) 189 final:

European Commission (2004), *Proposal for a Directive of the European Parliament and of the Council on market access to port services*, COM/2004/0654.

European Commission (1997), Directorate-General for Mobility and Transport, *Green Paper on Sea Ports and Maritime Infrastructure*.

European Countries by 2020, Romania, January 2010.

European Union (2015), *Romania's General Transport Master Plan and Rail System, doi:10.2861/20058*.

First railway package (2001), Report of the Commission to the European Parliament, the Council, the European Economic and Social Committee and the Committee of the regions on the implementation of the first railway package – ANNEX 11 The Rail Freight Transport Market. For Report: *http://eur-lex.europa.eu/legal-content/EN/TXT/?uri=CELEX:52006DC0189*. For Annex 11: *http://ec.europa.eu/transport/modes/rail/doc/communication_implementation_1st_rail_pack_annexes.pdf*.

Fumitoshi Mizutani and Shuki Uranishi (2013), "Does vertical separation reduce cost? An empirical analysis of the rail industry in European and East Asian OECD Countries", *Journal of Regulatory Economics* 43, pp. 31-59, *DOI 10.1007/s11149-012-9193-4*.

Government of Romania (2015), *General Transport Master Plan*, Chapter 5, Railway Transport. *http://eur-lex.europa.eu/legal-content/EN/TXT/?uri=CELEX:52006DC0189*.

Halder, M. (2015), "Technical measures for dedicated use of the electrical brake and the effect on energy consumption", presentation held at the UIC workshop on energy recovery held on 29 September 2015 in Madrid.

International Energy Agency (IEA) (2015), *Railway Handbook 2015 Energy Consumption and CO_2 Emissions*, IEA, Paris.

International Union of Railways (UIC) (2010), *Developing Infrastructure & Operating Models for Intermodal Shift (Diomis)*, Evolution of intermodal rail/road traffic in Central and Eastern

Koske, I., I.Wanner, R. Bitetti and O. Barbiero (2014), "The 2013 update of the OECD product market regulation indicators: Policy insights for OECD and non-OECD countries", *OECD Economics Department Working Papers*, OECD, Paris.

Lodge, Tony (2013), *Rail's Second Chance – Putting competition back on track*, Centre for Policy Studies, London, pp 36-37.

OECD (2014), "Evaluation of competitive impacts of government interventions", Working Party No. 2 on Competition and Regulation, DAF/COMP/WP2 (2014)7, 24 February 2014.

OECD (2014), "Evaluation of competitive impacts of government interventions", Working Party No. 2 on Competition and Regulation, DAF/COMP/WP2(2014)7, 24 February 2014.

OECD (2013), *Recent Developments in Rail Transportation Services*, DAF/COMP(2013)24.

OECD (2011), *Competition in Ports and Port Services*, Policy Roundtable, OECD, Paris.

OECD (2000), *Policy Roundtables – Competition Issues in Road Transport*: *www.oecd.org/regreform/sectors/2379173.pdf*.

Pittman, Russell (2005), "Structural Separation to Create Competition? The Case of Freight Railways", *Review of Network Economics*, Vol. 4, de Gruyter, Berlin, pp.181-196.

Pollitt, Michael G. and Andrew S.J. Smith (2002), "The restructuring and privatisation of British Rail: Was it really that bad?", *Fiscal Studies*, Vol. 23/4, Institute for Fiscal Studies, London, pp. 463-502.

Price, Waterhouse, Cooper (2013) Impact assessment on: "Measures to enhance the efficiency and quality of port services in the EU", submitted to: European Commission Directorate-General for Mobility and Transport Unit B3 Ports & Inland Navigation, *http://bit.ly/1QJnEbd*.

PricewaterhouseCoopers (PwC), Study aimed at supporting an impact assessment on: "Measures to enhance the efficiency and quality of port services in the EU", submitted to: European Commission Directorate-General for Mobility and Transport Unit B3 Ports & Inland Navigation, 2013.

PwC (2013), Study aimed at supporting an impact assessment on: "Measures to enhance the efficiency and quality of port services in the EU", submitted to: European Commission Directorate-General for Mobility and Transport Unit B3 Ports & Inland Navigation.

Statista (2016), "Leading ship operator's share of the world liner fleet as of 18 January, 2016", at *http://bit.ly/1Ws2ORL* (accessed on 16 January 2016).

SvitzerWijsmuller A/S and Adsteam Marine LTD, *A report on the proposed acquisition by SvitzerWijsmulle of Adsteam Marine Ltd*, Competition Commission, 2007

ANNEX 3.A1

Plates

Recommendation

The provision should be abolished and any information requirements related to the vehicle's dimensions should be dealt with in documentation such as the vehicle identity card or the *periodical technical inspection* certificate, which should be carried by the vehicle driver.

Estimates of the benefits arising from abolishing the provision

The provision regarding displaying the plate came into effect on 1 January 2014 and was applied to the total number of freight vehicles with a maximum weight > 3.5 tonnes registered in Romania in 2014.

According to the data provided by the RAR, they performed measuring operations for a number of 153 630 vehicles in 2014. According to the NIS, lorries transporting goods represent 63% of the total freight vehicles with maximum weight > 3.5 tonnes, road tractors represent 8% and trailers and semi-trailers represent 9% of the total freight vehicles with maximum weight > 3.5 tonnes (See Table 3.A1.1).

Table 3.A1.1. **Total number of plates by category of vehicle (2014)**

	2014
Total freight vehicles with maximum weight > 3.5 tonnes, of which:	153 630
Lorries[1]	96 725
Road tractors	12 792
Trailers and semi-trailers	44 113

1. According to the NIS, lorries transporting goods include both light commercial vehicles (70%) and specialised vehicles (30%).

Source: RAR, NIS, Registered road vehicles (end of the year), by category of road vehicle, by type of ownership, by macro regions, development regions and counties (database), *http://bit.ly/21YNinL*, Eurostat, Road transport equipment – Stock of vehicles (database), *http://bit.ly/1vbibQq*.

Thus, in order to comply with the plate requirement, Romanian transport operators were equipped with plates generating a total cost of approximately EUR 6.3 million (See Table 3.A1.2). This figure refers to a one-time operation that took place in 2014.

Savings may be achieved by abolishing the plate requirement, given that this requirement also applies to newly registered freight vehicles with a maximum weight > 3.5 tonnes. As this figure does not exist, we referred to Eurostat data available until 2012

Table 3.A1.2. **Registered road freight vehicles with maximum weight > 3.5 tonnes**

	Number of freight transport vehicles with maximum weight > 3.5 tonnes	Tariff for measuring operations (LEI)	Tariff for measuring operations (EUR)	Tariff for plate (LEI)	Tariff for plate (EUR)	Total cost (LEI)	Total cost (EUR)
Light commercial vehicles	67 708	92.20	20.49	43	9.56	9 154 122	2 034 625
Specialised vehicles	29 017	199.80	44.40	43	9.56	7 045 328	1 565 757
Road tractors	12 792	199.80	44.40	43	9.56	3 105.898	690 256
Trailers and semi-trailers	44 113	169.60	37.69	43	9.56	9 378.424	2 084 339
Total cost						28 683 771	6 374 978

Source: NIS, Registered road vehicles (end of the year), by category of road vehicle, by type of ownership, by macro regions, development regions and counties (database), *http://bit.ly/21YNinL*, Eurostat, Road transport equipment – Stock of vehicles (database), *http://bit.ly/1vbibQq*, RAR's website, *http://bit.ly/1U3fEYT* (accessed on 13 April 2016),Musliu şi Asociaţii calculations.

showing that the total number of freight vehicles with a maximum weight > 3.5 tonnes corresponds to approximately 30% of the total number of freight transport vehicles in circulation.[1] Therefore, we used the 0.3 Eurostat coefficient, applying it to the total number of newly registered freight transport vehicles in 2015.[2] According to this coefficient, a total of 26 710 vehicles with a maximum weight > 3.5 tonnes were registered in Romania in 2015. These vehicles were equipped with plates generating a total cost of approximately EUR 1.14 million (mln) a year (see Table 3.A1.3). Assuming that this figure stays the same in the future, EUR 1.14 mln annually corresponds to the savings for Romanian freight transport operators coming from abolishing the plate requirement for newly registered vehicles with a maximum weight > 3.5 tonnes.[3]

Table 3.A1.3. **New vehicles registered for freight transport in 2015**

	New registrations of freight transport vehicles in 2015	New registrations of freight transport vehicles with maximum weight > 3.5 tonnes in 2015	Tariff for measuring operations (LEI)	Tariff for measuring operations (EUR)	Tariff for plate (LEI)	Tariff for plate (EUR)	Total cost (LEI)	Total cost (EUR)
Light commercial vehicles	34 688	10 406	92.20	20.49	43	9.56	1 406 937	312 653
Specialised vehicles	14 866	4 460	199.80	44.40	43	9.56	1 082 854	240 634
Road tractors	13 862	4 159	199.80	44.40	43	9.56	1 009 708	224 380
Trailers and semi-trailers	25 616	7 685	169.60	37.69	43	9.56	1 633 788	363 064
Total cost							5 133 288	1 140 731

Source: NIS, *New registrations of vehicles for transport of goods, by macro regions, development regions and counties*, *http://bit.ly/1YvKLvP*, RAR's website, *http://bit.ly/1U3fEYT* (accessed on 13 April 2016).

Notes

1. Eurostat, Road transport equipment – Stock of vehicles (database), *http://bit.ly/1vbibQq*.
2. NIS, *New registrations of road vehicles for transport of goods* (database), *http://bit.ly/1Ohytzt*.
3. According to RAR, some freight vehicles are already equipped with the manufacturer plate, so the savings might be smaller than estimated.

ANNEX 3.A2

Copy of road transport licence

Recommendation

The provision should be modified. Where the licence is issued for a 10-year period, there is no need to impose an annual renewal. The copy should be issued at the same time as the licence and it should be made available for the same period of time as the duration of the licence to which it refers, i.e. 10 years. Furthermore, there is no reason to require specific copies for the registration number of the vehicle. Moreover, the cost of the copy should not exceed the administrative cost of issuing it.

Estimates of the benefits arising from modifying the provision

Methodology: comparison with data from other similar product markets in Romania.

One copy of the road freight transport licence currently costs RON 260 (approximately EUR 57.8).[1] The cost of issuing a copy of the licence should reflect the actual cost to be incurred by the Romanian Road Transport Authority (ARR) for delivering this service, including, for example, the cost of the paper, photocopying and the workforce, while excluding the cost of other inputs such as, for example, document verification given that the ARR is in charge of issuing the original road transport licence.

A possible comparator test can be obtained by reviewing the cost carried by the National *Trade Register Office (NTRO) when issuing certified copies, for example, registration of a company's Statute of Incorporation, in accordance with Government Decision* No. 425 of 20 May 2014. These copies are issued at a tariff of RON 4 + RON 0.2/page, resulting in a total cost of RON 4.2 (approximately EUR 1) for a page.

Taking as a benchmark the cost sustained by the NTRO *when issuing a certified copy, this results (in our sample case) in an overcharge for freight transport operators of approximately EUR 57/copy of licence.*

$$\mathbf{RON\,260 - RON\,4.2 = RON\,255.\,8} \tag{3}$$

$$\mathbf{RON\,255.8\,/\,4.5\frac{EUR}{RON}}\left(\boldsymbol{average\ exchange\ rate}\right) = \mathbf{EUR\,56,8 \approx EUR\,57} \tag{4}$$

As shown in Table 3.A2.1 below, the average number of the copies of road freight transport licence issued by ARR over the period 2012-2014 was 124 611.[2]

FTOB (freight transport operators benefit) = EUR 57 (the overcharge/copy of licence) * 124 611 (the average number of copies of road freight transport licence issued by ARR) = EUR 7.1 million (5)

Table 3.A2.1. **Copies of road freight transport licence (end of year: 2012-14)**

	2012	2013	2014
Copies of road freight transport licence issued bv ARR	119 898	123 979	129 956
Average number of freight transport vehicles		124 611	

Source: Data provided by ARR.

The benefits from modifying the provision are estimated at around EUR 13.13 million a year. This figure results from multiplying the average number of freight transport vehicles by the maximum weight > 3.5 tonnes registered in Romania over the past three years with the overcharge paid by freight transport operators for one copy of the licence.

The benefits arising from modifying the provision should have a significant impact on freight transport operators' costs and may lower the overall cost of freight transport services if these savings are passed on to customers. Moreover, extending the validity of the copy of the licence for the entire duration of the transport licence, i.e. 10 years, will remove an unnecessary administrative burden for freight transport operators who are currently forced to renew the copy of their transport licence annually.

Notes

1. Romanian Road Authority – ARR.
2. Our first estimates were based on data of NIS and Eurostat which are not in line with the data provided by ARR.

ANNEX 3.A3

Braking energy

Recommendation

Create appropriate legal framework: Compensation for regenerative braking energy should be introduced in the Romanian Law on Energy No. 123/2014, due to its ability to save energy consumption costs for railway freight transport operators. All metered train operators should pay for net energy consumption after taking into account the regenerated energy. This should imply changes to the existing infrastructure and acquisition of new locomotives.

Estimates of the benefits arising from creating an appropriate legal framework

Methodology: effects of regulatory reform elsewhere

Set forth below are some rough data about electricity supply and consumption in the Romanian rail freight transport sector, as well as a summary of the European experience in savings generated by regenerative braking.

In Romania, electricity for rail transport operators is supplied exclusively by CFR Electrificare, a subsidiary of CFR SA, which operates as the only supplier of traction electricity for the entire rail network as of 1 September 2014. The company also provides other services such as electrified railroad maintenance and operation of electrification facilities. Therefore, the turnover of CFR Electrificare does not correspond completely to the activity of energy supply, but also includes revenues from other services. Hence, we took into account in our analysis only the revenues from the account related to the sales of goods. According to its Profit & Loss Statement for the year 2014, this company generated revenues from sales of goods of approximately EUR 23.5 million (see Table 3.A3.1). We assume that these revenues cover only the revenues generated from supplying electricity to railway transport operators during the months of September to December 2014, the other revenues being derived from services and being in another account. The significant difference between the revenues obtained by CFR Electrificare from sales of goods in 2013 compared with those obtained in 2014, when CFR Electrificare became the exclusive supplier of energy for railway transport operators in Romania, supports our conclusion.

Table 3.A3.1. **Revenues from sales of goods of CFR Electrificare**

	2013 (RON)	2014 (RON)	2014 (EUR)
Revenues from sales of goods (acc. 707) CFR Electrificare	10 876	105 663 899	23 585 691

Source: CFR Electrificare Profit & Loss financial statement, available on *www.electrificarecfr.ro*.

The estimated value of the annual energy consumption of rail operators (both freight and passengers) is approximately EUR 70.7 million (See Table 3.A3.2). This estimated figure is obtained by multiplying the revenues from sales of goods obtained by CFR Electrificare in the period covering September to December 2014 (4 months) by 3 in order to estimate the annual revenues.

Table 3.A3.2. **Estimated revenues from traction energy of CFR Electrificare for 1 year**

	1 Sep-31 to Dec 2014 – 4 months (RON)	1 year (RON)	1 year (EUR)
Revenues from traction energy (freight and passengers)	105 663 899	316 991 697	70 757 075

Source: Musliu şi Asociaţii calculations.

As shown in Table 3.A3.3 below, the share of rail freight transport in Romania is around 25% of total railway traffic, the balance of 75% being represented by rail passenger transport. In Table 3.A3.3 below, we have used the above coefficient of 24.4%/75.6% between rail freight and passenger transport to calculate the estimated value of the annual energy consumption of rail freight transport operators. This corresponds to approximately EUR 17.26 million.

Table 3.A3.3. **Railway traffic in Romania in the period 2006-14 by type of train**

Railway traffic in Romania by type of train (thousand train-kilometres)	2006	2007	2008	2009	2010	2011	2012	2013	2014	Average percentage of traffic by type of train
Total	104 374	95 134	92 865	88 994	86 271	92 556	90 124	82 431	77 802	100%
Freight trains	35 743	25 873	23 061	17 200	19 088	21 464	20 844	18 922	17 749	24.4%
Percentage of freight trains	34.25%	27.20%	24.83%	19.33%	22.13%	23.19%	23.13%	22.95%	22.81%	
Passenger trains	68 631	69 261	69 804	71 794	67 184	71 092	69 280	63 509	60 053	75.6%
Percentage of passenger trains	65.75%	72.80%	75.17%	80.67%	77.88%	76.81%	76.87%	77.05%	77.19%	

Source: Eurostat, *Train movements* (database), *http://bit.ly/1yussbN*.

Table 3.A3.4. **Estimated revenues from traction energy for freight trains of CFR Electrificare**

	1 year (EUR)
Revenues from traction energy (both freight and passengers)	70 757 075
Revenues from traction energy (freight)	17 264 726
Revenues from traction energy (passengers)	53 492 349

Source: Musliu şi Asociaţii calculations.

It is a fact that regenerative braking reduces energy consumption, since through this form of braking rail operators put energy back into the network.

In our research covering European experience of this form of braking, we found that savings vary in accordance with the type of rolling stock used by operators – regional traffic, long distance or freight traffic (Halder, 2015). Generally, the potential of regenerative braking in freight trains is lower than in passenger trains as freight trains have the disadvantage of being much longer and heavier, carrying a larger mass to brake by unpowered axles. According to a measurement made by the Deutsche Bahn Group in the German rail network regarding freight trains, in 2011 this company saved 5.1% of its annual energy consumption by recouping energy produced during braking (DB Schenker, 2012).

Also, in 2015, London finished testing a system that collects and recycles energy generated by its underground trains when braking and Transport for London, the London transport authority stated that it is saving up to 5% on its annual energy bill.[1] On the basis of these findings, the creation of an appropriate legal framework for energy compensation through regenerative braking may lead to benefits for rail freight operators in Romania of around EUR 0.9 million.

$$\text{FTOB} = \mathbf{0.05 \times EUR\,17\,264\,726 = EUR\,863\,236.3} \quad (5)$$

Notes

1. UK Government, *http://bit.ly/1U3m76b*.

ANNEX 3.A4

Pilotage services

Recommendation

Create appropriate legal framework: Pilotage services shall not be granted through direct entrustment, but instead they should be tendered based on fair and non-discriminatory terms to guarantee competition for the market. Charges may be established by the port authority but shall be cost-oriented. Once the charges are established, they shall be validated by an independent regulatory body. Moreover, the law should not impose a minimum number of pilots per port, but instead it should require a minimum service level, such as maximum ship waiting time for pilots to be on board.

Estimates of the benefits arising from creating an appropriate legal framework

Methodology: comparison with data from other geographic markets and effects of the regulatory reform elsewhere.

Set forth in Table 3.A4.1 below are the tariffs for pilotage services applied in different ports of Europe located in Romania, Bulgaria, Italy, Spain, Turkey and Slovenia expressed in EUR currency for 6 different categories of ship gross tonnage – 5 000, 10 000, 38 000, 75 000, 90 000 and 120 000 tonnes.

Table 3.A4.1. **Pilotage tariffs throughout different ports in Europe by gross tonnage**

Gross tonnage (GT)	Consţanta	Burgas	Varna	Mersin	Genoa	Napoli	Valencia	Barcelona	Koper	Average tariff
5k	593	350	404	381	305	293	60	228	221	319
10k	883	525	618	680	502	483	106	275	308	493
38 k	2 179	2 415	2 298	2 473	979	998	351	694	648	1 472
75 k	3 903	4 912	4 518	-	1 908	1 530	676	1 190	1 080	2 465
90 k	4 583	5 930	5 418	-	2 140	1 663	807	1 419	1 188	2 893
120 k	5 933	7 950	7 218	-	2 837	2 062	1 069	1 559	1 512	3 768

Source: Relevant port websites: *http://bit.ly/1QJpHw6*, *http://bit.ly/1TLkDxw*, *http://bit.ly/1V9lEik*, *http://bit.ly/2522pvA*, *http://bit.ly/21tjHwV*, *http://bit.ly/1YVR8bM*, *http://bit.ly/21tkMoC*, *http://bit.ly/1TLmxOJ* accessed on 7 January 2016.

The tariffs are based on the ship's registered tonnage.

According to Figure 3.A4.1, the tariffs for pilotage services charged in Consţanta are 2 or 3 times higher than those charged in other EU similar ports in terms of the volume of the goods handled, such as Barcelona, Valencia and Genoa (see Figure 3.A4.2).

Currently, Compania Naţională Administraţia Porturilor Maritime S.A. (CN APM) provides pilotage services through four pilotage operators, although services are ultimately

Figure 3.A4.1. **Pilotage tariffs throughout different ports in Europe**

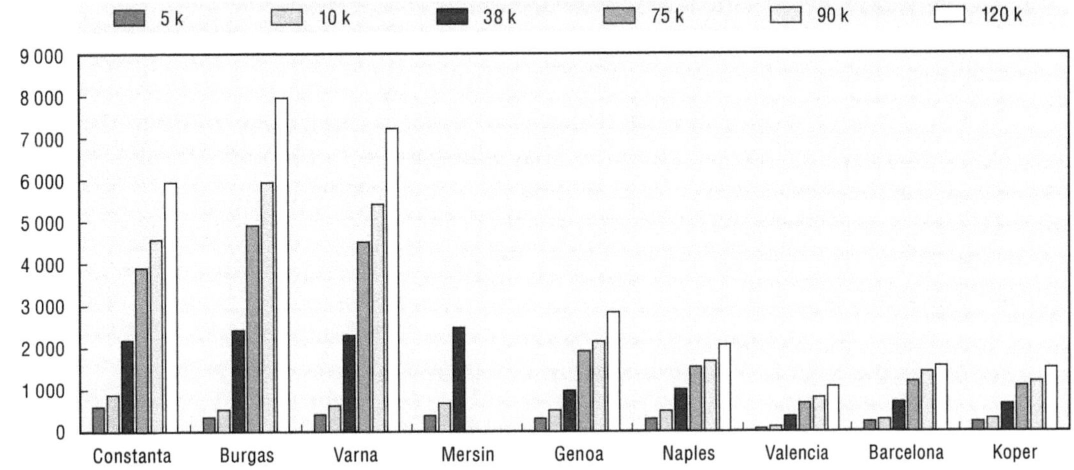

Note: For Burgas and Varna, an average tariff has been determined based on the tariffs of the two port areas for Burgas/for the five port areas for Varna. For Mersin an average is also used between the tariffs for container vessels and the tariffs for other cargo vessels. For Valencia and Barcelona the tariffs used are the maximum rates set by the port authorities.

Source: Relevant port websites: *http://bit.ly/1QJpHw6*, *http://bit.ly/1TLkDxw*, *http://bit.ly/1V9lEik*, *http://bit.ly/2522pvA*, *http://bit.ly/21tjHwV*, *http://bit.ly/1YVR8bM*, *http://bit.ly/21tkMoC*, *http://bit.ly/1TLmxOJ* accessed on 7 January 2016.

StatLink http://dx.doi.org/10.1787/888933361697

Figure 3.A4.2. **Volume of goods handled in different ports in Europe in 2014**

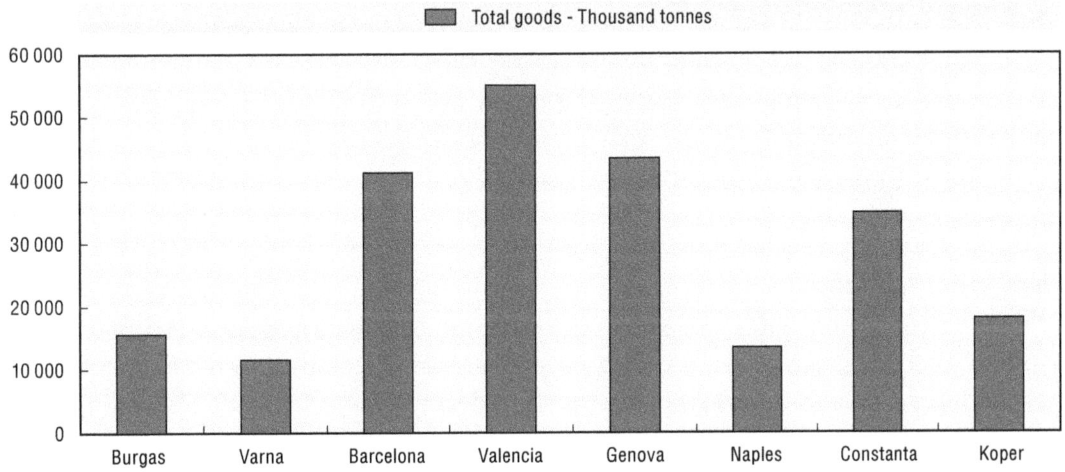

Source: Eurostat, Goods (gross weight) – Annual data – All ports – by direction (database), *http://bit.ly/1yussbN*.

StatLink http://dx.doi.org/10.1787/888933361708

billed to freight shippers directly by CN APM. The pilotage tariffs are set artificially by CN APM without the charges applied being supported by any study on the costs involved for delivering these services.

The introduction of a more transparent procedure such as public tendering in order to hire pilotage services should ensure more reliable, better quality services for freight shippers and lower costs for CN APM. Furthermore, the establishment of an independent regulatory body to monitor the activity of CN APM when setting pilotage tariffs may contribute to further reducing these tariffs. For the full scope of this recommendation to be applied and the savings to be passed on to freight shippers, a cost-based approach should be implemented.

A European Conference of Ministers of Transport (ECMT) paper (ECMT, 2007) on competitive tendering of rail service showed that in Germany following tendering procedures the special regional authorities which were responsible for planning, managing and procuring regional rail transport realised savings of 20%.

The total turnover of pilotage operators in 2014 was approximately EUR 12.9 million (see Table 3.A4.2). Taking into consideration that pilotage services are billed by CN APM and it retains 25% of the services value for providing the right for pilotage operators to carry out pilotage services in the Port of Consţanta, the total turnover of pilotage operators represents 75% of the pilotage market value. Therefore, in 2014, the market value was approximately EUR 17.2 million.

Table 3.A4.2. **Pilotage market value in the period 2012-14**

Year	Pilotage operators total turnover (million EUR)	Pilotage market value (million EUR)
2012	11.6	15.4
2013	12.6	16.8
2014	12.9	17.2

Source: Ministry of Finance, *http://bit.ly/1QxjYPO*, Musliu şi Asociaţii calculations.

The freight shipper's benefit is calculated as follows:

$$FSB = \left(\rho + \frac{1}{2}|\epsilon|\rho^2\right)R \qquad (6)$$

where FSB is the freight shipper's benefit, ρ is the percentage change in price related to restriction, R is the sector revenue and |∈| is absolute value of elasticity of demand.

For the price change we use the relevant estimation for the experience with competitive tendering in Germany (20%) provided by ECMT (2007).

In order to assess the elasticity of demand for pilotage services, we used two different approaches.

The "wide" approach

The starting point in this approach is the substitutability between ports. Firstly, it should be noted that freight shippers' demand for port services is derived from the demand for transportation of goods from a point of origin to a destination point. The point of origin and the destination point are those that mainly set the substitutability between ports. There are also others factors to be considered when establishing the substitutability of ports, such as the ability to handle different freight loads and water depth in the port basins.

Given the geographical context, the Port of Consţanta may face competitive constraints, especially from Bulgarian or Turkish ports, for situations where the destination point is a landlocked country in Central or Eastern Europe. Actually, few constraints are likely to come from Bulgarian ports because of the low level of modernisation, limited capacity and their lack of ability to handle certain cargos (OECD, 2011). Also, the water depth in the port basins in the Port of Varna is almost two times lower than the water depth in the Port of Consţanta.

Within the *ATENCO: Analysis of the Cost Structure of the main TEN-Ports*, research project for the European Commission (2001), port elasticities were estimated for the container sector. The price elasticities for selected northwest European container ports are shown in Table 3.A4.3.

Table 3.A4.3. **Price elasticities of 10% change in port dues**

Port	Price elasticity
Bremen ports	4.4
Hamburg	3.1
Rotterdam	1.5
Antwerp	4.1
Le Havre	1.1

Source: ATENCO (2001).

There is a substantial divergence of elasticities among the various ports. Since no estimations on elasticity of the Port of Consţanta exist in the literature, $|\epsilon|=2$ will be assumed. As pilotage services represent only a small proportion of the overall port costs, in order to determine the elasticity of pilotage services separately, the elasticity of the port will be multiplied by the share of pilotage services in total port costs. A study prepared for the Directorate-General for Transport and Mobility of the European Commission (Price Waterhouse Cooper, 2013) estimates pilotage services as representing 6% of total port costs. Accordingly, the elasticity of pilotage services is estimated at approximately 0.12, resulting from multiplying 0.06 (the share of pilotage services in total port costs) by 2 (the port elasticity coefficient).

Assuming that market value remains constant for the future and that CN APM will pass on the savings to its customers, the freight shippers' savings arising from the creation of a new legal framework for pilotage services will be approximately EUR 3.48 million a year. Currently there is no significant passenger traffic in the Port of Consţanta (Eurostat, Maritime transport, Passengers [database]). This figure results from the application of Formula 6 mentioned above, using the 20% price change percentage provided by the ECMT Paper and the 0.12 elasticity coefficient for pilotage services estimated above.

The "narrow" approach

According to this approach, the demand for pilotage services in the Port of Consţanta is made up of freight shippers calling into the port; the geographic market for pilotage services is thus limited to the Port of Consţanta.

This approach is based on the fact that, for port services, markets are often defined more narrowly. For example, during a merger investigation, the UK Competition Commission defined the relevant geographic market for towage services as being restricted to individual ports (SvitzerWijsmuller, 2007). Other cases also indicate that the geographic market for port services is limited to a single port. In Porto di Genova v Siderurgica Gabrielli[1] the Court of Justice held that the organisation of port activities at a single port constitute a relevant market; and in Corsica Ferries[2] it reached the same conclusion in relation to the provision of pilotage services at the same port.

In this case, we consider the elasticity of demand coefficient to be 0 (zero) as pilotage services are compulsory for freight shippers in ports and there is no substitute for these services. Thus, the formula becomes:

$$\mathrm{FSB} = \rho \mathrm{R} \qquad (7)$$

For the price change, we use the relevant estimation for the experience with competitive tendering in Germany (20%) provided by ECMT (2007).

$$\mathrm{FSB} = 0.2 * \mathrm{EUR}\ 17.2\ \mathrm{million} = 3.44\ \mathrm{EUR\ million} \qquad (8)$$

Assuming that the market value remains constant for the future and that CN APM will pass on the savings to its customers,, the benefits to freight shippers arising from introducing public tendering into the pilotage services market are estimated at approximately EUR 3.44 million a year.

Notes

1. Case C-179/90 [1991] ECR I-5889.
2. Case C-18/93 [1994] ECR I -1783.

ANNEX 3.A5

Towing services

Recommendation

Create appropriate legal framework: Towing services shall not be granted through direct entrustment, but instead they should be tendered based on fair and non-discriminatory terms to guarantee competition for the market. Charges may be established by the port authority but shall be cost oriented. Once the charges are established, they shall be validated by an independent regulatory body in charge of the promotion of competition in port services. Moreover, the law should not impose a minimum number of tugboats per port, but instead it should require a minimum service level, such as the maximum ship waiting time for a tugboat.

Estimates of the benefits arising from creating an appropriate legal framework

Methodology: comparison with data from other geographic markets

Set forth in Table 3.A5.1 below are the tariffs for towing services applied in different ports of the European Union located in Romania, Bulgaria, Italy, Spain, Turkey, Slovenia and Greece expressed in EUR currency for 6 different categories of ship with different gross tonnage and length overall.

Table 3.A5.1. **Towing tariffs throughout different ports in Europe by gross tonnage**

Reference ship	LOA (length overall)	GT	Consţanta	Burgas	Varna	Genoa	Napoli	Valencia	Barcelona	Koper	Piraeus	Average tariff
Starlink Hope	110	3 593	780	1 391	980	737	595	500	541	374	470	708
Guo Rui	154	14 743	1 310	6 838	2 358	1 624	1 354	2 209	1 283	533	860	2 020
KANG QIANG	190	28 613	1 595	9 308	3 081	1 866	1 527	4 486	2 205	652	1 150	2 874
MSC Natalia	244	40 177	1 915	14 003	3 701	2 148	1 706	6 442	2 974	652	1 335	3 875
Regina Maersk	318	81 488	2 815	19 748	5 820	2 546	2 053	13 066	4 957	704	1 450	5 907
CMA CGM Alaska	366	140 259	2 815	30 588	8 868	3 140	2 603	22 489	4 957	704	1 670	8 648

Source: Relevant port websites: *http://bit.ly/1U4laew*, *http://bit.ly/1QUCX3H*, *http://bit.ly/1S1UYNQ*, *http://bit.ly/1QV3QG7*, *http://bit.ly/1MkqOkv*, *http://bit.ly/1Pa4Gcs*, *http://bit.ly/1QUETcD*, *http://bit.ly/1WnzIDl* (accessed on 7 January 2016).

According to Figure 3.A5.1, the towing tariffs charged in the Port of Consţanta are similar to those charged in the other ports taken into consideration in our analysis. Actually, in some cases, tariffs charged in the Port of Consţanta are below the average tariffs charged by the other ports.

Figure 3.A5.1. **Towing tariffs throughout different ports in Europe**

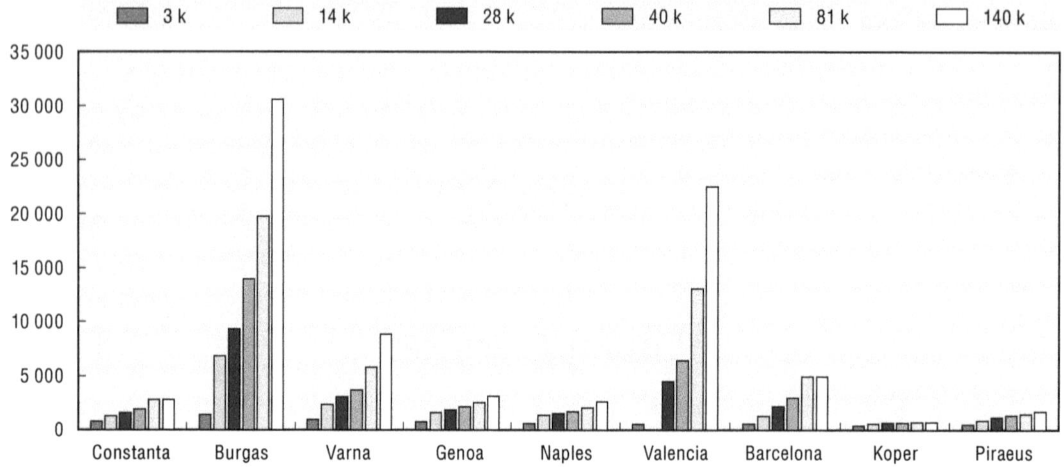

Note: For Burgas and Varna, an average tariff has been determined based on the tariffs of the three port areas of each port. For Valencia and Barcelona, the tariffs used are the maximum rates set by the port authorities.
Source: Relevant port websites: *http://bit.ly/1U4laew*, *http://bit.ly/1QUCX3H*, *http://bit.ly/1S1UYNQ*, *http://bit.ly/1QV3QG7*, *http://bit.ly/1MkqOkv*, *http://bit.ly/1Pa4Gcs*, *http://bit.ly/1QUETcD*, *http://bit.ly/1WnzIDl* (accessed on 7 January 2016).

StatLink http://dx.doi.org/10.1787/888933361711

However, the organisational framework for the provision of towing services is similar to that established for pilotage services. CN APM provides towing services through one towing operator and sets the tariffs without supporting the charges applied by any study on the costs involved in delivering these services.

The introduction of public tendering procedures, the establishment of a cost-oriented mechanism to set tariffs and the introduction of an independent regulatory body to review the competitiveness of these tariffs, once established by the port authority, should lead to significant cost benefits for maritime transport operators using Romanian ports. According to the MoF, Logistic Remo Services SRL, the only operator that performs towing services in the Port of Consţanta, had a turnover of approximately EUR 14.1 million in 2014. This figure does not correspond to the total market value as the towing services are billed by CN APM and it retains a certain amount of these revenues for providing the right to perform towing services in the Port of Consţanta (EUR 0.004 x gross tonnage unit of towed vessel). Based on our own calculation covering certain ships having different gross tonnages, as presented in Figure 3.A5.1, we estimate that CN APM has a 10% share of the total value of the towing services market in the Port of Consţanta. Therefore, the turnover of Logistic Remo Services represents 90% of the value of the towing market and in 2014 the market value was approximately EUR 15.66 million.

Taking into account the estimation of a 20% price reduction from the experience with competitive tendering in Germany provided by ECMT (2007) and applying the "narrow" approach previously adopted for pilotage services (reasoning and arguments are also identical), introducing tendering procedures for towing services should generate savings for freight shippers of approximately EUR 3.14 million a year. Using the "wide" approach, the freight shippers' benefits are estimated at EUR 3.16 million a year (we should note in that respect that towing services elasticity is estimated at 0.12 as towing services are also estimated at 6% of the total port costs, Price Waterhouse Cooper, 2013)

ANNEX 3.A6

Waybills and records of incoming-outgoing wood transport

Recommendation

The provision should be modified. Romania shall liberalise the provision of this service to all printing companies interested in performing such an activity.

Estimates of the benefits arising from modifying the provision

According to the data provided by Imprimeria Naţională, the number of waybills and records sold by Imprimeria Naţională are the following:

Table 3.A6.1. **Number of waybills and records sold in 2014-15**

Year	Number of waybills sold	Number of records sold
2014	102 822	14 001
2015	83 552	8 729

Source: Data provided on request by Imprimeria Naţională.

One block of waybills (one block contains 150 waybills) costs RON 66 (approximately EUR 14.7; source Imprimeria Naţională's website) and one record of 100 pages costs RON 54 (approximately EUR 12; source Imprimeria Naţională's website). Therefore, the total revenues of Imprimeria Naţională for the year 2015 are estimated at approximately EUR 1.22 million from the activity of issuing waybills and around EUR 100 000 from the activity of issuing records.

Table 3.A6.2. **Revenues of Imprimeria Naţională obtained from the sale of waybills and records**

Year	Number of waybills sold	Price of one waybill (EUR)	Total revenues from waybills (EUR)	Number of records sold	Price of one record (EUR)	Total revenues from records (EUR)
2014	102 822	14.7	1 511 483	14 001	12	168 012
2015	83 552	14.7	1 228 214	8 729	12	104 748

Source: Musliu şi Asociaţii calculations.

Introducing competition into the activity of issuing material forms from wood, an activity currently performed exclusively by Imprimeria Naţională, should lead to a cost reduction. The OECD study "Evaluation of competitive impacts of government interventions" (2014) estimates at around 23% the price reduction arising from the introduction of a pro-competitive market structure in order to replace a monopolistic one.[1] In accordance with this study, the benefits arising from liberalising the provision of this service to all printing companies interested in performing such an activity are therefore estimated at approximately EUR 0.3 million a year (see Table 3.A6.3).[2]

Table 3.A6.3. **The estimated benefits from the liberalisation of printing waybills and records**

Year	Total revenues from waybills and records (EUR)	Average price reduction from introducing competition into the marketplace	Benefits (EUR)
2015	1 332 962	0.23	306 581

Source: Musliu şi Asociaţii calculations.

Notes

1. A caveat should be noted. The price reduction of 23% is an average estimation of price change based on a number of findings from *ex post* studies of pro-competitive regulatory reforms, i.e. a conservative estimate.
2. In order to estimate the benefits arising from modifying this provision, we used the 2015 data as the quantity of wood exploited decreased significantly in 2015 compared with 2014 (as a consequence, the number of the waybills sold also decreased) due to extensive investigation of the Public Prosecutor's Office into illegal logging.

Chapter 4

Food processing

The food processing sector generated EUR 1.4 billion of GVA in 2013, representing approximately 10% of total GVA generated by manufacturing and 1% of Romania's total economy. Although food prices are relatively low in Romania, regulatory reforms could bring efficiency gains that would benefit Romanian households. Constraints that could be addressed are over-training of staff that do not pose a threat to food safety, reducing the separate areas for sale of baked goods in shops, excessive requirements for licences and control measures for food market operators, discrimination against importers and undue competitor collaboration (as in the milk industry) and ambiguous and outdated legislation.

4.1. Economic overview of the Romanian food processing sector

Definition of the relevant sector and areas of investigation

Food processing[1] includes activities in which raw agricultural products undergo chemical, mechanical or physical transformation into new products suitable for human or animal consumption. The production process involves various preserving and packaging techniques, such as canning and freezing. The manufacturing sector does not include agricultural activities, such as producing crops or raising livestock, or food services, such as preparing meals or snacks to customers' order for immediate consumption.

The value chain from food production to consumption includes the following stakeholders and activities:

- producers that research, grow, and trade crops, animal products, fishing or aquaculture products, hunting products, etc.;
- processors, both primary and value added, that process, manufacture, and market food products using inputs from the producers;
- distributors, including wholesalers, retailers and the hospitality industry that market and sell food products with varying degrees of processing; and
- consumers who shop, purchase and consume food.

Measuring economic activities related to food processing faces some challenges. For example, 1) some food products undergo limited processing that is not registered as a distinct economic activity, thus appearing to flow directly from production to distribution (e.g. raw agricultural products sold in bulk, such as some meat and fish products); 2) vertical integration is common for certain types of food products (e.g. meat products, milk) and therefore it may be difficult to measure economic activity strictly related to food processing; 3) production for self-consumption in rural households is widespread; this food processing activity, although often subject to regulation and monitoring,[2] is not registered in the accounts of companies active in the industry and therefore may distort the quantification of the food processing sector.

Development of the food processing sector

Value added of the sector/subsectors[3]

From 2005 until 2013, the food processing sector represented on average 1.13% of total gross domestic product (GDP). In 2009, its share of total economic output reached a peak of 1.25%, and has since then steadily decreased, representing 0.98% in 2013. (Figure 4.1)

The value added by the food processing sector relative to the value added by all manufacturing sectors decreased between 2009 and 2013. It represented only 10% in 2013 (Figure 4.2).

The processing and preserving of meat and the production of meat products is the largest subsector within the food processing sector. With a manufacturing value of more

Figure 4.1. **Food processing: Value added at factor cost (millions of EUR) and % of GDP**

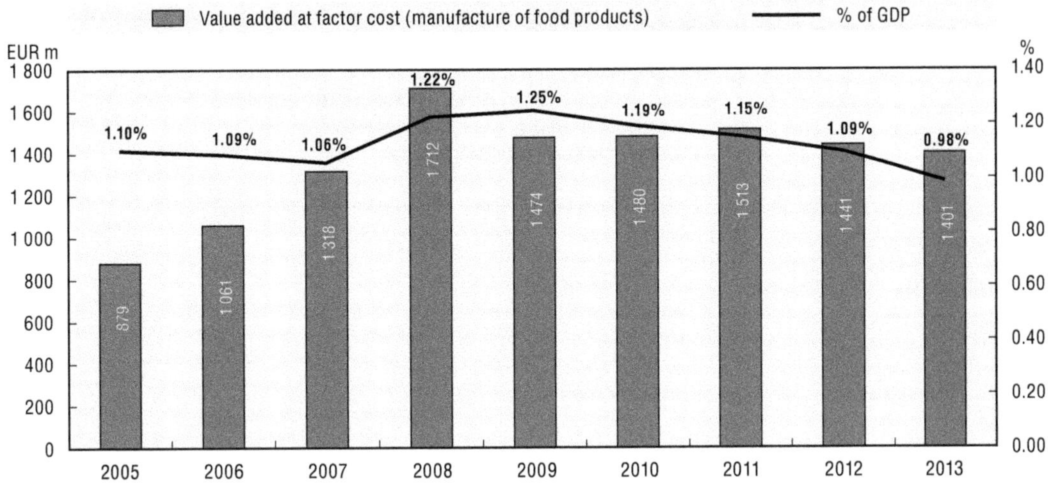

Source: Eurostat, codes: sbs_na_ind_r2 and nama_gdp_c at *http://ec.europa.eu/eurostat/en/data/database* (accessed on 11 February 2016) and Deloitte calculations

StatLink http://dx.doi.org/10.1787/888933361725

Figure 4.2. **Share of value added of food processing in total manufacturing**

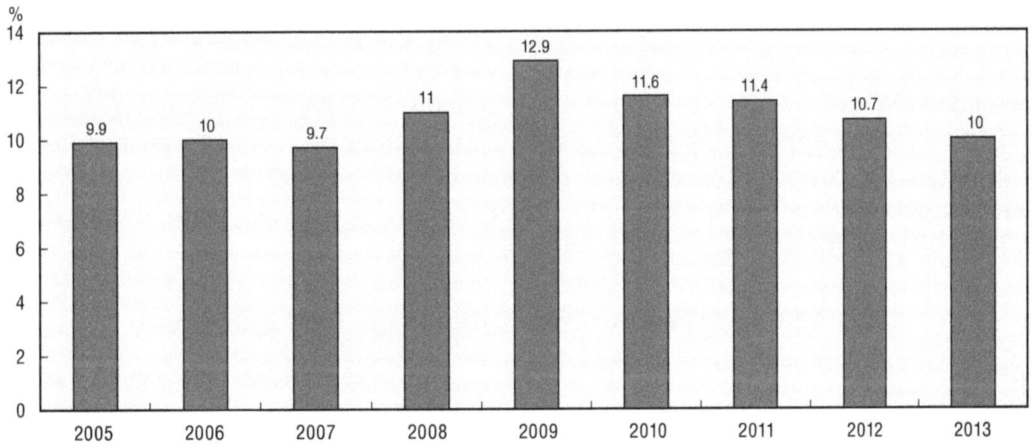

Source: Eurostat, code sbs_na_ind_r2 at *http://ec.europa.eu/eurostat/en/data/database* (accessed on 11 February 2016).

StatLink http://dx.doi.org/10.1787/888933361737

than EUR 400 million at factor cost in 2013, it represented a share of over 30% of the entire sector. The second largest subsector is the manufacture of bakery and farinaceous products with a manufacturing value of approximatively EUR 357.1 million added at factor cost, representing 25% of the sector's value added. This is followed by the manufacture of dairy products with EUR 144 million value added, representing 10% of the sector's value added. The manufacture of vegetable and animal oils and fats (4%), the manufacture of prepared animal feeds (3%) and the processing and preserving of fish, crustaceans and molluscs (1%) represent less significant economic activities within the subsector.

Food prices and inflation

Since 2005, food prices have generally increased.[4] Over the last five years (2010-15), food prices increased by approximatively 20%, with an average annual increase of

Figure 4.3. **Value added at factor costs of each subsector**

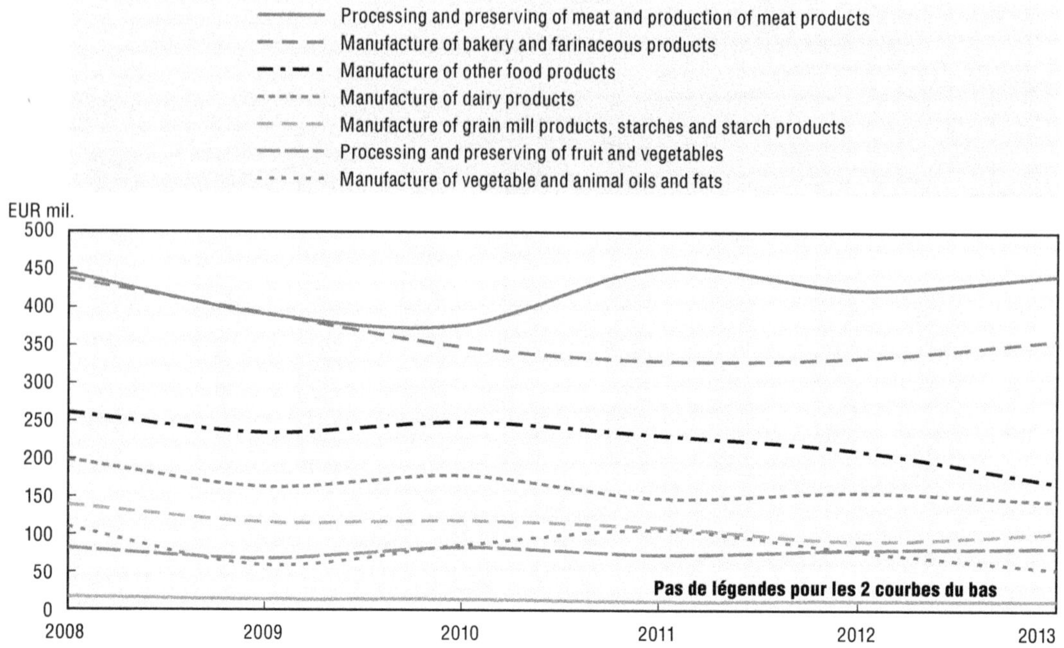

Source: Eurostat, code sbs_na_ind_r2 at *http://ec.europa.eu/eurostat/en/data/database* (accessed on 11 February 2016), and Deloitte Calculations.

StatLink http://dx.doi.org/10.1787/888933361740

approximatively 4%. During the same period, general price levels have increased by 13% (and on average by approximatively 2.3% each year). Food prices reached a peak of 126.95% in January 2013, compared to prices in the base month (June 2010). The cost of food in Romania decreased 6.95% in September 2015, compared with the same month in the previous year, in line with general price trends.[5]

Figure 4.4. **Consumer Price Index in the food industry**

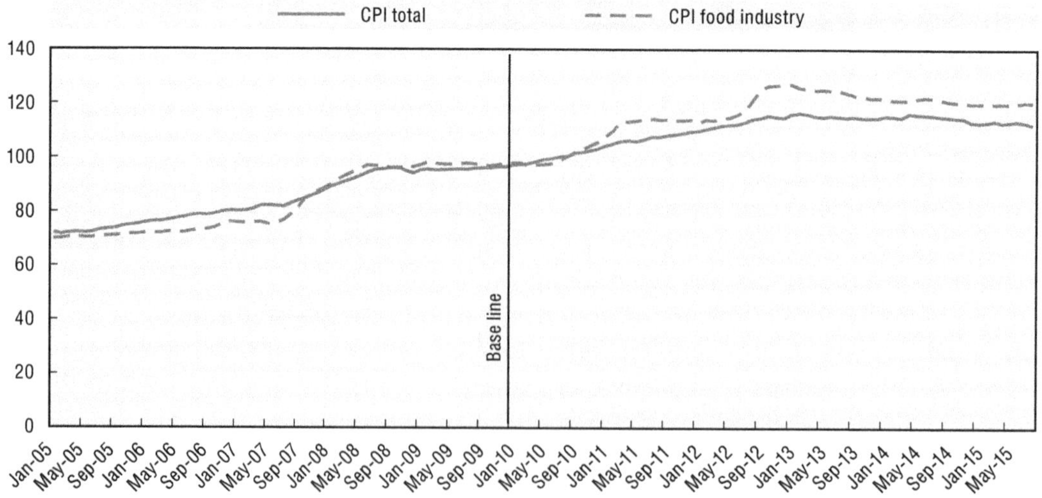

Source: NIS, *http://statistici.insse.ro/shop/index.jsp?page=tempo3&lang=en&ind=PPI103T* (accessed on 8 December 2015).

StatLink http://dx.doi.org/10.1787/888933361751

Main characteristics and indicators of the food processing sector

The main sources of supply for the food processing industry are the domestic agriculture/aquaculture industry and imports of input products.

Processed food products are sold through three main channels: food retailers, gastronomy and exports.

The largest demand comes from food retailers, including hypermarkets, supermarkets, discount shops, boutiques, grocery stores and kiosks. Table 4.1 shows the top ten retailers in terms of 2014 turnover:

Table 4.1. **Top 10 food retailers in Romania based on 2014 turnover**

Place	Retailer	Turnover 2014 (EUR mil.)	Turnover 2013 (EUR mil.)
1	KAUFLAND ROMANIA SCS	1 800	1 643
2	CARREFOUR ROMANIA SA	1 026	971
3	AUCHAN ROMÂNIA SA	848	521
4	MEGA IMAGE SRL	634	530
5	REWE (ROMANIA) SRL	525	497
6	PROFI ROM FOOD SRL	415	330
7	ROMANIA HYPERMARCHE SA	385	-
8	BILLA ROMANIA SRL	317	308
9	ARTIMA SA	200	185
10	SUCCES NIC COM SRL	75	80

Source: Credit Info and Deloitte calculations.
Note: Credit Info is a Romanian company that provides data for companies in the industry: *www.creditinfo.ro/?PageId=0718f876-7eb8-11e3-bfa2-005056867cb9.*

A comparison of the main indicators in the food processing sector, namely the number of companies, number of employees and turnover (in EUR million) in Romania and at the European level between 2008 and 2012/13 shows broadly similar trends, although with more pronounced changes in Romania. In Romania, the number of companies decreased throughout 2010 and has steadily recovered since 2011. In Europe, the number of companies dropped in 2009, but recovered already in 2009 and 2010 and has since then been rather stable. The number of employees in Romania in the food processing sector has decreased from 173 600 in 2008 to 162 700 in 2013. The number of employees in Europe slightly increased over a similar time period from 3.8 million in 2007 to 3.85 million in 2012. The turnover followed the same trend both in Europe and Romania with a sharp drop in 2009, followed by an increase since then.

These data indicate that the food processing sector in Romania has become more consolidated and productivity has increased during the relevant period. Both trends have been more pronounced in Romania than in Europe.

Romania has been a net importer of food products since 1991. Both exports and imports have increased over time. Until 2008 imports were increasing at a higher rate than exports. Since then, this trend has been reversed and, accordingly, the negative trade balance in this sector has decreased slightly.

International comparisons

A comparison between prices in Romania and in other European countries in 2014 for selected processed food products (in EUR) shows that Romanian prices are lower for white bread, loaf (1 kg) and fillets of chicken breast (1 kg) (Eurostat, 2014). The price for milk,

Figure 4.5. **Evolution of main indicators in the food processing sector**

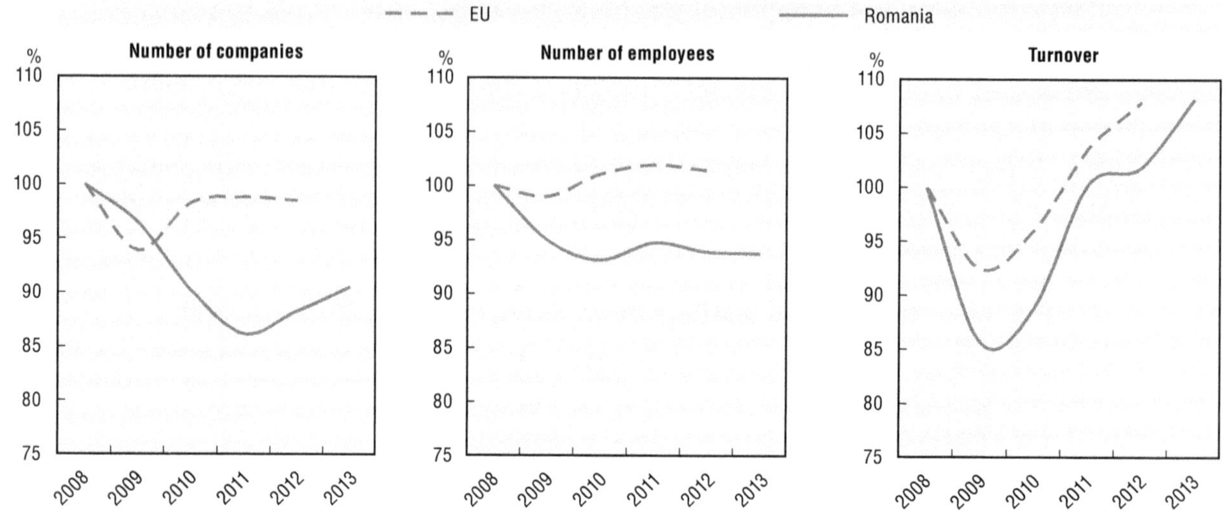

Source: Eurostat, code sbs_na_ind_r2 at *http://ec.europa.eu/eurostat/en/web/products-datasets/-/SBS_NA_IND_R2* (accessed on 11 February 2016) and Deloitte calculations.

StatLink http://dx.doi.org/10.1787/888933361768

Figure 4.6. **Imports, exports and trade balance in the food processing sector**

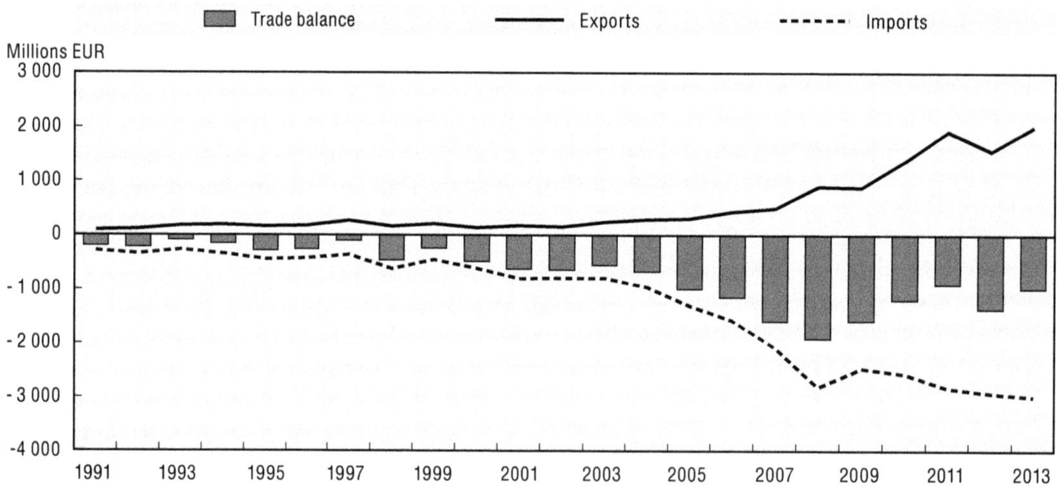

Source: NIS, *http://statistici.insse.ro/shop/index.jsp?page=tempo3&lang=en&ind=EXP101F* and *http://statistici.insse.ro/shop/index.jsp?page=tempo3&lang=en&ind=EXP102F* (accessed on 27 November 2015) and Deloitte Calculations

StatLink http://dx.doi.org/10.1787/888933361772

however, is higher in Romania. In fact, the price of EUR 1.08 for 1 litre (L) of fresh, unskimmed milk puts Romania among the more expensive countries in Europe.

A comparison of the amount of money spent on food consumption in absolute terms shows that Romania had one of the lowest per capita expenditures in the European Union (EU), significantly below the EU average. However, household consumption expenditure on food products in Romania represented 28.1% of total household expenditure, which was by far the highest share in the European Union.

Relevant legislation

In total, 170 legislative and non-legislative acts have been reviewed for the project.

Figure 4.7. **Prices for 1kg of white bread, loaf, across Europe (2014)**

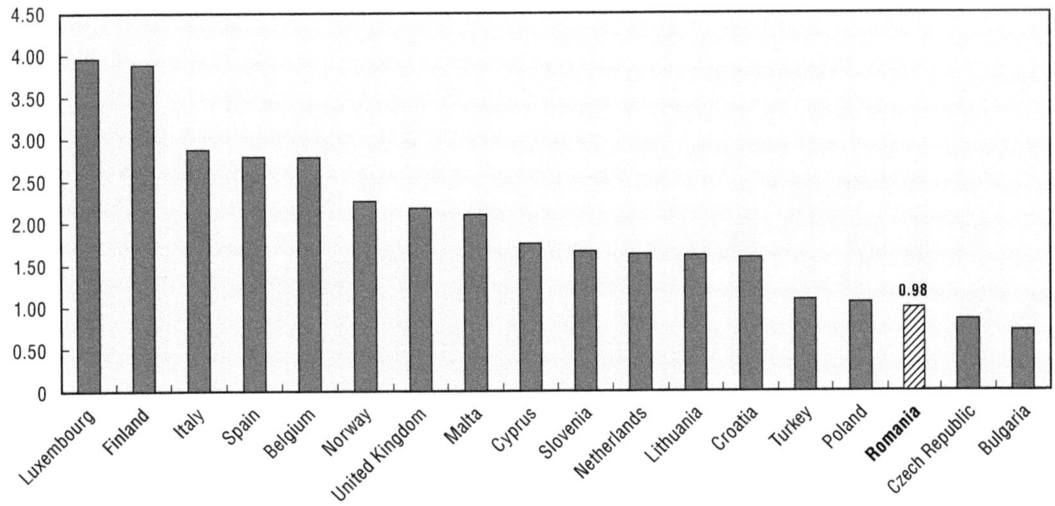

Source: Eurostat, code prc_dap14 at *http://ec.europa.eu/eurostat/en/data/database* (accessed on 11 February 2016).

StatLink http://dx.doi.org/10.1787/888933361782

Figure 4.8. **Prices for 1kg of fillets, chicken breast, across Europe (2014)**

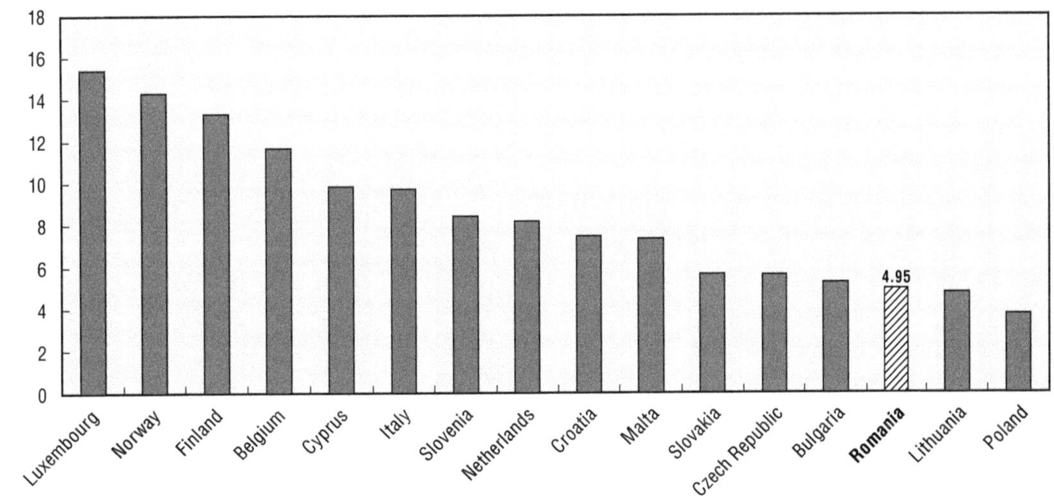

Source: Eurostat, code prc_dap14 at *http://ec.europa.eu/eurostat/en/data/database* (accessed on 11 February 2016).

StatLink http://dx.doi.org/10.1787/888933361793

The legislation applicable to the food processing sector is for the most part harmonised with EU legislation. In certain situations, however, domestic legislation which had been adopted before the accession of Romania to the European Union with the purpose of aligning the national legislation to EU legislation in preparation for accession has not been repealed.[6] As a result, there are certain cases where the domestic legislation has not been officially repealed, although directly applicable EU regulations supersede all domestic legislation.

The national regulatory regime applicable to the food processing sector covers:

- framework legislation, covering a wide range of provisions with respect to the establishment and operation of undertakings in the sector;
- processing and preservation of meat products;

Figure 4.9. **Prices for 1L of fresh, unskimmed milk across Europe (2014)**

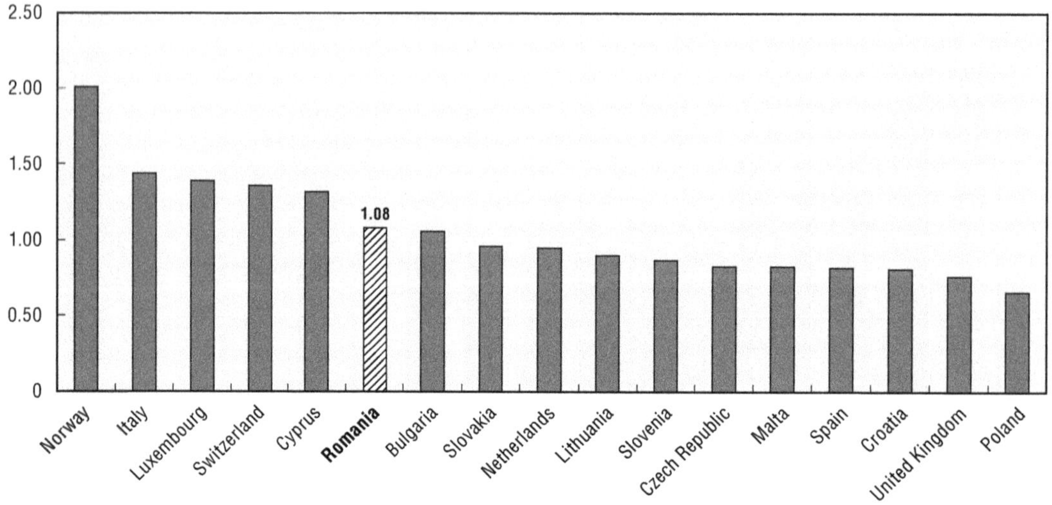

Source: Eurostat, code prc_dap14 at *http://ec.europa.eu/eurostat/en/data/database* (accessed on 11 February 2016).

StatLink http://dx.doi.org/10.1787/888933361805

Figure 4.10. **Household consumption expenditure in EU on food products (absolute terms, per capita, in EUR) in 2013 (2012 for Romania)**

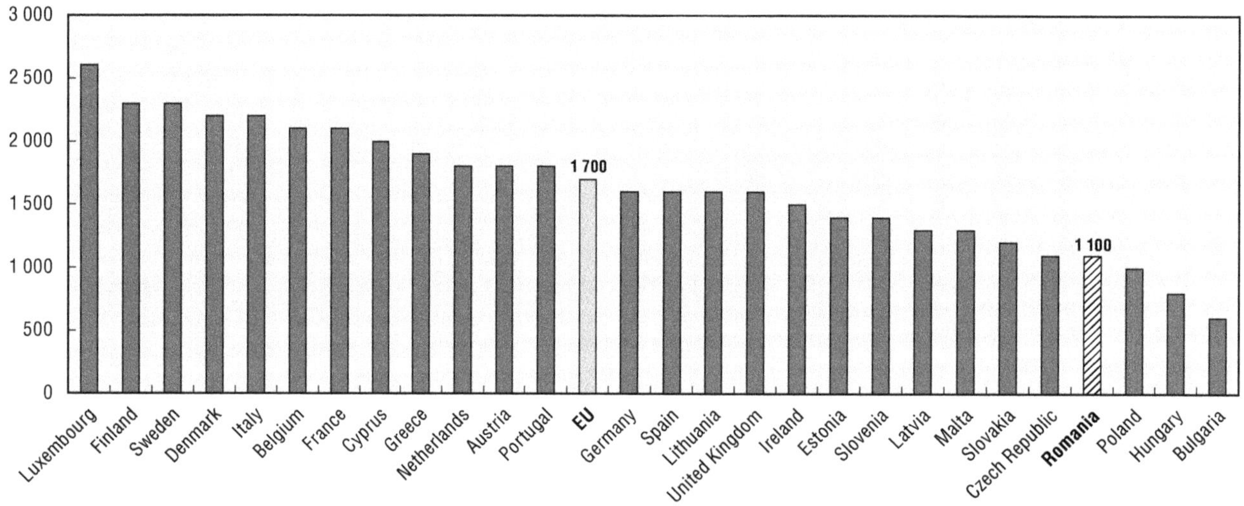

Source: Eurostat, code nama_10_co3_p3 at *http://ec.europa.eu/eurostat/en/data/database* (accessed on 11 February 2016).

StatLink http://dx.doi.org/10.1787/888933361812

- processing and preservation of fish, crustaceans and molluscs;
- processing and preservation of fruit and vegetables;
- production of milk and processing of dairy products;
- production and processing of grain mill products and starch products;
- manufacture of bakery and farinaceous products;
- manufacture of vegetable and animal oils and fats;
- manufacture of other food products for human consumption; and
- manufacture of prepared animal feed.

Figure 4.11. **Household consumption expenditure in EU on food products (percentage of total household expenditure) in 2013 (2012 for Romania)**

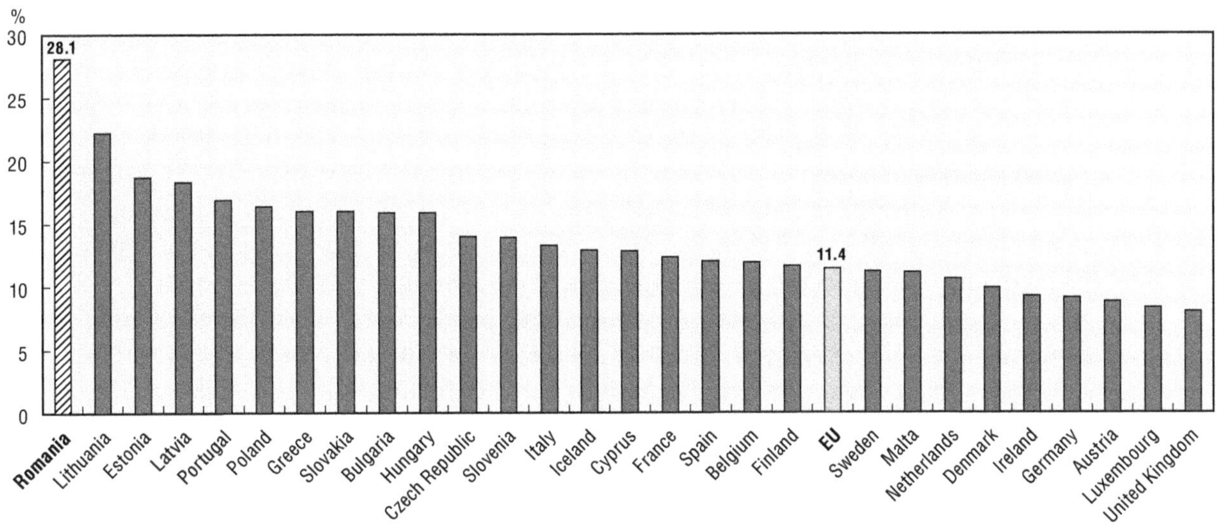

Source: Eurostat, code nama_10_co3_p3 at *http://ec.europa.eu/eurostat/en/data/database* (accessed on 11 February 2016).

StatLink http://dx.doi.org/10.1787/888933361829

In addition, a number of provisions such as the Tax Code and environment protection legislation are relevant in the food processing sectors, although they apply to other economic activities as well.

The Codex Alimentarius contains a series of international food standards, guidelines and codes of practice which aim contribute to the safety, quality and fairness of international food trade. While they contain recommendations for voluntary application by members, Codex standards serve in many cases as a basis for national legislation, including in Romania. The reference made to Codex food safety standards in the World Trade Organization's Agreement on the Application of Sanitary and Phytosanitary Measures (SPS Agreement) means that the Codex has far reaching implications for resolving trade disputes. WTO members who wish to apply stricter food safety measures than those set by the Codex may be required to justify these measures scientifically. Codex members cover 99% of the world's population.

Authorisations and licences in the food processing sector

The economic operators entering the food processing sector are required to obtain certain authorisations and licences from several authorities, such as:

- **The Ministry of Health** which issues authorisations for economic operators in the food processing industry, ensuring compliance with sanitary legislation.
- **The Sanitary-Veterinary and Food Safety National Authority (SVFSNA)** which issues the **Sanitary-Veterinary Authorization (SVA)** for all economic operators who produce, process, store, transport[7] and/or distribute[8] foodstuffs of animal origin.[9] For newly built facilities within the abovementioned categories, the SVFSNA issues a **temporary conditional SVA** and an **intra-community exchange licence,** before issuing the **definitive SVA.** Companies that are not required by law to obtain a SVA[10] but produce and sell animal/ non-animal foodstuffs are required to have a **SV Registration** and are also subject to SVFSNA controls. The issue of each type of SVA mentioned above is preceded by a SVFSNA control. Controls are also periodically performed on all economic

operators who are either authorised or registered. All controls and tests performed by SVFSNA staff are subject to fees.[11]

- **The Ministry of Agriculture and Rural Development (MARD)** is the central public authority that, in addition to being responsible for implementing government strategy and policies in the field of agriculture, rural development, fishing and aquaculture, also has authority over food production; it is responsible for issuing the following official documents:
  - **Manufacturing licences** for economic operators producing foodstuffs (per category of product).[12] A licence is issued for each type of product the facility is producing. A manufacturer is allowed to carry out technological testing for the equivalent of 3 days of production before being granted the licence, assuming a positive outcome of the technological test. **Certificates for traditional products** for all meat foodstuffs produced and sold as being "traditional". A traditional product must be produced in Romania, must contain local raw materials, may not include any food preservatives, must be produced either following a traditional recipe or through a traditional production/processing method, and can be distinguished from other similar products. A control precedes the issuance of the certificate.
  - **Certificates for products based on a well-known Romanian recipe:** a product is considered to be produced based on a well-known Romanian recipe if it can be proven that the recipe is more than 30 years old, measured from entering into force of Order 89/2014. A control precedes the issuance of the certificate.
  - **Ecological product certificate** for foodstuffs produced and sold as **"ecological".** An accredited inspector from the National Authority for Ecological Products (NAEP)[13] will perform a control and certify that the respective products may be sold as "ecological" and may be labelled with the ***ae*** logo.
  - **Deposit licences for cereal and seeds storage facilities:** economic operators who own seed storage facilities may request a storage licence,[14] provided that they fulfill the required financial and technical performance conditions. The licence is issued free of charge, but the costs of the verifications made in order to issue the licence are charged to the economic operator.
  - **Authorisation for quality self-control and for using the Community logo** (fruit and vegetables) is issued through MARD's State Inspection for the Technical Control on Producing and Exploiting Vegetables and Fruits. Authorisations are issued to economic operators who have equipment for performing a conformity check on the applicable quality standards as well as for packing and labelling, employ qualified staff with relevant degrees, and commit to performing conformity checks on fruit and/or vegetables as well as keeping a record of their control activities.
  - **Certificate of acknowledgement by the Dairy Producers' Association** is issued to legally established associations of dairy producers who request to be acknowledged as such by the MARD.
  - **Accreditation** by the MARD for economic operators producing **beetroot sugar** and/or **raw cane sugar**, producing **isoglucose** as well as those that use sugar and/or the isoglucose as raw materials for producing alcohol, rum, drugs and other pharma products, plastic materials, etc.
- **The National Authority for Consumer Protection (NACP)** which is the authority in charge of developing and implementing the national strategy for consumer protection in order

to prevent and combat practices that harm the life, health, safety and economic interests of consumers. Its operations are co-ordinated by the prime minister. The NACP has inspection and controlling powers over all types of producers, processors, distributors, transporters, sellers and re-sellers, service providers, etc. in the food sector. It can also impose sanctions and may initiate the removal or termination of certain licences and authorisations by the issuing authorities. In the food processing sector, the NACP supervises selling conditions and the labelling of products. Furthermore, through one of its subordinated entities, LAREX, it **issues certificates of conformity** for products that follow certain standards of quality.

- **The National Commission for Nuclear Activity Control (NCNAC)** which is the national authority under the prime minister, with responsibility for the regulation, authorisation and control of nuclear activities in Romania. The NCNAC is tasked with the enforcement of Law 111/1996 on safe deployment of nuclear activities, with subsequent completions and modification. In relation to the food processing sector, the NCNAC grants authorisations and performs inspections for facilities which use ionizing radiation for the treatment of food products.
- **The National Agency for Medicine and Medical Devices (NAMMD)** which is a public institution under the Ministry of Health, whose objective is to help protect and promote public health. In relation to the food processing sector, the NAMMD grants authorisations for the manufacturing of products based on medicinal plants, aromatic plants and hive products, which are promoted and qualify as medicine. Such authorisations are issued only to applicants who are based in an EU Member State or have their main activity in Romania.
- **The National Agency for Environment Protection within the Ministry of Environment, Water and Forests (NAEP/MEWF)** which is a specialised institution within the MEWF responsible for the implementation of policy and legislation in the field of environment protection. Economic operators performing certain types of food processing activities must obtain the following authorisations from NAEP: environment authorisation, integrated environmental authorisation, authorisation for activities with genetically modified organisms (GMOs), and greenhouse gas effect authorisation.

Fiscal aspects

Fiscal legislation applies across all economic sectors, with no specific provisions applicable only to the food processing industry.

Businesses within the food processing industry have complained about unfair fiscal treatment of the industry. The main issues are related to i) outdated legislation, ii) legislation that is difficult to apply, iii) discrimination against the food sector compared to other industry sectors, and iv) the lack of specific regulations for the food sector.

Outdated legislation

Part of fiscal legislation seems to be outdated with regard to food processing. This is the case, for example, of deductibility for the depreciation of fixed assets and value added tax (VAT) adjustments for loss of perishable goods:

- Deductibility for depreciation in case of fixed assets is computed based on a standard useful life provided for types of assets under a catalogue adopted by the Ministry of Finance and last updated in November 2008.[15] Depending on the specifics of each industry, different depreciation periods are applicable. For certain industries, depreciation periods may be considered outdated and inconsistent with the real economic useful life for which the companies actually use those assets. This significantly affects the food processing industry, where animals and birds used as fixed (biological) assets have a depreciation period of between 2 to 4 years, whereas in practice they can be efficiently used for less than one year.

- Losses of perishable goods are tax deductible and VAT adjustments should be made for such goods depending on standard percentages which are established by legislation last updated in 2004. The percentages admitted for deductibility/VAT adjustment purposes are differentiated by type of product or processes. No VAT deductibility is granted for quantities in excess of the statutory thresholds, and for items not falling exactly within the legislative categories. Given that undertakings in the food processing industry incur many losses of perishable goods, in practice the inadequate regulation of these products may lead to increased costs for the industry, due to VAT and profit tax which needs to be paid for what is not considered as being perishable goods.

Legislation is difficult to apply

Various fiscal provisions are difficult to apply to the food processing industry. For example, the exemption from payment of excise duties is hardly applied in practice in the food industry, although in theory the premises for its application are very often met.

As a general rule, fuel used for producing electricity is exempt from excise duty.[16] In the food processing industry the rule might apply to refrigerator trucks used for transportation of food products, as fuel is used for producing the electricity needed for refrigeration. However since the tax legislation does not contain methodological norms for application of the excise duty exemption, refrigerator trucks hardly benefit from such exemption.

Potential discrimination in relation to other sectors

The VAT rate in Romania is 20%. However, for certain products there is a reduced VAT rate of 9%. This includes food and beverages (except alcohol) for human and animal consumption, living domestic animals and birds, seeds, plants and ingredients used in food processing.

In some cases, the fiscal legislation conditions the application of the reduced quota of VAT of 9% for specific food products (versus the VAT of 20%) by the proof of their further use for human or animal consumption, while for other food products, the application of the reduced rate is not conditioned by their further use/destination. Conditioning the application of the reduced rate upon proof of use for some food products and not for others, may create discrimination.

Losses related to goods returned to the manufacturer by customers will generally be non-deductible as they can no longer be sold. However, the tax legislation provides for certain exceptions (such as the deductibility of expenses for publications returned to the editor) in which situation the losses would be deductible. No mention is made of goods returned to the manufacturer from consumers in the food processing industry, although the value and the volume of the returns is significant in the food processing industry. There could conceivably be similar arguments with those which provided the exception in other sectors (e.g., non-usage of the respective goods by consumer after a certain period of time).

Legislation creating an additional burden

In certain circumstances, the application of legislation by the competent authorities may create certain barriers to entry, even if the relevant tax legislation does not contain provisions which in themselves might qualify as potentially altering free and fair competition in the market. For example:

- No VAT should be charged for expired food products, the value of which can no longer be recovered and which are granted free of charge to non-profit organisations for social purposes. [17]Given the lack of further provisions regarding food products which may qualify for the application of this provision, discrimination may appear between producers within the food industry, as the tax authorities may not apply this provision to certain food products, such as sweets.
- Service expenses are deductible from the payment of corporate income tax provided that their necessity and actual performance can be justified with supporting documentation.[18] The justification process is very burdensome as it not only requires the accounting documents, but also operational/procedural documents.[19] No clear guidance on which standard documents are accepted for tax deductibility purposes is provided by the law. Considering certain practices in the food processing industry where producers may receive services from retailers, it is very difficult to provide the proper documentation of costs related to such services. This may result in non-deductible costs and non-deductible VAT for producers, which in turn may create barriers for producers of food products sold in retail chains. Separately, the lack of a clear procedure increases the discretion of tax authorities when controlling the respective undertakings, creating uncertainty for market participants.
- The tax legislation allows for the deduction of different types of costs with stock losses and provides that no VAT adjustment should be made[20] if such losses are properly documented. The documentation requirements are again very burdensome as companies should be able to prove that perishable losses occurred due to natural causes, document whether the losses have occurred in production, warehousing, sale or transportation, and present calculations for each deducted amount. Food processers/manufacturers are particularly affected by these provisions as many of their products are highly perishable. This burdensome procedure may lead to higher costs for producers/manufacturers of food products because they are not able to deduct the costs/ adjust the VAT.

Subsector view: Processing and preserving of meat and meat products (C10.1)[21, 22]

The processing and preserving of meat and meat products involves activities such as chilling and freezing, cutting, mincing, canning, smoking, etc. of any type of meat suitable for human consumption. Depending on the raw material used, meat products can be classified as: pork products, beef products, sheep products, poultry products, products that use other type of meat (such as rabbit, camel, lamb, mutton, etc.), and products that use more than one type of meat. Depending on their processing and preserving, there are different types of meat products:

- Fresh meat, which can be sold as pieces of fresh meat or minced (as fresh sausages, fresh minced meat, skewers);
- Processed meat with heat treatment; in this category are included:
  - pieces (salted, boiled and smoked) as baked ham;
  - minced (as sausages, salami), which are also boiled and smoked also;

- canned (usually hams or a mix of meat and different vegetables), using a hard heating treatment.

According to Eurostat, the gross value added from processing and preserving of meat and production of meat products was EUR 442.2 million in 2013, which represented an increase of 4.4% from the previous year.

Table 4.2 shows that the activities generating the highest percentage of the sector's revenue are the processing and preserving of meat and the production of meat and poultry meat products. Together, they represented over 86% of sector turnover and number of employees in 2014.

Table 4.2. **Structure of the processing and preserving of meat and meat products subsector**

Activity/Subsector	NACE Code		Turnover 2014 (EUR m)	Employees 2014
Processing and preserving of meat	C 1011	Abs.	1 153.89	18 243
		Percentage	*42.91%*	*43.40%*
Processing and preserving of poultry meat	C 1012	Abs.	358.21	4 873
		Percentage	*13.32%*	*11.59%*
Production of meat and poultry meat products	C 1013	Abs.	1 177.23	18 914
		Percentage	*43.77%*	*45.00%*
Processing and preserving of meat and production of meat products	*C 101*	*Abs.*	*2 689*	*42 030*
		Percentage	*100%*	*100%*

1. For companies with a turnover higher than EUR 50 000 in 2014.
Source: Credit Info and Deloitte calculations.

The supply for the processing of meat products comes from producers who grow and trade animals, as well as from imports. Since 2009, the production of unprocessed pig and poultry meat remained relatively stable, the production of beef meat decreased, and the production of sheep and goat meat increased.

Figure 4.12. **Evolution of tonnes of meat from cattle, pigs, sheep, goats and poultry in Romania (thousands of tonnes)**

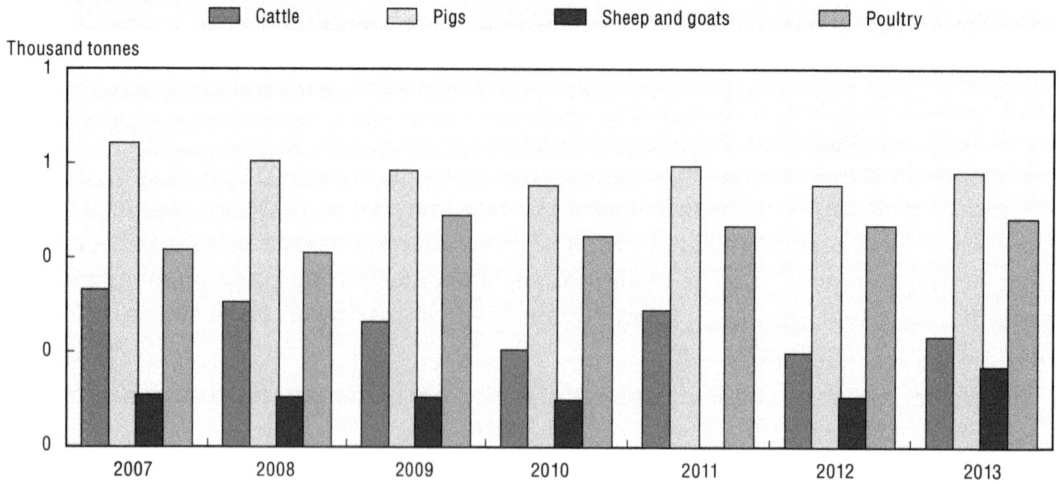

Source: MARD, *www.madr.ro/cresterea-animalelor.html* (accessed on 15 February 2016).

StatLink http://dx.doi.org/10.1787/888933361837

From 2001 to 2013, meat production increased, on average, 10.7% each year. The production of meat products, however, decreased between 2009 and 2013. The strong growth of meat production is explained by the increasing trend of importing living animals, especially the importation of pigs, which increased on average by 55% annually between 2007 and 2012.

Figure 4.13. **Production of meat, meat products and tinned meat (thousands of tonnes)**

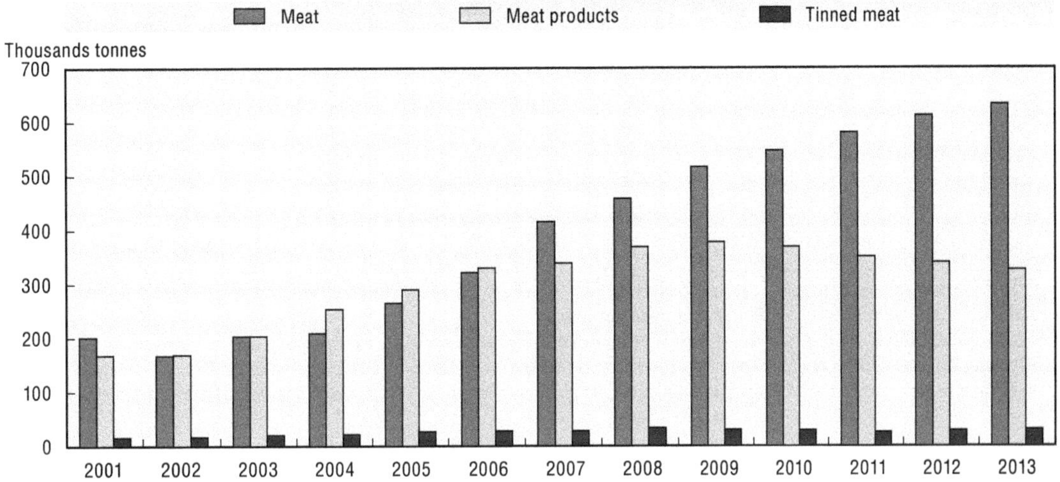

Source: NSI, *http://statistici.insse.ro/shop/index.jsp?page=tempo3&lang=en&ind=IND106C* (accessed on 26 November 2015).

StatLink http://dx.doi.org/10.1787/888933361845

Part of the processed and preserved meat and produced meat products is also exported, with a significant growth in exports since 2008. From 2003 until 2012 Romania had a ban[23] on exporting pigs and pork products. Since 2012,[24] however, Romania has been able to export raw pork meat and pork products to other Member States under certain conditions. This explains the increased export of processed meat in 2012.

Figure 4.14. **Exports of processed meat (thousands of EUR)**

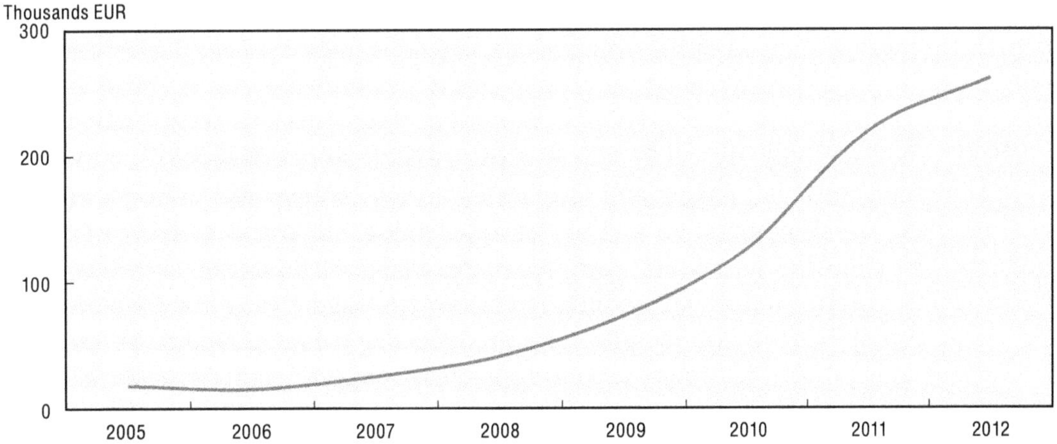

Source: NSI, *http://statistici.insse.ro/shop/index.jsp?page=tempo3&lang=en&ind=EXP101F* (accessed on 27 November 2015).

StatLink http://dx.doi.org/10.1787/888933361858

The top ten companies in terms of turnover in the processing and preserving of meat and meat products subsector are presented in Table 4.3:

Table 4.3. **Top 10 players in the processing and preserving of meat and meat products subsector**

No.	Company	NACE Code	Description NACE	Turnover 2014 (EUR m)	Market share 2014[1]
1	SMITHFIELD PROD SRL	C 1011	Processing and preserving of meat	180.16	6.61%
2	UNICARM SRL	C 1013	Production of meat and poultry meat products	149.03	5.47%
3	AAYLEX PROD SRL	C 1012	Processing and preserving of poultry meat	86.81	3.18%
4	AGRICOLA INTERNATIONAL SA	C 1012	Processing and preserving of poultry meat	79.57	2.92%
5	CAROLI FOODS GROUP SRL	C 1013	Production of meat and poultry meat products	78.39	2.88%
6	ELIT SRL	C 1011	Processing and preserving of meat	70.65	2.59%
7	DIANA SRL	C 1013	Production of meat and poultry meat products	64.75	2.37%
8	RECUNOSTINTA PRODCOM IMPEX SRL	C 1013	Production of meat and poultry meat products	62.14	2.28%
9	SCANDIA FOOD SRL	C 1013	Production of meat and poultry meat products	50.87	1.87%
10	ALDIS SRL	C 1013	Production of meat and poultry meat products	42.38	1.55%
TOTAL				*864.75*	*31.72%*

1. References to "market characteristics", "market shares" or "markets" in general, included in this report, do not reflect the same definitions used for the purposes of applying competition law.

Source: Credit Info, ANAF, *https://www.anaf.ro/indicatori/indfinanciari.html* (accessed on 11 February 2016) and Deloitte calculations. ANAF provides the data for GDP and GVA in the construction industry in RON m. For calculating the figures in EUR m, the medium annual exchange rate (RON/EUR) from the National Bank of Romania was used, *www.bnr.ro/Cursul-de-schimb-3544.aspx* (accessed on 11 February 2015).

The subsector is highly fragmented, with the top ten companies in the processing and preserving of meat and meat products subsector jointly accounting only for 31.72% of the sector's turnover. "SMITHFIELD PROD SRL" is the top player in the industry, representing 6.61% of the sector's turnover in 2014.

In terms of industry concentration, according to ANAF data in 2014, 12.59% of the companies active in this subsector accounted for more than 80% of its turnover.

The turnover in the subsector declined in 2009, but then recovered and surpassed the 2008 level in 2011. This development is consistent with the trend in Europe. However, the number of companies and employees in the subsector was slower to recover and has not yet reached the 2008 level. Another decoupling can be seen between the number of companies and the number of employees: in 2011 when the number of companies reached its lowest point for the period observed, the number of employees slowly increased; since then, the number of companies slowly increased, while the number of employees recorded a slight decrease and then a plateau.

Subsector view: Manufacture of bakery and farinaceous products (C10.7)[25]

The manufacturing of bakery and farinaceous products involves the preparation of raw materials, dough preparation and processing, baking, chilling and storage of finite products. This subsector uses as its main raw materials wheat flour, vegetable fats, grain mill products, starches and starch products (glucose syrup), as well as other food products (e.g. sugar, cocoa), but can also include dairy products (such as milk and/or butter). The products resulting from this activity can be classified into salty (e.g. bread, pasta, biscuits) and sweet products (cakes, sweet snacks, etc.).

According to Eurostat, gross value added from the bakery and farinaceous products subsector was EUR 357.1 million in 2013, increasing on average by 4% (annually) in 2012 and 2013.

Figure 4.15. **Evolution of main indicators (base year 2008) in the processing and preserving of meat and production of meat products subsector**

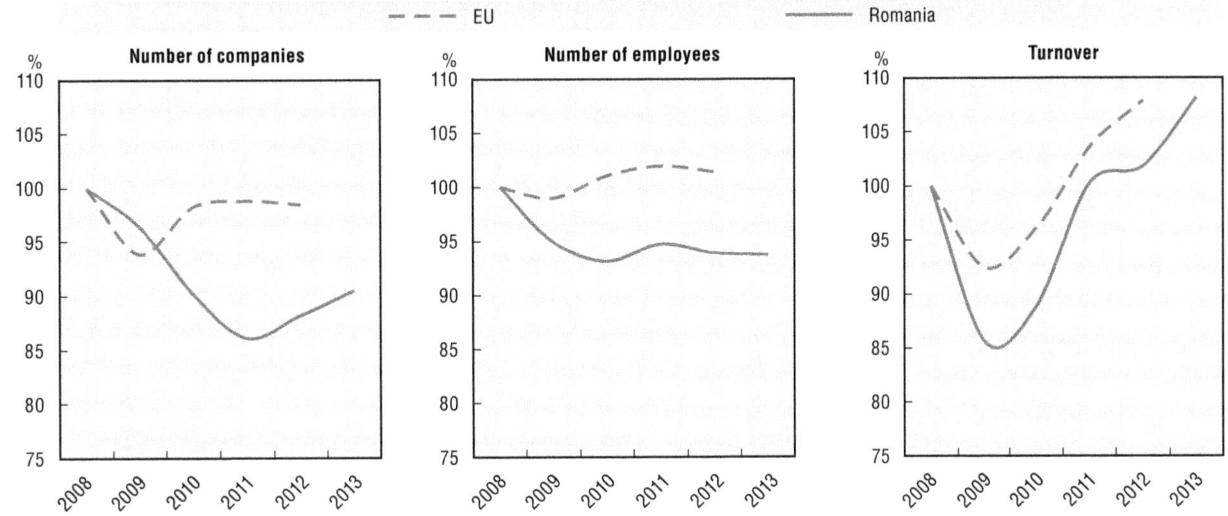

Source: Eurostat, code sbs_na_ind_r2 (accessed on 11 February 2016) and Deloitte calculations.

StatLink http://dx.doi.org/10.1787/888933361864

Table 4.4. **Structure of the bakery and farinaceous products subsector**

Activity/Subsector	NACE Code		Turnover 2014 (EUR m)	Employees 2014
Manufacture of bread; manufacture of fresh pastry goods and cakes	C 1071	Abs.	980.53	44 345
		Percentage	*78.12%*	*88.07%*
Manufacture of rusks and biscuits; manufacture of preserved pastry goods and cakes	C 1072	Abs.	247.06	5 502
		Percentage	*19.68%*	*10.93%*
Manufacture of macaroni, noodles, couscous and similar farinaceous products	C 1073	Abs.	27.56	507
		Percentage	*2.20%*	*1.01%*
Manufacture of bakery and farinaceous products	*C 107*	*Abs.*	*1 255*	*50 354*
		Percentage	*100%*	*100%*

Note: Considering companies with a turnover of more than EUR 50 000 in 2014.
Source: Credit Info and Deloitte calculations.

The main activity in terms of turnover and the number of employees is the manufacture of bread, fresh pastry goods and cakes (78.12% of subsector turnover and 88% of the number of people employed). The manufacture of rusks and biscuits, preserved pastry goods and cakes is a distant second (19.7% of the turnover and 11% of the number of employees). The manufacture of macaroni, noodles, couscous and similar farinaceous products represents the smallest share in the subsector.

Imports are an important source of raw materials. The main product imported as raw material is cane or beet sugar, and chemically pure sucrose in solid form. Imports of this raw material declined from 2011 to 2013.[26] On the other hand, imports of products such as chocolate and other food preparations containing cocoa, sugar confectionery not containing cocoa, including white chocolate, have increased over the last years.[27]

Total production in the subsector has increased on average by 10% annually from 2001 until 2008. In following years, it decreased on average by 5%.

The manufacture of bakery and farinaceous products is not very concentrated. Together, the top ten players accounted for 21.37% of total turnover of the subsector. The

Figure 4.16. **Production of confectionery and pastry products (thousands of EUR)**

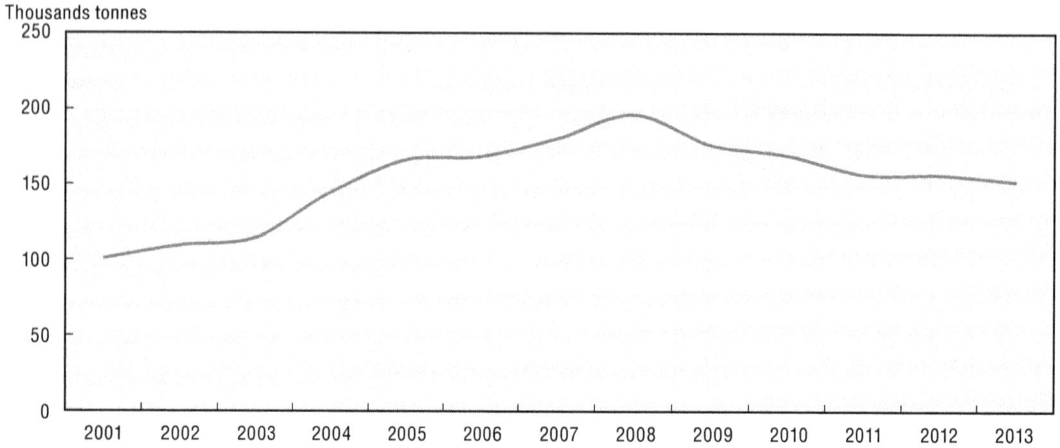

Source: NIS, *http://statistici.insse.ro/shop/index.jsp?page=tempo3&lang=en&ind=IND106C* (accessed on 26 November 2015).

StatLink http://dx.doi.org/10.1787/888933361872

company with the highest turnover in 2014 was "CHIPITA ROMANIA SRL" with 5.13% of turnover, which was followed by "VEL PITAR SA" (5.01%). According to ANAF data, 14.05% of the companies active in this subsector account for over 80% of total turnover.

The top ten companies in the manufacture of bakery and farinaceous products subsector in terms of turnover from 2014 are presented in Table 4.5:

Table 4.5. **Top 10 players in the manufacture of bakery and farinaceous products subsector**

No.	Company	NACE Code	Description NACE	Turnover 2014 (EUR m)	Market share 2014[1]
1	CHIPITA ROMANIA SRL	C 1072	Manufacture of rusks and biscuits; manufacture of preserved pastry goods and cakes	70.32	5.13%
2	VEL PITAR SA	C 1071	Manufacture of bread; manufacture of fresh pastry goods and cakes	68.68	5.01%
3	CROCO SRL	C 1072	Manufacture of rusks and biscuits; manufacture of preserved pastry goods and cakes	25.88	1.89%
4	FORNETTI ROMANIA SRL	C 1071	Manufacture of bread; manufacture of fresh pastry goods and cakes	23.20	1.69%
5	SAMMILLS DISTRIBUTION S.R.L.	C 1072	Manufacture of rusks and biscuits; manufacture of preserved pastry goods and cakes	21.87	1.60%
6	TRANS AGAPE SRL	C 1071	Manufacture of bread; manufacture of fresh pastry goods and cakes	19.15	1.40%
7	PHOENIXY SRL	C 1072	Manufacture of rusks and biscuits; manufacture of preserved pastry goods and cakes	18.60	1.36%
8	TECSA BUSINESS SRL	C 1072	Manufacture of rusks and biscuits; manufacture of preserved pastry goods and cakes	16.78	1.23%
9	LIDO GIRBEA SRL	C 1071	Manufacture of bread; manufacture of fresh pastry goods and cakes	15.65	1.14%
10	LA LORRAINE SRL	C 1071	Manufacture of bread; manufacture of fresh pastry goods and cakes	12.55	0.92%
TOTAL				*292.68*	*21.37%*

1. References to "market characteristics", "market shares" or "markets" in general, included in this report, do not reflect the same definitions used for the purposes of applying competition law.

Source: Credit Info, ANAF, *www.anaf.ro/indicatori/indfinanciari.html* (accessed on 11 February 2016) and Deloitte calculations.[28]

The number of companies active in the manufacture of bakery and farinaceous products has increased in Romania from 2008 to 2009. It then decreased until 2011, followed by a recovery in the last two years. In Europe, the number of companies decreased in 2009 compared to 2008, increased in 2010, and remained relatively stable in the years following. The number of employees decreased in Romania, whereas it increased until 2010 and remained relatively stable in the years following in Europe. Turnover decreased from 2008 to 2009, without any clear trend thereafter. In Europe, the turnover has increased since 2009.

Figure 4.17. **Evolution main indicators (base year 2008) in the manufacture of bakery and farinaceous (flour-based) products subsector**

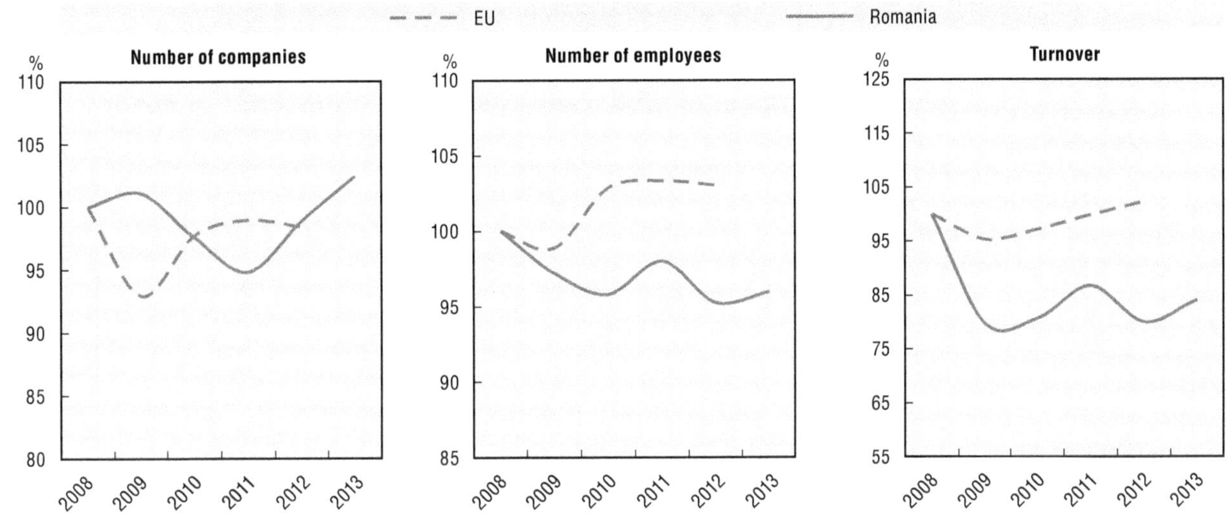

Source: Eurostat, code sbs_na_ind_r2 at *http://ec.europa.eu/eurostat/en/data/database* (accessed on 11 February 2016) and Deloitte calculations.

StatLink http://dx.doi.org/10.1787/888933361886

Subsector view: Manufacture of dairy products (C10.5)[29]

The manufacture of dairy products subsector involves processing of milk and the production of dairy products, such as milk powder, cheese, cream, butter, ice cream, etc. The main processes involved in milk production are the filtration of raw milk, separation of milk fat, pasteurisation, homogenisation, packing and delivery or storage, including cold storage. Other dairy products are generally obtained from the processing of pasteurised milk. Usually they are classified as follows:

- Fresh products: fresh milk for direct consumption and fresh fermented products (yogurt, kefir, fresh cheese);
- Long processed products (white cheese, fermented cheese, Emmental cheese).

According to Eurostat, gross value added from the manufacture of dairy products subsector was EUR 144.3 million in 2013, which represents a decrease of 7.32% from the previous year.

The operation of dairies and cheese making is the most important activity in the subsector, representing over 90% of subsector turnover and over 75% of the people employed.

The supply of raw materials for this subsector comes from domestic milk production. Imports play a very limited role, as raw milk is a perishable product.

Figure 4.18 shows the evolution of the number of cows bred for milk production (in thousands of heads).

Table 4.6. **Structure of the manufacture of dairy products subsector**

Activity/Subsector	NACE Code		Turnover 2014 (EUR m)	Employees 2014
Operation of dairies and cheese making	C1051	Abs.	921.24	9 845
		Percentage	*90.89%*	*76.25%*
Manufacture of ice cream	C1052	Abs.	92.34	3 066
		Percentage	*9.11%*	*23.75%*
Manufacture of dairy products	*C105*	*Abs.*	*1 014*	*12 911*
		Percentage	*100%*	*100%*

1. For companies with a turnover higher than EUR 50 000 in 2014.
Source: Credit Info and Deloitte calculations.

Figure 4.18. **Evolution of number of milk cows in Romania (thousands of head)**

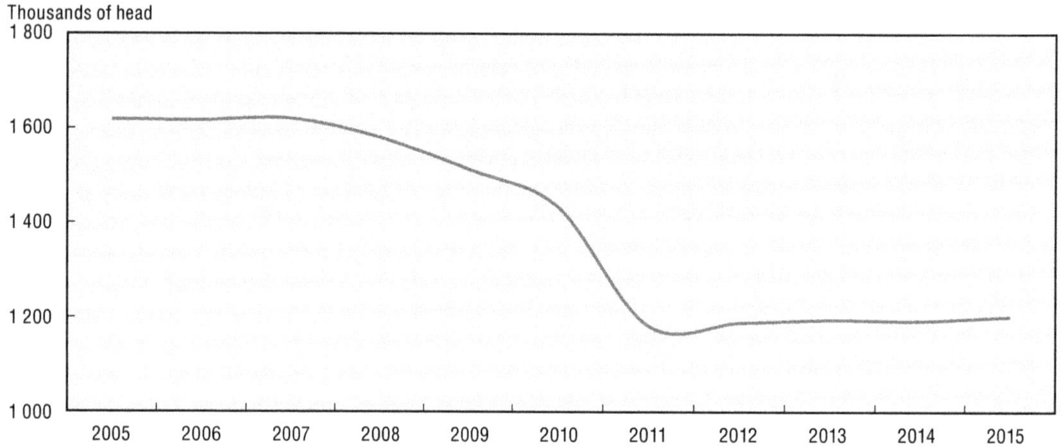

Source: NIS, *http://statistici.insse.ro/shop/index.jsp?page=tempo3&lang=en&ind=AGR201E* (accessed on 29 October 2015).
StatLink http://dx.doi.org/10.1787/888933361895

Figure 4.19 below shows the production of milk for consumption. Even though the number of milk cows has declined from 2006 to 2011, the amount of milk produced for consumption has continuously increased between 2001 and 2013, mainly due to increased imports of milk.

Figure 4.19. **Milk production in Romania (thousands of litres)**

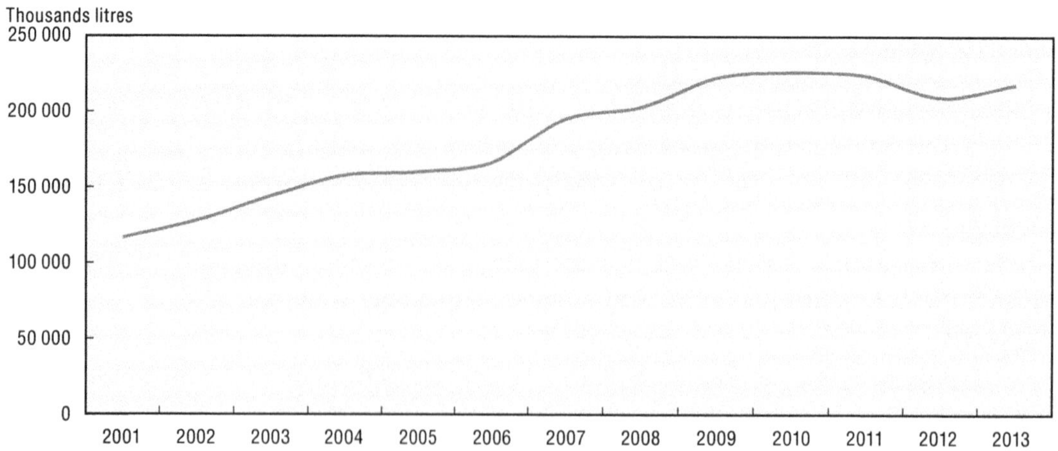

Source: NIS, *http://statistici.insse.ro/shop/index.jsp?page=tempo3&lang=en&ind=IND106C* (accessed on 26 November2015).
StatLink http://dx.doi.org/10.1787/888933361909

Through processing, raw milk is either converted into consumable milk or it is used in the production of other dairy products. The production of cheese products and the production of fresh milk products have been increasing, while the production of butter remained relatively stable.

Figure 4.20. **Production of fresh milk products, cheese products and butter**

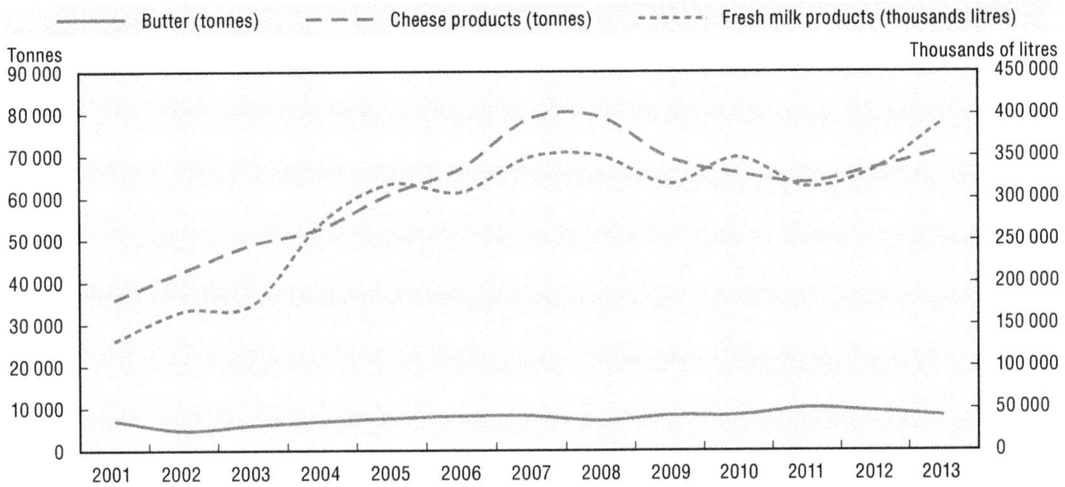

Source: NIS, *http://statistici.insse.ro/shop/index.jsp?page=tempo3&lang=en&ind=IND106C* (accessed on 26 November 2015).
StatLink http://dx.doi.org/10.1787/888933361919

Since 2009, exports of dairy products have been expanding. This was mainly caused by an increase in exports of cheese and curd which became the most exported dairy products in 2013. Imports have also been increasing, with cheese and curd also the most imported dairy product (in terms of thousands EUR).

Figure 4.21. **Exports of dairy products (thousands of EUR)**

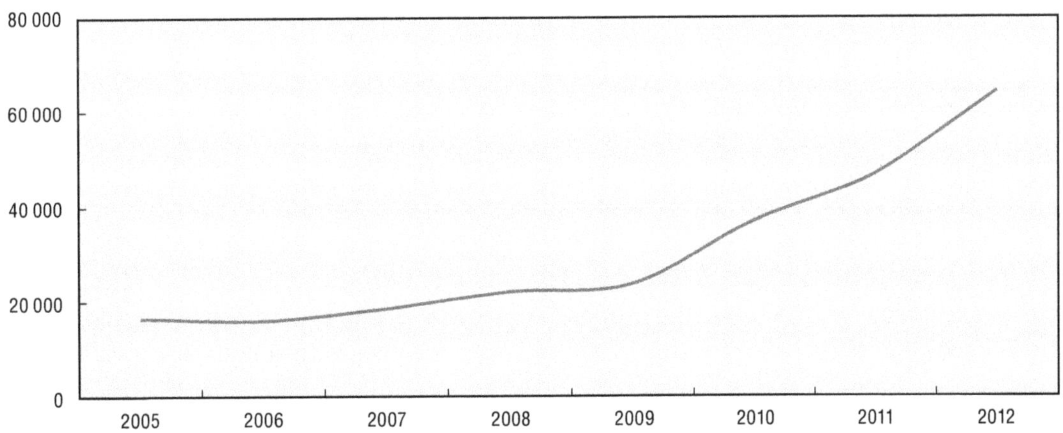

Source: NIS, *http://statistici.insse.ro/shop/index.jsp?page=tempo3&lang=en&ind=EXP101F* (accessed on 29 October 2015).
StatLink http://dx.doi.org/10.1787/888933361927

The manufacture of dairy products subsector is slightly more concentrated than other food processing subsectors, with the top three companies representing nearly 30% of total turnover. The top ten companies accounted for 59.27% of subsector turnover in 2014.

Figure 4.22. **Imports of dairy products (thousands of EUR)**

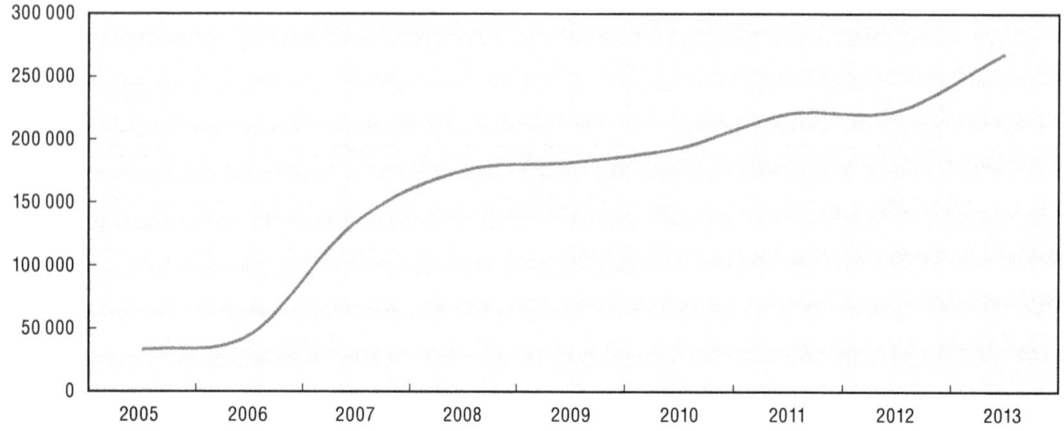

Source: NIS, *http://statistici.insse.ro/shop/index.jsp?page=tempo3&lang=en&ind=EXP102F* (accessed on 5 January 2016).
StatLink http://dx.doi.org/10.1787/888933361931

According to ANAF data, 5.81% of the companies active in this subsector make up over 80% of turnover in this subsector.

Table 4.7. **Top 10 players in the manufacture of dairy products subsector**

No.	Company	NACE Code	Description NACE	Turnover 2014 (EUR m)	Market share 2014[1]
1	ALBALACT SA	C 1051	Operation of dairies and cheese making	106.85	10.44%
2	DANONE - PRODUCTIE SI DISTRIBUTIE DE PRODUSE ALIMENTARE SRL	C 1051	Operation of dairies and cheese making	102.67	10.03%
3	FRIESLANDCAMPINA ROMÂNIA S.A.	C 1051	Operation of dairies and cheese making	90.14	8.80%
4	FABRICA DE LAPTE BRASOV S.A.	C 1051	Operation of dairies and cheese making	68.56	6.70%
5	NAPOLACT SA	C 1051	Operation of dairies and cheese making	51.28	5.01%
6	HOCHLAND ROMÂNIA SRL	C 1051	Operation of dairies and cheese making	48.97	4.78%
7	DORNA LACTATE SA	C 1051	Operation of dairies and cheese making	40.80	3.99%
8	INDUSTRIALIZAREA LAPTELUI MURES SA	C 1051	Operation of dairies and cheese making	38.71	3.78%
9	COVALACT SA	C 1051	Operation of dairies and cheese making	34.99	3.42%
10	SIMULTAN SRL	C 1051	Operation of dairies and cheese making	23.88	2.33%
TOTAL				*606.86*	*59.27%*

1. References to "market characteristics", "market shares" or "markets" in general, included in this report, do not reflect the same definitions used for the purposes of applying competition law.

Source: Credit Info, ANAF, *www.anaf.ro/indicatori/indfinanciari.html* (accessed on 11 February 2016), and Deloitte calculations. ANAF provides the data for GDP and GVA in construction industry in RON m. For calculating the figures in EUR m, the medium annual exchange rate (RON/EUR) from the National Bank of Romania was used, *www.bnr.ro/Cursul-de-schimb-3544.aspx* (accessed on 11 February 2015).

Turnover in the subsector decreased in 2009. It has slowly recovered since then, without reaching its 2008 level. The number of companies and the number of employees in the subsector declined sharply from 2008 to 2010, and has only slightly increased since then.

Subsector view: Manufacture of grain mill products and starch products (C10.6)[30]

The manufacture of grain mill products, starches and starch products subsector includes the transformation of cereals into flour or pearl cereals in the first case, or in starches and glucose syrup in the second. The milling process is dry one and generally involves cereal grinding followed by sifting. These are used on cereals such as wheat, rye and corn. Rice processing is different; the kernels are not ground, only polished on their surface.

Figure 4.23. **Evolution of main indicators (base year 2008) in the manufacture of dairy products subsector**

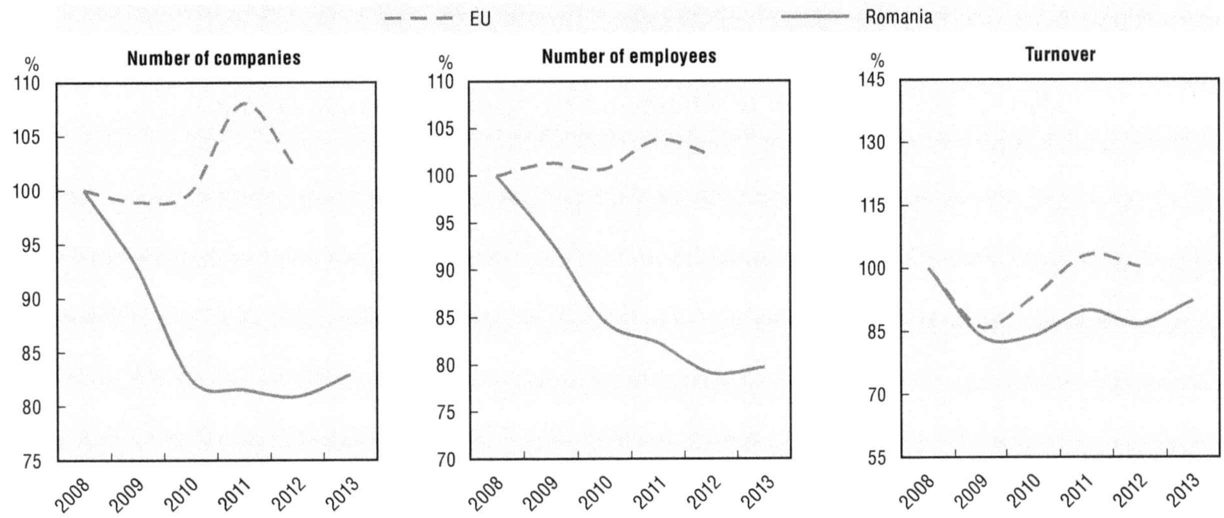

Source: Eurostat, code sbs_na_ind_r2 at *http://ec.europa.eu/eurostat/en/data/database* (accessed on 11 February 2016) and Deloitte calculations.

StatLink http://dx.doi.org/10.1787/888933361946

In the starch process the main raw material is corn, which is softened with water for a period of time, then ground after a long process of separation of the corn starch from corn protein. Finally, these products are dried. The main product is corn starch but corn protein is also a valuable by-product.

These products will further be used in the manufacture of bakery and farinaceous products subsector. The main cereals used as raw materials in this subsector are wheat, corn, barley, rice and rye. The main output of this subsector is wheat flour, manna croup, rye flour, corn flour, decorticated rice or pearl barley, native corn starch and glucose syrup.

According to Eurostat, the gross value added from the manufacture of grain mill products, starches and starch products subsector was EUR 102.7 million in 2013, increasing by 11.8% from 2012.

The main activity of the subsector is the manufacture of grain mill products, which accounts for 93.69% of subsector turnover and 95.98% of the number of employees. In 2014, the manufacture of starches and starch products activity accounted for 6.31% of subsector turnover and 4% of the number of people employed.

Table 4.8. **Structure of the manufacture of grain mill products, starches and starch products subsector**

Activity/Subsector	NACE Code		Turnover 2014 (EUR m)	Employees 2014
Manufacture of grain mill products	C 1061	Abs.	697.74	9 876
		Percentage	*93.69%*	*95.98%*
Manufacture of starches and starch products	C 1062	Abs.	46.97	414
		Percentage	*6.31%*	*4.02%*
Manufacture of grain mill products, starches and starch products	*C 106*	*Abs.*	*745*	*10 290*
		Percentage	*100%*	*100%*

Note: Considering companies with a turnover of more than EUR 50 000 in 2014.
Source: Credit Info and Deloitte calculations.

The subsector sources its supplies mainly from domestic production, but relies also on imports. Corn is the top grain produced by surface area in Romania, followed by wheat and millet.

Output in the sub-sector increased until 2010, followed by a decline since then.

Figure 4.24. **Production of wheat and rye flour (thousands of tonnes)**

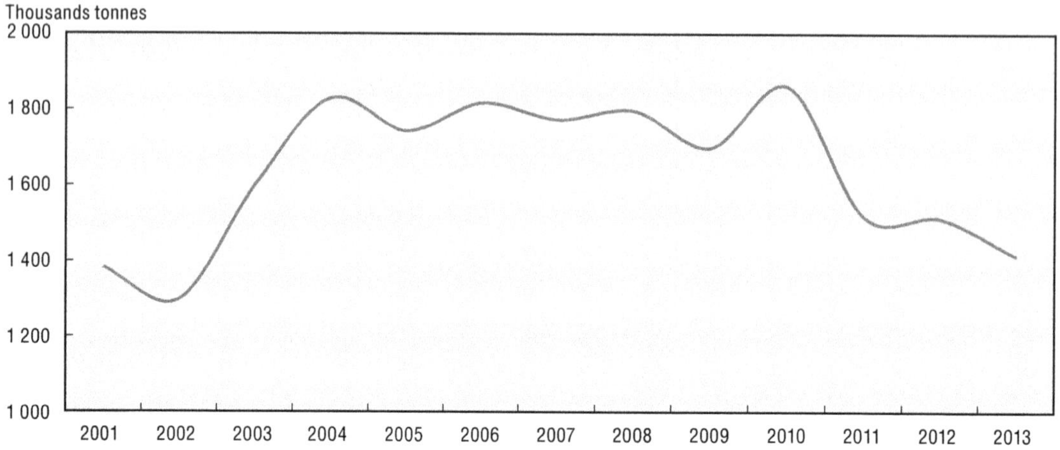

Source: NIS, *http://statistici.insse.ro/shop/index.jsp?page=tempo3&lang=en&ind=IND106C* (accessed on 26 November 2015).

StatLink http://dx.doi.org/10.1787/888933361951

Exports have increased, mainly because of an increase in the export of cereal grains, groats, meal and pellets.

Figure 4.25. **Exports of main grain mill, starches and starch products (thousands of EUR)**

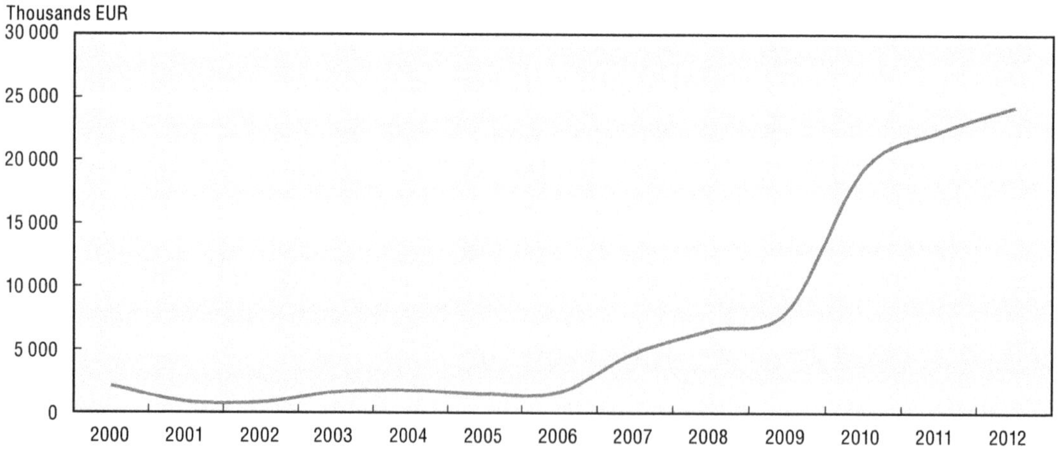

Source: NIS, *http://statistici.insse.ro/shop/index.jsp?page=tempo3&lang=en&ind=EXP101F* (accessed on 30 October 2015).

StatLink http://dx.doi.org/10.1787/888933361964

The top ten players in 2014 in the manufacture of grain mill products, starches and starch products subsector account for 56.95% of subsector turnover. The company that had the highest share of turnover for the subsector in 2014 was "SAM MILLS SRL" (11.99%), followed by "GOODMILLS ROMANIA S.A." (9.15%) and by "BOROMIR IND SRL" (7.05%).

The number of companies and the number of employees have decreased in Romania; this is similar to a trend in Europe over the period analysed. Turnover in the subsector has tended to increase since 2009, both in Romania and in Europe.

Table 4.9. **Top 10 players in the manufacture of grain mill products, starches and starch products subsector**

No.	Company	NACE Code	Description NACE	Turnover 2014 (EUR m)	Market share 2014[1]
1	SAM MILLS SRL	C 1061	Manufacture of grain mill products	91.68	11.99%
2	GOODMILLS ROMANIA S.A.	C 1061	Manufacture of grain mill products	70.02	9.15%
3	BOROMIR IND SRL	C 1061	Manufacture of grain mill products	53.93	7.05%
4	SAPTE SPICE SA	C 1061	Manufacture of grain mill products	49.87	6.52%
5	PAMBAC SA	C 1061	Manufacture of grain mill products	38.54	5.04%
6	MOARA CIBIN SA	C 1061	Manufacture of grain mill products	29.77	3.89%
7	DOBROGEA GRUP SA	C 1061	Manufacture of grain mill products	29.37	3.84%
8	M.P. BANEASA - MOARA SA	C 1061	Manufacture of grain mill products	25.49	3.33%
9	OLTINA IMPEX PROD COM SRL	C 1061	Manufacture of grain mill products	23.67	3.09%
10	BOROMIR PROD SA	C 1061	Manufacture of grain mill products	23.22	3.04%
TOTAL				*435.56*	*56.95%*

1. References to "market characteristics", "market shares" or "markets" in general, included in this report, do not reflect the same definitions used for the purposes of applying competition law.

Source: Credit Info, ANAF, *www.anaf.ro/indicatori/indfinanciari.html* (accessed on 11 February 2016), and Deloitte calculations. ANAF provides the data for GDP and GVA in construction industry in RON m. For calculating the figures in EUR m, the medium annual exchange rate (RON/EUR) from the National Bank of Romania was used, *www.bnr.ro/Cursul-de-schimb-3544.aspx* (accessed on 11 February 2015).

Figure 4.26. **Evolution of main indicators (base year 2008) in the manufacture of grain mill products, starches and starch products subsector**

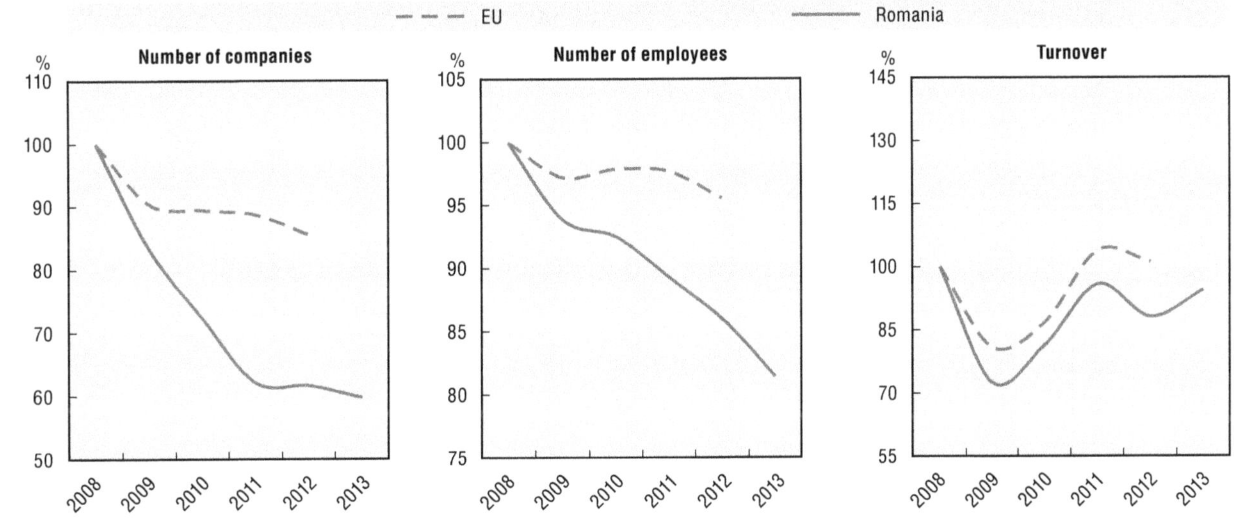

Source: Eurostat, code sbs_na_ind_r2 at *http://ec.europa.eu/eurostat/en/data/database* (accessed on 11 February 2016) and Deloitte calculations.

StatLink http://dx.doi.org/10.1787/888933361977

Subsector view: Processing and preserving of fruit and vegetables (C10.3)[31]

The processing and preserving of fruit and vegetables subsector involves activities such as sorting, washing, cleaning and dividing, as well as steaming, boiling, frying and cooling of fruit and vegetables.

The production of fruit and vegetables in Romania relies primarily on family businesses. A considerable share of production is either used for home consumption or sold to customers without being processed or preserved (Department of Agriculture, Netherlands, 2009). This high rate of self-consumption and direct sales of agricultural products makes it difficult to accurately determine the quantities of raw fruit and vegetables subject to processing and preserving.

According to Eurostat, the gross value added from the processing and preserving of fruit and vegetables subsector was EUR 82.7 million in 2013, an increase of 3.9% from 2012.

The main activity in the subsector, the processing and preserving of fruit and vegetables, represents 55.46% of the total turnover and 66% of the number of employees in the subsector. The processing and preserving of potatoes accounts for 43.45% of total turnover and 32.04% of the number of employees in the subsector.

Table 4.10. **Structure of the processing and preserving of fruit and vegetables subsector**

Activity/subsector	NACE Code		Turnover 2014 (EUR m)	Employees 2014
Processing and preserving of potatoes	C 1031	Abs.	155.51	1 289
		Percentage	*43.45%*	*32.04%*
Manufacture of fruit and vegetable juice	C 1032	Abs.	3.88	78
		Percentage	*1.08%*	*1.94%*
Other processing and preserving of fruit and vegetables	C 1039	Abs.	198.49	2 656
		Percentage	*55.46%*	*66.02%*
Processing and preserving of fruit and vegetables	*C 103*	*Abs.*	*358*	*4 023*
		Percentage	*100%*	*100%*

Source: Credit Info and Deloitte calculations.

In this subsector the supply comes from the farmers who grow and trade fruit and vegetables, or from imports. The internal source of supply is highly dependent on the agriculture industry. The main vegetable grown in Romania (based on agricultural surface covered) is potatoes, followed by tomatoes and white cabbage.

The development of imports was determined primarily by imports of fresh or chilled citrus fruit.

Figure 4.27. **Imports of fruit and vegetables (thousands of EUR)**

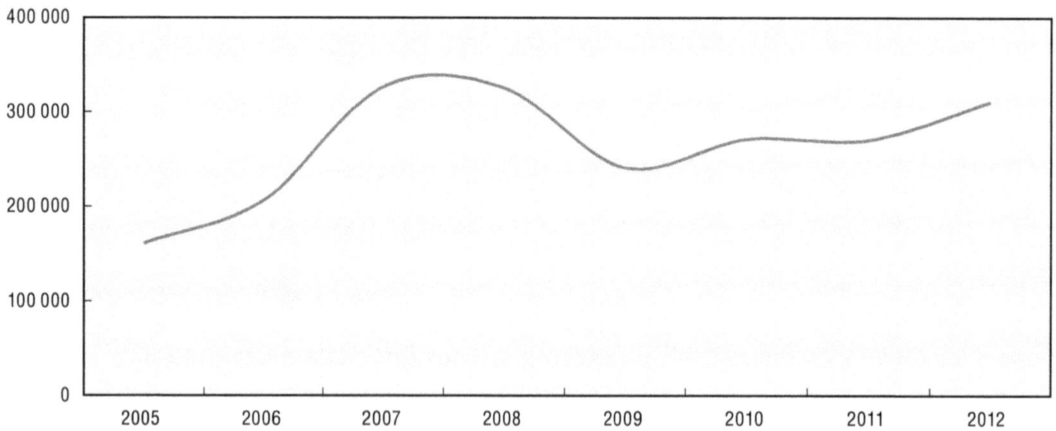

Source: NIS, *http://statistici.insse.ro/shop/index.jsp?page=tempo3&lang=en&ind=EXP102F* (accessed on 28 October 2015).

StatLink http://dx.doi.org/10.1787/888933361987

The production of tinned vegetables represents by far the largest share of output in this subsector. On average, the production of tinned vegetables increased over the past 12 years (57% total increase from 2001 until 2013). The production of tinned fruit, although less significant in absolute terms, has increased on average by 20% each year, despite a sharp decline in 2008.

Figure 4.28. **Production of tinned fruit and vegetables (tonnes)**

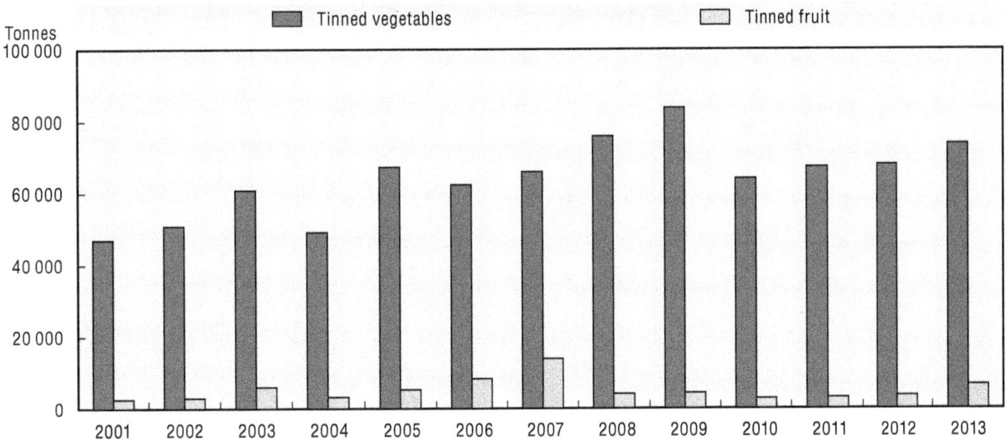

Source: NIS, *http://statistici.insse.ro/shop/index.jsp?page=tempo3&lang=en&ind=IND106C* (accessed on 26 November 2015).

StatLink http://dx.doi.org/10.1787/888933361994

Five top companies accounted for more than 59% of subsector turnover in 2014. "STAR FOODS E.M. SRL" is the top player, alone accounting for more than 25% of total turnover. "INTERSNACK ROMANIA SRL" represented over 16% of subsector turnover.

Table 4.11. **Top 5 players in the processing and preserving of fruit and vegetables subsector**

No.	Company	NACE Code	Description NACE	Turnover 2014 (EUR m)	Market share 2014[1]
1	STAR FOODS E.M. SRL	C 1031	Processing and preserving of potatoes	91.92	25.28%
2	INTERSNACK ROMANIA SRL	C 1031	Processing and preserving of potatoes	60.92	16.75%
3	EFES EXPORT S.A.	C 1039	Other processing and preserving of fruit and vegetables	27.28	7.50%
4	CONTEC FOODS SRL	C 1039	Other processing and preserving of fruit and vegetables	20.96	5.76%
5	ANNABELLA FABRICA DE CONSERVE RAURENI SRL	C 1039	Other processing and preserving of fruit and vegetables	13.97	3.84%
TOTAL				*215.06*	*59.14%*

1. References to "market characteristics", "market shares" or "markets" in general, included in this report, do not reflect the same definitions used for the purposes of applying competition law.

Source: Credit Info, ANAF, *www.anaf.ro/indicatori/indfinanciari.html* (accessed on 11 February 2016, and Deloitte calculations. ANAF provides the data for GDP and GVA in construction industry in RON m. For calculating the figures in EUR m, the medium annual exchange rate (RON/EUR) from the National Bank of Romania was used, *www.bnr.ro/Cursul-de-schimb-3544.aspx* (accessed on 11 February 2015).

The number of companies active in the processing and preserving of fruit and vegetables subsector in Romania has decreased from 2008 until 2011, and has recovered in the last 2 years of analysis. The number of employees in Romania did not follow a specific trend between 2008 and 2013. Turnover has increased in Romania by approximatively 20% from 2008 until 2013, and in Europe (by 10% from 2008 until 2012).

Subsector view: Manufacture of vegetable and animal oils and fats (C10.4)[32]

Traditional oil extraction includes various preliminary operations such as cracking, shelling, dehulling, etc., after which the crop is ground to a paste. The paste, or the whole fruit, is then boiled with water and stirred until the oil separates and can be collected. Modern methods of extraction involve crushing and pressing, as well as dissolving the crop in a solvent, most commonly hexane. The main activities involve processing of different vegetable[33] or animal products.[34]

Figure 4.29. **Evolution of the main indicators (base year 2008) in the processing and preserving of fruit and vegetables subsector**

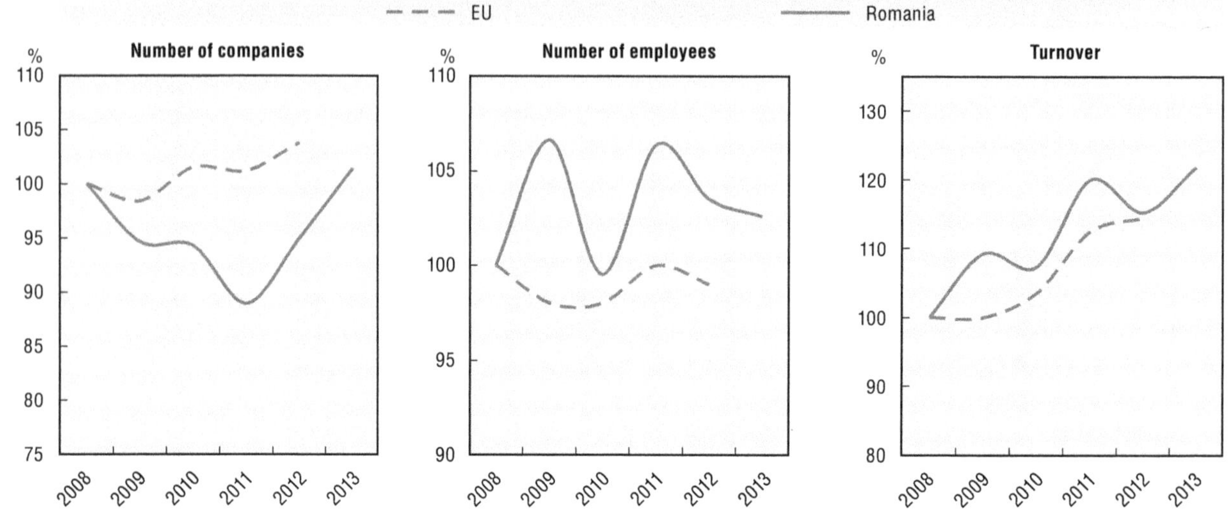

Source: Eurostat, code sbs_na_ind_r2 at *http://ec.europa.eu/eurostat/en/data/database* (accessed on 11 February 2016) and Deloitte calculations.

StatLink http://dx.doi.org/10.1787/888933362004

According to Eurostat, gross value added from the manufacture of vegetable and animal oils and fats subsector was EUR 54.1 million in 2013, a decrease of 30% from 2012.

The main activity of the subsector is the manufacture of oil and fats,[35] followed by the manufacture of margarine and similar edible fats.[36]

Table 4.12. **Structure of the manufacture of vegetable and animal oils and fats subsector**[1]

Activity/subsector	NACE Code		Turnover 2014 (EUR m)	Employees 2014
Manufacture of oils and fats	C 1041	Abs.	876.46	2 789
		Percentage	*94.61%*	*87.93%*
Manufacture of margarine and similar edible fats	C 1042	Abs.	49.92	383
		Percentage	*5.39%*	*12.07%*
Manufacture of vegetable and animal oils and fats	*C 104*	*Abs.*	*926*	*3 172*
		Percentage	*100%*	*100%*

1. For companies with a turnover higher than EUR 50 000 in 2014.
Source: Credit Info and Deloitte calculations.

The subsector sources input products from domestic production as well as imports. The main grain oilseed cultivated and used in edible oil production is sunflower, followed by rapeseed. These also oilseeds represent the main imports.

The production of edible oils has generally declined, while the production of margarine has remained relatively stable.

The exports of oils and fats increased from 2009 to 2011, but declined in 2012.

The subsector is more concentrated than other subsectors, with the top three producers accounting for more than 70% of total output. The largest company in 2014 was "BUNGE ROMANIA SRL", alone accounting for more than 30% of subsector turnover, followed by "EXPUR SA" with 26.37% and "PRUTUL SA" with 17.9% of subsector turnover.

Figure 4.30. **Production of vegetable oils (thousands tonnes)**

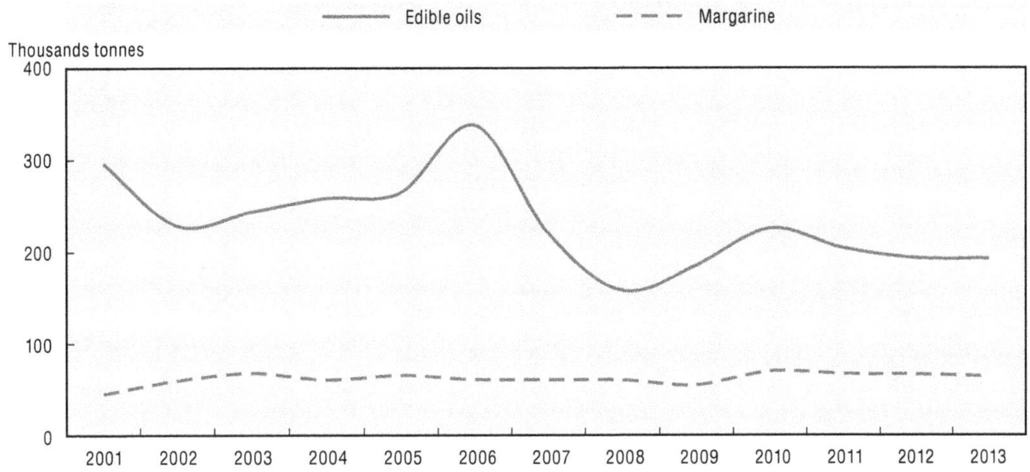

Source: NIS, *http://statistici.insse.ro/shop/index.jsp?page=tempo3&lang=en&ind=IND106C* (accessed on 26 November 2015).
StatLink http://dx.doi.org/10.1787/888933362014

Figure 4.31. **Exports of main vegetable and animal oils and fats (thousands EUR)**

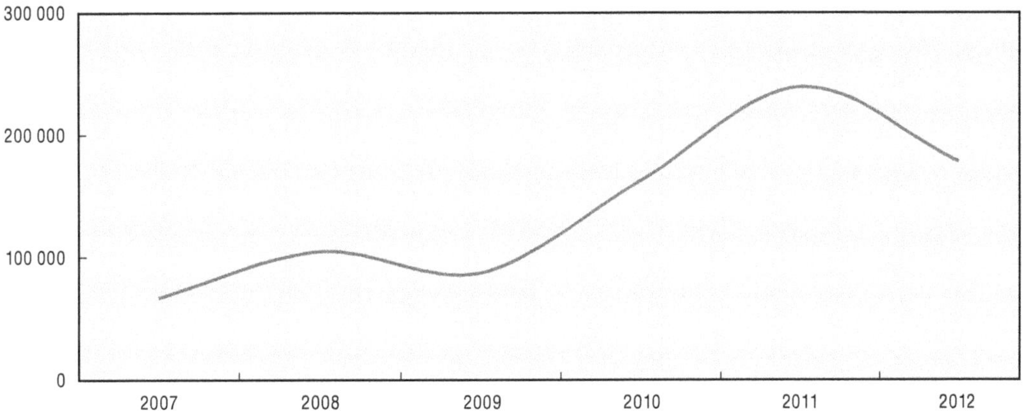

Source: NIS, *http://statistici.insse.ro/shop/index.jsp?page=tempo3&lang=en&ind=EXP101F* (accessed on 29 October 2015).
StatLink http://dx.doi.org/10.1787/888933362023

The following table presents the top players in the manufacture of vegetable and animal oils and fats subsector:

Between 2008 and 2013 the number of companies manufacturing vegetable oils and animal fats decreased in Romania and Europe.[37] However, the number of employees in the subsector shows different trends in Romania and Europe. In Romania, the number of employees decreased between 2008 and 2013,[38] whereas in Europe the number of employees increased by 6% in 2012 compared to 2008. Turnover has increased in Romania by approximately 45% in 2012 compared to 2008, and a similar trend can be observed in Europe.

Subsector view: Manufacture of prepared animal feeds (C10.9)[39]

Animal food can be either of plant origin (grains, oilseeds, fruit and fruit products, molasses and sugar, alfalfa products or other plant products – e.g. banana peels), of animal origin (animal waste, dairy products, marine by-products, by-products of slaughtered animals), of mixed origin (fats and oils), or of mineral, microbial or synthetic origin (drugs, non-protein nitrogen, minerals, vitamins, direct-fed microorganisms, flavours, enzymes, etc.).

Table 4.13. **Top 5 players in the manufacture of vegetable and animal oils and fats subsector**

No.	Company	NACE Code	Description NACE	Turnover 2014 (EUR m)	Market share 2014[1]
1	BUNGE ROMANIA SRL	C 1041	Manufacture of oils and fats	283.05	30.19%
2	EXPUR SA	C 1041	Manufacture of oils and fats	247.21	26.37%
3	PRUTUL SA	C 1041	Manufacture of oils and fats	167.79	17.90%
4	ARDEALUL SA	C 1041	Manufacture of oils and fats	51.42	5.49%
5	ARGUS SA	C 1041	Manufacture of oils and fats	39.70	4.23%
TOTAL				*789.18*	*84.18%*

1. References to "market characteristics", "market shares" or "markets" in general, included in this report, do not reflect the same definitions used for the purposes of applying competition law.

Source: Credit Info, ANAF, *www.anaf.ro/indicatori/indfinanciari.html* (accessed on 11 February 2016, and Deloitte calculations. ANAF provides the data for GDP and GVA in construction industry in RON m. For calculating the figures in EUR m, the medium annual exchange rate (RON/EUR) from the National Bank of Romania was used, *www.bnr.ro/Cursul-de-schimb-3544.aspx* (accessed on 11 February 2015)

Figure 4.32. **Evolution of main indicators (base year 2008) in the manufacture of vegetable and animal oils and fats subsector**

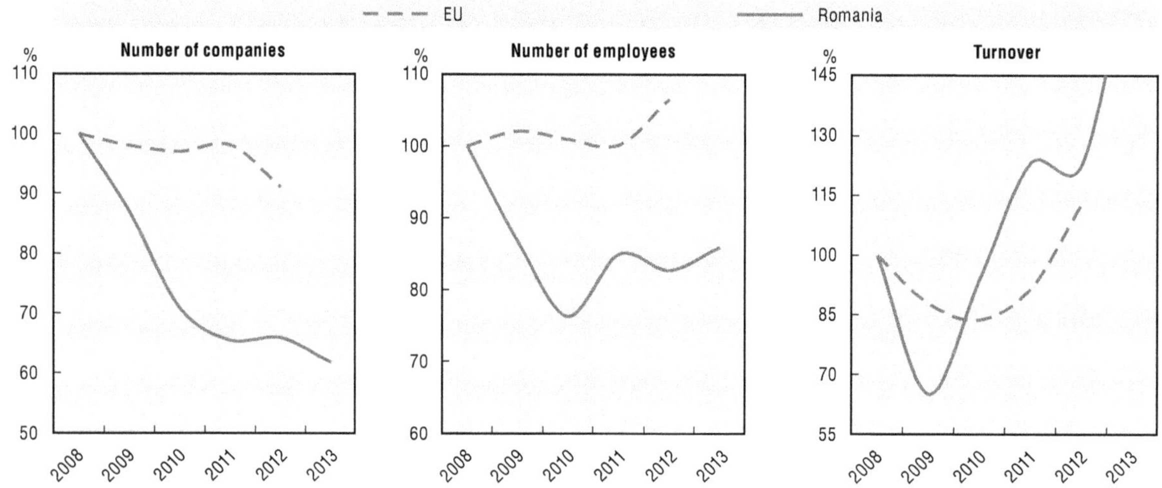

Source: Eurostat, code sbs_na_ind_r2 at *http://ec.europa.eu/eurostat/en/data/database* (accessed on 11 February 2016) and Deloitte calculations.

StatLink http://dx.doi.org/10.1787/888933362031

According to Eurostat, the gross value added from the manufacture of prepared animal feeds subsector was EUR 36.8 million in 2013, a decrease of almost 32% from 2012.

Table 4.14 shows that the main activity of the subsector is represented by the manufacture of prepared feeds for farm animals.[40]

Table 4.14. **Structure of the manufacture of the prepared animal feeds subsector**

Activity/Subsector	NACE Code		Turnover 2014 (EUR m)	Employees 2014
Manufacture of prepared feed for farm animals	C 1091	Abs.	303.92	1 499
		Percentage	*96.22%*	*92.08%*
Manufacture of prepared pet food	C 1092	Abs.	11.93	129
		Percentage	*3.78%*	*7.92%*
Manufacture of prepared animal feeds	*C 109*	*Abs.*	*316*	*1 628*
		Percentage	*100%*	*100%*

Source: Credit Info and Deloitte calculations.

As the origins of animal feed are diverse, the supply comes from various areas. As in the case of food products manufactured for human consumption, the supply for this subsector can come from the agriculture industry (both animal and vegetable areas).

The top five players in this industry make up 42% of subsector turnover. The company recording the highest share of sector's turnover in 2014 is "SAM MILLS FEED SRL" (10.9%), followed by "NUTRIENTUL SA" (8.91%). According to ANAF, in the subsector 10.77% of the companies make up over 80% of subsector turnover.

Table 4.15. **Top 5 players in the manufacture of prepared animal feeds subsector**

No.	Company	NACE Code	Description NACE	Turnover 2014 (EUR m)	Market share 2014[1]
1	SAM MILLS FEED SRL	C 1091	Manufacture of prepared feed for farm animals	34.98	10.90%
2	NUTRIENTUL SA	C 1091	Manufacture of prepared feed for farm animals	28.59	8.91%
3	PROVIMI ROMÂNIA SRL	C 1091	Manufacture of prepared feed for farm animals	27.26	8.50%
4	NUTRIMOLD SA	C 1091	Manufacture of prepared feed for farm animals	24.64	7.68%
5	G&M GRUP IMPORT EXPORT SRL	C 1091	Manufacture of prepared feed for farm animals	119.25	6.00%
TOTAL				*134.72*	*42.00%*

1. References to "market characteristics", "market shares" or "markets" in general, included in this report, do not reflect the same definitions used for the purposes of applying competition law.

Source: Credit Info, ANAF, *www.anaf.ro/indicatori/indfinanciari.html* (accessed on 11 February 2016, and Deloitte calculations. ANAF provides the data for GDP and GVA in construction industry in RON m. For calculating the figures in EUR m, the medium annual exchange rate (RON/EUR) from the National Bank of Romania was used, *www.bnr.ro/Cursul-de-schimb-3544.aspx* (accessed on 11 February 2015).

In Romania, the number of companies active in this subsector increased in 2009, followed by a sharp reduction until 2012 and a gradual increase since then. The number of employees has generally increased, with the exception of a sharp drop in 2010.[42] Turnover has increased since 2010. From 2009 to 2012 development in Europe was relatively stable, with a slight increase in turnover.

Figure 4.33. **Evolution of main indicators (base year 2008) in the manufacture of prepared animal feed subsector**

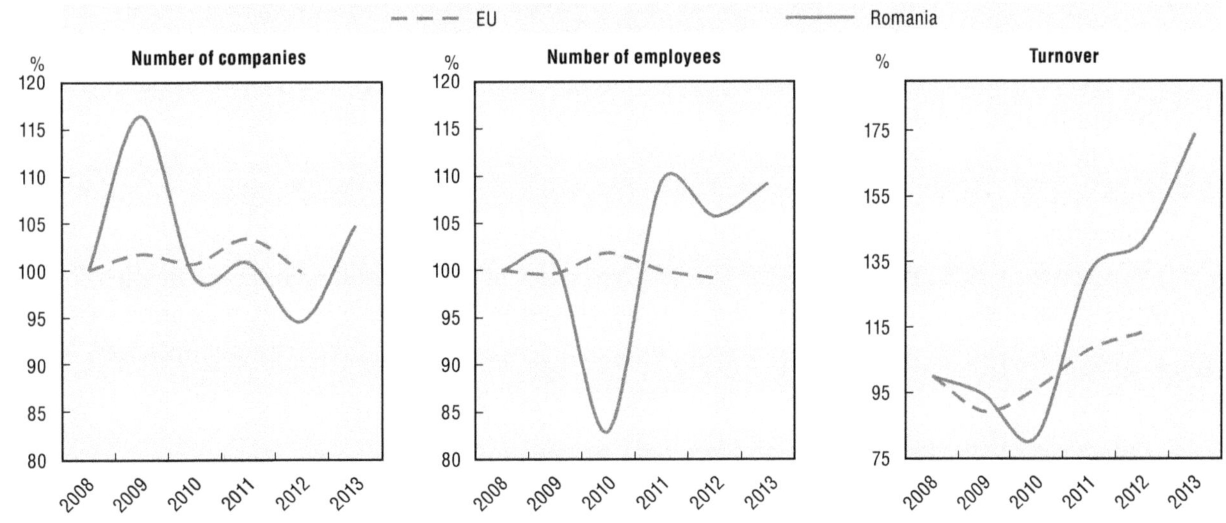

Source: Eurostat, code sbs_na_ind_r2 at *http://ec.europa.eu/eurostat/en/data/database* (accessed on 11 February 2016) and Deloitte calculations.

StatLink http://dx.doi.org/10.1787/888933362049

Subsector view: Processing and preserving of fish, crustaceans and molluscs (C10.2)[43]

The processing and preserving of fish, crustaceans and molluscs subsector involves several activities such as: refrigerating, freezing, salting, pickling, smoking and canning of fish, crustaceans and molluscs.

According to Eurostat, the gross value added from this subsector was EUR 12.8 million in 2013, a similar value to 2012.

Supplies for this subsector come primarily from fishing,[44] aquaculture and imports. According to the Operational Program for Fisheries of MARD,[45] fish catches have decreased over time.[46]

The production of semi-tinned fish has generally increased since 2001, while the production of tinned fish has decreased slightly.

Figure 4.34. **Production of processed fish products (thousands of EUR)**

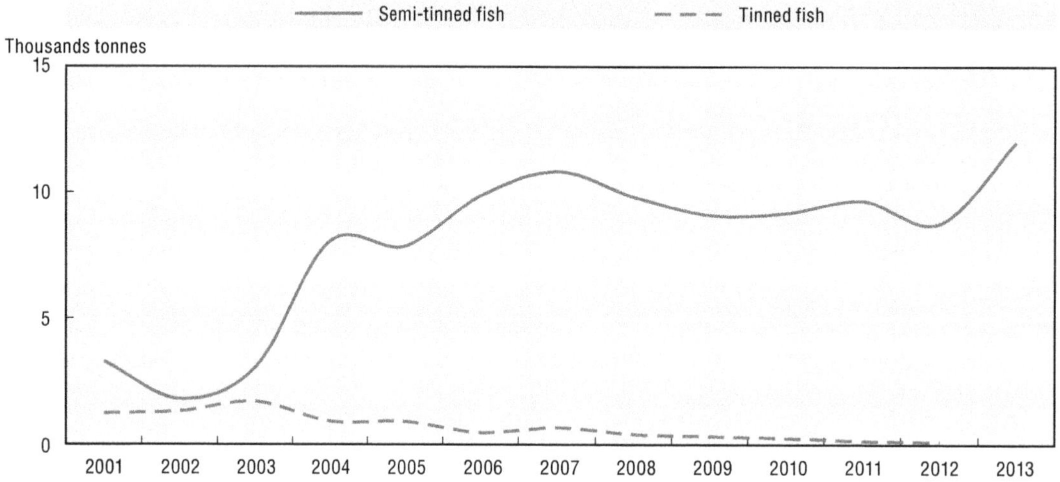

Source: NIS, *http://statistici.insse.ro/shop/index.jsp?page=tempo3&lang=en&ind=IND106C* (accessed on 27 November 2015).
StatLink http://dx.doi.org/10.1787/888933362051

As shown in Figure 4.35, exports of the main processed fish products, crustaceans and molluscs have increased.[47]

In 2014, the top five players in the subsector accounted for over 82% of subsector turnover. Together, the two top players account for more than 62% of turnover in this subsector.

Between 2008 and 2013 the number of companies in the processing and preserving of fish, crustaceans and molluscs subsector decreased in Romania, with the exception of 2012. The number of employees also declined. In Europe both indicators remained relatively stable, however, turnover has increased in Romania more than in Europe.

Subsector view: Manufacture of other food products (C10.8)[48]

This subsector includes the processing of raw materials into a variety of products such as sugar, cocoa and chocolate, tea and coffee, condiments and seasonings, prepared meals, etc. The manufacture of sugar involves sugar beet and sugarcane. For the manufacturing of cocoa, chocolate and sugar confectionery, the raw materials include cocoa beans, sugar, glucose, milk powder, condensed milk, as well as oils and fats such as cocoa butter,

Figure 4.35. **Exports of processed fish, crustaceans and molluscs (thousands of EUR)**

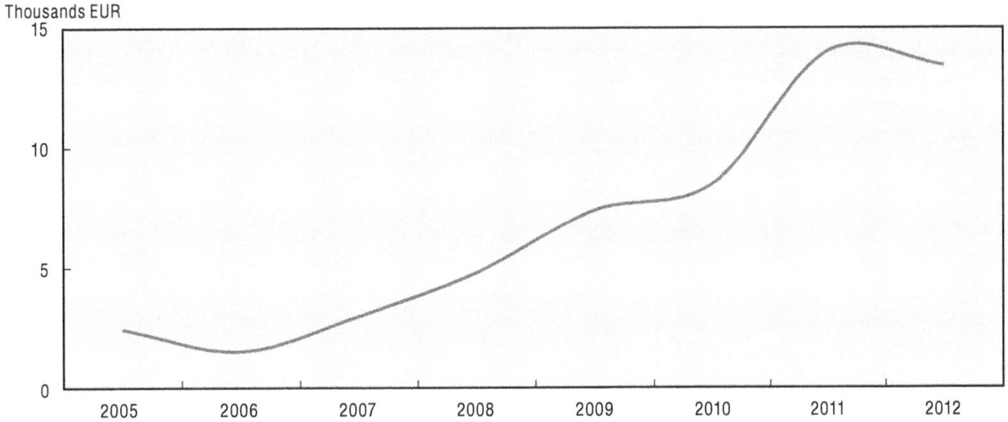

Source: NIS, *http://statistici.insse.ro/shop/index.jsp?page=tempo3&lang=en&ind=EXP101F* (accessed on 27 November 2015).

StatLink http://dx.doi.org/10.1787/888933362064

Table 4.16. **Top 5 players in the processing and preserving of fish, crustaceans and molluscs subsector**

No.	Company	NACE Code	Description NACE	Turnover 2014 (EUR m)	Market share 2014[1]
1	OCEAN FISH SRL	C 1020	Processing and preserving of fish, crustaceans and molluscs	26.85	31.43%
2	NEGRO 2000 SRL	C 1020	Processing and preserving of fish, crustaceans and molluscs	26.79	31.35%
3	PESCADO GRUP SRL	C 1020	Processing and preserving of fish, crustaceans and molluscs	8.88	10.40%
4	ROLUX SRL	C 1020	Processing and preserving of fish, crustaceans and molluscs	4.09	4.79%
5	SABIKO-IMPEX SRL	C 1020	Processing and preserving of fish, crustaceans and molluscs	3.61	4.23%
TOTAL				*70.22*	*82.20%*

1. References to "market characteristics", "market shares" or "markets" in general, included in this report, do not reflect the same definitions used for the purposes of applying competition law.

Source: Credit Info, ANAF, *www.anaf.ro/indicatori/indfinanciari.html* (accessed on 11 February 2016, and Deloitte calculations. ANAF provides the data for GDP and GVA in construction industry in RON m. For calculating the figures in EUR m, the medium annual exchange rate (RON/EUR) from the National Bank of Romania was used, *www.bnr.ro/Cursul-de-schimb-3544.aspx* (accessed on 11 February 2015).

margarine and butter made from cow's milk. Condiments and seasonings generally are produced from the dried parts of plants (roots, leaves or strains, peels, flowers or buds, bulbs, fruit or seeds). Tea and coffee are made from tea plants and coffee beans respectively.

According to Eurostat, the gross value added from the manufacture of other food products subsector was EUR 168.4 million in 2013, a decrease of 20% from 2012.

The main activity of this subsector in terms of turnover is the manufacture of sugar (34.65%), followed by the manufacture of cocoa, chocolate and sugar confectionery (23%), processing of tea and coffee (11.23%) and the manufacture of condiments and seasonings (11.2%). In terms of the number of employees, the top activity is the manufacture of cocoa, chocolate and sugar confectionery (35.44%), followed by the manufacture of sugar (accounting for 11.28% of employees in the subsector).

The input for this subsector comes from domestic production and imports.

Chocolate and other foods containing cocoa have been exported most frequently and recorded a significant increase from 2005 to 2013.

The top five companies accounted for over 44% of subsector turnover. The largest company in terms of 2014 turnover is "AGRANA ROMANIA SA" which is active in the

Figure 4.36. **Evolution of the indicators (base year-2008) in the processing and preserving of meat and production of meat products subsector**

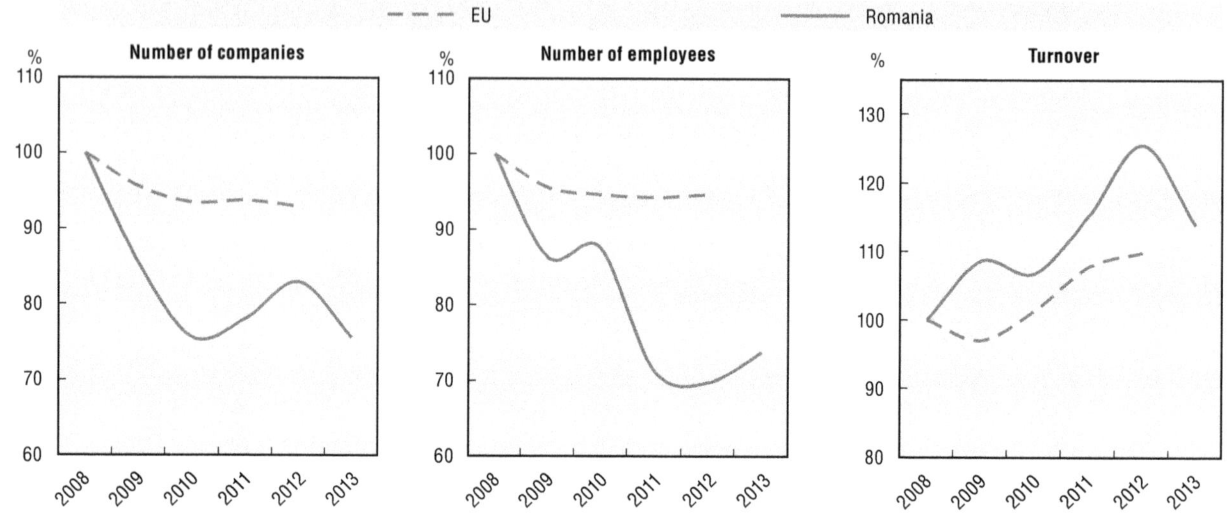

Source: Eurostat, code sbs_na_ind_r2 at *http://ec.europa.eu/eurostat/en/data/database* (accessed on 11 February 2016) and Deloitte calculations.

StatLink http://dx.doi.org/10.1787/888933362075

Table 4.17. **Structure of the manufacture of other food products subsector**

Activity/subsector	NACE Code		Turnover 2014 (EUR m)	Employees 2014
Manufacture of sugar	C 1081	Abs.	411.88	1 469
		Percentage	*34.65%*	*11.28%*
Manufacture of cocoa, chocolate and sugar confectionery	C 1082	Abs.	274.20	4 616
		Percentage	*23.07%*	*35.44%*
Processing of tea and coffee	C 1083	Abs.	133.48	1 394
		Percentage	*11.23%*	*10.70%*
Manufacture of condiments and seasonings	C 1084	Abs.	133.18	1 504
		Percentage	*11.20%*	*11.55%*
Manufacture of prepared meals and dishes	C 1085	Abs.	2.61	159
		Percentage	*0.22%*	*1.22%*
Manufacture of homogenised food preparations and dietetic food	C 1086	Abs.	7.41	178
		Percentage	*0.62%*	*1.37%*
Manufacture of other food products (n.e.c.)	C 1089	Abs.	225.97	3 703
		Percentage	*19.01%*	*28.43%*
Manufacture of other food products	*C 108*	*Abs.*	*1 189*	*13 023*
		Percentage	*100%*	*100%*

Note: The companies that recorded in 2014 a turnover higher than EUR 50 000.
Source: Credit Info and Deloitte calculations.

manufacture of sugar (16.97% of turnover), followed by "NESTLE ROMANIA SRL" which is active in the manufacture of cocoa, chocolate and sugar confectionery (11.45%).

From 2009 to 2013 the number of companies and the number of employees in the manufacture of other food products subsector declined in Romania. Turnover increased from 2010 to 2012, but declined again sharply in 2013. In Europe, all three indicators have increased over time.

Figure 4.37. **Sugar beet production (thousands of tonnes)**

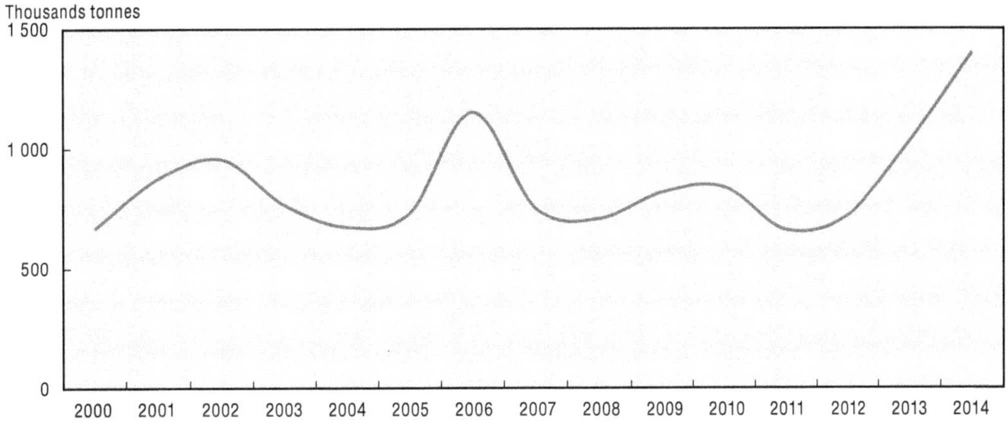

Source: NIS, *http://statistici.insse.ro/shop/?page=tempo3&lang=ro&ind=AGR109A* (accessed on 4 November 2015).
StatLink http://dx.doi.org/10.1787/888933362085

Figure 4.38. **Exports of main products from the manufacture of other food products subsector (thousands of EUR)**

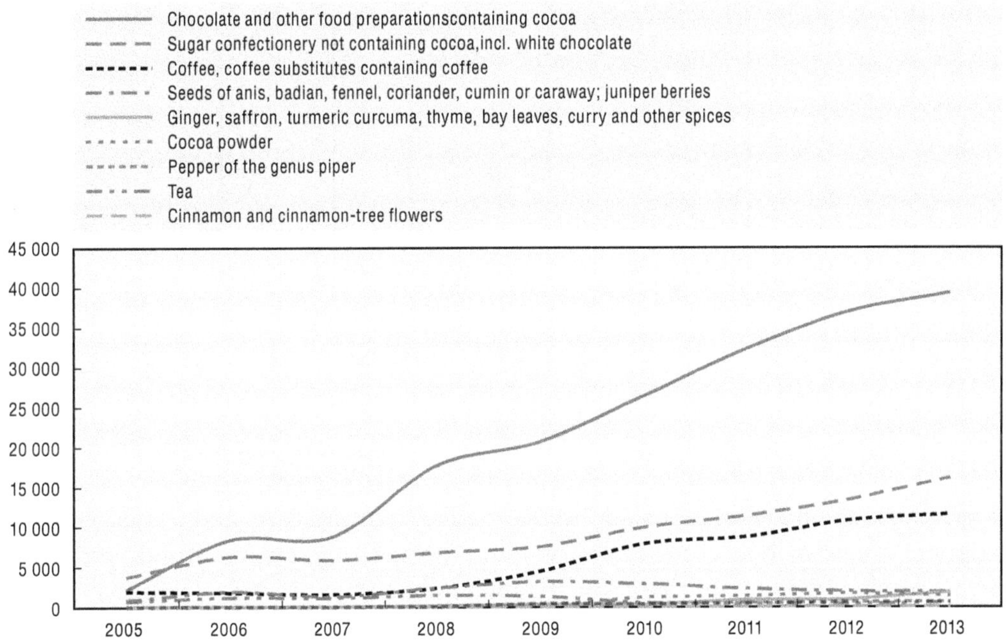

Source: NIS, *http://statistici.insse.ro/shop/index.jsp?page=tempo3&lang=en&ind=EXP101F* (accessed on 4 November 2015).
StatLink http://dx.doi.org/10.1787/888933362096

4.2. Restrictions to competitiveness in food processing

Overview

Using the methodology outlined in the Competition Assessment Toolkit (OECD, 2011a and 2011b), the OECD has examined the regulatory environment applicable to food processing in Romania. A total of 170 laws and regulations have been examined for this report.

The regulatory environment is characterised by several framework laws and regulations, in particular those on the establishment and operation of firms in the sector; they are designed to ensure compliance with food safety and hygiene standards. There are

Table 4.18. **Top 5 players in the manufacture of other food products subsector**

No.	Company	NACE Code	Description NACE	Turnover 2014 (EUR m)	Market share 2014[1]
1	AGRANA ROMANIA SA	C 1081	Manufacture of sugar	215.03	16.97%
2	NESTLE ROMANIA SRL	C 1082	Manufacture of cocoa, chocolate and sugar confectionery	145.11	11.45%
3	ZAHARUL ORADEA SA	C 1081	Manufacture of sugar	81.34	6.42%
4	EUROPEAN FOOD SA	C 1089	Manufacture of other food products (n.e.c.)	71.88	5.67%
5	STRAUSS ROMANIA SRL	C 1083	Processing of tea and coffee	53.99	4.26%
TOTAL				*567.35*	*44.78%*

1. References to "market characteristics", "market shares" or "markets" in general, included in this report, do not reflect the same definitions used for the purposes of applying competition law.

Source: Credit Info, ANAF, *www.anaf.ro/indicatori/indfinanciari.html* (accessed on 11 February 2016, and Deloitte calculations. ANAF provides the data for GDP and GVA in construction industry in RON m. For calculating the figures in EUR m, the medium annual exchange rate (RON/EUR) from the National Bank of Romania was used, *www.bnr.ro/Cursul-de-schimb-3544.aspx* (accessed on 11 February 2015).

Figure 4.39. **Evolution of main indicators (base year 2008) in the manufacture of other food products subsector**

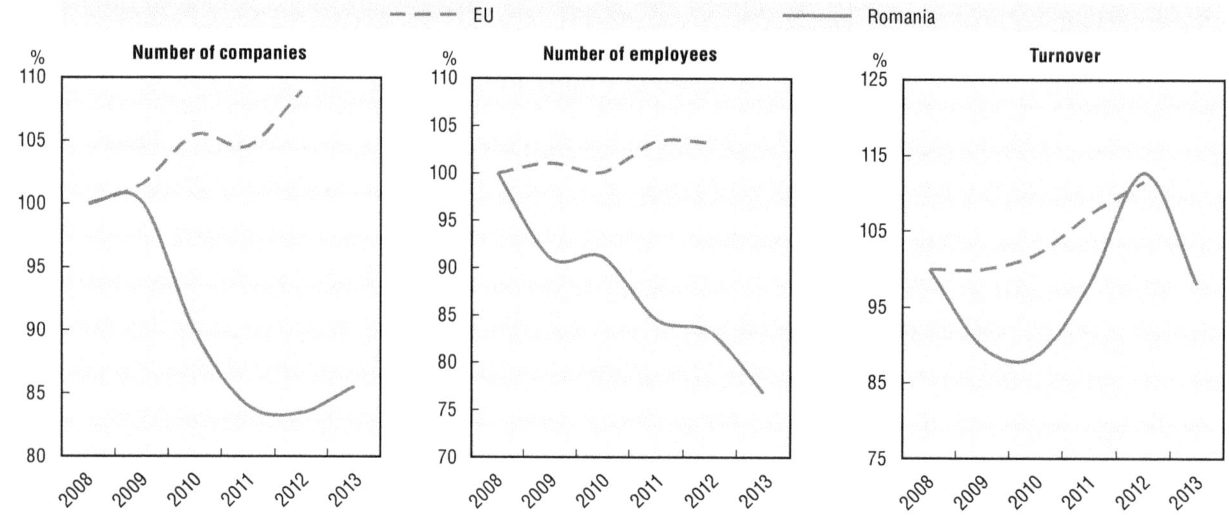

Source: Eurostat, code sbs_na_ind_r2 at *http://ec.europa.eu/eurostat/en/data/database* (accessed on 11 February 2016) and Deloitte calculations.

StatLink http://dx.doi.org/10.1787/888933362101

also specific laws and regulations applicable to particular products and usage. They cover a variety of issues such as conditions governing the sale of raw agricultural products and their processing, the sale of raw milk, establishment of production facilities, and food preparation and distribution. Several rules exempt small players from certain regulatory requirements. Hygiene and food safety represent the over-riding policy goals for laws and regulations on food processing.

The legislative/regulatory framework is strongly influenced by EU legislation on food safety.[49] Of particular importance is the package of EU regulations on food safety and hygiene of 2004. The package includes:

- Regulation (EC) 852/2004 on the hygiene of foodstuffs
- Regulation (EC) 853/2004 laying down specific hygiene rules for food of animal origin
- Regulation (EC) 854/2004 laying down specific rules for the organisation of official controls on products of animal origin intended for human consumption.

The regulations adopt an integrated approach, following the production chain from primary production to delivery to the consumer. Food and feed businesses carry full responsibility for the safety of products they produce, import, process, place on the market or sell. The regulations also offer greater flexibility for food produced in remote areas and for traditional production and methods.

Regulation 852/2004 is the centrepiece of EU food safety legislation, setting out general hygiene rules for all businesses that produce or process food. It includes detailed rules on hygiene and safety, such as measures to prevent contamination, rules on cleaning and disinfecting technical equipment and training of workers.

The EU food safety regulations are directly applicable in Romania, although the report has identified several instances in which a national law that had been adopted before Romania's accession to the European Union has not yet been repealed. These cases are briefly discussed at the end of this chapter.

In addition to the EU regulatory framework, Romanian rules governing the food processing sector have also been influenced by the international standards codified in the Codex Alimentarius, a collection of internationally recognised standards, codes of practice, guidelines, and other recommendations relating to foods, food production, and food safety.[50]

This report has identified several instances in which current laws and regulations can be considered to restrict competition and where revisions of currently applicable rules should reduce costs for market players and contribute to a more efficient market place. This would ultimately benefit consumers in Romania.

However, only a few of these restrictions appear significant, in the sense that the restriction does not effectively serve any legitimate policy goal and its removal is likely to result in substantial benefits to the economy. This result can be explained in particular by the fact that the rules applicable to the food processing sector have been largely harmonised with EU legislation and internationally recognised best practices. As explained above, the impact of domestic rules that are aligned with EU legislation and/or internationally recognised standards have not been examined in the report. The absence of substantial restrictions to competition might also be explained in part by the fact Romania's market economy is still comparatively young and that special interest groups have not been able to effectively lobby over time for rules that protect their economic interests.

Several Romanian norms that reflect EU or *Codex Alimentarius* standards appear on the face of it to limit competition when examined in light of the OECD toolkit. Examples include rules on the types of fruits that can be used in canned fruit mixtures, and rules limiting the locations in which the first sale of fish products may occur. However, in these instances the report has refrained from recommending any changes to national norms as they reflect international standards and it can be assumed that they are necessary to attain legitimate policy goals.

Case studies

This report will first present four case studies of restrictions that can be considered obstacles to the functioning of more efficient food processing markets in Romania. It will then provide a more systematic overview of the remaining restrictions in the food processing sector that can be considered to limit competition.

Staff training

Description of the obstacle. According to Emergency Ordinance 97/2001 on regulating the production, circulation and marketing of food, all foodstuffs may be produced, processed, stored, transported and sold only by staff with specific qualifications. Accordingly, all staff must have sufficient knowledge of public health, food hygiene and work hygiene. These qualifications must be attested by a certificate issued after completion of a training course and passing of an examination. The course and exam, which costs approximately EUR 20 per person, must be repeated every three years. The ordinance does not differentiate between staff working with packaged foods and those working with non-packaged food. Nor are the requirements adjusted for workers merely transporting foods or those working in food processing and distribution in an administrative capacity.

Harm to Competition. Although the annual costs of course and examination are relatively insignificant per employee, the training requirement appears to be overly broad as it applies across the board to all firms active in food processing and retailing and to their employees. This imposes costs on market participants that go beyond what appears necessary to attain the legitimate policy goals of ensuring a high level of food safety. The costs consist not only of the fees for the course and examination, but also the costs of absent personnel. Market investigations for this report suggest that smaller operators consider themselves substantially affected by these requirements.

Policy makers' objective. The policy objective pursued by the ordinance is to ensure that all who come in contact with food products are aware of, and observe in practice, the food safety rules. It appears, however, that this objective can be effectively pursued with lesser costs for market players.

Recommendation and benefits. The current scope of the ordinance should be reviewed in order to consider ways to apply it in a more targeted fashion only to those employees who could in fact pose risks to food safety because they come in direct contact with foodstuff. For example, employees transporting only packaged food, or employees working largely in administrative capacities, should be exempted.[51]

The report has attempted to quantify the costs of this measure and the potential benefits of a more targeted norm that applies only to personnel who could in fact pose food safety concerns. Considering the annual training costs per employee and the average firm size in the sector, the annual compliance costs per firm range from EUR 358 and EUR 448. This results in total, sector-wide costs between EUR 3.55 million (mln) and EUR 3.63 mln. Excluding personnel who are not involved in activities that imply direct contact with foods (such as technical and administrative personnel), would result in a total cost saving of between EUR 0.53 mln and EUR 0.73 mln annually.

Minimum sales areas for bakery products

Description of the obstacle. According to Order No. 392/2013 establishing the conditions to be met by business operators marketing bakery products in Romania,[52] bakery products must be sold in specially designated, separated areas of stores that, as regards to bread, must have a minimum area of 10 square metres (m^2).

Harm to competition. The minimum space requirements impose extra costs on firms selling bread. In addition, they may prevent certain market participants, in particular owners of small stores, from selling bread as their stores do not offer sufficient space to create the required separate sales area for bread. In this respect the restriction can be considered a barrier to entry.

Policy makers' objective. The goal of the provision is to prevent contamination of bakery products, in particular those that are regularly sold without packaging. Although concerns about possible contamination may appear legitimate as such, the norm appears to be overly broad in several respects. In particular, the norm does not differentiate between sales of packaged and unpackaged bread products. If a store considers selling only packaged bread products, the risks of contamination are not apparent. Moreover, the 10 m^2 minimum space requirement appears to be too extensive and inflexible.

Recommendation. The relevant provisions in Order 392/2013 should be amended. It is not clear why a minimum sales area can ensure greater food safety than the compliance with general food safety rules that apply also when stores are selling bread. Stores that can ensure safe selling conditions for bread should therefore not be required to also comply with minimum space requirements.

A more flexible norm requiring firms to ensure safe conditions when selling unpackaged bread without a mandatory minimum sales area could effectively serve the same policy goal. This would allow smaller stores in particular to sell bread under safe conditions, in light of the individual conditions of each store.

Licensing the storage of edible seeds

Description of the obstacle. According to Law No. 101/2014 on regulatory measures for the storage of edible seeds and their storage certificate regime, operators of facilities for storage of edible seeds must obtain a licence in order to obtain deposit certificates. Those certificates are particularly useful in obtaining bank loans.

The licence can be granted only by the Ministry of Agriculture and Rural Development following the proposal of a commission composed of 15 members. Only four commission members are designated by the ministry, whereas 11 members are designated by industry associations representing producers, storage providers, sellers, and processors and commodities exchanges.

Harm to competition. This provision can create entry barriers. Incumbent players are represented through trade associations that designate the majority of commission members, and can thus decide when potential rivals will be able to obtain deposit certificates. This does not constitute an absolute entry barrier as new entrants may decide to operate without certificates and bank loans. However, decisions by the commission have the potential of limiting entry opportunities in particular for smaller rivals without the necessary, independent financial resources, and therefore will affect the competitive conditions under which new players might enter the market. This creates an apparent conflict of interest as trade association members may be inclined to issue licences in light of their own commercial interest, rather than in the public interest in creating liberal market access.

Policy makers' objective. While a licence system may be beneficial to ensure that storage operators are likely to observe food safety standards when storing edible seeds and have the necessary financial resources, it is unclear why specific industry knowledge would be required to decide on the licences.

Recommendation. The law should be amended to eliminate potential conflict of interest. These licences should be granted directly by the ministry. If a commission is required for such a decision,[53] the majority of commission members should be appointed by the ministry.

Food inspections at the Romanian border for food imports

Description of the obstacle. Order No. 145/2007 approving the norms of food safety sets out the conditions for import/export operations, transit and intracommunity trade of non-animal food products subject to the supervision and control of food safety. It authorises the authorities to perform laboratory analysis to verify compliance with the feed and food law, in particular when foodstuffs are crossing the border into Romania.

In principle, the order is in line with EU legislation.[54] Its implementation in practice, however, deviates from the practice in other European Union Member States where the transported products are released immediately after sampling and the importer is allowed to deposit the products in warehouses until the laboratory results have been issued. In contrast, Romanian inspectors require importers to hold their goods at the border until the results of the analysis are available. This requires importers to keep their goods in (more expensive) refrigerated trucks for the duration of the analysis, which can take anywhere from three to seven days, rather than storing them in a more cost-efficient manner.

Harm to competition. This practice imposes unnecessary costs on importers of foodstuffs subject to inspection and analysis requirements. It may also incentivise operators to avoid Romanian borders for products in transit and instead pass through neighbouring countries.

Policy makers' objective. The rules on inspection of food products aim to ensure that harmful products do not enter the food chain. To achieve these goals, preventing the release into commerce of products for which compliance with safety requirement has not yet been established appears to be a necessary complementary measure. This, however, does not justify the current practice of holding products at the border pending the completion of laboratory tests and preventing their more cost-effective storage in designated storage facilities.

Recommendation. The Romanian government should ensure through internal instructions or guidelines that practices during border inspections and analysis are aligned with practices in other European Union member states and allow operators to store imported products in a more cost-efficient manner pending analysis of the imported food products.

Modalities of sales and food preparation

In addition to the abovementioned rule imposing minimum space requirements for the sale of bread, this report has identified two additional instances where Romanian law regulates modalities of sales or food production that appear to go beyond what would be necessary to ensure the safe handling of food.

Sales of fishery products

Description of the obstacle. Ministerial Order No. 100/2004[55] regulates the conditions under which fish and similar products can be sold. It prohibits the sale of fishery products outside of built and authorised areas and in the same units or specially designated spaces together with other animal or vegetable products.

Harm to competition. The two prohibitions impose higher costs on operators, as they require operators to set aside designated areas for the sale of fish and use dedicated personnel for only one activity. This prevents operators from using selling space and personnel more efficiently.

Policy makers' objective. Although the prohibitions pursue legitimate policy goals related to food safety and the prevention of contamination, it is unclear whether the scope of the prohibitions is in fact required to attain those goals. For example, when fishery products are sold in pre-packaged form, there is no contamination risk.

Recommendation. Ministerial Order 100/2004 should be reviewed to determine whether the safe handling of fishery products can be assured in a less restrictive manner. This could be accomplished, for example, by limiting the restrictions concerning separate sales areas to unpackaged fishery products.

Ambiguity in legislative provisions

The report has identified several instances where rules related to the handling and selling of food products include unnecessarily ambiguous terms. Frequently, the norms seek to establish exceptions for smaller operators from generally applicable rules for the relevant sector. They therefore pursue the legitimate policy goal of avoiding an unnecessary regulatory burden on small market players as the risk to public health posed by small operators is limited. However, ambiguity in rules creates uncertainty for operators as the scope of the rules remains unclear and leaves unnecessary discretion to the authorities. In the worst case, ambiguous provisions that provide wide discretion to authorities may encourage corrupt practices.

Selling vegetables by small producers

Description of the obstacle. Law No. 312/2003 on the production and use of vegetables contains rules on selling of vegetables, melons and mushrooms in traditional markets, street markets, or markets organised for special occasions. Small producers and natural persons are not required to comply with the rules on classification of the products they sell, and they are exempt from the requirement to issue receipts for their sales. The term "small producer," however, is not defined in the law.

The economic activities of farmers who are natural persons are also regulated by Law No. 145/2014 for establishing measures to regulate the market for agricultural products. Law 145/2014 considers as "small producers" those natural persons who produce agricultural products on their own farm for sale to the public (i.e., beyond their own consumption needs). The quantities traded by small producers must remain below certain thresholds foreseen by the Fiscal Code.

Harm to competition. The application of different laws governing the same activity creates uncertainty for market players, thus increasing the costs of compliance. It also creates the risk that authorities may apply one or both laws in an arbitrary fashion.

Policy makers' objective. Reducing regulatory burdens on small market players appears to be a legitimate policy goal of Law 312/2003. That goal is undermined, however, when the beneficiaries of a small producer exemption are not clearly identified.

Recommendation. Romania should ensure greater consistency between the two laws. For example, Law No. 312/2003 should be amended so as to use the same concepts and terms as those applicable under Law No. 145/2014 for establishing measures to regulate the market for agricultural products. As a result, one concept of "small producer", accompanied by clear output thresholds that small producers must not exceed, would apply across all relevant legislation. This would limit the discretion of authorities and provide greater certainty to market players.

Control scheme for vegetable and fruit producers and dealers

Description of the obstacle. Order No. 420/2008 establishing State inspection powers for the technical control of vegetable and fruit production and use regulates the control of quality standards for fruits and vegetables under the authority of the Ministry of Agriculture and Rural Development. It authorises authorities to establish a "simplified" control scheme for those traders dealing with fruit and vegetable exports if they meet a set of requirements, including "sufficient" guarantees of a constant and high rate of conformity. The order does not specify, however, what a simplified control scheme means, or under what conditions it can be granted. Apparently the authorities interpret these concepts in practice in line with Order 390/2009 establishing the Licensing methodology for self-control of operators in the fruit and vegetable sector. They therefore assume that Order 420/2008 also allows operators to self-certify their conformity with legal requirements, without the need for additional controls by authorities.

Harm to competition. The lack of clear norms raises the risk of arbitrary decisions. This creates uncertainty for market operators and increases the cost of compliance.

Policy makers' objective. The goal of reducing the regulatory burden for exporters with a prior compliance record is legitimate, and consistent with relevant EU legislation.[56] The regime should be maintained. The uncertainty created under Order 420/2008 and the lack of a clear link between the two related Orders 420/2008 and Order 390/2009 limits the benefits envisaged in Order 420/2008 as market players, in particular new entrants, may not be aware under which conditions that can benefit from a simplified control regime.

Recommendation. Order 420/2008 should be amended to define more closely terms such as "high conformity rate" and "simplified control scheme." A reference to Order 390/2009 to incorporate relevant provision in Order 420/2008 may be sufficient to achieve these goals.

Licensing of fodder producers

Description of the obstacle. Order No. 358/2003 governs the conditions under which fodder producers can operate in Romania.[57] Among other requirements, producers must obtain a licence from the local branch of the Directorate for Agriculture and Food Industry. However, the order does not provide for a deadline by which authorities must act on an application for a licence. The rules of general administrative law provide for a 30-day deadline by which authorities must respond to any petition applications. But it is not clear whether this rule applies to applications for licences under Order 358/2003.

Harm to competition. As the licence is a mandatory requirement for operators, the lack of a deadline for authorities to act upon an application creates uncertainty for operators. It also creates the risk of arbitrary decisions and abuse. This situation can be considered an entry barrier for new market entrants.

Policy makers' objective. The licence requirement seeks to ensure that fodder producers can comply with applicable animal feed safety rules. However, this goal can be attained without granting the authorities discretion as to when they issue a decision on the application.

Recommendation. Order No. 358/2003 should be amended to provide for a mandatory deadline by which the authorities must act upon an application for an operating licence.

Licensing facilities used in connection with products of animal origin

Order No. 57/2010 governs the operation of facilities used for the production, storage, distribution and other activities related to products of animal origin. Two provisions in the order raise the same issue as those discussed above in connection with Order No. 358/2003: authorities must issue licences for the construction of such facilities, and for any modifications to the initially approved technological workflow. In both cases, the order does not provide for a deadline by which the authorities must act upon an application.

The order does provide for a 15-day period within which authorities must react on a request for a sanitary-veterinary authorisation. But this provision does not apply to applications for licences for the construction of facilities or for modifications of workflows, even though in practice the authorities appear to respect the same 15-day deadline.

In addition, Order No. 57/2010 requires the operator of facilities to obtain a number of different licences from ANSVSA, including a statement of conformity, a conditional operating licence, a licence related to operations in intra-Community trade, and a regular operating licence. The Order is ambiguous with respect to the sequence in which these licences must be obtained. It is also unclear whether each licence is obligatory and whether certain licences may be combined. Moreover, each request for a licence must be supported by similar documentation.

Harm to competition. As discussed above, the lack of a deadline for authorities to act upon an application creates uncertainty for operators, even if in practice authorities may comply with an internal deadline. Moreover, the ambiguous regime governing various licensing operators leaves room for different interpretations which again results in uncertainty for operators. The need to submit the same documentation with each application for a licence imposes unnecessary costs on operators.

Policy makers' objective. The licence requirement seeks to ensure that facilities meet food safety standards, and that these standards are maintained when production workflows change. However, this goal can be attained without granting the authorities discretion as to when they issue a decision on the application.

The licence regime is consistent with EU legislation, namely Regulation 882/2004. However, the licensing regime can be equally effective if it is implemented with greater transparency and clarity for business. Re-submitting identical documentation for every application for a licence is not required to attain the policy objectives.

Recommendation. Order No. 57/2010 should be amended to explicitly extend the 15-day deadline also to applications for licences related to the construction of facilities and the modifications of workflows.

The licensing regime should be implemented with greater transparency, in particular by publishing, on ANSVSA`s web-page, instructions for local sanitary-veterinary authorities that clarify the application of Order No. 57/2010. The requirement to re-submit previously submitted documentation should be abolished.

Licensing of producers of farm feed

Description of the obstacle. Order No. 109/2010[58] sets forth licensing and registration requirement of facilities involved in farm feed. It requires operators of facilities for the production of farm feed and those transporting farm feed to obtain a licence. A licence can be revoked by the authorities when violation of legal requirements has been registered on "several occasions," and if the facility does not offer "proper safeguards" to ensure future compliance.

Harm to competition. The undefined and unclear conditions under which a licence can be revoked create uncertainty for operators and the risk of abuse. This situation can raise costs for operators.

Policy makers' objective. The possibility of revoking a licence aims to ensure that operators comply with the applicable animal feed safety rules. However, this goal can be attained without granting the authorities discretion as to when the conditions exist under which a license can be revoked.

Recommendation. Order No. 109/2010 should be amended to provide for greater legal certainty as to the conditions under which operating licences can be withdrawn.

Commercialisation of raw cow's milk

Description of the obstacle. Order No. 721/2009 on the approval of the Measures plan to improve the quality of raw cow's milk governs the conditions and requirements under which raw milk can be marketed in Romania. Producers that sell "small quantities" of raw milk directly to consumers are exempted from certain requirements and standards that apply to the rest of the industry. The concept of "small quantities", however, is not defined in the order.

The same small producer exemption can be found in Regulation (EC) 853/2004, which also does not apply to producers that sell small quantities of food products directly to consumers.[59] EU legislation requires Member States to regulate safety standards for small producers not covered by the regulation.[60]

These Member State obligations are not met through Order No. 721/2009, but through a separate ANSVSA Order No. 111/2008. This order, which requires small producers selling small quantities of milk to the public to register with the public authorities, defines the concept of "small quantities" and imposes the relevant food and safety standards on small producers.

Harm to competition. The lack of a definition of the term "small producer" in Order No. 721/2009 creates uncertainty and introduces the risk of abuse. First, producers of small quantities of raw milk may face uncertainty as to whether they can benefit from the exemption or must comply with the standards set forth in EU law. Legal uncertainly may be seen as an entry barrier as small producers who would be entitled to the exemption may be reluctant to rely on it and instead prefer to remain outside the market.

Second, larger producers may attempt to rely on the exemption under Order No. 721/2009 even though they should not be able to benefit from it, thus gaining an unjustified advantage over similarly situated competitors.

Policy makers' objective. Reducing the regulatory burden on small producers is a legitimate policy goal. The benefits of a small producer exemption are reduced, however, if the group of beneficiaries cannot be clearly identified and, in addition, larger producers might find a way to benefit from the exemption even though this was not intended by the legislator.

Recommendation. A clear definition of the term "small producer" should be applicable. This could be accomplished by referring in Order No. 721/2009 to the ANSVSA Order No. 111/2008 and the definition of "small quantities" contained therein. Alternatively, one legal instrument should be created that regulates all aspects of the sale of small quantities raw cow's milk.

Double control

Assigning overlapping responsibilities to more than one authority to control compliance with food safety norms has no direct effect on competition as such. However, such a situation results in uncertainty for businesses, and, if more than one authority controls the same business, in additional costs for those subject to multiple controls. Moreover, if standards of control and strictness in enforcement diverge, some businesses may be put at a competitive disadvantage vis-à-vis their rivals that are subject to more lenient controls.

Controls of operators marketing bakery products

Description of the obstacle. Operators of facilities used to market bakery products are subject to two control regimes, with different authorities in charge of controls: Order No. 392/2013, which establishes the conditions to be met by business operators marketing bakery products, and Order No. 976/1998 approving the hygiene norms concerning the production, processing, storage, preservation, transport and marketing of food. Compliance with Order No. 392/2013 is verified by the National Authority for Consumer Protection, while compliance with Order No. 976/1998 is verified by inspectors from the Public Health Directorate.

Harm to competition. Subjecting operators to controls and verification by two different authorities which both seek to ensure compliance with rules on hygiene and food safety imposes unnecessary costs on operators and may create uncertainty about the relevant standards that the operators have to observe.

Policy makers' objective. Controls of suppliers of baking products pursue the legitimate policy goal of ensuring compliance with food safety rules. However, subjecting operators to two similar controls by two different authorities is not required to attain this policy objective.

Recommendation. The current rules on controls should be amended so that compliance with rules on hygiene and food safety by operators of facilities used to market bakery products can be ensured by a single authority. This could be accomplished by eliminating those controls from the remit of one of the authorities, or by requiring the relevant authorities to co-ordinate their activities so that each individual operator is subject to control by only one authority.

Discrimination based on nationality/product origin

Rule that discriminate between domestically produced and imported products can have a direct impact on competition in the relevant sector, as it limits the ability of a group of suppliers to compete. If importers face a higher cost burden than domestic producers, competitive constraints on domestic producers will be reduced, which could allow them to charge higher prices than they could otherwise.

Costs for testing of animal feed

Description of the obstacle. Government Decision No. 1156/2013 on sanitary veterinary actions to prevent animal diseases[61] requires the testing of animal feed. For domestically produced animal feed, the costs of control are borne by the public authorities. Importers, however, must cover the costs of controls.

Harm to competition. The rule on the costs for control of animal feed that require only importers to bear the costs of such controls impose greater costs on importers, thus putting them at a disadvantage vis-à-vis their domestic rivals. This puts importers at a competitive disadvantage and provides a certain protection for domestic producers against competition by importers. This situation results in discrimination of certain market players, and can be seen as an entry barrier for foreign producers.

Policy makers' objective. Testing animal feed pursues the legitimate policy goal of ensuring compliance with animal food safety rules. Rules on who should bear the cost of control are a necessary component of such rules. Applying these rules in a discriminatory fashion, however, is not required to attain these policy goals.

Recommendation. Government Decision No. 1156/2013 should be amended to treat domestic and foreign producers equally. This could be achieved by having the government always bear the cost of controls. Since these controls are in the public interest, allocating related costs to the government appears to be the most consistent reform. Alternatively, the decision could be amended so that domestic producers bear the costs of controls to the same extent as their foreign rivals.

Rules encouraging competitor collaboration

Voting rights in milk producer associations

Description of the obstacle. Order No. 1186/2014 concerning milk production and milk products manufacturing organizations[62] regulates, among other things, the allocation of voting rights in associations of milk producers. It provides that voting rights should be allocated according to each member's contribution to the association's total output. Any association member is prohibited from controlling more than 49% of the association's voting rights. Order No. 1186/2014, however, does not regulate how voting shares should be determined.

Harm to competition. In the absence of any specific rules on how voting shares should be established, Order No. 1186/2014 creates the risk that the allocation of voting shares will lead to an exchange of competitively sensitive information, as each member may have to disclose current output or production capacity to the entire membership. Exchanging this information may help members to reach an understanding of how future production should be allocated among them, or it could be used to monitor compliance with an already established understanding of how production should be allocated among members.

Policy makers' objective. The purpose of this rule is to prevent large producers from gaining undue influence over producers' associations. This, in principle, appears to be a legitimate policy goal, as it will ensure that smaller members can prevent the adoption of rules or standards that will disadvantage them vis-à-vis their larger rivals. This policy goal can be achieved, however, without permitting a regime that could enable competitors to exchange sensitive business information.

Recommendation. Amendments to Order No. 1186/2014 should ensure that the allocation of voting shares cannot be used to exchange competitively sensitive information about individual market positions. To achieve this, the order should provide either that only historic output data (for example, output data from the previous year) should be used to allocate voting rights, or that the producer association must develop rules that prevent such an exchange of information among its members, for example by ensuring that only the association has full information about individual members' production or production capacity and allocates voting rights for certain classes of members according to ranges of production shares.

Rules imposing unnecessary costs on operators

Financial guarantees provided by grain warehouse operators

Description of the obstacle. Government Decision No. 699/2009 establishing the measures contained in common market organisation in the grain sector imposes an obligation on grain warehouse operators to provide financial guarantees for grain stored by the Payment and Agriculture Intervention Agency (PAIA) following an intervention in the grain market.[63] The financial guarantee can be provided by wire transfer, a bank letter guarantee in favour of PAIA covering 200% of the value of the grain, or an insurance policy for the value of the grain. The requirement that a bank guarantee, which may be the most cost effective way for warehouse operators to provide the necessary guarantees, covers 200% of the grain stored by the PAIA is remarkably high.

Harm to competition. The requirement that a bank guarantee covers 200% of the grain stored by the PAIA imposes additional costs on warehouse operators. Other forms of financial guarantees do not require covering more than the value of the stored grain. For example, when an operator provides the required guarantee by wire transfer, the government's interests are protected only in the amount represented by the transfer. No additional protection is available should grain prices rise at a later stage. The costs for bank guarantees can be considered a barrier to entry for new players, effectively reducing competition in the market and limiting the choice of the PAIA when selecting a warehouse to store grain following a market intervention.

Policy makers' objective. The requirement of substantial financial guarantees has been designed to ensure that the PAIA is able to recover losses resulting from a deterioration of the grain stored in a warehouse. High fluctuation rates in grain prices and the risk of significant losses may justify financial guarantee requirements. To attain this objective, however, it is not necessary to discriminate against one particular form of guarantee.

Recommendation. The provision requiring that bank guarantees cover 200% of the grain stored by the PAIA should be reviewed and it should be considered whether a lesser degree of coverage, as required with respect to other forms of financial guarantees, would be sufficient to protect the interests of the government while reducing disincentives for warehouses against offering their storage services to the PAIA.

Outdated legislation

Description of the rules. The report has identified several instances in which rules contained in domestic legislation are redundant in light of EU regulations with the same regulatory content that became effective when Romania joined the European Union. The domestic rules typically predate EU accession. Thus, initially valid domestic legislation should have been abolished when Romania became an EU Member State.

Harm to competition. In these instances market operators are subject to two legal rules with largely identical content, which may create uncertainly about the relevant legal regime.

Policy makers' objective. The norms identified below pursue legitimate policy goals related to food safety and hygiene. They have become unnecessary, however, once EU regulations covering the same issues have become effective in Romania.

Recommendation. The report lists below the instances in which domestic laws appear redundant in light of EU regulations. As the policy goals pursued by Romanian legislation appear legitimate, there is no need to alleviate the regulatory burden on market operators. The recommended action is simply to abolish the redundant domestic norms to create greater legal certainty.

Domestic regulation	EU regulation(s)	Recommendation
Government Decision No. 924/2005 on the approval of the general rules for food hygiene	Regulation (EC) No. 852/2004 regarding food hygiene	Abolish
Order No. 91/2005 approving the Sanitary veterinary norm laying down the rules applicable to regular checks on the general state of hygiene, carried out by facility operators, in accordance with the Sanitary veterinary norm on health conditions for production and marketing of fresh meat, approved by Order No. 401/2002, and with the Sanitary veterinary norm on health problems regulating the production and marketing of fresh poultry meat, approved by Order No. 402/2002	EU legislation on hygiene and safety of foodstuffs, including Regulation (EC) No. 178/2002, Regulation (EC) No. 852/2004, Regulation (EC) No. 853/2004, Regulation (EC) No. 2073/2005, and Regulation (EC) No. 882/2004.	Abolish
Order No. 78/2003 approving the Sanitary veterinary norm regarding exceptions to the Sanitary veterinary norm on health conditions governing the production and marketing of meat products and of other animal origin food products used for certain products containing other foodstuff and only a small percentage of meat or meat products	EU legislation on hygiene and safety of foodstuffs, including Regulation (EC) No. 178/2002, Regulation (EC) No. 852/2004, Regulation (EC) No. 853/2004, Regulation (EC) No. 2073/2005, and Regulation (EC) No. 882/2004.	Abolish
Law No. 150/2004 on safety of aliments and food for animals	Transposes Regulation (EC) No. 178/2002	Abolish those parts that are also regulated by EU regulation

Domestic regulation	EU regulation(s)	Recommendation
Order No. 976/1998 approving the Hygiene norms concerning the production, processing, storage, preservation, transport and marketing of food	Same objective as Regulation (EC) No. 852/2004	Abolish
Order No. 43/2003 for approval of Sanitary veterinary norms regarding the criteria applicable for meat-producing enterprises that do not have an industrial structure or production capacity	EU legislation on hygiene and safety of foodstuffs, including Regulation (EC) No. 178/2002, Regulation (EC) No. 852/2004, Regulation (EC) No. 853/2004, Regulation (EC) No. 2073/2005, and Regulation (EC) No. 882/2004.	Abolish

Notes

1. The statistics and financial definitions of the food processing sector rely on the Statistical Classification of Economic Activities in the European Community (NACE) which groups all food processing activities under group C Manufacturing, subgroup C10 Manufacturing of food products.
2. For example, the Sanitary Veterinary Norm in regards to animal protection during slaughter and killing of 22 September 2006, regulates the circumstances under which animals can be slaughtered, even if the meat is used for self-consumption.
3. Value added at factor costs is the gross income from operating activities after adjusting for operating subsidies and indirect taxes. Value adjustments (such as depreciation) are included. It can be calculated from turnover, plus capitalised production, plus other operating income, plus or minus the changes in stocks, minus the purchases of goods and services, minus other taxes on products which are linked to turnover but not deductible, minus the duties and taxes linked to production.
4. All prices presented in the figure are compared to the prices from the base month, which is considered to be June 2010.
5. The recent price drop appears to be largely the result of the reduction of the VAT rate from 24% to 9% for food products in June 2015. According to a study from the Embassy of the Kingdom of the Netherlands in July 2015, food prices decreased, on average, by 8.2% in June 2015 compared to the previous month, and by 6.4% compared to the same month in 2014. (Popescu, 2015).
6. For example, Law No. 150/2004 on food and feed safety, republished, Government Decision No. 924/2005 on the approval of the general rules for food hygiene.
7. All means of transportation.
8. Open/covered markets, fisheries, etc.
9. Pork, beef, cattle, ovine, poultry, venison, molluscs, fish, milk, eggs, escargots, etc.
10. Butcheries, in-farm poultry slaughter houses, venison collection centre, in-farm milk processing units, small milk processing units, small fish collection centres, fishing boats, on the shore fish collection centres, small fisheries, honey collection centres, apiaries, honey selling points, eggs collection centre, restaurants, pizza restaurants, cantinas, confectionery and pastry shops, inns, food shops, hypermarket/supermarket, internet markets, catering units, food deposit, washing point for foodstuffs vehicles.
11. Set by Order 96/2014.
12. Examples of products and activities the MARD issues licences for: production of milk and dairy products, butter, ice-cream, canned milk products, cheese, poultry slaughter, poultry & fish products, canned meat and fish, production of flour, corn flour, rice, bread, pasta, biscuits, canned fruit and vegetables, production of oils and mayonnaise, production of sugar and sweets, production of beverages, food packaging, etc.
13. MARD's specialised service.
14. Having a licensed storage facility enables the economic operator to issue storage certificates to the farmers which store their cereal and seed production in such facilities. Together with the guaranteed storage of their cereal and seed, the farmers may can the storage certificates to access bank credit. In case the cereals or seed for which a storage certificate has been issued, become stale, the farmer can be compensated by The Deposit Certificates Compensation Fund.
15. The Catalogue regarding classification and normal functioning duration of fixed assets approved through Government Decision No. 2139/2004 and amended through Government Decision No. 1496/2008.
16. See Article 339 par. 1 letter c) of Law No. 227/2015 regarding the Fiscal Code.

17. See Article 291 par. 2 letter e) of Methodological Norms for application of the Law No. 227/2015 regarding the Fiscal Code. This has all been said in the main text. You just need the reference which follows.

18. This applies to all types of services, including marketing or services provided by retailers for the benefit of the producers active in the food industry. With respect to VAT, the legislation does not provide for any additional supporting documentation except the invoice. Nevertheless, in practice the tax authorities request the same supporting documentation (as requested for corporate income tax purposes) in order to prove the actual performance of the services. See Article 25 par. 1, par. 4 letter f), Article 297 par. 4 and Article 299 par. 1 of Law No. 227/2015 regarding the Fiscal Code.

19. E.g. e-mail correspondence, signed reports, timesheets, pictures, minutes of meetings, etc.

20. Perishables, losses in production, expired goods, damaged goods that are destroyed, goods insured, etc. See Article 25 par. 3 d) and e), Article 25 par. 4 letter c) of Law No. 227/2015 regarding the Fiscal Code and Article 304 par. 2 letter a) of Methodological Norms for application of the Law No. 227/2015 regarding the Fiscal Code.

21. Composed according to the standard international classification of the following activities: C10.1.1 – Processing and preserving of meat, C10.1.2 – Processing and preserving of poultry meat and C10.1.3 – Production of meat and poultry meat products.

22. The order of the sections is according to the highest GVA recorded in the subsectors.

23. As a consequence of Council Directive 2001/89/EC of 23rd October 2001 on Community measures for the control of classical swine fever and extended in 2008.

24. Through amendment 2012/702/EU of Commission Decision of 3 November 2008 concerning animal health control measures relating to classical swine fever in certain Member States.

25. Composed according to the standard international classification of the following activities: C10.7.1 – Manufacture of bread; manufacture of fresh pastry goods and cakes, C10.7.2 – Manufacture of rusks and biscuits; manufacture of preserved pastry goods and cakes and C10.7.3 – Manufacture of macaroni, noodles, couscous and similar farinaceous products.

26. According to NIS data, imports of cane or beet sugar and chemically pure sucrose in solid form decreased by 3.7% in 2012 compared to 2011, followed by a 29.12% decrease in 2013 compared to 2012.

27. According to NIS data, on average, imports on each type of product increased by 13% each year (over the last 5 years).

28. ANAF provides the data for GDP and GVA in construction industry in RON m. For calculating the figures in EUR m, the medium annual exchange rate (RON/EUR) from the National Bank of Romania was used, *www.bnr.ro/Cursul-de-schimb-3544.aspx* (accessed on 11 February 2015)

29. Composed according to the standard international classification of the following activities: C10.5.1 – Operation of dairies and cheese making and C10.5.2 – Manufacture of ice cream.

30. Composed according to the standard international classification of the following activities: C10.6.1 – Manufacture of grain mill products and C10.6.2 – Manufacture of starches and starch products.

31. Composed according to the standard international classification of the following activities: C10.3.1 – Processing and preserving of potatoes, C10.3.2 – Manufacture of fruit and vegetable juice and C10.3.9 – Other processing and preserving of fruit and vegetables.

32. Composed according to the standard international classification of the following activities: C10.4.1 – Manufacture of oils and fats and C10.4.2 – Manufacture of margarine and similar edible fats.

33. Crude vegetable oils are obtained without further processing other than degumming or filtering. To make them suitable for human consumption, most edible vegetable oils are refined to remove impurities and toxic substances, a process which involves bleaching, deodorisation and cooling (to make the oils stable in cold temperatures). Vegetable oils have a wide variety of food uses including salad and cooking oils, as well as in the production of margarine, shortening and compound fat: they also enter into many processed products, such as mayonnaise, mustard, potato chips, French fries, salad dressing, sandwich spread and canned fish.

34. Animal oils and fats are obtained in the course of dressing the carcasses of slaughtered animals (slaughter fats), or at a later stage in the butchering process when meat is being prepared for final consumption (butcher fats). Processed animal fats include lard obtained by melting raw pig fat and tallow obtained from raw fat of other animal species. Animal fats are largely used in the production of margarine, shortening and compound fat. They also enter into many processed food products such as mustard, potato chips, French fries, salad dressing, sandwich spread and canned fish.

35. With almost 95% of subsector turnover and 88% of the number of people employed.
36. This activity accounted for 5.4% of the subsector turnover and 12% of the number of people employed.
37. However, in Romania the reduction of this indicator was greater than eat the European level.
38. The number of people employed in the sector decreased by 24% from 2008 to 2010. A slight increase in the number of employees was observed as a trend starting in 2011.
39. Composed according to the standard international classification of the following activities: C10.9.1 – Manufacture of prepared feed for farm animals and C10.9.2 – Manufacture of prepared pet food.
40. In 2014 recording 96.22% of subsector turnover and 92.08% of the subsector's number of employees.
41.
42. However, this indicator recovered in 2011.
43. Represented according to the standard international classification by the following activity: C10.2.0 – Processing and preserving of fish, crustaceans and molluscs.
44. Raw materials for the processing and preserving of fish, crustaceans and molluscs are provided through the commercial fishing activity in the Black Sea, the Danube, the Danube Delta and in other rivers and lakes in Romania (inland fishing).
45. MARD – Operational Program for Fisheries, Romania. Available at: *www.madr.ro/docs/fep/2014/program-operational-2007-2013/Operational-Programme-for-Fisheries-2007-2013.pdf*.
46. The main species captured on the territory of Romania are the Crucian carp, bream, the Danube herring and the common carp.
47. The main exported products are living, fresh, chilled, frozen, dried or salted molluscs.
48. Composed according to the standard international classification of the following activities: C10.8.1– Manufacture of sugar, C10.8.2 – Manufacture of cocoa, chocolate and sugar confectionery, C10.8.3 – Processing of tea and coffee, C10.8.4 – Manufacture of condiments and seasonings, C10.8.5 – Manufacture of prepared meals and dishes, C10.8.6 – Manufacture of homogenised food preparations and dietetic food and C10.8.9 – Manufacture of other food products (n.e.c.).
49. See, e.g., Tobias Baumgartner & Wesselina Uebe, "European Union" in *Global Food Legislation: An Overview* (Evelyne Kirchsteiger-Meier & Tobias Baumgartner eds. 2014).
50. The Codex is developed and maintained by the developed and maintained by the *Codex Alimentarius* Commission, a body established by the Food and Agriculture Organization (FAO) of the United Nations.
51. There is also a question whether Emergency Ordinance 97/2001 has been, at least in some parts, superseded by EU food safety regulations, including Regulation (EC) 1333/2008, Regulation (EC) 853/2004, and Regulation (EC) 1881/2006). If Romania were to decide to repeal the entire ordinance and apply instead only directly applicable EU regulations, including those applicable to staff training, the issue discussed in the text would become moot.
52. In conjunction with Order No. 976/1998 approving the Hygiene Norms concerning the production, processing, storage, preservation, transport and marketing of food.
53. The report also notes the high number of commission members, which appears difficult to justify in light of the issues the commission has to decide upon. However, since the number of commission members has no impact on competition and does not directly impose costs on market participants, the report makes no recommendation in this regard.
54. Regulation (EC) No. 882/2004 of the European Parliament and of the Council of 29 April 2004 on official controls performed to ensure the verification of compliance with feed and food law, animal health and animal welfare rules, OJ L 165, 30.4.2004.
55. Ministerial Order No. 100/2004 approving the sanitary veterinary norm laying down the additional conditions on the sanitary veterinary control of fishery products, crustaceans, molluscs, gastropods and batrachians for direct marketing to the final consumer or for food processing for human consumption.
56. Article 6 of Regulation (EC) 852/2004 and Article 31 of Regulation (EC) 882/2004.
57. Order No. 358/2003 approving the Norms on quality and sanitation parameters for the production, import, quality control, marketing and use of simple concentrated fodder, combined feed additives, premixes, energetic substances, minerals and special fodder.

58. Order No. 109/2010 approving the Sanitary veterinary norm on the sanitary veterinary licensing/registration of facilities involved in farm feed and means of transport of farm feed.

59. Regulation (EC) 853/2004, Article 1(3)(c).

60. Regulation (EC) 853/2004, Article 1(4).

61. Government Decision No. 1156/2013 approving sanitary veterinary actions included in the Programme for surveillance, prevention, control and eradication of animal diseases, of those transmissible from animals to humans, animal and environmental protection, identification and registration of bovines, swine, sheep, goats and equines, of the actions stipulated in the Programme for food safety supervision and control, and related charges.

62. Order No. 1186/2014 approving the technical implementation norms for the Methodological Norms for enforcement of Law No. 297/2013 on establishing contractual relations in the milk and milk products sector, as well as acknowledgement of milk and milk products manufacturing organisations approved by Government Decision No. 441/2014 on specific conditions to be met by manufacturing organisations from the milk and milk product/producer organisation associations in contractual relations, as well as the technical criteria for their acknowledgment for negotiation purposes, provided by Regulation (EU) No. 1308/2013 of the European Parliament and Council of 16 December 2013 establishing a common organisation of agricultural product markets and repealing EEC Regulations No. 922/72 and No. 234/79, EC Regulations No. 1037/2001 and No. 1234/2007.

63. The term "intervention" refers to the buying-in of cereals and rice into public storage by national authorities.

References

A. Popescu, July 2015, "Romania: VAT reduction on food – initial effects after 2 months of application", available at: *www.agroberichtenbuitenland.nl/roemenie/wp-content/uploads/sites/22/2015/08/imgm5jzoxif.pdf* (accessed on 15 February 2016).

Department of Agriculture, Nature and Food Quality (2009), "The Romanian food sector and the use of EU funds for Investments", Embassy of the Kingdom of the Netherlands in Romania, available at: *www.dbrochure.nl/romanian%20food%20sector/files/food%20sector%20report.pdf*.

Baumgartner, Tobias Wesselina Uebe (2014), "European Union" in Global Food Legislation: An Overview (Evelyne Kirchsteiger-Meier & Tobias Baumgartner eds. 2014), Wiley, U.K.

OECD (2011a), *Competition Assessment Toolkit: Principles*, OECD, *www.oecd.org/competition/assessmenttoolkit.htm*.

OECD (2011b), *Competition Assessment Toolkit: Guidance*, OECD, *www.oecd.org/daf/competition/45544507.pdf*.

ANNEX 4.A1

Staff qualifications

Emergency Ordinance No. 97/2001 on regulating the production, circulation and marketing of food, Art. 7.

Foodstuffs may only be produced/processed/stored/transported and sold by staff with specific qualifications, meaning "sufficient" knowledge of public health, food hygiene, work hygiene, attested by a certificate issued after completion of a training course and passing of an exam (e.g. the cost of the training course and the exam fee approximately EUR 20 while the duration could be up to 17 hours). The course should be repeated every three years.

The **key objective** of the analysis is to estimate the cost of complying with the regulation, by employee, company and throughout Romania in the food processing industry in 2014. The costs of complying with the regulation are composed of both the cost of training and the costs to personnel[1] who are obliged to obtain the specific qualification.

Training and accrediting all staff significantly increases costs for the employers and also limits the employment market. The impact is with respect to those traders who are not dividing people based on attributions and thus are obliged to train the entire personnel force, thus creating **harm to competition**. The text does not differentiate between staff working with packaged/non-packaged foodstuffs – i.e. the same requirements apply to those coming in direct contact with packaged and non-packaged foodstuffs, for those involved in the food processing chain and for those merely transporting the foodstuffs.

The **policy maker's objective** is to protect public safety, as there are people coming in contact with food products and who might risk contaminating the products they handle.

The **recommendation** is to abolish the conditions for employees not coming in direct contact with non-packaged foodstuffs. For that purpose, clear defined activities which do not involve direct contact with foodstuffs should be regulated.

The **results** show that in order for each employee to obtain the certificate, the equivalent yearly cost to the employer, per employee, is EUR 18.4; the yearly compliance costs per company range between EUR 358 EUR and 448 EUR and the total costs for 2014 to the companies in the food industry that have to comply with this regulation range between EUR 3.55 million (m) and EUR 3.63 m. EUR. If the technical, economic and socio-administrative personnel (TESA personnel), who are not involved in activities that imply direct contact with foodstuffs, were to be exempt from obtaining the certificate, the total saving in costs (for the entire industry) would range between EUR 0.53 m and EUR 0.73 m. If the entire cost reduction were to be transmitted entirely as a price reduction, the consumer benefit would be between EUR 0.55 m and EUR 0.73 m.

First, the cost of training is, on average, EUR 23.31 per employee (Table 4.A4.1).

Table 4.A4.1. **Cost of obtaining a compulsory food hygiene certificate (EUR)**

Source	Provider	Cost per training (EUR)	
		Bucharest-Ilfov	Other cities
www.accepthoreca.ro/cursuri-notiuni-fundamentale-igiena/	S.C. MILLENIUM BUSINESS LUXURY S.R.L	22.50	29.25
http://cursuridecalificare.ro/cursuri-de-igiena-obligatorii.php	Centrul de Formare Profesionala Eurodeal SRL	22.50	22.50
http://curs-igiena.blogspot.ro/2014/11/insusirea-notiunilor-fundamentale-de.html	AXEL – Centrul de consultanta si formare profesionala	-	22.50
www.securitatesisanatate.ro/curs-igiena.php	SC Volum Serv SRL	-	22.50
http://deratizaresidezinsectie.ro/curs-igiena/	SC FOR L EXIM SRL	22.27	-
AVERAGE		22.42	24.19
AVERAGE TOTAL		23.31	

Source: Websites and Deloitte calculations and analysis.

The personnel cost to the company includes both the average gross salary and the contributions paid by the employer as social benefits, representing 28% of the gross salary. Therefore, the gross salary hourly average is:

$$\textit{Average monthly gross salary}\,2014 = \text{EUR}\,348.96\,/\,\textit{employee} \quad (1)$$

$$\textit{Average monthly personnel cost to company} = \textit{average monthly gross salary}{*}128\%$$
$$= \text{EUR}\,446.67\,/\,\textit{month}$$

$$\textit{Average daily personnel cost to company} = \frac{\textit{average monthly personnel cost to company}}{\textit{number of working days}}$$
$$= \frac{\text{EUR}\,446.67}{21\ \textit{days}} = \text{EUR}\,21.27\,/\,\textit{day}$$

$$\textit{Average personnel cost to company for 1 hour} = \frac{\textit{average daily personnel cost to company}}{\textit{number of working hours}}$$
$$= \frac{\text{EUR}\,21.27}{8\ \textit{hours}} = \text{EUR}\,2.66\,/\,\textit{hour}$$

$$\textit{Average personnel cost to company per training}$$
$$= \textit{average personnel cost to company for 1 hour}{*}\textit{duration of the training} =$$
$$= \text{EUR}\,2.66{*}12\ \textit{hours} = \text{EUR}\,31.91\,/\,\textit{training}\,/\,\textit{employee}$$

(1) For the food processing industry; Source: National Institute of Statistics.

The cost is estimated per employee, per company and overall in Romania in the food processing industry, for 2014. The formulas for calculating the total cost (for each employee, of each company and total in Romania) are the following:

$$\textit{Annual training cost per employee} = \frac{\textit{training cost}}{\textit{number of years}} = \frac{\text{EUR}\,23.32}{3\ \textit{years}}$$
$$= \text{EUR}\,7.77\,/\,\textit{employee}\,/\,\textit{year}$$

$$\textit{Annual training personnel cost per employee}$$
$$= \frac{\textit{average personnel cost to company per training}}{\textit{number of years}} = \frac{\text{EUR}\,31.91}{3\ \textit{years}} =$$
$$= \text{EUR}\,10.64\,/\,\textit{employee}\,/\,\textit{year}$$

$$\text{Total annual cost per employee} = \text{annual training cost per employee} + \text{annual training personnel cost per employee} = \text{EUR}7.77 + \text{EUR}10.64 = \text{EUR}18.40 / \text{year} / \text{employee}$$

$$\text{Annual training cost per company} = \frac{\text{training cost per employee*average number of employees per company*}(1 + \text{employee turnover rate})}{3 \text{ years}}$$

The employee turnover rate in 2014 for the fast-moving consumer goods (FCMG) industry was 23.40%.[2]

$$\text{Annual training personnel cost per company} = \frac{\text{average personnel cost of company per training * average number of employees per company * } (1 + \text{employee turnover rate})}{3 \text{ years}}$$

$$\text{Total annual cost per company} = \text{annual training cost per company} + \text{annual training personnel cost per company}$$

$$\text{Annual total cost from training} = \text{anuual training cost per company * number of companies}$$

$$\text{Annual total personnel cost} = \text{anuual training personnel cost per company * number of companies}$$

$$\text{Annual total cost} = \text{annual total cost from training} + \text{annual total personnel costs}$$

Table 4.A4.2. **Annual costs of compliance (EUR)**

	Data source[1]	
	ANAF	Eurostat
Average number of employees per company	15.76	19.71
Number of companies	9,939	8,119
Annual training cost per employee	7.77	7.77
Annual training personnel cost per employee	10.64	10.64
Annual total cost per employee	*18.40*	*18.40*
Annual training cost per company	151.08	188.98
Annual training personnel cost per company	206.83	258.71
Annual total cost per company	*357.91*	*447.69*
Annual total cost of training	1 501 585.30	1 534 313.30
Annual total personnel cost[2]	2 055 672.18	2 100 476.85
Annual total cost	*3 557 257.49*	*3 634 790.15*

1. The differences in the data source are for the average number of employees per company and the number of companies in 2014.
2. 15% and 20% respectively.

Source: ANAF, *www.anaf.ro/indicatori/indfinanciari.html* (accessed on 25 January 2016), Eurostat, code: sbs_na_ind_r2 (accessed on 25 January 2016), and Deloitte calculations.

If 15% of the personnel represents technical and administrative staff who do not have direct contact with the foodstuffs, the average number of employees per company who have to obtain the certificate is lowered by 15%, generating a total annual cost saving of between EUR 0.533 m and EUR 0.545 m (Table 4.A4.3). If 20% of the personnel represents technical and administrative staff who do not have direct contact with the foodstuffs, the average number of employees per company who are obliged to obtain the certificate is lowered by 20%, generating a total annual cost saving between EUR 0.711 m and EUR 0.726 m (Table 4.A4.4).

Table 4.A4.3. **Annual cost savings if 15% of the personnel are exempt from obtaining the certificate (EUR)**

TESA personnel	Data source	
15%	ANAF	Eurostat
Average number of employees per company who do not have to obtain the certificate	2.36	2.96
Number of companies	9 939	8 119
Annual training cost saving per employee as fees	7.77	7.77
Annual training cost saving per employee as salary	10.64	10.64
Total annual cost saving per employee	*18.40*	*18.40*
Annual training cost saving per company as fees	22.66	28.35
Annual training cost saving per company as salary	31.02	38.81
Total annual cost saving per company	*53.69*	*67.15*
Annual training total cost saving from training as fees	225 237.80	230 146.99
Annual training total cost saving as salary	308 350.83	315 071.53
Total annual cost saving	*533 588.62*	*545 218.52*

Source: Deloitte calculations and analysis.

Table 4.A4.4. **Annual cost savings if 20% of the personnel are exempt from obtaining the certificate (EUR)**

TESA personnel	Data source	
20%	ANAF	Eurostat
Average number of employees per company who do not have to obtain the certificate	3.15	3.94
Number of companies	9 939	8 119
Annual training cost saving per employee as fees	7.77	7.77
Annual training cost saving per employee as salary	10.64	10.64
Total annual cost saving per employee	*18.40*	*18.40*
Annual training cost saving per company as fees	30.22	37.80
Annual training cost saving per company as salary	41.37	51.74
Total annual cost saving per company	*71.58*	*89.54*
Annual training total cost saving from training as fees	300 317.06	306 862.66
Annual training total cost saving as salary	411 134.44	420 095.37
Total annual cost saving	*711 451.50*	*726 958.03*

Source: Deloitte calculations and analysis.

$$\textit{Average number of employees per company who have to obtain the certificate} \\ = \textit{average number of employees per company} * \textit{percentage of reduction (1)}$$

(1) 15% and 20% respectively.

Consumer benefit

If the recommended solution is implemented and if it is assumed that the entire value of the cost savings is translated to a lower sales price, the benefit of the regulation change will be transmitted to the final consumers. In this case, the consumer benefits can be estimated using the following formula:

$$CB = \left(\rho + \frac{1}{2}|\epsilon|\rho^2\right)R_r$$

where:

- - CBs : standard measure of consumer harm

- - ρ : percentage change in price related to restriction
- - R : sector revenue
- - |∈|: absolute value of elasticity of demand

As the absolute value of elasticity of demand is unknown, this index is assumed to take the value of 2. In this case, the consumer benefits formula can be simplified as follows:

$$CB = \left(\rho + \rho^2\right) R_r$$

Sector revenue (turnover in the food processing industry), according to Eurostat, was EUR 9 050.3 m in 2013 (last available year). Moreover, percentage change in price related to restriction can be estimated based on the two earlier mentioned assumptions, exempting 15% (ρ_1) and 20% respectively (ρ_2) of the personnel from obtaining the certificate.

$$\rho 1 = \frac{\text{total annual cost saving from the restriction in the} 15\% \textit{reduction case}}{\textit{secto turnover}} = \frac{EUR 0.545 m}{EUR 9050 m} = 0.006\%$$

$$\rho 2 = \frac{\text{total annual cost saving from the restriction in the} 20\% \textit{reduction case}}{\textit{sector turnover}} = \frac{EUR 0.727 m}{EUR 9050 m} = 0.008\%$$

In this case, the consumer benefits for each case can be calculated, resulting in a range between EUR 0.55 m and EUR 0.73 m.

$$CB1 = \left(\rho 1 + \rho 1^2\right) * R = \left(0.006\% + 0.006\%^2\right) * EUR 9050.3 m = EUR 0.55 m$$

$$CB2 = \left(\rho 2 + \rho 2^2\right) * R = \left(0.008\% + 0.008\%^2\right) * 9050.3 mil. EUR = 0.73 mil. EUR$$

Notes

1. Personnel costs are considered in the calculation as during the training the employee does not produce any value for the company; they are composed of gross salaries and contributions paid by the employer.
2. *www.zf.ro/eveniment/angajatii-romani-din-retail-si-bunuri-de-larg-consum-au-cea-mai-mare-rata-de-renuntare-la-joburi-din-europa-de-est-13800017.*

ANNEX A

Methodology

This study covers three sectors of the Romanian economy: food processing, transport with a focus on freight transport, and construction with a focus on public procurement. The assessment of laws and regulations in the three sectors has been carried out in four stages. The present chapter describes the methodology followed in each of these stages.

Stage 1 – Mapping the sectors

The objective of Stage 1 of the project was to identify and collect all sector-relevant laws and regulations. As a prior condition, it was necessary to define the scope of the three sectors in detail. Whenever possible, we adopted a definition consistent with the Statistical Classification of Economic Activities in the European Community (NACE classification) in order to ensure consistency with international practice and to facilitate comparisons with other European countries.

The task of collecting the relevant legislation for each of the three sectors was conducted by the OECD team using a variety of sources. The Sintact legal database was the main tool used to identify the applicable legislation. In addition, in order to ensure that all important pieces of legislation were covered by the study, input was solicited from all the competent line ministries involved in the selected sectors, from the members of the High Level Committee composed of senior government officials and from stakeholders in the three sectors. Following this process, the relevant legislation was organised under thematic categories, such as framework regulation applicable across the sector, regulations that deal with specific economic activities within the sector and so on. In total, during Stage 1, 803 different pieces of legislation were identified, including laws, (emergency) government ordinances, government decisions and ministerial orders. This number increased slightly to 895 pieces in Stage 2 of the project, as several additional relevant pieces of legislation were discovered during the scanning of the legislation, while other pieces were found to no longer be in force. Some of the additional pieces had not been published in the *Official Gazette of Romania* or the ministries' websites and were difficult to access.

A very important task that started during Stage 1 and was continued through further stages was the establishment of contact with the market through the main associations active in the three sectors. The interviews with market participants contributed to a better understanding how the sub-sectors under investigation work in practice and helped in the discussion of potential barriers deriving from the legislation or misinterpretation of specific provisions.

Stage 2 – Screening of the legislation and selection of provisions for further analysis

In the second stage of the project, the main work was the screening of the legislation to identify potentially restrictive provisions as well as providing an economic overview of the relevant sectors. Every piece of legislation was scanned by two team members ("four-eyes-principle"). In addition, we started to compile economic papers and reports which were considered relevant for the three sectors covered by the study.

The legislation collected in Stage 1 was analysed using the framework provided by the OECD *Competition Assessment Toolkit*. This toolkit, developed by the Competition Division at the OECD, provides a general methodology for identifying unnecessary obstacles in laws and regulations and developing alternative, less restrictive policies that still achieve government objectives. One of the main elements of the toolkit is a "Competition checklist" that asks a series of simple questions to screen laws and regulations that have the potential to unnecessarily restrain competition.

Box A.1. **Competition checklist**

Further competition assessment should be conducted if a piece of legislation answers "yes" to any of the following questions:

A) Limits the number or range of suppliers

This is likely to be the case if the piece of legislation:

1. grants a supplier exclusive rights to provide goods or services
2. establishes a licence, permit or authorisation process as a requirement of operation
3. limits the ability of some types of suppliers to provide a good or service
4. significantly raises the cost of entry or exit by a supplier
5. creates a geographical barrier to the ability of companies to supply goods, services or labour, or invest capital.

B) Limits the ability of suppliers to compete

This is likely to be the case if the piece of legislation:

1. limits sellers' ability to set the prices of goods or services
2. limits the freedom of suppliers to advertise or market their goods or services
3. sets standards for product quality that provide an advantage to some suppliers over others or that are above the level that some well-informed customers would choose
4. significantly raises the costs of production for some suppliers relative to others (especially by treating incumbents differently from new entrants).

C) Reduces the incentive of suppliers to compete

This may be the case if the piece of legislation:

1. creates a self-regulatory or co-regulatory regime
2. requires or encourages information on supplier outputs, prices, sales or costs to be published
3. exempts the activity of a particular industry or group of suppliers from the operation of general competition law.

Box A.1. **Competition checklist** *(cont.)*

D) Limits the choices and information available to customers

This may be the case if the piece of legislation:

1. limits the ability of consumers to decide from whom they purchase
2. reduces the mobility of customers between suppliers of goods or services by increasing the explicit or implicit costs of changing suppliers
3. fundamentally changes the information required by buyers to shop effectively.

Following the methodology of the toolkit, the OECD team compiled a list of all the provisions which answered any of the questions in the checklist positively. Ministry experts were also involved in this task. The final list consisted of 227 provisions across the sectors, broken down by the sectors as follows:

- Construction: 95
- Transport: 85
- Food Processing: 47.

The collection of economic studies had the aim of identifying: i) analyses of relevant regulatory policy changes that had taken place in other countries ii) empirical and theoretical papers on the areas of interest emerging from the screening of legislation; and iii) competition cases and reports in the sectors covered by the study in other OECD countries. The main sources for the compilation of relevant literature included academic journals and publications, competition authorities in other countries, international bodies and associations, and the EU and OECD websites.

For each of the three sectors, we also prepared an extensive economic overview, covering industry trends and main indicators, such as output, employment and prices, including comparisons with other EU Member Countries where relevant. We also analysed summary statistics on the main indicators of the state of competition typically used by competition authorities, especially information on the market shares of the largest players in each sector. Where possible, these statistics were broken down by sub-sector. The analysis conducted in this stage aimed at giving background information to better understand the mechanisms of the sector, providing an overall assessment of competition as well as explaining the important players and authorities.

Stage 3 – In-depth assessment of the harm to competition

The provisions carried forward to Stage 3 were investigated in order to assess whether they could result in harm to competition. In parallel, the team researched the policy objectives of the selected provisions so as to better understand the regulation. An additional purpose in identifying the objectives was to prepare, in Stage 4, alternatives to existing regulations, taking account of the objective of the specific provisions when required.

The in-depth analysis of the harm to competition was carried out qualitatively and when possible quantitatively, and involved a variety of tools, including economic analysis, research into the regulations applied in other OECD and European Member Countries and econometric and data analysis.

First, all provisions were analysed qualitatively, relying on economic theory, findings from the literature survey and the guidance provided by the OECD's *Competition Assessment Toolkit*. Interviews with ministry experts held in several workshops complemented the analysis by providing crucial information on the lawmakers' objectives as well as the actual implementation and effects of the provisions.

Second, whenever feasible and appropriate for the analysis of the issue under consideration, the OECD team gathered data that could be used for the quantification of the effects. For instance, when possible, variables were collected for a sample of countries to compare prices. As the expected impact of a regulatory restriction could generally not be modelled directly because of the lack of sufficient data, we relied on the standard methodology of measuring the effect of policy changes on consumer surplus. In particular, we followed the approach as suggested in the OECD (2015), Competition Assessment Toolkit, Volume 3, which derives a formula for changes in consumer benefit when only sector revenue and the average price effect of the restriction found are available. This is explained in Box A.2 below.

Box A.2. **Measuring changes in consumer surplus**

The effects of changing regulations can often be examined as movements from one point on the demand curve to another. For many regulations that have the effect of limiting supply or raising prices, an estimate of consumer benefit or harm with the change from one equilibrium to another can be calculated. Graphically, the change is illustrated by a constant elasticity demand curve. Er shows the equilibrium with the restrictive regulation, Ec shows the equilibrium point with the competitive regulation. The competitive equilibrium is different from the restrictive regulation equilibrium in two important ways: lower price and higher quantity. These properties are a well-known result of many models of competition.

Figure A.1. **Changes in consumer surplus**

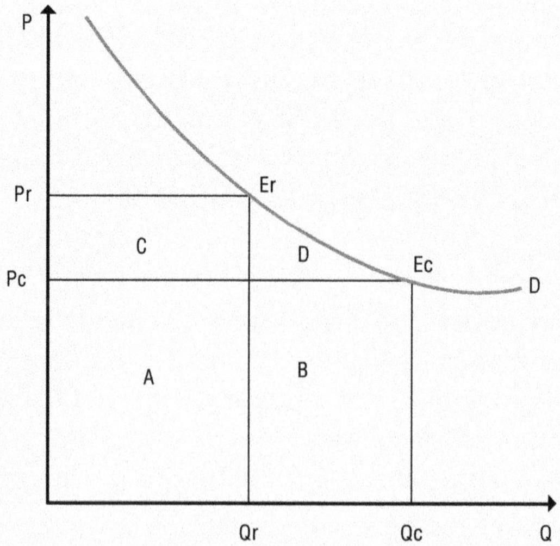

Source: OECD (2015), *Competition Assessment Toolkit*, Volume 3, OECD, Paris. *www.oecd.org/daf/competition/COMP_Toolkit_Vol.3_2015.pdf*.

Box A.2. Measuring changes in consumer surplus *(cont.)*

Under the assumption of constant elasticity of demand the equation for consumer benefit is:

$$CB = C + D \approx (P_r - P_c)Q_r + \frac{1}{2}(P_r - P_c)(Q_c - Q_r)$$

where price changes are expected, a basic formula for such a standard measure of consumer benefit from eliminating the restriction is:

$$CB = \left(\rho + \frac{1}{2}\epsilon\rho^2\right)R_r$$

where CB represents consumer harm, ρ represents the percentage change in price related to the restriction, R represents sector revenue and ∊is the demand elasticity.

When elasticity is not known, it is worth noting that if |∊|=2, which would correspond to more elastic demand than in a monopoly market, but also far from perfectly elastic as in a competitive market, the expression above simplifies to:

$$CB = \left(\rho + \rho^2\right)R_r$$

Source: OECD (2015), *Competition Assessment Toolkit*, Volume 3, OECD, Paris, *www.oecd.org/daf/competition/COMP_Toolkit_Vol.3_2015.pdf*.

Stage 4 – Formulation of recommendations

Building on the results of Stage 3, we developed recommendations for those provisions which were found to restrict competition. The present report is the result of Stage 4.

We tried to find alternatives which were less restrictive for suppliers while still aiming at the initial objective of the policy maker. In this process, we relied on international experience whenever available. In addition, the OECD asked the ministry experts for their views on recommendations.

Some provisions have been superseded by more recent legislation but have not been explicitly removed from the body of legislation. For these provisions, even if they may not result in actual harm to competition, we recommend that they be explicitly repealed in order to improve legal certainty and transparency. In other cases, we found that relevant legislation had not been published or that formulations were unclear, leaving room for wide discretion and possibly discrimination between market participants. Finally, we consider that some provisions constitute an administrative burden for suppliers. Even when we do not find evidence of harm to competition resulting from these provisions, we recommend that they be reviewed and simplified to the extent possible.

In total, 152 recommendations were submitted to the Romanian Chancellery:

- Construction: 72
- Transport: 46
- Food Processing: 34.

Capacity building

Another important work stream in the project was to provide assistance in building up the competition assessment capabilities of the Romanian administration. To this end, officials from the line ministries and relevant authorities involved in this project were appointed by the Romanian Chancellery in order to gain exposure to the application of the OECD *Competition Assessment Toolkit*. Experts were appointed from the Ministry of

Transport, the National Company of Highways and Roads, the Ministry of Economy, Commerce and Relations with the Business Environment, Ministry of Environment, Waters and Forests, Inspectorate of State Construction, National Authority for Mineral Resources, National Standardization Authority, National Agency for Public Procurement (Before: ANRMAP: National Regulatory and Monitoring Authority for Public Procurement), Ministry of Regional Development and Public Administration, Ministry of Agriculture and Rural Development, National Sanitary Veterinary and Food Safety Authority, Ministry of Health, Ministry of Public Finance, Ministry of Foreign Affairs and the National Authority for Consumer Protection.

The selected ministry experts were involved in all the stages of the project and provided insights into the complexity of the legislation in their sectors of expertise.

More specifically, at the beginning of the project in March 2015, we organised a workshop which gave an introduction to competition policy as well as the OECD *Competition Assessment Toolkit*. The workshop explained the tasks in Stage 1. The ministry experts provided a significant contribution in ensuring that the legislation collected was comprehensive.

In May 2015, we held an additional 2-day workshop in the town of Sinaia and provided substantive training on the OECD *Competition Assessment Toolkit*. Subsequently, ministry experts had the opportunity to gain hands-on experience in the screening of the legislation using the toolkit as they were invited to help with the scanning work conducted in Stage 2 of the project.

The capacity-building process continued in Stage 3 with the identification of the objectives of the legislation in their sectors of expertise. For that, we held two workshops in September and October 2015, one with members of Romanian Competition Council and one with ministerial experts, on qualitative and quantitative analysis of restrictive provisions. Additionally, we organised a workshop on public procurement and bid riggings. In November and December 2015 we held several small workshops with the ministerial experts to explain our assessment of the harm to competition with reference to specific provisions and to obtain important feedback on possible alternatives to achieve the same policy objectives while minimising harm.

Finally, throughout the project we provided updates to the members of the High Level Committee on the status of our work, including on co-operation with their staff, and discussed with them our preliminary views on the relevant legislation. They were thus able to provide feedback at all stages of the process.

References

OECD (2015), *Competition Assessment Toolkit*, Volume 3, OECD, Paris. *www.oecd.org/daf/competition/COMP_Toolkit_Vol.3_2015.pdf*.

OECD (2011a), *Competition Assessment Toolkit: Principles*, OECD Publishing, Paris.

OECD (2011b), *Competition Assessment Toolkit: Guidance*, OECD Publishing, Paris.

OECD, *Competition Assessment Toolkit Volume III: Operational Manual* (The manual is only available online *www.oecd.org/daf/competition/COMP_Toolkit_Vol.3_2015.pdf*).

ANNEX B

Legislation screening by sector

Sector: Construction/Procurement

No.	No and title of Regulation	Article	Thematic category	Brief description of potential obstacles	Keyword	Policy maker's objectives	Harm to competition	Recommendations
1	**Law No. 50/1991 regarding authorisation of construction works execution**	Art. 15 letter c)	Public procurement	A concession is an agreement according to which a natural or legal person can obtain a right to exploit a good owned by the state in exchange for a fee. Generally, under Law No. 50/1991, the conceding of land belonging to the state should be conducted through a public tender. However, in accordance with Art. 15 letter c) of Law No. 50/1991, no public tender procedure is required for concession of lands which are to be used by the concessionaire to build houses for young people under 35 years of age. E.g. The municipality provides a concession of a piece of land to a constructor who builds houses and rents/sells them to young people under the age of 35. There is no tender procedure for the concession of the land to the constructor/real estate developer.	Discrimination	The objective of this provision resides in a social policy meant to encourage real estate developers to build houses which will subsequently be sold/rented to young people under the age of 35.	This provision is likely to create advantages for real estate developers building houses to be sold/rented to young people contrary to other real estate developers. Large and valuable areas can be leased to developers without any public tender procedure. There is a risk of discrimination, corruption, concession and under-pricing while providing no guarantee that real estate developers will pass on their cost-savings to the young people.	Abolish and introduce the tender procedure as indicated under Law No. 50/1991.
2	**Law No. 50/1991 regarding authorisation of construction works execution**	Art 15 letter e)	Public procurement	A concession is an agreement according to which a natural or legal person can obtain a right to exploit a good owned by the state in exchange for a fee. Generally, under Law No. 50/1991, the conceding of land belonging to the state should be conducted through a public tender. However, in accordance with Art. 15 e) of Law No. 50/1991 regarding authorisation for the execution of construction works, no public tender is applicable for leasing private terrain owned by public authorities, if they are to be used by the initial owner of a building for extending the existing building on nearby terrain. E.g. An undertaking owning a building may ask for a concession on an adjacent land under the property of public authorities in the case where it plans on extending the existing construction. There is no tender procedure for the concession of the nearby terrain.	Public procurement	The objective of this provision is to allow an existing company to expand on nearby land.	An undertaking wanting to prevent a competitor from developing its business might buy/lease property around the land owned by the competitor and then concede the nearby terrain directly from the public authority. The public entity might concede the adjacent land at a lower price compared to the price which would have been paid in case a public procedure applied. There is also a certain risk of corruption.	1) Abolish and introduce the tender procedure as indicated under Law No. 50/1991. This avoids underpricing of the lease and granting of preferential rights. 2) Grant the owner of the existing building a special pre-emption right and the possibility of matching the best offer under the tender procedure. In this case, the new participant can win the tender only if a new participant is offering a higher price than the neighbour.
3	**Law No. 50/1991 regarding authorisation of construction works execution**	Art. 16	Public procurement	Information regarding tender procedures for terrain on the private property of the state/ municipality is to be disclosed by the city hall only by publishing it at its headquarters and in two major newspapers 20 days prior to the procedure. No reference is made to the requirement to publish the information online or to use other means of communication.	Public procurement	Tender procedures are duly publicised at the time of enactment of the legal provision. However, traditional communication channels have changed, making newspapers and notice boards less used/relevant as communication channels.	Considering that currently the information is available only through local communication means, undertakings located outside the city may not have access to information and might not be aware of future tender procedures. Thus, the number of potential bidders might be reduced.	This provision should be amended in order to include other means of communication, including the online environment (including the city hall's website, where possible).

Sector: Construction/Procurement *(cont.)*

No.	No and title of Regulation	Article	Thematic category	Brief description of potential obstacles	Keyword	Policy maker's objectives	Harm to competition	Recommendations
4	**Emergency Ordinance No. 84/18.09.2003 for the establishment of the National company for highways and roads in Romania – Joint stock company**	Art. 12.1	Public procurement	Upon the execution of works contracts covering construction, rehabilitation, expansion or modernisation of roads (as well as the execution of addenda to such contracts), the general contractor must constitute a pledge in favour of its subcontractors or suppliers having as its object any amount due by the National Company for Highways and National Roads in Romania (CNADR) to the general contractor. The amounts to be recovered by subcontractors or suppliers consist of the value of their works/services provided to the general contractor. No other form of guarantee is allowed (such as a bank guarantee).	Public procurement	The objective of the provision is to protect subcontractors and suppliers from delivering works/goods for which they are not paid. The pledge established by the general contractor would confer on the subcontractors the same assurance as the general contractor receives. Considering that the payment due under the public agreement is carried out with public funds, setting a pledge in favour of the subcontractors over the sums owed by CNADR to the general contractor gives the subcontractors a reasonable certainty that in the end the general contractor will pay them.	This provision interferes with commercial contracts between general contractors and subcontractors who might in practice use different commercial measures in order to protect their interests. In addition, the measure of not allowing insurance policies is seen by the business community as excessive financial guarantees in certain cases.	Keep the principle of the provision as far as work of subcontractor is guaranteed. Additionally, the provison should be amended to allow all types of commercial guarantee instruments to be used in the commercial relationship between general constructors and their subcontractors.
5	**Decision No. 1364/ 2001 for approving the methodological norms for the application of Government Ordinance No. 20/1994 on measures to mitigate the seismic risk of existing buildings**	Art. 83 letter a) corroborated with Art. 112 letter a)	Public procurement	Intervention works on buildings with a seismic risk are carried out by state authorities based on a technical solution issued by a designer. During the public procurement procedure for drafting technical solutions, the criterion used is exclusively the criterion of the lowest price. Also, the same criterion is to be used during the public procedure for the acquisition of technical expertise concerning the buildings. Thus, the second criterion under the procurement legislation, the economically most advantageous bid, is automatically excluded.	Public procurement	Considering that the costs are supported from public resources, the state wanted to limit the financial effort of the contracting authority.	By automatically excluding the criterion of economically most advantageous tender (which is a derogation from framework legislation on public procurement) a disadvantage is created for operators having new technology, for example, and who would prefer this criterion. This is also likely to affect the quality of the performance, as the economic operators would look to using cheaper technologies in order to cut costs. Also, a cheaper technical solution might not be appropriate especially when it comes to seismic risk.	Amend to allow all criteria foreseen by the legislation in force.

Sector: Construction/Procurement *(cont.)*

No.	No and title of Regulation	Article	Thematic category	Brief description of potential obstacles	Keyword	Policy maker's objectives	Harm to competition	Recommendations
6	**Government Emergency Ordinance (GEO) No. 34/2006 on assigning public procurement contracts, public works concession contracts and service concession contracts**	Art.3 letter k) and Art. 15	Public procurement	The special or exclusive right is the right arising from any form of authorisation granted under the law or through the issuance of administrative acts, by a competent public authority, with the purpose of reserving exploitation of public services to only one or to a limited number of undertakings, substantially affecting the ability of other to conduct such activity. The contracting authority has the possibility of awarding exclusive/special rights to exploit certain public services to an undertaking without applying any procurement procedure regulated by Government Emergency Ordinance 34/2006. Special rights are currently granted to Regia Autonomă de Distribuţie a Energiei Termice, Regia Autonomă de Transport Bucureşti, Regia Autonomă Apă- Canal Timişoara, Compania Naţională de Transport al Energiei Electrice "Transelectrica" S.A, Compania Naţională Administraţia Porturilor, which are strategic decisions of the Romanian state. We have not identified any exclusive rights in the construction field.	Foreclosure	The provisions transposes Art. 3 and Art. 18 from Directive 2004/18/CE. Special or exclusive rights in the field of public services can be granted based on special normative acts, provided they are compatible with the treaty, and the selection of the economic operator is based on criteria established by these special normative acts which are authorised by the responsible authority.	Considering that we have not identified any application of these special rights in the construction field, no harm to competition has been identified.	No recommendation for change.

Sector: Construction/Procurement *(cont.)*

No.	No and title of Regulation	Article	Thematic category	Brief description of potential obstacles	Keyword	Policy maker's objectives	Harm to competition	Recommendations
7	**Emergency Ordinance No. 34/2006 on assigning public procurement contracts, public works concession contracts, and service concession contracts**	Art. 12 index 1 par. 1 and par. 2	Public procurement	The general thresholds provided by GEO No. 34/2006 are: i) For supply and servicing agreements below EUR 30 000 the contracting authority does not have an obligation to apply a public procedure; (for works agreements, the threshold is EUR 100 000). ii) For supply and servicing agreements above EUR 30 000 and below EUR 130 000, the contracting authority has the obligation to apply a public procedure, including calls for tenders; (for works agreements, the range is between EUR 100 000and EUR 5 000 000). iii) For supply and servicing agreements above EUR 130 000, the contracting authority has the obligation to apply a public procedure, excluding calls for tenders; (for works agreements, the threshold EUR 5 000 000). As an exception from the above, the public procurement procedure is not applicable for "structures of the contracting authority functioning outside Romania" (including undertakings which qualify as contracting authorities because they are state owned) when the value of the public procurement agreement is lower than: a) for a supply agreement, EUR 130 000; b) for a servicing agreement, EUR 130 000; and c) for a works agreement, EUR 5 000 000. GEO No. 34/2006 does not provide clear criteria to be applied by the "structures of the contracting authority functioning outside Romania" when awarding an agreement without applying a public tender, such as conditions to be met by the economic operators (i.e. qualification, reputation, experience, or guidelines for the contracting authorities to be followed when choosing the economic operator). GEO No. 34/2006 solely provides very general principles to be followed, such as non-discrimination, transparency, etc.	Discrimination	The exception is motivated by the difficulty of carrying out the procedure of requesting an offer outside national territory.	State owned companies qualify as contracting authorities under the national legislation even if their market activities are similar to other private undertakings. In situations when the object of the agreement concluded by a contracting authority located outside Romania (supply, service, works) is to be executed exclusively on the territory of Romania, this provision is likely to cause discrimination between economic operators in terms of costs and timeline. While the undertakings not having a subsidiary abroad are obliged to follow the procurement procedure under GEO NO. 34/2006 when exceeding the general thresholds (respectively 30,000 EUR for supply agreement and servicing agreement and 100,000 EUR for works agreement) or applying the procedure of request of offers, undertakings having a subsidiary abroad may purchase the work/services through that subsidiary, thus avoiding having to apply GEO No. 34/2006.	The procurement procedure governed by the Romanian piece of legislation should apply in all situations involving public money, including to contracting authorities located outside Romania, when the objective of the procedure is the acquisition of works and/or services to be delivered within Romania.

Sector: Construction/Procurement *(cont.)*

No.	No and title of Regulation	Article	Thematic category	Brief description of potential obstacles	Keyword	Policy maker's objectives	Harm to competition	Recommendations
				For example, a state-owned company which qualifies as the contracting authority requires the performance of services/works (which are carried out exclusively on the territory of Romania) through a subsidiary from another state. In such a case the procurement procedure under GEO 34/2006 is not applicable. The procedure for performing works outside the territory of Romania is established at a national level and is not governed by the European directives. The same procedure is also provided in a similar manner in the new proposed public procurement legislation. While the current procedure governed by GEO NO. 34/2006 solely provides general principles to be followed when awarding contracts below the aforementioned thresholds, the new proposed public procurement legislation expressly states that below the thresholds (i.e., when the public procedures are not applicable), methodological norms (which have not been issued yet) will further establish rules covering general principles, such as transparency or equality.				

Sector: Construction/Procurement *(cont.)*

No.	No and title of Regulation	Article	Thematic category	Brief description of potential obstacles	Keyword	Policy maker's objectives	Harm to competition	Recommendations
8	**Emergency Ordinance No. 34/2006 on assigning public procurement contracts, public works concession contracts, and service concession contracts**	Art. 107 par. 2	Public procurement	For the competitive dialogue procedure, the timeframe in which the participants can elaborate and submit their final offer is set by mutual agreement of the parties (contracting authority and the selected participants from the first stage of the procedure), which is the same for all economic operators. Competitive dialogue procedure is an exceptional procedure which is applied by the contracting authority if a tender procedure is not likely to be sufficient for awarding the agreement and if the agreement is by its nature very complex. This procedure contains three steps: a) publication of a participation notice and preselection of candidates following their application; b) open dialogue with each selected participant with respect to the technical solutions, the future agreement, etc.; c) submission of final offers and selecting the winning offer. This procedure is applied more often in technical areas which require issuance of technical solutions. According to the newly proposed legislation in the field of public procurement, the contracting authority must simultaneously send to all selected candidates the invitation to submit the final offer (Article 88 para. 10 corroborated with Article 90 par. (5)). There is no mention of how the contracting authority sets such a term; the provision regarding the mutual agreement of the parties has been eliminated.	Discrimination	The provision is a transposition of Art. 29 from Directive No. 2004/18/EC. It is important to underline that according to Art. 106 of GEO No. 34/2006, during the procedure the authority must apply the equal treatment principle to all participants. This means the contracting authority does not have the right to offer information in a discriminatory manner which might create unfair advantages for some participants. The contracting authority has the possibility to set the deadline for submitting the final offers, taking into account the complexity of the identified solutions. The deadline is the same for all participants, thus ensuring the principle of non-discrimination. The purpose of this procedure is to obtain the best technical solution by allowing a certain degree of flexibility during negotiations.	There is no minimum time limit for the authority to respect when establishing the term for submitting the final offers, as the deadline is exclusively established through mutual agreement of the parties. E.g., following the negotiations regarding the technical solutions, one economic operator may need additional time to elaborate the final offer while others may not. Thus, considering that the contracting authority negotiates with each selected participant, in practice, this may lead to discrimination and a lack of visibility among the participants. Considering that the mutual agreement of the participants was eliminated under the proposed new draft, the risk has been removed.	No recommendation for change, provided that the provision under the proposed draft is enacted as such.

Sector: Construction/Procurement *(cont.)*

No.	No and title of Regulation	Article	Thematic category	Brief description of potential obstacles	Keyword	Policy maker's objectives	Harm to competition	Recommendations
9	**Emergency Ordinance No. 34/2006 on assigning public procurement contracts, public works concession contracts, and service concession contracts**	Art. 202 par. 1 index 1	Public procurement	GEO No. 34/2006 establishes that an offer is classified as having an unusually low price if the price contained in the offer is lower than 80%, excluding VAT (abnormally low tenders), of the estimated value of the agreement. In this case, the contracting authority has the obligation to request further information (including information with respect to prices, stocks, salary, organisation, etc.) and clarifications from the economic operator. Upon consultation with market operators, it is our understanding that in practice the contracting authorities do not challenge the justifications received from market participants and do not reject such low tenders. According to the new proposed legislation in the field of public procurement, the contracting authority will reject abnormally low tenders only when the proof submitted by the economic operators does not justify the low price level/proposed costs, taking into consideration the clarifications offered during the investigation. However, the new legislation does not provide any criteria for rejection of a bid and there is no threshold provided under which the offer is presumed to be abnormally low (Directive 2014/24, similarly, does not provide such thresholds).	Foreclosure	This current practice of the contracting authorities may be the result of a lack of specific and objective criteria to justify rejection of an offer. Authorities might also fear a potential challenge by an economic operator against the rejection decision. The objective of the proposed recommendation is to allow contracting authorities to reject an offer due to a greatly underestimated price. Such offers are unlikely to cover the costs necessary and thus unlikely to be implemented in practice.	Considering that in practice the contracting authorities do not reject the justifications and are still awarding the project to the bidder offering the lowest price, this may facilitate price dumping. Companies may win with non-sustainable offers which cannot be implemented or will require amending of the contract at a later date.	Amend the legislation to provide the contracting authorities with clear criteria and examples of when to reject an offer based on a lack of justification for an abnormally low price.
10	**Emergency Ordinance No. 34/2006 on assigning public procurement contracts, public works concession contracts, and services concession contracts**	Art. 225 letter a)	Public procurement	The contracting authority may impose on the concessionaire the obligation to sub-contract 30% of the value of the concession agreement for public works to third parties. The legislation does not provide for the following clarifications: i) if the contracting authority may impose such an obligation in the situation where the company can perform the work itself and ii) if the company decides itself who will be the third party for the sub-contract work or services or whether such third parties are imposed by the contracting authority. No similar provision has been identified in the newly proposed legislation in the field of public procurement.	Discrimination	The provision transposes Art. 60 from Directive 2004/18/EC. The objective of this provision is to allow small and medium-sized enterprises access to public works concession agreements.	The unclear wording of the legislation grants the contracting authority arbitrary power regarding the request for sub-contracting 30% of the value of the agreement. This may prejudice the economic operator who has the capabilities to provide the service or perform the work itself. Separately, in cases when the authority indicates who will be the third party, the economic authorities are not free to decide with respect to such a subcontractor. Upon discussions with market participants, we understand that there have been no situations where the contracting authorities have imposed a third party.	No recommendation for change, provided that the provision under the proposed draft is enacted as such.

Sector: Construction/Procurement *(cont.)*

No.	No and title of Regulation	Article	Thematic category	Brief description of potential obstacles	Keyword	Policy maker's objectives	Harm to competition	Recommendations
11	**Emergency Ordinance No. 34/2006 on assigning public procurement contracts, public works concession contracts, and services concession contracts**	Art. 188 par. 1 a), 2 a) and 3 a)	Public procurement	For certain public procurement agreements, the contracting authority may request that economic operators submit proof of their prior professional experience in the last three years (for supply and service agreements) or in the last five years (for works agreements). The contracting authorises may request proof of professional experience as a participation condition considering the nature and complexity of the public agreement. The contracting authorities are free to decide whether to request proof of professional experience or not on a case-by-case basis.	Discrimination	The purpose of the provision is to ensure proper experience of the bidders and to diminish the risk of non-fulfilment or inappropriate execution of contract. The provision is in line with Annex XII of Directive 2014/24. According to the National Agency for Public Procurement (ANAP), they are currently working on drafting instructions regarding the requesting of proof of professional experience.	Discretionary power is granted to contracting authorities which are allowed to request proof of professional experience, on a case-by-case basis, depending on the complexity of public agreements. Due to a lack of any guidance when taking the decision whether to request proof of professional experience or not, the contracting authorities decide on a case-by-case basis when to apply the provisions. Therefore, contracting authorities might take different decisions in similar situations. This might qualify as a barrier to entry onto the market and leads to an unpredictable business environment for private investors.	Draft guidelines to give market participants and contracting authorities a sufficient level of predictability and transparency regarding situations in which the contracting authorities may require proof of professional experience.
12	**Emergency Ordinance No. 34/2006 on assigning public procurement contracts, public works concession contracts, and services concession contracts**	Art. 271 index 1 par. 1 and par. 4	Public procurement	To challenge the actions undertaken by the contracting authority under the awarding procedure, the plaintiff must pay an amount representing a guarantee of good conduct. The amount of the guarantee varies depending on the value of the public procurement agreement and can reach a maximum of EUR 100 000. This provision was deemed unconstitutional by the Romanian Constitutional Court in January 2015. Thus, in practice, the plaintiff has to pay the guarantee but the amount is reimbursed irrespective of the outcome of the challenge. The new proposed legislation in the field of public procurement does not contain a similar provision regarding the guarantee. Any persons who consider themselves injured (irrespective of whether it is part of the tender procedure) can challenge the decisions of the contracting authorities. However, the appeals/complaints which are to be settled by the courts of law have a similar effect as stamp duty. The taxes are established according to the value of the public procurement agreement.	Limitation	The objective of the regulation is to avoid deferral of the tender procedure without just cause, to protect the contracting authority against any abusive appeals introduced, for example, by an economic operator only for the purpose of delaying the procedure, who was not selected/whose offer was deemed unacceptable. This guarantee was introduced to balance the contracting authority's interest in carrying out the tender procedures within a reasonable timeframe and the protection of the third party's rights affected by irregularities of the public procedures.	Despite the fact that the amount is reimbursed in the end, access to justice of any interested person is still affected, considering that the obligation to pay the guarantee is still incumbent upon the plaintiff.	No recommendation for change, provided that the provision under the proposed draft is enacted as such.

Sector: Construction/Procurement *(cont.)*

No.	No and title of Regulation	Article	Thematic category	Brief description of potential obstacles	Keyword	Policy maker's objectives	Harm to competition	Recommendations
13	**Emergency Ordinance No. 34/2006 on assigning public procurement contracts, public works concession contracts, and service concession contracts**	Art. 122 c)	Public procurement	The contracting authority may allow the start of negotiations under the tender procedure without the prior publication of a participation notice in cases of extreme urgency, resulting from unforeseeable situations which cannot be a result of the misconduct of the contracting authority. Moreover, in cases of force majeure/duly justified cases, the contracting authority may order the beginning of the works/services in parallel with the initiation of the negotiation without the prior publication of a participation notice procedure (i.e., before the execution of the public procurement agreement). The provision is similarly contained in the newly proposed public procurement legislation (Art. 104 par. 1 corroborated with par. 4 of the same article). This provision has no significant effect in the construction field but more in the case of service agreements awarded by public authorities (e.g., awarding agreements in December for cleaning the streets of snow).	Discrimination	The objective of the regulation is to eliminate bureaucratic procedures/reduce waiting time in cases of extreme urgency resulting from unforeseeable situations which cannot be a result of the misconduct of the contracting authority. This is in line with Art. 32 of Directive 2014/24. There is a document published on the ANAP website regarding the general applicability of Art. 122 mentioned above, but it does not provide adequate instructions and concrete examples for contracting authorities and market participants as regards the application of these exceptional situations.	Considering that the notions of "extreme urgency" and "duly justified cases" are not properly defined in legislation, the contracting authorities have broad powers to decide, on a case-by-case basis, when to apply the exception (thus avoiding the publication of the participation notice). Upon discussions with market participants, it is our understanding that, in practice, the contracting authorities use the lack of definitions in order to avoid procurement even in cases where, in reality, the situation of requesting the application of the exception is not the result of an unforeseeable situation.	1. Define more clearly notions of "extreme urgency" and "duly justified cases" . 2. Draft guidelines with examples of what situations may be considered to be of "extreme urgency" or "duly justified cases", based on European and national case law and practical experiences from the past. Ensure that such materials are published and accessible to all contracting authorities (including local ones) and are dully applied.

Sector: Construction/Procurement *(cont.)*

No.	No and title of Regulation	Article	Thematic category	Brief description of potential obstacles	Keyword	Policy maker's objectives	Harm to competition	Recommendations
14	**Emergency Ordinance No. 34/2006 on assigning public procurement contracts, public works concession contracts, and service concession contracts**	Art. 75, 76 and 224	Public procurement	The public procurement legislation provides various deadlines for the publication of a participation notice, award notices, etc. in SEAP and in the Official Journal of the European Union. As regards the submission of offers, the legislation provides for a minimum of 20 days for calls for tenders or 52 days for an open procedure. In practice, those minimum deadlines are applied as fixed terms and are not extended. The obligation to submit offers in 20 days for calls for tenders or 52 days for an open procedure was considered insufficient by the business community, and, in practice it may represent a potential impediment for economic operators in submitting sound offers, especially for undertakings participating in more complex projects or for small firms. In practice, it has been considered that the offers that are submitted within this timeframe are either of low quality or come from operators who might have had advance knowledge of the calls, leading to the suspicion that they might have been favoured by the contracting authority in question. The newly proposed public procurement legislation establishes shorter minimum terms, in accordance with Directive 2014/24. For example, the minimum term for an open procedure was reduced to 35 days (compared to 52 days according to the legislation in force), a term which can be even shortened in certain instances by up to 20 days to a minimum of 15 days. Similarly, for the restrictive tender procedure, the minimum term for the receipt of tenders shall be 30 days	Discrimination/ Corruption	The deadlines prescribed by the law are minimum periods to be respected by the contracting authority, which might be extended depending on the complexity of the contract and the time required for drawing up and submitting bids. According to ANAP, considering the multitude of public procedures undertaken annually and the particularities of each tender documentation, it is difficult to implement generally applicable rules to be considered when establishing the deadlines.	Since in practice the contracting authorities are using minimum terms as fixed ones, economic operators are impeded in submitting sound offers for more complex projects. This leaves room for discrimination and corruption. If the authorities used longer deadlines, in practice, more offers could be submitted.	Draft instructions giving practical examples for contracting authorities how deadlines should be set in accordance with the complexity of the contract and project.

Sector: Construction/Procurement *(cont.)*

No.	No and title of Regulation	Article	Thematic category	Brief description of potential obstacles	Keyword	Policy maker's objectives	Harm to competition	Recommendations
				from the date the invitation to the tender was sent, a term which can be even shortened in certain instances by up to 20 days to a minimum of 10 days (the current legislation provides a minimum term of 37 days for contracts over certain thresholds – for which the participation notice must be published in the Official Gazette of the European Union – and a minimum term of 20 days for contracts below certain thresholds – for which the participation notice is published in the national gazette – SEAP). For calls for tenders, the newly proposed legislation does not contain a similarly defined procedure, but rather a general provision stating that a simplified procedure will be applicable below certain thresholds, which are to be detailed in the methodological norms (it is not clear at this moment the minimum term for this new procedure replacing the former calls for a tender procedure).				
15	**Emergency Ordinance No. 18/2009 for increasing energy performance of housing blocks**	Art. 15 from the Methodological Norms corroborated with Art. 122 i) from GEO 34/2006	Public procurement	The parties may conclude addenda to agreements for intervention works to enhance the performance of residential buildings constructed after 1990 and which are awarded under a tender procedure if the value of the addenda do not exceed the value of the initial agreement by more than 10%. This provision derogates from the general procurement procedure, according to which the public procurement agreement for additional works/services could be awarded to the initial winner if the value of the additional works does not exceed 20% of its initial value.	Discrimination	The objective of the provision is to cover costs for potential unidentified and imminent works. No official answer has been received from the authorities with respect to this derogation from the general public procurement legislation.	The derogation from the general public procurement legislation may lead to delays in executing the works.	Abolish and apply the general procurement procedure.

Sector: Construction

No.	No and title of Regulation	Article	Thematic category	Brief description of potential obstacles	Keyword	Policy maker's objectives	Harm to competition	Recommendations
1	**Law No. 50/1991 regarding authorisation for execution of construction works**	Art. 9	Administrative burden	The experts (architects or engineers) preparing technical documentation to be submitted for issuance of the building permit must have a degree recognised by the Romanian state. The recognition of a diploma is made according to a procedure of the Ministry of Education.	Discrimination	The objective is to ensure proper qualification of individuals and a homogenous approach of standards in the construction field. The legislation foresees all necessary mechanisms for the recognition of qualifications and professions. There is no procedure at the EU level for automatic recognition of diplomas.	Architects or engineers who have obtained a degree in another state and have not taken the required steps for recognising the diploma in Romania, are not allowed to directly provide services in Romania. This provision may potentially reduce the number of specialists active in the market; however, in practice, there are substantial providers for such services. Thus, the competition impact is very low.	No recommendation for
2	**Law No. 50/1991 regarding authorisation for execution of construction works**	Art. 11 par. 2	Different treatment for the same set of facts	As a general rule, the execution of construction works is possible exclusively after obtaining a building permit. Among the exceptions to this rule, construction works for placing stalls for distribution and trading of newspapers, books and flowers are exempted from the obligation to obtain a building permit. This exception is applied in cases where the stalls are affixed directly on the ground, without having foundations or platforms, and without being supplied with any public utilities except electricity.	Discrimination	The objective of this provision is to reduce the administrative burden for simple constructions having low complexity.	Limitation of categories of products that can be sold in stalls may potentially limit the development of businesses of market participants. They are i) those who already have the stalls are limited to trading only in newspapers, books and flowers and ii) those who are interested in street trading in products other than newspapers, books and flowers do not benefit from the exception, resulting in potentially higher costs for them compared to the "preferred traders".	We recommend extending the exemption from the obligation to obtain a building permit for all stalls which are directly affixed to the ground, without foundations or platforms and that only need to be supplied with electricity. We recommend that each city issue a public policy with respect to street trading and conditions under which such businesses are permitted without a building permit. First, the availability of spaces to be used for street trade should be up to each city hall. Second, each city hall should implement limits in order to ensure that the undertakings carrying out commercial activities on public land are not abusing this right. The legislation should provide, for example, the following types of limitations for a stall:

Sector: Construction *(cont.)*

No.	No and title of Regulation	Article	Thematic category	Brief description of potential obstacles	Keyword	Policy maker's objectives	Harm to competition	Recommendations
								• It shall not lead to or cause congestion or blocking of pedestrian traffic on the sidewalk (establishing thus maximum sizes of the stall), • The commercial activities would involve a short transaction period necessary for completing the sale or rendering the service, • It shall not cause undue noise or offensive odours, etc.
3	**Law No. 50/1991 regarding authorisation of construction works execution**	Annex 1, section 2.5.2	Administrative burden	The technical documentation submitted when requesting a building permit has to be verified by project verifiers. Project verifiers are experts, hired by the investor who plans to obtain a building permit, and who checks that the initial solution prepared by the experts (e.g. architects) observes the norms on quality of construction based on national standards. These project verifiers are authorised by MDRAP. Project verifiers who have obtained a degree in another state and have not taken the necessary steps for their diploma to be recognised, cannot directly offer services in Romania.	Discrimination	The objective is to ensure proper qualification of individuals and a homogenous approach of standards in the construction field. The legislation foresees all necessary mechanisms for the recognition of qualifications and professions. There is no procedure at the EU level for automatic recognition of diplomas.	Project verifiers who have obtained a degree in another state and have not taken the required steps needed for recognising the diploma in Romania, are not allowed to directly provide services in Romania. This provision may potentially reduce the number of specialists active in the market; however, since in practice there are substantial providers for such services, the competition impact is very low.	No recommendation for change.

Sector: Construction *(cont.)*

No.	No and title of Regulation	Article	Thematic category	Brief description of potential obstacles	Keyword	Policy maker's objectives	Harm to competition	Recommendations
4	**Law No. 50/1991 regarding authorisation for execution of construction works**	Annex 1, section 2.5.6	Administrative burden	Among the documents that must be submitted when applying for a building permit, in certain situations there is also the neighbours' approval, expressed in authentic form. Such situations include: i) erecting a new construction adjacent to another building or in the immediate neighbourhood, if there are necessary measures for protecting such adjacent/ neighbouring buildings, ii) construction works which are necessary for changing the purpose of an existing building and iii) erecting new buildings having a different purpose than the surrounding buildings (e.g., erecting an office building where the surrounding buildings have a residential purpose).	Approval	The objective of the provision is to protect existing owners from potential abuses/discomfort caused by incompatibilities between the pre-existing and proposed function. E.g., a building is raised to be used for concerts around a building used for personal purposes, office buildings or educational purposes (in general quiet activities).	The obligation to have the neighbours' approval with respect to the purpose of a building raises a barrier to entry on the market for new developers. According to discussions held with the business community, such provisions sometimes lead to abuses in practice, such as neighbours requesting money for their approval or using it to keep competitors away.	Keep the obligation to request the neighbours' approval in the cases described above. However, for those situations where the investor does not obtain the neighbours' approval, he should still be able to apply for the building permit. It is then up to the local authority to decide, taking into account (but not being bound by) the neighbour's opinion.
5	**Law No. 50/1991 regarding authorisation for execution of construction works**	Art. 1 par. 1	Administrative burden	The law establishes the obligation of obtaining a building permit for any type of construction prior to commencement of works by the developer. The entire process of obtaining a building permit is bureaucratic as it involves submission of a significant amount of documentation, which also include documents released by other state authorities involved in the process.	Licence	The building permit is important for the safety of constructions; thus the objective is the proper use of the regulations/norms in the field. MDRAP mentioned that it is working to simplify the bureaucracy and to implement e-government systems for issuing planning certificates and building permits. However, there are several conditions to be fulfilled at the local level tin order to make the systems functional, such as the necessary IT resources and availability of sufficient human resources with the required abilities.	A bureaucratic process needs to be followed in order to obtain the building permit, creating an administrative burden.	The process of obtaining a building permit should be less bureaucratic by the use of the electronic means available and direct communication between the public authorities involved in the authorisation process.

Sector: Construction *(cont.)*

No.	No and title of Regulation	Article	Thematic category	Brief description of potential obstacles	Keyword	Policy maker's objectives	Harm to competition	Recommendations
6	**Law No. 50/1991 regarding authorisation for execution of construction works**	Art. 2 par. 2.1	Administrative burden	The planning certificate is an informative document issued by the local public authorities ascertaining, among others, how land and existing constructions can be used in accordance with the current urbanistic plans and informing the applicant with respect to the approvals and notices necessary in view of obtaining the building permit. The issuance of a planning certificate is solely for information purposes and contains conditions that need to be met in terms of construction work, green space requirements and classification as a historical monument. The planning certificate will be used by the person/entity intending to erect a building in order to prepare the technical documentation on which he building permit will be based.	Licence	The objective of the planning certificate is to inform all those interested in the features of a certain piece of land/ building; it represents a first step in the dialogue between the authorities, the investors and the civic community. MDRAP mentioned that it is working to simplify the bureaucracy and to implement e-government systems for issuing planning certificates and building permits. However, there are several conditions to be fulfilled at the local level tin order to make the systems functional, such as the necessary IT resources and availability of sufficient human resources with the required abilities.	No direct harm to competition has been identified as the planning certificate only summarises all form of restriction and does not create new ones and needs to be obtained by each natural/legal person who erects a construction; however, the planning certificate often means additional bureaucracy in the already complicated process of obtaining a building permit.	Option 1. The process for obtaining the planning certificate could be made less bureaucratic through the use of the electronic means available. Option 2. The issuance of the planning certificate might be seen as a service provided by the public authority to the developers by informing them about the limits imposed under planning regulations. In such a case, obtaining a planning certificate should be an optional, not a mandatory step when requesting a building permit. However, in such a scenario the risk of non-issuance of the building permit is transferred to the applicant.
7	**Law No. 50/1991 regarding authorisation for execution of construction works**	Art. 8 par. 1	Administrative burden	The legislation imposes the obligation of obtaining a demolition permit prior to any demolition, removal or dismantling, partial or total, of a construction. The constructions that are subject to a demolition permit are not clearly defined in this piece of legislation, as the lawmaker also included the installations annexed to constructions, a notion which is not explained in the law.	Licence	The demolition permit is important for the safety of constructions. The object of the provision is to discourage any kind of demolition works without the permit, by including in the notion of constructions a large category of assets.	The law does not specify what "installation annexes to constructions" means. This might triggers arbitrary application and discrimination in practice.	We recommend defining the installations annexes to construction, that are subject to a demolition permit, taking into account what affects the structural stability of buildings.

Sector: Construction *(cont.)*

No.	No and title of Regulation	Article	Thematic category	Brief description of potential obstacles	Keyword	Policy maker's objectives	Harm to competition	Recommendations
8	**Law No. 50/1991 regarding authorisation for execution of construction works**	Art. 37 par. 2	Administrative burden	The reception of any work subject to a building permit is the last legal step in the execution of construction works, ascertaining that all the elements provided within the building permit were accomplished. The law establishes that, at the end of the construction work, the reception of works should be performed by a reception committee. Such a committee consists of at least five members and includes a representative of the investor, a representative of the local public authorities which issued the building permit, and other experts invited by the owner, one of whom may be from the SCI. The approval committee which concludes the approval protocol can only function in the presence of two-thirds of its members and all the members must be present physically at a meeting at the location of the construction.	Licence	The reception of work is important for the safety of constructions; thus the objective is the proper use of the regulations/norms in the field. Considering that the members of the reception committee have different specialities (structural engineer, plumber, architect, firefighter), it is SCI's opinion that by having a physical meeting, the potential issues can be addressed in a more timely matter by combining solutions from each area of expertise rather than having each one of the members bring their separate conclusion.	The procedure for carrying out approval of constructions by requiring that various entities involved in the process give their consent only in a physical meeting, at the location of the construction, triggers delays in delivery of construction.	No recommendation for change.
9	**Law No. 350/2001 on town and country planning and city planning**	Art 37 par. 3	Unclear provision	A private investor may request a derogation from the planning regulations already approved for a respective area. If agreed, the public authority would issue a new zonal urbanistic plan based on an opportunity notice received from a specialised structure of the public authority. The opportunity notice is based on a technical document generally called an "opportunity study" submitted by the private investor and it is further approved by the mayor. The decision to issue the opportunity notice is based on the input given by a consultative technical commission. The technical commission i) has no clear criteria when giving any input and ii) it is not organised in the same manner in all localities.	Co-regulatory regime	We have not been able to identify the objective of this provision.	The consultative technical commission is not organised in the same manner in all counties and, as it uses no clear criteria when giving any input for changing urbanistic plans or not, this can lead to arbitrary advice in granting opportunity notices.	1) Legislation should be amended to ensure that the technical commissions have the same organisational structure in all localities. 2) There should be a checklist and clear elements should be taken into consideration by the consultative technical commission.

Sector: Construction *(cont.)*

No.	No and title of Regulation	Article	Thematic category	Brief description of potential obstacles	Keyword	Policy maker's objectives	Harm to competition	Recommendations
10	**Law No. 350/2001 on town and country planning and city planning**	Art. 36, Art 37	Conflict of interest	The legislation does not mention the duration of the mandate of the members of the consultative technical commission advising on the granting of opportunity notices necessary for the modification of planning regulations. According to the discussions held with the business community, those members can easily be changed in practice at the discretion of the local or county council. In addition, we have not identified an express time limit for releasing the opportunity notice.	Discrimination	It was not possible to identify the objective of the provision from the relevant piece of legislation.	The provision is too vague, creating a danger of appointing non-objective experts to the commission. Also, there is a danger of an overlong waiting time for the release of opportunity notices.	1) Legislation should be amended in order to ensure that the members of the commission are given a fixed-term mandate. 2) The legislation should be amended in order to foresee a legal time limit for releasing the opportunity notice.
11	**Law No. 350/2001 on town and country planning and city planning**	Art. 31.3	Opportunity notice	A private investor may request a derogation from the planning regulations already approved for a respective area. If agreed, the public authority would issue a new zonal urban plan based on an opportunity notice received from a specialised structure of the public authority. Under the new zonal urbanistic plan, the initial coefficient of terrain usage may be exceeded by a maximum of 20% of the previously approved plan. This limitation does not apply for terrains located in areas destined for economic activity such as industrial parks, technological parks, supermarkets, hypermarkets, commercial parks, service areas and other similar areas, in that these areas can exceed the threshold by more than 20 %. The notion of "similar areas" is not defined by any criteria.	Discrimination	The objective of this provision is to allow economic and industrial development of certain areas in accordance with economic interests. The provision also takes into consideration the fact that a general urbanistic plan cannot provide details on all relevant aspects or that it may not be updated.	Uneven application of the law is possible through different meanings given to the notion of "similar areas"; thus discrimination may take place between market participants. Another issue that can lead to arbitrary decisions by the local authorities is the lack of a threshold for exceeding the coefficient of terrain usage for areas destined to have economic activity, such as industrial parks, technological parks, supermarkets, hypermarkets, commercial parks, service areas and other similar areas.	The legislation should be amended ensure that the technical commissions have the same organisational structure in all localities. Also, MDRAP should prepare a checklist and define clear elements used for establishing the opportunity of an investment. In order to limit the uneven application of the law through different meanings given to the notion of "similar areas", we recommend either to define the notion of "similar areas" or eliminate it from the exception. In all cases, the lawmaker should set a threshold for a usage coefficient for terrains located in areas destined for economic activity.

Sector: Construction *(cont.)*

No.	No and title of Regulation	Article	Thematic category	Brief description of potential obstacles	Keyword	Policy maker's objectives	Harm to competition	Recommendations
12	**Law No. 350/2001 on town and country planning and city planning**	Art 38	Administrative burden	All planning documentation (be it requested by a person wishing to perform specific works or prepared by the city hall) used for issuing a building permit must be confirmed by specialists qualified in the field with a university degree and who have signatory rights. Such signatory rights are granted by the Romanian Register of Urbanists (autonomous public institution) which charges its members for each document signed by them depending on the type and size of the respective planning documentation.	Co-regulatory regime	The objective is to ensure proper qualification of individuals and a homogenous approach of standards in the urbanism field. The fee requested by the Romanian Register of Urbanists is considered to be an equitable payment for the signature right granted, since it fairly reflects the usage level of the signature right and the complexity of the works performed. According to MDRAP, according to a project undertaken by the General Secretary of the Romanian Government, this payment system has been qualified as good practice because the professionals who do not work are not charged in any manner.	The procedure adds costs for professionals in relation to the signature usage right. It is not clear why the members have to pay the fee for each signed document.	No recommendation for change.
13	**Government Decision No. 525/1996 approving the general urbanism regulation**	Art. 5-9 of Annex 1	Administrative burden	In addition to obtaining a building permit, a developer who intends to raise buildings within forests, near water, in protected areas or in dangerous areas has to obtain a separate authorisation from the Ministries of Environment/Home Affairs/Agriculture/ Regional Development/ Culture.	Authorisation	The objective of the provision is to ensure agreement granted for the investment by all parties responsible for a certain domain and to ensure proper protection of the mentioned areas.	Excessive licensing may impede the development of the construction market.	No recommendation for change.
14	**Government Decision No. 525/1996 approving the general urbanism regulation**	Art. 20 of Annex 1	Administrative burden	When obtaining a building permit for construction works in the protection area of the railway infrastructure, an approval has to be obtained from the national railway company (national railway infrastructure company "CFR SA"), a private company owned by the state.	Authorisation	CFR SA is a private company, state-owned, that manages the railway system. We assume that a proper delegation document exists for the attributions of managing railway systems.	Possible risk of abuse since an undertaking is granting authorisations to other undertakings. In case where CFR SA will be privatised in the future, the situation would arise when a private undertaking grants authorisation to another undertaking. The terms of issuing such approval by CFR SA should be contained in the specific regulation of CFR SA and not in this general piece of legislation.	Move the legal provision into a specific regulation of CFR SA.

Sector: Construction *(cont.)*

No.	No and title of Regulation	Article	Thematic category	Brief description of potential obstacles	Keyword	Policy maker's objectives	Harm to competition	Recommendations
15	**Government Decision No. 525/1996 approving the general urbanism regulation**	Art. 28 of Annex 1	Different treatment for the same set of facts	All utility networks in the area of the public roads inside the built up area of a town (intra muros) must be built underground. Exceptionally, electronic communication networks and the associated infrastructure can be built above ground, inside or outside the built up area (intra and extra muros) of the administrative units consisting of villages, communes and towns pertaining to cities and municipalities. The exception was introduced on 30 December 2014, motivated by the necessity of covering the white areas.	Discrimination	In the context of Europe 2020 and the Digital Agenda, the objective of the provision is to encourage the development of electronic communication networks in rural areas by reducing the cost of investment for such networks. Due to the economic aspects, such as density of population and GDP per capita, the communication network providers choose to only cover urban areas, thus leaving rural areas with no or poor access to communication networks. As access to digital networks is a political priority, populations in rural or remote areas must also be provided with access in order for it to become a universal service. Therefore, it is considered necessary to expand electronic communication networks as much and as fast as possible, while assuring optimised costs, specific to rural areas.	The exemption discriminates among communications networks and other utility networks. The utility market might be seen as a whole and all the utility providers might be seen as potential competitors on the same market as they all envisage providing all utility services in the future (however, the timeframe for collectively achieving such a goal cannot be assessed).	No recommendation for change.

Sector: Construction *(cont.)*

No.	No and title of Regulation	Article	Thematic category	Brief description of potential obstacles	Keyword	Policy maker's objectives	Harm to competition	Recommendations
16	**Government Decision No. 525/1996 approving the general urbanism regulation**	Art. 33 of Annex 1	Unclear provision/ unguided discretion	When requesting a building permit for execution of construction works for a building that, by its purpose, requires parking places, the building permit can only be obtained if the parking places, in a minimum number mandatory by law, are placed outside the public areas (i.e. on private areas). Exceptionally, local public authorities can allow the building of parking places on public areas. Two issues arise as regards this legal provision, respectively: i) It is not clear under the legislation that it refers solely to new buildings. The legal provision might also be interpreted in the sense that the existence of a sufficient number of parking places is scrutinised by the authorities for an existing building each time a building permit is required for construction works to the respective buildings or when the owner changes its current purpose, ii) The local authorities may use the public areas for granting parking places at their sole discretion.	Discrimination	The objective of the provision is to provide a solution to an existing problem, specifically the lack of sufficient parking places, by allowing public land to be used for the necessary parking places, subject to certain conditions.	The wording of the legal provision may lead to an arbitrary application of the law on a case-by-case basis, thus leading to heterogeneous practices across various cities or inside the same city. On the one hand, it is not clear that the obligation to ensure parking places outside the public domain only applies to newly erected constructions. It seems to be at the sole discretion of local authorities from each city to decide to which type of construction such a requirement is applicable. If interpreted in the sense that the existence of parking places is also scrutinised by the authorities in each case when a building permit is required for construction works or when the owner changes its current purpose to a new one, the owners of existing buildings might be prevented from performing such works. On the other hand, due to a lack of any clear objective criteria, one undertaking could receive the parking place in the public domain (in exchange for an amount to be paid below the real costs of building a parking space) in contrast to another who would need to invest significant funds in building their own parking place.	We recommend amending the legislation in the sense that the requirement to ensure parking places in order to obtain the building permit is applicable only when erecting new buildings. Furthermore, in order to avoid discretionary application, the possibility of granting parking places on public land should be limited solely to areas such as city centres, protected areas or areas in which the buildings have no direct access to roads. It remains to each city hall to establish which areas fall under the exception.
17	**Government Decision No. 525/1996 approving the general urbanism regulation**	Annex 1, section 1.3.7	Outdated legislation	It is forbidden to locate constructions used for services in industrial areas – except for services provided in buildings integrated with other purposes. Instead, buildings destined for service provision can only be built in central, commercial, residential or recreation areas. For example, within an industrial area, one could not build a car wash or a shop, or a canteen (which is not integrated in the other existing facilities) to serve the workers in the industrial area.	Discrimination	The objective of the regulation might be preserving the health of the labour force in service provision. Most probably the provision comes from the communist era of Romania when there should have been dedicated areas for each purpose.	Although industrial activities should not be carried out in residential or service areas, it is not clear why this should not be possible the other way around.	Amend legislation in order to allow service provision in industrial areas as long as specific health and safety regulations for each activity are observed.

Sector: Construction *(cont.)*

No.	No and title of Regulation	Article	Thematic category	Brief description of potential obstacles	Keyword	Policy maker's objectives	Harm to competition	Recommendations
18	**Government Decision No. 525/1996 approving the general urbanism regulation**	Annex 1, section 1.6.6	Outdated legislation	Professional schools can only be built within 1 000 m of housing areas and neighbourhoods.	Discrimination	The provision establishes a maximum distance to be travelled by students. The limitation seems excessive considering the fast expansion of cities and transport means available to the population.	Operators wanting to build a school outside a housing area are prevented from doing so.	Abolish.
19	**Government Decision No. 525/1996 approving the general urbanism regulation**	Annex 1, section 1.7.4	Outdated legislation	Specialised medical assistance for functional recovery, chronic diseases, psychiatric diseases and disabled persons should be located in out-of-town areas. The law does not differentiate between contagious and non-contagious chronic diseases such as cancer.	Discrimination	This restriction is destined to protect the health of citizens and to offer a proper environment for recovery, which is more easily achieved if the facility is located outside the urban area, with green areas. Most probably, the provision comes from the communist era in Romania when there should have been dedicated areas for each purpose.	This provision is likely to affect private investors providing specialised medical assistance, which may have to bear additional costs for assuring all required conditions outside city areas, where access to utilities is limited, in contrast to all other medical service providers located within the boundaries of a city. In addition, providers of services already located within the boundaries of a city are prevented from developing their business by also offering services for chronic diseases.	The national legislation should be amended in order to apply solely to contagious diseases, if they require medical isolation, or if specific medical equipment used in curing the disease presents a risk for the surrounding population.
20	**Government Decision No. 1739/2006 approving the types of constructions for which a fire protection authorisation should be obtained**	Art. 1	Different treatment for the same set of facts	A fire protection permit certifies the implementation of fire safety measures provided by the law. This permit is mandatory, as a functioning condition, for undertakings owning buildings who carry out their activity in these buildings. Buildings under a specific size (determined in consideration of the number of square metres of a building and type and the purpose of a building) do not need a fire protection permit.	Discrimination	Most probably, the lawmaker considered that small buildings are easy to evacuate.	This provision might create advantages for those enterprises owning small-size buildings.	Abolish the exception.

Sector: Construction *(cont.)*

No.	No and title of Regulation	Article	Thematic category	Brief description of potential obstacles	Keyword	Policy maker's objectives	Harm to competition	Recommendations
21	**Government Decision No. 1364/1990 prohibiting the export of raw or semi-finished wood products**	Art. 1	Outdated legislation	Since 1991, the export of timber and related products has been forbidden for all private agents, except companies or other entities under the Ministry of Resources and Industry (original name). Such entities are required to obtain a licence from the government. From discussions with the business community, such a limitation is no longer applied in practice and the export of timber is possible, in accordance with Art. 35 of the Treaty of Functioning of the European Union – prohibition of export bans or equivalent. However, we have identified a draft of a law regulating the export ban with respect to wood which is currently under the legislative process of the Parliament. The proposed law mentions as objective the preservation of the Romanian woods. Also, the preamble of the proposed law specifies a limited applicability of the export ban for 5 years.	Monopoly	According to MDRAP, GD 1364/1990 does not appear to be currently applicable.	The provision qualifies as an export ban which triggers fragmentation of the market. Also, by granting the possibility to export solely to state-owned companies, a legal monopoly is created which has an impact on pricing. Even though it appears that this provision is not applied in practice, it might still confuse companies.	Abolish GD 1364/1990. In what regards the new proposal of law currently under legislative process, the lawmaker should consider the necessity of such a measure in the current context and the general policy of the state with respect to the preservation of woods and the environment.
22	**Law No. 85/2003 on mines**	Art. 11	Mines	Mining activities are forbidden on terrains with a special regime (with cultural or historical monuments, nature reserves, sanitary protection areas, etc.). Exceptions are allowed through a government decision and following the responsible authority`s opportunity assessment. The government decision is taken by all ministries responsible.	Discrimination	The objective is to allow mining activities when it concerns the national interest, even if usually mining activities would be forbidden on land with a special regime. The law provides for assessment by all authorities that have responsibilities and can express a point of view on the matter. A decision can be made with the agreement of all such authorities involved.	No harm to competition has been identified considering that the government decision is taken by all ministries involved.	No recommendation for change.
23	**Law No. 85/2003 on mines**	Art. 20	Mines	An exploitation licence can be granted for a maximum of 20 years and may be extended for consecutive periods of a maximum of five (5) years each, without a maximum number of prolongations being foreseen by the legislation.	Licence	The objective is to ensure continuity of investment. Mining requires large investments. The title holder of the licence who discovered the deposit of mineral resources carries out mining activities at his own risk and cost. If the discovery is very large it may require a long period of exploitation until the mineral resources are depleted.	Without having a maximum duration of time for the licence, other enterprises could be prevented from entering the market for an infinite time.	Amend the legislation in order to stipulate a maximum number of prolongations that can be granted.

Sector: Construction *(cont.)*

No.	No and title of Regulation	Article	Thematic category	Brief description of potential obstacles	Keyword	Policy maker's objectives	Harm to competition	Recommendations
24	**Law No. 227/2015 regarding the Tax Code**	Art. 474 (10)	Mines	The tax for issuing an authorisation for drilling and excavating is established by the competent local authority and may have any value between RON 0 and 15 per square metre occupied by the construction.	Authorisation	The objective of the provision is to allow local authorities to establish the value of the tax for issuing an authorisation for drilling and excavating, taking into account their local development policy. For example, if they want to attract investors, the local authorities could establish a lower tax rate.	Different decisions may be taken by different local authorities, leading to different costs for the companies requesting the authorisation, depending on the locality where the works are being developed.	No recommendation for change.
25	**Emergency Ordinance No. 36/2001 regarding regulated prices and tariffs, confirmed by the Competition Office**	Art. 1 corroborated with Annex	Mines	The maximum price for sand and rock products is imposed by law and adjusted yearly to the Consumer Price Index. Maximum prices are only set for raw materials and do not cover materials mixed with other products used in construction. There is currently a project on the parliament's agenda to eliminate the maximum price for sand and rock.	Discrimination	The responsible authorities (Ministry of Public Finance) state that through the heterogeneous dispersion of the enterprises in the field, premises for local monopolies can occur. The authority also invokes that this category of products has a significant impact on the costs of public works, a reason why they want to have a maximum price.	The mere existence of a maximum price for rock and sand creates the risk of having all producers align to the maximum price, thus creating a horizontal effect. Moreover, sand and rock can and are traded on the commodities market, thus establishing a transparent price, in accordance with free market rules.	Abolish.
26	**Law No. 85/2003 on mines**	Art. 23	Mines	Mining activities may be carried out by Romanian companies, which are registered according to the law and are specialised and certified for performing mining operations. Also, foreign companies may be granted mining permits and licences. However, according to the law, within ninety (90) days of the date when the licence entered into effect, the foreign company, which obtained the right to perform mining activities, must set up and maintain a subsidiary in Romania for the whole duration of the concession.	Subsidiary	Foreign entities performing mining activities should open subsidiaries due to the fact that mining activities are large operations which are carried out in Romania and should be monitored on a daily basis. Also, proper communication between the state and the investor should be ensured. However, the interdiction is not justified from a fiscal point of view.	Additional administrative barriers are incurred for foreign undertakings when requesting a subsidiary.	Provision to be amended to allow any type of representation in Romania, not necessarily a subsidiary.

Sector: Construction *(cont.)*

No.	No and title of Regulation	Article	Thematic category	Brief description of potential obstacles	Keyword	Policy maker's objectives	Harm to competition	Recommendations
27	**Order No. 202/2881/ 2348/2013 for approval of the Technical Instructions on implementation and monitoring measures set out in the environmental remediation plan, extractive waste management plan and environmental rehabilitation technical design, as well as the manner of operation of the financial guarantee for environmental rehabilitation of the environment affected by mining activities**	Art. 6, 7, 8	Mines	All mining operations need to include, at the end of the mining process, activities for closure and post-closure (e.g., greening activities). In order to ensure that those obligations under the permit will be fulfilled, undertakings performing mining activities have to establish a financial guarantee which must be provided exclusively in the form of a bank deposit. No other form of guarantee is accepted, such as a bank letter of guarantee or an insurance policy. The amount of the guarantee shall be put into an account established by the National Agency for Mineral Resources.	Barrier to entry	In the case of prospecting, the impact is not significant. The duration of a prospecting permit or exploitation permit is limited.	Considering that only a bank deposit is accepted for performing the specific activities mentioned, and no other form of guarantee is accepted, a high volume of liquidities is blocked for those subject to this obligation. This is likely to discriminate against small companies.	Amend the legislation in order to allow all legal types of guarantees (bank deposit, guarantee letter, insurance policies, etc.), so as to allow small companies to also access the market.
28	**Law No. 10/1995 regarding quality in construction**	Art. 15	Administrative burden	Laboratories for analysis and testing in the construction field should be authorised and accredited.	Professional certification	The authorisation of laboratories is very important for the safety of constructions and for the quality of the construction materials used.	The number of laboratories can be limited through the evaluation process. The limitation of service providers could decrease competition and, hence, raise prices for consumers; however, in practice there are substantial providers for such services, so the competition impact is very low.	No recommendation for change.

Sector: Construction *(cont.)*

No.	No and title of Regulation	Article	Thematic category	Brief description of potential obstacles	Keyword	Policy maker's objectives	Harm to competition	Recommendations
29	**Government Decision No. 861/2009 approving the Methodological Norms for granting, use and control of annual amounts intended for the sustainable management of forests which are the private property of individuals and legal entities and the public and private property of the administrative-territorial units and for approving the procedure of the Forest Service and carrying out background checks**	Art. 6	Forests	State aid is granted to owners of forests for the durable maintenance of property. This is subject to EC approval.	Possible state aid implications	The objective is to ensure the sustainable development of forest areas.	There are state-aid implications since the legislative act provides for the possibility of the state to finance the owners of forests.	No recommendation for change.

Sector: Construction *(cont.)*

No.	No and title of Regulation	Article	Thematic category	Brief description of potential obstacles	Keyword	Policy maker's objectives	Harm to competition	Recommendations
30	**Law No. 10/1995 regarding quality in construction**	Art. 20 par. 3	Different treatment for the same set of facts	The SCI is not entitled to control the observance of construction quality rules when residential constructions are built exclusively with a ground floor designed for a single family and household annexes located in rural areas and owned by individuals as well as temporary constructions which may be performed without a building permit. Observance of construction quality rules also involves certain obligations for companies active in the construction field (such as manufacturers or producers of building materials) with respect to the level of quality they should ensure. Depending on the location, certain rural areas in which quality in construction rules should be observed as a measure of protection for the population (such as rural areas exposed to earthquake risk) could be identified.	Discrimination	Lawmakers consider that small buildings are not complicated to build in terms of quality of construction, and the risk of demolition/earthquake is not too serious due to their limited surface. Moreover, according to MDRAP, small building design, including seismic design, is based on the technical requirements in force.	By establishing a different treatment towards enterprises active on the market, a framework for discrimination between companies on the market has been created. The consequences are not significant because of the location of buildings in rural areas or buildings which may be erected without a building permit.	No recommendation for change.
31	**Order of Ministry for Regional Development and Public Administration (MDRAP) No. 1369/2014 approving the Procedure regarding state control of the quality of construction by controlling the entities involved in the execution process – indicative PCE 001**	Art. 13	Administrative burden	Plumbing works in specific areas, such as gas or electrical power and on historic monuments, may only be performed by personnel authorised by specific authorities (Romanian Energy Regulatory Authority, Ministry of Culture, etc.).	Barrier to entry	Considering that quality is very important for the safety of works, the objective is the proper use of the regulations/norms in the field. Separately, the objective is to ensure a homogenous approach of standards in the construction field.	There is a possible risk of market foreclosure through limitation of the number of enterprises on the market for performing plumbing works. However, in practice there are substantial providers for such services, so the competition impact is very low.	No recommendation for change.

Sector: Construction *(cont.)*

No.	No and title of Regulation	Article	Thematic category	Brief description of potential obstacles	Keyword	Policy maker's objectives	Harm to competition	Recommendations
32	**Order No. 847/2014 of MDRAP approving the Procedure regarding state control with respect to the implementation of legal provisions regarding continuous and special monitoring of construction exploitation – indicative PCU 004**	Art. 16 par. 2	Administrative burden	Extensive control in the case of significant damages, extraordinary events or change of purpose of a construction may be performed only by certified experts (e.g. experts controlling fire events should be certified by the Inspectorate for Emergency Situations).	Barrier to entry	Considering that quality is very important for the safety of works, the objective is the proper use of the regulations/norms in the field. Separately, the objective is to ensure a homogenous approach of standards in the construction field.	There is a possible risk of market foreclosure through limitation of the number of enterprises on the market for performing controls in the case of significant damages. However, in practice there are substantial providers for such services, so the competition impact is very low.	No recommendation for change.
33	**Law No. 10/1995 regarding quality in construction**	Art. 13	Administrative burden	The implementation of construction projects and observance of quality in construction rules should be checked by specialists different to those who were involved in the projects bearing the same qualification as the specialists who were involved in the projects (architects, structural engineers, etc.). The specialists are certified by MDRAP in accordance with GD 925/1995.	Professional certification	Quality is very important for the safety of constructions. Using the 4-eyes principle, this provision does not allow the expert who elaborated the project to also verify it, thus avoiding biased opinions.	No harm to competition as regards the number of competitors on the market has been identified, as in practice the number of market players (i.e., providers of this service) is large.	No recommendation for change.
34	**Decision No. 925/1995 approving the regulation of verification and technical expertise of quality of projects, execution work and construction**	Art. 23	Conflict of interest	The construction works should be verified by quality experts (in all construction phases: before starting works, during the process and at the end). The certificate of quality experts can be suspended/ cancelled by MDRAP based on a report prepared by a group of three experts. One member of the group must be an expert recommended by a professional association active in the field.	Co-regulatory regime	Lawmakers established such a procedure due to their lack of experts in the construction field and considered that it is more convenient to base the suspension/cancellation decision on experts who are aware of the technical requirements.	Allowing a certificate of a market participant to be cancelled/suspended based on a report prepared by a competitor of the respective market participant, can lead to a conflict of interest between professional associations, establishes barriers to entry into the market or exclusion from the market and possible exchange of sensitive information.	The legislation should be amended by mentioning independency rules so as to avoid a possible conflict of interest. The issue could also be partially solved if the public authorities hire more independent experts (this would be a management decision, based on the available resources of the public authority).

Sector: Construction *(cont.)*

No.	No and title of Regulation	Article	Thematic category	Brief description of potential obstacles	Keyword	Policy maker's objectives	Harm to competition	Recommendations
35	**Government Ordinance No. 20/1994 on measures to mitigate the seismic risk of existing buildings**	Art. 4 corroborated with Art. 58 and Art 86 of the Norms	Conflict of interest	Intervention works to buildings with a seismic risk are carried out by state authorities based on a technical solution issued by a designer. Technical solutions are also reviewed by the National Commission for Seismic Risks, a technical body set up by the authority with the consultative role of analysing and giving advice. Members of the commission also include experts appointed by professional associations and employers' union representatives in the field. Even though formally the state authorities are independent in making the final decision, it is likely that they follow the advice of the National Commission for Seismic Risks (as its members are the ones providing technical input and expertise).	Co-regulatory regime	Lawmakers established such a procedure due to their lack of experts in the construction field and considered that it is more convenient to base the decision on experts who are aware of the technical requirements. The commission of experts have only an advisory role to play in the decision making process, which is entirely in the hands and the responsibility of public authorities.	In general, the involvement of a professional association in the field is a good thing as it comes with their expertise. However, from a competition perspective, the fact that a competitor is involved in the procedure of authorising a market participant can lead, in practice and with help of public authorities, to i) a conflict of interest of the professional associations as these provisions create the framework for professional associations to get involved in possible anti-competitive practices and establish barriers to entry on the market or exclusion from the market, ii) a possible exchange of sensitive information and iii) administrative barriers due to a tendency to standardise interests/actions in cases where the members of private associations may influence the attitude of the public authorities and the legislation in their favour.	The legislation should be amended by mentioning independency rules so as to avoid a possible conflict of interest. The issue could also be partially solved if the public authorities hire more independent experts (this would be a management decision, based on the available resources of the public authority).
36	**Law No. 372/2005 regarding energy performance of buildings**	Art. 27 par. 1	Administrative burden	Certification and energy audits for buildings are performed by energy auditors who are certified by MDRAP. There is no express recognition of EU certified auditors or inter-state provision of services.	Qualifications	The objective is to ensure proper qualification of individuals and a homogenous approach of standards in the construction field. Also, according to MDRAP, it has been taken into account that there is no unique methodology in this profession at the European level. Therefore, MDRAP follows the provisions of Law No. 200/2004 on the recognition of diplomas and professional qualifications for regulated professions in Romania.	By not offering the possibility of EU citizens/legal entities to be active directly in Romania, a discriminatory regime is implemented between Romanian nationals and non-Romanian nationals and the number of the auditors may be reduced with direct impact on competition for such services. However, in practice there are substantial providers for such services, so the competition impact is very low.	No recommendation for change.

Sector: Construction *(cont.)*

No.	No and title of Regulation	Article	Thematic category	Brief description of potential obstacles	Keyword	Policy maker's objectives	Harm to competition	Recommendations
37	**Law No. 372/2005 regarding energy performance of buildings**	Art. 31	Conflict of interest	Specialists appointed from professional associations in the construction field also participate in the checks carried out by the State Inspectorate in Construction in the field of energy performance of buildings.	Co-regulatory regime	Lawmakers established such a procedure due to their lack of experts in the construction field and considered that it is more convenient to base the decision on experts who are aware of the technical requirements.	In general, the involvement of a professional association in the field is a good thing as it comes with their expertise. However, from a competition perspective, the fact that a competitor is involved in the procedure of authorising a market participant can lead, in practice and with help of public authorities, to i) a conflict of interest of the professional associations as these provisions create the framework for professional associations to get involved in possible anti-competitive practices and establish barriers to entry on the market or exclusion from the market, ii) a possible exchange of sensitive information and iii) administrative barriers due to a tendency to standardise interests/actions in cases where the members of private associations may influence the attitude of the public authorities and the legislation in their favour.	The legislation should be amended by mentioning independency rules so as to avoid a possible conflict of interest. The issue could also be partially solved if the public authorities hire more independent experts (this would be a management decision, based on the available resources of the public authority).
38	**Law No. 372/2005 regarding energy performance of buildings**	Art.18 par. 1 and 2, heading X	Administrative burden	Obtaining an energy certificate is mandatory for all buildings that are built, sold, rented or subject to major renovations. The cost of obtaining such a certificate depends on the surface area of the building. The certificate triggers no obligation in relation to the insulation of constructions and no recommendations in relation to energy performance. Obtaining the energy certificate is a requirement under Directive 2002/91/EC of the European Parliament and of the Council on the Energy Performance of Buildings.	Barrier to entry	The objective of the regulation is to collect data at a national level regarding energy efficiency of privately owned buildings, to raise awareness and make countries comparable.	As regards the content of such a certificate, as long as the existence of the certificate triggers no obligation in relation to the insulation of constructions, its issuance is a mere administrative burden and adds costs to transactions involving buildings.	The legislation should be amended in order to regulate the energy certificate and should contain practical recommendations for improving the energy performance of buildings, if this is practically possible.

Sector: Construction *(cont.)*

No.	No and title of Regulation	Article	Thematic category	Brief description of potential obstacles	Keyword	Policy maker's objectives	Harm to competition	Recommendations
39	**Emergency Ordinance No. 18/2009 for increasing the energy performance of housing blocks**	Art. 1 par. 3	Unclear provision/ unguided discretion	In terms of aesthetics, the state must approve intervention works for housing flats located in the historic centres of localities, in the areas of protected historic monuments and/or protected areas. Aesthetic authorisation of works is made by the Ministry of Culture. There is no mention as to what "aesthetic" means or the rationale behind each decision.	Barrier to entry	Urbanism aspects are the basis of this regulation.	Possibility of abusive interpretation on a case-by-case basis which triggers discrimination between enterprises.	Option 1. Amend the legislation so that general principles/objective criteria are observed and detailed under the law in order to avoid discretionary decisions and uncertainty (for example whether to keep the same initial façade of the building). Option 2. All decisions of the Ministry of Culture should be published for transparency purposes in order to avoid uncertainty with respect to each decision.
40	**Emergency Ordinance No. 18/2009 for increasing the energy performance of housing blocks**	Art. 3 par. 8	Conflict of interest	When approving local programmes for increasing the energy performance of housing blocks, technical committees collaborate with representatives of professional associations of energy auditors. There might arise a possible conflict of interest, as the energy auditors would subsequently be involved in the controlling procedure of SCI (based on provisions of Order No. 3152/2012 approving Control procedures regarding the unitary application of the legal provisions regarding energy performance of buildings and the control of the heating/ air conditioning systems mentioned below).	Co-operation	The objective is to ensure sufficient technical expertise.	In general, the involvement of a professional association in the field is a good thing as it comes with their expertise. However, from a competition perspective, the fact that a competitor is involved in the procedure of authorising a market participant can lead, in practice and with help of public authorities, to i) a conflict of interest of the professional associations as these provisions create the framework for professional associations to get involved in possible anti-competitive practices and establish barriers to entry on the market or exclusion from the market, ii) a possible exchange of sensitive information and iii) administrative barriers due to a tendency to standardise interests/actions in cases where the members of private associations may influence the attitude of the public authorities and the legislation in their favour.	The legislation should be amended by mentioning independency rules so as to avoid possible conflict of interest. The issue could also be partially resolved if the public authorities hire more independent experts (this would be a management decision, based on the available resources of the public authority).

Sector: Construction *(cont.)*

No.	No and title of Regulation	Article	Thematic category	Brief description of potential obstacles	Keyword	Policy maker's objectives	Harm to competition	Recommendations
41	**Order No. 3152/2012 approving Control procedures regarding the unitary application of the legal provisions regarding energy performance of buildings and the control of the heating/air conditioning systems**	Art. 16	Conflict of interest	The professional associations of construction designers, plumbing engineers, energy auditors, architects and technical experts in air conditioning/ heating systems will participate in the control procedure in the field of energy performance of buildings undertaken by the SCI. The participation will be established by collaboration protocols to be concluded with the SCI.	Self-regulation	The objective is to ensure sufficient technical expertise.	This may trigger possible exchanges of sensitive information between competitors and create uncertainty regarding the power of professional associations in the control procedure as the regulation does not expressly provide for their role in the control; it only states that they should attend the control.	The legislation should be amended by mentioning independency rules so as to avoid possible conflict of interest. The issue could also be partially resolved if the public authorities hire more independent experts (this would be a management decision, based on the available resources of the public authority).
42	**Law No. 121/2014 regarding energy efficiency**	Art. 9 par. 11	Administrative burden	Operators who annually consume an amount of energy over 1 000 tonnes oil equivalent (toe) and who have implemented an energy and environment management system certified by an independent body according to relevant European or international standards do not need to carry out an energy audit every four years. This is an exception to the general rule establishing that all operators consuming a quantity of energy over 1 000 toe annually must proceed with an energy audit every four years.	Discrimination	Most probably such derogation comes from the fact that the respective operators have to implement a management system for energy, which appears to be a more complex procedure than the energy audit.	This obligation may discriminate among competing enterprises having the same size based on implementation of an energy and environment management system.	No recommendation for change.
43	**Government Decision No. 525/2013 approving the general and specific duties, the organisational structure and the maximum number of posts, and the rating for fleet and fuel consumption of the State Construction Inspectorate (SCI)**	Art. 3 par. IV	Conflict of interest	The SCI works with professional associations in order to develop expertise, research reports, find technical solutions and consolidate projects which are necessary when exercising its control activities.	Co-operation	The objective is to ensure sufficient technical expertise.	This provision emphasises the deep involvement of professional associations in the activity of the SCI, also corroborated by the other possibilities mentioned above. Professional associations are in an obvious conflict of interest. They may be consulted but they should stay clear of the decision making process, which must be entirely in the hands and the responsibility of public authorities.	The legislation should be amended by mentioning independency rules so as to avoid possible conflict of interest. The issue could also be partially resolved if the public authorities hire more independent experts (this would be a management decision, based on the available resources of the public authority).

Sector: Construction *(cont.)*

No.	No and title of Regulation	Article	Thematic category	Brief description of potential obstacles	Keyword	Policy maker's objectives	Harm to competition	Recommendations
44	**Order No. 1369/2014 of MDRAP approving the Procedure regarding state control of the quality of constructions by controlling the entities involved in the execution process indicative PCE 001**	Art. 11 par. 1 letter a) 2.	Unclear provision/ unguided discretion	The SCI decides on the type of control applicable to each construction process during the execution phase, taking into account the complexity of the works (i.e., current control or random control). The legislation in force does not prescribe any criteria for the SCI when deciding to pursue random control.	Discrimination	The lawmaker allowed the SCI to decide on the type of control applicable to each construction process during the execution phase in order to efficiently use its resources and prioritise. According to the SCI, a "system procedure" could be implemented containing the criteria for the type of control (a "system procedure" provides general rules in comparison to an "operational procedure" which provides detailed criteria).	Due to lack of clear criteria when assessing the type of control applicable, the SCI might discriminate between competing undertakings on the market. There is only limited predictability for the subjects of the control activities. Those operators subject to random control need to allocate supplementary time resources for controls from SCI.	Implement a system procedure to be used by the SCI when assessing the complexity of the works and when to apply random control.
45	**Order No. 848/2014 of MDRAP approving the Procedure regarding state control of the quality of constructions by controlling the entities involved in the design and execution process with respect to the organising and functioning of the quality management system - indicative PCS 003**	Art. 6 par. 1	Unclear provision/ unguided discretion	The SCI has the right to discretionarily decide on the type of control (verification of quality management system) applicable to each designer and contractor: current control or regular control). Quality management systems in constructions ensure that the construction project is successful by making sure that activities have the necessary resources, that accurate information is channelled to the right people at the right time so that they can make the right decisions and by ensuring that technical activities are performed within accepted limits.	Discrimination	The lawmakers allowed the SCI to decide on the type of control (verification of quality management system) applicable to each designer and contractor in order to avoid overheads due to a lack of experts in the construction field. According to SCI, a "system procedure" could be implemented regarding the criteria for the type of control (a system procedure would provide with general rules rather than an "operational procedure", which would provide with detailed criteria, inapplicable in this case).	Due to a lack of clear criteria when assessing the type of control applicable, the SCI might discriminate between competing undertakings on the market. There is only limited predictability for the subjects of the control activities. Those operators subject to random control need to allocate supplementary time resources for controls from SCI.	Implement a system procedure to be used by the SCI when assessing the complexity of the works and when to apply randon control.
46	**Order No. 1370/2014 of MDRAP approving the Procedure regarding state control of the determining phases with respect to the mechanical strength and the stability of the construction, indicative PCF 002-2014**	Art. 9 para. 3 d)	Administrative burden	The SCI controls the projects in the critical intermediate stages of execution. The control is carried out on the basis of the programme proposed by the engineering designer and approved by the SCI. Afterwards the construction process may continue only after obtaining the approval of the SCI for each critical construction phase during a meeting in which representatives of the authority and of the engineering designer and developer should participate.	Barrier to entry	Lawmakers intended to identify any deviations from the technical regulations/legislation applicable in force and establish remedies/terms/ responsibilities to address them. According to SCI, they will analyse the opportunity of allowing the various entities involved in the process to give their consent at different times, not necessarily in a physical meeting at the location of the construction.	Excessive approvals may impede the development of the construction market. In the absence of clear criteria and specific deadlines, there is a possibility of abuse and additional costs to investors.	In order to avoid delays on the delivery of the construction, assess the opportunity of allowing the various entities involved in the process to give their consent at different times, not necessarily in a physical meeting at the location of the construction.

Sector: Construction *(cont.)*

No.	No and title of Regulation	Article	Thematic category	Brief description of potential obstacles	Keyword	Policy maker's objectives	Harm to competition	Recommendations
47	**Law No. 597/2001 regarding certain protection and authorisation measures of construction in the coastal areas of the Black Sea**	Art. 6	Different treatment for the same set of facts	In the seaside resorts and the area of tourist beaches, it is prohibited to execute construction or maintenance works in between 15 May and 15 September. Starting in 2014, works within a project financed with non-reimbursable external funds, ongoing works, seasonal works, urgent works and works that do not affect tourist activities are exempt from the abovementioned prohibition, and therefore allowed. There are several issues arising from this provision: • The interdiction to carry out construction or maintenance works in coastal areas is applicable automatically, without a prior assessment of the execution period, location or risk of adverse health and safety of persons in each case. • This limitation raises discriminatory conditions for undertakings having tourist resorts outside the interdiction zone (i.e., resorts in the mountains or in the historical sites) for which there is no such prohibition. • The large number of exceptions may circumvent the application of the interdiction.	Discrimination	The objective of the provision is to keep construction works from interfering with tourism activity.	This limitation interferes with the business activity of undertakings due to the fact that the interdiction to carry out construction or maintenance works in coastal areas is applicable automatically, without a prior assessment. In addition, the legal provisions raise discriminatory conditions for market participants. Separately, the large number of exceptions may circumvent the application of the interdiction.	Abolish article 6 of Law 597/2001.
48	**Government Decision No. 766/1997 approving certain regulations regarding quality in construction**	Entire act	Double/ unpublished legislation	There are two pieces of legislation in force with the same object of regulating the legal framework, main elements, methodology and organisation of technical approval in the construction field. Order No. 1889/2004 approving certain procedures for technical approvals in the construction field has the same object as Annex 5 of GD 766/1997 (Regulation on the technical agreement for products, processes and equipment in construction); thus, dual pieces of legislation are applicable.	Barrier to entry	The two different pieces of legislation are not completely the same.	It is unclear for companies active in the field what legislation is in force.	Unify the entire legislation on the subject in a sole legislative act.

Sector: Construction *(cont.)*

No.	No and title of Regulation	Article	Thematic category	Brief description of potential obstacles	Keyword	Policy maker's objectives	Harm to competition	Recommendations
49	**Government Decision No. 766/1997 approving certain regulations regarding quality of construction**	Entire act	Double/ unpublished legislation	Annex 4 of Government Decision No. 766/ 1997 approving certain regulations regarding the quality of constructions regulate the same control activity as mentioned under Order No. 847/2014 approving the Procedure regarding control activities performed for enforcing the legal provisions related to the current and specialised monitoring of the serviceability of constructions. However, the control activity pertains to two different authorities, namely specialists of MDRAP and the SCI.	Barrier to entry	Each normative act regulates the control of a different author, namely the control of MDRAP and of the SCI.	It is unclear for companies active in the field what legislation is in force.	A sole control authority should be established. No double check should be allowed for the observance of the same obligations.
50	**Order No. 2190/2004 approving the Regulation regarding European technical approval**	Entire act	Double/ unpublished legislation	Two pieces of legislation are in force with the same objective of regulating the European technical agreement for construction products. Order 2190/2004 has the same objective as EU Regulation No. 305/2011 setting forth harmonised conditions for the marketing of construction products and repealing Council Directive 89/106/EEC. Therefore dual pieces of legislation are available.	Non-harmonised legislation	The domestic legislation stopped being applied once the European legislation came into force.	It is unclear for companies active in the field what legislation is in force.	Abolish.
51	**Government Decision No. 622/2004 approving the conditions to introduce construction products on the national market**	Entire act	Double/ unpublished legislation	Two pieces of legislation are in force with the same objective of regulating the harmonised technical approvals. GD 622/ 2004 has the same objective as European Regulation No. 305/2011 setting forth harmonised conditions for the marketing of construction products and repealing Council Directive 89/106/EEC. Therefore dual pieces of legislation are applicable in the field of harmonised technical approvals.	Non-harmonised legislation	Government Decision No. 622/2004 approving the conditions to introduce construction products on the national market implementing the Council Directive 89/106/EEC abolished through European Regulation No. 305/ 2011.	It is unclear for companies active in the field what legislation is in force.	Abolish the part of the legislation that is related to the harmonised technical approvals.

Sector: Construction *(cont.)*

No.	No and title of Regulation	Article	Thematic category	Brief description of potential obstacles	Keyword	Policy maker's objectives	Harm to competition	Recommendations
52	**Order MDRAP No. 1269/2011 approving the Regulation regarding the organising and functioning of the Standing Technical Council for Construction (CTPC)**	Art. 2 par. 3	Technical approval	The Permanent Technical Council for Constructions (CTPC) is a public supervisory body that i) authorises companies that develop the technical approvals to function and ii) approves the technical approvals issued by development companies in the case of non-harmonised building materials. CTPC works in technical commissions. The technical commissions are formed, among others, by specialists proposed by specialised private entities already authorised to issue technical approvals and/or members of professional associations, and employers' unions in the construction field.	Self-regulation	Most probably, the lawmakers established such a procedure due to their lack of experts in the construction field and considered that it is more convenient to base the decision on experts who are aware of the technical requirements.	This may generate i) potential exchange of sensitive information between competitors (such as costs) and ii) potential barriers to entry for companies requesting technical approvals as a competitor is involved in the approval process.	The legislation should be amended by mentioning independency rules so as to avoid possible conflict of interest. The issue could also be partially resolved if the public authorities hire more independent experts (this would be a management decision, based on the available resources of the public authority).
53	**Order No. 1269/2011 of MDRAP approving the Regulation regarding the organising and functioning of the Standing Technical Council for Construction (CTPC)**	Art. 3 and Art. 6 and Art. 3 par. 1 of Government Decision No. 622/2004 approving the conditions to introduce construction products on the national market	Technical approval	The development of technical approvals is made by companies authorised by a council functioning under the authority of the CTPC. This technical council, which is able to decide on the authorisation of new entities as well as approvals for new products (and subsequently to give favourable notice to the technical approvals), is made up of representatives of already authorised certifying entities, among others.	Conflict of interest	Most probably, the lawmakers established such a procedure due to their lack of experts in the construction field and considered that it is more convenient to base the decision on experts who are aware of the technical requirements.	This triggers i) exchange of information between competitors ii) potential barriers to entry for companies requesting technical approvals as a competitor is involved in the approval process iii) the Regulation does not provide the criteria/procedure that the certifying entities should use to designate their representative to the Technical Council, which might be seen as a barrier to entry.	The legislation should be amended by mentioning independency rules so as to avoid possible conflict of interest. The issue could also be partially resolved if the public authorities hire more independent experts (this would be a management decision, based on the available resources of the public authority).
54	**Order No. 1889/2004 approving procedures for technical approvals**	Art. 3.2.2 of Annex No. 2 on procedure regarding the empowerment of the bodies which approve the request for technical certification	Technical approval	The companies seeking authorisation for the elaboration of technical approvals must be Romanian legal persons or associations of Romanian legal persons. There is no express recognition under the legislation of EU certified companies for elaboration of technical approvals.	Discrimination	The objective is to ensure proper qualification of individuals and the homogenous approach of standards in the construction field, based on the domestic climate and seismic conditions.	Individuals or foreign legal persons are excluded, thus creating discrimination between foreign citizens and Romanian citizens. This may trigger i) a barrier to entry ii) high risk of market foreclosure in an area which is anyway very specialised. The provision restricts suppliers' choices and their incentives to compete.	No recommendation for change.

Sector: Construction *(cont.)*

No.	No and title of Regulation	Article	Thematic category	Brief description of potential obstacles	Keyword	Policy maker's objectives	Harm to competition	Recommendations
55	**Order No. 1889/2004 approving procedures for technical approvals**	Art. 10 par. 3, Art. 41 of Annex No. 1 on procedure regarding technical approvals	Technical approval	The prolongation or the amendment of technical approvals should be requested only of the entity who elaborated the initial technical approval (strict exceptions include: the issuing entity no longer exists, was suspended, etc.).	Barrier to entry	Most likely, the purpose of this provision was to ensure accountability between entities elaborating technical approvals.	This restriction affects competition between private companies authorized by CTPC to elaborate technical approvals because an undertaking intending to amend the initial technical approval or to prolong its duration is not free to choose the body that would make such amendments.	Abolish.
56	**Order No. 1889/2004 approving procedures for technical approvals**	Art. 29 par. 2, Art. 30 par. 4 of Annex No. 1 on procedure regarding technical approvals	Technical approval	Entities elaborating technical approvals may be suspended from functioning if during a 12-month period the CTPC rejects three technical approvals issued by them.	Discrimination	It is a matter of security as the entity has not been shown to be trustworthy.	The suspension of activity could qualify as an excessive sanction, likely to create unnecessary pressure on the market participant which bears contractual liability as well as the economic liability of a bad reputation.	No recommendation for change.
57	**Order No. 1889/2004 approving procedures for technical approvals**	Art. 31 of Annex No. 1 on the procedure regarding technical approvals	Technical approval	In case that the activity of an entity elaborating technical approvals is suspended, the CTPC may discretionarily distribute the contracts of the suspended entity to other entities elaborating technical approvals, if the producer (solicitor) cannot wait for the delay of the duration of the suspension of the activity (the duration of the suspension of the activity is three or six months). The law provides no criteria for CTPC's allocation of the suspended entity's contracts to other entities. The opinion of the undertaking requesting the elaboration is not requested.	Discrimination	It was not possible to identify the objective of the provision from the relevant piece of legislation.	Considering that the CTPC may discretionarily distribute the contracts to other entities issuing technical approvals, without criteria and without having to ask the producer, there is a risk of abuse and discrimination. Moreover, considering that representatives of elaborating bodies are members of the CTPC, the distribution of contracts may be dictated by the representatives' private interest.	The company requesting the elaboration of technical approval should be consulted when the project is allocated to another entity. The final decision on the allocation should remain with the requesting entities, and not with CTPC.
58	**Order No. 1889/2004 approving procedures for technical approvals**	Art. 35 par. 1 of Annex No. 1 of the procedure regarding technical approvals	Technical approval	The validity of a technical approval is three years, but it may be extended by the CTPC to 5 years for certain products, services or equipment that are "safe" and "without risks". The provision does not define those notions.	Discrimination	It was not possible to identify the objective of the provision from the relevant piece of legislation.	Possible risk of abuse and discrimination in practice due to unclear wording. There is no predictability among the enterprises with respect to the application of this legal provision.	The national legislation should be amended so that it clearly defines the notion of products, services or equipment "without risk" and the notion of "safe" products, services or equipment.

Sector: Construction *(cont.)*

No.	No and title of Regulation	Article	Thematic category	Brief description of potential obstacles	Keyword	Policy maker's objectives	Harm to competition	Recommendations
59	**Order No. 1889/2004 approving procedures for technical approvals**	Art. 5.7.2, Art. 6.6. of Annex II – pct. 6 of – procedure regarding the empowerment of the bodies that approve the request for technical certification	Technical approval	The number of previously issued technical approvals is a criterion taken into consideration by the CTPC in assessing the entity authorised to elaborate technical approvals for the purpose of prolonging/ preserving the authorisation. The ministerial experts confirmed that such a criterion is used in practice but it is not possible to identify how much this counts when a decision is taken not to renew an authorisation.	Barrier to entry	The objective of the regulation is to ensure continuity of activity and maintenance of expertise. This is a matter of trust in the market, as they have not been entrusted with any services.	This provision creates an unjustified barrier to entry for newly authorised entities or for small ones.	Option 1. Abolish. Option 2. Amend the legislation by mentioning that such information is required solely for statistical purposes.
60	**Order No. 2142/2013 approving Procedures for designating the technical assessment bodies for construction products**	Art. 6 par. 3	Technical approval	Technical Assessment Bodies (TAB) are private entities notified to and designated by MDRP in order to elaborate a European technical approval in the case of harmonised building materials. The duration of the appointment of the TABs by the MDRP is not always unlimited. There are no criteria to assess when the appointment would be limited.	Discrimination	It was not possible to identify the objective of the provision from the relevant piece of legislation.	Risk of discrimination and abuse, as the CTPC may discretionarily decide when to grant an unlimited designation (significant lower cost as the designation procedure involves several stages of preparation and audit).	Option 1. Legislation should stipulate the cases where the appointment is limited in time. Option 2. The word "generally" should be eliminated from the text of the legal provision, so that any appointment is granted for an unlimited period of time.
61	**Order No. 2141/2013 approving Procedures for designating the entities performing the assessment and verification of constancy of performance of construction products**	Art. 22 par. 2 Art. 17 l	Technical approval	In the case of revocation of designation for verification of the performance of construction products, the entities that perform the assessment and verification of constancy of performance of construction products are prohibited from requesting designation for a future period of five years. This sanction is applied when the designation is revoked for specific situations such as not allowing inspections by the SCI and non-observance of its attributions under European Regulation 305/2011.	Discrimination	The five year sanctioning period is equal to the period of validity of the accreditation cycle.	Risk of discrimination and abuse as this provision may limit the number of entities designated to perform the assessment and verification of constancy of performance of construction products. Such a severe sanction for a future period of five years should be justified.	Responsible authorities should assess whether this sanction applies solely for severe infringements and decide if there is a chance of reducing the sanction, if this is the case.

Sector: Construction *(cont.)*

No.	No and title of Regulation	Article	Thematic category	Brief description of potential obstacles	Keyword	Policy maker's objectives	Harm to competition	Recommendations
62	**Order No. 607/2005 of Ministry of Internal Affairs approving the control methodology regarding the monitoring of the market of construction products designed to protect constructions against fire**	Art. 19	Outdated legislation	The State Authority for Emergency Situations has the competency for solving unfair competition complaints.	Foreclosure	It was not possible to identify the objective of the provision from the relevant piece of legislation.	This may breach the Romanian Competition Council's exclusive competence in this area. A secondary norm cannot infringe a law that has superior legal force such as Law 21/1996, which provides the attributions of the Romanian Competition Council and Law 11/1990 regarding unfair competition. The existence of such legal provisions may create uncertainty regarding the state authorities' competency in solving competition issues among market participants. The Competition Council is also best placed to decide on such cases.	Abolish and refer to general competition law.
63	**Law No. 278/2013 on industrial emissions**	Art. 14 para. 4 and 5	Environmental legislation	BAT conclusions ("best available techniques conclusions"), as defined by Directive 2010/75, means the best available techniques, their description, information to assess their applicability, the emission levels associated with the best available techniques, associated monitoring, associated consumption levels and, where appropriate, relevant site remediation measures for certain fields involving industrial emissions. BAT conclusions introduce a minimum binding standard for EU Member States. According to Directive 2010/75, the Member States maintain the right to impose more restrictive conditions in which case the Member State must establish rules under which the competent authority may set such stricter conditions. Romanian Law No. 2792013 provides the possibility of the competent authority imposing authorisation conditions in the field of industrial emissions more restrictive than those applicable at the European level, but fails to provide categories of express cases when the competent authority may impose such restrictive conditions. Thus, it seems that authorities have unguided discretion to decide.	Barrier to entry	It was not possible to identify the objective of the provision from the relevant piece of legislation.	Risk of market foreclosure and discrimination among market participants due to a lack of clear situations when the competent authority may impose authorisation conditions more restrictive than the conditions resulting from BAT conclusions.	The national legislation should provide objective and transparent criteria for determining the situations in which the competent authority may impose authorisation conditions more restrictive than the conditions resulting from BAT conclusions.

Sector: Construction *(cont.)*

No.	No and title of Regulation	Article	Thematic category	Brief description of potential obstacles	Keyword	Policy maker's objectives	Harm to competition	Recommendations
64	**Law No. 278/2013 on industrial emissions**	Art. 25 para. 1	Environmental legislation	The national law provides that any interested third party, having a legitimate interest to do so, may appeal in court the decisions, omissions, or any other acts of the competent authority in the field of industrial emissions. However, the law fails to define legitimate interest in the field of public emissions.	Barrier to entry	Considering that there is a wide range of measures which can be contested by the public, resulting in delays in the authorisation process, Directive 2010/75 provided expressly that EU Member States must establish what constitutes a sufficient interest and breach of a right in this field, consistently with the objective of giving the public concerned wide access to justice.	Failing to establish specific examples of what constitutes a legitimate interest of a third party in the field of industrial emissions gives the authority, and the relevant courts of law a discretionary right, to appreciate the legitimacy of such potential claims of third parties.	Clear guidelines with examples should be implemented at the national level, stating when a third party has a legitimate interest in challenging a decision in the industrial emissions field.
65	**Law No. 104/2011 on ambient air quality**	Art. 57 para. 3	Environmental legislation	In the areas where emissions in the air for certain pollutants exceed the provision, the environmental authority will impose more restrictive emission limits for those pollutants, based on studies assessing their environmental impact.	Discrimination	It was not possible to identify the objective of the provision from the relevant piece of legislation.	The wording of this provision is unclear with two possible interpretations. One would be that the more restrictive conditions are imposed only to new pollutants. Another possible interpretation would be that more restrictive conditions may also be imposed on old pollutants.	The national legislation should be amended, in order to clarify how and to what type of pollutants the restriction applies.
66	**Order No. 863/2002 on the approval of methodological guidelines applicable to the frameworkprocedure for evaluating environmental impact**	Guideline, tables No. 2 and 3	Environmental legislation	After the economic operator submits certain data and information regarding its project to the environmental authority, the competent authority must decide whether the project will go to the evaluation procedure or not. In order to take such a decision, the authority fills in a control list consisting of questions based on the data provided by the economic operator. The possible answers for the economic operator are "Yes", "No", "Not applicable" or "Unclear". Then, the authority decides if the project must go to the evaluation procedure or not. The legislation does not provide clear criteria to be followed by the authority when taking such a decision. Order No. 863/2002 establishes that even a single "Yes" answer in the control list could trigger the decision to submit the project for further evaluation.	Discrimination	It was not possible to identify the objective of the provision from the relevant piece of legislation.	Risk of discrimination and abuse by the authority when deciding which project to further evaluate due to lack of criteria and thresholds for evaluation. Considering that the evaluation procedure involves time and costs for economic operators, the authorities must apply a more objective guideline in the screening stage.	Option 1. Draft guidelines which include criteria to be used by the authorities when deciding which project to further evaluate Option 2. Publish decisions of the authority on the website in order to bring transparency and predictability for the enterprises active on the market.

Sector: Construction *(cont.)*

No.	No and title of Regulation	Article	Thematic category	Brief description of potential obstacles	Keyword	Policy maker's objectives	Harm to competition	Recommendations
67	**Order No. 290/2000 regarding the technical acceptance of products and/or services for use in activities of building, upgrading, repair and maintenance of rail infrastructure and rolling stock for rail and metro**	Art. 2	Roads & highways	The Romanian railway authority (AFER) issues a railway technical approval for building materials made from processed/ mixed construction materials needed to achieve specific activities or processes when building, modernising or maintenance of the railway infrastructure and rolling stock.	Authorisation	The objective is to ensure safety of railway networks also through the use of proper materials.	The provision of quality approvals by AFER leads to additional costs and effort for producers.	No recommendation for change.
68	**Legislation that has not been published**	Entire act	Double/ unpublished legislation	We have identified the following piece of legislation which is not published in the Official Gazette of Romania, or in the case where it has been published, it is not generally available, except upon payment of a separate fee: Order No. 2360/2013 approving the technical regulation "Technical specification on products for construction. Key features, levels and performance classes" indicator ST 051-2013.	Lack of transparency/ barrier to entry	All these technical normative documents have a large number pages, so publication in the Official Gazette would be excessive in terms of cost. The technical regulations approved by ministerial orders may be used as legal documents only if published in the Official Gazette.	The legislation in force is unclear for companies active in the field and it may create uncertainty for enterprises willing to enter the market.	Publish such normative materials additionally on the dedicated websites in order to make the information available to all market participants.

Sector: Construction *(cont.)*

No.	No and title of Regulation	Article	Thematic category	Brief description of potential obstacles	Keyword	Policy maker's objectives	Harm to competition	Recommendations
69	**Legislation that has not been published**	Entire act	Double/ unpublished legislation	We have identified the following piece of legislation which is not published in the Official Gazette of Romania, or in the case where it has been published, it is not generally available, except upon payment of a separate fee: Order No. 615/2003 approving the technical regulation "Regulation regarding the organisation and conduct of traffic surveys, origin, destination. Preparing data for processing" (revision DD 506 – 1988), indicator DD 506 – 2001. Moreover, according to a list published by MDRAP on its website containing the technical enactments in force as of 1 January 2016 (the list was revised on 9 February 2016), the abovementioned regulation, identified as DD 506 – 2001, was replaced by another regulation (with the indicator DD 506-2015), in accordance with Decision No. 155/02.12.2015 of CNADNR. Neither the decision nor the new regulation were published in the Official Gazette of Romania, but only in a construction bulletin.	Lack of transparency/ barrier to entry	All these technical normative documents have a large number pages, so publication in the Official Gazette would be excessive in terms of cost. The technical regulations approved by ministerial orders may be used as legal documents only if published in the Official Gazette.	The legislation in force is unclear for companies active in the field and it may create uncertainty for enterprises willing to enter the market.	Publish such normative materials additionally on the dedicated websites in order to make the information available to all market participants.
70	**Legislation that has not been published**	Entire act	Double/ unpublished legislation	We have identified the following piece of legislation which is not published in the Official Gazette of Romania, or in the case where it has been published, it is not generally available, but one needs to pay a separate fee in order to obtain it: MTCT Order No. 622/2003 approving department Regulation on extra-urban highways design, code PD 162/2002.	Lack of transparency/ barrier to entry	All these technical normative documents have a large number pages, so publication in the Official Gazette would be excessive in terms of cost. The technical regulations approved by ministerial orders may be used as legal documents only if published in the Official Gazette.	The legislation in force is unclear for companies active in the field and it may create uncertainty for enterprises willing to enter the market.	Publish such normative materials additionally on the dedicated websites in order to make the information available to all market participants.

Sector: Construction *(cont.)*

No.	No and title of Regulation	Article	Thematic category	Brief description of potential obstacles	Keyword	Policy maker's objectives	Harm to competition	Recommendations
71	**Legislation that has not been published**	Entire act	Double/ unpublished legislation	We have identified the following piece of legislation which is not published in the Official Gazette of Romania, or, where it has been published it is not generally available, and payment of a separate fee is required to obtain it: Order No. 479/2003 approving the technical regulation "Guide on achieving cement concrete pavement with chippings of limestone nature" (Revision CD 170-1988), indicator CD 170-2003.	Lack of transparency/ barrier to entry	All these technical normative documents have a large number pages, so publication in the Official Gazette would be excessive in terms of cost. The technical regulations approved by ministerial orders may be used as legal documents only if published in the Official Gazette.	The legislation in force is unclear for companies active in the field and it may create uncertainty for enterprises willing to enter the market.	Publish such normative materials additionally on the dedicated websites in order to make the information available to all market participants.
72	**Legislation that has not been published**	Entire act	Double/ unpublished legislation	We have identified the following piece of legislation which is not published in the Official Gazette of Romania, or in the case where it has been published, it is not generally available, but one needs to pay a separate fee in order to obtain it: Order No. 618/2003 approving the technical regulation "Regulation on road concrete with added fly ash" (revision CD 147-1985), indicator CD 147 – 2002. Moreover, according to a list published by MDRAP on its website containing the technical enactments in force as of 1 January 2016 (the list was revised on 9 February 2016), the abovementioned regulation having the identification CD 147 – 2002 appears to be replaced by another regulation (with the indicator CD 147-2013), in accordance with the decision No. 1.282/12.09.2013 of CNADNR. It is unclear whether the new regulation actually abolished the old one, as we could not identify the regulation identified as CD 147 – 2002 in the list published by the Ministry.	Lack of transparency/ barrier to entry	All these technical normative documents have a large number pages, so publication in the Official Gazette would be excessive in terms of cost. The technical regulations approved by ministerial orders may be used as legal documents only if published in the Official Gazette.	The legislation in force is unclear for companies active in the field and it may create uncertainty for enterprises willing to enter the market.	Publish such normative materials additionally on the dedicated websites in order to make the information available to all market participants.

Sector: Construction *(cont.)*

No.	No and title of Regulation	Article	Thematic category	Brief description of potential obstacles	Keyword	Policy maker's objectives	Harm to competition	Recommendations
73	**Legislation that has not been published**	Entire act	Double/ unpublished legislation	We have identified the following piece of legislation which is not published in the Official Gazette of Romania, or in the case where it has been published, it is not generally available, but one needs to pay a separate fee in order to obtain it: Order No. 605/2003 approving the technical regulation "Regulation on design conditions and execution technology of asphalt coating works" (revision CD 16 – 1978), indicator CD 16 – 2000.	Lack of transparency/ barrier to entry	All these technical normative documents have a large number pages, so publication in the Official Gazette would be excessive in terms of cost. The technical regulations approved by ministerial orders may be used as legal documents only if published in the Official Gazette.	The legislation in force is unclear for companies active in the field and it may create uncertainty for enterprises willing to enter the market.	Publish such normative materials additionally on the dedicated websites in order to make the information available to all market participants.
74	**Legislation that has not been published**	Entire act	Double/ unpublished legislation	We have identified the following piece of legislation which is not published in the Official Gazette of Romania or, where it has been published, it is not generally available, but a separate fee is required to obtain it: Order No. 606/2003 approving the technical regulation "Regulation on design and execution of double reverse bituminous treatments on coatings with hydraulic binders " (Revision CD 16-1978), indicator PD 216 – 2001. Moreover, according to a list published by MDRAP on its website containing the technical enactments, in force as of 1 January 2016 (the list was revised on 9 February 2016), the abovementioned regulation identified as PD 216 – 2001 was replaced by another regulation (with the indicator PD 216-2008), in accordance with Decision No. 21/13.01.2009 of CNADNR. Neither the decision nor the new regulation were published in the Official Gazette of Romania, but only in a construction bulletin.	Lack of transparency/ barrier to entry	All these technical normative documents have a large number pages, so publication in the Official Gazette would be excessive in terms of cost. The technical regulations approved by ministerial orders may be used as legal documents only if published in the Official Gazette.	The legislation in force is unclear for companies active in the field and it may create uncertainty for enterprises willing to enter the market.	Publish such normative materials additionally on the dedicated websites in order to make the information available to all market participants.

Sector: Construction *(cont.)*

No.	No and title of Regulation	Article	Thematic category	Brief description of potential obstacles	Keyword	Policy maker's objectives	Harm to competition	Recommendations
75	**Legislation that has not been published**	Entire act	Double/ unpublished legislation	We have identified the following piece of legislation which is not published in the Official Gazette of Romania, or in the case where it has been published, it is not generally available, but one needs to pay a separate fee in order to obtain it: Order No. 613/2003 approving the technical regulation "Regulation on the performance at hot temperature of bituminous clothing for the bridge path" (revision AND 546 – 1999), indicator AND 546 – 2002. Moreover, according to a list published by MDRAP on its website containing the technical enactments in force as of 1 January 2016 (the list was revised on 9 February 2016), the abovementioned regulation identified as AND 546 – 2002 was replaced by another regulation (with the indicator AND 546-2013), in accordance with Decision No. 1.278/ 11.09.2013 of CNADNR. Neither the decision nor the new regulation were published in the Official Gazette of Romania, but only in a construction bulletin.	Lack of transparency/ barrier to entry	All these technical normative documents have a large number pages, so publication in the Official Gazette would be excessive in terms of cost. The technical regulations approved by ministerial orders may be used as legal documents only if published in the Official Gazette.	The legislation in force is unclear for companies active in the field and it may create uncertainty for enterprises willing to enter the market.	Publish such normative materials additionally on the dedicated websites in order to make the information available to all market participants.
76	**Legislation that has not been published**	Entire act	Double/ unpublished legislation	We have identified the following piece of legislation which is not published in the Official Gazette of Romania or, where it has been published, it is not generally available, but a separate fee is required to obtain it: Order No. 614/2003 approving the technical regulation "Regulation regarding the technical conditions and testing methodology of cationic over stabilized bituminous emulsions", indicator AND 581 – 2002.	Lack of transparency/ barrier to entry	All these technical normative documents have a large number pages, so publication in the Official Gazette would be excessive in terms of cost. The technical regulations approved by ministerial orders may be used as legal documents only if published in the Official Gazette.	The legislation in force is unclear for companies active in the field and it may create uncertainty for enterprises willing to enter the market.	Publish such normative materials additionally on the dedicated websites in order to make the information available to all market participants.

Sector: Construction *(cont.)*

No.	No and title of Regulation	Article	Thematic category	Brief description of potential obstacles	Keyword	Policy maker's objectives	Harm to competition	Recommendations
77	**Legislation that has not been published**	Entire act	Double/ unpublished legislation	We have identified the following piece of legislation which is not published in the Official Gazette of Romania, or in the case where it has been published, it is not generally available, but one needs to pay a separate fee in order to obtain it: Order No. 302/2003 approving the technical regulation "Regulation regarding the design of floors made of corrugated sheets – concrete", indicator N.E. 020-03.	Lack of transparency/ barrier to entry	All these technical normative documents have a large number pages, so publication in the Official Gazette would be excessive in terms of cost. The technical regulations approved by ministerial orders may be used as legal documents only if published in the Official Gazette.	The legislation in force is unclear for companies active in the field and it may create uncertainty for enterprises willing to enter the market.	Publish such normative materials additionally on the dedicated websites in order to make the information available to all market participants.
78	**Legislation that has not been published**	Entire act	Double/ unpublished legislation	We have identified the following piece of legislation which is not published in the Official Gazette of Romania, or in the case where it has been published, it is not generally available, but one needs to pay a separate fee in order to obtain it: Order No. 304/2003 approving the technical regulation"Regulation regarding calculation and composition of wood resistance structures located in seismic areas", (addendum P 100), Indicator N.E. 019-03. Moreover, following our check in the list published by MDRAP on its website containing the technical enactments in force as of 1 January 2016 (the list was revised on 9 February 2016), we could not identify the regulation having the indicator N.E. 019-03 (neither as being in force or abolished).	Lack of transparency/ barrier to entry	All these technical normative documents have a large number pages, so publication in the Official Gazette would be excessive in terms of cost. The technical regulations approved by ministerial orders may be used as legal documents only if published in the Official Gazette.	The legislation in force is unclear for companies active in the field and it may create uncertainty for enterprises willing to enter the market.	Publish such normative materials additionally on the dedicated websites in order to make the information available to all market participants.

Sector: Construction *(cont.)*

No.	No and title of Regulation	Article	Thematic category	Brief description of potential obstacles	Keyword	Policy maker's objectives	Harm to competition	Recommendations
79	**Legislation that has not been published**	Entire act	Double/ unpublished legislation	We have identified the following piece of legislation which is not published in the Official Gazette of Romania, or in the case where it has been published, it is not generally available, but one needs to pay a separate fee in order to obtain it: Order No. 303/2003 approving the technical regulation "Regulation on design of wood constructions", (revision NP 005-96)", indicator N.E. 018-03. Moreover, following our check in the list published by MDRAP on its website containing the technical enactments in force as of 1 January 2016 (the list was revised on 9 February 2016), we could not identify the regulation having the indicator N.E. 018-03 (neither as being in force or abolished).	Lack of transparency/ barrier to entry	All these technical normative documents have a large number pages, so publication in the Official Gazette would be excessive in terms of cost. The technical regulations approved by ministerial orders may be used as legal documents only if published in the Official Gazette.	The legislation in force is unclear for companies active in the field and it may create uncertainty for enterprises willing to enter the market.	Publish such normative materials additionally on the dedicated websites in order to make the information available to all market participants.
80	**Legislation that has not been published**	Entire act	Double/ unpublished legislation	We have identified the following piece of legislation which is not published in the Official Gazette of Romania or, where it has been published, it is not generally available, but a separate fee is required to obtain it: Order No. 903/2003 approving the technical regulation "Guide regarding performance criteria of quality requirements according to Law No. 10/ 1995 on constructions' quality, for electrical installations in buildings", indicator GT-059-03.	Lack of transparency/ barrier to entry	All these technical normative documents have a large number pages, so publication in the Official Gazette would be excessive in terms of cost. The technical regulations approved by ministerial orders may be used as legal documents only if published in the Official Gazette.	The legislation in force is unclear for companies active in the field and it may create uncertainty for enterprises willing to enter the market.	Publish such normative materials additionally on the dedicated websites in order to make the information available to all market participants.

Sector: Transport Horizontal Legislation

No.	No and title of Regulation	Article	Thematic category	Brief description of potential obstacles	Keyword	Policy maker's objectives	Harm to competition	Recommendations
1	**Ordinance No. 8/2013 on the medical and psychological examination of the personnel involved in transport safety and for amendment of the Law No. 95/2006 on healthcare reform and Order No. 1262/10.10.2013 on approval of the norms from 10 October 2013 on the procedure of acceptance of medical and/or psychological units as a means to examine transport personnel with duties in transport safety.**	Art. 12	Framework legislation	In order to do the health check and to issue the medical certificate and physiological evaluation of the personnel involved in transport safety, an approval certificate is needed for the specialised medical or psychological units. The approval authority is the Ministry of Transport. The medical units and the psychological units as well have to meet several mandatory requirements, such as the ownership of the necessary equipment needed to carry out medical investigations.	Authorisation	The criteria which must be fulfilled by the medical and/or psychological units are stipulated in the Order No. 1262/2013. The Ministry of Transport's (MoT) approval seems to be justified by the objective of the legal provision (public security and transport safety), so the criteria must be fulfilled. The criteria are clear and non-discriminatory, except the one referring to the obligation of the medical units to prove ownership over the necessary equipment for carrying out medical investigations that seems to be excessive. There is no justification for the medical units not to be allowed to rent or lease equipment when they are about to perform examination of the personnel involved in transport safety activities. According to the information posted on the Web page of MoT, there are about 25 psychological units and 16 medical units.	The provision reduces the number of players and raises administrative costs. The medical and psychological examination of the personnel involved in transport safety can be performed only by the specialised medical and/or psychological units which have certificates of approval issued by the Ministry of Transport. The medical and psychological units have to be the owners of the necessary equipment needed to carry out medical investigations in order to obtain the above mentioned certificate. As the equipment can be quite expensive – e.g., about EUR 50 000 for an ultrasound machine, such high costs represent a barrier to entry into the market.	Modify the provision: The requirement for the medical units to be the owners of the equipment should be modified – medical units should also have the right to use rented or leased equipment.

Sector: Transport Horizontal Legislation *(cont.)*

No.	No and title of Regulation	Article	Thematic category	Brief description of potential obstacles	Keyword	Policy maker's objectives	Harm to competition	Recommendations
2	**Law No. 86/2006 on the Customs Code of Romania**	Art. 31 para. 5	Framework legislation	Any person may appoint a representative when dealing with the customs authority, to draw up the documents and to perform formalities laid down by customs regulations. The representative shall be established in Romania. "Customs representative" means any person appointed by another person to carry out the acts and formalities required under the customs legislation in his or her dealings with customs authorities.	Discrimination	This provision could be justified by the fact that the customs representative shall have an established office inland, so it can be easily checked by the Romanian authorities. Also, the restriction is justified for fiscal reasons resulting from the nature of the customs representative activity. Still, notice should be taken of the fact that the Union Customs Code (UCC) was adopted on 9 October 2013, as Regulation (EU) No. 952/2013 states. It entered into force on 30 October 2013 but its substantive provisions will apply starting on 1 May 2016. The Regulation is binding in its entirety and directly applicable in all Member States, including Romania. According to article No.18 of the Regulation, customs representative shall be established within the customs territory of the Union and a customs representative who complies with the criteria laid down in the Regulation shall be entitled to provide such services in a Member State other than the one where he or she is established.	This provision seems to discriminate against operators who do not have an established office in Romania.	Abolish: the requirement for a customs representative to be established in Romania should be removed and replaced by the counterpart provision of the Regulation No. 952/2013 laying down the Union Customs Code.

Sector: Transport Horizontal Legislation *(cont.)*

No.	No and title of Regulation	Article	Thematic category	Brief description of potential obstacles	Keyword	Policy maker's objectives	Harm to competition	Recommendations
3	**Law No. 86/2006 on the Customs Code of Romania**	Art. 32 para. 1	Framework legislation	The Customs Authority grants the status of authorised economic operator only to undertakings established in Romania. Customs authorities shall, on the basis of recognition of the status of an authorised economic operator for customs simplification and provided that the requirements related to a specific type of simplification in the customs legislation are fulfilled, authorise the operator to benefit from that simplification. Customs authorities shall not re-examine those criteria which have already been examined when granting the status of an authorised economic operator.	Discrimination	This provision could be justified by the fact that the customs representative shall have an established office inland, so it can be easily checked by the Romanian authorities. Also, the restriction is justified for fiscal reasons resulting from the nature of the customs representative activity. Still, notice should be taken of the fact that the Union Customs Code (UCC) was adopted on 9 October 2013, as Regulation (EU) No. 952/2013l. It entered into force on 30 October 2013 but its substantive provisions will apply starting on 1 May 2016. The Regulation is binding in its entirety and directly applicable in all Member States, including Romania. According to article 38 of the Regulation in order to obtain the status of authorised economic operator, the operator shall be established within the customs territory of the Union. The status of the authorised economic operator shall consist in the following types of authorisations: a) that of an authorised economic operator for customs simplifications; or b) that of an authorised economic operator for security and safety. Subject to the provision of the Regulation, the status of authorised economic operator shall be recognised by the customs authorities in all Member States (para. 4). Customs authorities shall not re-examine those criteria which have already been examined when granting the status of authorised economic operator (para. 5).	This provision seems to discriminate against operators who do not have an established office in Romania.	Abolish: the requirement for a authorised economic operator to be established in Romania should be removed and replaced by the counterpart provision of the Regulation No. 952/ 2013 laying down the Union Customs Code.

Sector: Transport Horizontal Legislation *(cont.)*

No.	No and title of Regulation	Article	Thematic category	Brief description of potential obstacles	Keyword	Policy maker's objectives	Harm to competition	Recommendations
4	**Law No. 86/2006 on the Customs Code of Romania**	Art. 87 para. 2	Framework legislation	The customs declaration should be done by a declarant established in Romania. "Declarant" means the person lodging a customs declaration, a temporary storage declaration, an entry summary declaration, an exit summary declaration, a re-export declaration or a re-export notification in his or her own name or the person in whose name such a declaration or notification is lodged.	Discrimination	This provision may be justified by the fact that the person who makes the declaration shall have an established office in the country, so that it can be checked by the authorities. Also, the restriction may be justified for fiscal reasons. Still, notice should be taken of the fact that the Union Customs Code was adopted on 9 October 2013 as Regulation (EU) No. 952/2013. It entered into force on 30 October 2013 but its substantive provisions will apply starting on 1 May 2016. The Regulation is binding in its entirety and directly applicable in all Member States, including Romania. According to article 170 para. 2 of the Regulation, the declarant shall be established in the customs territory of the Union.	This provision seems to discriminate against operators who do not have an established office in Romania.	Abolish: the requirement for a declarant to be established in Romania should be removed and replaced by the counterpart provision of the Regulation No. 952/2013 laying down the Union Customs Code.
5	**Law No. 86/2006 on the Customs Code of Romania**	Art. 116 para. 3 lit. a, b	Framework legislation	Within a transit procedure, there is a so-called "main debtor" who is the holder of the transit procedure and the one responsible for ensuring payment of the customs duties for goods in transit. The main debtor has to provide a single or a global warranty for the payment of customs duties. A global warranty covers several transit operations and is permitted to be used only subject to Customs Authority authorisation. Such an authorisation is issued only if the main debtor meets the following requirements: (i) established in Romania, (ii) a frequent user of the transit system or having the capacity to pay and (iii) has not committed serious or repeat offenses against customs rules (as Article 116 (3) of the Customs Code stipulates).	Discrimination	This provision may be justified by the fact that the person who is responsible for providing the warranty for the payment of customs debts shall have an established office inland, so it should be easily checked by the Romanian authorities. Still, notice should be taken of the fact that the Union Customs Code was adopted on 9 October 2013 as Regulation (EU) No. 952/2013. It entered into force on 30 October 2013 but its substantive provisions will apply starting on 1 May 2016. The EU Regulation is binding in its entirety and directly applicable in all Member States, including Romania. According to Article No. 95 of the Regulation the authorisation shall be granted only to guarantors who are established in the customs territory of the Union.	This provision seems to discriminate against operators who do not have an established office in Romania.	Abolish: the requirement for a guarantor to be established in Romania should be removed and replaced by the counterpart provision of the Regulation No. 952/2013 laying down the Union Customs Code.

Sector: Transport Horizontal Legislation *(cont.)*

No.	No and title of Regulation	Article	Thematic category	Brief description of potential obstacles	Keyword	Policy maker's objectives	Harm to competition	Recommendations
6	**Law No. 86/2006 on the Customs Code of Romania**	Art. 121 para. 3	Framework legislation	The management of a customs' warehouse is subject to an authorisation issued by the Customs Authority. The authorisation is granted only to persons established in Romania. Customs warehousing allows the owner to hold imported Non-Community goods in the Community and choose when to pay the duty or re-exports the goods.	Discrimination	This provision may be justified by the fact that the person who fulfils the declaration shall have an established office inland, to be easily checked by the Romanian authorities. Also, the restriction may be justified for fiscal reasons. Under customs' warehousing procedure, imported goods are stored under customs' control in a designated place (a customs warehouse), without payment of import duties and taxes. Still, notice should be taken of the fact that the Union Customs Code was adopted on 9 October 2013 as Regulation (EU) No. 952/2013. It entered into force on 30 October 2013 but its substantive provisions will apply starting on 1 May 2016. The EU Regulation is binding in its entirety and directly applicable in all Member States, including Romania. According to Article 211, para. (3) of the EU Regulation, the authorisation for the activity of storage, which shall comprise customs warehousing, shall be granted only to persons who are established in the customs territory of the Union.	This provision seems to discriminate against operators who do not have an established office in Romania.	Abolish: the requirement to be established in Romania in order to carry out the management of a customs warehouse should be removed and replaced by the counterpart provision of the Regulation No. 952/ 2013 laying down the Union Customs Code.

Sector: Transport Horizontal Legislation *(cont.)*

No.	No and title of Regulation	Article	Thematic category	Brief description of potential obstacles	Keyword	Policy maker's objectives	Harm to competition	Recommendations
7	**Law No. 86/2006 on the Customs Code of Romania**	Art. 137 lit. a	Framework legislation	Authorisation for performing active processing operations is granted only to persons established in Romania. Processing operations means any of the following a) the working of goods, including erecting or assembling them or fitting them to other goods; b) the processing of goods; c) the repair of goods, including restoring them and putting them in order; d) the use of goods which are not to be found in the processed products, but which allow or facilitate the production of those products, even if they are entirely or partially used up in the process. The active processing operations are performed in Romania.	Discrimination	This provision may be justified by the fact that the active processing operations imply an economic activity which is operated in Romania. Thus, the undertaking which performs this activity shall have an established office inland, so it can be checked by the customs authorities. Also, the restriction is justified for fiscal reasons. Still, notice should be taken of the fact that the Union Customs Code was adopted on 9 October 2013 as Regulation (EU) No. 952/2013. It entered into force on 30 October 2013 but its substantive provisions will apply starting on 1 May 2016. The EU Regulation is binding in its entirety and directly applicable in all Member States, including Romania. According to article. 210 (d) and article 211 para. (3) of the EU Regulation authorisation for the activity of processing, which shall comprise inward and outward processing, shall be granted only to persons who are established in the customs territory of the Union.	This provision seems to discriminate against operators who do not have an established office in Romania.	Abolish: the requirement to be established in Romania in order to carry out processing, which shall comprise inward and outward processing should be removed and replaced by the counterpart provision of the Regulation No. 952/2013 laying down the Union Customs Code.

Sector: Transport Horizontal Legislation *(cont.)*

No.	No and title of Regulation	Article	Thematic category	Brief description of potential obstacles	Keyword	Policy maker's objectives	Harm to competition	Recommendations
8	**Law No. 86/2006 on the Customs Code of Romania**	Art. 153 lit. a	Framework legislation	The authorisation for processing products under customs control is granted only to persons established in Romania. The definition of "processed products"/ "processing operations" is provided by Article No. 5 of EU Regulation No. 952/ 2013 (coming into force on 1 May 2016). Thus, "processed products" means goods placed under a processing procedure which have undergone processing operations. "Processing operations" means any of the following: a) the working of goods, including erecting or assembling them or fitting them to other goods; b) the processing of goods; c) the destruction of goods; d) the repair of goods, including restoring them and putting them in order; e) the use of goods which are not to be found in the processed products, but which allow or facilitate the production of those products, even if they are entirely or partially used up in the process (production accessories).	Discrimination	This provision may be justified by the fact that the processing under the customs control implies an economic activity which is operated in Romania. Thus, the operator who performs this activity shall have an established office in the country, so that it can be checked by the authorities. Also, the restriction may be justified for fiscal reasons. Still, notice should be taken of the fact that the Union Customs Code was adopted on 9 October 2013 as Regulation (EU) No. 952/2013. It entered into force on 30 October 2013 but its substantive provisions will apply starting on 1 May 2016. The EU Regulation is binding in its entirety and directly applicable in all Member States, including Romania. According to recital (50) of the Regulation, the inward processing suspension procedure should be merged with processing under customs control, so that the latter no longer exists as such. According to article 210 (d) and article 211 para. (3) of the EU Regulation the authorisation for inward processing shall be granted only to persons who are established in the customs territory of the Union.	This provision seems to discriminate against operators who do not have an established office in Romania.	Abolish: the requirement to be established in Romania in order to carry out inward processing should be removed and replaced by the counterpart provision of the Regulation No. 952/ 2013 laying down the Union Customs Code.

Sector: Transport Horizontal Legislation *(cont.)*

No.	No and title of Regulation	Article	Thematic category	Brief description of potential obstacles	Keyword	Policy maker's objectives	Harm to competition	Recommendations
9	**Law No. 86/2006 on the Customs Code of Romania**	Art. 168 lit. a	Framework legislation	The authorisation for performing outward processing operations is granted only to persons established in Romania. Processing operations means any of the following: a) the working of goods, including erecting or assembling them or fitting them to other goods; b) the processing of goods; c) the repair of goods, including restoring them and putting them in order; d) the use of goods which are not to be found in the processed products, but which allow or facilitate the production of those products, even if they are entirely or partially used up in the process. The outward processing operations are performed outside Romania. Outward processing procedure allows community goods to be temporary exported from the Community customs territory in order to undergo improvement processing operations and that the products resulted from the improvement to be released for free circulation with total or partial relief from import duties.	Discrimination	This provision may be justified by the fact that the processing under customs control implies an economic activity which is operated in Romania. Thus, the operator who performs this activity shall have an established office in the country, so that it can be checked by the authorities. Also, the restriction may be justified by fiscal reasons. Under the outward processing procedure goods may be temporarily exported from the customs territory of Romania in order to undergo processing operations. The processed products resulting from those goods may be released for free circulation with total or partial relief from import duty upon application by the holder of the authorisation or any other person established in the customs territory provided that that person has obtained the consent of the holder of the authorisation and the conditions of the authorisation are fulfilled. Still, notice should be taken of the fact that the Union Customs Code was adopted on 9 October 2013 as Regulation (EU) No. 952/2013. It entered into force on 30 October 2013 but its substantive provisions will apply starting on 1 May 2016. The EU Regulation is binding in its entirety and directly applicable in all Member States, including Romania. According to article 210 (d) and article 211 para. (3) of the Regulation the authorisation for outward processing shall be granted only to persons who are established in the customs territory of the Union.	This provision seems to discriminate against operators who do not have an established office in Romania.	Abolish: the requirement to be established in Romania in order to carry out outward processing should be removed and replaced by the counterpart provision of the Regulation No. 952/ 2013 laying down the Union Customs Code.

Sector: Transport Horizontal Legislation *(cont.)*

No.	No and title of Regulation	Article	Thematic category	Brief description of potential obstacles	Keyword	Policy maker's objectives	Harm to competition	Recommendations
10	**Decision No. 707/2006 for approval of the Implementing regulation of the Customs Code of Romania, as further amended and supplemented**	Art. 563 from the Regulation	Framework legislation	The customs agent must be a Romanian legal person.	Discrimination	This provision is justified by the fact that the customs agent shall have an established office inland, so it can be checked by authorities. Also, the restriction is justified for fiscal reasons resulting from the nature of the customs agent activity. Still, notice should be taken of the fact that the Union Customs Code was adopted on 9 October 2013 as Regulation (EU) No. 952/2013. It entered into force on 30 October 2013 but its substantive provisions will apply starting on 1 May 2016. The EU Regulation is binding in its entirety and directly applicable in all Member States, including Romania. The regulation does not contain any provision regarding "customer agent" the term closest in meaning is "representative". According to article 18 of the Regulation, the customs representative shall be established within the customs territory of the Union and a customs representative who complies with the criteria laid down in the Regulation shall be entitled to provide such services in a Member State other than the one where he or she is established.	This provision seems to discriminate against foreign operators.	Abolish: the requirement to be established in Romania in order to carry out outward processing should be removed and replaced by the counterpart provision of the Regulation No. 952/ 2013 laying down the Union Customs Code.

Sector: Road transport

No.	No and title of Regulation	Article	Thematic category	Brief description of the potential obstacle	Keyword	Policy maker's objective	Harm to competition	Recommendations
1	**Order of the Ministry of Transport (MoT) No. 980/2011 approving the Methodological Norms on the application of the provisions regarding the organisation and performance of road transport and related activities established by Government Ordinance (GO) No. 27/2011 on road transport, as further amended and supplemented**	Art. 3 from the Norms	Road freight transport	Road transport for hire or reward can be performed only by authorised road transport operators. They must be registered with the Romanian Road Authority. This provision applies only to transport operators established in Romania.	Authorisation/ registration	This provision complies with Articles 10, 11 and 16 of EC Regulation No. 1071/2009. All Member States apply the same requirement to transport operators established in their country. The scope of this provision is to enable law enforcers to verify compliance of the transport operators with public policy objectives such as safety, civil liability and prevention of fraud and crimes.	The requirements to obtain an authorisation and to register with the Romanian Road Authority create an entry barrier which reduces the number of operators.	No recommendation.
2	**MoT No. 980/2011 (same as above)**	Art. 8 from the Norms	Road freight transport	In order to obtain registration in the road freight transport Electronic National Register and the transport licence (Community licence), an undertaking must fulfil the following requirements: a) have an effective and stable establishment in Romania; b) be of good repute; c) have appropriate financial standing; and d) have the required professional competence.	Licence	These requirements are in line with Art. 3 of EC Regulation No. 1071/2009. They are reasonable and enable verification of compliance by road hauliers with legislation related to road transport. Also, they try to prevent socio-economic damages by, for example, refusing a licence to operators who lack professional qualification concerning road safety.	The requirements to register and obtain a licence create an entry barrier which reduces the number of hauliers available in the market.	No recommendation.
3	**MoT No. 980/2011 (same as above)**	Art. 9 from the Norms	Road freight transport	To obtain a transport licence, companies must have a registered seat in Romania, where they maintain all records related to their activity. Vehicles must be registered in Romania and be subject to technical inspection in an operating centre established in Romania. It is applied only to hauliers established in Romania.	License	These requirements are in line with Art. 5 of EC Regulation No. 1071/2009. They are reasonable and enable verification of compliance by road hauliers with legislation related to road transport, since there is no European Electronic Register concerning road transport operators and their vehicles which can be accessed by Romanian law enforcers.	The requirements to have a registered seat in Romania and to use only vehicles registered and inspected in Romania, in order to obtain a transport licence, may prevent acquisition of vehicles from abroad and the provision of inspection services by foreign operators. These requirements may also increase costs for hauliers since they are forced to comply with the national requirements.	No recommendation.

Sector: Road transport *(cont.)*

No.	No and title of Regulation	Article	Thematic category	Brief description of the potential obstacle	Keyword	Policy maker's objective	Harm to competition	Recommendations
4	**MoT No. 980/2011 (same as above)**	Art. 10 from the Norms	Road freight transport	One of the requirements needed to obtain a transport licence is to have good repute. The State Inspectorate for Road Transport Control (ISCTR) is in charge of enforcing this requirement.	License/ Discrimination	The requirement of good repute is in line with Art. 6 of EC Regulation No. 1071/2009. The Romanian rules on good reputation may be enforced only against drivers registered in Romania. The ISCTR enforcement procedure is established in a document entitled "Ediţia I, Revizia 0 – Cod PO 89" recorded with the ISCTR No. 2508/ 30.01.2014 and refers to an internal administrative procedure which does not need to be published. Infringements of good repute are recorded in a local database and should be reported in the ERRU database (Europe-wide system). Decisions taken by the ISCTR concerning good reputation may be appealed before administrative courts.	The requirement of good repute is in line with Art. 6 of EC Regulation No. 1071/2009. However, ISCTR enforcement procedure verifying compliance with the good repute requirement is not published.	Make provision clearer: The ISCTR procedure related to compliance with good repute by transport operators shall be published to enable monitoring of the ISCTR exercise of power and enable operators with the ability to present their view before a potentially negative decision is taken.
5	**MoT No. 980/2011 (same as above)**	Art.14 from the Norms	Road freight transport	To obtain a transport licence, undertakings shall have appropriate financial standing. They shall demonstrate, on the basis of annual accounts certified by an auditor or a duly accredited person, that, every year, they have at their disposal capital and reserves totalling at least EUR 9 000, when only one vehicle is used, and EUR 5 000 for each additional vehicle used. Also, undertakings can demonstrate their financial standing by means of a certificate such as a bank guarantee or insurance from one or more banks or other financial institutions, including insurance companies.	Licence	The provision is in line with Art. 7 of EC Regulation No. 1071/2009. The capital requirement or bank guarantee is reasonable if compared with the total costs of a truck, approximately EUR 200 000. This capital may be used, for example, to cover liabilities incurred by transport operators.	The financial standing requirements in order to obtain a Community transport licence may represent a barrier to entry into the market for those operators who cannot afford them.	No recommendation.

Sector: Road transport *(cont.)*

No.	No and title of Regulation	Article	Thematic category	Brief description of the potential obstacle	Keyword	Policy maker's objective	Harm to competition	Recommendations
6	**MoT No. 980/2011 (same as above)**	Art.15 from the Norms	Road freight transport	In order to obtain a transport licence, undertakings must have the required professional competence. In this respect, undertakings shall appoint a transport manager who has a certificate of competence, fulfils the requirement regarding good repute, permanently leads the transport activities of the undertaking, is an employee/director/owner/shareholder or manager of the undertaking. Also, the transport manager must reside in the European Union. A natural person can be a transport manager in only one single undertaking.	License	This restriction could be explained for reasons related to the quality of the transport manager services, since in the case that the transport manager works for several separate undertakings, he may not always be available to brief drivers, e.g. about the characteristics of the goods transported or over which route to choose to avoid delays or additional charges. The requirements of the Romanian legislation are in line with European Regulation No. 1071/2009, but the obligation of the transport manager to lead only one single undertaking is more stringent. Thus, according to Art. 4 of European Regulation No. 1071/2009, transport managers can either be direct employees or persons so closely linked to the business that they have a real, direct connection with the operator. They can also be independent third parties, such as transport consultants, in the case that the operator does not have a transport manager with a genuine link to the undertaking. As per Art. 4 para. (2), a transport manager without a genuine link to the undertaking may serve up to four separate transport operators, as long as their combined fleet does not exceed 50 vehicles. The European Regulation provides that Member States may decide to lower the number of undertakings and/or the size of the total fleet of vehicles which the manager may manage. However, even if the Member States can determine the maximum number of transport operators led by a manager, the Romanian provision makes no link to the total combined fleet of operators, which seems to be the relevant criterion to pursue the EU policy objective.	The obligation to be a transport manager in only one single undertaking could make it more difficult for transport managers to expand their business by covering more than one undertaking. If such a restriction is lifted, the costs of hiring transport managers for a single undertaking may become lower, whereas earnings of transport managers may become higher.	We recommend modifying the relevant Romanian legislation by inserting the provision from the EU legislation: Based on Art. 4 EC Regulation No. 1071/ 2009, transport managers may serve up to 4 separate transport operators as long as their combined fleet does not exceed 50 vehicles. More restrictive provisions are not justified, notably due to the fact that Romanian freight hauliers generally have small fleets.

Sector: Road transport *(cont.)*

No.	No and title of Regulation	Article	Thematic category	Brief description of the potential obstacle	Keyword	Policy maker's objective	Harm to competition	Recommendations
7	**MoT No. 980/2011 (same as above)**	Art. 17 from the Norms	Road freight transport	Undertakings may operate road transport services for their own account only after registration with the Romanian Road Authority and the issuance of a certificate of own-account transport. Requirements for engagement in the occupation of own-account road transport are as follows: The undertaking and transport manager shall be of good repute and the transport manager shall have the required professional competence. This provision only applies to transport operators established in Romania. Further, it applies only to vehicles whose overall weighting load exceeds 3.5 tonnes.	License	This restriction is justified for reasons of public safety. Vehicles with load exceeding 3.5 tonnes may be used to cover very long distances and to carry all kinds of goods including dangerous goods. Requesting compliance with good repute and professional competence is done in order to verify the compliance of transport operators with public policy objectives such as preventing bankruptcy, infringements related to commercial law, drug traffic, etc. or ensuring compliance with labour remuneration rules with respect to staff (see Art. 6 EC Regulation No. 1071/2009).	The requirement to register with RRA and to obtain a licence creates an entry barrier which reduces the number of own-account hauliers.	No recommendation.
8	**Government Ordinance (GO) No. 27/2011 on road transport, as further amended and supplemented**	Art.11	Road freight transport	Undertakings performing road transport for hire or reward are exempted from the application of the licensing requirements if they are exclusively engaged in national transport operations having only a minor impact on the transport market because of: a) the nature of the goods carried; or b) the short distances involved. Such an exemption is granted to all vehicles with an authorised maximum gross tonnage not exceeding 3.5 tonnes.	Discrimination	According to EC Regulation No. 1071/2009, EU Member States have discretion about which regime to choose for vehicles whose gross maximum tonnage does not exceed 3.5 tonnes. This exemption may be justified by the fact that transport operations listed in this article have only a minor impact on the transport market. Furthermore, vehicles whose maximum gross tonnage do not exceed 3.5 tonnes are only used to cover short distances.	This provision may favour one or more operators vis-à-vis others. It creates additional costs and an administrative burden for those who may not benefit from this exemption.	No recommendation: No such licences are required by EU legislation and no complaints are known from those operators under the obligation to get such a licence, against the excepted ones. Also, information obtained through research, indicates that in some European countries the relevant provisions are the same. Thus, for example, in the UK, operators do not need a licence if they carry out road freight transport using vehicles that have an authorised maximum gross tonnage under 3.5 tonnes.

Sector: Road transport *(cont.)*

No.	No and title of Regulation	Article	Thematic category	Brief description of the potential obstacle	Keyword	Policy maker's objective	Harm to competition	Recommendations
9	**GO No. 27/2011 on road transport, as further amended and supplemented**	Art. 19	Road freight transport	Undertakings performing own-account road transport may be exempted from the application of the provisions related to obtaining a certificate of own-account transport and the provisions related to registration with the Romanian Road Authority if they are exclusively engaged in national transport operations having only a minor impact on the transport market because of: a) the nature of the goods carried; or b) the short distances involved. Such an exemption is granted to all vehicles having an authorised maximum gross tonnage not exceeding 3.5 tonnes.	Discrimination	EC Regulation No. 1071/2009 does not cover own-account transport. Thus, EU Member States enjoy discretion on how to regulate this type of transport at national level. This exemption is justified by the fact that transport operations listed in this article are carried out for the own interest of the undertaking and have only a minor impact on the transport market. Furthermore, vehicles whose maximum gross tonnage does not exceed 3.5 tonnes are used only to cover short distances.	This provision may favour one or more operators vis-à-vis others. It creates additional costs and administrative burden for those who may not benefit from this exemption.	No recommendation: No such licences are required by EU legislation, nor are any complaints known from those operators under the obligation to get such a licence, against the excepted ones. Also, information obtained through research indicates that in some European countries the relevant provisions are the same. Thus, for example, in the UK, operators do not need a licence if they carry out road freight transport using vehicles that have an authorised maximum gross tonnage under 3.5 tonnes.
10	**GO No. 27/2011 on road transport, as further amended and supplemented**	Art. 25	Road freight transport	National and international road transport for hire or reward can be carried out only with vehicles registered in Romania. This provision applies only to undertakings established in Romania.	Discrimination	The provision is in line with Art. 5 of EC Regulation No. 1071/2009. The restriction is reasonable given that a transport operator needs to use a vehicle that is registered in an EU Member State in order to enable inspection of its record. Also, there is no European electronic database, accessible by law enforcers, related to the record of vehicles used for freight transport. The absence of a European electronic database makes a compelling case for the registration of vehicles in the country where the transport operator is established.	These requirements may prevent hauliers to buy cheaper vehicles from abroad as they face the extra burden of mandatory registration with ARR.	No recommendation.
11	**Law No. 92 of 10 April 2007 on local public transport services**	Art.1 para.(4), Art 17 para. (1)	Road freight transport	Public authorities shall consult representatives of trade associations in order to establish the strategies regarding local public transport, ways of functioning of this service and for elaborating and approving local norms and regulations.	Consultation	Public authorities consult representatives of trade associations in order to gain from their experience and take appropriate decisions to ensure the good quality of public transport services for consumers.	These provisions may facilitate exchange of sensitive commercial information among competing undertakings which may lead to collusive behaviour in the market.	No recommendation.

Sector: Road transport *(cont.)*

No.	No and title of Regulation	Article	Thematic category	Brief description of the potential obstacle	Keyword	Policy maker's objective	Harm to competition	Recommendations
12	**Law No. 51 of 8 March 2006 on public utility services**	Art. 14 para. (4) in conjunction with Art. 17 para. (1), para. 4 & para. (5)	Road freight transport	The Regulatory Authority of Public Transport Community Services – ANRSC – shall consult professional associations of road transport operators and authorised carriers in order to operate its competences. Professional associations of road transport operators and authorised carriers appoint representatives in the Consultative Council which is part of ANRSC.	Consultation	Public authorities consult representatives of trade associations in order to gain from their experience and take appropriate decisions to ensure the good quality of public transport services for consumers.	These provisions may facilitate exchange of sensitive commercial information among competing undertakings which may lead to collusive behaviour in the market.	No recommendation.
13	**Law No. 265/2008 of 7 November 2008 on the management of traffic safety on road infrastructure and Order No. 358 of 4 May 2012 on the approval of Guidelines related to measures to improve traffic safety on road infrastructure, implementing Directive No. 2008/96 /EC on road infrastructure safety management**	Art.11 para. (2) and para. (3) from Law and 13 para. (1) and (2) from Order	Road freight transport	Auditors/inspectors of road safety are professional individuals in charge of verifying road construction projects from a safety point of view. They also periodically verify existing road infrastructure. The appointment of auditors/inspectors of road safety is made for territorial areas and gives preference to individuals residing in those areas or close to those areas where the auditor/inspector needs to be appointed.	Discrimination/ Entry barriers	This restriction may be necessary in order to make the deployment of auditors/inspectors more efficient.	These provisions create an entry barrier which may be unnecessary (reduces the number of operators) or discriminatory (favours one or more operators vis-à-vis others).	Abolish: appointment of auditors/inspectors of road safety should not be linked to the domicile of the auditor/inspector.
14	**Law No. 92 of 10 April 2007 relating to local public transport services**	Art. 1	Road freight transport	Only authorised transport operators may operate local public transport of goods.	Authorisation	This authorisation may be necessary in order for public authorities to have a record of all public transport operators. Indeed, public authorities have exclusive competence in relation to the establishment, organisation, co-ordination and financing of local public transport.	The requirement to obtain an authorisation creates an entry barrier which reduces the number of operators.	No recommendation.
15	**GO No. 27/2011 on road transport, as further amended and supplemented**	Art. 49	Road freight transport	National own-account road transport can be carried out only by vehicles registered in Romania. This provision applies only to undertakings established in Romania.	Discrimination	The registration requirement is justified in order to subject vehicles to regular inspections. Absence of a European electronic database for vehicles that can be accessed by law enforcers makes a compelling case for registration at national level.	The registration requirement may increase costs for hauliers established in Romania which are forced to register vehicles acquired abroad even when those vehicles are used for transport in their own interest.	No recommendation.

Sector: Road transport *(cont.)*

No.	No and title of Regulation	Article	Thematic category	Brief description of the potential obstacle	Keyword	Policy maker's objective	Harm to competition	Recommendations
16	**MoT No. 181/2008 on the approval of Regulations concerning the conditions for installation, repair and verification of tachographs and speed limitation devices, as well as for the authorisation of the economic operators carrying out such activities – RNTR 8**	Art. 24 lit. (m)	Road freight transport	Those authorised to carry out the activity of installation, repair and/or verification of tachographs and speed limit devices must use only spare parts provided by the manufacturer of tachographs and speed limit devices or by the supplier appointed by the manufacturer.	Exclusivity	There is no official recital for this particular provision. The objective of the provision is to ensure road safety. A speed limitation device is the equipment used to limit the top speed of a vehicle. A tachograph is a device intended for installation in road vehicles to display, record, print, store and output automatically or semi-automatically details of the movement, including the speed of such vehicles, and details of certain periods of activity of their drivers. A tachograph, moreover, provides vital information to road traffic inspection regarding the transport operators' compliance with the regulations, mainly their observance of working hours and possible overwork in road transport. Strict adherence to these regulations is stressed as a crucial factor in road safety and accident prevention. Taking into consideration the importance of these devices for road safety, it is mandatory to eliminate every possibility of their manipulation by the operators. If the market for spare parts were to be opened, there would be huge possibilities for manipulation of these devices. Moreover, even if the tachograph spare parts aftermarket were opened, its impact on competition and on the transport operators' costs would be reduced as tachographs generally have a longer life span than that of the trucks and the spare parts for the tachographs aftermarket volume would be small.	This obligation is likely to foreclose other producers of these spare parts. It may also raise costs for operators.	No recommendation: Even though this restriction is likely to foreclose other producers of spare parts for tachographs and speed limit devices, and also raises costs for freight hauliers, its purpose is to promote road safety and the restriction is proportional to the objective served.

Sector: Road transport *(cont.)*

No.	No and title of Regulation	Article	Thematic category	Brief description of the potential obstacle	Keyword	Policy maker's objective	Harm to competition	Recommendations
17	**GO No. 43/1997 on the road regime, as further amended and supplemented**	Art. 41^{1} para. (1)	Road freight transport	Managers of national roads apply tariffs additional to the RO vignette for authorising access to the national road network, for vehicles registered in a foreign country, not member of the EU. These tariffs are established during bilateral agreements between Romania and third countries.	Discrimination	This restriction is justified for reasons of public interest. During bilateral talks with third countries, Romania negotiates these additional tariffs together with the number of authorisations which are granted to third-country hauliers, taking into consideration the interests of Romanian hauliers.	This provision authorises Romania to charge differential tariffs to third-country hauliers as opposed to Romanian and EU hauliers. It may therefore lead to discriminatory treatment of third-country hauliers.	No recommendation.
18	**MoT No. 1513/2014 for approving the methodological norms on the allocation and use of ECMT permits for international cargo road transport in the year 2015**	Art. 10 para 2 lit. (d).	Road freight transport	The allocation of CEMT authorisations is carried out by the CEMT Commission. The CEMT Commission includes among others, two representatives of unions and professional freight transport associations. CEMT authorisations are limited in number. The procedure for the allocation of CEMT authorisations is not included in a law but only in orders which are renewed every year. The allocation of CEMT licences is done within the OECD. The allocation of CEMT authorisations refers to international freight transport with countries which are not EU Member States.	Information exchange/ Decision	The limited number of CEMT licences is established at international level by the International Transport Forum thus, this issue is outside the scope of this project. The Romanian allocation system is fair, transparent and non-discriminatory. Licences are allocated in accordance with an algorithm. Any transport operator may participate as an observer of the allocation process. The allocation criteria are subject to regular changes and do not necessarily need to be included in a law.	Allocation of CEMT authorisations may discriminate against some hauliers vis-à-vis others. The methodology established for the allocation of CEMT authorisations may be subject to regular changes given that it is not included in a law. The current system may lead to legal uncertainty. It may also lead to an exchange of strategic information among hauliers such as those related to vehicle fleets, etc.	No recommendation.
19	**GO No. 27/2011 on road transport, as further amended and supplemented**	Art. 73 para. (1)	Road freight transport	Transport operators are obliged to display on vehicles a plate containing information related to the dimensions and maximum weight authorised for the vehicle. The total cost generated by the obligation to display such a plate on vehicles is approximately EUR 60/vehicle. If the vehicle has a trailer and/or a semi-trailer, it is necessary to have a plate for each, besides the plate for the vehicle (the vehicle, trailer and semi-trailer are measured separately), thus multiplying the EUR 60 charge for each additional trailer or semi-trailer. Approximately EUR 50 of this sum corresponds to the fee charged by the Romanian Automotive Register for measuring the vehicle's dimensions. The balance corresponds to the price of the plate.	General levy	In Romania as well as in Europe, heavy goods vehicles must comply with certain rules on weights and dimensions for road safety reasons and to avoid damaging roads, bridges and tunnels. These rules are established by European Directive No. 96/53 and Romanian legislation. The obligation to display a plate is required by law enforcers in order to verify the compliance of the transport operators with the abovementioned legal provisions. Art. 6 of Directive No. 96/53/EC authorises Romania to opt for a regulatory system whereby information related to the vehicle dimensions and maximum weight can result also from a document issued by the competent authorities of the Member State in which the vehicle is registered or put into circulation.	The requirement to display on vehicles a plate containing information related to the dimension and maximum weight authorised for the vehicle may lead to a rise of costs for national operators compared to foreign operators.	We recommend repealing this provision: The objective of the provision to verify the compliance of the transport operators with the rules on weights and dimensions can be achieved through documentation such as the vehicle identity card or the periodical technical inspection certificate, which should be carried by the vehicle driver. The vehicle identity card is the single document through which the vehicle is registered and put into circulation. It is issued by the Romanian Automotive Register and contains

Sector: Road transport *(cont.)*

No.	No and title of Regulation	Article	Thematic category	Brief description of the potential obstacle	Keyword	Policy maker's objective	Harm to competition	Recommendations
								the same headings and information as that appearing on the plate (the manufacturer's name, identification number, dimensions and weights of the vehicle). The transport operator should keep the original vehicle identity card or a certified copy of it in case the operator is not the owner of the vehicle (for instance, in the case of a lease). The periodical technical inspection certificate is issued automatically and free of charge by the Romanian Automotive Register or by a body authorised by the Romanian Automotive Register to carry out periodical technical inspection. It is issued after the performance of the mandatory technical inspection that can also include measuring the vehicles. The periodical technical inspection certificate does not currently contain the information referring to the vehicle's dimensions and weight, but it can be inserted by the issuer. Both the vehicle identity card and the periodical technical inspection certificate should also be kept for trailers and semi-trailers. Carrying an identity card

Sector: Road transport *(cont.)*

No.	No and title of Regulation	Article	Thematic category	Brief description of the potential obstacle	Keyword	Policy maker's objective	Harm to competition	Recommendations
								or a periodical technical inspection certificate by the vehicle driver would be in line with EU legislation regarding the vehicle's dimensions and maximum weight.
20	**Emergency Government Ordinance (EGO) No. 195/2002 regarding traffic on public roads, as further amended and supplemented**	Art. 122	Road freight transport	Only operators authorised by MoT are able to carry out the following activities: • periodic technical inspections of vehicles: • training of drivers for vehicles and agricultural/forestry tractors and trams; • repairing, adjusting, reconstructing and dismantling of vehicles	Authorisation	The first two authorisation requirements are reasonable. The first one is necessary to ensure public safety and is in accordance with EU legislation (Directive No. 2009/40/CE). The second one is necessary to ensure the quality of the training course and, thus public safety, and it is in accordance with EU legislation (Directive No. 2003/59/CE). Regarding the last indent, the requirement to obtain an authorisation in order to carry out the activity of repairing, adjusting, reconstructing and dismantling of vehicles is based on national legislation and not on EU legislation. There is no official recital for this particular provision. However, the objective of the provision seems to be public safety on roads, since garages need infrastructure, technical equipment, knowledgeable personnel, etc. Legal frameworks from other European countries such as France, the UK and Spain, do not require an authorisation in order to run a vehicle repair garage. In France, starting up a garage is subject to proving the professional qualifications of the person who leads the activity of the operator. Such a person must possess a certificate of professional competence, a certificate of professional studies, a degree or the equivalent of a degree issued by a national directory of professional certifications, or have three years of relevant experience working in the European Economic Area.	The authorisation requirement reduces the number of operators and raises administrative costs.	No recommendation: The purpose of the first two restrictions is to ensure public safety and quality of the training course. Thus, the restrictions seem proportional to the objective served. Moreover, they are in accordance with EU law. Abolish the last intent: The appropriate quality of the repairs carried out by the garages could be ensured by requiring the manager of the garage to possess a certificate of professional studies or a degree issued (for instance by the RAR) in case the manager does not have a certificate of professional studies. Also, the employees directly involved in repairing, adjusting, reconstructing and dismantling vehicles should have a certificate of professional studies.

Sector: Road transport *(cont.)*

No.	No and title of Regulation	Article	Thematic category	Brief description of the potential obstacle	Keyword	Policy maker's objective	Harm to competition	Recommendations
						Also, French legislation establishes the obligation of the garages to be registered in the National Register of Professions. In order to be enrolled in the abovementioned register, the manager of the garage must have attended a preparatory course that can be organised by the regional Chambers of Craft. For the registration, the manager of the garage must lodge the following documents: i) a statement of intent for creating the garage, ii) a statement concerning the criminal record of the manager iii) the certificate granted by the Chamber of Craft, attesting the passing of the preparatory course, iv) a copy of the identity card of the manager. In the UK, it seems that there is no obligation for the manager of a garage or for the employees directly involved in repairing vehicles to pass an exam or to have a diploma in order to prove their professional qualification. For the customers to be convinced when checking if a garage is reputable, garages join a trade association with codes of practice that have been approved by the Trading Standards Institute or a trading standards approved scheme such as "Buy With Confidence". The membership inspection regime to which garages voluntarily submit ensures they are monitored in terms of their premises, equipment, technical training, customer care and operation of the code of practice and to their individual ability to quickly remedy any problem, as it arises, to their customers' satisfaction.		Moreover, the policymakers' objective – public safety on roads – is supposed to be achieved through periodic technical inspection. According to G O No. 81/2000 all vehicles and trailers must be inspected at regular intervals by the Romanian Automotive Registry or by bodies authorised by the Romanian Automotive Registry. The Ordinance provides a basis for checking that vehicles throughout Romania are in a roadworthy condition and meet the same safety standards as when they were first registered. Therefore, no authorisation should be required for the garage to operate. Instead, the garage should be checked by the Romanian Automotive Registry in order to prove that its manager possess a certificate of professional studies or a degree issued by the Romanian Automotive Registry and its employees have certificates of professional studies.

Sector: Road transport *(cont.)*

No.	No and title of Regulation	Article	Thematic category	Brief description of the potential obstacle	Keyword	Policy maker's objective	Harm to competition	Recommendations
21	**GO No. 43/1997 on the road regime, as further amended and supplemented**	Art. 58	Road freight transport	MoT and the Ministry of Regional Development and Public Administration (MRDPA) develop regulations mandatory for natural and judicial persons who own roads open to public traffic. Both institutions should respect regulations regarding the autonomy of local government and ownership.	Co-regulatory regime	CNDNAR states that there is no co-regulatory regime given that MoT manages the national road whereas MRDPA manages regional and municipal road.	Overlapping of competence between several institutions may lead to legal uncertainty and increase administrative costs for operators.	No recommendation.
21	**MoT No. 733/2013 for the approval of norms regarding driving schools and driving school instructors**	Art. 2	Road freight transport	Only operators authorised by MoT can carry out training in the road transport sector.	Authorisation	This authorisation is reasonable and aims at ensuring proper training based on the accomplishment of experience as well as fulfilment of safety standards.	The requirement to obtain an authorisation creates an entry barrier which reduces the number of operators.	No recommendation.
23	**MoT No. 640/2007 for the approval of Norms regarding training and professional attestation of drivers for the carriage of dangerous goods by road, with further amendments**	Art. 1 para. (2)	Road freight transport	Only operators authorised by MoT can carry out the activity of training and further training of the personnel operating in the field of road freight transport of dangerous goods.	Authorisation	The authorisation is reasonable to ensure the quality of the training course. The conditions that shall be fulfilled by operators are reasonable and refer to their good repute, material resources and professional competence.	The requirements to obtain an authorisation create an entry barrier which reduces the number of operators.	No recommendation
24	**MoT No. 597/2003 on the approval of Norms establishing the conditions for obtaining the professional attestation by drivers carrying out road haulage with vehicles whose maximum authorised tonnage exceeds 3.5 tonnes, etc.**	Art. 4 para. (2) from the Norms	Road freight transport	Only operators authorised by MoT can carry out the activity of training of personnel operating in the field of road transport with vehicles whose maximum authorised gross tonnage exceeds 3.5 tonnes,etc. Romania currently gives different training modules to transport operators of vehicles which do not exceed 3.5 tonnes from those which exceed 3.5 tonnes. The former modules do not include training on how to carry dangerous goods.	Authorisation	The authorisation is reasonable to ensure the quality of the training course. The conditions that shall be fulfilled by operators are reasonable and refer to their good repute, material resources and professional competence.	The requirements to obtain an authorisation create an entry barrier which reduces the number of operators.	No recommendation.
25	**MoT No. 42/2006 on the conditions for the initial and continuous professional training of certain categories of drivers, as further amended**	Art. 5 para. (2)	Road freight transport	Only operators authorised by MoT can carry out the activity of training and further training of the personnel operating in the field of road transport.	Authorisation	The authorisation is based on point 5 of Annex 1 of Directive No. 2003/59/EC. It ensures quality of training.	The requirements to obtain an authorisation create an entry barrier which reduces the number of operators.	No recommendation.

Sector: Road transport *(cont.)*

No.	No and title of Regulation	Article	Thematic category	Brief description of the potential obstacle	Keyword	Policy maker's objective	Harm to competition	Recommendations
26	**MoT No. 761/1999 on the designation, training and professional attestation of persons who permanently and effectively lead road transport activities, etc.**	Art. 3 para. (2)	Road freight transport	Only operators authorised by MoT can carry out the designation, training and attestation of persons who permanently and effectively lead road transport activities.	Authorisation	This authorisation is in line with Art. 8 (4) and (5) of EC Regulation No. 1071/2009. It ensures quality of training.	The requirements to obtain an authorisation create an entry barrier which reduces the number of operators.	No recommendation.
27	**Government Decision No. 470/2014 for the approval of Norms regarding the origin, movement and sale of timber materials, storage regime of timber materials and regime of the round timber processing plants, as well as of measures for the implementation of Regulation (EU) No. 995/2010 laying down obligations for operators who place timber and timber products on the market**	Art. 9 para. (1) of Norms	Road freight transport	The waybills for the transport of wood materials are to be printed only by the Imprimeria Nationala SA – a State-owned company. In order to purchase these waybills, operators must provide to Imprimeria Nationala some documents, including a certificate issued by the Regional Forest Guard attesting the right of the operator to trade wood. Drivers need to have with them the waybills when transporting wood materials. The waybills for the transport of the wood materials are documents under special regime, provided with specific security elements. They are printed in blocks with 150 sheets, consisting of 50 sets of three sheets each, carbonless copy paper, with the security elements applied on the first copy. The characteristics of the security elements contained in the waybills are established on the basis of a protocol with the Imprimeria Nationalǎ. The characteristics of the security elements are not public. An Integrated Informational System of Tracking Wood Materials (SUMAL) was established for the tracking of the traceability of timber harvested from the woods and for providing statistical information.	Exclusive rights/ limitation of number of suppliers	The objective of the provision is to prevent illegal deforestation and smuggling of Romanian wood.	This provision sets up a monopoly over the printing forms of waybills related to wood. It may therefore lead to higher costs for operators who sell and transport wood material and are required to purchase the waybills.	Modify provision: We recommend opening the market. The monopoly position held by Imprimeria Naţională on printing waybills market is unable to lead to the achievement of the policymakers' objective, namely to prevent illegal deforestation and smuggling of Romanian wood. Instead, this monopoly leads to higher costs for the operators that transport wood material. Even if the Romanian legislation should further provide the obligation to obtain specific waybills for transport of wood material, Romania must liberalise the provision of the printing service to all companies aiming to carry out such activity. Also, the waybills do not need to be printed with security elements as the unique code generated by the application SUMAL attests to the legal origin of the transported timber.

Sector: Road transport *(cont.)*

No.	No and title of Regulation	Article	Thematic category	Brief description of the potential obstacle	Keyword	Policy maker's objective	Harm to competition	Recommendations
				The waybill is issued by the operator which sells and transport wood material at the transport origin point. The operator has to upload the standardised information in the application SUMAL, online or using any electronic terminal that runs this application, which necessarily must exist at the transport origin point. The information uploaded refers among others to the series and number of the waybill for the transport of the wood materials, the point of unloading of the timber, the vehicle registration number, the species, type and volume of the timber. After receiving the information, SUMAL generates a unique code, as well as the date, hour, minute and second of the registration. The law requires writing in the waybill the unique code generated by SUMAL. Also, the unique code, as well as the date, hour, minute and second of the registration are recorded in the Register of input-output wood materials kept by the operator. The unique code attests the legal origin of the transported timber.				

Sector: Road transport *(cont.)*

No.	No and title of Regulation	Article	Thematic category	Brief description of the potential obstacle	Keyword	Policy maker's objective	Harm to competition	Recommendations
28	**Government Decision No. 470/2014 (same as above)**	Art. 21 from the Norms	Road freight transport	The record of incoming-outgoing wood material is to be printed only by the Imprimeria Nationala SA – a State-owned company. In order to purchase this record, transport operators must provide to Imprimeria Nationala some documents, including a certificate issued by the Regional Forest Guard attesting the right of the operator to trade wood. Operators need to hold the record of incoming-outgoing wood material at their headquarters. The Registers of input-output wood materials are documents under special regime that are printed in blocks of 100 sheets. The legal provisions do not stipulate whether the registers contain security elements.	Exclusive rights/ limitation of number of suppliers	The objective of the provision is to prevent illegal deforestation and smuggling of Romanian wood.	This provision sets up a monopoly over the printing forms of waybills related to wood. It may therefore lead to higher costs for operators who sell and transport wood material and are required to purchase the waybills.	Modify provision: We recommend opening the market. The monopoly position held by Imprimeria Națională on printing waybills cannot achieve the policymakers' objective, namely to prevent illegal deforestation and smuggling of Romanian wood. Instead, this monopoly leads to higher costs for the operators who transport wood material. Even if Romanian legislation should further provide the obligation to obtain specific waybills for transport of wood material, Romania must liberalise the provision of the printing service to all companies aiming to perform such activity. Also, the waybills do not need to be printed with security elements as the unique code generated by the application SUMAL attests the legal origin of the transported timber.

Sector: Road transport *(cont.)*

No.	No and title of Regulation	Article	Thematic category	Brief description of the potential obstacle	Keyword	Policy maker's objective	Harm to competition	Recommendations
29	**Order of the Minister of Economy (OME) No. 971/2014 for the approval of the list of bodies designated to issue the agreement certificates and the certificates of conformity with the prototype according to the European Agreement concerning the International Carriage of Dangerous Goods by Road (ADR), etc.**	Annex to Order	Road freight transport	Only one undertaking, named IPROCHIM, is on the list of bodies designated to issue certificates of conformity with respect to superstructures fitted on vehicles transporting dangerous goods as well as packaging of dangerous goods. The main shareholder of IPROCHIM is the Ministry of Economy with 72.99% of shares. The Order of the Minister of Economy, Trade and Business Environment (MoE) No. 2737/2012 on the procedure related to the appointment of institutions performing checks on superstructure built on top of vehicles transporting dangerous goods as well as packaging sets the conditions which must be fulfilled by operators in order to carry out the activity of checking on superstructures built on top of vehicles transporting dangerous goods as well as packaging applicable to the freight transport of such goods. Among these conditions there are the following: operators should be registered with the National Trade Registry and have their headquarters in Romania. As of today, only one operator has been authorised to carry out this activity, IPROCHIM. The Ministry of Economy is the authority which authorises bodies designated to issue certificates of conformity.	Authorisation		Actual conflict of interest leads to higher costs for transport operators who shall obtain a certificate of conformity with respect to superstructures fitted on vehicles transporting dangerous goods as well as packaging of dangerous goods.	No recommendation: the conditions for authorising the performance of this activity set in MoE Order No. 2737/2012 are clear. Moreover, those operators whose application was rejected may always appeal the rejection decision before a competent court.
30	**GO No. 43/1997 on the road regime, as further amended and supplemented**	Art. 21 para. (5)	Road freight transport	The manager of a national road (e.g. the municipal council) which crosses a municipality can impose taxes in addition to those established by the Government (RO vignette). Payment of this additional tax is normally done directly at the municipality by the truck driver.	Co-regulatory regime	The main objective of local taxes is to regulate local traffic and to avoid congestion in municipalities. Also, taxes are aimed at ensuring infrastructure investment and maintenance and thus a high level of road quality and safety providing drivers with an appropriate network of national, county and local roads.	Additional taxes may increase the costs of operators. According to the industry, these taxes are not levied in a transparent manner and may lead to uncertainty and discrimination of some operators vis-à-vis others.	Make legal provisions more transparent and the tax payment system more efficient: We do not recommend abolishing the local road taxes. However, we recommend that the Romanian government should introduce an appropriate legal framework in order to ensure the transparency and efficiency of the

Sector: Road transport *(cont.)*

No.	No and title of Regulation	Article	Thematic category	Brief description of the potential obstacle	Keyword	Policy maker's objective	Harm to competition	Recommendations
								payment system for local road taxes. Local authorities should also find a way to ensure transparency of the tax requirements, notably by making the application of these taxes more transparent for hauliers. County and local councils need to publish these charges and make them easily accessible since they are likely to apply not only to local operators, but also to operators coming from other regions of Romania, as well as from abroad. In particular, the information related to local taxes should also be made available in English, in order to ensure easy access for foreign operators. To guarantee transparency of local taxes, a good measure might be to publish all road taxes on the websites of the Ministry of Transport, and Ministry of Regional Development and Public Administration. Also, an online payment system of taxes might be introduced through a new legal framework. An efficient payment system might involve payment with mobile phones and/or through wireless devices, as, for example, is currently implemented

Sector: Road transport *(cont.)*

No.	No and title of Regulation	Article	Thematic category	Brief description of the potential obstacle	Keyword	Policy maker's objective	Harm to competition	Recommendations
								in cities such as London and Milan – but also in Romania, e.g. for the toll bridge at the Fetești-Cernavodă station on the A2 București- Consțanta highway, introduced by Emergency Government Ordinance No. 8/2015. There, the enforcement of tax payment is achieved through a closed-circuit television (CCTV) system, which records the plate of each vehicle entering and exiting the city centre perimeter.
31	**MoT No. 42/2006 on the conditions for the initial and continuous professional training of certain categories of drivers, as further amended**	Art. 1 para. (1) and para. (2)	Road freight transport	In order to carry out the activity of road transport of goods, drivers must obtain a certificate of professional competence and a certificate showing a continuing professional qualification.	Certification	The provision is in line with Art. 6 and 7 of Directive No. 2003/59/EC on the initial qualification and periodic training of drivers of certain road vehicles for the carriage of goods or passengers. This certification is reasonable to ensure public safety.	The certification requirement may represent a barrier to entry into the marketplace.	No recommendation.
32	**MoT No. 1214/2015 on the approval of norms establishing the conditions for obtaining a professional attestation by road transport staff.**	Art. 1 from the Norms (Annex No. 5)	Road freight transport	In order to carry out the activity of road transport of goods with vehicles exceeding an applicable length or weight limits, so-called abnormal load transport, drivers must obtain a certificate of professional competence.	Certification/ Discrimination	There is no official recital for this particular provision. However, it seems that the objective of the provision is to ensure public safety on the roads. This provision is based on national legislation and is not established in accordance with EU law.	The professional certificate for abnormal load transport affects drivers and operators, causing less flexibility in replacing the drivers for these types of transport. For instance, an operator needs a driver with an additional certificate in order to transport goods with abnormal vehicles. Also, the provision increases the administrative burden of road transport operators. Moreover, the provision applies only to the drivers who carry out transport operations with vehicles registered in Romania. Therefore, besides the additional cost and administrative burden, it discriminates in favour of foreign transport operators with drivers operating vehicles registered in other countries.	Abolish: Romania seems to be the only EU country requiring an abnormal load transport certificate. Professional qualification can be addressed by considering the training undertaken for the issuance of the certificate certifying the initial qualification.

Sector: Road transport *(cont.)*

No.	No and title of Regulation	Article	Thematic category	Brief description of the potential obstacle	Keyword	Policy maker's objective	Harm to competition	Recommendations
33	**MoT No. 980/2011 approving the Methodological Norms on the application of the provisions regarding the organisation and performance of road transport and related activities established by the Government Ordinance No. 27/2011 on road transport, as further amended and supplemented**	Art. 20 from the Norms	Road freight transport	Road transport operators must obtain a copy of the transport licence (Community licence) for each vehicle of their fleet, which must be renewed annually, although the road freight transport licence issued to transport operators has a validity for a period of 10 years. The copy of the Licence cannot be transferred, i.e. it applies only to one registered vehicle. In accordance with the Order No. 2156/2005, a copy costs 260 lei/year, approximately Euro 60. A copy of the Community licence must be carried on the vehicle on all journeys and must be presented to any enforcement official on request. Each copy has the registration number of the vehicle and cannot be used for any other vehicle of the same transport operator's fleet.	Authorisation	The imposition of such an obligation may be justified in order to permit ISCTR inspectors to verify the compliance of transport operators with the provisions regarding authorisation. Information obtained through research indicates that in some European countries the validity of the copy of the Community licence is the same as the validity of the licence. For example, in Estonia, a copy of the licence is issued for 10 years if the applicant does not require it for a shorter period, and not for longer than the term of validity of the Community licence (10 years). In the UK and Spain the Community licence is issued for a five year period, as well as the copy of the Community licence, and it is not specific to one vehicle – it does not contain the vehicle registration number. Also, in Spain a copy costs EUR 5.99 for five years.	The requirements to obtain a copy of the licence is in line with Art. 4 of EC Regulation No. 1072/2009. However, the fact that the copy costs approximately EUR 60/vehicle/year and that it applies to only one registered vehicle (i.e. it cannot be used for others vehicles which are part of the operator's fleet) increases costs for hauliers established in Romania.	Make provision clearer: The obligation to carry a copy of the transport operator's licence does not need to be subject to such high costs. There is no need to impose annual renewal, where the licence is issued for a 10-year period. Further, there is no reason to impose the vehicle's specific copies, since different vehicles may belong to the same licence owner. The licence and the copy, should be issued at the same time and it shall be made available for the same period as the duration of the licence to which it refers, i.e. 10 years. The costs of the licence should be re-evaluated.

Sector: Rail transport

No.	No and title of regulation	Article	Thematic category	Brief description of potential obstacles	Keyword	Policy Maker's Objective	Harm to competition	Recommendation
1	**Government Decision No. 1696/2006 approving the Regulation on railway infrastructure capacity allocation**	Art. 4	Railway freight transport	MoT may grant special rights to CFR SA, the infrastructure administrator, with respect to capacity allocation where it is indispensable to ensure good execution of public railway transport services or for the efficient use of the infrastructure. The Government Decision states that the conditions to obtain these special rights will be established under Ministerial Order. However, the referenced Ministerial Order has never been published. This provision is likely to be at odds with Art. 7(1) and (2) of the Rail Recast Directive No. 2012/34; these European provisions require independence of the essential functions of an infrastructure manager from its service operating activities.	Special rights discrimination	This provision is meant to transpose ARt. 5 Directive No. 95/19/EC and aims at ensuring adequate public services or efficient use of infrastructure capacity. There is no official justification for not publishing the Order mentioned in Art. 4 para. 2.	The conditions for the exercise of these special rights are unclear. CFR SA may take undue advantage of these special rights to favour CFR Marfă, which is under the same ownership of CFR SA, over CFR Marfă competitors.	Make provision clearer: the provision should be redrafted clarifying i) what these special rights are and ii) in which instances they can be triggered by the infrastructure manager to allocate capacity. The Order of the Ministry of Transport settling the conditions for granting CFR SA special rights to allocate public rail way infrastructure should also be published in the Official Gazette.
2	**Government Decision No. 1696/2006 approving the Regulation on railway infrastructure capacity allocation**	Art. 7 para. 2	Railway freight transport	Requests of infrastructure capacity allocation will be subject to a financial and technical analysis by CFR SA. CFR SA has the right to reject a route allocation requested by railway operators when statistics related to freight transport operating on that route show a use of under 20% compared to the timetable in force. The right and the threshold as such are also mentioned in CFR SA Network Statement – Art.7(1)(b) of Annex XV.	Restriction discrimination	This provision transposes art. 27(2) of Directive No. 2001/14/CE, which states that the railway infrastructure manager is entitled to optimise the use of infrastructure and may terminate a route allocation in case of under-performance of a railways operator's utilisation rate compared to the operational plan. This provision therefore enables CFR SA to make efficient and optimal use of its infrastructure capacity. This provision effectively deals with minimising sub-optimal use of capacity and is legitimate if it is spelled out in the Network Statement. Similar provisions exist across the EU.	This provision is unclear. Any refusal to access the railway infrastructure by CFR SA may represent a serious limitation to market entry, unless objectively justified. Further, CFR SA may try to favour CFR Marfa over its competitors given that these two companies, although separate, belong to the same holding group under MoT.	Make provision clearer: Railway undertakings must be provided with guidelines, which should be included both in the Regulation on Railway Infrastructure Capacity Allocation and in CFR SA Network Statement, describing with detail i) instances that can be accounted to trigger the 20% under-performance threshold by the infrastructure manager as well as ii) instances which fall outside the application of this threshold since they cannot be placed under the responsibility of the railway operator. These instances should also be quantified to the greatest possible extent in order to facilitate calculation of the under-utilisation rate by railway enterprises. These clarifications must be reflected in the information to be presented by the railway enterprise in its operational timetable plan.

Sector: Rail transport *(cont.)*

No.	No and title of regulation	Article	Thematic category	Brief description of potential obstacles	Keyword	Policy Maker's Objective	Harm to competition	Recommendation
3	**Order No. 290/2000 of Ministry of Transport on technical acceptance of products/services for use in building activities, modernisation, maintenance and repair of railway infrastructure and rolling stock for rail and metro**	Art. 1 para. 1 & para. 2	Railway freight transport	Only authorised enterprises are allowed to provide products and services to be used for building, modernising, maintaining and repairing the railway infrastructure and rolling stock. The authorisation is issued by the National Rail Transport Authority (AFER).	Authorisation	This authorisation is justified for safety reasons. This is a common requirement across the EU and the authorisation conditions are reasonable. There is no shortage of suppliers for these products and services given that every enterprise which has fulfilled the authorisation conditions has received an authorisation from AFER. However, a new piece of legislation is to be issued as some provisions (other than Art. 1 para 1&2) are not in line with Romanian transport legislation transposing EU Directives.	This regulatory entry barrier may unnecessarily reduce the number of operators and raise administrative costs. Further, it may discriminate against one or more operators vis-à-vis others.	No recommendation.
4	**Order of Ministry of Transport No. 535/2007 on the approval of procedures related to granting the licence and safety certificate necessary to carry out rail transport services in Romania**	Art. 1 para. 3	Railway freight transport	A transport licence and a safety certificate are needed to carry out railway services. The conditions for obtaining the licence and the safety certificate can be found in Annex 1 and 2 of the MoT. They mainly refer to honourability, financial capacity, professional competence and civil liability coverage. Rejections may be challenged in court under Art. 28.	Authorisation	All the required conditions are in line with Articles 4(3) and (5) of Directive No. 95/18/CE on the licensing of railway enterprises as well as with Articles 2(1), (8) and (10) of Directive No. 2004/49/CE on the safety of EC railways. These are common requirements across the EU.	This regulatory entry barrier may unnecessarily reduce the number of operators and raise administrative costs. Further, it may discriminate against one or more operators vis-à-vis others.	No recommendation.
5	**Government Ordinance No. 89/2003 – on the allocation of railway infrastructure capacity and the levying of charges for the use of railway infrastructure and safety certification, with further amendments**	Art. 5 para. 1	Railway freight transport	Annex 2 recital 2 sets the services to which access must be granted by the infrastructure administrator. These include access to a power supply system, fuel supply, freight terminals, etc. The infrastructure administrator can reject a request for access to the facilities mentioned in Annex 2 of the GO if there are alternative options in the marketplace. These "alternative options" are not specified.	Exclusive rights discrimination	The provision transposes Art. 5 of Directive No. 2001/14/CE and is justified for reasons of efficient allocation of capacity.	This provision is unclear. It may be used by the infrastructure administrator CFR SA to favour CFR Marfă over its competitors.	Make provision clearer: A definition of "viable alternative" is necessary to provide further guidance to railway undertakings. This definition should be made available in the Network Statement, in accordance with Art. 27 and Annex IV of Directive No. 2012/34. Such a definition can be found, for example, in Section 2.23 *et seq.* of the UK Guidance on Appeals to Office of Rail Regulation under the Railways Infrastructure.

Sector: Rail transport *(cont.)*

No.	No and title of regulation	Article	Thematic category	Brief description of potential obstacles	Keyword	Policy Maker's Objective	Harm to competition	Recommendation
6	**Order of Ministry of Transport No. 340/1999 on the approval of rules for granting authorisations to railways stations which are in operation or for building, repairing or modernising such stations**	Art. 2 para. 1	Railway freight transport	Owners of railway stations must obtain an authorisation which proves that the station fulfils the technical conditions required to ensure safety of railway transport. This authorisation is issued by AFER. The conditions required for the authorisation are stipulated in the Annex of the Order. They refer mainly to technical issues and training of employees.	Authorisation	This authorisation is in line with the provisions of Directive No. 2004/18/CE on the licensing of railway enterprises as well as with Directive No. 2004/49/CE on safety on the Community's railways. The provision enables a public authority to verify that the working station belonging to rail operators has the minimum facilities required for operating public transport.	This regulatory entry barrier may unnecessarily reduce the number of operators and raise administrative costs. Further, it may discriminate against one or more operators vis-à-vis others.	No recommendation.
7	**Order of Ministry of Transport No. 410/1999 concerning the authorisation for testing and certifying railway products used in construction activities, modernisation, operation, maintenance and repair of rail infrastructure and rolling stock, railway and subway**	Art. 1 & Art. 6, Art. 4 align 2 of Annex 1 of Order No. 410/1999	Railway freight transport	In order to verify and monitor rail transport safety, the testing of railway products shall be done by authorised laboratories. The authorisation is issued by AFER. The conditions to be met so that the authorisation can granted are supposed to be mentioned in the Annexes of Order No. 410/1999. However, these annexes are not published but can be requested from AFER.	Authorisation	Guidance on how to obtain an authorisation can be found on the AFER website. This authorisation is a common requirement across EU countries.	This lack of transparency may lead to unclear conditions for operators and raise administrative costs.	Make regulatory framework more transparent: Annexes of Order No. 410/1999 must be published in order to make all the authorisation requirements known to interested operators. To this extent, they should be published both in the Official Gazette and on the AFER website.
8	**Order of Ministry of Transport No. 410/1999 concerning the authorisation for testing and certifying railway products used in construction activities, modernisation, operation, maintenance and repair of rail infrastructure and rolling stock, railway and subway**	Annex 1 Art. 4 (2)	Railway freight transport	In order to ensure safety of rail transport, testing of railway products shall be done only by authorised laboratories. The authorisation is issued by AFER for a 10-year period and is subject to a mandatory renewal every two years, at the end of which authorised independent testing laboratories need to show their ability to fulfil all the authorisation requirements once again.	Authorisation	This authorisation is a common requirement across EU countries justified for safety reasons. However, the two-year renewal is not standard practice in EU Member States. Art. 10 of EC Regulation No. 402/2013 establishing common safety standards for testing railway products allows Member States to establish an authorisation renewal not exceeding five years.	The two-year mandatory renewal represents an unnecessary administrative burden for independent testing laboratories, as other EU countries (e.g. Italy) require renewal after 5 years. This unnecessary regulatory burden reduces the incentive for independent testing laboratories to invest resources for entering into or staying in the business, since there is a risk that their authorisation will not be renewed at the end of the two year period.	Create appropriate legal framework: the renewal should be extended to cover a period not to exceed 5 years, in line with Art. 10 EC Regulation 402/2013. Introducing a longer renewal period may increase market entry and create more appetite for investment as well as for competition with respect to prices and quality of rail product testing services.

Sector: Rail transport *(cont.)*

No.	No and title of regulation	Article	Thematic category	Brief description of potential obstacles	Keyword	Policy Maker's Objective	Harm to competition	Recommendation
9	**Order of Ministry of Transport No. 410/1999 concerning the authorisation for testing and certifying railway products used in construction activities, modernisation, operation, maintenance and repair of rail infrastructure and rolling stock, railway and subway**	Annex 1 Art. 5 and Art. 6	Railway freight transport	The conditions to be met in order to obtain the authorisation for testing and certifying railway products are set in Annexes No. 1-3. Requests can be submitted only by undertakings having Romanian legal personality.	Authorisation discrimination	There is no justification for requesting enterprises to have Romanian legal personality. However, CFR SA claims there is no discrimination.	Competitors with a legal entity registered abroad may be kept out of the market.	Amendment: the legal requirement should be for the operators to be registered in the EU, ensuring alignment with the Single European Rail Area objectives and the provisions of the Technical Pillar of the Fourth Rail Package.
10	**Emergency Government Ordinance No. 12/1998 on freight railway transport and on the reorganisation of the Romanian National Railways Company**	Art. 1 para. 9	Railway freight transport	In order to operate as a railway transport operator, the company must have Romanian legal personality and needs to obtain a licence. This licence is issued by MoT. The conditions to be met for the licence are stipulated in Art. 2 and in MoT No. 535/2007, as modified by Order No. 884/2011 and Order No. 1502/2014.	Licence/ discrimination	With respect to the licence requirement, the conditions to be met are in line with the provisions of Articles 4-9 of Directive 2004/18/CE on the licensing of railway enterprises as well as with Articles 1 and 8 of Directive No. 2004/49/CE on the safety of EC railways. Paragraph 2.2.2. of the Romanian Network Statement provides that there should be no discrimination against foreign operators. However, CFR SA claims there is no discrimination.	This provision may discriminate against foreign companies.	Amendment: the legal requirement should be for the operators to be registered in the EU, ensuring alignment with the Single European Rail Area objectives and the provisions of the Technical Pillar of the Fourth Railway Package, mainly the ones concerning the new requirements of the vertical integrated undertakings (VIU) (the proposal COM (2013) 29 for a Directive to amend Directive No. 2012/34/EU, the new Art. 7 as stipulated within the proposal).

Sector: Rail transport *(cont.)*

No.	No and title of regulation	Article	Thematic category	Brief description of potential obstacles	Keyword	Policy Maker's Objective	Harm to competition	Recommendation
11	**Emergency Government Ordinance No. 12/1998 on freight railway transport and on the reorganisation of the Romanian National Railways Company**	Art. 9	Railway freight transport	This provision grants exclusive rights to CFR SA to manage the national public railway infrastructure. The concession to CFR SA is granted for 49 years.	Concession	Granting exclusive rights to an infrastructure manager is in line with Art. 7 of Directive No. 2012/34/CE. The monopoly regime which this concession grants is still very common across the EU and its duration is not unreasonable if compared with other EU countries (e.g. Italy, where the concession to the infrastructure manager, RFI, is granted for 60 years). CFR SA is a 100% state-owned company and the 49-year term is the maximum term stipulated in Romanian law regarding the granting of concessions for public services.	CFR SA may establish more advantageous conditions for CFR Marfa over its competitors, since it may grant the latter better terms for accessing its infrastructure or providing its essential services.	No recommendation.
12	**Emergency Government Ordinance No. 12/1998 on freight railway transport and on the reorganisation of the Romanian National Railways Company**	Art. 18(3)	Railway freight transport	Access to infrastructure and services provided in terminals and ports linked to the railway infrastructure can be restricted when there are "viable alternatives" in the marketplace. There is no definition of these "viable alternatives".	Concession	There is no justification for the lack of definition by CFR SA of what are these "viable alternatives" which may be used as grounds for refusing access to its infrastructure.	The infrastructure administrator may deter competition by rejecting access requests to essential services without an objective justification.	Make provision clearer: CFR SA must provide a comprehensive definition of what these "viable alternatives" are that may justify a refusal to access its infrastructure. This definition should be included in the Romanian Network Statement, in accordance with Art. 27 and Annex IV of Directive 2012/34.
13	**Government Decision No. 643/2011 approving the Rental Conditions by the National Railway Company "CFR" SA of some parts of the non-interoperable railway infrastructure, as well as their management**	Annex 1 Art. 15 para. 3	Railway freight transport	CRF SA, the railway infrastructure administrator, has the right to rent parts of the infrastructure which are not inter-operable to private operators, selected through public tender. The provisions of the rental contract are not negotiable. The rental contract must stipulate as mandatory several clauses provided in Art. 15(1) letter b) f. Private operators are permitted to negotiate only the precise moment when they are effectively taking over the infrastructure as well as the assets and/or activities that will be taken over.	Barrier to entry	It is common across EU countries to have general standard terms applying to all contracts concluded by railway infrastructure managers with railway operators. Generally these terms are non-negotiable. Further, CFR Marfa obtains access to the CFR SA infrastructure in accordance with conditions which are similar to those applied to other private operators.	It is unclear which issues are not negotiable. CFR SA may use its discretion to favour CFR Marfa over its competitors by granting it more favourable treatment over standard terms.	No recommendation.

Sector: Rail transport *(cont.)*

No.	No and title of regulation	Article	Thematic category	Brief description of potential obstacles	Keyword	Policy Maker's Objective	Harm to competition	Recommendation
14	**Government Ordinance No. 7/2005 on approval of the Regulation over railway transport in Romania**	Art. 4 para 5 and art. 51 para. 2 of the Regulation, Annex of GO	Railway freight transport	Foreign operators may rent their transport vehicles and loading devices on the basis of tariffs customarily used in international traffic. These rental tariffs are called RIV and are established in an international agreement called COTIF to which Romania is party. National railway operators apply RIV tariffs every time their rent wagons belonging to foreign railway operators transporting freight are to be delivered in Romania. In these instances, the national railway operator will charge its customers the RIV tariff (which the national operator reimburses to the foreign owner of the wagon) + an extra charge, which is the object of negotiation with the freight customer. Although Art. 4 of this Regulation stipulates for every transport operator the obligation of publishing its RIV + extra tariffs, CFR Marfă is de facto the only operator which does so. The information published by CFR Marfa concerning its rental tariffs of foreign wagons may well act as a focal point in an oligopolistic market such as the Romanian freight railway market, favouring tacit collusion among market players.	Discrimination	The restriction imposing RIV charges is established in an international agreement to which Romania is bound. It has primacy over Romanian law. RIV tariffs are set to a relatively high-margin level in order to push the national railway operator to give the rented wagon back to the foreign railway operator with the shortest possible delay. On the other hand, the obligation for CFR Marfa to publish its additional rental charges concerning foreign wagons makes no sense also to CFR and puts CFR at a disadvantage vis-à-vis all the other operators who do not publish such tariffs.	The effect of this provision is two-fold: i) it establishes RIV as a fix charge to be reimbursed always to the foreign owners of a wagon; ii) it increases market transparency providing a focal point for the price freight railway transport operators intend to charge their customers. Thus, on the one hand it introduces unnecessary rigidity in the prices charged for renting foreign wagons. On the other hand, it introduces unnecessary transparency in a market with oligopolistic characteristics which may favour tacit collusion among existing players.	Abolish: With respect to freight transport, national railway operators should not be under an obligation to publish their RIV + extra charge tariffs.

Sector: Rail transport *(cont.)*

No.	No and title of regulation	Article	Thematic category	Brief description of potential obstacles	Keyword	Policy Maker's Objective	Harm to competition	Recommendation
15	**Government Decision No. 581/1998 on setting up the National Railway Company "CFR SA"**	Annex No. 1 Art. 19 (o)	Railway freight transport	CFR SA provides access to several essential services including, for example, freight terminals. Access tariffs for such services are established unilaterally by CFR SA and could give rise to some form of discrimination against operators competing with its affiliated company, CFR Marfă. Furthermore, ownership of some of these CFR SA terminals was transferred to CFR Marfă. Access to these terminals by competing operators may be either foreclosed or subject to unfair terms.	Discrimination	CFR SA tariffs are the same for every transport operator. CFR Marfa is free to choose with whom it wants to do business.	CFR SA may use this provision to confer on CFR Marfa an undue advantage over its competitors. CFR Marfa may refuse access to its terminals and discriminate against its competitors.	Make provision clearer: CFR SA shall publish guidelines explaining the methodology it uses to calculate its tariffs, notably with reference to the costs related to each of its essential services. If terminal ownership by CFR Marfa continues and as long as CFR Marfa is a state-owned company, CFR Marfa shall be under the same obligation of CFR SA with respect to the terms applicable for accessing its terminals by competing railway operators. Notably, both CFR SA and CFR Marfa need to provide fair, transparent and non-discriminatory conditions for accessing their terminals (so called FRAND terms). Compliance with FRAND terms must be ensured by an independent regulatory body.
16	**Order of Ministry of Transport No. 443/2011 on the approval of Norms concerning the authorisation for the functioning of a newly build or modernised industrial railway**	Art. 5	Railway freight transport	In order to build or modernise an industrial railway, an authorisation has to be obtained from the Romanian National Safety Authority, an administrative body within AFER and MoT.	Authorisation	This provision is in line with Articles 1 and 2 of Directive No. 2004/49/CE related to the safety of EC railways. This is a common requirement across the EU.	The authorisation requirement may prevent access to the marketplace by other economic operators.	No recommendation.

Sector: Rail transport *(cont.)*

No.	No and title of regulation	Article	Thematic category	Brief description of potential obstacles	Keyword	Policy Maker's Objective	Harm to competition	Recommendation
17	**Regenerative braking**		Railway freight transport	Romania lacks the legal framework for introducing regenerative braking by railway operators. Regenerative braking leads to energy consumption savings and is already installed in the locomotives of most railway operators. The infrastructure of the European Transport Network Corridors of Romania has already been modernised to allow regenerative braking. The current state of play puts operators having locomotives capable of generating this form of energy saving at a competitive disadvantage vis-à-vis other railway operators.	Discrimination	Introduction of regenerative braking requires dedicated rules concerning electricity pricing, infrastructure financing (dedicated storage facilities are necessary) and access conditions. Thus, before introducing this form of braking, the existing regulatory framework, assets and infrastructure system need to be adjusted.	The non-introduction of this form of braking discriminates against those operators who have this technology already installed in their locomotives. For these operators, the non-introduction of this form of braking increases electricity costs.	Create appropriate legal framework: Compensation for regenerative braking energy should be introduced in Romanian Law on Energy no 123/2014, due to its ability to save energy consumption for railway freight transport. All metered train operators should pay for net energy consumption after taking into account the regenerated energy. This should lead to changes to the existing infrastructure and acquisition of new locomotives. A good example of a legal framework for regenerative braking discounts is in the UK, namely Art. 8 of Traction Electricity Rules issued by the Office of Rail Regulation.

Sector: Maritime and inland waterways

No.	No and title of regulation	Article	Thematic category	Brief description of the potential obstacle	Keyword	Policy maker's objective	Harm to competition	Recommendations
1	**Order of Ministry of Transport (MoT) No. 547/2014 concerning the authorisation of economic operators for the operation of shipping related activities – security service piloting ships into and out of ports, between the piers of the same port and inland waterways**	Art. 1	Sea and coastal freight water transport	Vessel piloting services can be provided only by authorised economic operators under NACE Code 5222.	Authorisation	The authorisation requirement is necessary for safety reasons and is applied in all EU Member States.	The authorisation requirement restricts market access of economic operators.	No recommendation.
2	**Order of MoT No. 547/2014 concerning the authorisation of economic operators for the operation of shipping related activities – security service piloting ships into and out of ports, between the piers of the same port and inland waterways**	Art. 2	Sea and coastal freight water transport	Port authorities and/or authorities managing maritime canals may operate piloting services without an authorisation, unlike private operators for whom authorisation is mandatory.	Discrimination	Port authorities are obliged by law to provide piloting services. Port authorities have the possibility of providing piloting services either directly according to the current law or outsourcing them to private operators.	Competition may be distorted if in a port area the pilotage of vessels is conducted by both private operators and port authorities (state operators) because only state operators can carry out the activity without obtaining authorisation. This may confer on state operators an unfair competitive advantage.	Create appropriate legal framework: Port authorities (state operators) and private operators shall not be subject to different legal and administrative regimes when performing the same services in competition. Piloting services may therefore either be operated by the port authority or they can be outsourced. When outsourced, the contracts shall be granted through a tendering process subject to fair and non-discriminatory terms.

Sector: Maritime and inland waterways *(cont.)*

No.	No and title of regulation	Article	Thematic category	Brief description of the potential obstacle	Keyword	Policy maker's objective	Harm to competition	Recommendations
3	**Order of MoT No. 547/2014 concerning the authorisation of economic operators for the operation of shipping related activities – security service piloting ships into and out of ports, between the piers of the same port and inland waterways**	Annex 1 Art. 1	Sea and coastal freight water transport	To be authorised, piloting service providers should have a minimum number of pilots per port. Order No. 547/2014 requires companies to have a minimum number of 8 pilots in Consţanta, 4 pilots in Midia and 2 in Mangalia. However, port authorities unilaterally establish general terms and conditions for the provision of piloting services, contradicting the letter of this order. For example, for the ports of Consţanta, Mangalia and Midia, the port authority requires companies to have at least 21 pilots servicing these three ports. The port authority has cancelled an agreement with four piloting companies which according to RCC share all their revenues, without giving any consideration to which of them has actually delivered the services.	Authorisation	Minimum number of pilots is justified by the fact that piloting services should be regularly provided 24 hours a day, 7 days a week.	The minimum number of pilots may restrict market access or preserve the status quo, limiting the business of smaller firms.	Create appropriate legal framework: Piloting services shall not be granted through direct entrustment but instead they should be tendered based on fair and non-discriminatory terms to guarantee competition for the market. Abolish the provision: The law should not impose a minimum number of pilots per port but should instead guarantee a minimum service level (e.g. maximum ship waiting time for pilots to be on board).
4	**Government Ordinance No. 42/1997 on civil navigation**	Art. 12	Sea and coastal freight water transport	Professional training for the seafarers may be provided by CERONAV (Romanian Maritime Training Centre) or trainers accredited by MoT. The accreditation requirements are not specified in the text of the law.	Authorisation	The accreditation criteria can be found in Order No. 1354/2007 and aim at reasonably ensuring safety and professional competences.	The lack of criteria for accreditation leaves wide discretion to CERONAV or the Ministry of Transport and may lead to possible discrimination of certain trainers vis-à-vis others.	No recommendation.
5	**Government Ordinance No. 42/1997 on civil navigation**	Art. 25 and Art. 26	Sea and coastal freight water transport	The Romanian Naval Authority (ANR) or any other institution with whom the ANR has concluded an agreement are responsible for issuing certificates of compliance with the technical rules related to shipbuilding. The criteria for appointing such institutions in charge of issuing certificates of compliance are unclear. Further, under EC Regulation No. 391/2009, once appointed by ANR, these accreditation bodies must be ratified by the European Commission (EC). However, ANR is under no obligation to conclude agreements with those accreditation bodies which have been recognised by the EC.	Authorisation	The provision is in line with EC Regulation 391/2009. The authorisation is aimed at complying with technical requirements.	In the absence of clear criteria for the appointment of such institutions, the ANR, which is owned by MoT, may distort competition by regulating access to the marketplace, foreclosing entry of new competitors as well as charging supra-competitive fees for its services.	Create new legal framework: The criteria for the appointment of institutions in charge of issuing certificates of compliance with shipbuilding rules must be published in the law and should be fair and non-discriminatory. The ANR must be under an obligation to conclude agreements with accreditation bodies recognised by the EC in accordance with EC Regulation no. 391/2009.

Sector: Maritime and inland waterways *(cont.)*

No.	No and title of regulation	Article	Thematic category	Brief description of the potential obstacle	Keyword	Policy maker's objective	Harm to competition	Recommendations
6	**Order of MoT No. 548/2014 concerning the authorisation of economic operators for the operation of shipping related activities – security service towage for manoeuvring ships in ports**	Art. 1	Sea and coastal freight water transport	Safety towing services in ports can be provided only by authorised operators holding NACE 5222 Code. The conditions under which such authorisation may be obtained are not clearly set out in the text of the Order.	Authorisation	The provision does not represent a restriction, the conditions for authorisation can be found in Annex 1 of Order No. 548/2014. This restriction is justified for reasons of compliance with safety standards.	The lack of clarity over the conditions under which the authorisation can be obtained may deter market access of economic operators and thus distort competition.	No recommendation.
7	**Order of MoT No. 548/2014 concerning the authorisation of economic operators for the operation of shipping related activities – security service towage for manoeuvring ships in ports**	Art. 2, para. 4	Sea and coastal freight water transport	Port authorities which are state-owned operators can carry out towage activity without having an authorisation, unlike private operators for whom authorisation is required.	Discrimination	The port authorities are obliged by law to provide towing services. Port authorities can provide these services directly or can grant them to private operators.	Competition may be distorted if towage is conducted in a port area by both private operators and port authorities (state operators) because state operators can carry out the activity without obtaining authorisation. This may confer on state operators an unfair competitive advantage.	Create appropriate legal framework: Port authorities (state operators) and private operators shall not be subject to different legal and administrative regimes when performing the same services in competition. Towing services may therefore either be operated by the port authority or they can be outsourced. When outsourced, the contracts shall be granted through a tendering process subject to fair and non-discriminatory terms.

Sector: Maritime and inland waterways *(cont.)*

No.	No and title of regulation	Article	Thematic category	Brief description of the potential obstacle	Keyword	Policy maker's objective	Harm to competition	Recommendations
8	**Order of MoT No. 548/2014 concerning the authorisation of economic operators for the operation of shipping related activities – security service towage for manoeuvring ships in ports**	Annex 1	Sea and coastal freight water transport	Issuing an authorisation for towing services is subject to several criteria including safety certificates concerning the ship and its equipment issued by the ANR. In order to have this authorisation an operator needs to have a minimum number of tugboats, depending on the length of the ship and its maximum gross tonnage. For example, the law requires at least one tugboat with a hook traction strength of minimum 5 tonnes for towing ships up to 120 metres long and 1 000 tonnes; 4 tugboats for towing ships over 250 metres, etc. Although Order No. 548/2014 is in force, port authorities unilaterally establish general terms and conditions for the provision of towing services in their ports, contradicting the letter of this order. For example, for the ports of Constanta, Mangalia and Midia, the port authority requires companies to have at least 17 towing vessels servicing these three ports. It currently has concluded a contract only with one single company, which is a joint venture formed among the previous three largest towing operators in the marketplace.	Authorisation	The minimum number of towage vessels is requested in accordance with the specific characteristics of each port in order to ensure the safety of navigation.	The minimum number of tugboats may limits competition by restricting access to the market for some players and preserve the status quo.	Create appropriate legal framework: Towing services shall not be granted through direct entrustment but instead they should be tendered based on fair and non-discriminatory terms to guarantee competition for the market. Abolish the provision: Instead of regulating the number of tugboats per port, MoT should regulate the minimum service level (e.g. the maximum length of time a ship would need to wait for a tugboat).
9	**Government Ordinance No. 22/1999 on the management of ports and waterways, the usage of freight water transport infrastructures belonging to public ownership and the development of freight water transport activities in ports and inland waterways**	Art. 19 para. 3	Sea and coastal freight water transport	All economic operators that provide shipping activities are subject to authorisation by the ANR, except for the port administration and operators which carry out such activities in their own interest.	Discrimination	The lack of authorisation for shipping activities carried out by the ANR and the other port authorities but also by private operators who undertake these activities on their own account is justified by the fact that they do not provide these services for third parties.	The law establishes a differential treatment for public and private operators as well as more favourable conditions for operators engaged in shipping activities in their own interest.	No recommendation.

Sector: Maritime and inland waterways *(cont.)*

No.	No and title of regulation	Article	Thematic category	Brief description of the potential obstacle	Keyword	Policy maker's objective	Harm to competition	Recommendations
10	**Decree No. 298/1948 of the Ministry of Foreign Affair for the ratification of the Convention regarding the Regime of Navigation on the Danube signed in Belgrade on 18 August 1948 along with its two Annexes and the Supplementary Protocol (Belgrade Convention)**	Art. 41	Sea and coastal freight water transport	Discounts over port services tariffs given by port authorities to ship-owners are not regarded as discriminatory if they are in accordance with customary industry use and are proportionate to the volume of services rendered or the nature of the cargo.	Permissive legislation	The Belgrade Convention regarding the Regime of Navigation on the Danube stipulates that "the amounts that will be paid for services rendered shall be established without any discrimination. The advantages granted by commercial usage, with the volume of work and the nature of the goods shall not be regarded as discrimination". The Belgrade Convention prevails over Romanian legislation.	This provision may be applied in a discriminatory manner, favouring one or more operators vis-à-vis the others.	No recommendation.
11	**Government Ordinance No. 22/1999 on the management of ports and waterways, the usage of freight water transport infrastructures belonging to public ownership and the development of freight water transport activities in ports and inland waterways**	Art.50 and Art. 52	Sea and Costal freight water transport	Tariffs for using port infrastructure lack transparency.	Discrimination	Economic operators authorised in this field pay the same price for using the infrastructure.	The application by port authorities of this provision may lead to differential tariff treatment and discrimination among operators.	Create appropriate legal framework: Port authorities should set their charges based on a transparent methodology which must be cost-oriented and/or by comparison with other ports. Furthermore, the port authorities' autonomy in setting charges should be balanced by the ability to review these charges, given to an independent regulator having the mandate to ensure that competition among port operators is promoted.

Sector: Maritime and inland waterways *(cont.)*

No.	No and title of regulation	Article	Thematic category	Brief description of the potential obstacle	Keyword	Policy maker's objective	Harm to competition	Recommendations
12	**Government Ordinance No. 22/1999 on the management of ports and waterways, the usage of freight water transport infrastructures belonging to public ownership and the development of freight water transport activities in ports and inland waterways**	Art. 51	Sea and coastal freight water transport	Piloting services in and out of Sulina, Tulcea, Galați and Brăila ports must be provided by the Regia Autonoma "Administrația Fluvială a Dunării de Jos" – AFDJ, (Galați Lower Danube River Administration – public undertaking entrusted with special tasks and rights), by pilots authorised by AFDJ or with whom AFDJ has concluded a framework contract or by concession agreements.	Authorisation Exclusive rights	The provision complies with Art. 31 and Art. 33 of the Belgrade Convention of 1948, ratified by Romania by Decree No. 298/1948.	The coexistence of these two forms of pilotage service provision to vessels, i.e. by port administration and by third parties (either by pilots authorised by port administration under a contract for services concluded or by concession agreement) is likely to distort competition. AFDJ may abuse its exclusive rights granted by the law in order to organise the piloting and harbour manoeuvres. As AFDJ is the gate keeper, it may reduce the number of authorised operators and their incentive to compete against AFDJ services.	Establish conflict of interest regulation: The port authority must not act as both regulator and service provider in the same port. Piloting services shall either be offered by the port authority or outsourced to private companies. If outsourced, the right to provide piloting services shall be tendered based on fair and non-discriminatory terms in order to promote competition for the market.
13	**Government Ordinance No. 22/1999 on the management of ports and waterways, the usage of freight water transport infrastructures belonging to public ownership and the development of freight water transport activities in ports and inland waterways**	Art. 36 and Art. 37	Sea and coastal freight water transport & fluvial freight water transport	Port tariffs lack transparency. Romanian-flagged vessels may benefit from large discounts compared to foreign-registered vessels. For example, the price list regarding pilotage services available on the Port Administration website states that pilotage tariffs will be reduced by 50% for ships registered in Romanian maritime ports.	Exclusive rights Restricts the geographic flow of goods	The authorised economic operators are paying the same price for using the infrastructure.	The lack of transparency in the calculation of port charges may lead to large-scale abuses by port authorities. Discounts granted to Romanian flagged vessels are in sharp contrast with the principle of non-discrimination based on the grounds of nationality established by EU law. We are aware that, for example, in the port of Consțanta vessels pay very high charges which do not exist in other ports.	Create appropriate legal framework: Port authorities should set their charges based on a transparent methodology which must be cost-oriented and/or in comparison with other ports. Furthermore, the port authorities' autonomy in setting charges should be balanced by the ability to review these charges given to an independent regulator, having the mandate to ensure that competition among port operators is promoted.

Sector: Maritime and inland waterways *(cont.)*

No.	No and title of regulation	Article	Thematic category	Brief description of the potential obstacle	Keyword	Policy maker's objective	Harm to competition	Recommendations
14	**Government Decision No. 83/2003 on authorising commercial companies which provide services of selection and placement of seafarers and inland waterway vessels flying the Romanian or foreign flag, and the establishment of financial security measures in case of withdrawal outside of Romania**	Art. 2, para. 3 lit. f) from the Annex	Sea and coastal freight water transport	Those operators who wish to act as agents of seafarers must receive an authorisation to do business. In order to receive such authorisation it must show that it has already concluded a contract or a pre-contractual agreement with a shipowner. This is chicken-and-egg situation because it is also difficult to get a contract with a shipowner without being a recognised agency.	Authorisation	The requirement is necessary to protect seafarers from bankruptcy or liability.	The requirement of having concluded a contract or a pre-contractual agreement with a shipowner may discourage new entrants in the marketplace by those agents who have the required professional competence to act as seafarers' crewing agents but do not have a contract or a pre-contractual agreement with a shipowner.	Abolish: There is no match between the authorisation requirement and the policy objective since shipowners may always cause liability to seafarers even if these have been employed through an authorised crewing agent.
15	**Order of MoT No. 1447/2008 on technical requirements for inland waterways**	Art.7	Sea and coastal freight water transport	The ANR can grant derogations from the application of all or part of the provisions of the Order to certain categories of inland waterway vessels, depending on vessel capacity.	Authorisation	This provision complies with Art. 7 of Directive No. 2006/87/EC establishing technical requirements for inland waterway vessels. The Directive enables the Member State to grant derogations to certain categories of vessel, but the Romanian law transposing the Directive does not specify any criteria to be met in order to obtain derogation.	The derogation may grant preferential treatment to some operators vis-à-vis others.	Make provision clearer: The law must expressly state the criteria of this Order that a market operator needs to fulfil in order to be granted a derogation from the provisions of this Order.
16	**Order of MoT No. 37/2014 concerning the authorisation of economic operators to carry out public transport of passengers and/or goods by inland waterways**	Art. 2 Annex 1	Sea and Costal freight water transport	The ANR shall establish minimum technical requirements for providing authorisation to freight transport on inland waterway canals.	Authorisation	These technical requirements have been laid out in Order No. 1447/2008 of the Ministry of Transport, with subsequent amendments, which transposes Directive No. 2006/87/EC. This restriction is justified for safety reasons.	The authorisation requirements may prevent market access by economic operators.	No recommendation.
17	**Order of MoT No. 250/2011 on the compliance by Romania with its State flag obligations**	Art. 3 (1)	Sea and Costal freight water transport	Before authorising the use of the Romanian flag, the ANR may take "all necessary measures" to ensure that the ship respects safety provisions established under the applicable international provisions.	Authorisation	These provisions are in line with Art. 4 of EU Directive No. 2009/21/EC regarding state flag obligations for vessels.	The ANR enjoys unnecessary discretion when carrying out this task. This discretion may lead to abuse of power and place some market operators at a competitive disadvantage vis-à-vis others.	Make provision clearer: The law must expressly indicate the activities that the ANR is entitled to implement in order to verify compliance with safety rules by vessels.

Sector: Maritime and inland waterways *(cont.)*

No.	No and title of regulation	Article	Thematic category	Brief description of the potential obstacle	Keyword	Policy maker's objective	Harm to competition	Recommendations
18	**Order of MoT No. 249/2011 on the inspection, technical supervision and certification of maritime vessels under the Romanian flag and carrying out international voyages**	Art. 4 (3)	Sea and coastal freight water transport	The ANR may limit the number of contracts authorising operators to provide technical inspection and surveillance activities for ships flying the Romanian flag.	Barrier to entry	This provision transposes Art. 4 from EU Directive No. 2009/15/CE and is justified to ensure safety and quality of services, but the limitation of the number of authorisations to be issued is not a mandatory requirement.	This provision may act as an unnecessary entry barrier, reducing the number of operators or raising costs. It may also discriminate among shipowners.	Abolish: There should not be any limitation on the number of authorised operators which may provide technical inspection and surveillance activities for ships travelling under the Romanian flag. Make provision clearer: The criteria required in order to become an authorised body shall be published in order to increase transparency.
19	**Order of MoT No. 249/2011 on the inspection, technical supervision and certification of maritime vessels under the Romanian flag and carrying out international voyages**	Art. 6 (1)	Sea and Costal freight water transport	The ANR may suspend or terminate the execution of the special mandate contract concluded with a recognised authorised organisation in charge of inspecting vessels even if this organisation regularly meets the minimum criteria established for such activity under Annex I of EC Regulation No. 391/2009.	Restriction in number of suppliers	The provision transposes Directive No. 2009/15/CE.	The law does not state expressly in which instances the ANR may suspend or terminate the mandate of an organisation authorised to provide inspection services on Romanian-flagged vessels. The Romanian provision imposes requirements, but without specifying them and that may lead to lack of transparency, predictability and possible abuses by the ANR.	Make provision clearer: The law must specify the instances where the ANR is entitled to suspend or terminate the mandate of an organisation authorised to provide inspection services on Romanian-flagged vessels.
20	**Order of MoT No. 251/2011 on establishing the commissions for the coordination of maritime and inland waterway vessel movement in Galați, Brăila and Tulcea ports**	Art. 5	Sea and Costal freight water transport	Economic operators which ensure loading and unloading of goods in the ports of Brăila, Galați and Tulcea must establish their plan for loading and unloading rail wagons on a daily basis with CFR Marfă. Currently, there are other rail freight operators operating in the ports of Galați, Brăila and Tulcea in addition to CFR Marfă and they do not participate in setting the timetable for the activities of loading and unloading of wagons. Therefore, they have to comply with the timetable established by their competitor, CFR Marfă.	Exclusive rights	This provision is not related to ANR competencies. This exclusive right is justified in order to ensure a more efficient use of port logistics.	Other railway operators may be disadvantaged by the fact that the timetable for loading and unloading rail wagons in the ports mentioned is established by CFR Marfă, their competitor.	Abolish: The provision should be abolished and the timetable for loading and unloading rail wagons should be established by committees co-ordinating the movement of maritime and inland waterway vessels and ships in the ports of Gala?i, Br?ila and Tulcea so that all rail freight operators transporting goods in these ports may benefit from equivalent and non-discriminatory conditions.

Sector: Maritime and inland waterways *(cont.)*

No.	No and title of regulation	Article	Thematic category	Brief description of the potential obstacle	Keyword	Policy maker's objective	Harm to competition	Recommendations
21	**Government Decision No. 1105/2007 approving the Methodological Norms for enforcement of the provisions of Appendix VI to the International Convention for the Prevention of Pollution from Ships MARPOL 1973/1978**	Art. 49 and Art. 50	Sea and coastal freight water transport	If an authority included in the MARPOL list establishes that inadequate fuel has been supplied from Romania, the ANR may, before suspending or withdrawing its authorisation, warn the supplier to adopt remedies in order to bring the fuel to the required standard.	Standards for product quality	The warning measure was not intended to be a form of preferential treatment for bunkering companies. Warning is administered depending on the gravity of the situation and is done for the purpose of gradually remedying the damage produced by the bunkering company.	This provision may provide a more advantageous treatment for bunkering companies and seems to grant the ANR unnecessary discretion on whether a company may be sanctioned for supplying inadequate fuel.	Amend the provision: Art. 50 para. 2 should be amended in order to clearly establish the instances in which a warning is a measure proportional and adequate to be taken, as well as the instances that require the suspension or withdrawal of the company's authorisation, as the current provision may lead to a discretionary use of power by the ANR.
22	**Order of MoT No. 1894/2002 on the approval of the guidelines on State control for ships flying the Romanian flag**	Annex	Sea and Costal freight water transport	The rules concerning the development of the control activity of Romanian-flagged vessels are not published and access is restricted.	Lack of transparency	These rules are published in MO 750 bis/2014.	This provision grants unguided discretion to the ANR which may lead to discriminatory treatment of operators and abuse of power by the ANR.	No recommendation.
23	**Order of MoT No. 558/2003 on the replacement of the appendix to the Order of MoT No. 1894/2002 on the approval of the guidelines on the State control on ships flying the Romanian flag**	Annex	Sea and Costal freight water transport	The rules concerning the development of the control activity of Romanian flagged vessels are not published and access is restricted.	Lack of transparency	These rules are published in MO 750 bis/2014.	This provision grants unguided discretion to the ANR which may lead to discriminatory treatment of operators and abuse of power by the ANR.	No recommendation.
24	**Order of MoT No. 288/1999 on the approval of the technical guidelines on maritime constructions**	Annex	Sea and coastal freight water transport	The technical standards for shipbuilding are not published and access is restricted.	Lack of transparency	These technical standards are published on the ANR website (*http://portal.rna.ro/Pagini/Legisla%C8%9Bie/Certificare-tehnica-nave.aspx*).	This provision may lead to discriminatory treatment of operators and abuse of power by the competent authority.	No recommendation.
25	**Decision No. 492/2003 on the organisation and functioning of the Lower Danube River Administration A.A. Galați**	Art. 5	Sea and coastal freight water transport	Although the legislation establishes the obligation for AFDJ to ensure navigable conditions of the Danube, often it does not fulfil this task. Thus, the circulation of vessels on the Danube is hampered, especially in periods when its water level is low. AFDJ Galați operates as an autonomous administration under the MoT and serves as a waterways authority on the Romanian sector of the Danube.	Poor quality of infrastructure	Dredging the Danube is difficult because most of this river belongs to both Romania and Bulgaria. Port authorities do dredge their ports in order to respect the depth indicated in safety threshold rules established by the ANR. The ANR is also responsible for granting derogations over safety issues related to the navigation of the Danube.	Navigational conditions on the Danube vary from one period to another, depending on weather conditions particularly due to dry seasons. If the Danube is not dredged, competition may be distorted. A low depth sailing line favours ships with low draft over those with higher draft.	Create appropriate legal framework: MoT must provide an enforcement system, including sanctions, against failure to dredge the Danube by the designated authority.

Sector: Food

No.	No and title of Regulation	Article	Thematic category	Brief description of potential obstacles	Keyword	Policy maker's objectives	Harm to competition	Recommendations
1	**Law No. 312/2003 on the production and use of vegetables**	Art. 9, Art. 10 par. 2 and Art. 11	Food processing framework legislation	Selling of vegetables, melons and mushrooms in traditional markets, street markets or markets organised on special occasions triggers the following consequences: i) small producers are not obliged to comply with the rules on classification of products in accordance with commercial standards and ii) small producers, natural persons, are not required to issue invoices for the products sold (instead, they use a trading booklet). Notions of small producer, traditional market and street market are different from the terms used by Law No. 145/2014 for establishing measures to regulate the market sale of agricultural products.	Discrimination	Law No. 145/2014 for establishing measures to regulate the market of agricultural products is a recent piece of legislation and most probably the law maker did not make reference to the old legislation in force.	Lack of corroboration between two pieces of legislation and usage of different notions for similar aspects, in practice, triggers uncertainty among producers/ traders. While we have no issues with respect to exempting small producers from some obligations in order to avoid excessive burdens on their part, lack of definition of the terms "small producer", "traditional markets", "street markets" might lead to arbitrary and possibly abusive interpretation in practice.	Ensure a unitary regulation of these notions and amend Law No. 312/2003 on the production and use of vegetables in order to use the same wording as under Law No. 145/2014 for establishing measures to regulate the market of agricultural products.
2	**Law No. 491/2003 on medicinal and aromatic plants and hive products**	Art. 3 par. 5	Food processing framework legislation	The legal provision contains a drafting error and makes reference to an article which does not relate to the subject matter i.e. Art. 695 instead of Art. 699 of Law No. 95/2006 regarding health system reform.	Barrier to entry	The correct reference has not been updated after republishing of Law No. 95/2006 regarding health system reform.	Economic operators are unable to identify the applicable legal provisions.	Amend the legislation and make the correct reference to Art. 699 of Law No. 95/2006 regarding health system reform.
3	**Emergency Ordinance No. 97/2001 on regulating the production, circulation and marketing of food**	Art. 7	Food hygiene	Foodstuffs may only be produced/ processed/ stored/ transported and sold by staff with specific qualifications, meaning "sufficient" knowledge of public health, food hygiene, work hygiene, attested by a certificate issued after completion of a training course and passing of an exam (e.g. the cost of the training course and the exam fee is approximately EUR 20 while the duration could be up to 17 hours). The course should be repeated every three years. Upon discussions with MADR, it appears that the domestic legislation has the same provisions as various CE Regulations (such as CE Regulation 1333/2008, CE Regulation 853/ 2004, CE Regulation 1881/2006).	Excessive measure	The policy maker's objective is to protect public safety, as there are persons coming in contact with food products and who might risk contaminating the products they handle. Moreover, the official recital received from the authorities states that Emergency Ordinance No. 97/2001 on regulating the production, circulation and marketing of food should be entirely abolished since it represents domestic legislation that was not expressly abolished after entry into force of EC Regulations which are directly applicable in Romania as of 1 January 2007. For example, the definition of food additives foreseen by the considered domestic piece of legislation is also to be found in EC Regulation 1333/2008, the definition of foodstuffs of animal origin is also foreseen by EC Regulation 853/2004.	Having all staff trained and accredited significantly increases the costs for the employers and also limits the employment market. The impact is with respect to those traders who are not dividing people based on attributions and thus have to train all personnel. The text does not differentiate between staff working with packaged/non-packaged foodstuffs – i.e. the same requirements apply to those coming into direct contact with packaged and non-packaged foodstuffs, for those involved in the food processing chain and for those merely transporting the foodstuffs.	Abolish provisions which are double regulated. For employees not coming in direct contact with the unpackaged foodstuffs, the conditions should be abolished. Maintain the obligation to follow public health, food hygiene, work hygiene training courses only for employees coming in direct contact with the unpackaged foodstuffs. For that purpose, clearly define activities which do not involve direct contact with foodstuffs (e.g. transportation, storage and sales personnel).

Sector: Food *(cont.)*

No.	No and title of Regulation	Article	Thematic category	Brief description of potential obstacles	Keyword	Policy maker's objectives	Harm to competition	Recommendations
4	**Government Decision No. 924/2005 on the approval of the general rules for food hygiene**	Entire act	Food hygiene	Upon discussions with MADR, it appears that the domestic legislation has the same objective as Regulation (EC) No. 852/2004 regarding food hygiene, thus dual pieces of legislation are applicable. The EU Regulation is directly applicable in Romania and, as such, there is no need for transposition into the domestic legislation.	Dual regulation	Domestic legislation was not expressly abolished after entrance in force of EC Regulation No. 852/2004 which is directly applicable in Romania as of 1 January 2007.	It is unclear for companies active in the field what legislation is in force.	Abolish provisions which are redundant in light of EU legislation. The abolishment of the provisions which are double regulated shall not interfere with the possibility of having a code of conduct for market participants.
5	**Government Decision No. 1156/2013 approving sanitary veterinary actions included in the Programme for surveillance, prevention, control and eradication of animal diseases, of those transmissible from animals to humans, animal and environmental protection, identification and registration of bovines, swine, sheep, goats and equines, of the actions stipulated in the Program for food safety supervision and control, and related charges**	Chapter II, Section 1, par. 3	Food processing framework legislation	The veterinary testing of animal feed is mandatory; non-compliance with such an obligation being sanctioned with a fine. Costs for sampling, transport and analysis of probes for veterinary tests are borne by the Sanitary Veterinary and Food Safety National Authority (ANSVSA) for locally produced animal feed, but the same cost for imported animal feed is borne by the importer.	Discrimination	The policy maker's objective is to encourage use of animal feed coming from domestic producers.	Producers of animal feed from EU Member States are at a disadvantage compared to domestic producers as Romanian farmers are more inclined to opt for domestic animal feed given the exemption from paying the testing costs (e.g. farmers are more inclined to use domestic animal feed as the costs for the veterinary testing are borne by the ANSVSA while for imported animal feed, the testing costs are borne by the farmers themselves). There are possible state aid implications for the farmers who use domestic animal feed.	Option 1. Amend the legislation to have equal treatment for all animal feed produced in EU Member States and sold to Romanian farmers, thus the government would also pay for the imported animal feed. Option 2. Abolish the provision, thus making all operators pay the tax.
6	**Order No. 43/2003 for approval of Sanitary veterinary norms regarding the criteria applicable for meat producing enterprises that do not have an industrial structure or production capacity**	Entire act	Food hygiene	Upon discussions with MADR, it appears that the order contains provisions which have the same objective as EU legislation on hygiene and safety of foodstuffs which is directly applicable in Romania, namely EC Regulation 178/2002, EC Reg. 852/2004, EC Reg. 853/2004, EC Reg. 2073/2005 which provide the microbiologic criteria for the foodstuffs, as well as for sampling for laboratory analysis. The official controls carried out in the food processing sector are regulated by EC Regulation 882/2004. The EU Regulation is directly applicable in Romania and as such, there is no need for transposition into domestic legislation.	Dual regulation	Domestic legislation was not expressly abolished after entry into force of EC Regulation No. 852/2004 which is directly applicable in Romania as of 1 January 2007.	It is unclear for companies active in the field what legislation is in force.	Abolish provisions which are double regulated.

Sector: Food *(cont.)*

No.	No and title of Regulation	Article	Thematic category	Brief description of potential obstacles	Keyword	Policy maker's objectives	Harm to competition	Recommendations
7	**Order No. 43/2003 for approval of Sanitary veterinary norms regarding the criteria applicable for meat producing enterprises that do not have an industrial structure or production capacity**	Art. 1	Food hygiene	Enterprises producing less than 7.5 tonnes of meat per week or 1 tonne of fatty liver per week shall benefit from derogations in Art. 9 par. 1 and 2 of Sanitary veterinary norms regarding health conditions for production and commercialisation of meat products and other animal products, approved by Order No. 322/ 2003, issued by the Ministry for Agriculture and Rural Development. However, the norms including the derogations referred to in the legal provision have been abrogated and we have not been able to identify any equivalent derogations in the legal provisions in force. It is our understanding that currently, such derogations do not apply in practice. Furthermore, ANSVSA is currently the regulating authority in the sanitary-veterinary field and not the Ministry for Agriculture and Rural Development, as stated in the Order.	Barrier to entry	The Order was issued prior to Romania's accession to the EU and it has not been subsequently amended.	Considering that such derogations are not applicable in practice and reference is made to a normative act which has been abolished, the mere existence of a legal provision mentioning a derogation creates uncertainty among market participants. Abolishing the derogation does not interfere with the factual situation on the market as it is not currently applicable.	Abolish.
8	**Order No. 91/2005 approving the Sanitary veterinary norm laying down the rules applicable to regular checks on the general state of hygiene, carried out by facility operators, in accordance with the Sanitary veterinary norm on health conditions for production and marketing of fresh meat, approved by Order No. 401/2002, and with the Sanitary veterinary norm on health problems regulating the production and marketing of fresh poultry meat, approved by Order No. 402/2002**	Entire act	Food hygiene	Upon discussions with MADR, it appears that the Order contains provisions which have the same objective as EU legislation on hygiene and safety of foodstuffs which is directly applicable in Romania, namely EC Regulation 178/2002, EC Reg. 852/2004, EC Reg. 853/ 2004, EC Reg. 2073/2005 which provide the microbiologic criteria for the foodstuffs, as well as for sampling for laboratory analysis. The official controls carried out in the food processing sector are regulated by EC Regulation 882/2004.The EU Regulation is directly applicable in Romania and as such, there is no need for transposition into the domestic legislation.	Dual regulation	Domestic legislation was not expressly abolished after entrance in force of EC regulations which are directly applicable in Romania as of 1 January 2007.	It is unclear for companies active in the field what legislation is in force.	Abolish provisions which are double regulated.

Sector: Food *(cont.)*

No.	No and title of Regulation	Article	Thematic category	Brief description of potential obstacles	Keyword	Policy maker's objectives	Harm to competition	Recommendations
9	**Order No. 91/2005 approving the Sanitary veterinary norm laying down the rules applicable to regular checks on the general state of hygiene, carried out by facility operators, in accordance with the Sanitary veterinary norm on health conditions for production and marketing of fresh meat, approved by Order No. 401/2002, and with the Sanitary veterinary norm on health problems regulating the production and marketing of fresh poultry meat, approved by Order No. 402/2002**	Annex I, Art. I par. 2	Food hygiene	The frequency of testing in factories of low production and factories without continuous activity may be lower, as decided by the official veterinary doctor. There is no definition for factories of low production.	Discrimination	Some exceptions are necessary in order to avoid excessive burdens in case of factories of low production.	Establishing what factories have low production with the veterinary doctor without establishing clear directions may lead, in practice, to arbitrary decisions.	Abolish as indicated under point above but assess the possibility of keeping such an exemption under another piece of legislation, if this is the state decision.
10	**Order No. 203/2006 on the approval of the Sanitary veterinary norm laying down special conditions for the marketing of aquaculture animals species and their products deemed not susceptible to certain diseases**	Annex 2 letter g)	Aquaculture animals	A transport document must be obtained for the transportation of aquaculture animals (any aquatic animal at all stages of its life, including eggs and gametes grown in a farm or in a shellfish farming area) and their products. With the exception of naval transport, the document for all other types of transport is valid for a fixed 10-day time period. In case of naval transport, the validity period is extended over the navigation period.	Geographical division of market	The order transposes the provisions of EC Decision 2003/390/CE which under letter g) Annex II establishes the same validity term of 10 days for the transport permit, with the exception of naval transport for which the validity term is prolonged for the duration of the transport.	Discrimination with regard to the validity period of the transport document favours naval transport for long distances in case of international transports. This is detrimental to all other types of transports. Considering that storage conditions may be implemented which ensure adequate preservation of aquaculture animals and their products, the discrimination seems arbitrary and unjust.	No recommendation for change.
11	**Order No. 78/2003 approving the Sanitary veterinary norm regarding exceptions to the Sanitary veterinary norm on health conditions governing the production and marketing of meat products and of other animal origin food products used for certain products containing other foodstuffs and only a small percentage of meat or meat products**	Entire act	Products of animal origin	Upon discussions with MADR, it appears that the Order contains provisions which have the same objective as EU legislation on hygiene and safety of foodstuffs which is directly applicable in Romania, namely EC Reg.178/2002, EC Reg. 852/2004, EC Reg. 853/2004, EC Reg. 2073/2005 etc. The EU Regulation is directly applicable in Romania and as such, there is no need for transposition into domestic legislation.	Dual regulation	Domestic legislation was not expressly abolished after entry into force of EC Regulations which are directly applicable in Romania as of 1 January 2007.	It is unclear for companies active in the field what legislation is in force.	Abolish provisions which are double regulated.

Sector: Food *(cont.)*

No.	No and title of Regulation	Article	Thematic category	Brief description of potential obstacles	Keyword	Policy maker's objectives	Harm to competition	Recommendations
12	**Order No. 78/2003 approving the Sanitary veterinary norm regarding exceptions to the Sanitary veterinary norm on health conditions governing the production and marketing of meat products and of other animal origin food products used for certain products containing other foodstuffs and only a small percentage of meat or meat products**	Art. 1 and Art. 2	Products of animal origin	Products containing meat ingredients up to 10% are granted exceptions regarding the sanitary veterinary authorisation conditions applicable to enterprises producing and commercialising meat products. The conditions under which the exception is granted are contained in Order No. 322/2003 which has been abolished. In their place new norms have been adopted for transposition of EU Directive No. 2002/99/EC.	Barrier to entry	The Order was issued prior to Romania's accession to the EU and it has not been subsequently amended.	It is unclear for the economic operators what legislation is applicable, considering the abolishment of Order No. 322/2003.	Abolish as indicated under point 11 above.
13	**Ministerial Order No. 100/2004 approving the Sanitary veterinary norm laying down the additional conditions on the sanitary veterinary control of fishery products, crustaceans, molluscs, gastropods and batrachians for direct marketing to the final consumer or for food processing for human consumption**	Art. 5	Fish products	The sale of fishery products i) outside of built and authorised areas or ii) in the same units or specially designated spaces together with other animal or vegetable products is prohibited.	Barrier to entry	The policy maker's objective is to ensure no contamination between food products takes place. Due to the high risk of perishability, keeping separate flows from other foods, as well as minimum standards on marketing are essential to protect public health.	The prohibitions may represent barriers to entry on the market as they entail higher costs for commercialising fish products than for other types of food products. The interdiction is not justified as regards the packaged products which do not present a risk of contamination.	The interdiction should be eliminated as regards the packaged products as long as risks of contamination are not present.
14	**Emergency Ordinance No. 23/2008 regarding fishing and aquaculture**	Art. 41, Art. 2 point 22 and Art. 64 h)	Fish products	The first sale of fish products on the national territory can only take place through authorised centres of first sale (private enterprises within which natural persons or companies, authorised for commercialisation of fish products, purchase the fish products and issue a sale note containing the quantity purchased and the purchase price), approved by Order of the Ministry of Agriculture and Rural Development. The purchasers of the fish products or the manager of the authorised centre must report all sales notes monthly to the National Agency for Fishing and Aquaculture. Although the legal provision makes reference to the Ministry of Agriculture and Rural Development, the public authority responsible in the field is ANSVSA. The authority is under the control of the Ministry of Agriculture and Rural Development.	Price fixing	This provision is in line with the requirements of the Common Fisheries Policy approved by Council and Parliament effective from 1 January 2014. This states that the first sale must take place at the first sale centres authorised by the competent authorities. This provision aims at tackling illegal, unregulated and unreported (IUU) fishing practices.	The trading of fish products might be limited.	No recommendation for change.

Sector: Food *(cont.)*

No.	No and title of Regulation	Article	Thematic category	Brief description of potential obstacles	Keyword	Policy maker's objectives	Harm to competition	Recommendations
15	**Order No. 420/2008 establishing State Inspection Powers for the Technical Control of Vegetable and Fruit Production and Use**	Art. 6 par. 3	Fruit and vegetables	State Inspection of Technical Control in Production and Trade of fruit and vegetables (subordinated to the Ministry of Agriculture and Rural Development), in charge of controlling quality standards, may establish a "simplified" control scheme for those traders dealing with fruit and vegetable exports if they meet a set of requirements, including offering "sufficient" guarantees of a constant and high rate of conformity. There is no clear indication to what a simplified control scheme means. However, upon discussions with MADR it is our understanding that it should be read as a "self-control" procedure as it is regulated under Order 390/2009 establishing the licensing methodology for self-control of the operators in the fruit and vegetable sector.	Discrimination	The lawmaker aimed to ensure the possibility of allocating a different level of resources for controlling activity by the merchant, based on their prior compliance with imposed standards. The provision is in line with Art. 6 of EU Reg. 852/2004 and Art. 31 of EU Reg. 882/2004.	In practice, the legal provision may leave room for abuses and corruption as it does not clearly indicate what the terms "high conformity rate", "sufficient guarantees" or "simplified control scheme" mean. Lack of corroboration between this piece of legislation and Order 390/2009 establishing the licensing methodology for self-control of operators in the fruit and vegetable sector creates uncertainty among undertakings.	Amend the legislation in order to clearly link it with Order 390/2009, when the simplified control scheme applies and to stipulate criteria for establishing sufficient means in terms of the conformity rate.
16	**Law No. 297/2013 on establishing contractual relations in the milk and milk products sector, as well as acknowledgement of milk and milk products manufacturing organisations**	Art. 3	Raw milk	For the first sale of raw milk for collection, storage, processing and packaging, the seller and the buyer must sign a contract with a mandatory duration of 6 months. The mandatory 6-month duration may be waived with the consent of the seller.	Limitation of options	The minimum 6-month period of a contract is in accordance with the provisions of EC Reg. 1308/2013, Art. 148 para. (4) that stipulates this minimum term. The necessity for this minimum 6-month period comes from the inferior and dependent position that farmers have vis-à-vis the first buyers of milk. The provision was introduced to balance the asymmetry of bargaining power between farmers and processors, because milk is perishable and it cannot be stored.	The buyer in the first sale of raw milk is forced by the legal provisions to sign a contract valid for 6 months. Due to such provisions, the buyer cannot freely change the provider of raw milk unless he obtains the consent of the producer. However, the duration of the agreement in itself does not guarantee any placement of orders by the buyers unless quantities have been agreed under the agreement.	No recommendation for change.
17	**Order No. 721/2009 on the approval of the Measures plan to improve the quality of raw cow's milk**	Art. 1	Raw milk	For ensuring an appropriate quality of raw milk for commercialisation, economic operators active in the production, collection and processing of milk must fulfill certain obligations for compliance with quality and safety standards provided by Regulation (EC) No. 853/2004. Producers of milk are not held to the same standards are allowed to sell small quantities of raw milk to consumers without observing such obligations. Separately, the term "small quantities" of raw milk is not defined in the legislation. As mentioned under EC Regulation 853/2004, Community rules should not apply where small quantities of primary products or of certain types of meat are supplied directly by the food business operator producing them for the final consumer or to a local retail establishment, a case where public health should be protected through national law.	Discrimination	Small producers were exempted from some obligations in order to avoid excessive burdens from their side. Moreover, according to ANSVSA Order 111/2008, small producers selling small quantities of milk directly to final consumers have to be registered with the state authorities in order to perform this activity. The same piece of legislation foresees all obligations and standards that have to be respected by the small producers and it defines what small quantities of milk refer to.	In the absence of a clear definition, there could be a technical problem in determining what quantities may be seen as small quantities that are not proportionate or justified. The lack of proportionality may limit certain suppliers from providing their products and create barriers to entry.	Make reference to the provisions of Order No. 111/2008 enacted by ANSVSA which define the notion of small quantities.

Sector: Food *(cont.)*

No.	No and title of Regulation	Article	Thematic category	Brief description of potential obstacles	Keyword	Policy maker's objectives	Harm to competition	Recommendations
18	**Order No. 1186/2014 approving the technical implementation norms for the Methodological Norms for enforcement of Law No. 297/2013 on establishing contractual relations in the milk and milk products sector, as well as acknowledgement of milk and milk products manufacturing organisations approved by G.D. No. 441/2014 on specific conditions to be met by manufacturing organisations from the milk and milk product/ producer organisation associations in contractual relations, as well as the technical criteria for their acknowledgment for negotiation purposes, provided by (EU) Reg. 1308/2013 of the European Parliament and Council of 16 December 2013 establishing a common organisation of agricultural product markets and repealing EEC Reg. No. 922/72, EEC 234/79, EC 1037/ 2001 and EC 1234/2007**	Art. 2 par. 4 c)	Dairy products	Voting rights in a producers' organisation are determined proportionately to the contribution of each producer to the organisation's production. However, members of a producers' organisation are prohibited from controlling more than 49% of all voting rights in the organisation. It is not mentioned under the legislation how often this information is exchanged, most probably the statute of each organisation regulates how often/ when such an exchange of information occurs.	Discrimination/ excessive restriction	The policy maker's objective was to prohibit the control of a producers' organisation by a single undertaking, as in such a case the purpose of protecting the interests of all the members of the organisation may be undermined.	When assessing collectively the voting rights in order to determine the contribution of each member, in practice, the provision might trigger exchanges of sensitive information between milk producers with respect to their production capabilities.	Option 1. Amend the legislation so as to be used in calculation solely historical data concerning the previous year. Option 2. The voting might be done based on thresholds established by the associations.

Sector: Food *(cont.)*

No.	No and title of Regulation	Article	Thematic category	Brief description of potential obstacles	Keyword	Policy maker's objectives	Harm to competition	Recommendations
19	**Government Decision No. 699/2009 establishing the measures contained in common market organisation in the grain sector**	Art. 10 par. 4	Grain mill products, starches and starch products	Grain warehouse operators must ensure grain is stored by the Payment and Agriculture Intervention Agency (PAIA) following an intervention on the grain market, with a wire transfer, a bank letter guarantee in favour of PAIA for 200% of the value of the grain, or an insurance policy for the value of the grain.	Barrier to entry	The intention was to ensure that the PAIA would be able to recover all its losses if the grain stored deteriorated or was destroyed. The official stand is that the value of the warranty is a reasonable one for Romania to make up for the losses incurred. The arguments taken into consideration by the authorities when establishing this level of guarantee are: a) The price of the grain eligible for the intervention measure has fluctuated in the last 10 years between 80% of the intervention price up to values of almost 3 times higher than the same intervention price; b) The high stock value of the grain and the high risks of quantitative or qualitative losses during storage; c) The lack of experience in implementing intervention measures and the fact that in Romania, traditionally, technological losses higher than the 0.2% accepted by EU legislation; d) The fact that the value of the lost cereals is set in accordance with Annex X and XI of EC Reg. 884/2006 (5% is added to the current market value); e) The value of the lost grain is reimbursed to the European Commission or it is diminished from the value that the Member State is entitled to receive; Moreover, the grain house operators subject to this provision must undergo a procurement procedure and adhere to a contract. Hence, it is not a mandatory provision for all warehouse operators.	Taking into account that grain warehouses generally have large and very large capacities, the condition of submitting a guarantee of 200% of the value of the goods in storage involves extremely high costs and may severely limit access to the market for new economic operators. There is no explanation why the insurance policy may be concluded for the value of the grain but other guarantees need to equal the value of 200 % of the quantity.	Assess the opportunity to decrease the value of the guarantee from 200 % so as not to constitute a barrier to entry on the market.
20	**Order No. 392/2013 establishing the conditions to be met by business operators marketing bakery products in Romania and Order No. 976/1998 approving the Hygiene Norms concerning the production, processing, storage, preservation, transport and marketing of food**	Order No. 392/2013 – Art. 8 Order No. 976/1998 – Art. 50 par. 6	Bakery products	Bakery products must be sold in specially designated areas of the stores and must be distinctly separated from other food products. Moreover, as regards bread, any area designated for sale should be a minimum of 10 m^2. The legislation does not differentiate between packaged and unpackaged bakery products. The provision might be too strict considering that other products, from which contamination might come, are generally packaged and as such, contamination is highly unlikely.	Barrier to entry	The policy maker's objective was to safeguard public health, avoiding contamination of bakery products, which are regularly sold without packaging, from other food or chemical products.	Requiring bakery products to be sold in specially designated areas with a predetermined minimum area size, may create barriers for operators which sell bakery products as well as discrimination between producers of bakery products and producers of other food products. Operators which sell bakery products might be disadvantaged by imposing the obligation to arrange a special area for commercialisation of bakery products. Producers of other food products might be disadvantaged in comparison with producers of bakery products by granting bakery products special status among food products due to their distinct marketing.	Amend the legislation so as to abolish the minimum size of 10m^2 of the specially designated area for sale of bakery products.

Sector: Food *(cont.)*

No.	No and title of Regulation	Article	Thematic category	Brief description of potential obstacles	Keyword	Policy maker's objectives	Harm to competition	Recommendations
21	**Order No. 392/2013 establishing the conditions to be met by business operators marketing bakery products in Romania and Order No. 976/1998 approving the Hygiene Norms concerning the production, processing, storage, preservation, transport and marketing of food**	Art. 9	Bakery products	Compliance with rules on bakery products is verified by the National Authority for Consumer Protection, while compliance of observance of rules on bread is verified by inspectors from Public Health Directorates.	Barrier to entry	We were not able to identify the objective of such a provision.	With respect to the verification of compliance with the legal provisions, two different authorities with such competence may create confusion for market participants.	A sole control authority should be decided, no double check should be allowed for the observance of the same obligations.
22	**Order No. 358/2003 approving the Norms on quality and sanitation parameters for the production, import, quality control, marketing and use of simple concentrated fodder, combined feed additives, pre-mixes, energetic substances, minerals and special fodder**	Art. 33	Mixed fodders	In order to be able to operate the production of fodder, the producers must have a manufacturing licence. This licence is issued by the General Directorate for Agriculture and Food Industry in the county where they are based. However there is no deadline specified for the approval of the application. It is our understanding that in practice, the general administrative deadline is used (i.e. 30-day term), during which the public authorities should respond to any petition.	Unclear legal provision	The Ministry of Agriculture and Rural Development has not received any complaints as to delays for issuing the licence in 30 days.	The manufacturing licence is mandatory for a fodder producer in order to operate. Not having a deadline for approving applications might generate abusive behaviour from the issuing authority, thereby creating a barrier to entry into the market for new operators.	Amend the legislation and stipulate a maximum period during which the producer's application would be analysed and the licence would be issued.
23	**Law No.101/2014 on regulatory measures for the storage of edible seeds and their storage certificate regime**	Art. 4 par. 2, Art. 6 par. 1	Warehousing	Operators running facilities for storage of edible seeds must obtain a licence in order to obtain deposit certificates useful in obtaining further bank loans. The licence is granted by the competent ministry at the proposal of a commission composed of 15 members (4 members designated by the ministry and 11 members designated by industry associations and the commodities exchanges), which verifies the reports and documentation regarding the technical and financial conditions for the issuance of the licence.	Licence	The Commission also has other attributions such as approving the average price of edible grains on the market, designating administrators of the deposits, etc. To cover such a large sector as well as for transparency reasons, the Commission is made up of representatives of stakeholders across the sector (producers, storage providers, sellers, processors, stock exchange markets, ANSVSA, etc).	This provision may trigger i) exchanges of information between competitors ii) potential barriers to entry on the market as a competitor is involved in the approval process and iii) administrative barriers due to a tendency of standardisation of interests/actions in cases where the same associations are dictating their own interests. In addition, a commission formed of 15 members seems to be too much for issuance of a licence.	The legislation should be amended to avoid possible conflicts of interest, for example, by authorising the Ministry to issue the deposit licences or by ensuring that the majority of Commission members are appointed by the Ministry.
24	**Law No.101/2014 on regulatory measures for the storage of edible seeds and their storage certificate regime**	Art. 14 par. 3	Warehousing	Entities operating storage facilities for edible seeds must ensure the publication and update of the deposit fees used at every deposit location.	Disclosure	Publishing the fees ensures transparency and allows those interested to choose the preferred storage facility. In addition, publication of such a fee protects farmers against local market power.	Publication of fees for deposit may favour alignment between operators of deposits of edible seeds and as a consequence distort the fees determined by the market.	No recommendation for change.

Sector: Food *(cont.)*

No.	No and title of Regulation	Article	Thematic category	Brief description of potential obstacles	Keyword	Policy maker's objectives	Harm to competition	Recommendations
25	**Law No. 150/2004 on safety of aliments and food for animals**	Entire act	Food and animal food safety	The law transposes Regulation (EC) No. 178/2002 laying down the general principles and requirements of food law, establishing the European Food Safety Authority and laying down procedures in matters of food safety. Thus, two pieces of legislation are applicable, with the same objective. The EU Regulation is directly applicable in Romania and as such, there is no need for transposition into domestic legislation.	Barrier to entry	Law 150/2004 partially transposes EC Reg. 178/2002 and was issued to set the legal framework for setting up the competent authority in the field of food safety (ANSVSA) and to establish that this authority is the liaison institution for the Food Safety European Authority.	It is unclear for companies active in the field what legislation is in force.	Abolish provisions which are double regulated.
26	**Order No. 113/2008 on the approval of Instructions for the organisation and performance of official control activity in manufacturing, processing, storage, transport, exploitation and marketing facilities food products and sub-products of non-animal origin**	Art. 8, Art. 9, Art.14	Products of non-animal origin	The Sanitary Veterinary and Food Safety Department (ANSVSA) is responsible for the controls related to sanitary veterinary authorisations. ANSVSA charges the economic operators for the official controlling activity, thus generating extra budgetary income used for covering the costs of ANSVSA related to the controlling activity performed. There is no provision referring to the possibility of carrying out the controls with another laboratory. The Order is in force until December 2016.	Controls	The applicable control procedure is in line with EU Regulation No. 882/2004. The general principle stated in the EU regulation when referring to coverage of costs for official controls is that the Member States must ensure financial resources through any means they consider necessary, including taxation or fees, as mentioned in align. (32) of the Regulation preamble. The objective of the provisions is the safety of the foodstuffs and the general health of the population. The objective of the request for fees in exchange for mandatory controls is to ensure a sufficient workforce across all regions of the country and also to ensure coverage of costs for lab tests.	The law establishes a cost borne by the economic operator for a mandatory control that, under normal circumstance, the operator might not have requested.	No recommendation for change.

Sector: Food *(cont.)*

No.	No and title of Regulation	Article	Thematic category	Brief description of potential obstacles	Keyword	Policy maker's objectives	Harm to competition	Recommendations
27	**Order No. 57/2010 approving the Sanitary veterinary norm regarding the sanitary veterinary licensing of facilities for the production, storage, transport and/or distribution of products of animal origin**	Annex- Norm Art.3, Art. 4	Products of animal origin	The law establishes the obligation to obtain a sanitary veterinary licence from ANSVSA for facilities for the production, storage, transport and/or distribution of products of animal origin. Following the licensing process, the licensed units are subject to controls. An undertaking amongst those that are the objective of the norm, in order to be operational, must obtain from ANSVSA: * a statement of conformity before being built (for new facilities) * a conditional licence * a licence to be able to operate intra-community * a regular licence (after the conditional one) valid as long as the sanitary veterinary regulations are observed. Each time a licence is requested, the company must submit similar documents to the same authority and pay a fee.	Licence	The licences mentioned are foreseen by EU legislation, namely Art. 31 of EU Reg. No. 882/2004. According to discussions held with MADR, local sanitary-veterinary authorities have received instructions from ANSVSA for clarifying the content and the application of Order No. 57/2010. Moreover, national guides of good practice can be developed according to Art. 8 of EC Regulation 852/2004. When these national guides are developed, according to the same article, they are developed and disseminated by food business sectors in consultation with representatives of parties whose interests may be substantially affected, as defined by the regulation. National guides are developed under the aegis of a national standards institute. Member States shall forward to the Commission national guides. The Commission shall set up and run a registration system for such guides and make it available to Member States. These guides are to be found in the Register for National Guides to Good Practice together with other guides issued by the EC – *http://ec.europa.eu/food/food/biosafety/hygienelegislation/good_practice_en.htm.*	The law is ambiguous regarding the procedure for obtaining a sanitary-veterinary licence. The law refers to different types of sanitary veterinary licences that may be issued by the ANSVSA, and it is not clear which should be obtained first, which second, which is optional (if any). The lack of clarity may leave room for different interpretations. Also, it is not clear whether the conditional licence and the licence to be able to operate intra-community can be combined, or whether they are alternatives.	Publish on ANSVSA`s web-page the instructions sent to the local sanitary-veterinary authorities meant to clarify the content and the application of Order No. 57/2010 for economic operators. Eliminate requests for documents previously requested/issued by ANSVSA.
28	**Order No. 57/2010 approving the Sanitary veterinary norm regarding the sanitary veterinary licensing of facilities for the production, storage, transport and/or distribution of products of animal origin**	Annex – Norm – Art. 3 par. 4-6	Products of animal origin	Before building any of the facilities mentioned by the Norm, a formal, written statement of conformity needs to be obtained from ANSVSA. Conformity with sanitary veterinary legislation is sought with regard to the planned location of the facility, the activities to take place in the facility, the building plan of the facilities, workflows, equipment and machinery. No deadline is set for granting/denying such approval. In practice the same deadline is applied as the one provided under Art. 6 of the same piece of legislation which states that the authorisation request will be settled 15 working days from the date of registration of the request).	Licence	No policy maker objective has been identified. According to the discussions held with MADR, instructions have been sent to the local sanitary-veterinary authorities regarding the application of Order No. 57/2010.	No deadline is set for granting/denying the written statement of conformity for new facilities which might lead to various time limits for various companies and a discriminatory approach.	Amend legislation in order to make it clear that the request for a written statement of conformity must be settled by the authority in the term provided for responding to the authorisation request.

Sector: Food *(cont.)*

No.	No and title of Regulation	Article	Thematic category	Brief description of potential obstacles	Keyword	Policy maker's objectives	Harm to competition	Recommendations
29	**Order No. 57/2010 approving the Sanitary veterinary norm regarding the sanitary veterinary licensing of facilities for the production, storage, transport and/or distribution of animal origin products**	Annex – Norm – Art. 3 par.7	Products of animal origin	Any modifications to the initial approved technological workflow of the facilities mentioned by the Norm must be further approved by ANSVSA. No time limit is set for granting/denying such approval. In practice the same deadline is applied as the one provided under Art. 6 of the same piece of legislation which states that the authorisation request will be settled 15 working days from the date of registration of the request).	Licence	No policy maker objective has been identified.	No deadline is set for granting/denying the approval of modifications to the workflow which might lead to various time limits for various companies and a discriminatory approach.	Amend legislation in order to make it clear that the request for granting/denying approval of modifications to the workflow must be settled by the authority in the terms provided for settling the authorisation request.
30	**Order No. 64/2007 approving the Sanitary veterinary norm regarding the organisation and performance of the official sanitary veterinary control activities carried out by specialised personnel in facilities producing animal origin foodstuffs**	Annex. 2. Art. 2	Fees	The service provision contract template used by ANSVSA when performing sanitary veterinary control specifies as the date of end of contract 31 December 2007.	Tariffs	The end date is prolonged yearly through an order of ANSVSA but the legal provision was not updated.	Economic operators are unable to identify the applicable legal provisions.	Update the template in Annex No. 2 so as to allow parties to fill in the end date of the contract or to fix the term in number of months so as to avoid yearly modification of Order 64/2007.
31	**Order No. 35/2011 on the approval of the Minimum operating conditions of small capacity slaughterhouses**	Art. 3, par. 2 b)	Slaughter-house	If animals are to be transported more than 50 km before reaching the slaughtering unit, small slaughterhouses must hold, as minimum equipment, a paddock.	Restrictions	The objective of the provision is to avoid the presence of hormones in the processed meat due to anxiety of the animals being slaughtered. Also, the provision is in line with EU regulations in the field and with the international food safety standards of Codex Alimentarius. The Code of hygienic practice for meat, Chapter 6.2 mentions that holding of animals should take into consideration their physiological condition which should not be compromised, e.g., animals should be adequately rested and not overcrowded and protected from weather where necessary. Furthermore, the Order was drafted based on the exceptions permitted under Art. 10, pt. 4b) of EC Regulation 853/2004, destined to encourage small slaughterhouses. The order establishes the minimum conditions a small slaughterhouse should fulfill, taking into consideration that they benefit from certain exceptions regarding space and equipment (exceptions from Annex III of EC Reg. 853/2004).	The provision seems to discourage new competitors on the slaughterhouses market by establishing a standard that creates a disadvantage for small businesses at the beginning of their activity.	No recommendation for change.

Sector: Food *(cont.)*

No.	No and title of Regulation	Article	Thematic category	Brief description of potential obstacles	Keyword	Policy maker's objectives	Harm to competition	Recommendations
32	**Order No. 34/2008 approving the Sanitary veterinary and food safety norm for granting exemptions to facilities producing foodstuffs with traditional characteristics according to the requirements of the European Parliament and Council Regulation No. 852/2004/EC on the hygiene of foodstuffs, and laying down the procedure for granting exemptions and sanitary veterinary registration, and for food safety from facilities producing foodstuffs with traditional characteristics**	Art. 9 par. 3 Norms	Traditional products	In case traditional production units "repeatedly" fail to meet the requirements established by the norms, they are removed from the list of authorised production units. The term "repeatedly" is not defined. According to MADR Order 690/2004, Art. 2 a traditional product is one obtained from traditional raw materials, has a traditional composition or a traditional production/ processing method and it can clearly be distinguished from other similar products.	Exemptions	The Order was drafted based on the exceptions allowed by Art. 7 of EC Regulation 2074/2005 for the units producing traditional foodstuffs. The exceptions refer to certain requirements regulated under Annex II of EC Reg. 852/2004. The provisions under Art. 9 (3) were set based on Art. 54 of EC Reg. 882/ 2004. The Order was referred to and accepted by the European Commission.	The provision leaves room for different interpretations of the word "repeatedly", which might lead to discriminatory approaches.	No recommendation for change.
33	**Order No. 34/2008 approving the Sanitary veterinary and food safety norm for granting exemptions to facilities producing foodstuffs with traditional characteristics according to the requirements of the European Parliament and Council Regulation No. 852/2004/EC on the hygiene of foodstuffs, and laying down the procedure for granting exemptions and sanitary veterinary registration, and for food safety from facilities producing foodstuffs with traditional characteristics**	Art. 12, Art. 13 Norms	Traditional products	The law foresees a list of minimum hygiene requirements for facilities producing foodstuffs with traditional characteristics in general. Specifically, hygiene requirements for sheepfolds are lighter. For example, in the case of sheepfolds, working staff does not have to disinfect their hands, as washing is considered enough. Sheepfolds do not have to have a separate area or a closed cabinet for storing sanitary materials and/or protection equipment.	Exemptions	The provision is in line with EU Regulation 852/2004. Exceptions to certain requests of Annex II of EC Regulation 852/2004 need to be approved by the local sanitary veterinary authorities.	The legal provision seems to establish standards that offer advantages to sheepfolds compared to other type of facilities.	No recommendation for change.

Sector: Food *(cont.)*

No.	No and title of Regulation	Article	Thematic category	Brief description of potential obstacles	Keyword	Policy maker's objectives	Harm to competition	Recommendations
34	**Order No. 34/2008 approving the Sanitary veterinary and food safety norm for granting exemptions to facilities producing foodstuffs with traditional characteristics according to the requirements of the European Parliament and Council Regulation No. 852/2004/EC on the hygiene of foodstuffs, and laying down the procedure for granting exemptions and sanitary veterinary registration, and for food safety of facilities producing foodstuffs with traditional characteristics**	Art. 12 (n), Art. 13 (l)	Traditional products	In case of facilities producing foodstuffs with traditional characteristics and that are requesting derogations from the general health and safety framework, personnel in charge of preparing and handling raw materials and food products have to show proof that they are in good health by presenting a medical certificate. The law does not elaborate on how often the document must be submitted, nor does it mention what are the measures to be taken if the personnel have health issues. The law does not stipulate whether work health and safety legislation is applicable or if more strict rules are applicable. However, all these requirements are stipulated under EU regulation 852/2004.	Exemptions	The provision is in line with EU Regulation 852/2004 (Annex 1, Art. 4, letter E stipulates the obligation to ensure that staff handling any type of foodstuffs in primary production are in good health). The objective of the provision is to ensure safety of foodstuffs in the production chain. More provisions regarding the hygiene and health of staff handling foodstuffs are foreseen in Chapter VIII, Annex II of the same regulation. The representatives of the Public Health Departments are responsible for applying the legislation elaborated by the Ministry of Health regarding staff hygiene and health. Moreover, undertakings in the food sector have the obligation to prepare and implement specific procedures regarding the hygiene and health of the staff. These procedures are verified by the local sanitary-veterinary authorities and their implementation is supervised by official veterinarians.Lack of conformity with the procedures is sanctioned by the local bodies of ANSVSA (local sanitary-veterinary authorities).	No harm to competition has been identified. However, the legal provision establishes unclear and incomplete standards, thus leaving room for discriminatory approach between competitors.	No recommendation to change.
35	**Order No. 976/1998 approving the Hygiene norms concerning the production, processing, storage, preservation, transport and marketing of food**	Entire act	Food processing framework legislation	After discussions with MADR, it appears that the domestic legislation has the same objective as Regulation (EC) No. 852/2004 regarding food hygiene, thus dual pieces of legislation are applicable. The EU Regulation is directly applicable in Romania and as such, there is no need for transposition into domestic legislation.	Dual regulation	Domestic legislation was not expressly abolished after entrance into force of EC Regulation No. 852/2004 which is directly applicable in Romania as of 1 January 2007.	It is unclear for companies active in the field what legislation is in force.	Abolish provisions which are double regulated.
36	**Order No. 976/1998 approving the Hygiene norms concerning the production, processing, storage, preservation, transport and marketing of food**	Art. 17	Food processing framework legislation	Public catering units and production units with high risks for consumers may hire only qualified personnel. However, clear criteria for determining units with high risks for consumers are not defined. Minimum criteria for personnel of public catering units and production units is established in Annexes I & II of EC Regulation No. 852/2004.	Unclear legal provision	The lawmaker did not have to define notions under obsolete legislation.	Since the provision does not set standard criteria for determining the rate of risk for food production units and/or catering units by sector, it is hard for these units to self-determine their level of risk. Also it is difficult for those units to establish, before entering the market, their cash flow and working capital needs concerning future personnel costs.	Abolish as indicated under point 35 above.

Sector: Food *(cont.)*

No.	No and title of Regulation	Article	Thematic category	Brief description of potential obstacles	Keyword	Policy maker's objectives	Harm to competition	Recommendations
37	**Order No. 976/1998 approving the Hygiene norms concerning the production, processing, storage, preservation, transport and marketing of food**	Art. 19	Food processing framework legislation	Food industry units must request an authorisation when increasing a production plan over the normal capacity of the unit. With this authorisation, the sanitary authorities can establish special clauses. It is not defined by the law what the special clauses are and what they refer to. The procedure to be applied when increasing the production plan over the normal capacity of the unit is covered by Art. 6 of EC Regulation No. 852/2004.	Unclear legal provision	The lawmaker did not have to define notions under obsolete legislation.	Since the legal provision does not include details on the types of special clauses that are applicable in this situation, one may assume that they might be favourable for some competitors while being restrictive to others.	Abolish as indicated under point 35 above.
38	**Order No. 976/1998 approving the Hygiene norms concerning the production, processing, storage, preservation, transport and marketing of food**	Art. 31 par. 3	Food processing framework legislation	Depending on the type of catering unit, annexes must exist to the actual kitchen. Cold dishes must be prepared in a separate room (salads, mayonnaise, products with gelatine, sandwiches, and cold appetizers), completely separated from the actual kitchen. Provisions regarding the cold chain of foodstuffs also appear under chapter IX of EC Regulation No. 852/2004.	Unreasonable restriction	The lawmaker did not have to define notions under obsolete legislation.	The provision could limit the possibility for some catering units to offer a certain type of product, cold dishes in this case, in case the space does not meet this standard, aiming to promote certain types of suppliers that are more likely to meet this standard. Also this standard may significantly raise the investment costs of location.	Abolish as indicated under point 35 above.
39	**Order No. 976/1998 approving the Hygiene norms concerning the production, processing, storage, preservation, transport and marketing of food**	Art. 37 f)	Food processing framework legislation	Duck eggs are not to be used in public catering units. We have not identified such a recommendation under a piece of legislation applicable at the EU level. However, it appears that such a interdiction in using duck eggs is also applied in other EU countries (e.g. the United Kingdom and Ireland) due to the high risk of salmonella and the perishable nature of the foodstuff..	Unreasonable restriction	Duck eggs have a high risk of salmonella and a perishable nature.	The provision may limit the ability of duck-egg suppliers to provide their goods to the catering market.	Abolish as indicated under point 35 above and assess whether to keep the interdiction under a different piece of legislation.
40	**Order No. 976/1998 approving the Hygiene norms concerning the production, processing, storage, preservation, transport and marketing of food**	Art. 38 (d)	Food processing framework legislation	In case there is only one room for storing perishable and non-perishable raw materials, it is required that the supply of perishable goods (meat and dairy products especially) in catering units does not exceed the quantity needed to cover supply needs for one operating day. Provisions regarding the cold chain of foodstuffs also appear under chapter IX of EC Regulation No. 852/2004.	Unreasonable restriction	The lawmaker did not have to define notions under obsolete legislation.	The provision may generate additional supply costs for the catering units. On the other hand, it may limit the ability of suppliers of perishable goods to provide their goods on the catering market.	Abolish as indicated under point 35 above.
41	**Order No. 976/1998 approving the Hygiene Norms concerning the production, processing, storage, preservation, transport and marketing of food**	Art. 62	Food hygiene	Selling of unwrapped ice cream in case of small fixed vendors is allowed only indoors.	Unreasonable restriction	Safety perspective	The provision limits the ability of a certain type of ice cream vendor to sell their products.	Abolish as indicated under point 35 above and assess whether to keep the interdiction under a different piece of legislation if this is necessary from a safety perspective.

Sector: Food *(cont.)*

No.	No and title of Regulation	Article	Thematic category	Brief description of potential obstacles	Keyword	Policy maker's objectives	Harm to competition	Recommendations
42	**Order No. 321/2004 approving the Norm on the nature, content, production, quality, packaging, labelling, marking, storage and transport of canned fruit mixtures**	Norm, Annex 1, Art 2 -3	Standards	When preparing canned fruit mixtures, only 5 named fruits can be used. The law also indicates which ones may be left out if only 4 fruits are used.	Unreasonable restriction	The provision is in line with international food safety standards of Codex Alimentarius-Codex standard for canned fruit cocktail Codex Stan 78-1981.	Prevents the economic operators who produce canned fruit mixtures from using recipes that contain other types of fruits than those mentioned in the norm, thus limiting innovation and offerings of different products for which there might be a market segment.	No recommendation for change.
43	**Order No. 321/2004 approving the Norm on the nature, content, production, quality, packaging, labelling, marking, storage and transport of canned fruit mixtures**	Norm, Annex 2, Table 1	Standards	The norm establishes set proportions of the fruits a producer may use in his canned fruit mixture recipe.	Unreasonable restriction	The provision is in line with the international food safety standards Codex Alimentarius-Codex standard for canned fruit cocktail Codex Stan 78-1981.	Prevents the economic operators who produce canned fruit mixtures from using recipes that contain different proportions of fruits than the ones mentioned in the Norm, thus limiting innovation and restricting product offerings.	No recommendation for change.
44	**Order No. 321/2004 approving the Norm on the nature, content, production, quality, packaging, labelling, marking, storage and transport of canned fruit mixtures**	Norm, Annex 4, Table 3	Standards	Standards are set for the dimensions and types of fruit cuts allowed in canned fruit mixtures.	Unreasonable restriction	The provision is in line with the international food safety standards of Codex Alimentarius-Codex standard for canned fruit cocktail Codex Stan 78-1981.	Prevents the economic operators who produce canned fruit mixtures from using different cuts (shape or size), thus limiting innovation and restricting product offerings.	No recommendation for change.
45	**Order No. 242/2008 on the distortion of surplus sugar stocks for use in animal feed**	Art. 3 par. 2	Sugar	Only sugar intended for animal feed is eligible for a denaturing/distortion process. Distortion of sugar refers to the process of transforming sugar in animal feed through different mixtures, in different proportions, as set by the legislation. According to Romanian legislation, a minimum quantity of 10 metric tonnes of white sugar may be distorted per day in a single location. In accordance with the Act of Accession to the EU of Romania, quantities of stocks of sugar or isoglucose exceeding the normal carry-over stock had to be eliminated from the market by 30 April 2008 at the latest, including through distortion for use in animal feed. Currently, the licensed sugar producers do not have surplus stocks according to data held by the Ministry. Following the 2006 reform of the sugar regime that introduced changes to the Union sugar sector, Regulation (EU) No 1308/2013 is now applicable for the sugar market, establishing the sugar quotas for each country.	Obsolete provision	According to Art. 19-21 of EC Regulation 100/1972, the minimum quantity to be denatured per day in any one place shall be 20 metric tonnes. However, Member States may fix another minimum quantity. Even if currently no surplus stocks appear to be held by the producers, in case such surplus stocks should appear, the provision should be in force.	Considering that it is not applied in practice for surplus sugar stocks, the mere existence of legal requirements creates uncertainty among market participants.	No recommendation for change.

Sector: Food *(cont.)*

No.	No and title of Regulation	Article	Thematic category	Brief description of potential obstacles	Keyword	Policy maker's objectives	Harm to competition	Recommendations
46	**Order No. 109/2010 approving the Sanitary veterinary norm on the sanitary veterinary licensing/registration of facilities involved in farm feed and means of transport of farm feed**	Art. 14 par. 8 b)	Farm feed	Facilities involved in farm feed and means of transport of farm feed cannot operate unless they are authorised/registered with the competent local health and veterinary authority. The competent local health and veterinary authority can lift the granted authorisation/registration when "on several occasions", breach of legal provisions is reported and if the facility continues not to offer "proper safeguards" with regards to future production. The list of authorised units is available on the ANSVSA website (*www.ansvsa.ro/?pag=814*)	Unclear legal provision	The lawmaker aims to insure that the authorisation/registration is, at all times, based on compliance with all legal provisions and quality standards. Upon discussions with ANSVSA it is our understanding that ANSVSA is currently drafting an Order to modify / complete/abolish parts of Order 109/2010, in order to clarify certain issues which, in the current version, may leave room for interpretation.	The legal provision establishes unclear and incomplete conditions for lifting authorisation, thus making it difficult for competitors to comply and leaving room for discrimination.	Amend the legislation so that it clearly defines phrases such as: "on several occasions", "proper safeguards".
47	**Order No. 145/2007 on approval of the Norm for food safety which sets out the conditions in case of import-export operations, transit and intra-community trade of non-animal food products subject to the supervision and control of food safety**	Art. 9 par. 1 c)	Taxation	In case of food products of non-animal origin, the authorities can perform laboratory analyses to verify compliance with the feed and food law. In such cases, in practice, importation is delayed at the border by sanitary veterinary controls. During the laboratory analysis for verification of compliance with the feed and food law, the products are kept at the border in refrigerator trucks until the issuance of the laboratory results (between 3 and 7 days). This involves significant costs for the undertaking in relation to rental of the trucks, salary of the driver, fuel used, etc. In other EU Member States the products are released from customs immediately after sampling. Operators are avoiding Romania borders when entering into EU through other Member States (e.g. Bulgaria) to reduce transportation time and costs.	Excise duties	The domestic legislation is in line with EU legislation. Also, there is no mention under Order 145/2007 in the sense that the transports are held at the border until the finalisation of the analysis. However, this is the practice of the authorities which do not issue the necessary documents.	The practice of holding transports at the border until the finalisation of the laboratory analysis whereas in other Member States the transports are released immediately after sampling distorts the patterns of trade within the common European market as economic operators avoid Romanian borders and pass through neighbouring countries instead. The economic operators are adding significant costs due to this practice which could be reduced in cases where they could deposit the products in their own warehouses until the issuance of laboratory results.	Guidelines should be issued in order to ensure that the authorities are applying the legal provisions and are not keeping trucks at the borders without justification.

ORGANISATION FOR ECONOMIC CO-OPERATION AND DEVELOPMENT

The OECD is a unique forum where governments work together to address the economic, social and environmental challenges of globalisation. The OECD is also at the forefront of efforts to understand and to help governments respond to new developments and concerns, such as corporate governance, the information economy and the challenges of an ageing population. The Organisation provides a setting where governments can compare policy experiences, seek answers to common problems, identify good practice and work to co-ordinate domestic and international policies.

The OECD member countries are: Australia, Austria, Belgium, Canada, Chile, the Czech Republic, Denmark, Estonia, Finland, France, Germany, Greece, Hungary, Iceland, Ireland, Israel, Italy, Japan, Korea, Luxembourg, Mexico, the Netherlands, New Zealand, Norway, Poland, Portugal, the Slovak Republic, Slovenia, Spain, Sweden, Switzerland, Turkey, the United Kingdom and the United States. The European Union takes part in the work of the OECD.

OECD Publishing disseminates widely the results of the Organisation's statistics gathering and research on economic, social and environmental issues, as well as the conventions, guidelines and standards agreed by its members.

OECD PUBLISHING, 2, rue André-Pascal, 75775 PARIS CEDEX 16
(24 2016 01 1 P) ISBN 978-92-64-25742-9 – 2016

www.ingramcontent.com/pod-product-compliance
Ingram Content Group UK Ltd.
Pitfield, Milton Keynes, MK11 3LW, UK
UKHW051456290926
15471UKWH00008B/1239

9 789264 257429